Praise for *The Su*

"An entertaining story."

"An absorbing account."

"With dry wit, Parrish distills a large subject into a compelling popular narrative that draws the reader in slowly . . . using the best unclassified historical scholarship while also seeking out testimony from the deckplates. Parrish has set himself a task that, in lesser hands, would effectively please no one. A fascinating ride."
—*The San Diego Union-Tribune*

"A compelling and fascinating subject . . . [*The Submarine*] makes for excellent entertainment."
—*New York Post*

"An astounding compilation truly marking the significance of the evolution and recognition of perhaps the greatest asset to naval forces. Parrish makes his narrative unique by infusing the history of the submarine with a thorough analysis of its political and diplomatic effects, as well as the personal motives and actions of the crews, inventors and leaders that charted the submarine's course through history. With this personal interest, Parrish eloquently unveils the complicated details surrounding the invention and evolution of this ship in a definite, readable manner that adds interest to history by charting the real-life drama and landmarks left in the wake of the submarine during the past two centuries."
—*Sea Power*

"A magnificent narrative history of the submarine. A fascinating chronological account of the growth in size and complexity of these boats . . . Parrish makes an excellent case for his contention that the twentieth century's most significant military innovation was the submarine. Parrish is particularly masterful in depicting the events in Germany prior to and during World War I. Parrish's coverage of these and many other episodes are presented in such fascinating and suspenseful prose that the reader quickly forgets that this is actually history. . . . Entertaining and informative."
—*The Roanoke Times*

"Parrish does a superior job of research . . . this book should be included in every serious submarine historian's library and referred to often."
—*Navy Submarine Base*

"To a minutiae-ridden subject, Parrish brings a superb general treatment."
—*Booklist*

"Smooth and even witty writing . . . a most respectable book . . . it should set the new armchair submariner sailing off into the extensive and up-to-date bibliography."
—*Publishers Weekly*

"A superb history of the submarine . . . this brilliant, dramatic account of submarines and the men who sail them is a required acquisition for every military history collection."
—*Choice*

PENGUIN BOOKS

THE SUBMARINE

Thomas Parrish is the author of a number of highly respected books on twentieth-century history, including *Berlin in the Balance*, *The Cold War Encyclopedia*, *The American Codebreakers*, and *Roosevelt and Marshall*. He also created and edited the acclaimed *Simon and Schuster Encyclopedia of World War II* and the six-volume *Men and Battle* series. He lives in Berea, Kentucky.

THE SUBM

THOMAS PARRISH

ARINE

PENGUIN BOOKS

A HISTORY

PENGUIN BOOKS
Published by the Penguin Group
Penguin Group (USA) Inc., 375 Hudson Street, New York, New York 10014, U.S.A.
Penguin Group (Canada), 10 Alcorn Avenue, Toronto, Ontario, Canada M4V 3B2
(a division of Pearson Penguin Canada Inc.)
Penguin Books Ltd, 80 Strand, London WC2R 0RL, England
Penguin Ireland, 25 St Stephen's Green, Dublin 2, Ireland (a division of Penguin Books Ltd)
Penguin Group (Australia), 250 Camberwell Road, Camberwell, Victoria 3124, Australia (a division of
Pearson Australia Group Pty Ltd)
Penguin Books India Pvt Ltd, 11 Community Centre, Panchsheel Park, New Delhi—110 017, India
Penguin Group (NZ), cnr Airborne and Rosedale Roads, Albany, Auckland, 1310 New Zealand
(a division of Pearson New Zealand Ltd)
Penguin Books (South Africa) (Pty) Ltd, 24 Sturdee Avenue, Rosebank, Johannesburg 2196, South Africa

Penguin Books Ltd, Registered Offices:
80 Strand, London WC2R 0RL, England

First published in the United States of America by Viking Penguin,
a member of Penguin Group (USA) Inc. 2004
Published in Penguin Books 2005

10 9 8 7 6 5 4 3 2 1

Copyright © Thomas Parrish, 2004
All rights reserved

Insert Credits: Mark Stein: p. 1, p. 10, p. 14; Mc Lure's, February 1899: p. 2 top, p. 3, p. 4 top and bottom;
Courtesy U.S. Naval Institute and Submarine Force Museum: p. 2 bottom; Courtesy Submarine
Force Museum: p. 5 top and bottom, p. 7 top, p. 27, p. 28 top; McLure's, January 1899: p. 6 top and bottom;
Sharkhunters: p. 8 top; Darren Milford: p. 7 bottom, p. 8 bottom, p. 9 top; U.S. Naval Institute
Photo Archive: p. 9 bottom, p. 11 top and bottom, p. 16, p. 17 top and bottom, p. 20, p. 24 bottom, p. 25
top, p. 26, p. 29 top and bottom, p. 31; National Archives: p. 12 top and bottom, p. 13, p. 15 top and
bottom, p. 18 bottom, p. 19 top and bottom, p. 24 top, p. 25 bottom; Robert Hall Collection: p. 21 top
and bottom, p. 22, p. 23 top and bottom; Courtesy Robert Rowe: p. 18 top; Courtesy Syracuse
University Library: p. 28 bottom; Robert Brancaccio: p. 32 top; Getty Images: p. 32 bottom.

Drawings on insert p. 30 by William Clipson.
Reprinted by permission from Norman Polmar's The Naval Institute Guide to the Ships and
Aircraft of the U.S. Fleet (Annapolis: Naval Institute Press, © 2001).

THE LIBRARY OF CONGRESS HAS CATALOGED THE HARDCOVER EDITION AS FOLLOWS:
Parrish, Thomas (Thomas D.)
    The submarine : a history / Thomas Parrish.
        p.   cm.
    Includes bibliographical references and index.
    ISBN 0-670-03313-8 (hc.)
    ISBN 0 14 30.3519 3 (pbk.)
    1. Submarines (Ships)—History. I. Title.
    V857.P37 2004
    359.9'383—dc22   2003070515

Printed in the United States of America
Designed by Carla Bolte • Set in Bembo

NEITHER TIMID NOR RECKLESS MEN SHOULD GO TO SEA.

—Arleigh A. ("31-Knot") Burke, Admiral, U.S. Navy

PREFACE

From time to time in the following pages, you will see mention of the American naval historian and philosopher Alfred Thayer Mahan, whose famous book *The Influence of Sea Power upon History*, published in the closing years of the nineteenth century, created an intellectual revolution among people in every country who concerned themselves with naval affairs and national policy. The captain's insights and arguments gave his readers a new way of looking at issues and questions either that they had never thought much about or that they had believed long settled. In a similar if far more modest way, the present book seeks, in telling its story, to show the remarkable influence the submarine has exerted on the history of the world in the last hundred years. To put it another way, the book presents this history from the point of view of the submarine. It was fortunate that this theme, with its dimensions and implications, declared itself; otherwise, such a vast subject as the history of the submarine might well have sunk into an ocean of general information and become merely a catalogue of unrelated facts instead of a genuine narrative.

Although it had a colorful past in the minds of dreamers, the submarine reached its form and developed genuine usefulness only at the beginning of the twentieth century, and it went on to play dominant and diversified parts in the three great conflicts of the century: World War I, World War II, and the Cold War. In the first war (aptly called the Great War by most Europeans), it exercised decisive *political* influence (a startling realization for people at the time), even though it was still a brand-new part of the world's navies. Was it a warship that should fight other warships—one good and proper soldier against another—or was it a wide-ranging highwayman, a commerce raider operating outside all conventions to attack merchant shipping? Once realizing the question, politicians and admirals endlessly argued it. In the second war the submarine played a central *economic* role, seeming to offer victory to one side in the struggle only to withdraw the prize and then, in another ocean, present it to the opponents. In the Cold War the submarine became the direct agent of strategy as the guarantor of the strange two-sided peace that ended in the 1990s when the world returned to its state of normal chaos. In each of the three conflicts, of course, the submarine played more than one part, but its dominant influence exerted itself in these three differing ways.

The story of the submarine is also a story of boats and people: those who created the boats (including the early dreamers), those who employed them, and those who fought against them. Influences can hardly exist in a realm apart from the personal and concrete and technical (for instance, the character of a chief like Admiral Isoroku Yamamoto or of a daring skipper like Lieutenant Commander Mush Morton; the effectiveness of torpedoes or the development of nuclear propulsion).

Lastly, and specifically, the story of the submarine is a story featuring a cast of heroes—many more than could find mention here. There are villains, too, and some of them are the same as the heroes.

■ ■ ■

The names of cities, islands, and other geographical entities are given as they were at the time under discussion (Surabaya, Formosa), with clarification supplied where it seemed needed.

The Notes, which begin on page 519, give the sources of all quotations and of other material in the main body of the book. In some instances the Notes present background information or give further details about particular points.

CONTENTS

LIST OF MAPS

CHARLESTON 2000-1864

1

THE PERIPATETIC COFFIN

On the sunny morning of Tuesday, August 8, 2000, the city of Charleston gave itself a party. Men in Civil War uniforms and women in dresses of the period—some in the symbolic black of widows—mixed with other residents and tourists, while out in the harbor and beyond more than two hundred boats of all sizes rode the swell, their owners waiting for a special moment. Crews from the broadcast TV networks, the History Channel, and German TV had come for the occasion, and even a team from Fox Sports, though, as a reporter commented, "they weren't exactly sure why." A place on the media boat went for $150.

About four and a half miles out from the Battery, a huge crane began raising a steel superstructure and the sling that hung from it, and at 8:39 a strange-looking object broke the water—a 40-foot cigar, encrusted with corrosion and marine growths, that had lain on the bottom, just thirty feet below the surface, for 136 years. Hesitating, carefully timing his move against the swell, the crane operator deftly deposited the 23-ton object on the barge that would carry it into the harbor. A great wave of sound arose from sirens, whistles, and bells, and the thousands of people began applauding as the tugs maneuvered the barge shoreward. Then, as it passed the Maritime Center, with members of the recovery team constantly wetting it with garden hoses to protect it from the air, Confederate battle reenactors fired a twenty-one-gun salute.

At Waterfront Park, a woman said, "I can't even find the words to describe what I felt when they went by. We don't have heroes like that any more."

The cradle holding this strangest of cigars bore the sign:

HUNLEY.COM

3

■ ■ ■

At the outset of the Civil War, President Lincoln had ordered a blockade of the Confederate coast, and the navy, unprepared for such a responsibility, cobbled together a scratch force that even included the Staten Island ferry.

For a year or more the blockade proved ineffective, but as the Union navy grew, it stood guard in ever greater force outside Confederate ports. The Reverend Franklin Smith, a Tennessee inventor as well as preacher, published a letter, widely reprinted across the South, in which he proposed a new kind of weapon against the tightening Yankee hold—a cigar-shaped craft that could move underwater to attack enemy ships.

A group of like-minded New Orleans citizens, including a planter and merchant named Horace L. Hunley, began working to create such a vessel. By 1863 the group had moved to Mobile, with Hunley as one of the designers as well as the chief contributor. Their work produced a craft that was constructed from a converted iron boiler and was only about five feet in diameter. When put to the test in July 1863, this tiny vessel performed perfectly, as its "torpedo," a trailed explosive charge, sank a coal barge. After the test the Confederates shipped the vessel, named for the man who financed it, to Charleston, where the blockading Union ships were almost shutting down the port, giving the North a symbolic as well as an economic victory. Charleston merchants put a $50,000 bounty (presumably in Confederate currency) on each blockading Union ship.

The military commander in Charleston, General P. G. T. Beauregard, took the *H. L. Hunley* over from its private owners, but army proprietorship immediately proved disastrous. After bumbling soldiers allowed it to be swamped by a passing ship, with the loss of five members of the crew, the general permitted Hunley himself to take control of the vessel, but the financier also proved incompetent as a skipper. Two months later, a hatch mistakenly left open caused the submarine to sink again, taking Hunley and his seven crewmen to their deaths. General Beauregard, who saw the *Hunley* brought up, said that "the spectacle was indescribably ghastly. The unfortunate men were contorted into all sorts of horrible attitudes." The *Hunley,* raised and re-paired, became known as the "peripatetic coffin."

The motive power of the boat came from the muscles of the crew, who turned cranks attached to a drive shaft; she could achieve a speed of about 4 knots. Night after night in January 1864, the laboring crew-men would crank the boat out into the bay in search of a Union vic-tim, but, warned by Southern turncoats, the Union commander, Admiral John Dahlgren, had spread iron booms to protect his ironclads. Then, at the beginning of February, a new Union ship arrived, the wooden-hulled steam sloop *Housatonic,* which, most conveniently for the hard-working crew of the *Hunley,* anchored closer in to the harbor than the other Union ships, just about 4 miles out.

On the cold night of February 17, the *Hunley* set out from Breach Inlet, near Charleston, heading toward the *Housatonic,* which lay at an-chor just 6 miles from Fort Sumter, where the war had started. The submarine would employ a new mode of attack; instead of trailing the black-powder charge, she would now assault the enemy with the tor-pedo mounted on a 15-foot spar protruding from the bow. At about 8:45, a deckhand on the *Housatonic* spotted the approach of what looked to him like a dolphin swimming on the surface. But as suspi-cion spread among the crewmen, they began peppering the craft with small arms fire. Others slipped the anchor chain and tried to get the ship moving away from the impending attack.

But they had not moved quickly enough. The *Hunley* plunged the point of her spar into the wooden hide of the *Housatonic,* forward of the mizzenmast on the starboard side and just in line with the powder magazine, as if administering a lethal injection with a hypodermic nee-dle. Then, backing the boat away under the small arms fire to a dis-tance probably considerably less than the desired 150 feet, the skipper, Lieutenant George Dixon, pulled on the rope trigger that detonated the torpedo. A large explosion resulted, sending the *Housatonic* heeling to port and sinking stern first. When she went down, the tops of her masts remained above water, and sailors took refuge in the rigging. Only five of them died. Meanwhile, having done her work, the *Hunley* sailed away into a lasting mystery. She sank about half a mile seaward of her victim, carrying nine men to their deaths, but no one knew why. Before disappearing, she flashed the blue lantern, the agreed-upon signal of success, and a soldier on shore at Breach Inlet lit a bonfire to guide her home. But she never arrived.

In her one brief engagement, however, the *Hunley* had entered history by becoming the first submersible craft ever to sink an enemy ship. The world and the submarine itself would undergo vast changes before such an event occurred again.

THE UNDERWATER PIONEERS

The little cigar-shaped vessel . . . may or may not play an important part in the navies of the world in the years to come.

—*New York Times* (May 17, 1897)

2

DREAMERS AND SOME DOERS

Something about the surface of the earth has always made us try to leave it. Our ancestors scanned the heavens and sought to break away, flying toward the sun, into a new and temptingly close upper dimension, and they also cherished the dream of escaping the familiar surface by diving beneath it, into the depths of the sea. But for all the strength of their dreams, and all the legends that surrounded them, the ancients and their successors for many centuries lacked the means to make practical progress toward translating their visions into reality. When Leonardo da Vinci drew his famous flying machine, he was expressing only an idea; of course, Leonardo tried his hand at the submarine, too. He professed to have discovered the secret of remaining under water for a "protracted period of time" but refused to reveal it to anybody. "I do not publish or divulge [my method]," he declared, "because of the evil nature of men who practice assassination at the bottom of the sea."

A sixteenth-century English mathematician, William Bourne, went further than Leonardo and appears to have been the first person known to have designed a submarine in some detail. In 1578 Bourne described a submersible, a rowboat that would consist of a wooden skeleton covered by an oiled leather skin. But though Bourne gave the dream some specific form, he took no steps to build such a craft. Some forty-five years later, however, Cornelis Drebbel, a Dutchman living in London, produced an actual boat, which featured the kind of frame and covering described by Bourne; hence Drebbel (also known as Cornelius van Drebel) has sometimes been hailed as the builder of the first submarine, though "submersible craft" might be a more apt characterization. Drebbel's craft is said to have maneuvered successfully in the

9

Thames at depths of about 15 feet; one account even has King James I coming aboard for a brief excursion (a daring venture that perhaps inspired the presidents of France and the United States to make comparable gestures almost three hundred years later).

In England the eighteenth century saw many inventors proposing various ideas for submersible craft. A martyr to the cause, a wagon maker named John Day, devised an effective way to cause an old sailing vessel to sink by the use of ballast, but unfortunately failed to survive the demonstration, which took place in June 1774; the courageous Captain Day stayed down with the ship. But it was a young American, David Bushnell, who in 1775 became the first of all the dreamers to produce a submersible that, though inescapably primitive, could with some legitimacy be termed a submarine. The definition of the submarine is simple enough: a vessel that, like all others, can propel itself on the surface of the water but, unlike any other, can propel itself under the surface as well. It can sink at will, operate and flourish underwater, and return to the surface when the operator wishes; it is therefore unique. Bushnell, a student at Yale (and classmate of Nathan Hale), had developed his ideas concerning submersible craft during the years of increasing tension leading up to the outbreak of the Revolutionary War, and in July 1776 the adoption of the Declaration of Independence found the inventor ready to put his creation into the fight. The Americans chose as the target H.M.S. *Eagle,* the flagship of Vice Admiral Lord Howe, commander of the British fleet blockading New York. The inventor had received counsel from Benjamin Franklin and the project had the support and personal involvement of George Washington himself.

Bushnell's underwater vessel, called the *Turtle,* was a one-man craft, only 6 feet long, often described as being shaped like two bathtubs clamped together, with a small viewing hole in the upper part (with its double shell, it could also have been called the *Oyster).* The limited technology of the day enabled Bushnell only to create a submersible driven by direct human power—in this case, a crew of one, who would turn a crank or work pedals that turned a propeller. Even so, in designing this primitive, pioneering boat the inventor had faced and dealt with important issues. In creating a submarine, Bushnell and all of the inventors who would follow him had to devise a method (or methods) of causing the vessel to sink beneath the surface as desired, to stay level underwater, to go where desired, and to return to the surface on command. While on the surface, a submarine or any other vessel exists in a state of positive buoyancy: It is lighter than the water it displaces, and thus it floats. Inventors before Bushnell had seen the need for ballast tanks filled with water, which by increasing the weight of the vessel produce negative buoyancy, causing it to sink. When the boat is completely underwater, it is in a state of neutral buoyancy. Bushnell's particular contribution was to supply the ballast tanks with pumps, so that the operator could empty them when he wished to surface; he also devised a depth gauge. Operation of this vessel made enormous demands on its single crew member. He had no simple way of taking on and expelling small amounts of ballast to keep the boat at the desired attitude, or angle, in the water ("in trim"), a problem that would concern inventors for years to come; further, he had to keep the boat at the right depth, keep the propeller shaft turning, steer his craft to the desired spot, and carry out a planned attack.

In going after the *Eagle,* the operator would have to attempt to place a 150-pound charge of black powder under the hull of the enemy warship, where she lay at anchor off Staten Island, in New York harbor. The task called for fastening this "torpedo" to the keel with a screw and setting a timer that would activate the fuse after the *Turtle* had moved out of harm's way. Overall, the task imposed requirements that would have tested the dexterity of a trained octopus. Some subsequent commentators have considered them to have been impossible of fulfillment, and perhaps the details of the *Turtle*'s mission that have been repeated through the years should be considered examples of submarine stories made up more of legend than of fact. In any case, David Bushnell, not robust enough to meet the physical demands of piloting the submarine himself, had to yield that honor to his brother Ezra, whose illness then forced postponement of the operation. An army sergeant, Ezra Lee, volunteered to do the job, and on September 6, after a period of training, he set forth from lower Manhattan to attempt history's first attack by a submarine on an enemy vessel.

The plan called for Lee to drill a hole in the keel of the *Eagle* with an auger that would also serve as the supporting screw for the torpedo; then the timer would start to do its work. But the sergeant did not succeed in attaching the torpedo to the warship, and he appears to have returned to his comrades reporting failure. No one could have considered this result surprising, since any of many possibilities could have gone wrong. Perhaps Lee did reach the desired position and begin the operation with the auger, only to find the wood of the keel unyielding. As an example of the kinds of legends in the chronicle of the submarine, one may note that writers have often ascribed the failure of Lee's attempt to drill into the keel of the *Eagle* to the resistance of the ship's copper bottom. Though the Admiralty frequently provided its ships with copper sheathing as a protection against worm infestation, in 1776 the *Eagle* had not yet received this treatment. It is also possible that Lee did not in fact reach the target, and it is likely that, whatever he did, he was rendered somewhat non compos by excessive inhalation of carbon dioxide and therefore did not return fully aware of exactly what he had done.

Like a succession of subsequent submarine dreamers turned builders, Bushnell attacked practical problems and produced practical results, but he could not resolve the central if unstated problem: His ideas ran far in advance of the technical possibilities of his day. After him in the line of submarine dreamers came another American, one of the most remarkable personages of his time, a man who would win the kind of special and lasting fame that comes to inventors credited with the creation of basic and universally employed devices and processes. The invention with which history would forever associate this pioneer would not be the submarine, however, but the powered vessel that runs on top of the water, the steamboat. Yet, as a very practical man as well as a dreamer, the inventor would make a memorable place for himself in the annals of the submarine as well.

Born in 1765 in southeastern Pennsylvania, Robert Fulton as a schoolboy gave the world a glimpse of the future when, it was said, he grew tired of rowing a small boat the local youngsters used for fishing and devised a set of paddlewheels for it (though it still required human power to operate). He began his working life as an artist, however, leaving the Lancaster area to learn and work in Philadelphia. There he evinced a pronounced trait of his personality that would often play a decisive part in his life: a kind of automatic ability to win the favor and liking of persons of wealth and influence and to go on to build close friendships with them. In 1787 a benefactor provided the money for a trip to England, where Fulton, who in Philadelphia had achieved a measure of success as a portrait painter, intended to take up the serious study of art. He carried a letter of introduction to a fellow Pennsylvanian and artist, Benjamin West, who had won great renown in London, having become court painter to George III and cofounder of the Royal Academy. West, a notably generous man, befriended the newcomer (his list of other American protégés included Gilbert Stuart and Samuel F. B. Morse) and introduced him into a varied circle of friends and acquaintances.

A slim, good-looking six-footer, Fulton with his engaging ways could move with success in various groups, and some of these contacts led him not toward developing as a painter but toward the tinkering he had done as a boy. Although the nineteenth century was coming on, Fulton and his fellows still mostly dwelt in a Ben Franklin–eighteenth-century world, in which a polymath could glide from one broad realm to another and do well in all, and Fulton became involved with various British establishment figures preoccupied with the creation of canals as the key to future national commercial prosperity. Drawing on his native mechanical talent—particularly a sort of editorial flair for seeing what a system or a device lacked and how this need could be met—and on his ability as a draftsman, Fulton developed and presented designs for canal-digging equipment as well as plans for the canals themselves, producing in 1796 a substantial book called *A Treatise on the Improvement of Canal Navigation*. In 1797, in search both of a patent on his canal system and of financial backing, Fulton—the prototypical man of ideas with no money of his own—made the short but for him epochal journey across the English Channel to France, which then functioned under the government called the Directory and which was at war with England. Early in his stay in France, Fulton became involved in a close and unusual relationship with an American couple, Joel and Ruth Barlow; Joel Barlow, a writer (he produced the once-celebrated epic *The Columbiad*), diplomat, and all-around dabbler, insisted that Fulton share their lodgings and, some evidence suggests, their connubial life as well.

After three years of living in Paris in a series of furnished rooms (the trio was a movable ménage à trois that actually seemed most often to be a ménage a deux, as Barlow spent much of his time away), they settled into a large stone house that "Hub," as Barlow liked to be called (for "Hubby"), had been able to pick up at a bargain price because the member of the nobility who had built it had fled the country to escape the Revolution. The mansion on the rue de Vaugirard, just across from the northwest corner of the Luxembourg Gardens, had a ground floor and two upper stories, with servants' attics above, and a four-windowed façade presenting an imposing appearance, especially to a visitor approaching the great bronze gate, with its gatehouse.

Thus, after three years in Paris, the American inventor found himself living in comfortable if unlikely circumstances, though his business affairs continued to be as episodic as ever. During this time, perhaps influenced by new friends, Fulton—an engineer at heart and thus generally more interested in process and technique than in specific subject matter—had directed his energies away from canals and had begun talking and writing about still another new interest, naval warfare. As a convinced disciple of Adam Smith he had developed the idea, even before receiving his canal patent, that national navies represented an economic evil, because they interfered with the practice of free trade, and therefore the world should rid itself of them. All the friendships he had built up in England seemed to have exerted little moderating influence on Fulton's outlook, since it was at this point that, carrying his philosophy much further than his Scottish intellectual master would have sanctioned, he introduced into his discussions a term (although with idiosyncratic spelling) and a proposed invention that would have resonance for at least the next two centuries. If the Directory would pay him a bounty for each English ship sunk, he said in a new proposal, he would build a "Mechanical Nautulus," a submarine vessel that would destroy the British fleet and thus free the world from a great and persisting economic menace.

Fulton's proposal came at what seemed a particularly appropriate time, since the Directory was contemplating an invasion of England, to be led by their young star commander Napoleon Bonaparte, but there ensued a series of frustrating dealings with French political officials who moved in and out of office as governments changed, until Napoleon took effective power in November in the famous 18th Brumaire coup of 1799. Some of these officials raised prescient points about the use of this new kind of "plunging" craft in warfare. If France employed such submersibles, would not England simply counter with submarines of her own? And the illegality of this underhanded new weapon was obvious, though Fulton resisted any such charges of immorality. Instead, he maintained, by literally making naval warfare impossible the submarine would prove itself to be a truly humane weapon. "The liberty of the seas," he reportedly was fond of declaring, "will be the happiness of the earth." Friends, or former friends, in England did not subscribe to this logic, which Fulton confusingly expanded on by patriotically declaring that his invention would serve to protect the United States because it would lead to the destruction of both the British and the French navies. For one writer in London, who can be regarded as having established the standard for much future commentary on the character of submariners, Fulton had shown himself "a crafty, murderous ruffian."

Regardless of the course of his rationalizations, Fulton by the end of 1799 had succeeded in attracting official French support, with financing apparently arranged by Joel Barlow, and by the following spring the copper-sheathed *Nautilus* (with spelling corrected) had taken shape in a shipyard on the Seine. The inventor presumably knew about Bushnell's *Turtle* (for one thing, Barlow and Bushnell, though not classmates, had been at Yale at the same time), but Fulton did not adopt the blob design favored by Bushnell; instead, he created a classic cigar-shaped vessel, 24.5 feet long and thus large enough to carry several crew members. The mast and sail, needed for ordinary operating on the surface, could be struck when the time came to submerge, a maneuver accomplished with the aid of diving planes, an innovation of prime importance; the vessel could be *aimed* downward instead of merely sinking because of increased weight from ballast. Underwater, hand cranks rather than a foot pedal, as Bushnell had probably used, turned the screw.

On June 13, 1800, at a point in the Seine just above the present-day Pont Alexandre III, with spectators lining the river walks and the quays below, Fulton and his assistant, carrying the lighted candle that would provide interior light, climbed into the boat, which moved out into the middle of the river and then thrilled the crowds by disappearing beneath the surface—not far under, but still out of sight. Some twenty minutes later it reappeared a good distance downstream, having been carried along by the current; it then returned upstream to its starting point, just opposite the golden dome of the Hôtel des Invalides on the Left Bank.

The trial had proved remarkably successful and the government's official observer produced a glowing report, but the shallowness of the Seine at Paris and the speed of the current meant that neither for the diving ability of the *Nautilus* nor for its maneuverability could the test be considered definitive. Hence in July and August Fulton conducted new trials at Rouen and Le Havre, and in September he took the boat to sea, out in the English Channel, and in a pair of pioneering incidents frightened away two English ships whose masters had apparently heard about the new underwater menace.

Yet how much of a threat could Fulton's little boat actually present to a ship? Bushnell, Fulton, and all other early submariners had to answer a basic question: What means could they use to bridge the space between the attacking boat and the target with destructive force? How could they make an underwater craft into a genuine menace, one that could actually sink an enemy man-of-war? Bushnell had tried to accomplish the feat by bringing the two craft together and affixing the line attached to an explosive charge. Fulton, who increasingly became more interested in explosives than in submarines themselves, turned away from Bushnell's idea and took a crack-the-whip approach, in which a bomb would be towed behind a vessel, which would then make a sharp turn and swing the torpedo into the target ship; a contact exploder would detonate the bomb. Again, the inventor produced a test that impressed the official French observer.

But fundamentally, though Fulton continued to add improvements to the *Nautilus*—a periscope and a compressed air tank to produce a good supply of oxygen—he and the French government were not fated to develop a partnership. Ingenious as the inventor's work had been, he had not produced a boat that had enough speed, endurance, and killing power to give it any practical usefulness. In his submarine efforts Fulton resembled a composer whose genius, though remarkable, could not enable him to create a concerto for an instrument that did not yet exist.

■ ■ ■

In 1848 Bavaria and other German kingdoms and principalities found themselves involved in a war that had the unlikely purpose of repelling aggression by Denmark, which was attempting to annex the adjacent duchies of Schleswig and Holstein. The German states fought off the Danes on land, but King Frederick VII's navy succeeded in clamping a tight blockade on Schleswig. After each side had won an important battle or two, the contending parties brought this vest-pocket war to an end by concluding an armistice and in July 1850 signing a peace treaty intended to reestablish the antebellum status quo.

The effectiveness of the Danish blockade had made a great impression on an obscure Bavarian soldier, an artillery corporal named Wilhelm Bauer, who in January 1850 resigned from the army and enlisted under the colors of the provisional government of Schleswig-Holstein. Although his own landlocked country lay hundreds of miles from any sea and therefore had few naval pretensions, Bauer had given himself the mission of breaking the Danish blockade, which still continued. Having quickly created the design of a submarine, the corporal found the Schleswig authorities receptive to his ideas and received a subsidy to support the building of a working model. Though this little copper-sheathed craft, about 28 inches long, powered by a clockwork mechanism, performed satisfactorily, the government treasury proved to have no money to support the building of an actual boat. But a public subscription produced the needed funds, and on December 1 the submarine Bauer called *Brandtaucher* (difficult to translate neatly, but "Fire Diver" comes close) slid down the ways of a shipyard at Kiel.

8

THE SUBMARINE

About 26.5 feet long, the *Brandtaucher* carried a crew of three and, unlike the model, drew its propulsive force not from clockwork but, like Bushnell's and Fulton's machines, from human power (two men operating a treadmill). To dive, the boat would take on water in a ballast tank, which a pump would empty when the operator wanted to surface. In one of the most important details, Bauer tried to solve the problem of adjusting the trim by means of a weight moving forward or backward along a track.

As soon as he moved out of the harbor on his first sea trial, he later noted, the Danish fleet began moving out, anchoring again farther from the shore. As a result, on February 1, 1851, Bauer created a historic first in submarine annals. Heading farther out than in the earlier trial, he took the *Brandtaucher* down, intending to go somewhat deeper than before. But apparently some of the plates became sprung, admitting water, and when the trim-adjusting weight slid forward the boat began a plunge all the way to the bottom, about 60 feet beneath the surface. Now Bauer displayed not only remarkable coolness but also, for a landsman, remarkable insight into this strictly maritime problem that had arisen. The boat had clearly stuck itself on the bottom and the crew had no hope of forcing a hatch open against the pressure of the water. The only answer, Bauer told his companions, was not to prevent any more water coming in but to allow it to continue. It was all, he said cheerfully, a matter of air pressure. When the pressure inside the hull equaled the pressure outside, they could open a hatch and rise to the surface in the bubble of air that remained. More than six hours later, events unfolded just as Bauer had foretold, and the three men survived, in history's first escape from a disabled submarine.

With the war having wound down, Bauer set out to peddle his creation elsewhere, beginning in his home country; the Bavarian authorities, however, having no coastline and no ports, displayed little interest in submarines, and the inventor began traveling across Europe. In England he received support from Prince Albert, the leading evangelist for science in high British circles. Recognizing the need for a genuinely effective propulsive system, and the fatal limitations of treadmills and hand cranks, Bauer began experimenting with an engine that would run on gas produced by the combustion of a mixture of sulfur, saltpeter, coal, and ammonia. Severely injured in the perhaps inevitable explosion that followed, Bauer then found himself out of favor with the Admiralty, and departed to try to sell his wares elsewhere. Like Robert Fulton, he looked for any buyers he could find.

In Russia, then fighting against Britain and France in the Crimean War—one of the most mysteriously pointless of the nineteenth-century European conflicts—Bauer received immediate support. By November 1855 a St. Petersburg shipyard had produced the *Seeteufel* ("Sea Devil"), which represented no technical advance; it ran on human power and employed the earlier sliding-weight device to adjust the trim. It made, according to Bauer's later account, 134 dives and it also foundered, creating the need for another escape via air bubble. It also served as history's first and perhaps last underwater stage; on September 6, 1856, in celebration of the first anniversary of the accession to the throne of Czar Alexander II, the *Sea Devil* dived beneath the waters of the harbor carrying with it four musicians of the Imperial Guard, whose rendition of the imperial hymn reached the ears of observers on the surface for several hundred feet in all directions. But aside from serving as the platform for this unique and impressive concert, the *Sea Devil* with its technical limitations had little real significance. For all his doggedness, Bauer had not succeeded in crafting the first U-boat.

During this same era, Spain produced two submarine dreamers who attempted to make the leap into functioning underwater reality. Narcisco Monturial, whose career is enveloped in the usual amount of legend that submarine pioneers attracted, found himself moved by the problems of coral fishers; a submersible craft, he thought, might be just what these hard-working men needed in their trade. Working with another engineer, he moved from this original concept to develop a submersible warship, the *Ictineo,* about 20 feet in length, which was launched in 1862. It apparently carried a cannon but had as its main weapon of attack the device Bushnell had pioneered: an auger to drill holes in the hull of an enemy vessel. But Monturial's contribution was to make the auger steam powered; how a steam engine would function if the boat dived beneath the surface, however, remains an interesting question. The craft had room for five or six crew members, who, like their counterparts in the earlier inventions, drove the boat by muscle power. In 1868 Monturial, in *Ictineo II,* apparently tried steam as the motive power—for operating on the surface—but in 1868, out of money, he had the boat broken up and the metal sold for scrap.

This was the period in which the C.S.S. *Hunley* attacked and sank the *Housatonic* off Charleston, but this feat, though unique in history to that time, did not involve any technical advance on the work of Robert Fulton. In many ways the encounter represented a clash of times and cultures—a human-powered craft like a Roman galley assaulting a steamship, winning a surprising victory over the symbol of modernity but then perishing itself.

Perhaps the most striking idea of the era came from a Dr. J. Lacomme, who in 1869 won the approval of the Emperor Napoleon III for a submarine cross-Channel train, to be powered by compressed air. If necessary, declared the inventor, the submarine could drop its wheels and rise from the track to the surface of the water. Alas for Dr. Lacomme, however, the emperor lost his throne before the submarine railroad could make any move off the drawing board.

The best-known submarine creator during the middle of the nineteenth century produced no tangible boat at all and made no attempt to do so. In 1870 Jules Verne, the prolific French novelist who founded modern technofiction, furnishing his tales with realistic descriptions of devices that would not exist for many years, gave ample evidence that he had been following the work of the submarine experimenters across Europe with his famous story, destined to enjoy perpetual popularity, *Twenty Thousand Leagues Under the Sea.* In a tribute to Robert Fulton, who, after all, had created his submersible craft in Paris, Verne named the submarine in his story *Nautilus.* (And if he had lived half a century or so longer—he died in 1905—he would have seen much of his incredible underwater vision come true.)

The idea of using steam power came to the fore in the 1880s in the work of an English clergyman, George Garrett, who equipped a submersible boat with a steam engine and retractable smokestack. The craft could thus move about on the surface, but of course the crew would have to put out the fire before diving, and then they would swelter in the boiler room. Garrett developed his ideas in several boats, in association with a Swedish engineer and arms merchant named Thorsten Nordenfelt.

Also during the 1880s, more important ideas came from the second and more significant of the Spanish submarine pioneers, the engineer Isaac Peral, a navy lieutenant who took an interesting step toward illustrating the possibilities of a true submarine by creating a craft deriving its motive power from a bank of the newly developed storage batteries; this boat could make 8 knots underwater. Not only did Peral move toward the use of a practicable if limited source of motive power, he also showed how the submarine could become a truly effective delivery system for an explosive charge, bridging the space between itself and the target, by demonstrating the effectiveness of an invention produced by an English engineer working in Austria. During most of the nineteenth century and in earlier times, as in David Bushnell's day, the term *torpedo* had applied to what is more generally known as a mine, an anchored or floating device designed to explode on contact with the hull of a ship. (These were the kinds of devices that caused Admiral David Farragut to deliver his famous Civil War command, "Damn the torpedoes.") Some warships had also made use of "spar torpedoes," explosives placed on the ends of long poles that were swung at enemy vessels, a variation on Robert Fulton's crack-the-whip idea.

But all that began to change in the 1860s. Taking up the idea of an Austrian naval officer for a self-propelled rather than static torpedo, Robert Whitehead, an English engineer who managed a factory in Fiume, developed it into the first "automobile" torpedo, a tube having a detonator on the front and powered by a compressed air engine that spun a propeller in the rear; it carried an 18-pound charge of dynamite, the potent explosive invented by the Swedish chemist and manufacturer Alfred Nobel at exactly this time. A hydrostatic valve that operated fins to maintain the proper depth controlled the running of the torpedo. Typically for a new invention, the weapon had flaws; it was unreliable, lacking accuracy and precision, but for all its infant imperfections it seemed likely to exert a revolutionary impact both on the design of ships and on naval tactics. "The Whitehead torpedo was all

right as far as the idea went," thought a young Prussian naval officer
and pioneer torpedo specialist, Alfred Tirpitz, and he and his subordinates set out to increase its reliability, producing models of their own.

In the most successful part of his whole demonstration before the
Spanish queen-regent, Peral, firing dummy automobile torpedoes,
scored three hits on a cruiser in three tries. The Spanish government,
however, gave this unorthodox display no encouragement and some
officials even seemed jealous of the inventor; certainly the bureaucracy
offered no response, though if Lieutenant Peral had lived into the
twentieth century he would have seen his government bestow his
name on his country's first commissioned submarine.

■ ■ ■

For all their appeal and charm, and for all their looking to the future,
the drawings, models, and devices produced by the submarine dreamers
through the centuries exerted no influence on great events. Many
problems were recognized, but nobody succeeded in producing a true,
functioning submarine—an underwater craft that had practical value.
Some of the approaches had begun to come close to the goal, in a way
analogous to the promise shown by steamboat experiments before
Robert Fulton created his synthesis and thus became crowned as the
inventor: They had demonstrated or at least had suggested possibilities.
Now, in the closing years of the nineteenth century, what Fulton had
done for surface boats in the opening years, but had been unable to do
for submersible craft, was about to happen. The submarine found its
Fulton; in fact, it found two of them.

THE DREAM REALIZED: HOLLAND AND LAKE

One day in May 1897 the editor of the *New York Evening Sun* dispatched a reporter to a shipyard in Elizabethport, New Jersey, to cover the launching of a strange new craft—a submarine. "This event," the reporter said many years later, "was regarded as of so little importance as to be almost disregarded by the other papers." Actually, however, the launching attracted a bit more attention than the *Sun's* reporter remembered. Showing some sense of the future, although hedging his bet, a writer in the *New York Times* described that submarine as "the little cigar-shaped vessel, owned by her inventor, which may or may not play an important part in the navies of the world in the years to come."

The inventor, John P. Holland, who had come to America from Ireland in 1873, had been drawn across the Atlantic in good part because he saw the United States as a promising place to develop his ideas and create a weapon that might be able to threaten the mighty Royal Navy. (The Americans had produced the submarine pioneer David Bushnell and in the recent Civil War had created the ironclad *Monitor* and also an interesting if useless submersible nicknamed the *Intelligent Whale*.) As a survivor of the famine that marked his childhood years, as well as of the cholera and smallpox epidemics that followed the great disaster, Holland brought with him to America no love of the English oppressor. Mild mannered and, unlike his two brothers, not a political activist, he nevertheless hoped to help break England's hold on Ireland through weakening the symbol and visible agency of that oppression, the Royal Navy.

On May 22, 1878, a large wagon pulled by sixteen horses was slowly backed up to the edge of the Passaic River in Paterson, New Jersey, and the watching crowd saw a work crew unload a curiously shaped object that to a later generation would have resembled, in profile, a World War I tank. The local people had created the rumor that "the professor," as they called John Holland, had devised a "wrecking boat" to destroy other ships—and, unlike many rumors, this one was perfectly sound. Within five years of his arrival in America, Holland had taken a great step forward in the world of the submarine; he had designed and built a boat that represented a move away from human motive power, the limiting feature that made the submarine appear to most observers as nothing much more than an interesting novelty, something increasingly anachronistic in a world that had enjoyed steam-powered travel on the surface for more than half a century. Taking advantage of a recent invention, Holland had fitted out his boat with four-horsepower "petroleum" engines.

Unfortunately, after the *Holland I* floated out into the river it began to sink, and it quickly disappeared. But the lines attached to it rendered recovery simple enough, and an easily repaired leak turned out to be the cause of the foundering; a few days later Holland presided over the boat's first test. Now a more serious problem occurred: The gasoline engines simply did not work. Feeling that he could not afford to accept failure, Holland attached a hose to a valve on the boiler of a steam launch and ran it to one of his engines, and with this stopgap rig he proceeded to maneuver the boat. In particular, he tested his method of submerging, by which, instead of simply flooding ballast tanks and settling in the water, the boat went down at an angle, directed by diving planes or fins in cooperation with ballast tanks. Though dissatisfied with the immediate results, he held to the principle and refined its application, as his work developed, moving the planes from amidships to the stern. On the other hand, however, he abandoned the idea of requiring the operator to affix any screws to the hull of an enemy ship for the detonation of a torpedo. As Ezra Lee had apparently discovered in New York harbor, operating a submarine made demands enough with no explosives involved; Holland observed succinctly, "One man could never manage it."

Having received the approval of his backers, Holland went on to produce a second and much larger submarine (31 feet long, with a displacement of 19 tons), which quickly acquired the nickname the *Fenian Ram* (because the inventor's financial support came from members of the Irish-nationalist Fenians). This boat, begun in May 1879, was built at an ironworks in Manhattan and launched two years later. The inventor designed it for a crew of three: (1) the operator, (2) the engineer, who had charge of the valves and gauges relating to the ballast tanks and the compressed air reservoirs, and (3) the gunner, who would load a projectile with a 100-pound charge into an 11-foot tube and then open a valve that would allow compressed air to rush into the tube. Despite the boat's nickname, Holland had not created it to serve as a ram; the gun would provide the offensive punch. (In test firings, in an almost eerie glimpse of the future seventy-five years off, the projectiles traveled underwater and then rose into the air, reached their apogee, and descended in a neat ballistic arc.) A greatly improved gasoline engine powered the *Ram,* which the inventor put through successful trials in the Hudson and later in New York Bay, diving more than 60 feet below the surface of the Narrows and once spooking a ferryboat captain who turned and fled for home, apparently believing that he had sighted a metal-sheathed form of the Loch Ness monster.

While engaged in adventures with the *Ram,* Holland supervised the building of a third submarine, a small (1-ton) replica of the boat that he could use for experiments. But trouble came when the Fenians who funded him began splitting into feuding factions. One night in November 1883 a group of dissidents appeared with a tug at the shipyard, waved a forged pass at the night watchman, and simply kidnapped the *Ram* and its smaller sister, which was tethered to it. Incompetent sailors, they allowed the baby *Ram* to be swamped and sunk in the bay. When they appeared at New Haven with the big boat, the harbormaster found them such a menace to navigation that he banned them from the water. Thus, abruptly, ended the easygoing, kindly Holland's association with his revolutionary backers; he simply washed his hands of the whole affair. The *Fenian Ram* never sailed again, a strange fate for a boat that did everything asked of it; more than any other, this streamlined marvel, designed with the porpoise contours Holland favored, came close to ranking as the first functioning submarine.

Now without backers and therefore without money, Holland needed a job. A navy officer who admired his work tried to arrange an appointment for the inventor as a navy draftsman, but the department moved so slowly that Holland felt that he had to accept an offer from Lieutenant Edmund Zalinski, a well-known ordnance expert who had his own gun company. Zalinski, an inventor in his own right, hoped to use a submarine to demonstrate the value of such boats as gun platforms. Holland produced for him a wooden boat, called the *Zalinski Boat*, that suffered fatal damage during the launch, and the project died with it.

By this time, in 1887, Holland, whose deep disgust at the failure of the Navy Department to pay attention to the submarine had led him to try to directly influence naval and public opinion, had written a tribute to the power of the submarine titled "Can New York Be Bombarded?" In fact, even though Holland felt that "the navy doesn't like submarines because there's no deck to strut on," the department was moving in its slow-footed way toward facing the submarine issue, an event that took place in 1888 with the announcement of a competition for the design of a "submarine torpedo boat." Though Holland of course took part, neither he nor any of his competitors—a group that included Thorsten Nordenfelt and George Garrett with a steam-powered vessel and another extremely interesting inventor, Professor J. H. L. Tuck, of San Francisco—reaped any rewards; the navy, though accepting Holland's design (no details of which are known today), did not make the arrangement official because Holland's designated builder would not guarantee to meet the set specifications.

Like Robert Fulton, Professor Tuck, who enjoyed the financial backing of a Broadway vaudeville producer and thus could employ a New York ironworks to build a submarine to his design, presented his work as a deterrent to war. "I call this boat the *Peacemaker*," he declared at a banquet, "because it will abolish war. No naval vessels will dare approach our shores once the power of this defensive weapon is realized." Like Holland, the professor believed that a submarine should be able to attain speed underwater as well as on the surface and favored a similar porpoise profile, though, unlike Holland, he held to the conventional wisdom of the day in submarine circles that a boat must submerge on a level keel. It was the source of power that made the *Peacemaker* unique: Tuck employed steam to drive the boat, but the steam came not from the combustion of oil or coal but from caustic soda; engineers of the time spoke of its "encaustic engine." It produced 14 horsepower.

When Tuck's boat made its first dive, on November 23, 1886, a remarkably intrepid *New York Herald* reporter went along, while three crowded excursion boats followed the "iron shark"up the Hudson. After an excursion that included being stuck underwater for a time that "seemed to have lasted about a week" but actually was fifteen minutes, the boat returned its passengers to the mother ship, which provided the setting for the congratulatory banquet at which Professor Tuck made his utopian pronouncement. Opposite the professor sat the designer of the Civil War *Monitor,* the eighty-six-year-old John Ericsson, whose deafness apparently kept him from hearing Tuck's lofty thoughts about the end of war. "Gentlemen," Ericsson responded with enthusiasm, "land wars are old-fashioned; future wars will be fought in the air and under the seas." Despite the small problem the *Peacemaker* had encountered, the *Herald* reporter came away enormously impressed by Tuck's achievement, and until the end of his days in the midtwentieth century this observer considered the professor the true inventor of the submarine. But in an audition for naval officers, the *Peacemaker,* for all its genuine merits, performed erratically, and its encaustic engine could not be considered a long-range answer to the central question of power.

In 1889 Holland met fresh disappointment at the hands of the government when, though reaffirmed as the competition winner, he saw the climate in Washington change with the departure of the Cleveland administration. The money set aside to support submarine experiments now went instead to surface ships, and Holland spent the years of the Harrison presidency supporting himself by designing dredging equipment, while sketching plans for aircraft and trying to push the development of a reliable and powerful gasoline engine that could power submarines.

These developments did not occur in a vacuum. Even though the Harrison administration had shown no interest in submarines, the wave of imperialism that had swept Europe in the preceding decade, sending the ships of the powers out to all corners of the earth to claim colonies or simply to establish coaling stations on scattered islands, had created in America a rising tide of official and general awareness of the country's almost total naval weakness. (At one point, in fact, even Chile, a country that had bought three ironclads, told an American admiral, in the words of one congressman, that "if he did not mind his own business, they would send him and his fleet to the bottom of the ocean.") As Holland had divined in the 1860s when assaying the might of the Royal Navy, a submarine vessel might serve as an equalizer, enabling the weak to stand up to the strong. So, too, thought influential Democrats—neither they nor the Republicans had any idea of building a huge battle fleet to rival Britain's. When the second Cleveland administration took office in March 1893, Holland's prospects immediately improved, although he still had to endure two years of procrastination, congressional suspicions, and Gilded Age Washington machinations before the company he and his new backers had established received a contract for $200,000 for the delivery of a submarine torpedo boat, as the 1888 announcement had called it. During one meeting in Washington, Holland had taken note of a pleasant young man named Simon Lake, who it seemed was his chief competitor. When he selected a shipyard to build his boat, which was to be called the *Plunger,* Holland abandoned the New York area and chose a Baltimore firm, the Columbian Iron Works, which already had a submarine contract; it was building Lake's experimental *Argonaut.*

During the previous decade Holland had developed, or at least moved a long way toward defining, a set of basic principles that for him would govern submarine design. As he had learned from his experience with *Holland I:* (1) A boat must have positive buoyancy, so that, left to itself, it would always rise to the surface; (2) it would submerge not by filling ballast tanks and settling in the water but by being driven downward, directed by the plates or fins fixed aft and powered by the engine; (3) it must have a fixed center of gravity below the boat, for stability; (4) it should have the hull lines of a porpoise; (5) it should have the ability to submerge quickly and should be highly maneuverable; and (6) it should be able to fire a missile of some kind. But as work proceeded on the *Plunger,* Holland found himself trapped by impossible navy requirements. He intended to solve the power dilemma by employing two sources: steam and electricity, surfaced and submerged. (Though he did not originate this idea, he most clearly envisioned its possibilities.) Thus, he could draw on storage batteries to drive the boat when it was underwater.

But specifications called for a boat capable of doing 15 knots on the surface. None of the gasoline engines Holland had worked with could produce the 1,000 to 1,500 horsepower necessary to reach such a speed; steam power offered the only option. Steam, indeed, had established itself as the world's standard source of energy; it had powered the factories, steamships, and railroads that transformed Europe and North America in the nineteenth century. But steam's need for flaming furnaces and bulky boilers militated against Holland's chances of meeting another requirement, which called for a boat capable of submerging in one minute. Even if the fire could be damped, the smokestack aperture blocked by its sliding panel, and the hatches secured in the permitted time, the crewmen unfortunate enough to find themselves sealed up in this steamy cylinder would quickly turn into lobsters. (On a test run at only two-thirds power, the temperature in the boiler room reached 137°.) Beyond that, even Holland's inventive genius simply could not overcome the essential fact that a steam plant did not belong in an underwater vessel. Holland experienced no more success than his predecessors had found in trying to reconcile this source of power with this unique function.

As navy technicians hung over Holland's shoulder, continually calling for revisions in his plans, "the outcome," said a later colleague of Holland's, became "a boat that departed far from the ideas over which Holland had labored. It was improved to such an extent that it failed." The navy representatives even insisted that the boat have two vertical screws: propellers that would be aimed upward to enable the submarine to submerge on an even keel, an idea completely at variance with Holland's principle of submerging by diving. The builders did finish the boat, but it did not live up to anybody's expectations or hopes, and like the author of a rejected manuscript (though gracefully) Holland returned the advance given the company by the navy. Next time, he declared, he would build his own boat to his own design, free of inter-ference from people who presumed to tell him what to do because they represented the source of the financing.

Thus came Holland's defining project, the *Holland VI*, laid down in 1896 and launched on May 17, 1897, as described in the New York newspapers. Just over 53 feet long and 10 feet wide at its greatest diam-eter, the boat displaced 63 tons on the surface and 74 submerged; it could dive to 75 feet. No longer did Holland have to struggle with adapting steam engines to the needs of the submarine, thanks to the kind of luck that all invention requires at one time or another. Drop-ping by Madison Square Garden to look at the displays in an exhibition of electrical equipment, he sighted a generator-and-engine combination designed to light a country home; the generator was driven by a new 45- to 50-horsepower Otto gasoline engine (named after the inventor of the internal combustion engine). "That is what I want for my boat!" Holland exclaimed, bought the engine on the spot, and had it hauled to the shipyard for installation on the submarine. The engine would give the boat a top speed on the surface of 8 knots, and a 75-horsepower electric motor would drive it at 5 knots when submerged. The boat would have a range of 1,000 miles on the surface; the batter-ies could produce 30 miles submerged on one charge but, owing to the new engine, they could be recharged; the engine could even recharge the battery while the boat was under way. For armament, Holland fit-ted the boat with an 18-inch torpedo tube. Overall, he had produced a remarkably sophisticated submarine that embodied all of his principles of design and performance, some of which were so advanced that they would not find acceptance for another half-century.

Bound to no deadline, Holland could play the perfectionist as he presided over the fitting out of his boat. But before the craft had the chance to show what it could do in trials, a piece of serious and im-mensely fateful bad luck intervened. One of the stock figures of mate-rial tragedy, the careless workman, entered the story, making his negative contribution as he finished his day's work by leaving one small valve open. During the night the *Holland VI* took on enough water to send it to the bottom of its slip, and when workers raised it the next day the inventor saw that the feared and expected result had indeed occurred:

Corrosion had corrupted the electrical system. To remove and repair it would call for major surgery, cutting into the hull of the boat itself, but a month of trying to dry it out by keeping stoves burning night and day produced no results. In desperation Holland and his associates sought help from the manufacturer of the dynamos, the Electro-Dynamic Company of Philadelphia, which promptly sent over Frank T. Cable, a young man who not only cleverly solved the problem but developed such an interest in the project that major consequences would follow, not only for Holland and his company but for the general future of the submarine.

Holland conducted tests of the boat during February and March 1898, and in the later phases he had at his right hand Frank Cable, who had agreed to serve the company as the permanent electrician. The timing of the official trials, which took place on March 27, could hardly have been better; within four days the United States would go to war with Spain. Theodore Roosevelt, the assistant secretary of the navy, told the secretary: "I think the Holland submarine boat should be purchased. Evidently she has in her great possibilities for harbor defense." This endorsement produced no magic results, however; instead, the inspectors suggested modifications, with more trials to follow. Here several factors came together. Frank Cable's talk about the *Holland* aroused the interest of another Philadelphian, Isaac Rice, a combination patent lawyer and business tycoon, who was president of the Electric Storage Battery Company, which controlled most of the battery market (and had supplied those used on the *Holland*). Rice agreed to help the cash-hungry Holland Company out of a tight corner by financing the required modifications.

While the seemingly endless ballet continued between Holland and the Navy Department, company officials, having found New York harbor too crowded to serve as a satisfactory site for trials, moved operations out to Peconic Bay, at the end of Long Island. One Sunday afternoon the *Holland* cruised around the bay, stopping at the old port of Sag Harbor, where a crowd rushed to take in the novel sight. A notable spectator, Clara Barton, founder of the American Red Cross, accepted an invitation to come aboard (and may have been treated to an underwater ride) and then lectured Holland for creating such a terrible weapon. The inventor, unruffled as usual, replied with an answer straight out of Robert Fulton and Professor Tuck: The very effectiveness of the submarine would serve to prevent war. (Later, however, he called the submarine a "sea-devil"; more lightheartedly, the *New York Herald* described it as a "steel fish with revolving tail.") At any rate, the seventy-seven-year-old Clara Barton ended the afternoon as the first woman known to have sailed in a submarine. Later in the season, two other important visitors, German naval officers, came to look the *Holland* over, with one of them receiving a submerged ride. This event caused a U.S. Navy officer, on hand as an official observer, to worry that the Germans might proceed to outdo the United States in what, in view of the navy's sluggishness during the past decade and more, could hardly be called the submarine race. A near tragedy also marked the summer, when crew members were overcome by fumes from a leak in the exhaust system; Holland responded to the problem, which always posed a threat, with the most effective technical countermeasure available at the time, the purchase of a cage and several white mice.

Isaac Rice proved to be far more than simply a source of funds for the Holland Company. An astute and aggressive operator in a national business climate that had been largely created by such types, he not only provided cash but took over the playing field, buying a boat-building firm, the Electric Launch Company, and combining it with Electro-Dynamic and with the Holland Company to create a new entity called the Electric Boat Company. Rice also showed himself an imaginative salesman and lobbyist when he took the *Holland* to Washington and showed it off to crowds, including congressmen and government officials lining the banks of the Potomac. One of the witnesses, Admiral George Dewey, the naval hero of the war with Spain, declared to a congressional committee that "if the [Spanish] had two of those things in Manila, I could not have held it with the squadron I had." (Holland had ideas of his own about participation in the Spanish-American War. In an imaginative piece of salesmanship, he had proposed to the secretary of the navy that he be allowed to take the *Holland* to Cuba, where it could attack and sink the Spanish squadron bottled up by U.S. warships in the harbor of Santiago. The Navy Department declined the offer.)

Finally, on April 4, 1900, the company offered the *Holland* to the navy for $150,000, with other boats to follow at $170,000. The authorities agreed to the terms, and six months later, on Columbus Day, the boat became the U.S.S. *Holland,* thereby becoming the first submarine commissioned in the United States Navy, but not the first in the service of any country. Fourteen years earlier the Greek government, always keeping an eye on the Turks, had bought a Nordenfelt steam-powered boat and the Turks had riposted by commissioning a British shipyard to build two boats to a Nordenfelt design; in 1888 the Russians had joined this game, but their purchase, the *Nordenfelt IV,* was wrecked off the coast of Denmark en route to Russia. Even the boats that entered service, however, proved to have no value; steam-powered, they quickly became filled with gases and vapors, and their lack of longitudinal stability caused them to buck up and down almost constantly. Another deficiency would have seriously limited the usefulness of one of these boats even if it had performed perfectly in every other respect: it could not take to sea until the reservoir was fully heated, a process that required three days.

Later, retrospectively, the *Holland* received the historic designation SS-1, marking it as the U.S. Navy's first commissioned submarine. It could also validly claim to be the world's first functional, operational, nonexperimental submarine. Four months after the navy took delivery, the *Holland* showed in a war game what a submarine could do. Surfacing close to the flagship of the enemy fleet, the boat signaled: "You're blown to atoms." Within three years the navy had bought seven more of these pioneering craft (actually modified and expanded *Holland*s, longer and fitted with more powerful, four-cylinder engines: *Adder, Grampus, Moccasin, Pike, Porpoise, Shark,* and a successor *Plunger* to the earlier failed boat), which were designated A-class boats after the first-named; their mission was harbor defense.

During the next fourteen years, as Electric Boat worked to improve its product, the navy, moving slowly, would buy twenty-four more submarines from the company. In 1905 Theodore Roosevelt, the true-believing big-navy apostle who had become president in 1901, gave the company an infusion of positive publicity, and exhibited his own unquestioned daring, by welcoming the *Plunger* to a cove near his house at Oyster Bay, Long Island, and then taking a two-hour plunge in her. This ride did not make TR the first head of state ever to go down in a submarine, however, and not even the first head of state to take such a plunge in three hundred years; President Émile Loubet of France had claimed that distinction in 1901.

In improving its products, Electric Boat devoted attention to increasing their size and speed, but at the same time a number of other features planned by Holland were met with disapproval by Frank Cable and by the firm's new chief designer and architect, a former navy lieutenant from Ohio named Lawrence Spear. Holland, who controlled neither the company nor his creations, had been removed as general manager and given the title of chief engineer. As a pioneer of servomechanisms and automatic controls, he erupted in fury when he saw that the more conservative Spear had removed devices for controlling steering and diving from an A-boat: "You might expect this from a young whippersnapper from the Navy. He has ruined my life's work!" Though much younger, Spear actually had a substantial background. A trained engineer, he had received a degree from the University of Glasgow as well as his engineering bachelor's from the Naval Academy, and also had served as superintendent of construction of the shipyard that built Admiral Dewey's flagship. A good part of the normally placid Holland's rage no doubt came from his frustration and awareness of his powerlessness: He had lost his own company (he owned only about half of one percent of the stock of the new Electric Boat combine). Rice and the other backers had brought in Spear as Holland's boss; they wanted a manager now, not an inventive genius.

This scene apparently took place in 1902, and in 1904, responding to the pressure forcing him out and literally to the approaching expiration of his contract, Holland, "demoted, isolated, and undervalued," became one more of history's underfunded and defeated idea men. Resigning from the firm, he declared his intention of once again building his own kind of boat to his own design. He soon found, however, that because all his patents had been sold to various European countries, few foreign corporations would deal with him. A Japanese builder, however, responded to Holland's idea for a submarine that would do 20 knots submerged, proceeded to buy the plans from him, and produced two boats under contract for his government (which had just ordered five A-class boats from Electric Boat). Otherwise, however, Holland had little luck; he was even sued by Electric Boat, which claimed the exclusive right to use the name "Holland" and also declared that Holland had agreed never to compete with the company. Electric Boat never produced any such document, however, and the courts ultimately dismissed the suits, but the cloud of litigation dampened the interest of potential backers. In 1907, with the financial panic of that year administering the coup de grâce, Holland took himself out of the submarine business. His once kindly and optimistic outlook now darkened by bitterness at the way his former associates had stripped him not only of his company but also of his standing in the world, he turned for solace to religion. Ever the inventor, however, he continued to develop ideas for aircraft and actually worked on building one in the barn behind his house on Long Island, out near the old test site of *Holland No. 6*.

■ ■ ■

As it attempted to sell its products to the U.S. Navy, the Electric Boat Company found itself facing a dogged competitor, the Lake Torpedo Boat Company, located not far away along Long Island Sound in Bridgeport, Connecticut. A native of New Jersey, the state to which fate had directed John Holland, Simon Lake, fifteen years younger than Holland, came from a family long established in the area; his grandfather had served in the state legislature and had founded Ocean City, and young Simon, a red-haired lad with a boisterous sense of humor, grew up in nearby Pleasantville. His father had invented a window shade roller, which he manufactured, and owned an iron foundry and machine shops; thus fortune had favored the son with the perfect background to nurture his genius, and after studying mechanical drawing at the Franklin Institute in Philadelphia he became a partner in his father's foundry.

By the age of twenty-three, having received patents for various nautical devices including a steering gear for ships, Lake had moved to Baltimore and set himself up in business to manufacture his inventions. He also found himself competing with John Holland, Professor

Tuck, and others in the U.S. Navy's frustrating rounds of submarine competitions; one of his problems, some said, was that he had not built a boat but merely submitted designs. But by 1894, still just twenty-eight, he had produced his first submarine, the little *Argonaut Junior,* which he made out of pine boards. He followed this experimental effort with the senior *Argonaut,* the boat that the builders in Baltimore worked on side by side with Holland's *Plunger;* it was 36 feet long and 9 feet across at its greatest diameter, and powered by a 30-horsepower gasoline engine.

A romantic who entered the submarine world because, he said, *"Twenty Thousand Leagues Under the Sea* inspired me," Lake saw these craft through Jules Verne's eyes as devices for exploration and for such commercial uses as searching for sunken treasures. He fitted his first models with wheels—a pair in the front and a third aft, for steering—so that they could run along the bottom of the ocean; together with the stubby appearance of the boats as compared with Holland's flowing designs, the wheels gave a Lake boat a quaint look somewhat reminiscent of an old-fashioned Gypsy caravan. The inventor also provided an airlock, which would enable treasure hunters, for example, to step outside in their diving suits and walk along the sea bottom. Unlike Holland, he did not dream of a boat that could emulate the grace of a fish underwater; he took as his model, it was said, the less glamorous crab.

Lake later summed up the technical virtues of the *Argonaut.* She was, he said, "the first submarine successfully to navigate over the bed of the ocean; she was also the first submarine to be fitted with internal combustion engines and, as rebuilt in 1898, she was the first submarine to be built as a combination submarine and surface vessel with a large reserve of buoyancy in the form of a heavy pressure-resisting inner hull surmounted by a buoyant outer hull of light-weight material and of shipshape form"—that is, she was designed for better performance on the surface than "the previous cigar-shaped submarines" (or, he might have put it, Holland's "dolphin-shaped" boats). The innovation of the double-hull concept would have fundamental importance in the evolution of the submarine.

To show what the *Argonaut* could do, however, Lake asked the authorities at Fort McHenry, the bastion of the republic given eternal fame by Francis Scott Key, to allow him to make an approach, unseen, to the minefields protecting the fort and sever some of the cables holding the mines. Whether he seriously expected to receive such permission was not recorded, but the bureaucrats had no trouble turning him down. Undeterred, he proceeded to sail into the minefield and succeeded in reaching its center without being detected. The *Argonaut,* however, did not compare for naval purposes to the *Holland,* which her inventor had never envisioned as anything except a warship, and in more or less due course the navy made the 1900 deal with Electric Boat.

Lake then came back with a new boat, the *Protector,* which was 65 feet long with a displacement of 130 tons (twice that of the *Holland*) and could carry torpedoes (three tubes); he also offered it to the navy. In its now established tradition of moving at a glacial pace when dealing with submarine inventors, the department could not make up its mind about the *Protector;* the Russian government had no such problem, however, and this sale marked Lake's entry into the world of international navies and competition for sales. It also involved a bit of intrigue. Since Russia was at war with Japan at the time and the United States was neutral, Lake arranged for the boat to be picked up in Long Island Sound and smuggled out of the country on the deck of a Russian collier. (Electric Boat engaged in a similar escapade with the Russians, involving the Holland-designed, Spear-modified *Fulton,* a sister of the A-boats; Electric Boat tagged the submarine with the cover name *Madame,* which pleased the buyers so much that they kept it. They also purchased licensing rights to build five more of the type, while Lake sold seven more boats to these welcome customers.)

Despite naval interest in his boats, Lake continued to think of them in much broader terms than as instruments of war. Working with the Russians, for example, he sought to perfect boats that could turn ice-bound northern ports into year-round ice-free ports. He also worked with the Arctic explorer Sir Hubert Wilkins on a project, incredibly daring for its day, of reaching the North Pole by submarine. To Lake's keen disappointment, however, Sir Hubert abandoned the trip on the eve of his scheduled departure (he would try again some twenty-five years later).

The rivalry between Electric Boat and Lake could at times turn into a white collar version of a scrap with brass knuckles, as happened in March 1908 when a congressman named Lilley accused Electric Boat of "lobbying," apparently a damning charge in itself, though what he meant, as he made plain, was that political contributions to the campaigns of both parties were helping the company make excessive profits off building submarines for the navy. In April, as Lilley continued to charge that Electric Boat used improper methods to influence legislation, expert students of handwriting and typing testified that the anonymous letters and documents the congressman had presented in making his charges had been written in the office of the Lake Torpedo Boat Company. The affair ended in nothing stronger than recriminations, and somehow, through it all, Simon Lake himself managed to remain out of the public eye and uninvolved.

Despite all his determined efforts, Lake would not succeed in selling a submarine to his own government until 1912. But his *Protector* nevertheless played an important role in the early history of the submarine, because it marked the beginning of a distinction the navy would later draw between what would be called "Holland-type boats" and "Lake-type boats"—between the plunging boats Holland created and the level-keel submerging principle favored by Lake. More concerned with the functioning of the boat on the surface and less with streamlining, Lake fitted his boats out with superstructures of the kind that later, adopted for Electric Boat submarines under Lawrence Spear's direction, gave these boats what became the standard profile of the submarine: a torpedo or a cigar hidden inside a yacht with a bridge.

■ ■ ■

Of the European maritime countries, France had made the earliest entry into the submarine arena. Believing that they could never rival their traditional British enemy on the surface of the sea, younger officers saw some years before 1900 that this new weapon might bring them an effective new way of commerce raiding—attacking enemy cargo vessels. With such interest behind it, the development of the sub-marine proceeded more rapidly in France than anywhere else. Gustave Zédé built a pioneering electrically powered boat in 1888, and in 1892 saw his contributions acknowledged with the building of a larger boat named after him.

Far more important than these electric boats and a steam-driven boat produced in 1899 was the creation in 1900 by Maxime Laubeuf of the *Aigrette*: A diesel engine supplied its motive power, and this de-velopment represented the wave of the future—at least, for the next half-century. Rudolf Diesel got his patent in 1892, but much experi-menting and adaptation were required to fit the engine into a subma-rine. Because his engine used the heat produced by air compression, rather than spark plugs, to produce the explosion in the cylinder, it did not require volatile gasoline with its vapors; in fact, Diesel originally intended for the engine to run on coal dust, as the cheapest imaginable fuel, but in the next year he produced an oil-burning version that be-came standard. Not only was the diesel engine much safer than previ-ous internal-combustion engines, it also worked with high efficiency; besides, it ran without requiring a great deal of attention from me-chanics. But before it could go to sea, it had to be reduced in bulk, a project that proceeded in the first decade of the new century and that was capped by the development of mechanical fuel injection in 1910. Until the engineers had completed the adaptation of the diesel engine to the demands of the submarine, the development of underwater craft had hung on the cusp. Now, however, the submarine could grow from a curiosity into a warship, and this new warship could perform effec-tively because of the development, during the same years, of the gyro-scopic compass and the periscope.

Electric Boat and Lake performed alike as true practitioners of free enterprise, both in finding customers wherever they could, with na-tionalistic feeling playing little part in their operations, and in getting government help whenever possible. They had found effective if dif-fering solutions to three vital aspects of the submarine: dive control, mobility, and power source—in particular Holland, with his diving planes—and the rest of the world took increasing notice of American progress in this new and puzzling realm. Looking across both the

Channel and the Atlantic, the *Times* declared on behalf of Britain that when "a particular weapon has found favour with a nation as shrewd as the Americans and as ingenious as the French, it behooves us not to neglect it ourselves."

British business had, in fact, already begun to act on this principle. Just a few days after the commissioning of the U.S.S. *Holland,* Vickers, the renowned shipbuilding and armament firm, had signed licensing agreements with Electric Boat to manufacture Holland submarines in England, and a Holland boat thus became the first submarine commissioned in the Royal Navy; by 1903 five had come into service. Though Electric Boat and Vickers remained allies and, in some senses, partners in world markets for many years, after 1903 the Admiralty produced its own designs, which were then executed by the Vickers Company.

In Germany Krupp's Germaniawerft at Kiel, freely borrowing Holland's designs, became both the chief designer and the chief builder of submarines. This was not at first the great plum it might seem to be; Krupp could fill this role because the state secretary of the navy, Admiral Alfred von Tirpitz, though a visionary in many ways, like many other officers at the time followed the guidance of intellectual influences that favored the battle fleet above all and thus had played a large part in thrusting Germany into a naval arms race with Great Britain. Earlier experiences with Nordenfelt boats had not given the German naval authorities any reason to have faith in the potential of the submarine, although Simon Lake later described an interesting response he had received in 1905, when he was attempting to acquire the German Navy as a customer. When the inventor submitted two models, one of a small boat intended for "defensive" use and the other of a larger "offensive" boat, Admiral von Tirpitz waved away the small model, declaring "I am more interested in your larger boat, for that is for offensive purposes." Tirpitz bought neither from Lake, however, and gave his navy funds only for a small research program, thus largely leaving the field to German private enterprise. Indeed, the Imperial Navy acquired *U-1* (*Unterseeboot-1* or *U-boot-1*), its first commissioned submarine (139 feet long, 238 tons' surfaced displacement), only in 1906.

■ ■ ■

Long forgotten in the swirl of developments and activities in the beginning years of the twentieth century was an engineer and inventor
from forty years earlier, during the Civil War—an American named Alstitt. He was the first person to see that the submarine (or, in his case,
the semisubmersible) did not have to limit itself to a single source of
power; indeed, Alstitt saw that it could prove feasible only if it drew on
two sources: one for the surface, one for underwater. This inventor accordingly turned to steam and electricity, but unfortunately his boat
suffered from flaws in design that rendered it unmanageable, and hence
it experienced no success at all. Inventors many decades later therefore
had to re-create Alstitt's insight, while he receded into such obscurity
that even his first name faded from the record.

THE GREAT WAR:
THE U-BOATS AND MR. WILSON

Westwards we cruised in our boats, throughout the months and years. There stood our enemy, England: there, where the sun sank daily into the sea: there, where the trade-routes lay, the very arteries of the British Empire: there was the wide and storm-tossed battlefield of the U-boats. Westwards we sailed—always westwards.

—Commander Ernst Hashagen, Imperial German Navy

PART II

4

"THOSE DAMNED ENGLANDERS"

On Sunday morning, June 28, 1914, in Sarajevo, Bosnia, a young Serb nationalist shot and killed the heir to the Austrian throne, the Archduke Franz Ferdinand. An officer of the imperial household had the grim task of bringing the news to the aged Emperor Franz Josef, whose life had been marked by a series of such personal tragedies: His brother had fallen before a Mexican firing squad, his son had committed suicide, and his wife had been fatally stabbed by an Italian anarchist. Now, told about this latest violent death, the old man was heard to say, "Horrible, horrible! No sorrow is spared me."

Franz Josef had chosen the right word. Many years earlier, the founding chancellor of the German Empire, Otto von Bismarck, had declared that "the next war will come out of some damned business in the Balkans." The Iron Chancellor had produced a deadly accurate forecast, but in his grave now for sixteen years, he could not have foreseen how horrible the next war would prove to be—a cataclysm far beyond his experience with nineteenth-century wars, a seemingly endless struggle characterized by ever expanding scope and by new methods, new weapons, and new kinds of issues. Draped with gold lace and hung with decorations, the helmeted and plumed sovereigns of the empires marched the Continent into the transformative struggle that would quickly earn the name the Great War and would quickly become the great modern tragedy of Europe.

. . .

The German Empire went to war in 1914 with a navy that in many respects could claim to be the best in the world. Unlike Britain's Royal Navy, which embodied a tradition hundreds of years old, the *Kaiserliche*

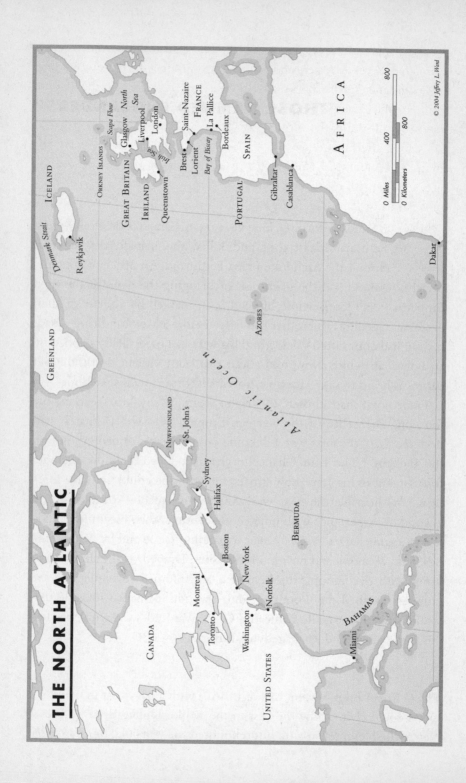

THE NORTH ATLANTIC

CANADA

UNITED STATES

Toronto
Montreal
Washington
New York
Norfolk
Boston
Halifax
Sydney
St. John's
NEWFOUNDLAND

Miami
BAHAMAS

BERMUDA

GREENLAND

ICELAND
Reykjavik
Denmark Strait

ORKNEY ISLANDS
Scapa Flow
Glasgow
Liverpool
London
Irish Sea
GREAT BRITAIN
IRELAND
Queenstown

North Sea

Brest
Lorient
Saint-Nazaire
FRANCE
La Pallice
Bordeaux
Bay of Biscay

SPAIN

PORTUGAL

Gibraltar
Casablanca

AFRICA

Dakar

AZORES

Atlantic Ocean

0 Miles   400   800
0 Kilometers   800

© 2004 Jeffrey L. Ward

Marine (Imperial Navy) had barely emerged from adolescence when war came. Yet its planners and builders had produced ships outstanding in design and remarkably sturdy in construction, and in efficiency of gunnery and quality of explosives the High Seas Fleet clearly exceeded its great rival across the North Sea. But the Germans faced a problem for which they could see no solution: They had built a fleet large enough to count as a major factor in all calculations of power, but not large enough to defeat the British fleet in a general engagement. In 1912 Winston Churchill, the First Lord of the Admiralty and thus the political head of the navy, had called it a "luxury" fleet in contrast to the Royal Navy, which Britain's worldwide commitments made "necessary."

The Kaiser and his admirals saw the picture differently, naturally enough, and they had a measure of logic on their side; they, too, had oceanic trade and colonial commitments. The *Risikoflotte* (risk fleet) was supposed to deter Britain from risking war with Germany. But if the German fleet was "big enough to constitute a provocation and a worry to the British, but not big enough to defeat the Royal Navy," what then might it do now that war had come?

Much of the reason for the navy's quality and power could be traced back to an event that had taken place seventeen years earlier, in June 1897, when the Kaiser brought an important new figure, Rear Admiral Alfred Tirpitz, into high German councils. The admiral had always shone as a naval rising star. In 1865, at the age of sixteen, he had become a cadet in the "modest aggregation of frigates known as the Prussian Navy," and four years later, as a newly minted lieutenant, he had been assigned to make himself thoroughly informed about a brand-new invention, Robert Whitehead's self-propelled torpedo; only two years later, at the age of twenty-two, Tirpitz became chief of the torpedo division of the navy ministry. "My rise," he once said, "is bound up with the development of the torpedo arm."

The invention of the torpedo created a new vulnerability for the vital parts of a ship that previously could be attacked only by ramming, and its range—almost half a mile, even at first—enabled a small vessel to exert potent destructive force against a much larger opponent. There followed, inevitably, the development of the torpedo boat, especially designed to exploit these new offensive possibilities, and Tirpitz, as a pioneer torpedo specialist, received command of the first German flotilla of these boats. Taking a handful of insignificant mosquito craft, "he discovered officers peculiarly adapted to the needs of torpedo tactics, and by dint of restless example and enthusiasm welded them into an aggregation of experts."

From that point Tirpitz's career moved upward, receiving a significant boost in 1887, when he became acquainted with the Kaiser, then Prince Wilhelm. In 1892, now on the throne, Wilhelm chose Tirpitz as chief of staff of the naval executive command at Kiel, on the Baltic Sea; the appointment followed an evening-long after-dinner conversation in which the admiral captivated the Kaiser with ambitious talk about the future development of the navy.

The Kaiser's choice of Tirpitz as secretary of state in the navy ministry in 1897 represented far more than a simple shuffle in the governmental bureaucracy. In the German Empire (the "Second Reich," established in 1871), no real dividing lines separated the political and the military spheres, nor did the Kaiser feel much pressure to heed the wishes of the Reichstag, which, though a parliamentary body in name, had little real power. As a government, the empire, an idiosyncratic creation designed by Bismarck to his own personal specifications, functioned as a blend of oligarchy and dictatorship. It resembled a car designed to be driven by only one person and, after its great chauffeur's dismissal in 1890, would never find anybody else who could operate it with much success. The selection of Tirpitz as professional head of the navy thus represented a significant political event, all the more so as it was one of several ministerial changes intended to make the imperial administration more effective. More important were Tirpitz's own character and personality. A man of intelligence and experience with a measure of political skill, he was described at the time by a fellow officer as "an honorable, energetic, independent, and ambitious character," one who, however, had "shown a tendency to look at matters one-sidedly, and devote his whole energies to the achievement of some particular end. . . ."

Neither Tirpitz nor anybody else could ever be another Bismarck, and the admiral, though a physically large man like the chancellor, certainly did not look the part: A bushy fork beard gave him the innocuous look of a fusty old Victorian squire, and he embellished the picture by speaking in a squeaky voice. But he nevertheless had notable similarities with Bismarck. The Iron Chancellor had been driven by one great obsession—the creation and preservation of a new German empire; the admiral likewise had developed a dominating dream—the creation of a great imperial German navy. He could now devote his whole energies to achieving this end.

Tirpitz would not have to pursue the dream unaided. Though even as a young officer he had displayed "his amazing capacity for initiative and his ability to impose his ideas on superior and inferior alike," he would not find himself having to employ these persuasive qualities to convert Kaiser Wilhelm to his ideas; the emperor already sang in the same choir. In good measure monarch and admiral had been drawn together because both had become disciples of a remarkable American naval officer, Alfred Thayer Mahan, a historian whose writings, beginning in 1890 with *The Influence of Sea Power upon History,* were winning him not only respect as a student of strategy but acclaim as a prophet. ("I am just now not reading but devouring Captain Mahan's book," the Kaiser wrote in a letter, "and am trying to learn it by heart.")

A prophet not without problems, Mahan did not derive his insights and principles from successful practical experience. As a skipper, he "grounded, collided, or otherwise embarrassed" every ship except one that he ever commanded; a shipmate said of Mahan that he "had one navigational obsession—fear of collision." Not only an incompetent seaman and a poor sailor, "he feared and hated the sea, its storms, its moods, its loneliness." Egotistical and contentious, he engaged in frequent battles over doctrine, and many of his fellow officers disliked him. Except for literally a few minutes at the beginning of the Civil War, he never heard a shot fired in anger, but he took a stern approach to war, arguing, for instance, that hospital ships at the scene of a battle should not be treated as neutral, and as a U.S. delegate to the Hague conference of 1899 he opposed arbitration and arms-limitation agreements.

The new wave of European expansion that had made Americans aware of their naval weakness and thus had led to the navy's sponsoring of submarine competitions had continued to cause concern in Congress, with some members fearing that even in the Caribbean the United States could do little to stop any European naval power that might want to pick up a few islands as outposts and bases. Imperialism flourished in the world, with Rudyard Kipling as its poet laureate, and Mahan, whose followers read him for his ideas and did not care how poorly he performed as a sailor, explained that Great Britain had achieved its dominance in the world because of the sea power it had developed in the preceding centuries. In fact, Mahan said, all of the great empires of the past had owed their success to control of the sea; not one to put a case lightly, he declared that only by control of the sea could a nation could grow healthy and strong and that a nation losing such power fell into decay.

Two years later, in *The Influence of Sea Power on the French Revolution and Empire, 1793–1812,* Mahan buttressed his argument by showing how the decline of the French Navy in that era had allowed the elimination of the French merchant marine from the seas and produced the loss of the French colonies; the lesson for the Americans, if the country did not develop a sizable merchant fleet, was obvious. Other books and articles followed, all eagerly read in navy ministries around the world, and in his writing and his teaching Mahan told American leaders that they must create a strong navy that could fight an enemy on its own terms, even across the ocean, and that the country must control the Caribbean to protect the great isthmian canal that was surely coming. "The Caribbean will be changed from a terminus, and place of local traffic . . . into one of the great highways of the world. Along this path a great commerce will travel, bringing the interests of the other great nations, the European nations, close along our shores, as they have never been before. With this it will not be so easy as heretofore to stand aloof from international complications." Failure to rise to the challenge as the Caribbean became a New World Mediterranean Sea, Mahan said in effect, would reduce the country to second-class status. All this proved a potent dose for many Americans, reared in a tradition of idyllic isolationism, but soon a prominent congressman, Champ Clark, calling for a reinvigorated Monroe Doctrine, issued a warning to the rest of the world to "keep their hands off the

Western Hemisphere on the penalty of being thrashed within an inch of their lives."

As Germany made its belated entrance into the colonial scramble, the leaders took as their guide Mahan's teaching that a merchant marine must be backed up by a battle fleet; Germany could not count for much in the world if its lifelines to its colonies had to exist on the sufferance of the British. Tirpitz set out to build a battleship navy, with widespread support from a coalition of interests public and private, and then, after 1905, had to begin reconstituting the fleet when the British redefined the battleship by introducing the "all-big-gun" *Dreadnought.*

What followed for the next decade were an arms race and a cold war with Britain. The British government established a new body, the Committee of Imperial Defence, to keep a high-level eye on events across the North Sea, and Parliament passed a stringent security bill, the Official Secrets Act; the government established a register of aliens living in Britain, and the Post Office began making wholesale interceptions of some categories of mail. The public during these years suffered from continual invasion jitters stirred up alike by serious articles and popular thrillers, the most famous of the latter being the outstanding novel *The Riddle of the Sands.* Whatever else the Kaiser and Admiral von Tirpitz (Wilhelm endowed him with the *von* in 1900) accomplished with their luxury fleet, they managed to infect the British with a chronic case of nerves.

Theodore Roosevelt's secretary of state, Elihu Root, declared that "the tendency is toward war, not now but in a few years' time." The prospect of a major war did not seem to cause great perturbation among the members of the European ruling classes; many, indeed, saw war as a much needed moral tonic that could purify society after decades of peace and softness. It was an age of giant Continental armies and burgeoning navies, great, costly bodies informed by a spirit of naiveté and innocence, commanded by men who had no useful precedents to serve them as guides.

As for the Americans who, like Elihu Root, observed this European scene, they took a coolly transatlantic view: They considered it none of their business.

The development of the submarine had for the first time given the world's navies the capacity to fight their enemies in three dimensions, but in the years leading up to 1914 nobody had seen very clearly how this new way of waging war might be employed. A British admiral sneered at submarines as "underhand, unfair, and damned un-English," and, showing little more enthusiasm for this new kind of craft, most other officers conceded only that it might serve as a coast defense watchdog or simply argued that it should take its place in the fleet just like all the other ships. Curiously, officers in all navies tended to ignore the most remarkable quality of the submarine, the trait that actually defined it: its ability to submerge at will and return to the surface. They had no notion of the submarine as a device that could extend sea war into a new dimension, unlike John Holland, Simon Lake, and their predecessors, for whom the underwater capability had served as the driving vision. But Holland was the dreamer and inventor, of course, not a practical operative or bureaucrat who had suddenly had this innovation thrust at him. No more than people in general did naval officers appreciate being forced to change their ways, and sometimes it was only necessity that could drive them to it.

■ ■ ■

From the moment the first patrol of Prussian Uhlans, brandishing their long lances, trotted into Luxembourg following the declarations of war between the great European powers at the beginning of August 1914, the task of the Allied armies was perfectly clear, even if the method to be employed was not: They were to defend France against the invading Germans. Allied naval commanders, on the other hand, did not have the benefit of such an unambiguous assignment. The French, essentially, would look after matters in the Mediterranean Sea, leaving the British with a vast field of action: the English Channel, the North Sea, and the Atlantic Ocean, north and south. But what ought the Royal Navy seek to accomplish? Overall, of course, it should seek to control the sea and the approaches to the islands, ensuring the uninterrupted flow of vital supplies to Britain; otherwise the island kingdom could not survive, much less wage war. Beyond that, the admirals did not know what they would try to do. The British had traditionally made

blockade their weapon, but a new factor had entered the equation. Although still untried, the submarine with the threat of its torpedoes
made the classic close blockade of enemy ports seem impossible; the
world would see no more close investment of ports, like the blockades
the Royal Navy had mounted in the American Revolution, the War of
1812, and the Napoleonic wars or those the North had very effectively
clamped on the South in the American Civil War. If Germany was to
be blockaded, a new method must be found.

The presence of the submarine affected other calculations as well.
During the years leading up to the war, German officers had drunk to
der Tag—"the day" the German fleet would confront the British in the
North Sea. Very well, thought many observers, let the Royal Navy give
them what they had asked for: Sail Britain's twenty-eight modern battleships into German waters and force the High Seas Fleet out of its harbors; fight the great battle, get it over with, and end the Kaiser's boasting
once and for all. But Admiral Sir John Jellicoe, who took command of
the Grand Fleet at the beginning of the war, quickly scotched this idea.
The Germans could sow their home waters with mines and they could
concentrate their submarines, with their deadly torpedoes, in this area
of the North Sea. Hence, if any fleet action was to occur, it should take
place not in German waters but across the North Sea, closer to Britain.

Jellicoe, a cautious and methodical commander, also offered another
caveat. He would exercise extreme restraint in pursuing the enemy
during such an engagement, he told his superiors at the Admiralty in
London, because what might appear to be an enemy withdrawal could
actually be simply a tactic to lure the British battle fleet into a nest of
U-boats. The admiral clearly felt that in expressing such passive ideas
he hardly measured up to the heroic image of Lord Nelson, the victor
of Trafalgar, who for a century had set the standard of command
against which no British admiral could escape being measured. "I feel
that such tactics, if not understood, may bring odium on me," Jellicoe
defensively explained to his superiors, who offered no opposing
thoughts but hastened to assure him that he enjoyed their "full confidence." (Taking no chances on becoming the victim of any future re-
visionism, the canny admiral forwarded the Admiralty's letter of
endorsement to his bank for deposit in the vault.)

The German naval high command likewise harbored no aspirants for heroic stature. Admiral Friedrich von Ingenohl, the commander in chief of the High Seas Fleet, lived in constant consciousness of the fact that he commanded the smaller fleet, although the Germans' qualitative superiority lessened the difference between the antagonists, perhaps more than anybody on either side realized. Already, merely by the British declaration of war, the High Seas Fleet had failed in its mission of deterrence: The *Risikoflotte* had not, after all, proved large enough to keep the British from running the great risk. "If we had made more progress with our fleet," Tirpitz self-servingly lamented, "England wouldn't have risked it."

Yet, in actual fact, the Germans had made remarkable progress with their fleet in a short span of years. But what should it do now? Even more cautious than Jellicoe, Admiral von Ingenohl reflected the fears of his master, Kaiser Wilhelm, to whom the light blue dreadnoughts— *Friedrich der Grosse, König, Kaiserin*, and their sisters—were precious as babies. His "darlings," he called them, and he insisted that they be kept safe in their nursery in the Jade Bay, even when the British moved in to establish the expected, traditional kind of close blockade of the coast.

Such a blockade, however, did not wear the fearsome aspect that would have marked it in an earlier war. Now, the Kaiser and the naval staff believed, submarines and torpedo boats would damage and sink enough British vessels to make a close blockade ineffective, without demanding the involvement of the big ships. Thus the German analysis exactly paralleled British thinking; why then did the Germans feel that their enemies would fail to draw the obvious conclusion and adopt an alternative strategy? The explanation perhaps lies in the profound German respect for the Royal Navy with its proud tradition of carrying the fight to the foe. As it was, the Germans placed their two U-boat flotillas, twenty-eight "overseas" boats in all, at the fortified island of Heligoland, where, with torpedo boats, they would form part of the advance warning and attack system. The battle fleet would await the arrival of the British behind its defenses (minefields, shore-mounted heavy guns), prepared to whittle away at the British fleet until, perhaps, it had achieved something approaching parity with the foe. Altogether, a general engagement between the two navies seemed most unlikely, either in 1914 or in the foreseeable future, even though the impatient Churchill declared in a speech that if the German fleet refused to come out and fight, "it would be dug out like rats from a hole." King George V grumped at such bombast as "hardly dignified for a Cabinet Minister," and naval officers found it annoying and embarrassing.

To his frustration and growing dismay, Tirpitz, now that war had come, found himself unable to affect events; although he had conceived and nourished the High Seas Fleet—the battleships might have been the Kaiser's darlings, but the entire fleet was Tirpitz's child—the Grand Admiral had nothing to command. Ingenohl led the fleet, and the naval staff (*Admiralstab*), under Admiral Hugo von Pohl, planned and directed operations under the direct gaze of the Kaiser; thus, for all the devotion he had poured into the fleet through the years, Tirpitz had failed to write himself into the war script. Both the High Seas Fleet and its creator seemed condemned to sit on the sidelines as the Great War began the destruction of classical Europe by shot and shell.

Then, four weeks after hostilities began, the British offered sudden evidence that the German admirals who expected a close blockade might after all be right, though because of the increased range of guns, no blockade could move in as close as in earlier days. On August 28 the Royal Navy mounted an operation off Heligoland, right on Germany's doorstep, with light British forces sweeping across the Bight of Heligoland from east to west and in a sharp action sinking three light cruisers while suffering relatively little damage.

Though only a minor operation, this display of Royal Navy aggressiveness won acclaim across Britain at a time when the Allied armies were continuing to fall back before the German advance in France. It so upset the Kaiser, who could turn hysterical even on a quiet day, that he tightened the strings still further on his darlings—an order that produced what amounted to a shouting match between Wilhelm and Tirpitz, which the admiral predictably lost. Among the British, "everybody cheered like mad," reported one of the commanders, and Churchill "fairly slobbered over me." But Commodore Roger Keyes, who had dreamed up the operation, told a fellow officer that "an absurd fuss was made over that small affair." If Keyes had possessed any way of knowing the reaction of Wilhelm II, however, he might well have allowed himself to express real satisfaction, because the sweep at Heligoland in reality had nothing to do with the mounting of a close blockade but, by Keyes's own account, had a psychological aim: to implant in German naval minds the thought that "when we go out those damned Englanders will fall on us and smash us."

Yet to be tried, aside from its employment in a few inconclusive cruises in the North Sea, was the new factor of marine warfare, the boat that could move in the third dimension, under the surface of the sea.

5

"THE DREADED LITTLE SUBMARINE"

On September 5 a 650-ton submarine of the Imperial German Navy, the *U-21*, commanded by Kapitänleutnant (Lieutenant) Otto Hersing, arrived off the Firth of Forth on a pioneering mission that called for her to invade the home base of the British battle cruiser force. In the middle of the afternoon, during a strong storm, Hersing sighted a target—not one of the big ships but, instead, a small cruiser, the 2,900-ton *Pathfinder*. An aristocratic officer who would become one of the most acclaimed of all U-boat commanders, Hersing fired one torpedo, which streaked straight to its target through the turbulent sea as if moving through calm waters. The deadly hit detonated the magazine of the cruiser, which quickly went down by the bow, taking most of her crew with her.

Thus came history's second sinking of a warship by a submersible craft, a little more than fifty years after the *Hunley*'s attack on the *Housatonic* but the first sinking ever by a submarine acting as a true undersea boat. This landmark event attracted little notice, however, because, for all the tragedy of her loss, the *Pathfinder* counted as only a minor target. That would not be the case, however, in another U-boat attack that would take place a little more than two weeks later.

■ ■ ■

"I could see their gray-black sides riding high over the water," remembered Kapitänleutnant Otto Weddigen, describing the tempting vision that presented itself to him in the early daylight hours of September 22 as his boat, the *U-9*, cruised some 18 miles northwest of the Hook of Holland. After sighting three British armored cruisers steering north-northeast at a sluggish 10 knots, Weddigen had the *U-9* running at periscope depth. What were the cruisers doing there? Could they form part of the screen of a battle fleet engaged in a major operation?

Weddigen had posed himself a logical question, but actually the cruisers were at sea on their own. At the outset of hostilities, the Admiralty had assigned these ships, designated the 7th Cruiser Squadron but known in the fleet by the nickname the "live-bait squadron," to North Sea duty as watchdogs, with orders to start their barking if the Germans attempted to approach the eastern English coast or the English Channel. In carrying out their patrolling duties, the cruisers, accompanied by destroyer flotillas, tended to sail methodically on their courses, like troops marching on a drill field. These coal burners were good-sized cruisers at 12,000 tons but carried a main battery of only two 9.2-inch guns; having come from an earlier era of ship design, they had now declined into obsolescence. The three (*Aboukir, Cressy,* and *Hogue*), together with a sister ship (the flagship, absent on September 22 along with the admiral), seemed likely, in the ironic humor of the Grand Fleet, to attract the attentions of modern German ships that could make quick work of them. The routine they followed did not help. Because they ravenously consumed coal at any speed much over 12 knots, they proceeded slowly, and since they had never seen a U-boat their admiral had early on decided to dispense with the evasive tactic called zigzagging, designed to make it difficult for a submarine to achieve a firing position. Certainly the navy had not intentionally spread the cruisers before the enemy as bait of any kind, but the admiral later offered the astonishing testimony that he did not know why the patrol had been formed and had received no instructions concerning it.

During the first weeks of the war Commodore Keyes had urgently told an Admiralty official that "the Germans must know [the cruisers] are about, and if they send out a suitable force, God help them." Ill fitted for their patrolling task, these three elderly ships (named after victorious battles in British history) were not bait at all, but because heavy weather had kept their destroyer flotillas in harbor, they lacked any protection against submarines. They were simply comatose sitting ducks, more vulnerable than ever, prey for any prowling opportunist.

Now Lieutenant Weddigen prepared to capitalize on this remarkable opportunity. Although playing the role of the marauder, his U-boat by all conventional warship standards ranked as an insignificant vessel: small, slow, and unarmored, with no defense against an attack, carrying a crew of just twenty-six. But her ability to submerge cloaked her in invulnerability, and inside her frail envelope she carried six torpedoes, with two tubes forward and two aft, enabling the skipper to shoot at target ships either ahead or astern. Even so, the state of the torpedo art in these beginning days of the submarine war did not guarantee Weddigen success. His missiles might fail to detonate or, even if perfectly aimed, might veer off course and bypass the target (characteristics, in fact, that to some degree would plague torpedoes for years to come). Besides, if a target ship made efforts to zigzag, a slow submarine would have further trouble in achieving a good firing position. But the admiral commanding the live-bait squadron had forsworn that newfangled tactic.

"When I first sighted them," said Weddigen, who had quickly realized that the three cruisers were all alone, "they were near enough for torpedo work, but I wanted to make my aim sure, so I went down and in on them." Submerging completely, the *U-9* moved into the center of the line-ahead but roughly triangular formation in which the British ships were sailing. "I soon reached what I regarded as a good shooting point," said Weddigen. "Then I loosed one of my torpedoes at the middle ship. I was then about twelve feet underwater and got the shot off in good shape, my men handling the boat as if she had been a skiff." Weddigen then ordered the *U-9* to periscope depth to check the result; he immediately saw that the coolness and professionalism of the crew in this pioneering effort had produced immediate success. "The shot had gone straight and true, striking the ship, which I later learned was the *Aboukir*, under one of her magazines, which in exploding helped the torpedo's work of destruction.

"There was a fountain of water, a burst of smoke, a flash of fire, and part of the cruiser rose in the air. Then I heard a roar and felt reverberations sent through the water by the detonation." Weddigen stayed at periscope depth long enough to note the bravery of the *Aboukir*'s crew, who "even with death staring them in the face kept to their posts, ready to handle their useless guns"—useless because the captain quickly took the U-boat down. But he had stayed on top long enough to take in a surprising sight. The other cruisers turned and began steaming "full speed to their dying sister, whose plight they could not understand."

When the *Aboukir's* skipper, Captain J. E. Drummond, who also commanded the squadron in the absence of the admiral, felt the explosion, he immediately ordered the *Cressy* and the *Hogue* to come to the aid of his stricken ship and of the hundreds of men who had gone into the water and were swimming or clinging to wreckage. Despite Weddigen's charitable thought that the British would not know what had caused the catastrophe, Drummond's action could only be considered ill judged: If the explosion had not come as the result of collision with a mine, then a torpedo had to have been the agent. But, of course, no ship of any size in any navy had ever been sunk or even damaged by a torpedo from a submarine.

To his credit, Drummond quickly realized that a torpedo had been the agent of destruction and he reversed his order to the *Cressy* and the *Hogue*. But, driven by "chivalrous simplicity," their commanders ignored him. Each cruiser stopped dead and lowered all its boats to pick up survivors. But now the *U-9* had maneuvered to put the *Hogue* between her and the wounded *Aboukir,* which was still above water. "As I reached my torpedo depth," said Weddigen, "I sent a second at the nearer of the oncoming vessels, which charge was for the *Hogue.*" Among the crew, "the spirit of the German navy was to be seen in its best form. With enthusiasm every man held himself in check and gave attention to the work in hand. The attack on the *Hogue* went true," the torpedo slamming into the cruiser amidships just as the *Aboukir* turned over and slid beneath the water. Within ten minutes the *Hogue* followed her.

"By this time," said Weddigen, "the third cruiser knew, of course, that the enemy was upon her"; indeed, the captain of the *Cressy* already knew it, but, in this new kind of situation, he had let his humanitarian impulses control his conduct. The *Cressy* "loosed her torpedo defense batteries of both starboard and port," Weddigen noted, "and stood her ground as if more anxious to help the many sailors who were in the water than to save herself." Coming to the surface for a better look before laying his course for the *Cressy,* Weddigen saw "how wildly the fire was being sent from the ship. Small wonder that was when they did not know where to shoot, although one shot went unpleasantly near us." Striking once again, the *U-9* fatally wounded the British cruiser, which "began sinking by the head. Then she careened far over, but all the while her men stayed at the guns looking for their invisible foe. They were brave and true to their country's sea traditions." After a boiler explosion the *Cressy* turned turtle and "with her keel uppermost she floated until the air got out from under her and then she sank with a loud sound, as if from a creature in pain."

Having no desire to encounter any British destroyer patrols, Weddigen did not linger on the scene but set his course for home. In less than two hours' time, at the touch of a few buttons, twenty-six men in a craft of only a few hundred tons had sent 36,000 tons of warships to the bottom of the sea, and with them had gone sixty-two officers and 1,397 men. Captain Robert Johnson of the *Cressy* was among them.

A gust of reaction to this news swept through Britain. It seemed inconceivable that so great a loss of life could have been caused by a single tiny craft, and, indeed, the first reports from survivors told a different and falsely specific story, declaring that as many as five U-boats had taken part in the attack and that two of them had been sunk. It likewise came as a great shock to the public that such sizable vessels could so easily fall prey to submarines, however many might have taken part in the attack. "The loss of three armored cruisers is a disaster the meaning of which it would be foolish to minimize," wrote the naval correspondent of the *Daily Chronicle.* "The vessels were not new, they were even obsolescent, but they were still valuable." He added a potent point: "Wherever the disaster took place, the danger was not foreseen." The naval expert of the *Daily News* conceded that "it would be idle to deny that the exploit reflects the greatest credit on the German submarine service."

Amid the shock of this stunning tragedy, the British public experienced a brief countervailing surge of pride when survivors began landing at English ports. Albert Dougherty, the chief gunner of the

Cressy, told interviewers an exciting story. After the torpedoing of the *Aboukir* and the *Hogue,* he said, "we got closer to both ships to save as many of their men as we could, and the brave fellows calmly awaited our approach." Then someone nearby cried out: "Look out, sir, there's a submarine on our port beam!" Dougherty, by his detailed account, swung into immediate action. "She was about 400 yards away. Only her periscope showed above the waves. I took careful aim at her with a twelve-pound shot. It went over her by about two yards, and that gave me the range." Firing again, said Dougherty, "I hit the periscope and she disappeared. Up she came again, and this time part of her conning tower was visible, so I fired my third shot and smashed in the top of the conning tower. The men standing by shouted, 'She's hit, sir!' and then they let out a great cheer as the submarine sank."

Chief Gunner Dougherty embellished this remarkable story by describing how he and his crew had also shot at a trawler "which was 1,000 yards away and evidently a German boat in disguise, directing operations," and next had turned their fire on a second attacking submarine. Then, as the *Cressy* began to turn over, Dougherty said— speaking with the elevated diction that would soon become a casualty of the war, as the great struggle began to lose its heroic trappings and reveal itself as a mass brute collision of forces—the men had "acted like British sailors, and those who died died as a Briton should." Captain Johnson, who, according to Dougherty, was "loved by all his men," had performed on the same verbal level, telling the crew "in a steady voice" to "keep cool, my lads, keep cool."

Reaffirming a general observation, the gunner declared that altogether he "personally observed five submarines, and although the guns pegged at them, only one was hit as far as we know." The impression among survivors seemed to be that at least "two of the German submarines" accompanied the three cruisers to the bottom of the sea. This idea gained logical support from the undisputed fact that nobody claimed to have seen more than one submarine leaving the scene.

The press, the public, and the participants themselves at first met this tragedy in the North Sea with a strong element of denial added to the kind of exaggeration embodied in Dougherty's vivid report. Coming just a little more than two years after the most famous prewar maritime tragedy, the sinking of the *Titanic* (which, indeed, would become the most famous maritime event of all time and had been commemorated in a memorial dedicated in July, only a few days before the war began), the attack on the three cruisers produced a comparable loss of life. One frail submarine simply could not have brought about such appalling results, and therefore the mythical swarming U-boat pack came into being; eyewitnesses not only swore to its existence but even described having sunk one of its members. The language, like Dougherty's, immediately took on the lofty tone that marked narratives of the last hours of the *Titanic,* which in reality produced its great loss of life largely because of the incompetence and indecisiveness of its captain rather than to anyone's misguided faith in a myth of unsinkability but which quickly became a ship of legend whose captain had indeed gone down with it, dying—as was said in so many words—as a Briton should.

The mysterious "Dutch" trawler mentioned by Dougherty came into the story perhaps inevitably, because "trawler mania," as a new phenomenon would become known, spread the belief that fishing boats in the North Sea were actually serving as scouts and intelligence posts for the German navy, keeping in touch with home bases by wireless and carrier pigeons; this idea represented a continuation of the prewar invasion jitters. Land-based spies also constituted a danger, said the *Times*, which demanded that the government "institute a far more rigorous search for suspicious persons dwelling within fifty miles of the coast. We are by no means satisfied that sufficient precautions have been taken in this respect."

Spies, trawlers, a pack of submarines—all these formidable elements, and bad luck as well, appeared to have combined to create the tragedy, which, however, the navy seemed to have confronted with the kind of spirit the inspirational poet Sir Henry Newbolt had celebrated for many years; the lost sailors, all would have agreed, fully deserved honor "as long as waves shall break, To Nelson's peerless name." They had lived up to the voice of Newbolt's oft-quoted schoolboy: "Play up! play up! and play the game!" In the midst of all the racket produced by gunfire, boiler explosions, and general confusion, the captain of the *Cressy,* remarkably, was supposed to have reached his "lads" throughout the ship with the quiet admonition to "keep cool."

Quick study of the historical record showed that the number of deaths put the destruction of the three cruisers among the greatest naval tragedies of all time in British waters. The toll far exceeded that exacted in the Royal Navy's greatest victory, at Trafalgar in 1805, when the British lost 449 men, including, however, Lord Nelson himself.

Despite all the praise of heroism, all the words of comfort, and all the denial, some critics besides the naval expert of the *Chronicle* never-theless felt that the Royal Navy might not be completely blameless: Perhaps somebody, some identifiable person, had miscalculated, blun-dered, misused his authority, even deepened the tragic results of the attack. The critics did not have to look far to find their man. In a mar-velous piece of post hoc reasoning, Winston Churchill's instanta-neously notorious "digging out the rats" declaration now drew blame as a provocation. Since the attack on the cruisers immediately followed the speech, critics said that the Germans had mounted it as a direct re-sponse to the First Lord's remarks, unlikely as the Germans were to re-quire such a stimulus to action. Churchill, however, had played no part in putting the live-bait squadron in harm's way; that had been the do-ing of the professional sailors, not of the restless civilian head of the department.

Much more to the point, the Admiralty moved quickly to acknowl-edge the arrival of the powerful new factor in sea warfare. Within four days of the disaster, rules had appeared laying down procedures to meet the changed conditions. In publishing the reports of the surviving se-nior officers of the cruisers, the Admiralty commented that modern naval war was presenting "so many new and strange situations" that an error of judgment was pardonable; but the fact was that "the natural promptings of humanity" on the part of the *Cressy* and the *Hogue* had led to several losses that would have been avoided by a strict adherence to military considerations; a little less perceptively, with a slap of the whitewash brush, the admirals observed that the sinking of the *Aboukir* was "an ordinary hazard of patrolling duty." In any case, in future situ-ations involving enemy attack, military concerns must take precedence over saving lives; the ethics of the battlefield must govern the conduct of captains, with disabled ships being left to look after themselves. The war was still young, of course, and few people anywhere yet knew how to think and talk about it. But an admiral's flag lieutenant, for one, took a clear and unromantic view: "One ship was sunk by a submarine and the other stupid ships went to her assistance, simply asking to be sunk too."

Weddigen's triumph dominated the Berlin September 23 morning papers, with the German authorities quickly assuring the world that the three sinkings were the work not of a pack but of a single submarine. The press proudly gave the world details of the *U-9:* built in 1910 at Danzig, she was of 300 tons, and her armament consisted of three 18-inch torpedo tubes and two 1-pounder guns; she did 8 knots submerged and 13 on the surface—a tiny vessel, indeed, to have produced such damage. (Actually, the announced figure understated her displacement, which was about 500 tons; also, she had four torpedo tubes, not three.) This spectacular feat seemed to everybody to proclaim a new naval era. According to reports, German sailors in harbor, chafing at their forced inaction, received the news with particular pleasure; now they had something naval to cheer about. Kaiser Wilhelm's jubilation put him, it was said, in seventh heaven. In October, Weddigen would receive Germany's highest military decoration, the Pour le Mérite. (It amounted almost to a wedding present, since the skipper had been married just before leaving on the patrol that took him to the fateful encounter with the live-bait squadron.)

Talking with an American official in Berlin, the captain of the *U-9* made the surprising statement that, after torpedoing the first two cruisers, he had almost spared the *Cressy,* feeling great reluctance to send to the bottom the ship that could save the men from the other cruisers who were struggling in the water. He was about to turn away from the periscope and give the order to depart the scene when his first officer spoke up with a stiff reminder: "You know we have four navies fighting us." Nodding his acceptance of this point, Weddigen then returned to the periscope to give the order that finished the job.

"What wonder that men the world over began to predict the abandonment even of the dreadnoughts," commented a writer of the time, "for all their weight of armor on their sides will avail them not a whit against attack from below. As the ironclad sides of the *Merrimac* and the revolving turret of the little *Monitor* relegated to the scrapheap the 'wooden walls of England,' so the submarine, and its scarcely less sinister coadjutor, the airship, may put an end to the $12,000,000 floating forts of steel which the Powers have been building." The ranks of the forecasters shocked by the sinking of the three cruisers included the U.S. secretary of the navy, Josephus Daniels, who said, ruefully, that the U.S. government "like many other governments" had acted on the belief that "the most powerful sea fighters would be the huge dreadnoughts. But we are now learning from the war in Europe that the weapon of national defense on the sea in the future probably will be the dreaded little submarine." No comment could be forthcoming from John P. Holland. Just a little more than five weeks before Otto Weddigen gave the world his dramatic demonstration of the power of the submarine, the inventor, who had foreseen it all, had died at his home in Newark.

Despite the talk of airships, in the 1914 war neither the airplane nor the lumbering zeppelin would play an important naval role. But the submarine would take on central significance in determining the destiny of the nations at war. Yet this profound development would not come in the way everyone expected after the tragedy that struck the *Aboukir,* the *Cressy,* and the *Hogue.*

6

BLOCKADES FOR A NEW WAR

Some of the smallest events in history have cast the longest shadows. One such event in the Great War occurred just about a month after the sinking of the three British cruisers in the North Sea. At noon on Sunday, October 18, a small British steamer, the *Glitra*, departed from Grangemouth on the Firth of Forth, bound for Stavanger on the southern Norwegian coast with a load of coal and coke, oil, and iron plate. At half-past twelve on Tuesday afternoon the *Glitra*, having almost completed its trip, suddenly saw a U-boat that "popped out of the water to the starboard and stopped us." The submarine, the *U-17*, commanded by Lieutenant Feldkirchner, dispatched a boat with five men who, with revolvers drawn, came aboard and ordered the Red Ensign, the British merchant flag, hauled down— "threatening to shoot me," said the captain of the *Glitra*, "if I did not obey." When the flag had been lowered, a German officer took it from the captain's hands, threw it on the deck, and trampled on it, topping off this little ceremony, some said, with a mouthful of spit. Except for inflicting this indignity on the ship and its crew and their flag, and imposing a ten-minute limit for getting off, Feldkirchner fastidiously observed the international rules of engagement, which required that the passengers and crew of an intercepted ship be conducted to a "place of reasonable safety"—rules, supposed to guide the conduct of war at sea, that the nations had established for a world of surface ships. Making sure that all the crew were safe in the two lifeboats, which were towed some 500 yards away, Feldkirchner ordered the seacocks opened; the rear of the ship began to sink and, said her poor captain, "the *Glitra* disappeared quietly beneath the waves"; the German officers ordered the men in the lifeboats to row to shore, some ten miles distant. With a displacement of 866 tons, the *Glitra* was tiny—only about 300 tons more than the *U-17*—and unarmed; she had made an easy victim for the attacker. The most remarkable aspect of this fateful incident, history's first sinking of a merchant ship by a submarine, was that nobody had seized such an opportunity until the war had gone into its third month.

Just a week after the sinking of the *Glitra* came another first for the historical record. In the Strait of Dover the *U-24*, commanded by Lieutenant Schneider, without warning fired a torpedo at an unarmed merchant ship, the French steamer *Amiral Gentaume*. The target vessel, bound from the Pas de Calais to Havre and crammed to absolute capacity with 2,500 refugees who had fled the German invasion of Belgium, did not sink, but some forty of the passengers were lost. These unplanned attacks suggested that something new, a force not yet defined, had come to war on the sea.

At the outbreak of the war, however, those on both sides responsible for submarines focused on the possible uses of these boats not as commerce raiders but as warships to be put into some kind of action against other warships, though everybody—Allied and German—had only limited ideas of what these uses might prove to be. Cramped, smelly machines that crammed remarkable and unreliable complexity into their small envelopes, submarines should serve as scouts and otherwise support the main fleet, everybody agreed, but probably would prove useful only in narrow waters close to their home bases; their limited range and seaworthiness would rule out any role on the open ocean.

To begin with, the British and the Germans dispatched a few submarines across the North Sea on cross-checking missions: The British needed to make sure that the High Seas Fleet stayed in harbor, but the Germans had the more elaborate purpose of tracing the movements of the Grand Fleet, which operated from Rosyth on the Firth of Forth and Scapa Flow, in the Orkney Islands north of the Scottish mainland. One German objective was to discover whether the Royal Navy had established a picket line across the North Sea to ensure that, if units of the High Seas Fleet did emerge from their bases, they would still be bottled up in the North Sea. The U-boats had no success on this mission; if there was a trip wire line in northern waters, they could not find it.

But when it became clear that the British would not come thundering across the North Sea to dig them out of their well-protected holes, the Germans decided to seek other employment for their U-boat flotillas. Thus began the series of sweeps and patrols that led on September 5 to the sinking of the light cruiser *Pathfinder* by the *U-21* and a little more than two weeks later to Kapitänleutnant Weddigen's "exploit without parallel," as the press accurately characterized the triple sinking. Weddigen's feat made Admiral Jellicoe an immediate and confirmed believer in the power of the single U-boat, even though the losses involved older ships rather than elements of the fleet's first-line strength. (So great had Weddigen's reputation become that, after the sinking of the *Glitra,* he had to publicly refute the widespread story that he had done it with his *U-9.*)

The British had made their first submarine sinking of an enemy warship (and so avenged the *Pathfinder*) on the morning of September 13. During the previous night, Lieutenant Commander Max Horton, a brusque and aggressive young officer who enjoyed operating on his own initiative and was one of several commanders assigned to watch the High Seas Fleet, had taken his submarine, the *E-9,* into Heligoland Bight, where she spent the night sitting on the bottom, 120 feet down. Boats of the new and potent boat E-class, the first British oceangoing submarines, had a range of 2,600 miles or more; displacing 667 tons, they carried five torpedo tubes and a 12-pounder gun. At 6:30 the next morning, Horton brought the *E-9* up, saw that the day was misty, with a heavy rain, and retired for a time, returning at 7:15 to see Heligoland 5 miles off on his port bow, but closer, only about 2 miles away, he sighted a German light cruiser just moving out of a patch of fog. In twelve minutes, operating at periscope depth, he had taken position abeam of the enemy ship, some 600 yards off. He fired both bow torpedoes, noted one loud explosion, and immediately dived; the *E-9* spent the rest of the day dodging German destroyers, having briefly surfaced to note that the cruiser had disappeared. When the *E-9* returned to Harwich two days later, she did not enter the harbor anonymously. The Admiralty had issued an official announcement of this first-blood British sinking, and the crews of the warships in the harbor greeted Horton and his crew with loud cheers. Horton's sinking of the German cruiser, the *Hela,* represented the first success in a series of successes for this officer that would last the bulk of a lifetime.

▪ ▪ ▪

What worried Sir John Jellicoe more than submarine kills of older warships were sightings of periscopes in northern waters, in areas far beyond the presumed range of the U-boats. As the German submarines began to take on a mystique of ubiquity, imagined periscope sightings joined real contacts. On September 1, at its base inside the misty ring of islands that framed Scapa Flow, the Grand Fleet found itself engaged in the "First Battle of Scapa," when gunfire erupted across the harbor as the ships of the fleet fired at a ripple on the surface that later opinion declared to have been nothing more than one of the local seals enjoying a swim. On October 16 sightings of periscopes led to the equally bloodless "Second Battle of Scapa."

Deeply concerned, Jellicoe responded to each of the alarums at Scapa by ordering the fleet out of its base and around the top of Scotland, on the second occasion dispatching part of it all the way across the North Channel to Lough Swilly on the northern coast of Ireland. These moves represented a profoundly unsatisfactory answer to the U-boat problem; they put the big British ships hundreds of miles and many hours of steaming away from the arena of action, the North Sea. Thus it seemed to many that a handful of little U-boats might change the strategic proportions of power in the North Sea, because the restless high-speed steaming to which Jellicoe subjected the battleships created mechanical problems that at various times put several dreadnoughts out of action. "We are gradually being pushed out of the North Sea, and off our own particular perch," wrote Vice Admiral Sir David Beatty, the flamboyant commander of the battle cruiser force, in a private letter to Churchill.

The picture became even more urgent on November 23, when the *U-18* demonstrated the vulnerability of Scapa by penetrating Hoxa Sound, the passageway into the anchorage, although after being rammed it managed to limp only a few miles away before scuttling itself. Earlier, on September 25, following Weddigen's triumph, the gloomy and frustrated Admiral von Tirpitz had cheered up enough to applaud "the submarine successes" and to note, "Thank God we have more submarines for offensive purposes than England." But, having gone to war without plans for mounting any kind of underwater offensive, the Germans in reality had available only a handful of U-boats, which, together with newer submarines coming along to join the flotillas, would serve purposes the old admiral had never contemplated. The sinkings of cruisers and other warships in the autumn of 1914 made the headlines, dramatizing the arrival of the submarine as a powerful factor in war, but it was the fate of the tiny merchantman *Glitra* that showed what the future would hold for underwater vessels as the Great War unfolded.

The emerging central point was that, for all the enterprise and daring its commanders had shown the world, the U-boat had sharp limitations as a warship in a struggle against Britain. However inconvenient and even demeaning might have been Admiral Jellicoe's removal of the Grand Fleet from exposure at Scapa Flow, it nevertheless exerted no essential effect on the national life of Great Britain. If the Germans should decide to attack the island from across the North Sea, the admiral could bring back the entire gigantic array and turn it loose on the ships of the invaders. But when he chose to move his pieces off the board, then they would be safe from attack. Commercial shipping, on the other hand, presented quite a different picture. No strategic need and no problem of vulnerability could allow the authorities to remove merchantmen from the sea lanes for weeks and months at a time: Shipping constituted the bloodstream of Britain. The cargo ships and the tankers could exercise some choice of routes and some discretion with respect to timing, but these vital vessels, by the very definition of the sentence, could not avoid going in harm's way, into narrow waters where the U-boats could get at them. For the Germans the question therefore had to become, not what were they going to do, but how were they going to try to do it?

Now that submarines had gone to war in earnest for the first time, they found no tradition to guide them and no context specifically outlined for them in which to function. Commerce raiding presented particularly challenging questions. According to what appeared to be the general presumption, if submarines engaged in commerce raiding they must operate under rules, drawn up for surface vessels, that European naval powers had begun to formulate in the middle of the nineteenth century. At that time, the great growth of industrialism and the spread of liberal thought led the powers to make "a positive and vigorous attempt to curb the impact of war upon society," a movement whose immediate stimulus came from the pointless suffering that characterized the Crimean War, a conflict the mention of which has ever since brought to mind images of political obstinacy and spectacular military incompetence. By confining the fighting to the armed forces, discouraging wars of attrition, and localizing the fighting, the limitations that were adopted brought about the desired practical effects but also produced unexpected and ironic results, making wars frequent if short and favoring aggressors. (Bismarck took Prussia into three wars in just six years.) Hence, as a group of scholars noted, a bit acidly, the limitations proved "on the whole acceptable to military men as well as to liberals," and they enjoyed a fair measure of success.

Naval operations, in particular, seemed appropriate candidates for rules and limitations, because they frequently involved violations of the rights of neutral countries, as the fiery disputes between the United States and Great Britain had demonstrated in 1812 when they turned into war. In 1856, at the peace conference that followed the Crimean War, the powers in attendance produced the Declaration of Paris, which established a framework of rules for the conduct of operations involving warships and merchant vessels. No longer would national governments commission and support privateers (officially sponsored pirates), who traditionally had created many a controversy on the high seas. All enemy cargo carried in a neutral ship, except contraband of war, was exempt from seizure ("the flag covers the goods," as Mahan later put it) as were neutral goods, except contraband, carried in an enemy ship. Blockades, which in the past had caused great economic dislocation and hardship throughout the Continent, received precise discussion: To be acknowledged as legal, a blockade could not simply be declared but must be effective, actually sealing off the blockaded coast. Referring to an old English practice, Mahan observed that "there will be no more paper blockades"; a blockade demonstrates that it is "efficient" by constituting a "manifest danger to a vessel seeking to enter or leave the port." Thus a blockading force must form its cordon close to the invested port.

Through the ensuing decades, as weapons and war evolved, representatives of naval powers debated numerous questions (for instance, should maritime powers be allowed to bombard towns on the seacoast?) and attempted to work out refinements in the rules. Nobody had supposed that the abolition of privateers meant that merchant ships could henceforth ply the seas with no fear of interference from anything less than a battle fleet; a country had the right to put guns on merchantmen and thus convert them into cruisers. And the nature of blockade changed as definitions suitable for the age of sail and smoothbore cannon fell further and further behind new realities—not only the coming of the torpedo boat and the submarine, but the development of rifled guns and high explosives that would make it suicidal for a blockading fleet to lie immediately outside a harbor.

In an attempt to deal with such questions and bring an element of certainty into relations between belligerent naval powers and neutrals, maritime nations came together in 1908, but their efforts, published in the Declaration of London in early 1909, had not come into effect (though even the U.S. Senate had given its approval) because Great Britain, the acknowledged mistress of the seas, had declined to ratify the treaty and the other powers had therefore withheld their own ratification. During the deliberations in London, a comment by a member of the German delegation had offered a possible glimpse of the future. The conference should not adopt rules, said Baron Marschall von Bieberstein, "whose strict observance may be rendered impossible by the force of circumstances."

Thus matters stood at the time the Great War broke out in 1914.

■ ■ ■

Already, in October 1914, the Germans were raising complaints about the effect "the English method of carrying on the war" was having on German foreign trade. Imports in August had experienced only a small decline from the figure for the same month in 1913—eternally to be remembered everywhere as the last year of the normal, traditional world—whereas exports from Germany had undergone a huge decrease, of some 40 percent, from the previous year; the favorable German balance of trade had turned into a deficit. The deprivation the German people complained of here was financial—they could still buy most of what they wanted, through neutrals, but they were losing sales. This development, of course, had not come about by accident but had followed from the so-called English method of carrying on the war.

The impossibility of mounting a close blockade of Germany did not at all mean that the British had resigned themselves to allowing German commerce to enjoy the unimpeded flow of goods that characterized economic life in peacetime. At the outset of the war, German ships were swept from the ocean lanes as if by a giant vacuum cleaner. Most of the larger, faster vessels were bottled up in neutral harbors, avoiding the British, or they stayed at home. Within less than three months from the beginning of the war, some 130 of the German merchant skippers who did venture to sea had fallen into British hands. Thus the future of seaborne trade between Germany and the outside world would henceforth rest in the hands of neutrals. Instead of lying in wait outside enemy harbors, as in a traditional blockade, British ships were operating a "distant blockade" by intercepting neutral ships bound for ports in the two neutral areas to which Germany had access, the Netherlands and Scandinavia: The British would attempt to choke the Germans at arm's length rather than close up.

Ranking far and away as chief of the neutrals was the United States. "What made America's situation exceptional was the country's geographical remoteness [from Europe], pacifist and isolationist traditions, and enormous latent power. For the belligerents, these same distinguishing facts made the American problem one of unusual difficulty, delicacy, and danger. Never before had they faced a neutral so invulnerable, so awesomely powerful in potential, and so self-consciously detached from European politics."

Although various kinds of asserted rights and procedures would at different times come into contention, trade constituted the central and most contentious issue. How should the European powers seek to handle the United States? Could the transatlantic republic ever occupy a position to exercise a decisive or even strong effect on the war? Or could it safely be disregarded? The issue at first appeared only theoretical. Everybody from Whitehall to the Wilhelmstrasse expected the war to end by New Year's, because the universal belief held that peoples and economies could not long endure the unprecedented stresses this modern war imposed on them. But in September, when the German armies moving south in France came to a stop and then stepped backward, behind the River Aisne, the result was not an acknowledged stalemate and consequent peace negotiations. Instead, the two sides displayed a general determination to carry on the fight, marked by the institution of trench warfare, with two facing lines gouging a great scar across the earth from Switzerland to the English Channel. The struggle would continue, and for an unforeseeably long time. Thus, with a protracted war in prospect, the British would now have to decide how to deal with all the neutrals trading with Germany, with the Americans at the head of the parade.

For its part, the U.S. State Department moved within the first few days of the fighting to ask the nations at war whether they would abide by the rules contained in the Declaration of London. Without such guidelines, the Americans knew, dominant naval powers tended to conduct war according to their own interests without much concern for the rights of neutrals. The British, however, delivered a cautious and cloudy answer to the American question: They would act in accordance with the declaration, but "subject to certain modifications and additions." The British also soon invoked what was called the principle of continuous voyage (recognized in the Declaration of London), which meant that they would seize cargoes headed for the Netherlands and Scandinavia, on the grounds that these goods could simply be transshipped from the neutral countries to the Germans as the ultimate consumers. Altogether, the British plans fell short in several ways of meeting the treaty definition of an effective blockade. A quarter-century earlier, in 1890, Mahan had produced the relevant insight: "For two hundred years England has been the great commercial nation of the world. More than any other her wealth has been intrusted to the sea in war as in peace; yet of all nations she has ever been most reluctant to concede the immunities of commerce and the rights of neutrals."

The Liberal government, which had come into power in 1905 and which since 1908 had been presided over by H. H. Asquith, included a number of leading "talents," as the phrase went, and among these prominent national figures Sir Edward Grey enjoyed a high degree of respect. Perhaps curiously for a foreign minister, Grey disliked foreigners and abhorred travel abroad; he apparently had left his homeland only once, for a brief trip to Paris, and he spoke no language but English. For all that, he wielded great influence with his colleagues; criticized by some for not having made it clear to the Germans that Britain would fight beside France if war should come (he defended himself against the charge by declaring that he could not say what his country would do until the time for decision came), he had nevertheless led the country into the war, his notable speech after the Germans invaded Belgium having carried the House of Commons with him.

In the present situation, as Grey explained to Walter Hines Page, an early and influential political supporter of President Woodrow Wilson who now served as the U.S. ambassador in London, Britain simply could not follow the rules of the 1909 declaration; the navy would do what it must, and surely any small legal disputes between the United States and Britain could be settled amicably. "That made sense to Page," noted a biographer. "After all, the British were fighting for their lives against a group of heathens; [it was] certainly no time to become aroused about an unimportant technicality." But it did not make sense to the State Department or to American traders and shippers. On September 28 the department sent Page a starchy note to use in talks with Grey; Acting Secretary of State Robert Lansing told the ambassador to warn Grey that the British government must not allow the Royal Navy such a free hand that the American government would be forced to adopt an anti-British policy, which it did not wish to do.

Thus began what would prove to be a many-chaptered running story of British actions on the high seas and American objections to these actions. Almost immediately, the British took an innovative and certainly controversial step, declaring the entire North Sea a military area, in which neutral vessels risked being sunk by British mines or taken into British ports as "suspicious craft" (they might, it was alleged, be German minelayers). This act in effect cut off the approaches to Germany by forbidding these waters to all merchant shipping. Though relationships with the United States did not constitute the only factor in their calculations, Grey and his colleagues in the Cabinet fully realized their vital importance. The Cabinet believed that, while "blockade of Germany was essential to the victory of the Allies," the "ill-will of the United States meant their certain defeat." Hence, since an all-out quarrel with the Americans could produce fatal consequences for the Allies, the blockade would have to go, if the choices came to that. British policy therefore aimed at pushing American tolerance to the limit, "to secure the maximum of blockade that could be enforced without a rupture with the United States."

The German ambassador in Washington, Count Johann von Bernstorff, observed the workings of British policy with considerable respect. Often an insightful commentator on American thought and habits, Count Bernstorff noted the "extraordinarily skillful way" in which the British went about influencing American opinion in relation to the London rules. The English (Bernstorff, like most Continentals, invariably said "English" rather than "British") always proceeded "cautiously and gradually," he noted, first accepting the declaration in principle but making several alterations that seemed unimportant but actually had significant effects and thus "formed the basis for the gradual overthrowing of the Declaration of London." The "blockade was introduced after careful preparation in the Press; it was not at first described as a blockade, but was gradually and systematically tightened."

Captain Mahan had said that "in her secure and haughty sway of the seas England imposed a yoke on neutrals which will never again be borne." Indeed, the question would soon become: Just how much would President Wilson and the United States prove themselves willing to bear? In spite of his confidence in the strength of American sympathy with the Allies, Grey might have felt some twinges of perturbation had he been eavesdropping on a September conversation between Wilson and his confidential adviser, Edward M. House (always known as "Colonel," although he had no military background), in which the president, author of numerous books and scholarly articles, read aloud a page from his *History of the American People,* in which he had described how the War of 1812 began over controversies like those now arising with Britain. "The passage said," House noted, "that Madison was compelled to go to war despite the fact that he was a peace-loving man and desired to do everything in his power to prevent it, but popular feeling made it impossible." Then, carrying the similarities to a precise and personal point indeed, Wilson added: "Madison and I are the only two Princeton men that have become President. The circumstances of the War of 1812 and now run parallel. I sincerely hope they will not go further."

■ ■ ■

Privateers had long vanished from the oceans, but now the submarine had appeared as a possible modern analogue, seeming almost swash-buckling, roaming the sea lanes, always ready for sudden attack. But how should this new and ill-defined vessel conduct itself in relation to the Paris rules of 1856 or to the London rules of 1909, which had been widely discussed even if not formally ratified? The Kaiser's naval hero and mentor, Captain Mahan, had dismissed commerce raiding as "a delusion, and a most dangerous delusion" if depended on as a primary weapon—particularly against Great Britain with its large merchant marine and powerful navy—and, though surface raiders like the cruiser *Emden* had won early fame, the Germans had not entered the war with any plan for use of U-boats in this fashion. Yet a number of other individual successes, accomplished in accordance with the cruiser rules, had followed the sinking of the *Glitra* by the *U-17*—including Otto Hersing's sinking of a French steamer, the *Malachite*—while, for all the effort, ingenuity, and money that had gone into its creation, the High Seas Fleet was paying no dividends as it lay tucked up in its harbors.

Admiral von Tirpitz saw the situation as resulting from a kind of unsporting strategy in which England "kept her fleet back in order to deprive us of the opportunity of achieving a swift decision by force of arms" and, instead of engaging in a straightforward fight with Germany, aimed at destroying her economically. The proclamation of the entire North Sea as a war zone offered a striking example, which the British justified by describing it as "in effect a blockade adapted to the conditions of modern warfare and commerce." Certainly, because of their geographical situation, the Germans needed a short war, as their "resources would diminish the longer the hostilities continued." In peacetime "Germany bought 20 percent of her cereals and 40 percent of her fats from abroad; from France, Sweden, or Spain she bought 12,500 tons of iron ore; she also had to resort to importing all of her raw cotton, copper, rare metals, rubber, and petroleum." The German economy and even the health of the population depended on deliveries of supplies from neutrals.

But perhaps two could play at this game of blockade. If, in this new kind of war, the enemy could stretch the definition of a blockade, could not the Germans do some stretching of their own, basing their version of a blockade on what had proved to be an effective weapon against merchant vessels, the U-boat? And might not this disruption of neutral shipping lead the United States to insist that Britain abandon its so-called blockade?

On November 7 Admiral von Pohl showed Tirpitz a draft of a proposed declaration of a submarine blockade of the entire British Isles. Feeling that this subject still had legal complexities to be explored, and also that the Germans had too few submarines to mount such an ambitious effort, Tirpitz argued for starting small, perhaps with a blockade simply of the Thames, and watching to see how naval and political reactions developed. Like the British, the Germans kept a constant awareness of the need to take account of American opinion, and by avoiding the Atlantic side of the island, Tirpitz thought, they could avoid any problem that might arise from attacks on passenger ships.

Pohl, less patient than his senior, came back a few weeks later with another draft, in which he asked the Foreign Office to approve the opening of a submarine campaign at the end of January, with all the waters surrounding the British Isles defined as a war zone. Besides his previous objections, Tirpitz now added his fear of truly alienating neutral opinion by instituting so drastic a measure without even seeking to justify it as a blockade. Although Tirpitz had the right to be consulted on such decisions, Pohl, in a kind of backstage maneuver, won the assent of Chancellor Theobald von Bethmann Hollweg, a friend of the Kaiser's from student days—a politician of a philosophical turn once described as "a man who means well feebly"—and then of the Kaiser; on February 5, 1915, Tirpitz found himself confronted by a fait accompli with the publication of Pohl's declaration. In proclaiming the war zone, the text declared that every enemy merchantman encountered in these waters would be sunk and that the navy could not in every case assure the safety of the passengers and crew. Further, the British government's misuse of the flags of neutral countries meant that ships of such countries encountered in the area would also find themselves in danger through being mistaken for British vessels in disguise. The new campaign would begin on February 18; Pohl and Bethmann justified it as a retaliation for the illegal British effort to strangle "the economic life of Germany and finally through starvation doom the entire population of Germany to destruction." In January Tirpitz had noted the government's miscalculations in relation to the supply of grain, and in a few weeks the authorities would take steps to ration food, beginning with restrictions, at first relatively light, on the purchase of bread. On the other side of the coin, the timing of the German campaign coincided with the beginning of the arrival in British waters of ships carrying wheat from the Argentine harvest.

In principle, Admiral von Tirpitz believed strongly in the use of submarines as commerce raiders, and his reservations concerning the new policy did not keep him from speaking to an American interviewer about Germany's determination to wage a ruthless war on British merchant shipping. Yet for him it was a question of timing. Since the navy had just twenty-two boats available and could at most keep just six or seven on patrol in British waters at one time, the admiral considered this new declaration "a blustering flourish of trumpets and threats," likely to accomplish little besides further alienating neutrals who always tended to accept "almost anything the English did at sea."

After reflecting on the whole issue, State Department officials let reporters know that they planned no protest of the move, making the point that they could not raise the issue with Germany without making the same point with Britain; a close comparison of the two cases convinced officials that they rested on the same foundations. Altogether, in creating a "war zone" to offset Britain's "military area," the Germans, in the reported view of some State Department officials, had pulled off "a rather neat and clever diplomatic counterstroke."

President Wilson, however, expressed no admiration of the Germans' cleverness. Having warned the British not to make unauthorized use of the American flag, he pointed out to the Germans the deeply serious consequences that would result if a submarine should "destroy on the high seas an American vessel or the lives of American citizens." Americans, he said, must have "the full enjoyment of their acknowledged rights on the high seas," and the U.S. government would take whatever steps proved necessary to safeguard American lives and property. Indeed, the administration at times seemed almost obsessed with asserting the right of Americans to travel through war zones on the ships of belligerents, even if those ships might also be carrying war matériel. This was so even though relatively few Americans had any desire for any such travel or ever had any such opportunity.

Representatives of the most directly involved group, the shipping companies, seemed quite unalarmed, making light of the declaration by purporting to regard the whole thing as a great bluff. A Cunard official said simply, "This makes no difference at all to us," adding the world's oldest one-liner of commercial reassurance: "Our business will go on as usual." Others ladled out similar soothing syrup. A Holland-America official unwittingly reflected Admiral von Tirpitz's own view of the timing of the action: "The Germans haven't the ships to make such threats effective. Their submarines cannot do very much when their actions are compared with the magnitude of the field." In the circumstances, such good cheer perhaps had nothing surprising about it, but Philip Franklin, a White Star director, expressed himself more thoughtfully: "We have a new problem every day in war times and the situation is constantly changing"; the "full application and actual force" of the proclamation might not be seen at once. Franklin had a sound point: In early February 1915 nobody anywhere knew how many commerce-raiding U-boats would be required to make a real impact on the war.

"MY GOD, IT'S THE *LUSITANIA!*"

O n the morning of Saturday, May 1, 1915, various newspapers across the United States carried a curious advertisement:

NOTICE!

Travellers intending to embark on the Atlantic voyage are reminded that a state of war exists between Germany and her allies and Great Britain and her allies; that the zone of war includes the waters adjacent to the British Isles; that, in accordance with formal notice given by the Imperial German Government, vessels flying the flag of Great Britain, or any of her allies, are liable to destruction in those waters and that travellers sailing in the war zone on ships of Great Britain or her allies do so at their own risk.

IMPERIAL GERMAN EMBASSY
Washington, D. C., April 22, 1915

Wondering what to make of it, an editor at the *New York Times* (which had received its copy of the advertisement just the preceding evening) telephoned Charles P. Sumner, the local agent of the Cunard Line, who, in what appeared to have become the company's standard response to any sort of threat, made light of it. Only a few days previously, he said, Cunard had received letters from an extortionist who demanded $15,000 not to publish advertising that would harm the line. Hence, said Sumner, he found it hard to believe that the advertisement had really come from the German Embassy. Even after the editor pointed out that the text accurately summarized the official German proclamation of a war zone and that it clearly had been submitted by a representative of the embassy, Sumner expressed skepticism; he obviously did not believe that his business duties called for him to discourage transatlantic travel on his company's ships. The Germans no longer had any commerce-raiding cruisers in the Atlantic, he pointed out, and "as for submarines, I have no fear of them whatever."

Earlier, in the first week of February, the Cunard liner *Lusitania* had received another kind of unwelcome attention, though in this case her captain had been the cause of it.

■ ■ ■

On the morning of February 5, as the *Lusitania*, bound for Liverpool, arrived off Queenstown, on the southern Irish coast, she received a radio message from another passenger ship, the White Star Line's *Baltic,* which reported having sighted two U-boats in the Irish Sea. After some delay off Queenstown the *Lusitania* then headed for Liverpool at full speed, not even stopping to pick up a pilot and arriving at daybreak with, for all to see, the Stars and Stripes flying at the stern in place of the familiar Red Ensign and another American flag fluttering at the forepeak. It almost seemed that the liner's veteran captain, "Paddy" Dow, had decided to test the German war zone declaration even before he could have known about it. According to one passenger's report, Dow had claimed the right to fly the American flag because he had neutral mails and neutral passengers aboard. As illogical as that statement seemed—and surprised as Cunard officials in New York appeared to be by the whole thing when they learned of it—several shipping veterans commented that the captain had offered the only explanation that would make any sense, since no U-boat skipper could "for an instant" mistake the *Lusitania,* which was only a hundred feet shorter than the *Titanic,* for an American ship; the United States had no liners even remotely as large and only the British and French operated four-funneled vessels in the Atlantic passenger trade.

The incident had caused quite a ripple in New York and Washington, with some newspapers noting that if the British continued the practice of running up the American flag, the result could be danger to Americans traveling on actual American ships. The United States had no protest to make about it, however, and then, somewhat less than two months later, a U-boat sank a much smaller British steamer, the 4,800-ton cargo-passenger vessel *Falaba,* off Ireland with the loss of one American. A little more than a month after that, on May 1, off the Scilly Islands at the tip of Cornwall, a U-boat torpedoed an American oil tanker, the *Gulflight,* en route from Port Arthur, Texas, to Rouen. Although the ship stayed afloat and, under tow, ultimately managed to make her way into port, the radio operator and a seaman dived overboard and were drowned, and several hours later the captain suffered a fatal heart attack. Aside from these encounters with submarines, the Americans had seen two ships sunk by German mines and another (the tanker *Cushing)* bombed by an airplane, apparently in a case of mistaken identity and of poor aim as well, little damage having been done. Such incidents created and swelled a wave of indignation against the Germans, who, two historians declared at the time, "had entered upon a campaign of intimidation, citing these attacks and threatening others, in an avowed effort to compel Americans and American shipping to keep out of the 'war zone.' "

· · ·

At midday on May 1, with a light rain falling, the Cunard pier at the foot of West Fourteenth Street presented an unusually lively scene. Not only was the *Lusitania* departing, but she had suddenly been called on to take aboard 163 passengers from the Anchor Line steamer *Cameronia,* which just a few hours earlier had been commandeered by the British Admiralty; trucks and cabs convoyed the *Cameronia'*s passengers down from the Anchor Line pier at Twenty-fourth Street. At 12:30 the *Lusitania* cast off on her 101st crossing of the Atlantic with 1,388 passengers aboard, the largest number she had carried eastbound since 1914.

Her captain, William Turner, the senior Cunard Line skipper who had taken over when his previous ship, the *Aquitania,* had been removed from passenger service, commented that the Germans with their public notice did not appear to have "scared many people from going on the ship by the look of the pier and the passenger list." Calling the German action "a lot of tommyrot," an unworried passenger, Alexander Campbell of the Dewar's Scotch distillery pointed to what everybody seemed to consider the twin guarantees of the liner's safety: "The *Lusitania* can run away from any submarine the Germans have got, and the British Admiralty will see that she is looked after when she arrives in striking distance of the Irish coast." Neither the company nor the captain had told the passengers that, to conserve coal, six of the ship's twenty-five boilers would not be in use and the top speed would hence drop from 25 knots to 21. Besides that, the Royal Navy escort through the danger zone, of which Charles Sumner had spoken reassuringly, would not be forthcoming; it was not naval practice to escort the liners through St. George's Channel and the Irish Sea, because the navy lacked sufficient resources "to provide destroyer escorts for mail and passenger ships." When they reached home waters these vessels were on their own, just as they had been in the ocean passage.

None of the optimistic officers or passengers on the *Lusitania* offered any observations about the results produced since the proclamation of the German war zone had gone into effect. In the ten weeks since February 18, submarines and mines had sunk a reported sixty-eight ships. Most of these, of course, were not passenger ships—and certainly not large and luxurious liners—but steamers of 2,000 to 3,000 tons and upward, the kinds of freighters and tankers that kept Britain fed and fighting.

■ ■ ■

In the last week of April Fregattenkapitän (Commander) Hermann Bauer, commander of the two submarine flotillas (*Führer der U-boote*) under the control of the High Seas Fleet and based at Wilhelmshaven, issued special operational orders to three of his boats. They were to depart for English waters "as soon as possible" in order to intercept "large English troop transports" expected to sail from Liverpool, the Bristol Channel, and Dartmouth—bound presumably for the Mediterranean to take part in the Allied land campaign on the Gallipoli peninsula that had just begun that very week after the failure of attempts by warships to force the Dardanelles by bombarding the Turkish shore fortifications.

Commander Bauer assigned one of the boats, the *U-30* (widely known in the navy as a Jonah, a boat that was always getting into trouble), to the English Channel, off Dartmouth, on the south coast of England; the other two, the *U-20* and the *U-27*, he directed to take station in the Irish Sea, off the west coast. Though his order called for the boats to pursue the "fastest possible" route to station, Bauer believed, mistakenly, that minefields and nets had effectively barred the Strait of Dover and hence ordered all the boats to proceed to their destinations around the top of Scotland. The expected departure of the troop transports had provided the incentive for the operation, but the skippers were told to attack merchant ships and warships as well.

The *U-20*, commanded by Lieutenant Walther Schwieger, departed from Emden at seven o'clock in the morning on the last day of April, with express orders to patrol off Liverpool. A bit younger than some of the other U-boat skippers, Schwieger, at thirty, had won a reputation as an ace submariner. Tall and broad-shouldered, with well-cut features, he was good-looking enough to have done well in a silent film; he was no showboater, however, but rather a thoroughly methodical and professional officer who seemed to take an unemotional approach to his duties. A member of an old Berlin family, he "was very well educated, and had in the highest degree the gifts of poise and urbane courtesy," with "talk full of gayety and pointed wit."

Schwieger's boat, one of four in the *U-19* class, completed in 1913, had a surfaced displacement of 650 tons, which made her substantially larger than Weddigen's famous *U-9*. Like all the later (post-1908) U-boats, she was powered by diesel engines rather than the smoky and stinking kerosene motors German builders had employed previously to avoid having to use volatile gasoline. She could do 15 knots on the surface and a respectable 9 to 10 submerged, and as armament she carried four 20-inch torpedo tubes and an 86mm deck gun.

Although bigger than the *U-9*, Schwieger's boat hardly ranked as a luxury liner. She carried forty-nine men in all, including seven officers, crowded into her 210-foot hull; like all submarines she put every conceivable cubic centimeter of space to use for storage of food and other supplies. Water was severely limited, and the toilet facilities—never inviting—declined in appeal as a patrol continued. "Certain necessary matters," recalled a *U-19*–class skipper, "were dealt with behind a green curtain, and it was distinctly embarrassing to be disturbed

by an alarm while in this apartment." On occasion the plumbing re-
belled and began acting backward, with appalling results. Constipation
became the occupational disease of submariners, and a lust for any
fresh air they could get one of their most pronounced traits.

When the fresh air remaining in a submerged boat from its last run
on the surface was used up—a process taking six to eight hours—the
exhaled air was cleaned by being put through containers of potash. If
necessary, the crew could draw on the boat's oxygen cylinders, of
which, however, it could carry only a few. After about fifteen hours, either way, "things begin to get uncomfortable. The lungs work heavily
and a great weariness assails the crew." After running submerged for a
number of hours, as the crew sat at supper, "no one spoke, each man
stared in front of him and scarcely ate. No one had any appetite and
nothing pleased one's palate." Then oxygen would be introduced, for
perhaps ten minutes. "Air, air! The whole human system responded."
But such relief could only be brief. Three continuous days represented, at the outside, the longest span of time a submerged crew could
survive.

These *U-19*–class boats had the standard double hull, the inside,
cigar-shaped shell of nickel-steel called the *pressure hull,* because that
was exactly what it was designed to withstand, and an outer hull that
was only "tinplate," as the skipper said, which gave the boat the general
appearance of an ordinary ship, including a deck. German design had
been inspired by Simon Lake (indeed, many people believe that the
Imperial Navy had simply stolen the inventor's patents) and this
arrangement reflected Lake's ideas. The double hull had the advantage
of allowing the ballast tanks to be fixed outside the pressure hull; forward and aft hydroplanes permitted easy adjustment of trim. Like all
submarines of the time, these vessels with their combination of ballast
tanks and diving hydroplanes represented a blend of the ideas of Holland and Lake.

■ ■ ■

Though an efficient commander, Lieutenant Schwieger ran "one of
those jolly craft, loud with laughter and rollicking fellowship, with
more of the spirit of an old three-master, full of hearty shipmates, than

of an ultra-modern shell crammed with mechanisms of intricate and deadly precision." During Christmas night of 1914, the first in the war, Schwieger had taken his boat to the muddy bottom of the North Sea and there, out of the way of any possible patrolling enemy craft, had presided over a celebration complete with a wreath and an after-dinner concert (violin, mandolin, and accordion). Another time, after long days of subsisting on canned and dried food and hardtack, the *U-20* spotted fishing boats off the French coast. Schwieger brought the submarine up right in their midst. "It was dangerous for a U-boat to show its conning tower in those waters," one of the officers recalled, "but we were desperate men." Having heard stories about the U-boats, the fishermen "expected to be massacred at once. They laughed and cheered and got very busy when they discovered that all the U-boat wanted was some fresh fish." As a parting joke, the officers handed the fishermen a draft on the French government for payment.

As a practicing commerce raider, Schwieger did not seem to concern himself overmuch about the registry of a ship (whether it belonged to a belligerent or a neutral). Early in the morning of May 3, on rounding the Orkneys north of Scotland, his war diary reports, he spotted what was "probably a Danish passenger steamer: Copenhagen-Montreal" and did not attack it only because it was too far ahead for the *U-20* to be able to get into firing position (though his brief diary notation possibly meant just that, as an abstract tactical matter, he could not have attacked the steamer if he had wanted to do it); later, similarly, he could not make an attack on a small Swedish steamer. Nor did he consider any potential victim too insignificant to call for his attention.

On May 5, off southern Ireland, having sighted a small schooner, Schwieger warned its crew of his presence, allowed them to take to the boats, and then employed the deck gun to sink his quarry. (When possible, Schwieger, like other U-boat captains, preferred to employ gunfire rather than torpedoes; these big missiles came with a high price tag and a boat could carry only a limited supply of them.) He could follow this orthodox warning procedure because he had no fear either of gunfire from the schooner or of being rammed, the latter a possibility submariners always had to keep in mind and one that the British Admiralty encouraged ship captains to practice. Next day, now in St.

George's Channel in misty weather, Schwieger disposed of two ships, one by torpedo, the other by torpedo together with shelling by the deck gun. He failed, however, in an attempt to bag a middle-sized White Star liner.

Despite his orders to patrol off Liverpool, Schwieger noted in his log that his heavy fuel consumption led him to abandon the idea and remain south of the entrance to the Bristol Channel, which in any case he rightly saw—and no doubt preferred—as an area offering rich pickings. He now had only three torpedoes left, two of which he wished to save for the homeward voyage (a conservative practice favored by his superiors). The next morning, May 7, began in thick fog, but by eleven o'clock (like all German naval vessels, the *U-20* kept her chronometers on home time) the mist had burned off, leaving a clear, bright day. The captain found the day so fine that at 1:45 he noted the "very great visibility, very beautiful weather."

At 2:20 Schwieger sighted on the horizon "a forest of masts and stacks." At first he thought he might be looking at several ships but soon made the sight out to be a single vessel with four smokestacks and two masts, a large passenger steamer, coming from the southwest on a course perpendicular to that of the *U-20*. Immediately Schwieger took the submarine down to 35 feet and went ahead at full speed on a course converging with that of the steamer "in the hope that she would change her course to starboard along the Irish coast"; otherwise, she would probably outrun the U-boat. At 2:35 the ship obligingly made precisely that change. The *U-20* raced ahead and at 3:00 had taken her attack position, with the big steamer then less than half a mile away.

■ ■ ■

As was customary—war or no war (and, it seemed, warning or no warning)—a number of prominent and wealthy Americans had embarked on the *Lusitania*. Even if outshone by the galaxy that went down with the *Titanic,* the group of unworried travelers included such varied types as Elbert Hubbard, the founder of a well-known writers' and artists' colony in western New York and author of an inspirational essay, "A Message to Garcia," that for years appeared in all junior high school anthologies; Charles Frohman, a leading theatrical producer and entrepreneur in both New York and London; and Alfred Gwynne Vanderbilt, of the famous New York dynasty, commonly identified in the press as a "sportsman," his chief interests being horses and women, perhaps in that order.

Like their fellow travelers these gentlemen preferred the speed as well as the luxury of the big Cunard liner. Though the speed had been lacking on this trip, the passengers had enjoyed a smooth and comfortable crossing. Now, late in the afternoon of Thursday, May 6, the *Lusitania* had entered what mariners were generally calling the danger zone. Though no passenger liner had ever been torpedoed and Captain Turner gave no sign of expecting any trouble, he duly ordered the portholes closed and the lifeboats swung out. That night the Admiralty flashed warnings of submarine activity in St. George's Channel, and following earlier orders Turner swept wide around Fastnet Rock, at the southwest corner of Ireland, where U-boats had been reported operating. On encountering a light fog, Turner slowed the ship to 15 knots but then increased speed, though only to 18 knots. As he explained, he felt in no hurry, because he wished to reach the Mersey bar, outside of Liverpool, at high tide on the morning of the eighth so that he could go right in instead of having to loiter outside, a possible delay he deemed dangerous. Hugging the Irish coast, the *Lusitania* proceeded northeastward through the next morning and early afternoon, and at about two o'clock those on board sighted a standard landmark, the projecting cape known as the Old Head of Kinsale, just nine or ten miles away.

Many of the passengers were still sitting at lunch, while others enjoyed games or lounged in the shade of the awnings; Elbert Hubbard and his wife playfully tossed a tennis ball back and forth. Suddenly a cry from a lookout on the forecastle head—a lad named Leslie Morton, from New York—interrupted this tranquil scene. The boy shouted to the bridge that a torpedo was heading toward the starboard bow of the ship. At first, nobody seemed to hear him, while the torpedo ate up precious seconds on its course toward its target. Then, a moment later, came an echoing cry from a lookout in the crow's nest. But before the officers could make any move to take evasive action, as they might possibly have been able to do had they responded immediately to the first warning, the torpedo struck, smashing into the *Lusitania* well forward with an explosion that shattered portholes. A second and far greater explosion followed immediately, breaking the steam pipes and flooding the boiler room, creating a hissing geyser that burst through the deck and flung coal and debris high above the ship. This blow, which everybody on board took to mark a hit by another torpedo, cut off all power, which meant that the momentum of the ship could not be checked by reversal of the propellers.

Following the orders of Captain Turner—who, in presenting his ship so temptingly to the voracious U-boat, appeared to have violated every canon of Admiralty procedure—the crew attempted to launch the lifeboats, but the ship had already begun to list while still moving ahead at several miles an hour. These conditions, together with the crew's obvious lack of familiarity with the boats, made the task exceptionally difficult. Watching one boat being lowered, a Manhattan shipping executive heard an officer shout at the sailor on the bow rope to hurry up. The man "threw off a bight, lost control of the rope and the bow dropped, throwing the passengers into the water. A minute later a second boat, which seemed about to get safely away, also got out of control and fell upon the people struggling in the water." After passing out life preservers to several passengers, the executive, realizing that the ship was sinking fast, hesitated until the deck was just eight or ten feet above the water and then jumped, swimming hard to get clear of the great funnels, which now loomed just a few feet above the surface. A sudden vacuum sucked a woman swimming nearby into one of them, but moments later, like a human cannonball, she came hurtling out again, soaked and smeared with soot but not critically injured.

Robert Clarke, a fifteen-year-old cabin boy from Liverpool, stood farther toward the stern on the deck of the *Lusitania*, and thus higher in the air, trying to muster the courage to leap the distance of perhaps eighty feet to the water; having made the jump successfully, he watched the fantail of the great liner rise in the air just seconds before she began her final plunge. Mr. and Mrs. Hubbard were not among those in the water. After the explosions they had walked hand in hand into a stateroom and sat down to await the end, along with hundreds of other "helpless souls, caught like rats in a gilded trap." As Charles Frohman stood on deck talking with a group of acquaintances, a passenger overheard him greeting his final moments philosophically, saying "Why fear death? It is the most beautiful adventure that life gives us." After the two explosions, Alfred Vanderbilt had told his servant: "Find all the kiddies you can," and he busied himself putting life jackets on the youngsters, giving his own jacket to a woman. Although known as a sportsman, Vanderbilt could barely swim, if he could do so at all; shortly before scrambling off the sinking ship, as the *Lusitania* readied for her final plunge, the shipping executive saw the multimillionaire standing quietly in a passageway, waiting.

■ ■ ■

Through his periscope, a 20-foot steel tube with a prismatic lens, Lieutenant Schwieger had a close-up view of this incredible drama. At 3:10, leading his target like a hunter leading a duck, he had fired a "clean [*rein*] bow shot" at a range of about 255 yards with a very shallow depth setting of about 10 feet. The torpedo and the advancing liner needed less than a minute to meet at the point at which Schwieger had aimed. Then "there came a tremendous detonation, with a very dense smoke cloud reaching far above the forward funnel. Besides the torpedo explosion there must have been another (boiler or coal or powder?)." As Schwieger saw the scene before him, "the superstructure over the point of impact and the bridge was torn asunder. Fire broke out and smoke hid the high bridge." The big ship stopped immediately, Schwieger noted, and listed heavily to starboard and began sinking by the bow. It looked as if she might soon capsize. "Great confusion ensued on board. The boats were swung out and some of them lowered into the water, but panic must have reigned, since several boats filled with people slid down either stern or bow first and immediately were swamped. Fewer boats could be lowered on the starboard side, because of the heavy list."

Like all U-boat skippers, Schwieger had at his side a "war pilot," a civilian merchant officer who helped identify possible target ships and in this case recognized the big four-funneled liner as either the *Lusitania* or her sister ship, the *Mauretania* (as Schwieger could well have done on his own). Schwieger recalled the pilot's putting his eye to the periscope and then yelling, "My God, it's the *Lusitania!*" In function the two sister liners differed greatly at this stage of the war. After the *Mauretania* was withdrawn from the transatlantic service, she had been converted into a troop transport, whereas the *Lusitania,* though carrying munitions, was not, as various observers would claim, ferrying Canadian soldiers to France. Even if a U-boat commander and his war pilot should be inclined to concern themselves with such distinctions, however, they might easily lack full information, and in any case the British themselves had listed both ships as subject to being armed as merchant cruisers. Beyond that, Schwieger, as all his actions demonstrated, considered a liner as valid a target as any other vessel that entered the war zone his government had proclaimed. For him, the mission simply called for him to sink ships.

What had happened to the *Lusitania* seemed remarkable to the U-boat skipper; he had been forced to use two torpedoes to sink much smaller vessels, and yet with just one shot the great liner had heeled over, clearly doomed, sinking in just a few minutes. At 3:25 Schwieger took his boat to a depth of 80 feet and headed out to sea. There was nothing more to do here: "I could not have fired a second torpedo into that crowd of people struggling to save themselves"—people swimming amid a great swirl of dead bodies, deck furniture, and wreckage. It was, he later said, the most horrible sight he could remember.

The day remained clear and later, looking back, Schwieger noted, "There was no more of the 'Lusitania' to be seen." He could still see the shore and above it a lighthouse, which made a good marker for the location of the wreck. The young skipper of the *U-20* did not yet realize that, with his one torpedo, he had fired a shot that would truly be heard round the world—and across the Atlantic.

8

A PRESIDENT TOO PROUD

On hearing the news that Woodrow Wilson had won the 1912 presidential election, Kaiser Wilhelm had expressed surprise at the decision of the voters. "What will America ever accomplish," he asked an American acquaintance, "with a professor at its head?" Wilson had in fact won one of the most remarkable of all American presidential elections. For some time during the 1912 political season it had appeared that the Democratic Wilson's chief foe would be the incumbent Republican president, William Howard Taft. But these expectations had been upset by the actions of Taft's predecessor, the flamboyant Teddy Roosevelt, who had served almost two full terms as president (1901–1909) but found private life not nearly as much fun as the "bully pulpit" offered by the White House and therefore set out to shove his former protégé Taft aside and seize a third term for himself.

After Republican convention delegates loyal to Taft denied Teddy the nomination, he turned to direct action, creating the Progressive Party and, having declared himself "as strong as a bull moose," mounting a full-scale campaign, not winning but leaving Taft far behind in third place. If Roosevelt had sat in the White House in 1914, few could doubt what attitudes he would have held toward the belligerents in the Great War and what role he would have seen for the United States. As a private citizen, he became so public and active an advocate of intervention that he even accused President Wilson of making the United States shirk its duty to Belgium out of a "spirit of commercial opportunism." After the sinking of the *Lusitania,* Roosevelt urged full preparation for war.

94

But Woodrow Wilson and not Theodore Roosevelt sat behind the presidential desk, and in temperament, background, and mode of expression the president differed mightily from the colonel (the title by which Teddy was always known from his Spanish-American War exploits). If looking into Roosevelt's soul could be likened to gazing into a room through an open window, a search for the inner Wilson encountered veils and shades raised and lowered in ways that baffled any seekers. "The mind of man is a labyrinth," said one student of Wilson, "through whose complexities the biographer stumbles almost blindly in search of motives and true emotions." The strength of Wilson's faith in his own opinions, however, struck everybody. He was said by some to have "the faculty of seeing black as white and white as black if this optical illusion suited his mood."

Wilson sometimes expressed similar thoughts about himself; he was fond of saying "a Scotch-Irishman *knows* that he is right." A Jersey City Irish political boss who had played a central part in putting Wilson in the governor's mansion in Trenton in 1910 called him a "Presbyterian priest." (That was before Wilson, having won the election, broke with the party machine; what the boss then said about the newly elected governor can only be imagined.)

In the days immediately following the sinking of the *Lusitania*, people on all sides, however much they may have known about Wilson, wondered just what the president would in fact see when he looked at the picture. The Germans had begun the war by committing an act equivalent to political original sin: the invasion of Belgium, a country with which they had no conceivable quarrel and whose frontiers they (as the government of Prussia) had joined with Britain and France in guaranteeing in 1839 and further in 1870. Within the first week of the war the invaders had brought further opprobrium on themselves from all sides by the destruction of the heart of Louvain, a Gothic treasure of a town with a renowned medieval library; German soldiers torched it, supposedly in response to sniper attacks by *francs-tireurs*.

Though initially he fought to keep his personal beliefs and prejudices from influencing his official conduct with respect to the belligerents, Wilson culturally and indeed naturally favored the Allies and made no secret of it in talks with House and others close to him. He also shared the feelings of the millions revolted by the destruction of Louvain, at one point saying to Colonel House that "if Germany won it would change the course of our civilization and make the United States a military nation." On the other hand, Wilson seemed to look on the war as a terrible but essentially European event in which America should not become directly involved, a view unquestionably held by the great majority of the people. He ordered army and navy officers not to talk about the war in public and even urged moviegoers not to applaud for either side when film from the fighting fronts was shown. At the same time, a great purpose—perhaps a great ambition—had quickly taken shape in the president's mind. Not only must he maintain the neutrality of the United States, but he must also be ready "to aid in every possible way to bring peace again to the world."

The president was just finishing lunch on May 7 when Rudolph Forster, the executive clerk (a permanent member of the White House staff), brought him the news of the Lusitania, which had come from a newspaper bulletin. No one yet could be sure of the cause, and the first report erred wildly in declaring that no lives had been lost. Despite this seeming good news, the tragedy "greatly shocked and perturbed" Wilson, and he decided to cancel his scheduled golf game and remain in the office to deal with developments. Later in the afternoon more false information arrived in bulletins declaring positively that everybody on the ship had been saved. Only that night, after the president had gone to bed, did news come that "two torpedoes had been fired into the Lusitania by a submarine and that the Lusitania sank fifteen minutes afterward."

Journalists familiar with the president had no doubt that he would proceed carefully, making sure of the facts, before deciding on and announcing any course of action. However, the statement from London that the Lusitania had been torpedoed without warning clearly indicated that a delicate situation if not a crisis had developed, since the United States had earlier warned the Germans that they must follow the old rules, visiting and searching a merchant ship before taking her captive or sinking her. And matters became grimmer still when it became evident that many Americans, more than a hundred, had perished in the tragedy.

Most Londoners met the news with "stupefaction." "What is America going to do about the torpedoing of the Lusitania?" demanded the British theatrical producer Frederick Harrison, a close friend of Charles Frohman. Expressing his intense shock over the report that his American colleague had been lost with the ship, Harrison said, "What is Washington going to say about the drowning of American citizens? Is America going to take it lying down?"

■ ■ ■

On May 10 a coroner's jury in Kinsale found not only the crew of the U-boat but also "the Emperor and Government of Germany" guilty of wholesale murder. On the same day President Wilson took the train from Washington up to Philadelphia, where in the evening he was to deliver an address to a group of newly naturalized citizens. Crowds cheered him as he passed through the streets on his way to Convention Hall, where a throng of thousands, including four thousand new Americans, gave him an ovation. Fittingly enough for this kind of occasion, Philadelphia's Mayor Blankenburg spoke with a distinctly German accent in giving Wilson the simple introduction: "I present to you—God bless him!—the president."

After an eloquent exposition of his theme, "The Meaning of Americanism," the president, while making no reference to the tragedy that occupied all minds, declared that "the example of America must be a special example. The example of America must be the example not merely of peace because it will not fight, but of peace because peace is the healing and elevating influence of the world and strife is not. There is such a thing," he said in sentences that would become famous, "as a man being too proud to fight. There is such a thing as a nation being so right that it does not need to convince others by force that it is right." One of Wilson's advisers later produced a succinct summary of the president's message: "Humanity first."

Questioned by reporters after news came of the *Lusitania* tragedy, Colonel Roosevelt was characteristically blunt: Piracy was piracy, and that was what the sinking of the *Lusitania* represented. Newspapers soon featured further declarations by Roosevelt that the time for thought had passed and the time for action had arrived. Teddy seemed to find it hard to believe that the president could speak of a nation's being "too proud to fight."

Despite the heat of the disapproval, particularly in the East, President Wilson did not at this moment in history intend to allow the deed of a young man in command of a small boat to push him out of his neutral stance and into, or close to, war. Count Bernstorff had noted in his travels that the Americans, a people who looked "cheerfully into the future," generally displayed little interest in what went on in other countries, and a survey of newspapers from across the country, conducted in the first three days following the *Lusitania* sinking, showed that out of a thousand no more than half a dozen argued for a declaration of war. Instead, the situation "called for diplomacy." Thus, at this point, the followers of President Wilson and what seemed to be his policy of peace greatly outnumbered those lining up behind Colonel Roosevelt, who dwelt in visible frustration that at this gigantic moment in world history he had no power to guide events.

An angry American blamed the disaster on "British recklessness," which had brought about the loss of the *Titanic* and now of the *Lusitania*. The Americans who had perished in the *Lusitania,* said the writer, "had persisted in their journey, not with wanton disregard of their lives, but because of their reliance upon British assurances. And now we read in the London Times that there was not convoy or possibility of a convoy." In short, "the British have met the submarine with the same fatuous recklessness with which they met the iceberg, and with a like result." This writer had ample logic on his side. Although the official British inquiries praised the conduct of Captain Turner, the veteran master actually had behaved with an almost adolescent sense of immunity to danger, slowing his ship down and making a landfall in the middle of the day instead of at night, proceeding close to the coast instead of staying well away from headlands, and sailing in a straight line and forgoing zigzagging, the recently developed procedure intended to make it difficult for a U-boat to determine and take up a firing position. At the inquest in Kinsale, in answer to the coroner's question about zigzagging, Turner explained that he had not been following such a course because "it was bright weather and the land was clearly visible," although he conceded that it was "quite possible" for a submarine to approach the ship without being seen. He clearly had not understood the reasoning behind zigzagging.

At the later official inquiry conducted in London by Lord Mersey, as "wreck commissioner," Turner testified that he "understood that it was only when you saw a submarine that you should zigzag." Preoccupied not with a possible lurking U-boat but with getting a fix on the Old Kinsale light, in order to determine his exact position (a concern that in the circumstances puzzled one of his interrogators, who demanded, "Do you mean to say you had no idea where you were?"), the captain had sailed close offshore and he had made a fateful turn to starboard. In the hearing the attorney-general made it fairly evident that, if negligence was found, the government preferred to see it charged to Captain Turner rather than to the Admiralty. But neither side needed to worry; the Admiralty, the Board of Trade, the Cunard Line, and the captain all emerged unblemished. Lord Mersey, after all, had also presided over the inquiry into the *Titanic* disaster, and he had found no fault with any of the participants except the iceberg.

In a conversation with the American ambassador, James W. Gerard, the Kaiser declared that he would not have permitted the torpedoing of the *Lusitania* had he known it was going to happen and that "no gentleman would kill so many women and children." He also produced an insight into Captain Turner's conduct that, while thoroughly self-serving, did not lack shrewdness: "England was really responsible as England made the *Lusitania* go slowly so Germany could torpedo her and so bring on trouble." With this imperial opinion, Wilhelm II established himself as one of the pioneers of what would prove to be an eternally flourishing conspiracy theory about the destruction of the *Lusitania*.

▪ ▪ ▪

Washington observers believed that President Wilson and the State Department would combine the *Lusitania* case with those of the *Gulflight,* *Cushing,* and *Falaba* in a single demand for German acts of atonement.

These forecasters proved to be correct, and three days after the speech in Philadelphia the department cabled the text of a note to Ambassador Gerard for delivery to the German Foreign Office. It called attention to the different attacks, which constituted a "series of events which the Government of the United States has observed with growing concern, distress, and amazement," and emphasized Wilson's familiar theme that ships must be visited and searched and that none must be destroyed unless the safety of passengers and crew could be fully assured. "The Imperial German Government," the note declared, "will not expect the Government of the United States to omit any word or any act necessary to the sacred duty of maintaining the rights of the United States and its citizens and of safeguarding their free exercises and enjoyments."

But to the surprise of the ambassador, who had already begun packing to leave Berlin, the note did not announce the rupture of relations between the United States and Germany. Wilson had instead told his secretary that he would not be stampeded into war, but after a series of notes to Berlin failed to produce results, the State Department called Bernstorff to a meeting. Believing that it would be logical for the government to forbid American citizens to travel on ships of nations at war, Secretary of State William Jennings Bryan had refused to sign Wilson's second note, which had been sent off on June 10, and instead had resigned his office. (In discussing the threat to American neutrality brought by the flow of dollars in loans to arm and supply Britain and France, Bryan had warned the president that "money is the worst of all contrabands, because it commands everything else.") Bernstorff would now deal with Robert Lansing, a strong supporter of Britain and an interventionist even to the point of not carrying out the wishes of his superiors if these conflicted with his own views.

Bernstorff had no doubts about the magnitude of the disaster the sinking of the *Lusitania* represented for friendly German-American relations. Popular indignation had burst out with such strength that "even the German-Americans were terror-stricken by its violence. Not only did our propaganda collapse completely, but even our political friends dared not open their mouths." What the ambassador called

"Germanism" in America "may be said to have been absolutely killed by the *Lusitania* incident, and only gradually came to life again."

Even the attention-getting move that Count Bernstorff had considered a positive gesture had backfired in spectacular fashion. Since the American government had appeared to underestimate the danger to passengers sailing on British ships, and therefore not only had not forbidden U.S. citizens to travel on such ships, but also had not given them any kind of warning about the likelihood of trouble, Bernstorff and his colleagues had resolved to do the job themselves. The fateful warning to Atlantic travelers, bearing the date of April 22, had been scheduled to appear in newspapers on April 24 and on the following two Saturdays as well. Through a mixture of incompetence and bad luck not uncommon in history, however, the announcement had missed its scheduled first appearance and thus was first published on the morning the *Lusitania* sailed. Of course the warning applied to this reigning monarch of the Atlantic as well as to all other Allied vessels, but the accidental timing gave the world the false impression that the notice referred specifically to the *Lusitania*—and to this crossing—and that the sinking had all been arranged; to most people the threat and the execution seemed beyond question to constitute the two parts of a carefully drawn plan. The publication of the warning had even brought a stern rebuke from President Wilson, who pointed to the "irregularity" of the Germans' addressing the American public through the newspapers and declared that the issuing of a warning that an unlawful act would be committed did not constitute an excuse for the act.

In his own defense, Bernstorff could have explained that he and his colleagues had published the warning in an attempt to prevent the problem that had in fact developed. He could also have reminded the president that the *Lusitania* was not simply a passenger vessel but carried rifle cartridges (4,200 boxes, in fact—two rounds to be fired at each German soldier on the Western Front), 125 boxes of shrapnel shells, and other infantry equipment, and that a case could be made for not allowing the Americans to serve as shields or "guardian angels" for such munitions. He could have pointed to a statement made by Winston Churchill even before the war began that the Admiralty had developed a plan to arm merchant ships and that the *Naval Annual* listed the *Lusitania* and the *Mauretania* as "Royal Naval Reserved Merchant Cruisers," which meant that they had been or could be outfitted with guns. He also could have observed that governments often warned their citizens away from danger zones on land and that the ocean ought to be viewed in the same light.

Though the nations had been at war for just a year, Wilson's legalism already had an anachronistic air to many, for, as a writer of the time observed, "Before the war had proceeded very far international law had been as badly shot to pieces as the Cathedral at Rheims." The great struggle had "witnessed the rapid discarding, by both sides, of hampering restrictions. Germany violated the provisions of the Hague Convention regarding aerial bombardment and gas warfare and in self-defence the allies were obliged to do likewise. England rid herself of the handicaps imposed on her sea power by the Declaration of Paris of 1856 and that of London of 1909," and Germany replied with her submarine campaign. Whatever Bernstorff may have wished to say, however, he concentrated on influencing his home government to conciliate the American president, and as August began he saw progress being made.

But the climax to all these events came on August 19 with the torpedoing and sinking of a British liner, the *Arabic,* with the loss of two Americans. Bernstorff quickly reported to Berlin that diplomatic relations would definitely be broken if the government did not make a conciliatory statement to the Americans. In so thinking, the ambassador had read Wilson's intentions correctly, and after some discussion the Germans agreed—in what became known as the *Arabic* pledge— not to sink passenger ships without warning and without ensuring the safety of passengers and crews. Berlin issued the order on August 30, but one more British liner would be torpedoed before the pledge took practical effect. On September 4, in the familiar waters off southern Ireland, the hard-working *U-20* and her narrowly focused skipper, Lieutenant Schwieger, encountered the 10,000-ton steamer *Hesperian,* bound from Liverpool to Montreal, and sent her to the bottom. Whether or not Schwieger knew it, the *Hesperian* had been fitted with guns.

Thus ended what might be called the *Lusitania* season. It had begun with the German proclamation on February 4, had not involved the sinking of any American ship, had curiously brought about a ministerial change not in Berlin or London but in Washington, and now faded into a relative calm (though negotiations about compensation for the American losses dragged on for months) that both the Americans and Germany's chief representative in the United States could only hope would last.

How misguided had the Germans been in trying to break the new kind of British blockade with their own new kind of commerce raiding? Many Americans felt that the adoption of this campaign proved the Germans to be ruthless warmakers beyond the pale of civilization, and the sinking of the *Lusitania* seemed the maritime equivalent of the destruction of Louvain. Certainly the Germans had consistently displayed blundering ineptitude in the area of public relations, while the British proved themselves masters of the art, drawing on great ingenuity to paint themselves and the French as the defenders of civilization against the spike-helmeted apostles of *Kultur*. As a British historian later wrote, "the Allies, and particularly the British, managed to give the impression that they acted brutally or unscrupulously with regret; the Germans always looked as though they were enjoying it."

Germany had committed offenses more visual, more dramatic, and more immediately deadly than those of the British; inescapably, this new practice the submarine had created of sinking unarmed ships without challenge or any means of saving the crew went against the ancient practice of the sea. "Blockade and death by slow starvation are hallowed by use and wont," as a British commentator later observed. "Speedy death by drowning is not." Besides, the Americans looked on the Allies as democracies and, Count Bernstorff noted, Britain exerted special influence in the United States: "The Americans unconsciously borrow their thoughts and ideas from England, because it is the only nation whose literature and Press are accessible to them in the original tongue." Indeed, said the ambassador, "the English language exercises more absolute power in the United States than even in England itself."

Bernstorff, who favored the American arguments for freedom of the seas over his own country's practices (because he feared conflict with the United States and wished to secure American support in German efforts to ease the British blockade), had felt that at least the government in Berlin must decide on one policy or the other and then stick to it. Perhaps that had now happened. For his part, however, Admiral von Tirpitz had few illusions. He had earlier noted that the Americans would continue "supplying arms and munitions, and neither the Irish nor German Americans will alter that, for it is too good a business." Now, he said on August 22, "the difficulty lies in the question of how the unrestricted submarine campaign can be resumed against England when it has once been interrupted." As a British general would later observe, "Where participation in war is concerned, national interest is apt to override every other consideration."

But on September 18, 1915, the new chief of the German naval staff, Admiral Henning von Holtzendorff, ordered the fleet "to suspend all submarine activities of any sort on west coast [of England] and in Channel, and to carry on in North Sea only in accordance with Prize Order. Practically complete cessation of all employment of submarines." Made easier for the government because of a temporary shortage of available U-boats, such a sweeping order nevertheless gave eloquent proof of the power the submarine had demonstrated as a commerce raider in just a few months: In August alone, U-boats had accounted for 135,000 tons of British shipping; the total for the year would amount to 748,000. In the first test history had given it, the submarine had shown that not only could it inflict material damage on an enemy, it could create and alter currents of thought and thus could shape vital national policies. A handful of these small vessels at moments had threatened to change the entire course of the war. And, of course, they still might do that.

9

FROM FOLKESTONE TO DIEPPE

ount Bernstorff did not get to enjoy for long his satisfaction at the abandonment of the unrestricted U-boat campaign. The pressure to accede to President Wilson's demands had come from the civilian side of the imperial government, Chancellor von Bethmann Hollweg and Foreign Minister Gottlieb von Jagow, and had succeeded despite the hostility of the military and naval leaders. For the time being, Bethmann had talked the Kaiser into acquiescence, a development that had then led to the appointment of Admiral von Holtzendorff, an ally of Bethmann's, as chief of the naval staff.

In February and March, however, the U-boats came back to the vital waters surrounding the British Isles, this time with strict instructions to avoid any attacks on passenger ships inside the war zone and to commit no such sinkings anywhere without the warnings and assurances of safety of the passengers called for by the cruiser rules; armed enemy merchantmen were to constitute the prime targets. Both the German Admiralty and the civilian leaders had been slow to realize that during the preceding summer U-boats had accomplished most of their work not by torpedo attack without warning, as everybody seemed to assume, but by surface action with gunfire. The skippers had not acted out of political considerations but preferred the deck gun to the torpedo tubes for reasons of efficiency and economy.

Even so, the fleet commanders strongly opposed any restrictions on the freedom of action of their boats and crews, and during the winter they received the support of a potent new ally, General Erich von Falkenhayn, the chief of the General Staff. Previously Falkenhayn had not taken submarines with full seriousness as possible major contributors to German victory, but now, influenced by Tirpitz and other naval leaders, his view shifted. Increasingly the German people felt the squeeze of the British blockade, and Falkenhayn came to believe that the war must be won in 1916 and that the part the growing U-boat fleet could play outweighed any dangers that might result from American intervention. Germany found herself in a life-and-death struggle with an implacable England, Falkenhayn maintained, and he told Bethmann that the military leaders "had no right to refrain from the unrestricted use of U-boats" and that "the political authorities, therefore, were not justified in trying to prevent it."

Nevertheless, as Bethmann wished, the resumed campaign came with restrictions, at least at first, and after various discussions—including important meetings to which he had not been invited—Admiral von Tirpitz reached the limit of his frustrations and resigned as naval state secretary, the position in which he had long served like a member of an advisory board instead of as an executive with line authority. Once described as "the one minister of his imperious master who is not accustomed to yield," the admiral had declined into powerlessness, unable to influence the operations of the navy he had created. But after his departure the military and naval authorities continued to argue for the lifting of all restrictions on U-boat operations in British waters, so that any vessel found in the war zone would constitute fair game.

Meanwhile, a naval memorandum of March 13 had made plain the new responsibilities of an individual U-boat commander. In February, pointing to the continuing danger of problems with the United States, Bethmann insisted that submarine commanders must take great care to avoid creating troublesome incidents; they must, in effect, know what they were shooting at before they released a single torpedo. In practice, as the naval memorandum indicated, this requirement meant that a skipper, hurriedly peering into his periscope in varying conditions of weather and light, must be able to tell whether a possible target vessel was neutral or enemy, merchant or passenger, armed or unarmed. However practicable the high naval commanders believed such rules to be, nobody suggested how the individual skipper might develop the extraordinary powers of perception that full adherence to them would require. Skeptical and fatalistic observers, including some of the admirals who detested restrictions, hence had no doubt that an undesirable incident would not be long in coming.

Not only did the skeptics, with shocking speed, prove to be correct, but the expected incident had uniquely damning qualities; it seemed to be a sort of *Lusitania* through the looking glass. Three sinkings in the latter part of March led up to it, but details about them were slow in becoming known. Then came March 24.

■ ■ ■

In mid-December 1915 the Spanish composer Enrique Granados and his wife had come to New York for the world première of his opera *Goyescas,* an event originally planned to take place in Paris but canceled after the outbreak of the war. A musical re-creation of the world of Goya, based on the composer's popular suite for piano of the same name, Granados's opera duly made its bow on January 27 at the Metropolitan Opera House at Broadway and Thirty-ninth Street.

The forty-eight-year-old composer's stay in the United States took on an unplanned dimension when he accepted an invitation from President Wilson to pay a visit to Washington. Having been attracted by the attention given Granados, who was not only a pioneer in the development of a Spanish idiom in serious music but also the first important Spanish composer ever to visit the United States, the president played host at a White House recital by the distinguished visitor. Because his acceptance of the presidential invitation caused Granados to miss his scheduled sailing date, his return to Europe took place later than planned, and so, after their eastward transatlantic voyage, fate placed him and his wife at Folkestone, on the English Channel, at midday on Friday, March 24, ready to cross over to France and thence to make their way back home to Spain. Along with some 380 other passengers, they boarded the channel steamer *Sussex,* a shallow-draft 1,350-ton ferry boat, which departed at some minutes after one o'clock for her routine 80-mile crossing to Dieppe. Since the boat had only five private cabins, the passengers filled the decks and many crowded into the public rooms, which as usual had little space to spare because the ferry made only three crossings a week each way.

The skipper of such a vessel normally might concern himself with the possibility of encountering a floating mine in his Channel passage, but, because of the light draft of the *Sussex,* torpedoes did not constitute a serious concern. It was also true, in addition, that a craft as innocuous as a Channel ferry could hardly be considered a tempting target for a raiding U-boat. Attacking it would be as unsporting as shooting a sheep.

. . .

Besides the High Seas Fleet Flotillas under Commander Bauer, the *Führer der U-Boote,* the Imperial Navy also maintained the Flanders Flotilla, under Commander Bartenbach, working from Bruges in occupied Belgium via canals to two port towns, Ostend and Zeebrugge. This "lair," as the Flanders base became known, served as home for a new class of submarines, the UB boats, which at 127 tons were far smaller than the standard U-boats—"sewing machines," the men called them—but were deemed suitable for coastal operations and could be built quickly. Not surprisingly, their size soon began to increase, with a second generation, the UB IIs, having surfaced displacements from about 260 to about 280 tons (and much better handling qualities) and a third generation, the UB IIIs, almost doubling the UB IIs (most of the 1916 boats weighed in at 516 tons). These larger boats could carry deck guns and thus constituted a surface as well as underwater threat to enemy shipping.

March 24 saw one of the new UB IIs, the *UB-29,* with an able and active young skipper, Lieutenant Pustkuchen, operating in the English Channel. Though certainly familiar with the fresh orders governing U-boat operations, the eager lieutenant also had in mind an earlier order directing submarines to seek out troopships conveying soldiers from England to France. He apparently also believed that passenger ferries no longer ran between Folkestone and Dieppe and therefore that any ship he saw on that run would be fair game. If he encountered a vessel that seemed crammed with people, almost overflowing, he could thus presume it to be a British troop transport and therefore eminently deserving of a torpedo. (A few weeks previously, Colonel House, President Wilson's roving diplomatic operative, had crossed the

Channel both ways on such transports, but the UB IIs had not yet become active; here again, as in his 1915 voyage on the *Lusitania,* the adventurous colonel had demonstrated the eternal importance of luck and timing.)

A little before three o'clock in the afternoon of the twenty-fourth, out in the Channel, Pustkuchen sighted through his periscope a vessel that seemed to meet the qualifications; she was headed for Dieppe, and people were milling around on the decks. "The bridge is covered with people," Pustkuchen wrote in his log. "It is a transport."

At three o'clock the captain of the *Sussex* spotted a torpedo, about a hundred yards away, cutting through the water toward his boat. He immediately ordered evasive action but escape proved impossible. Hurling some of the passengers into the water, a loud explosion blew off the bow of the vessel and also wrecked the radio antenna, delaying the sending of calls for help (which, when they did go out over an improvised replacement, proved misleading, because the operator reported an incorrect position for the boat). Something of a panic ensued, and people who stepped or, in some cases, jumped into the lifeboats found, as one lady from New York commented, that the boats were "not all that might have been desired from the standpoint of safety." Not only "were the lifeboats insufficient in number, but they were unseaworthy and badly managed"; hers literally had holes in it and began to fill up with water, which she attempted to bail with a gentleman's commandeered derby hat. There were only four or five boats, she noted, "and these were largely filled with men."

Although the explosion had inflicted severe damage, the *Sussex* had not suffered mortal wounds—her watertight compartments kept her afloat—and just before midnight a ship took her in tow and set off for Boulogne. Some of the passengers had been taken aboard a sloop from Boulogne, and others by a British destroyer that took them to Dover. But the attack had killed or wounded about eighty passengers, with early reports putting the dead at fifty, from the explosion or from drowning. A number of the injured were among the twenty-five Americans who had been on board.

The explosion had blown Enrique Granados and his wife into the water, and several survivors reported that, when last seen, the couple were clinging to a small raft; the composer was striving to control it with a board he was using as a paddle. Others said they saw Granados plunge off the raft to try to save his wife, who was struggling in the water. A boat that came out to search could find no trace of them.

Instructed to ask the German government whether a U-boat had sunk the *Sussex,* Ambassador Gerard had to wait something over two weeks for a reply that, when finally delivered, amounted to a flat denial. A U-boat had sunk a British minelayer in the general location of the *Sussex* sinking and at about the same time, the note conceded, but that target vessel had gone up in a great explosion, proving that it was stuffed with munitions and therefore could not have been the Dieppe ferry. However, the Channel had been rendered extremely dangerous by the large numbers of mines, fixed and drifting, placed by both the British and the Germans. No doubt, the note implied, the *Sussex* had struck a mine. But rescued passengers, including a young researcher from Harvard, Samuel F. Bemis, had told the U.S. ambassador to France, William G. Sharp, that the explosion had unquestionably been caused by a torpedo; on the very next day, the French Ministry of Marine declared it as a fact. (Actually, since a deliberate attack on a Channel ferry would have represented disobedience to orders and, in the bargain, would have served no purpose, the German authorities for some time had trouble convincing themselves that it really had happened; they shared Pustkuchen's belief that he had attacked a transport. But, as Count Bernstorff glumly noted, "the discovery in the hull of the *Sussex* of a piece of a German torpedo placed the matter beyond all doubt.")

As always, President Wilson insisted on waiting for the full facts before taking action, meanwhile fending off efforts by his hawkish secretary of state, Lansing, to push him into demanding that the Germans totally cease the submarine campaign—no attacks against any merchant ships of any kind. The president found this approach not helpful (Lansing wanted to use words like "barbarian" in a formal diplomatic note), and after satisfying himself that a U-boat had indeed attacked the *Sussex,* he produced his own note. Stern but not insulting, as Lansing's proposed terms had been, it demanded the end not of all submarine attacks but of *unrestricted* submarine warfare. Unless the Imperial German Government "should now immediately declare and effect abandonment of this present method of submarine warfare against passenger- and freight-carrying vessels, the Government of the United States can have no choice but to sever diplomatic relations with the German Empire altogether." Wilson had now defined his issue and had finally issued the ultimatum that many had looked for after the sinking of the *Lusitania*. (Here, again, the vessel that had been attacked was not American, and this time no Americans had been numbered among the fifty passengers who had lost their lives, although for a long time it was believed that one American had been killed; but, of course, whatever the merits of the issue of principle involved, it did not turn on the severity of the injuries suffered by American passengers.)

After intense discussion and strong arguments with the Kaiser and the military and naval authorities, Chancellor von Bethmann Hollweg, who consistently sought to avoid a clash with the United States, won his case for bowing to Wilson's ultimatum and reverting to the traditional prize rules. Tirpitz, in retirement, sent a lengthy memorandum of protest, and Falkenhayn, still in power, continued to argue for unrestricted submarine warfare. What seemed obvious was that sooner or later in this life-and-death struggle—in which, despite the appalling slaughter and destruction like nothing ever seen before, each side persisted in believing it could win a worthwhile victory—either the British would soften their blockade or the Germans would resume and even extend unrestricted submarine warfare. Mitigation of the blockade would come only through some kind of forceful American intervention, which German civilian leaders hoped to earn by good behavior with respect to submarines. These leaders might have been surprised to learn that British naval authorities felt as much disgust with their civilian superiors as Tirpitz and his fellows expressed in relation to Bethmann; indeed, a cleavage between the "frocks" (frock-coated politicians) and the "brass hats" characterized all the warring countries. In December 1915, after vainly struggling for two hours to persuade Admiralty authorities to forget their worries about the United States and other neutrals and allow the navy to clamp the blockade even tighter on Germany, Admiral Jellicoe described the disheartening scene to Admiral Beatty, concluding with the observation: "The French politicians, they say, are worse than ours. Is that possible?"

Though some talk of peace negotiations came along from time to time, on the part of Wilson, House, Bernstorff, Grey, and Bethmann, the hope always foundered on hard and unyielding minimum demands and requirements put forth by either side, the Allies as well as the Central Powers.

After the German government formally accepted the American terms, the frustrated naval authorities once again whistled their boats home from the waters around Britain. Forbidden to make what he considered the best use of his submarines, the new commander of the High Seas Fleet, Admiral Reinhard Scheer, an able and aggressive officer who had no intention of allowing the war to be fought out without the navy's playing a central part in the action, turned his thoughts to the battleships and battle cruisers lying idly in harbor. Perhaps, in combination with U-boats employed as warships (operating with the fleet against enemy warships) rather than as commerce raiders, the big ships could lure portions of the Grand Fleet from their bases and begin to whittle it down to a point at which it would have lost its commanding numerical superiority.

This idea led, at the end of May, to the great but inconclusive clash called the Battle of Jutland, in which the U-boats did nothing to justify Scheer's hopes. On the surface the qualitative superiority of the Germans clearly told, with the Royal Navy suffering losses almost twice as great as those of the outnumbered High Seas Fleet, and in the immediate aftermath of the battle this relatively poor showing led to rumors of a serious British defeat. Some dockyard workers booed damaged ships returning with dead and wounded aboard, and the Kaiser joyously declared that his ships had beaten "the gigantic fleet of Albion," which had "surrounded itself with a nimbus of invincibleness." But this tactical victory for the Germans, though indicating that all was not well with the Royal Navy, did not change the strategic situation. At the end of the day Jellicoe's ships remained the masters of the North Sea, while Scheer's fleet once more sat buttoned up at its bases. The admiral advised the Kaiser that Germany's best hope now lay with the U-boat force.

10

IN THE MED

Looking back, a U-boat skipper called the summer months of 1916 "the dull season, the doldrums." But it was during that time, when the Atlantic offered no action for submariners, that this bold officer began to run up his tally of Allied ships sunk, the tally he modestly did not characterize as "remarkable" or "amazing."

Admiral von Holtzendorff's September order had effectively ended submarine operations not only in the Western Approaches to Britain—the areas in which the U-boats were most likely to encounter American vessels and subject Americans to danger—but also in the North Sea, because of the refusal of the High Seas Fleet commanders to risk their U-boats by making them act in accordance with prize rules. But European waters offered other targets the boats could pursue, far out of the view of the pesky Americans with their legalisms and their declarations. After Germany bowed to Wilson's threat to break off diplomatic relations in April 1916, these other targets took on even greater prominence.

"I was sent down to the Mediterranean," said the ecumenically named Lieutenant Lothar von Arnauld de la Perière (an eighteenth-century ancestor, a French soldier of fortune, had offered his sword to Frederick the Great and, having risen to the rank of general, had become solidly established in Prussia), "and there found the gunning very good." Important cargoes moved through the Mediterranean in both directions: raw materials coming from the east, troops and supplies from England and France going out to the large Allied army based at Salonika in Greece. Yet, compared with the situation in British waters, the Allied navies did not patrol the Mediterranean heavily, though its

more benign weather made it a far better arena for submarine operations than the volatile North Atlantic.

A tall, slender young man, Arnauld served in the surface fleet before
the war as torpedo officer on the cruiser *Emden,* which in the early
days of the fighting enjoyed what quickly became a storied career as a
raider. By that time, however, Arnauld had moved to the staff of Admiral von Pohl as aide-de-camp. When the war broke out, he had no
intention of missing the action and, failing in his search for a zeppelin
to command, turned in the direction of the other third dimension and
entered the submarine service.

Arnauld took command of the *U-35* in January 1916, the winter that
led into the season of "doldrums" following Holtzendorff's command
and then the abandonment of the second unrestricted campaign after
the *Sussex* fiasco. (Once again, the indefatigable Lieutenant Schwieger
had failed to get the word. Almost two weeks after the U-boats were
summoned home, Schwieger in the *U-20* torpedoed and sank the liner
Cymric in the Atlantic out from Ireland.) Arnauld's orders sent him
overland to the submarine base the navy had established at the fine harbor of Cattaro on the hilly Montenegrin coast of the Adriatic Sea.
There the twenty-nine-year-old lieutenant took command of the *U-35*
from one of the pioneer submarine officers in the Imperial Navy,
Korvettenkapitän (lieutenant commander) Waldemar Kophamel, who
had originally brought the boat down from Germany and through the
Strait of Gibraltar and who now became commander of the flotilla
based at Cattaro.

Commissioned in November 1914, the *U-35* belonged to a class of
eleven boats (*U-31–U-41*) turned out by Krupp's Germania shipyard at
Kiel. Slightly larger than Walther Schwieger's *U-20,* with a surfaced
displacement of 685 tons and submerged displacement of 878 tons, it
was 212.27 feet long with a beam of 20.73 feet (dimensions it shared
with eighteen other submarines in three classes produced between 1911
and 1915). It was double-hulled, as all Imperial Navy submarines had
been from the early days, and propelled by twin screws. When driven by
its diesels on the surface, it could attain a speed of more than 16 knots,
about one knot faster than the *U-20* and its classmates; underwater it
could do 9.7. It had four torpedo tubes (two at the bow, two at the stern)

and carried six torpedoes; importantly—perhaps most importantly—it mounted one deck gun, making it a threat on the surface without having to expend any of its torpedoes (the concern always on the minds of the skippers). These boats carried, as the standard complement, four officers and thirty-one men. Altogether, the *U-35* ranked among the most modern and effective of U-boats, demonstrating, as one naval historian commented, that "German submarine design had matured remarkably quickly."

Britain's workhorse submarines at the time, the E-class, were smaller (almost 30 feet shorter, though 2 feet broader in the beam, and displacing 667 tons surfaced); they were a knot slower than the U-31s. Fifty-five of these boats saw service during the war, Max Horton's *E-9* being one of the early stars of the class. E-boats also figured in adventures in the Mediterranean, for which their long range fitted them.

Horton, who had sunk the *Hela* off Heligoland in September 1914, pursued the German fleet through heavy defenses into the Baltic Sea, where he harassed these vessels during their training exercises. Horton and Commander N. F. Laurence in the *E-1* also found substantial targets in ships carrying iron ore from Sweden to Germany. Joined by others, these submarines produced such distress among German leaders that they, with a remarkable lack of self-consciousness, branded the skippers as pirates who employed "underhanded and criminal methods"; they singled out the daring Horton for special opprobrium, but admiring sailors also renamed the Baltic "Horton's Sea."

During the ultimately disastrous Allied 1915 Dardanelles campaign, which aimed at opening a pathway through the straits to the Black Sea and Russia, another E-boat skipper, Lieutenant Commander Martin Nasmith in the *E-11,* created a legend for himself with a series of remarkable exploits in the Sea of Marmara. Plunging through antisubmarine nets and under ranks of mines, he torpedoed a ship in the Golden Horn, the harbor of Istanbul (then Constantinople), sending the inhabitants into a panic, and sank a troop transport. He made two return trips, spending in all about three months on the doorstep of the capital the Turks had believed to be invulnerable, disrupting traffic and, with other submarines, making what turned out to be a vain contribution to the Dardanelles operation. In December 1915 the Allies abandoned the campaign, which had been poorly planned and halt-ingly executed; the submarines followed the departure of the troops with seeming reluctance. The boats had done well: thirteen of them, British and French, had accounted for a total of eight enemy warships, fifty-five transports and commercial steamships, and 148 sailing boats.

■ ■ ■

In a four-week period in July and August 1916, the period that Arnauld de la Perière had called the doldrums, the *U-35* under his command sank fifty-four ships totaling 91,150 tons, and it performed this ex-tended feat in a special way: The deck gun, firing 900 shells, did almost all the work; Arnauld used only four torpedoes.

On Arnauld's very first cruise, his adherence to established proce-dure almost cost him his boat. Having stopped a Dutch freighter with a shot across the bow, he took the *U-35* closer and closer to the steamer, while her crew scrambled into the lifeboats and rowed away. Warily, thinking the vessel might be a Q-ship (an armed vessel disguised as an ordinary steamer), he studied it through his periscope and then had his executive officer take a look. "Harmless," they agreed. Nevertheless, Arnauld steered over to the lifeboats, now lying almost half a mile astern of the ship. "If there were any hidden guns aboard the ship," he felt, "the gun crew would scarcely take so much chance of hitting their own people." Then, as he summoned the men in the boats to row closer, a clattering from the ship announced the running down of gun housings and, with a crack, a shell came whizzing overhead, and the British sailors began pulling away as fast as they could. "Those En-glishmen had their nerve—no doubt about it," Arnauld said. "But there was no time to stop and generously admire the enemy's courage." Hastily he took the submarine down, so fast that, though he had given the order for 20 meters, it went to 60 before the men at the controls could slow the descent. "Yes," Arnauld said with a measure of philos-ophy, "those Q-ships were no joke, especially as we had to warn all ships before sinking them."

Far more deadly proved a British submarine chaser, the *Primola,* with which Arnauld later fought a ferocious duel. A small craft, she was "scarcely worth a torpedo," but Arnauld knew that if "we did not get her she might possibly get us." Having loosed the torpedo and seen it smash into the chaser's bow, Arnauld stared in amazement as the enemy vessel, instead of beginning to sink by the head, reversed engines and backed up at full speed, intending to ram the *U-35 in reverse.* This "brilliant maneuver" had the notable side benefit of helping the *Primola* stay afloat, because in backing up she was literally running away from the water trying to pour into her shattered bow area. A second torpedo from the *U-35* missed its target, as the *Primola,* still reversing, managed to evade it and then resumed her attempt to ram the U-boat. "I'll get you yet," Arnauld muttered, but a third torpedo also missed; however, "that sort of thing could not go on forever." Finally a fourth torpedo hit home, sending the gallant sub chaser to the bottom but leaving Arnauld annoyed at having had to spend four torpedoes for "that tiny wasp." But such a stinger could put an end to the career of a commerce-raiding U-boat, and Arnauld definitely did not wish to "come up with any more Primolas."

Another sinking, however, which Arnauld termed "a frightful affair," seemed to haunt him. A skipper who knew a troopship when he saw one, he spotted a French transport, the *Gallia,* on course for Salonika, and as he later learned the vessel carried three thousand soldiers together with a number of pieces of field artillery. "I had only one torpedo left in a stern tube," Arnauld noted, and since his quarry was making perhaps 18 knots while zigzagging, "it seemed so impossible, in the first place, that we should hit her." But on one zig or zag the *Gallia* presented herself at an extremely difficult but not impossible angle, at a range of 900 yards. Considering this the only chance he would get, Arnauld gave the order to fire and then, since nobody expected a hit to be scored, put the *U-35* into a quick dive to avoid the possibility of being rammed. Then came a *ping!* and immediately afterward a rumbling explosion. Going up to periscope depth, Arnauld "looked through the eyepiece at an appalling sight." A great column of water had shot up into the air, and men were frantically lowering the lifeboats much too fast for safety; hundreds of soldiers had leapt into the water, and "the sea became a terrible litter of overturned lifeboats, overcrowded and swamped lifeboats, and struggling men."

As his crew crowded around him in the conning tower, Arnauld allowed them to take turns looking in the periscope: "Some gazed impassively, others grew pale, some grunted, others cried out in horror. *'Ach Gott!'* a deep guttural cry burst from the throat of the fat cook." Silhouetted against the setting sun, the *Gallia* began her final plunge, as her bow rose high into the air. She hung in that position for a moment, and then, almost in a flash, she disappeared. With this feat of marksmanship, Arnauld said, he had caused one of France's greatest naval disasters (he later learned that 1,852 officers and men were lost), but he could feel no elation.

What Arnauld liked to call his "fish story, a whopper" really amounted to a miracle at sea; either that, or it proved the primary importance of luck in war. Returning from a long patrol in the Mediterranean, the *U-35* sneaked through the cordon of Italian destroyers at the mouth of the Adriatic, and, with everybody eager to get home, Arnauld decided to run the rest of the way to Cattaro on the surface to make port by nightfall. He then went below for a nap, having left on the bridge his watch officer, who had for company no less a personage than the Kaiser's nephew, Prince Sigismund, who had embarked in the *U-35* to acquire submarine experience.

About half an hour later a loud banging and clanking awoke the captain. Rushing to the bridge he saw the executive officer and Prince Sigismund standing transfixed, "white as a pair of ghosts," staring over the side of the boat. Holding his questions about the noise that had drawn him from his bunk, Arnauld looked in the same direction and saw, next to the submarine, a periscope. He also saw the deadly streak of a torpedo heading straight for the *U-35*. Though "no earthly power" could have moved the submarine out of its path, Arnauld mechanically ordered "helm hard aport" and then, like the others, waited for frozen moments. But there came no crash, no explosion: the torpedo, set to run too low, had passed under the *U-35*. In a few seconds another streak rippled the water, but by this time the boat was swinging about in response to the captain's order and the torpedo passed alongside, almost close enough to touch. By the time another one came, the *U-35* was zigzagging away from that hot spot.

But what had caused the banging and rattling noise that woke him up? The watch officer and the prince told Arnauld a remarkable story. As they stood on the bridge they had spotted a periscope just visible above the surface and then the streak of a torpedo heading straight for the *U-35;* just as would happen again in a few minutes, no evasion was possible. The two men "stared aghast, petrified, gazing at certain destruction, which was right upon them." And then, when it was no more than a dozen yards away, the torpedo leapt from the water, as Arnauld said, like a flying fish. Popping up into the air, it came down in an arc and, landing on the deck, slid across it, making its way as if purposefully through the narrow space—no more than 4 feet—between the conning tower and the forward gun, splashed back into the water, and kept on going. A few inches either way had kept the missile's sensitive nose from encountering metal and detonating its explosive charge, thus saving the *U-35*. The attacking submarine commander had set the first torpedo for too shallow a run and overcompensated with the second torpedo, twice saving the *U-35*.

A miracle of such dimensions overwhelmed an old petty officer in the crew, who assured Arnauld that such goings-on as torpedoes bouncing on the deck was all simply too much. Next he would be seeing an entire British submarine leaping into the air and vaulting over the deck! Determined to avoid any further submarine-*v.*-submarine confrontations, he refused to go on the next patrol and won a transfer to shore duty. As for Arnauld, he ended the war as Germany's submarine ace of aces, with 194 ships sunk, representing more than 450,000 tons of Allied shipping sent to the bottom. Before he had been in command of the *U-35* more than a few months, he had received the Pour le Mérite. Since no future triumphs could win him a greater honor, the next time he came up for a medal he was given, at his own request, a signed photograph of the Kaiser.

■ ■ ■

In September 1917 another unusual young officer reported for duty to the commander of the Mediterranean Flotilla at Pola, the Austrian naval base at the head of the Adriatic. Though just graduated from the

Submarine School at Kiel, this officer, Lieutenant Wilhelm Canaris, had not arrived at this advanced stage of the war without having had some remarkable adventures and without having displayed remarkable and specific talents.

Unlike a great many officers in both German services, Canaris came from a family with no military tradition, and unlike most young men at the time, he felt powerfully drawn to what was still only the emerging Imperial Navy rather than to the army, the pride of the nation. Graduating from the naval academy at Kiel in 1907, he went off to the Caribbean and the South Atlantic on the cruiser *Bremen,* whose mission included among its purposes the maintaining of contacts with influential German emigrants to the countries along those shores. Although he tended toward shyness and reserve, his intelligence and efficiency quickly won him praise from his superiors, and his ability with languages—he spoke good English, workable French, and a measure of Russian and quickly mastered Spanish—led his captain to make him the designated negotiator in dealings with Latin American officials; he revealed "an almost unrivalled talent for dealing with foreigners" and also displayed a marked ability in handling people.

After a period of service in European waters, Canaris returned to Latin America at the beginning of 1914, aboard the cruiser *Dresden,* which found itself serving as a refuge for foreigners caught up in the violence of a revolution in Mexico and even ferried the overthrown President Victoriano Huerta to safety in Jamaica (although, following orders, Lieutenant Canaris had to draw on all his diplomatic skills to induce the reluctant tiger to leave the country). By this time it was late July, and before the *Dresden* could depart from the Caribbean on its scheduled return home, the war had begun; orders then came to stay in the Western Hemisphere and conduct cruiser warfare. This meant that, working as a lone eagle with no reliable communication with home, the *Dresden* would have to develop and weave together its own sources of information about the enemy navy. As the officer with the best contacts in the whole area, Canaris received this daunting assignment, to which he also brought a love of intrigue and a fondness for its trappings—aliases, ciphers, and secret inks. Although information from his network helped Admiral Graf Spee defeat a British squadron off the coast of Chile, Spee, unwisely emboldened by this success, soon led his ships into a collision with a superior British force, an engagement from which only the *Dresden* escaped.

For the next three months the cruiser devoted herself to scrabbling for coal while eluding the eyes of the British (aided by diversionary schemes produced by Canaris) until she was run to ground in a speck of an island hundreds of miles out in the Pacific. At the beginning of August, with his ship scuttled and his crew interned on an island off the central Chilean coast, the captain finally allowed Canaris to try to escape in a fishing boat. The attempt turned into the first stage of an adventure that included a trek across the Andes and through Argentina, where the young officer's fluent Spanish made it possible for him to acquire a fake passport as a Chilean national. By way of Uruguay, Brazil, Portugal, and even England, he finally returned to Germany, reaching home in October.

As they increased the attention they gave to submarine operations in the Mediterranean in the autumn of 1915, the German authorities, seeing the need to build up an information network in Spain, realized that the ideal officer to perform such a task had just been delivered to them. Still using his Chilean passport, Canaris traveled to Spain by way of France and proceeded to produce one of what had become his typical successes. Within two or three months he had turned the existing German naval intelligence effort in Spain into a flourishing network producing information on Allied naval operations. Canaris also did well at creating a supply network of ships that could act as tenders to U-boats.

Hungry for direct action—he had long wanted to command a torpedo boat—Canaris tried to return to Germany via Switzerland but, identified to French intelligence as no Chilean but instead an important German agent, found himself detained in Italy. He managed to escape, however, and returned to Madrid, but this time, preparing for an expanded submarine war, the naval authorities wanted his services badly enough to arrange for him to be picked up by a U-boat. The plan called for Canaris, in a small sailing boat, to be picked up off Cartagena by the distinguished Lieutenant Lothar von Arnauld de la Perière in the *U-35*. But other parties intended to appear as well; tipped off by a double agent, the French had dispatched a submarine and a Q-ship with the explicit mission of eliminating the German spymaster Canaris.

The sailing boat, the two French vessels, and the *U-35* came together, almost as if invited to have a meeting. Faced with the problem of extricating his prospective passenger from this complex situation, Arnauld, who had studied the scene through his periscope, surfaced on the side of the sailing boat away from the French vessels, so that the sail itself could veil the U-boat from the French on the Q-ship. Like Canaris, Arnauld had become accustomed to success, and in a quick three- or four-minute operation he took Canaris and two accompanying officers aboard and, to the accompaniment of blasts from the Q-ship's siren, ordered the U-boat down and away. Soon he was headed for Cattaro with his prize passenger, his daring mission accomplished except for the formality of negotiating his entrance into the Adriatic.

It was submarines and not torpedo boats that the naval authorities had in mind for Canaris, and after extensive training, and accompanied by the usual effusive reports from his superiors, he returned to the Mediterranean in September 1917, officially qualified to command a U-boat. His opportunity to shine came in January 1918 when he filled in for Johannes Klasing, the skipper of the *U-34*. Operating like a veteran, Canaris picked off a freighter out of each of two convoys and added one more, thus returning to Cattaro with a record that won him special praise for achieving such success as a beginner. He soon acquired a command of his own, the *UB-128,* but by the time the boat was ready and he and the crew had trained together and had come down from Kiel to Cattaro, the war—and with it the German Empire—was fading. So, also, was Canaris's temporary command, the *U-34,* which, once again skippered by Klasing, encountered the guns of a Q-ship on November 9 and thus, two days before the Armistice, became the last U-boat to be lost in the war. As for Canaris himself, his background of experience and his reputation made it most unlikely that history would see him fading away at the age of thirty-one.

11

"THE CURSED CROWD"

n late June 1916 a mystery was brewing out in the Atlantic off the Virginia Capes. On the twenty-eighth of the month a tug appeared in these waters at the entrance to Chesapeake Bay and, while appearing to be awaiting a vessel to tow, spent the day in obvious idleness. It returned the next morning for another uneventful session on station, an unproductive routine that stretched on and on, into thirteen days; the tug, the *Thomas F. Timmins,* would leave the scene only to go into Norfolk for coal.

When reporters questioned the captain after he had allowed several vessels bound for Baltimore to go by without offering them a tow, he replied, in interesting detail, that he was looking out for one particular ship, an Italian sailing vessel coming from Norway, loaded with saltpeter. A check of ship registries turned up no listing for any such vessel, and rumors, fed from various sources as the days went by, declared that the tug actually was waiting not for an Italian bark with a cargo of saltpeter but for a new and large German submarine. Veteran mariners, including U.S. Navy officers, however, hooted at the idea; even the Germans, efficient and daring as they were, could hardly have brought a submarine 4,000 miles across the Atlantic from its base in home waters. And what for?

On the other hand, a Dutch skipper, arriving in Nova Scotia on June 29, reported that five days earlier and two-thirds of the way across the Atlantic, his crew had sighted a large submarine westward bound, making about 15 knots. Apparently reacting to what it would have correctly presumed to be a sighting, the submarine had promptly dived. On Friday, June 30, reporters discovered that the *Timmins* had on board a German merchant skipper; he surely could be there only to direct the reception of the mysterious submarine. And, giving strong proof that the Allied navies put considerable stock in the submarine story, a British and a French cruiser patrolled offshore, obviously there to bar the harbor door to any such U-boat. These vessels had come even though the British naval attaché (who was also an intelligence officer) had told the world that no German submarine with transatlantic aspirations could get very far before being caught.

Finally, at about 1:45 in the morning of July 9, having eluded the patrolling cruisers, a large submarine slipped into U.S. territorial waters, surfacing just about a mile past the stations of the cruisers, and by eight o'clock on the stormy evening that followed it had engaged in an exchange with reporters on a press boat. To the question "Where do you come from and when?" an authoritative voice from the bridge cried back: "Heligoland. June 23." The arrival stirred such excitement throughout the area that the Baltimore chief of police called in reinforcements to handle the crowds.

Heading up Chesapeake Bay, "the big submarine presented a picturesque sight as she ploughed through the tumbling whitecaps. Time and again searchlights from excursion steamers played upon her, throwing even her darkly painted hull into bold relief against the blackness of a rainy night. She was riding high out of the water, and almost the whole ship's company walked about on the narrow deck. Most of the men wore oilskins, but the officer on the bridge stood regardless of the storm in his blue coat and white trousers." On either side of her bow the vessel bore the name: DEUTSCHLAND.

By ten o'clock that evening the submarine had dropped anchor in Baltimore harbor; after being cleared at Quarantine, she would move to her berth on the Patapsco River, near Locust Point. The news quickly spread that the new arrival belonged to a subsidiary of the North German Lloyd steamship line and thus had come to the United States not as a naval vessel but as something new, a merchant submarine, an underwater cargo ship—a striking reversal of the role as commerce raider that had won submarines their great notoriety during the past year and a half. The captain of the *Deutschland,* Paul König, former skipper of the Lloyd liner *Neckar,* explained that she carried a thousand tons of cargo, mostly dyestuffs (special German products whose absence had been felt in the United States), together with mail and a messenger with a letter from the Kaiser to President Wilson.

Discussing his transatlantic voyage, Captain König revealed that he had not taken the submarine around Scotland but had come straight through the Channel. In crossing the ocean he had sighted a great many merchant ships and one British cruiser, and had avoided detection by quickly submerging. During the previous night, he said, while creeping surfaced through the darkness he had sighted the patrolling Allied craft about 9 miles off the Capes and had passed them with no trouble, at one point proceeding within 500 yards of the French cruiser.

The *Deutschland* had, in fact, experienced a stressful time while still close to home in the North Sea, battling a storm that produced waterspouts and waves high enough to lift her into a *Kopfstand* (literally, to make her stand on her head) and then having to dive to elude a British destroyer.

As time had gone on from the summer of 1914, the British blockade had squeezed Germany more and more tightly. Swept off the seas in that first summer of the war, German merchant ships had never been able to return; the Royal Navy controlled the surface of the oceans; the all-encompassing blockade could not be run. But perhaps giant underwater merchant craft could at least loosen the noose. Hence the *Deutschland*.

The fate of this new kind of submarine in America would now rest in the hands of the State Department, which found itself presented with an entirely new problem in international and maritime law: Were submarines now to be divided into two categories, belligerent and merchant? And thus the department had to determine whether to treat the *Deutschland* as a merchant ship or as the warship of a belligerent power; if the latter, she would have to depart within twenty-four hours. If she was carrying a true cargo and had the proper documents and manifests, did not carry torpedoes, and had no armament stronger than quick-firing deck guns for defense, Washington observers said, the government would most likely treat her as a merchant vessel. In Baltimore, after an inspection that was "the most thorough and minute ever made at this port," the customs authorities gave her their stamp of approval, declaring that they "found her absolutely unarmed, save for five pistols she carried in her ship's stores for the use of her officers." She was then allowed to move to the berth at Locust Point, while local Germans in Baltimore declared her to be the first in a long line of such submarines that would engage in commerce with the United States. (Simon Lake, paying a call on Captain König, noted that the *Deutschland* had been berthed within a quarter of a mile of the spot at which he had first taken the *Argonaut* underwater in 1897.)

In style and manner, König, a forty-nine-year-old merchant officer who had never served in the navy and hence had never before now commanded or even set foot on a submarine, found much favor with reporters, who hailed him as "the typical modern ocean adventurer" and "modest about it all." Asked why the *Deutschland* had carried 300 tons of scrap iron ballast instead of supplementing the dyestuffs with other cargo, the captain said: "What else should we have brought—beer?" For reading matter the crew had, besides German authors, Shakespeare, Bret Harte, and Mark Twain. "We had all of Dickens," the captain noted, "but we left behind Jules Verne's 'Twenty Thousand Leagues Under the Sea.' It was too imaginative for us." The trip marked "the beginning of regular international commerce by means of submarines," König declared. "We have proved that their range is practically unlimited, that the British blockade, so called, cannot hinder them, and that they are economically feasible." It might in fact prove a slow way to combat the British "blockade" (neatly given implied quotation marks by König), but at least the Germans could consider it a beginning.

Impressed by the size of the *Deutschland,* reporters called her a giant and a supersubmarine and, given her surfaced displacement of 1,512 tons, she deserved the descriptions. Built at Krupp's Germania yards, she belonged to the U-151 class and was one of three large cruiser submarines converted from warship to commercial vessel (the others were the *Oldenburg* and the *Bremen)*. She had the orthodox arrangement of twin-screw diesel engines with electric motors for underwater running and could do 12.4 knots on the surface and 5.2 knots submerged. She was 213 feet long, though enthusiastic reporters credited her with another 102 feet. An official visitor, the assistant health officer in Baltimore, declared, "I never saw such a mass of machinery in my life." It was "an inexplicable tangle of burnished copper and glistening steel."

For Count Bernstorff, "the few days after the arrival of the *Deutsch-land* were the pleasantest I experienced in America during the war. Feeling on all sides was openly friendly, and Captain König was the most popular man in the United States." On his official visit to view the submarine, on a day with the thermometer standing at a hundred degrees, the ambassador had the company of the mayor of Baltimore, even "into the lowest parts of the submarine, which cost the stoutly-built gentleman considerable effort and a good deal of perspiration." At the mayor's banquet that evening the rooms were hung with German and American flags and the band played "Die Wacht am Rhein." For Bernstorff it all served as a cheery reminder of "the good days before the war."

Singlehandedly, Captain König seemed to have transformed the national hostility toward Germany produced by the destruction of the *Lusitania* into a semblance, at least, of the old friendship. Together with the increasing American annoyance at the restriction of U.S. trade caused by the British blockade, the success of the *Deutschland*'s mission yielded a public relations triumph that gave some of the German civilian leaders the hope that they might not have to face another round in the running battle of U-boats vs. Woodrow Wilson.

■ ■ ■

To Count Bernstorff's dismay, his countrymen soon produced a fresh PR nightmare. The glow from the deeds of Captain König and his boat had not yet faded when a conventional commerce-raiding U-boat, the *U-53*, arrived off the U.S. East Coast all on its own and, after pausing to refill its tanks at Newport, Rhode Island, sailed off to torpedo and sink five freighters: none American (though one was a Canadian ship en route to a U.S. port), and all in international waters and done according to the proper rules, but within the sweep of Nantucket Light, on the doorstep of the United States and so seeming like the slap of a gauntlet across the face of Woodrow Wilson.

Already scheduled for a meeting with the president on another matter, Bernstorff received a direct personal warning from Wilson that popular feeling in the United States might again, as after the loss of the *Lusitania,* turn "very bitter" against Germany if any more such U-boat attacks should occur. If that should happen, the president said, he could not be responsible for the state of public feeling. The ambassador needed no admonitions. With the election almost at hand and with Wilson being Germany's best hope for an outcome of the war that would at least be acceptable—even though he had made no progress in inducing the British to mitigate the blockade—the Germans must avoid any action, submarine or otherwise, that would harm the president politically. Nothing could really happen until the voters had spoken on November 7.

At the Democratic convention in June, astonishing scenes not only made the emotional temperature of much of the country dramatically plain for all to read but even shook the party managers. As the keynote speaker, a former New York governor, Martin Glynn, ran down a list of incidents in American history in which the country had refused to allow provocations to push it into war, the delegates bellowed, "What did we do? What did we do? *We didn't go to war!*" Party elders even feared that the fervor of this demonstration would make the Democrats look opposed to fighting under any circumstances.

The election between Wilson, for whom "He kept us out of war" became the signature slogan, and the Republicans' imposing, bearded candidate, Charles Evans Hughes, who had resigned from the Supreme Court to make the run, proved so tight that the tabulators could not determine the winner for three days; the decision came when the count gave California to the president by 3,775 votes. Wilson had received about 52 percent of the votes, making him now a majority president. With this victory in hand, he could move to take on the peacemaker role he cherished and work for mediation rather than armed intervention in Europe.

On January 22, addressing the Senate, Wilson, speaking "on behalf of humanity," uttered one of his most famous statements, the call for a "peace without victory." But looking back at the lives they had lost and the material and financial damage they had suffered, the Allies brusquely dismissed such notions. In a "laboriously drafted note" containing their reply to a note from the president, they demanded the evacuation of invaded territories by the Germans and reparations for damages that had been inflicted, but beyond that the Allies proclaimed sweeping intentions across the map. They would liberate non-Turkish peoples from Ottoman rule and would free from foreign domination the population of Alsace-Lorraine and all others in Central and Eastern Europe—Italians, Romanians, Czechs, Slovaks, Yugoslavs, and Poles. They were dying for ideals while Wilson merely talked about them. If there was to be no victory, then what had all the suffering been for? In its reply to the same note, the German government applauded the president's "noble initiative" but expressed a preference for direct dealings between the Central Powers and the Allies rather than a process of mediation directed by Wilson.

On both sides, it seemed, "even with the increasing war weariness, the governments were losing their sense of reality"; the unrelenting god of war appeared to have hypnotized every cabinet and every general staff. The Allies had made it plain that they aimed at victory and nothing less. Now the Germans had vital decisions to make.

In the evening of January 9, 1917, a so-called Crown Council gathered in one of the great rooms of Pless castle, Kaiser Wilhelm's Eastern Front headquarters in Silesia. "All stood around a large table," recalled the chief of the Imperial Civil Cabinet, "on which the Emperor, pale and excited, leaned on his hand." The other participants of high rank were Chancellor Bethmann Hollweg; Field Marshal Paul von Hindenburg, the most admired German soldier, who had replaced General von Falkenhayn as chief of the General Staff; General Erich Ludendorff, the field marshal's younger and in many ways dominant associate; and Admiral von Holtzendorff. The meeting came as the climax of weeks of deliberations and debates involving the military and civilian authorities, with a chasm developing between Bethmann and the Hindenburg-Ludendorff team, who had come to power the previous August and demonstrated increasingly the truth that, when a country puts a hero in a high position, it thereby puts itself in the hands of that hero; the team from the Eastern Front had advanced far toward establishing a de facto dictatorship in the German Empire. But, still, the niceties would be observed.

A visitor to Pless had noted with considerable surprise that, for the fulcrum of a great war, the place seemed an oasis of peace and quiet; gazing out of a window, he saw nothing more military than two officers on horseback cantering across a lawn in the distance. The *Schloss,* an enormous building of perhaps three hundred rooms with long marble corridors lined with the heads of aristocratically slain stags, sat in a great park landscaped with lakes and flower beds "arranged in the most artistic manner." Long-tailed golden pheasants walked across the lawns and swans floated on the lakes. The opulence of the remote setting contrasted strongly with the daily realities faced by the Kaiser's people during this winter of 1916–17, which would long be remembered as the "turnip winter." By a perhaps not altogether voluntary agreement with the British, even the Netherlands and Norway had greatly cut their delivery of food to the Germans, and at this stage of the war the shortage of fodder and fertilizer had resulted in greatly reduced agricultural production; the prospect for cereals and the vital potato crop in 1917 looked even worse. As the most eminent authority on the subject observed, "It was the food-shortage which was the dominant preoccupation of the enemy Governments and peoples." In fact, "it appeared probable that the harvest would be both late and bad, and meanwhile it was a question whether the available foodstuffs could be made to hold out until it was gathered." Food was not only in short supply but often could be considered not much better than inedible, and much of it had little nutritious value; bread, for instance, often consisted of husks and fungi with just a smattering of grain.

The High Command now proposed to produce comparable and even worse conditions in Great Britain, to counter one kind of thorough blockade with another. The military leaders bluntly affirmed that the adoption of unrestricted submarine warfare would bring victory to Germany; England would be starved out in six months, Admiral von Holtzendorff declared, before a single American soldier had set foot anywhere on the Continent. In relation to foodstuffs, Britain presented an ideal target for a blockade of one kind or another, as an island that, in the five years immediately preceding the outbreak of the war, had imported (in caloric value) about two-thirds of its annual consumption.

Though the Kaiser and Bethmann both had their doubts about the wisdom of the decision the council was about to make, they did not oppose it. In a private noon meeting with Hindenburg and Ludendorff, Bethmann had called the U-boat campaign "the last card" but had conceded that "if the military authorities consider the U-boat war essential, I am not in a position to contradict them." Hindenburg replied, "We need the most energetic, ruthless methods that can be adopted." In that meeting and in the Crown Council as well, Bethmann noted, as though only slowly grasping the point, "I had the feeling that I had before me men who no longer had any inclination to be diverted by persuasion from their already settled decisions."

For his part, the chancellor had not kept the military and naval leaders informed about any possibility of positive results from President Wilson's peace initiative; he seems to have presumed, and on obviously sound grounds, that the generals and admirals would have paid no attention to him. Besides, he shared "the distrust which the most influential statesmen felt towards the President." What animated Woodrow Wilson? What motives guided him? The German leaders were not the only ones who could not answer such questions. (A later commentator would observe that "the historian who tries to disentangle the motives and purposes of Wilson's actions from what he himself said—and sincerely believed—about those motives and purposes will find himself constantly baffled by the apparent incongruity and irrelevance of the pieces which he has to fit together.")

For a cluster of reasons, the High Command accepted the probability that the decision to adopt the unrestricted submarine campaign would bring the United States into the war; resuming the campaign would certainly represent a repudiation of the settlement reached after the *Sussex* incident, but in seeing little for a Continental, war-hardened power to fear from American intervention they were, by their own lights, not acting unreasonably: The United States had no real army, and the last time the country had gone to war (against Spain in 1898), it had put on a fumbling and farcical show for the amusement of the world's military observers.

But the problem for Hindenburg, Ludendorff, and their colleagues was precisely that their lights were limited; they knew little of the

United States, not having had the experience of a diplomat like Bern-storff, and thus had no comprehension at all of the enormous latent power of the country, of the energy with which that power could be organized, or of the self-righteous anger with which it could be exerted. Bethmann himself had said in his meeting with Hindenburg and Ludendorff that, if the United States should enter the war, her assistance to the Allies would consist of—that is, be limited to—"the delivery of food supplies to England, financial support, delivery of airplanes, and the dispatching of corps of volunteers."

The German nation had not understood, said Bernstorff, that "the most important battle of the war was taking place in Washington." Certainly the limited knowledge and insight that characterized the crucial meetings of January 9 provide a cautionary example of the level of ignorance that frequently governs the decision making of great nations. As Churchill noted a few years later, "Of all the grand miscalculations of the German High Command none is more remarkable than their inability to comprehend the meaning of war with the American Union."

The German armies everywhere stood on enemy soil, and thus might have appeared to have had the better of the great argument so far. But that would merely be a map speaking. The central fact was that bodies on both sides had piled up for two and a half years now, and the deadlock on land still existed. On a get-acquainted visit to the front in France, Hindenburg and Ludendorff had been shocked on realizing the dimensions and the pointlessness of the continuing slaughter; the Allies controlled the world's seaborne commerce, and the grip of the British blockade became steadily tighter. Hence, absolutely convinced that unrestricted submarine warfare offered the only chance of victory, the High Command got its way; with the Kaiser's acquiescence, the campaign would begin on February 1. Finally, the "cursed crowd of intriguers at Pless" had adopted the departed Tirpitz's prescription for beating England. In reality, however, the Germans had trapped themselves in a paradox: The only way they could win the war was by adopting a strategy that ensured their defeat. The chief of the Civil Cabinet saw the truth; he added to his notes of the meeting the laconic but ominous comment "Finis Germaniae." (And, acknowledging the fateful importance of timing in human affairs, Tirpitz commented later that if the German leaders could have foreseen the Russian Revolution, whose beginnings were only two months off, they would "perhaps not have needed to regard the submarine campaign of 1917 as a last resort"—a last resort because it came dangerously late; if the grand admiral had been able to have his way, the Germans would have launched the campaign much earlier.) In reaching for the submarine as his weapon the Kaiser "never seems to have realized that in the world's eyes he was wielding not a sword but a snake." But, at least to some extent, the Kaiser did see the point; the true failure of realization belonged to his generals.

The next day the military leaders told the Kaiser that he ought to dismiss the chancellor, and thus, after only a few months, departed the man, more bureaucrat than politician, who meant well feebly and who in his final weeks in office served as little more than a punching bag for Ludendorff. "It would have been better before history to have gone down with flag flying," commented Churchill. "His capitulation had availed him nothing." Within three weeks of the January 9 council, the Germans would produce evidence of a wholly unexpected kind that the generals and the admirals had no monopoly on ignorance of the United States and on incomprehension of American affairs generally.

■ ■ ■

American newspapers had hailed the appointment, on November 22, 1916, of Arthur Zimmermann as German foreign minister. Commentators not only spoke of him as a "warm friend of the United States" (the *New York Post* actually titled a column "Our Friend Zimmermann") but welcomed him as a possible symbol of an imperial government move toward liberalization, because he came not from the ranks of the Prussian Junkers but from the middle class. This idea represented little more than propaganda or wishful projection, though Ambassador Gerard gave it a degree of credibility with his characterization of Zimmermann as, at heart, a liberal whose "mental excitement caused by his elevation to the Foreign Office at a time of stress, made him go over to the advocates of ruthless submarine war, lock, stock and barrel." Germany "could not hold out a year on the question of food,"

Zimmermann explained to the ambassador. "Give us only two months of this kind of warfare and we shall end the war and make peace within three months."

In February President Wilson and his colleagues would learn the remarkable limitations of the foreign minister's understanding of America and of the overall situation in the Western Hemisphere. On the morning of January 17 a freshly intercepted German ciphered diplomatic dispatch had arrived in the British decrypting center known innocuously as Room 40. The two men on duty, both nonprofessionals doing wartime service as codebreakers (one a publisher, the other a preacher), went to work and in due course produced the substance of an English text they read with astonishment: The intended recipient of the message was Heinrich von Eckhardt, the German minister to Mexico, with the imperial embassy in Washington serving as the relaying station.

BERLIN TO WASHINGTON, W 158. 16 JANUARY 1917.

MOST SECRET FOR YOUR EXCELLENCY'S PERSONAL INFORMATION AND TO BE HANDED ON TO THE IMPERIAL MINISTER IN (?) MEXICO WITH . . . BY A SAFE ROUTE. WE PROPOSE TO BEGIN ON THE 1 FEBRUARY UNRESTRICTED SUBMARINE WARFARE. IN DOING THIS HOWEVER WE SHALL ENDEAVOUR TO KEEP AMERICA NEUTRAL . . . (?) IF WE SHOULD NOT (? SUCCEED IN DOING SO) WE PROPOSE TO (? MEXICO) AN ALLIANCE ON THE FOLLOWING BASIS:

(JOINT) CONDUCT OF WAR (JOINT) CONCLUSION OF PEACE . . . YOUR EXCELLENCY SHOULD FOR THE PRESENT INFORM THE PRESIDENT [I.E., OF MEXICO] SECRETLY (? THAT WE EXPECT) WAR WITH THE USA (POSSIBLY) (JAPAN . . .) AND AT THE SAME TIME TO NEGOTIATE BETWEEN US AND JAPAN . . . PLEASE TELL THE PRESIDENT THAT . . . OUR SUBMARINES . . . WILL COMPEL ENGLAND TO PEACE WITHIN A FEW MONTHS. ACKNOWLEDGE RECEIPT.

ZIMMERMANN.

This "Zimmermann telegram" gave the British official if inadvertent notice of the decision taken at Pless on January 9; Germany was staking everything—the outcome of the war, the future—on the U-boats. That news, though deeply unwelcome, would cause no great surprise. But proposing an alliance between the German Empire and Mexico, directed against the United States, was truly startling. Since President Wilson had for several years kept the United States embroiled in the turbulent Mexican political scene in furtherance of his curious desire to find and support a Mexican government on which he could bestow his approval, Zimmermann apparently believed that a full-scale war between the two countries would produce American involvement on a major scale, drawing considerable attention and effort away from war against Germany. But what could Germany contribute to the alliance, and what did Mexico stand to gain from it?

The latter question found its answer when further decryption revealed the German promise to help Mexico "regain by conquest her lost territory in Texas, Arizona, and New Mexico." But Zimmermann, who appears to have been the father of the scheme, had produced a wholly self-serving plan, which called for Mexico not to initiate hostilities against the United States but to take action only if Germany and the United States went to war with each other; if that did not happen, the lost provinces, as far as the Germans were concerned, would remain lost. The supposedly pro-American Zimmermann seemed not to have developed enough understanding of the United States to realize that, even if such a move were possible in terms of force, reintegrating Texas into Mexico would be as impossible as restoring the virginity of the Kaiserin (who as a good German *Frau* had borne the emperor seven children). Or, if Zimmermann made the offer only as bait for Mexican President Venustiano Carranza, he was showing contempt for Carranza's intelligence. Even so, the German foreign minister could not bring himself to include another lost province, California, in the offer.

But such considerations hardly ranked first with the codebreakers and their superiors, including the famous Admiral "Blinker" Hall, the director of naval intelligence and head of Room 40. What use should the British government make of this astonishing telegram? Perhaps it should simply be suppressed, to ensure that no reaction or leak would reveal to the Germans one of the great secrets of the war, the British ability to read their diplomatic cipher. In the realm of intelligence, much precedent existed for rejecting action in favor of discretion in such situations, but on this day, presented with this message, Hall without hesitation spent no time in such thinking. Fearing that his own political chiefs would simply dither and do nothing, he took it upon himself to pass the information on to an acquaintance at the U.S. embassy in London, who found Zimmermann's scheme so absurd that he suspected his British friends of having concocted the message, but once persuaded that it was genuine, got it on its way to Washington.

President Wilson, who had responded to the German declaration of January 31 by sending Count Bernstorff home and asking Congress for the authority to arm merchant ships (he really wanted Congressional endorsement, since he already possessed the authority), gave Zimmermann's message a curious reception. For a month now, commerce in the North Atlantic had been drying up as American freighters, afraid to venture out into the sea lanes, sat in port (in the first nineteen days of February only five American freighters sailed for forbidden ports), while in Congress those fearing moves toward war battled with those who favored such moves. As Zimmermann's telegram arrived, the president was preparing for his second inauguration, consequent on his reelection four months earlier as the leader who "kept us out of war," and arranging to go to Capitol Hill to deliver in person his message on the ship-arming bill.

Receiving Zimmermann's message in this context, Wilson, as would be expected, expressed outrage at the foreign minister's impudence. But in a message to Ambassador Page in London he made an extraordinary request. As though Arthur Balfour, the British foreign secretary, had gone out of his way to perform a selfless service for the United States, the president asked his ambassador to express thanks for "so marked an act of friendliness on the part of the British government." Whatever Wilson intended by this bit of disingenuousness, he could hardly have been so naive as not to realize that what Zimmermann had done, as Admiral Hall had immediately seen, was to hand the British what seemed an almost heaven-sent opportunity to give U.S. policy a shove toward intervention in the war. For Britain, passing the message to the Americans represented a simple act of self-interest.

The publication of the telegram in U.S. newspapers on March 1 created a nationwide sensation. "[N]o other event of the war to this point, not even the German invasion of Belgium or the sinking of the

Lusitania, so stunned the American people," no doubt because it concerned the United States directly and also, importantly, because it amounted to simply the latest and perhaps the greatest in the series of colossal psychological and public relations blunders the Germans had committed since the opening days of the war. Thus the telegram influenced American attitudes toward Germany, including Wilson's, even though the president did not base his subsequent actions on shock or anger at Zimmermann's plan. Most strikingly, perhaps, the message gave dramatic proof of how little the Germans understood the United States and the whole North American scene. Still, it was the work of the U-boats, Wilson's antagonists for two years now, that would lead the United States into the war.

On March 12 a German submarine sank an American cargo ship by shellfire, without warning but with no loss of life. Then, on March 18, came news that U-boats had pounced on three more American steamers in British waters, with fifteen members of one crew being drowned while launching the lifeboats. Just the day before, Washington had received confirmation of reports about a truly tremendous event, the overthrow of the czar of Russia and the establishment of a promisingly parliamentary regime in Petrograd. Thus the Western Allies could now, with more justice than formerly, claim to be fighting for fairness and democracy, a claim that had proved far from convincing in many circles while they were leagued with the world's greatest despotism.

On April 2, having summoned the recently adjourned Congress back in special session, President Wilson appeared before the senators and representatives, not to assert that the United States must defend the sea lanes for her own safety, but to declare, far more grandly, that "the world must be made safe for democracy" and that the day had come when America was "privileged to spend her blood and her might for the principles that gave her birth and happiness." He asked for a declaration of war on Germany, which both houses passed in joint resolutions, the Senate on April 4 and the House the next day; the effective date was April 6.

Thus a handful of U-boats, craft that had received little attention just three years earlier at the outbreak of hostilities, had performed what amounted to an unintentional miracle, the greatest political feat

of the war. Step by inadvertent step, they had succeeded where tradition and emotion, diplomatic efforts and strategic considerations, and
financial pressures had all failed. For the first time since 1812, an
American president had taken his country to war with a formidable
foreign foe.

12

THE FIGHT FOR SEA SHEPHERDS

On the sunshiny morning of May 4, 1917, four weeks after the United States entered the war, crowds of people, gathering as if summoned for some great ceremony, covered the hills enclosing Queenstown, the port off which the *Lusitania* had been torpedoed two years earlier. Presently, looking off to the west, watchers could discern a tiny smudge of smoke, followed soon by another and then still another. Before long, these three black spots took shape with three others as a flotilla of warships—destroyers—coming on fast and arriving, at the end of a transatlantic voyage, at almost the exact minute that had been foretold. Buildings on shore and boats in the harbor broke out the Stars and Stripes and people moved down toward the water; local officials shrugged themselves into their robes, getting ready to give the newcomers an official reception. How the public had learned of the event and its timing constituted a mystery, since the authorities did not tend to inform the newspapers about the movements of warships, but everyone in Queenstown seemed to have come to the harbor to welcome these new allies in the struggle with the German U-boats.

The destroyers had endured a rough crossing through a series of spring gales and hence needed overhauling, but the commanding officer, Commander Joseph K. Taussig, got matters off to a good start in Queenstown with a classic reply to a question from Vice Admiral Sir Lewis Bayly, the British commander in Irish waters. Notable even among Royal Navy admirals for taciturnity and crustiness, Bayly reflected the urgency of the situation by asking Taussig how soon he would be ready to go to sea. Taussig did not hesitate. "We are ready now, sir," he said, adding, "that is, as soon as we finish refueling."

The process of decision that produced the dispatch of the destroyer division to Britain had begun shortly before Woodrow Wilson's war speech to Congress. In late March, in view of the obvious imminence of war, the secretary of the navy had summoned Rear Admiral William S. Sims from the Naval War College at Newport and dispatched him on a special mission to London to assess the situation and suggest what part in the war the U.S. Navy should play as Britain's ally. By the time Sims arrived in England, on April 9, the United States had been at war for three days. Met by an admiral with a special train, Sims found himself whirled to London and almost straight into a conference with Admiral Jellicoe, who no longer commanded the Grand Fleet but now sat at the Admiralty as First Sea Lord.

From his days as a young lieutenant, Sims, a strong individualist, had found himself engaged in controversy brought on by his outspoken and unvarnished criticisms of naval institutions and practices, one of his most famous being his long campaign to call attention to the lamentable state of the navy's gunnery. Thanks to the backing of Theodore Roosevelt, then in the White House, Sims won the reputation, which became permanently associated with him, of being "the man who taught the navy how to shoot." Despite this background of often single-handed struggle against obsolescent customs and methods, the navy's "stormy petrel" continued to rise in rank and responsibilities, and, Secretary Josephus Daniels later said, "knowing how highly he was esteemed by the British Navy, I selected Admiral Sims to go to London in the certainty that he would secure the quickest and most cordial cooperation with the British Navy."

Sims had a high respect for the compactly built, keen-eyed Jellicoe; close contemporaries and acquaintances for many years, the two men had as fellow gunnery specialists kept up something of a regular correspondence. For his part, Jellicoe could not have hoped for a more compatible American representative than this strong Anglophile who had no intention of following the parting and richly metaphorical advice of the chief of naval operations, Admiral William S. Benson: "Don't let the British pull the wool over your eyes. It is none of our business pulling their chestnuts out of the fire. We would as soon fight the British as the Germans."

Almost immediately, the meeting with Jellicoe produced a revelation for Sims. Up to this point, even if somewhat better informed than the general newspaper reader, the U.S. admiral had not had the advantage of any inside sources of information about the effectiveness of Germany's U-boat operations and so, when he had sailed for England, he had "felt little fear about the outcome." Now Jellicoe made it plain to him: In creating or fostering reports that "the volume of British shipping is being maintained," that large numbers of U-boats were being sunk, and even that U-boats were voluntarily surrendering to Royal Navy ships, the Admiralty was simply spreading morale-boosting propaganda that had little to do with the facts. Reaching into a desk drawer, the First Sea Lord took out a paper and handed it to Sims. A record of ship tonnage losses, it showed total sinkings (British and neutral) for February, the first month of the new campaign, as 536,000 tons; for March the total amounted to 603,000 tons; and in April sinkings had begun at a rate projected to produce losses of almost 900,000 tons for the month. These figures were three or four times as great as the public could deduce from the carefully arranged totals that appeared in the press. Clearly, the U-boats were taking the lead in the race for victory. Never having "imagined anything so terrible," Sims did not hide his consternation.

"Yes," Jellicoe said quietly, "it is impossible for us to go on with the war if losses like this continue." Britain was making every effort she could, using every possible craft to fight the U-boats and building antisubmarine vessels as fast as could be done, but the situation was "very serious" and help was urgently needed. Still, the First Sea Lord seemed to have little hope of stopping these losses and thwarting the marauding U-boats. No one had ever characterized Jellicoe as an optimist ("he viewed things from the sober standpoint," said a fellow admiral), but as the season advanced, bringing long summer daylight hours and better weather, the great crisis of the war indeed appeared certain to be at hand. Even allowing for a measure of tactical exaggeration on Jellicoe's part, Sims could reasonably conclude that by November 1, the Allies might have lost the war.

In his first report back to the Navy Department, Sims, after outlining the critical nature of the situation he had encountered, "urgently" recommended, as his first specific proposal, the sending of the "maximum number of destroyers" accompanied by small antisubmarine craft; the destroyers would patrol in the ocean west of Ireland, based on Queenstown. The Navy Department, already engaged in other discussions of the problem, had come forth with an impressively quick response, the dispatch of Commander Taussig's flotilla to Ireland.

As Jellicoe summed up the issue in one statement, "there were only three ways of dealing with the submarine menace. The first, naturally, was to prevent the vessels from putting to sea; the second was to sink them after they were at sea; and the third was to protect the merchant ships from their attack." On becoming First Sea Lord in November 1916, Jellicoe had picked the second answer as the right one, and in pursuing it he sought incessantly for more and more antisubmarine craft—by manufacture, by conversion of vessels of various kinds, and now from the United States—and also for more freighters. As Sims reported to Washington, " 'More Ships! More Ships! More Ships!' is heard on every hand."

As the Admiralty had quite accurately concluded, the Germans entered on the unrestricted campaign with about 150 U-boats. This figure by no means represented an overwhelming number of vessels, especially when the average count of boats assigned to operational flotillas (*Frontboote,* as they were called, i.e., boats serving at the front) amounted to about 120. Only some ninety of these were available for operations in British waters and, on the average, only a third of them would be on actual patrol at any one time, with the others in transit or undergoing repairs and refit. Even so, that would be about twice as many, on the average, as in the previous year. But "could Germany have kept fifty submarines constantly at work on the great shipping routes in the winter and spring of 1917," Sims later said, "nothing could have prevented her from winning the war." Strangely enough, the German High Command, after choosing U-boats as the weapons that would win the war, made no push to turn out large numbers of them. In a characteristic bit of shortsightedness, they allowed their optimism to convince them that the war would be over before new boats could play a part in it. But another reason counted as well: Following the laws of territoriality and parochialism that tend to govern armed services everywhere, Hindenburg and Ludendorff refused to grant the shipyards the services of needed skilled workmen who were serving in the army.

By contrast, the U.S. Navy Department took a bold and in many ways selfless step, involving cooperation not just between services but between countries. As shown by the dispatch of Commander Taussig's flotilla to Queenstown to take part in Britain's antisubmarine efforts, the navy took the concept of alliance with great seriousness. The United States, after all, possessed a formidable navy, the third largest in the world, and traditionally a great naval power entering a war in such circumstances would have insisted on planning and carrying out its own fleet operations. "There were those," wrote Admiral Sims, "who believed that national dignity required that we should build up an independent navy in European waters, and that we should operate it as a distinct American unit." But the admiral, an unorthodox man, believed that the Americans should simply do what was most likely to produce the desperately needed results.

While Admiral Sims was engaged in his discussions in London, the British and French governments, not wanting to leave the decision about the nature and timing of American naval participation solely in American hands, had ordered their commanders in the Caribbean to Washington for conferences with U.S. authorities. Ever eager, Assistant Secretary Franklin Roosevelt wished to join Admiral Benson in sailing out to greet the visitors, but Secretary Daniels refused to give his permission; "he did not like it," the secretary noted drily.

The ensuing talks ran much like those in London between Sims and Admiralty officials, so much so that Secretary Daniels inscribed in his diary: "O for more destroyers!" The British representative expressed his gratification at the readiness of the Americans to take advice and at their clear wish to make a significant contribution to the naval war. For his part, the French admiral seemed unimpressed by the unprepared American officials—with one exception. He found Roosevelt "a convinced and active partisan of an immediate intervention on our coasts. He does not hide his sympathies in regard to France. . . ." And now that the United States was at war, the assistant secretary, a man who traditionally spent much of his summer sailing off the New England

144 · THE SUBMARINE

coast, intended to go ahead with a favorite project of his own, the creation of a flotilla of small—50-foot—submarine chasers.

■ ■ ■

During the preceding three years, the antisubmarine efforts of the
Royal Navy had taken a variety of forms: A mine barrage was stretched
across the Strait of Dover, and mines were laid in the Bight of Heligoland, in front of the U-boats' North Sea bases. A number of decoy
Q-ships sailed the ocean lanes. British submarines were used on antisubmarine patrol. Destroyers found their principal use gathered in
hunting flotillas, which would respond to reports of the presence of
U-boats by steaming to the area and patrolling it with the aim of keeping the enemy beneath the water until his batteries were drained and
then, when he had no choice but to surface, sinking him by gunfire.
Auxiliary vessels engaged in similar patrols. In addition, a new invention, the depth charge, had begun to come into use in 1916.

But all these methods had proved almost wholly ineffectual.
U-boats moved readily through the Dover mine barrier, and German
minesweepers rapidly cleared the waters around Heligoland, although
the barrier could give a U-boat some harrowing moments. "Suddenly
there is a scraping and an eerie scratching all along the boat's side," said
one German skipper. "We listen, holding our breath, and then it stops."
In a moment comes "a sharp tearing sound and an eerie tapping on the
side, like human fingers drumming a nervous tattoo." Finally, after a
long period of silence, the submarine could surface, and "again, we all
realize what pleasure it is to live and breathe."

As for all the deployment of destroyers and other antisubmarine
vessels, this effort had by the end of April 1917 produced the destruction of just one U-boat. The problem was simply that, after a sinking,
the U-boat did not wait around for an antisubmarine vessel to come
after it. Thus, no matter how strongly Sir John Jellicoe called for more
destroyers and more auxiliary vessels, such craft would not and could
not solve the problem. For every U-boat destroyed, seventy Allied or
neutral vessels were lost. In April one-fourth of all the ships sailing
from Britain never returned to complete their round trips, and in the
first three months of the campaign the U-boats reduced the world's

shipping tonnage by two million tons. Hence Jellicoe's quiet despair. On March 23 the War Cabinet even discussed, though it did not adopt, the idea of seeking a "reasonable peace" with Germany.

Did no solution exist? Jellicoe thought not, and the Admiralty staff supported him. But others were not so sure. Sims reported to Daniels on April 19 that critics were attacking the Admiralty for not taking "more effective steps and for failing to produce more substantial and visible results." In particular, said Sims, "one of the principal demands is for convoys of merchant shipping." But the Admiralty met the criticisms with the off-the-record answer that it lacked the ships needed to provide protection for convoys. But why not, Sims had asked, concentrate merchant shipping at chosen points of rendezvous and then convoy the vessels through the dangerous areas? "The answer is the same," Sims said, "the area is too large; the necessary vessels are not available."

The idea of convoy had nothing new about it. The gathering of ships under the protection of an escort held a long and honorable place in the annals of naval warfare, going back at least two thousand years; the first use of convoy in waters around Britain was by Julius Caesar, who in preparation for his invasion of the island assembled a collection of small boats to serve as escorts for his troop transports. The Romans also employed escorts to shield merchant ships from the depredations of Mediterranean pirates. In the Middle Ages the merchants of the Hanseatic League sailed their ships in convoy for defense against Viking freebooters in the Baltic Sea; the Venetians, though having no warships, clustered their vessels in groups for protection against "water thieves," as Shylock called the Mediterranean pirates of his day. Later, Spain used escorts to protect convoys of treasure ships in the Caribbean against British and French raiders. During the Napoleonic era Britain had achieved such remarkable success with "sea shepherds" (as convoy escorts have been called), cutting losses by about 90 percent as compared with the figures for ships sailing independently, that the government made it illegal for a merchantman to leave any port without escort.

In the present war, as had long been the practice, convoys under the protection of warships had carried British troops to Continental war theaters. And—of great significance—convoy had received the unassailable imprimatur of Captain Mahan, who declared that, properly organized, "it will have more success as a defensive measure than hunting for individual marauders—a process which, even when most thoroughly planned, still resembles looking for a needle in a haystack."

Officially, however, the Admiralty accepted neither the verdict of the great naval philosopher nor the collective witness of history nor the lessons of its own traditions. Convoy, it stiffly declared in January 1917, "is not recommended in any area where submarine attack is a possibility. It is evident that the larger the number of ships forming a convoy, the greater the chance of a submarine being able to attack successfully and the greater the difficulty of the escort in preventing such an attack."

But experience did not bear out what might have seemed the Admiralty's commonsense point. In actual fact, a U-boat did not find it much easier to sight a convoy of twenty or thirty ships than to spot a solitary freighter. "A single ship will probably be seen by a U-boat lurking within ten miles of its track," a British officer noted, but "a convoy of twenty ships is only two miles wide and so would be seen by a U-boat lying within eleven miles of the centre of the track of the convoy. Five convoys of twenty ships were not, therefore, very much more likely to be seen than five single ships and"—the telling point— "were obviously much harder to find than a hundred independents." In essence, convoy turned many targets into only one, and if a patrolling submarine was not in position to attack when it chanced on a convoy, it would then find itself alone on a shipless ocean, with no individual steamers to come along offering themselves for destruction. Besides that, the inevitable thinness of coverage resulting from the use of naval vessels on individual patrols could be seen in the frequency with which the crews of merchant ships sunk in the western approaches to England had to row for one or two days before being sighted and picked up.

Having controlled the seas for many generations, the British had discovered that the submarine had now left them with control only of the *surface* of the seas, and that even this control might do them little good. In February, the first month of the new campaign, the U-boats had sunk 260 ships (British, Allied, and neutral), with total tonnage of

469,000. In March the figures had risen to 338 ships and 524,000 tons; April was moving toward final totals of 430 ships and 852,000 tons— an appalling reckoning, and quite close to Jellicoe's gloomy forecast. But when various officers spoke up in favor of adopting convoy, the admirals at the top rebuffed them out of the obsessive belief that it would not work: Merchant skippers could not keep their ships in their places ("keep station"), a point on which some of the skippers agreed with the Admiralty; or the navy lacked the number of destroyers it would need; or there were just too many ships entering and leaving British ports each week.

On the last point, investigation revealed the appalling inadequacy of the Admiralty's staff work and statistical analyses. The navy, or at least some of its officers, believed that it had to protect the unmanageable total of 5,000 arrivals and departures a week, until a closer look revealed that this figure included all coastal and cross-Channel shipping (with some ships even being included several times as they hopped from port to port) as well as oceangoing traffic, which amounted to only 250 to 280. But Admiral Jellicoe was dead set against convoy, offering a succession of reasons for his stand, and, wrote another admiral, "the more experienced the Officer the more damning was the opinion expressed against mercantile convoy."

Jellicoe's opposition to convoy did not, however, lack sound supporting arguments. The method had some inherent drawbacks, notably its effect in limiting the productivity of shipping, because some ships had to delay their sailing so as to become parts of a group and, once at sea, a convoy could go no faster than the speed of its slowest participant. Convoy also diminished the efficiency of receiving ports because, by arriving en masse instead of singly, the ships tended to produce a feast-or-famine situation; the British would later estimate what might be called the negative efficiency factor of convoy at about 25 percent, but this calculation related only to effective carrying capacity and did not factor in a crucial point—the effectiveness of convoy in saving ships from being sunk.

Yet at this very time—more to the point than the squabbles in London—freighters bearing iron ore and other vital raw materials from Norway to Scottish ports, sailing in groups with the protection of destroyers and trawlers, had begun to show a remarkable decline in the rate of losses. This northern convoy effort received strong support from Admiral Beatty, who had succeeded Jellicoe in command of the Grand Fleet. Beatty believed that, while convoy appeared to be—and certainly was—a defensive device, with ships huddled together inside a ring of escorts, it could find its greatest value as a weapon of the offense, by attracting submarines to places where it was "easier to find and destroy them." This view, one shared by Admiral Sims, had some logic on its side but could also make convoy palatable to officers who tended to scorn the defensive because of their devotion to the naval traditions that emphasized taking the fight to the enemy.

Into the middle of this increasingly tense scene now strode the new prime minister, David Lloyd George, the charismatic and dynamic "Welsh wizard," who had little respect for form and hierarchy and always had an ear open to pick up backstairs information. Whatever might be held as official dogma, Lloyd George believed that if you were bleeding to death and the present treatment was failing completely, then you must demand that the doctors switch from tourniquet to transfusions or vice versa—try something new rather than simply allow you to expire. Lloyd George's assorted advisers, his backstairs informants, Admiral Sims, even Woodrow Wilson in far-off Washington—all saw that the "something new" was convoy. (Though claiming no expert knowledge and carefully avoiding interference in naval affairs, the president raised the convoy issue with Secretary Daniels just a few weeks after the Germans had begun the unrestricted campaign. Seeming puzzled at the British failure to adopt convoy, Wilson, saying simply that "the British ought to convoy," began showing doubts concerning the competence of the Admiralty authorities.)

Lloyd George made formal arrangements to review the situation in a visit to the Admiralty on April 30, but by the time the meeting took place the navy itself had stolen much of the prime minister's thunder, offering the grudging admission that, with the entrance of the United States having increased the supply of potential escort vessels, the picture had changed so that "an experiment in this direction should be made." The role played by the imminence of Lloyd George's intervention, as against the Admiralty's own evaluation of the situation, became and has eternally remained a subject of controversy, often bitter. But, however the factors may have combined to produce the result, the "experiment" not only took place but, as it more and more showed the desired results, convoy finally became established Allied policy, though the prime minister later noted that the top admirals "had been convinced against their will and at heart remained of the same opinion still."

On May 20, an experimental convoy that had been assembled at Gibraltar, with its merchant captains carefully coached in procedures by Royal Navy officers, arrived at an English port "in perfect condition"—no losses. This date, said Sims, "marked one of the great turning points of the war. That critical voyage meant nothing less than that the allies had found the way of defeating the German submarine." Confirmation came on June 8 with the arrival in England of a second experimental convoy, which had sailed from Hampton Roads on May 24. Though one of its merchantmen had been torpedoed and sunk, this attack came after the ship had dropped out of the group because it could not maintain the required speed. On June 14 Admiral Jellicoe officially declared the experiment a success and, though nothing came easily and many intricacies remained to be thrashed out, establishing convoy now became the official policy of the Admiralty.

It quickly became evident that the Allies must now extend protection southward from the North Atlantic. In June a familiar vessel, the 1,500-ton *Deutschland* (which, having no role to play as a commercial submarine because American ports were no longer open to her, had become a "submarine cruiser" and reverted to her original designation as the *U-155*), appeared off the coast of West Africa. It sank several ships, and during a cruise that lasted through July and until the end of August disposed of ten merchant steamers and seven sailing ships. Escort vessels had to be found to fend off the *U-155,* and they soon were.

The Allies had learned the central fact: The risk to a ship sailing in convoy was comparatively small. By the beginning of September everyone knew that, though losses continued, salvation had come.

13

IDEAS, METHODS, AND TRIUMPH

The U.S. Navy followed the dispatch of Commander Taussig's destroyer division to join the British in the war against the U-boats by sending a second flotilla of six ships, which arrived at Queenstown on May 17. Further reinforcements increased the total number of U.S. destroyers in British waters to twenty-eight by the end of June and thirty-seven a month later. During this time the navy took on another vital assignment, the shepherding of U.S. military forces to France. The Germans had been willing to run the risk of bringing the United States into the war because of their conviction that the issue would be settled before the Americans could produce enough troops to affect the outcome. Certainly no great American army existed in the spring and summer of 1917 to be transported across the Atlantic, but the French authorities, dismayed by the collapse of their great spring offensive and the consequent mutinies and desertions, called for the moral support of even a small U.S. force. In a true Allied spirit, the Americans cooperated by cobbling together a transport fleet from various sources and sending these vessels off to France in one great convoy, which arrived safely on June 25. The establishment of convoy produced marvelous results, but being part of a such a flock shepherded by warships could not always guarantee a merchant ship immunity from danger. One summer morning the *U-62*, a 1916 boat of 768 tons' surfaced displacement, capable of doing a bit more than 16 knots on the surface, overtook an American freighter, the *J. L. Luckenbach*, sailing without company; the freighter was truly a stray, having fallen almost a hundred miles behind her convoy.

"I sent a shot across her bow," recalled the *U-62*'s skipper, Commander Ernst Hashagen, "but instead of stopping she opened up with her own gun. All morning long we had a running fight with the *Luckenbach*. She did no serious damage to us. But a full dozen of our shells found her. One had even set fire to her cargo of cotton. Still those stubborn Yankees refused to surrender. Our gun outranged theirs, but still they kept on firing at us and flashing out SOS signals."

The crew of the U-boat worked with enthusiasm, said the captain, and were "almost pleased at the howling and crashing of the shells falling about us. At last, a fight in the daylight and fresh air. A brisk and lively fight, in which one can see the enemy and set about him."

Aboard the destroyer U.S.S. *Nicholson,* which formed part of the escort of an inward-bound convoy of British merchantmen, a sailor brought a radio message up to the bridge: WE ARE BEING SHELLED. The message gave longitude and latitude, as well as the name of the victim: *J. L. Luckenbach.* One officer on the bridge knew that ship, a 6,000-ton freighter. In a few minutes came another message: SHELL BURST IN ENGINE ROOM. ENGINEER CRIPPLED. In a few more minutes the senior officer of the group flashed an order to the *Nicholson* to proceed at once to the assistance of the *Luckenbach.* When the pummeled freighter received the word that help was on the way, her operator radioed back: OUR STEAM IS CUT OFF. HOW SOON CAN YOU GET HERE?

Ordering the engine room to make as much speed as the destroyer could, which he thought should be about 28 knots, the captain figured that they could cover the 82 miles within three hours. STICK TO IT he told the *Luckenbach*'s officers. The *Nicholson*'s crew began looking alive as oil smoke poured from the funnels, while the ship, rolling one rail down and then the other, reached 28, then 29, then 30, and even a bit more.

The messenger from the radio shack, a lanky lad in rubber boots, brought fresh word: A SHELL BELOW OUR WATER LINE. SETTLING, BUT STILL AFLOAT AND STILL FIGHTING. Twenty minutes later the *Luckenbach* reported: WATER IN OUR ENGINE ROOM; then FIRE IN OUR FOREHOLD, BUT WILL NOT SURRENDER. LOOK FOR OUR BOATS. And finally: THEY ARE NOW SHOOTING AT OUR ANTENNA.

Sailors removed the canvas caps from the *Nicholson*'s four guns—one forward, one aft, and two in the waist—and their crews were ordered to load and stand by. A chief gunner's mate made ready the torpedo tubes. Then a lookout reported smoke on the horizon, and in a few more minutes a watch officer in the foretop called that he could now see the ship, with shells splashing alongside her and smoke rolling from her hull. And where the *Luckenbach* was, there the U-boat was also.

With the forward gun trained on the horizon dead ahead and the U-boat now sighted, the gun crew opened up at a range of 11,000 yards, while the submarine, lying out of range of the *Luckenbach*'s guns, continued to shell her. The third shell from the *Nicholson,* observers on the bridge believed, landed close to the U-boat. And then, said one of them, "down she went and wasted no time at it. Before we could train and fire again she was gone." Three or four hours after he had first encountered the *Luckenbach,* said Commander Hashagen, "we saw a smudge in the distance. '*Was zum Teufel ist da los?*' I said to myself," and, indeed, it was what he thought: an American destroyer "popped over the horizon, hurrying to the aid of the *Luckenbach.* Those Yankee destroyers!" Hashagen gave his listener a rueful smile at the memory of those enemy boats. "Naturally," he said, "we commanders had no love for them."

The destroyer opened fire at once, said the skipper, and more accurately than her own officers realized: "Her second shell got us in the bow. That was our cue to get away from that place." As the U-boat dived, the captain received reassuring reports from crew members checking for damage from the hit; the pressure hull had remained intact. "The enemy has only removed a few ornaments, without doing any further damage. We breathe a sigh of relief."

As the *Nicholson*'s officers later learned, the U-boat had landed fifteen shells in the steamer, wounding nine of the crew, including three of the gun crew. One of these bluejackets, hit three times by fragments and shouting, "No damn German's going to hit me three times and get away with it!" continued carrying a shell to the gun and insisted that the gun pointer keep firing, even though his shots were falling half a mile short of the submarine.

With encouragement and help from the *Nicholson,* the crew of the *Luckenbach* patched things together, the engineer began to make steam, and by five o'clock in the afternoon the destroyer had rejoined its convoy, with the *Luckenbach* alongside. Looking at the freighter, a quartermaster on the *Nicholson* mused: "They must have had you checked up and counted in, a big ship and a three-million-dollar cargo, this morning, and here you are tonight—one they didn't get."

■ ■ ■

In the English Channel, during 1916 and the early months of 1917, German submarines and British antisubmarine forces had grappled in a sort of sub-war. Previously U-boats had rarely operated in the Channel, but now submarine minelayers began working off Dover and then moved down the coast, sowing mines. In attempting to counter these efforts, the Allied navies, as Admiral Sims observed, were in effect hopelessly blind and therefore had to cultivate other senses. Hearing obviously was the most important: The enemy could make himself invisible simply by submerging but he could make himself unheard only by stopping his engines, thus immobilizing himself. With the engines running underwater, the submarine, owing to the characteristics of these engines and to the peculiar shapes of hull and propellers, produced completely distinctive sound waves, like none that existed in nature. Both British and American engineers had for some time been working to take advantage of these sound patterns, through the development of detecting devices called hydrophones.

In the summer of 1916 the Royal Navy established a trawler hydrophone flotilla, but the hydrophones then existing had only limited effectiveness. It was only "by turning towards the sound [that they] ascertained in what direction the submarine was," noted an officer who had been involved in these activities, "after which they relied solely on the EYE"; they would then attack with depth charges, but "they were successful in the destruction of ONE submarine." One problem with the use of hydrophones came from the fact that every ship in the general area had to stop, in order to keep its engines from drowning out the pulsations from the U-boat.

In November 1916 the Admiralty supplied replacement but still crude hydrophones, which produced somewhat better results in fixing the location of the intruding U-boat. In March 1917 the authorities issued the Mark II, the first truly directional hydrophone, soon followed by a modification, dubbed the Fish, that incorporated an

American-designed amplifier and went a good way toward rendering irrelevant water noises inaudible.

American electrical engineers at General Electric and other companies had, on their own initiative, begun work on listening devices well before the United States entered the war. In 1917 the government established a special board to coordinate these efforts, with a headquarters for the work set up at New London, Connecticut. By the fall of 1917 the scientists had produced a number of devices that, on being tested in actual conditions in the Channel, proved "superior to anything in the possession of the Allies. The ease with which they picked up all kinds of noises, particularly those made by submarines," noted Admiral Sims, "astonished everybody who was let into the secret." Their greatest advantage lay in the accuracy with which they determined the direction from which the sounds of the submarine came. "The conviction that such a method of tracking the hidden enemy might ultimately be used with the desired success," observed Sims, "now became more or less general."

Still other possible approaches to solving the U-boat problem claimed attention in the corridors of London and Washington. As the second-ranking official of the Navy Department, Franklin D. Roosevelt involved himself in all aspects of naval activities. Eager for action and sometimes seeming almost too energetic as he brashly tried to circumvent the slow-moving Secretary Daniels, he liked to say, "I get my fingers into about everything and there's no law against it." (In one memo to himself, he noted that, happening into the secretary's office during the afternoon of July 27, he found his boss signing mail dated July 5.)

Though the admirals dismissed Roosevelt's idea of developing 50-foot boats as submarine chasers, the scheme by no means represented his only thought on antisubmarine warfare. On May 24, 1917, the assistant secretary handed a carefully written memorandum to a British visitor to Washington, Rear Admiral Sir Dudley de Chair. The admiral had arrived a month earlier as naval adviser to a special mission headed by the veteran statesman Arthur Balfour, who sought "to call to fresh vigor our life-long friendship" and, in the process, to make sure that the new American allies understood British ideas concerning the proper prosecution of the war. Since the submarine had become the successor of the great battle fleets of ancient times, Balfour told an audience in New York, it found "its natural prey in the destruction of defenseless merchantmen and the butchery of defenseless women and children," and as a menace to the future good of the world it must be stopped.

For Balfour's hosts the discussions involved immediate issues of some complexity and gravity: Should the Americans concentrate on the antisubmarine war or should efforts go toward creating a balanced fleet, if for no other reason, because of the possibility that the Allies might lose the war and the United States would thus find itself facing a hostile and powerful German navy? Not misled by his marked Anglophilia, Admiral Sims accurately saw the pressing danger as coming from U-boats in the Atlantic, and these U-boats must be defeated if the Allies wanted to avoid defeat themselves. The ultimate U.S. decision makers adopted this view.

In the document he handed Admiral de Chair (written before convoy had been put in practice on any scale and thus taking no account of it), Roosevelt summed up the antisubmarine means then in use: "a) patrol of coasts of France, England, Scotland and Ireland by armed patrol vessels; b) netting of harbors and narrow estuaries and straits; c) planting of mine fields, such as the one off Heligoland; d) sweeping in occasional localities with nets and towed bombs." But, said the assistant secretary, "it is certain that these methods combined are not successful, because the number of submarines thereby destroyed probably does not equal the production of new submarines by Germany." No one in London would have argued with Roosevelt about the unsatisfactory nature of the antisubmarine effort at this time when losses in the previous month had reached almost 900,000 tons, but what remedy did he propose?

Since, as he saw it at the time, it seemed impossible to destroy any significant number of submarines on the high seas, the Allies must seek to keep them from reaching the Atlantic. Because the effort to close the English Channel to them had largely proved successful, he said (this was actually an overly optimistic judgment) the Allies now needed to complete the job by cutting off the U-boats' passage around the north of Scotland and out into the open ocean. Acknowledging that the Admiralty had tried to lay mines and deploy nets between Scotland and the Shetland Islands and between the Shetland Islands and Norway, Roosevelt said, "It is clear to me, after talking with many British officers, that these attempts have been made on a small scale. It is true that they have failed, but it is also true that no great concerted effort has been made to place a barrier of nets, mines, or a combination of [the two], from Scotland to Norway." But such an effort, if successful, could bring a speedy end to the war.

For almost three years, Roosevelt noted, naval officers and concerned civilians in the United States and Britain had discussed the problem; as the plan's most devoted promoter, he declared that the time had come to carry it out. Such a gigantic, unparalleled barrage would in fact present great technical challenges and would exact huge costs in material. After the French naval attaché in Washington transmitted the Roosevelt memorandum to the Naval General Staff in Paris, he received a reply in which, after acknowledging the strategic merits of the plan, the chief of the staff listed several questions to be faced: Realization of the scheme would require several thousand anchors, nets, buoys, and steel cables; guarding the barrier would call for an enormous number of patrol vessels—possibly as many as four thousand—along its entire length and to a breadth of at least 50 miles; and, most important, bases for the supply and repair of this great fleet would have to be developed close to the barrier. Furthermore, said the French admiral, "Will it be possible to incur the responsibility of depriving all the coasts of England and France of their patrols, trusting to the absolute efficacy of this barrage?" To thrash out these questions, added the admiral, officers from all the navies concerned would have to come together to take an objective look at the project. In any case, he said, "the question is one which must be decided chiefly by the British Admiralty." Perhaps Admiral Sims could serve as intermediary.

In a message to Roosevelt of July 12, however, Admiral de Chair delivered a brisk if polite brush-off. The Board of Admiralty agreed that the placing of such a net was practicable but believed that "the difficulties attending its maintenance, and the prevention of submarines from passing through it or over it are so great as to render it of secondary value compared to present methods of dealing with the submarine menace." He found that such a barrier had already been tried in the Channel, said the admiral, as though he had not previously known of this effort, but it had not proved satisfactory; however, the Admiralty would continue to look at the question. When Roosevelt and de Chair had discussed the barrier project during the admiral's visit to Washington, the visitor had raised various objections to it, and during the six weeks that had elapsed since Roosevelt had produced his formal proposal, convoy had taken its first steps toward transforming the scene.

But Roosevelt, who combined a great deal of tenacity with what sometimes seemed his immature eagerness, had no intention of giving up. The French admiral had by no means overstated the challenges and difficulties that carrying out the project would involve, and Roosevelt, for his part, continued collecting technical information about mines and nets and methods of deployment in waters 250 feet deep or more—all questions that would require answers if high-level opinion turned favorable toward consideration of the project. Aside from technical factors, a cultural issue played a part in the whole discussion of the great barrier. It seemed natural to the Americans to plan an enterprise involving an enormous number of mines and a huge new fleet of antisubmarine vessels—that was what raw materials and production facilities were for—while, to the British, the barrier project appeared as something of a megalomaniac undertaking.

In September, despite all the objections to the project, Roosevelt's faith began to take on some justification. Far from serving as any kind of useful intermediary, Admiral Sims had reacted as negatively as Admiral de Chair and the Board of Admiralty, but now the American admirals in Washington were warming to the idea. The quest for an appropriate mine—one of the central issues—had now produced an effective model, which did not require direct contact between submarine and mine but would be detonated by a new kind of firing device: When a U-boat made contact anywhere along an antennalike wire that stretched upward from the explosive to a surface buoy, the mine would be triggered. In September, Admiral Jellicoe supported the project at an inter-Allied naval conference, and in October the General Board of the U.S. Navy gave its official approval. Though Daniels had his doubts, he noted that the admirals considered it "the only big thing" the United States and Britain could do. The United States would supply the needed mines, as many as a hundred thousand.

Actual laying of the "Northern Barrage," as it was called, began in June 1918 across some 250 miles of water between the Orkney Islands and Norway. The Americans put down the center section, the largest part; the British laid the section neighboring the Orkneys; and the section off the Norwegian coast was laid by both navies. The operation involved a total of about 70,000 mines, 57,000 of them laid by the Americans; U.S. factories produced about 1,000 a day. They all had their problems: Some of the American mines exploded on their own, shortly after being put in place, and some of the British mines were laid at such a shallow depth that they threatened surface shipping; minesweepers had to be deployed to skim them from the sea.

The operation of laying the great field had its dramatic aspects. "Ten mine-layers participated in each 'excursion' "—the sailors' nickname for the individual minelaying expedition—"all ten together laying about 5,400 mines at every trip," noted Admiral Sims, who mellowed toward the project as it developed. Showing no lights, the squadron would leave Moray Firth, usually on a foggy night, and rendezvous with destroyers, there to shield it from U-boats. "The absolute silence of the whole proceeding was impressive; not one of the destroyers showed a signal or a light; not one of the mine-layers gave the slightest sign of recognition." The "swishing of the water on the sides and the slow churning of the propellers were the only sounds that could possibly betray the ships to their hidden enemies." Then, at dawn, those in the squadron would see a force of battleships, with supporting vessels, cruising majestically past, setting up a wall of steel to protect the minelayers—defenseless boats that had begun life as holiday excursion steamers—from any attack by German surface forces.

A ship performing the actual minelaying called to mind some giant creature, swimming full speed through the water, releasing, at intervals of just a few seconds, giant black eggs, which rolled toward the tail, then fell headfirst into the water with a great splash, and disappeared beneath the waves. The sailors called the mines "nails in the coffin of the Kaiser."

Impressive and intricate as it was, this gigantic operation, something like building a great wall to protect a province or even an entire nation from barbarian assaults, would have little chance to prove itself. The navies finished laying the barrier in October, only a month before the end of the war came with the signing of the armistice on November 11. Even so, in its brief period of operation it accounted for six U-boats, and who could know, in the spring of the year, that the war would end that autumn? Certainly not the activist U.S. assistant secretary of the navy, who persisted during much of 1918, right up until what proved to be the final days, in trying to wangle his way into active duty at the front in France.

■ ■ ■

In the Mediterranean, in these same final days of the war, a young Imperial Navy officer displayed an innovative approach to tactics in his effort against Allied convoys. Born in Berlin into an old family of village mayors and landowners, clerics, and officers, Karl Dönitz had grown up "deeply conscious of the corporate spirit of the Prussian community" to which the family belonged, and his prewar service in foreign waters served to enhance his patriotism and sense of duty. During the first two years of World War I Dönitz had served on the cruiser *Breslau,* taking part in "cat and mouse" raids on the much stronger Russian fleet in the Black Sea, until called home in 1916 for training in submarines. (For Turkish diplomatic purposes, the *Breslau* carried the name *Midilli* during this service, and Dönitz and the rest of the crew, sporting fezzes in place of their normal headgear, nominally served in the Turkish navy.) In 1918, promoted to Oberleutnant zur See, Dönitz received command of the *UB-68,* one of the UB III boats, at 513 tons' surface displacement much larger than the early UBs; these boats carried ten torpedoes instead of the four or five of the earlier boats. Operating with the first flotilla out of Pola, at the head of the Adriatic, Dönitz patrolled the Mediterranean.

In October 1918 Dönitz and a senior fellow submarine skipper named Steinbauer hatched a plan for a new kind of tactic: They would join forces in a simultaneous attack on the surface, at night, "with the assistance of the new moon," on a British convoy near Malta. They would rely on the small silhouettes of their boats to keep them unseen by the destroyer escorts as they slipped through the protective screen and into the heart of the convoy. "Up till now," Dönitz reflected, "the U-boats had always waged war alone. They set forth and ranged the seas alone, they battled alone against the antisubmarine defenses, and they sought out and fought the enemy alone." Dönitz had performed creditably in his brief time as a U-boat commander, having sunk seven ships for a total of 17,000 tons; Steinbauer, a holder of the Pour le Mérite, had done extraordinarily well using orthodox methods; in command of two boats, the *UB-47* and the *UB-48,* he had sunk 185,000 tons of shipping—fifty-six ships. But now he was ready, with Dönitz, to test a new kind of cooperation.

The evening of October 3 saw Dönitz all set, waiting at the agreed meeting point off the southeast coast of Sicily, but Steinbauer did not appear (owing, as Dönitz later learned, to mechanical problems with the *UB-48*). Deprived of the chance to test the new tactic, Dönitz then attacked by himself in the traditional fashion, but his boat suffered troubles of its own. The failure of its longitudinal stabilizer forced him to surface in the middle of the convoy and its escorts, where shells from the steamer *Queensland* ended the career of the *U-68,* and just a month before the end of the war Dönitz found himself a prisoner of the British.

He had seen, close up, the vital importance and the success of convoy. From his prejudiced point of view, it had acted as a kind of spoilsport, having "robbed the U-boat arm of its opportunity to become a decisive factor" by assembling fifty or more ships into a huge concourse surrounded by a strong escort of warships. A lone U-boat might at best sink one or two of the vessels in a convoy—not much of a haul, as he saw it—but "the greater the number of U-boats that could be brought simultaneously into the attack, the more favorable would become the opportunities offered to each individual attacker." Further, in the darkness of night the confusion caused by sudden violent explosions and sinking ships would work to confound the escorting vessels and increase these opportunities. All in all, as he looked to the future, this serious and highly professional twenty-seven-year-old officer had given himself a great deal to think about.

■ ■ ■

When the twenty-one months of unrestricted submarine warfare wound down, the record showed that up until the end of October, the last full month, the U-boats had sunk 3,843 merchant ships, with a gross tonnage of 8,378,947, an average of just under 400,000 tons a month. But in that final month, the total—though certainly appalling—came in at a relatively low 112,427. The establishment of convoy by the Allies had truly trumped the U-boat aces of the plotters at Pless.

In November 1918 the Germans had 121 submarines at sea, manned by about 13,000 men. Overall during the war, U-boats had sunk 5,708 ships, amounting to the remarkable total of more than 11 million tons, one-fourth of all the world's shipping; more than half of the lost vessels were British. Although, for reasons of economy and convenience, U-boat skippers liked to sink ships by gunfire when they could, this method accounted for only about 32 percent of merchant tonnage sunk; the main weapon of destruction, just as the popular imagination would have supposed, was the sinister torpedo, which dealt the fatal blows to 60 percent of the total. The remaining ships sank in various accidents or after colliding with mines laid by U-boats.

Submarine service proved to be the most hazardous kind of sea duty. The Imperial Navy had sent 373 U-boats to sea from August 1914 until the end of the great struggle; 178 of them were lost, and with them had gone some 5,000 officers and crewmen—deaths, observed Admiral Sims, that "involved perhaps the most hideous tragedies of the war." But, while making its mark as a warship like the cruiser and the destroyer, the submarine had repealed the dictum of Captain Mahan by demonstrating its special and undreamed-of power as a commerce raider. In sinking thousands of freighters and tankers, it had shown itself capable of establishing mastery of the seas and winning wars. In particular, it had dramatized the vulnerability of island nations dependent on lifelines strung across oceans. Just fifty more submarines constantly at work, Sims had said, and Germany would have won. Instead, by finally goading the United States into belligerence, the U-boats had brought about their own defeat.

FROM WAR TO WAR

The period since 1914 has been crowded with events of world importance, with complex questions of war guilt, reparation, war debts, disarmament, reconstruction, national minorities, territorial readjustments, economic upheaval, and dictatorships. The mind is easily confused by the magnitude of some of the problems and by the technical aspects of others.

—Walter C. Langsam (1933)

PART III

14

BOATS AND BUILDERS I

s the Great War was raging in Europe, the Electric Boat
Company and the Lake Torpedo Boat Company continued
their battle for the U.S. Navy's submarine dollar, with Electric Boat occupying the dominant position. The navy itself stood on
the sidelines, operating no construction facilities of its own and showing little desire to spend much of its limited resources on the new invention whose very purpose remained obscure. Britain and Germany
presented a similar picture, with Electric Boat's de facto partner Vickers and Krupp filling comparable roles in their respective countries.
(Until after the war, Electric Boat did not itself build its submarines
but contracted to have them built, notably at the Fore River Shipbuilding Company in Quincy, Massachusetts.) Electric Boat also created a subsidiary, New London Ship and Engine Co. (Nelseco), to
build diesel engines for the boats. An American-Swiss partnership between Adolphus Busch, the St. Louis beer tycoon, and the engineering
firm Sulzer Brothers, Ltd., produced more satisfactory engines than
those from Nelseco, but under the rules of the game these went into
Simon Lake's submarines while navy policy allowed Electric Boat to
install its own engines in the submarines it sold the government. Engines and the complex problems associated with them would prove to
be a subject of continuing contention between the navy and Electric
Boat.

Having begun by providing the navy with the boats of the A series,
Electric Boat moved up to the F-class submarines; the *F-1* was the first
U.S. diesel boat (330 tons with a surfaced speed of 13.5 knots). This development came as a definite boon to crewmen, whose exposure to
gasoline fumes in the previous boats often required treatment with

smelling salts. The *G-1*, the first submarine the navy bought from Simon Lake, attracted particular notice by setting a depth record of 256 feet. Submarine production went on to skip through the alphabet with submarines labeled the H, K, L, M, N, O, and R classes, the last of this final group joining the fleet in 1919. Lake contributed a number of the Ns, Os, and Rs.

On October 3, 1915, the navy gave four K-boats (*K-3, K-4, K-7,* and *K-8*) what amounted to a pioneering endurance test, dispatching them from San Francisco to Oahu as replacements for boats that had not performed satisfactorily. The four submarines made the 2,100-mile voyage in eleven days, arriving at Pearl Harbor in the evening of October 14. The boats experienced no particular problems, their skippers reported, and the *K-7* pleased everybody by managing to complete the trip without once having had to stop its engines.

Most of the early U.S. boats were, in truth, primitive affairs, produced for only a year or two and in small numbers. They generally had a surfaced displacement of about 300 tons, with the size inching up to the 530 tons for all except a few of the R class. The most successful of the prewar U.S. submarines, however, were those of the L class, which displaced 450 tons, could turn off 14 knots on the surface, and carried a 3-inch deck gun.

Some of the navy's problems stemmed from the lack of interest in submarines on the part of most officers and, in fact, of navy higher-ups themselves. But in 1915 Assistant Secretary of the Navy Franklin Delano Roosevelt, the most hands-on civilian official concerned with naval affairs, made his own pronouncement about the importance of increasing the production of submarines. "The submarine has come to stay," Roosevelt declared. "It has taken its place, not as the whole weapon in naval offense and defense, but as an adjunct to other weapons. That it is useful for coast defense, for commerce destroying, especially in narrow waters, for scouting purposes, and as a part of the protection and attacking power of a battleship fleet is established." Taking a look at the future of the submarine, Roosevelt noted that "it would of course be most unreasonable to suppose that while the weapons for the destruction of underwater craft are being perfected, the improvement of the submarine itself will not continue. Without doubt its size will increase, its engines both surface and subsurface gain in horsepower and resulting speed, its radius of action grow and its sea-worthiness improve."

Experience showed, however, that the boats were far from ideal; no general agreement yet existed on the role of the submarine and hence on the most appropriate design. Some enthusiasts continued to see it replacing the battleship, while other observers considered it merely a minor auxiliary to the fleet. At the time, the navy divided submarines into two general and rather vague classes, offensive and defensive. Smaller submarines, particularly those of the N and O classes, had the basic coast defense mission assigned to them, while others—K and L boats—would be dispatched to European waters after the United States entered the war, in the hope that they could perform in an offensive role.

"In all navies data relating to submarine construction and operation are, as far as it is possible to do so, kept a Government secret," observed a writer in the *New York Times* in January 1916. "A visit to any American ship-building or naval yard, where submarines are under repair or in process of construction, will prove the correctness of this statement. The visitor will be welcomed on board dreadnoughts, cruisers, gunboats, and destroyers, but never on board the submarine. No matter how loyal the citizen, he can't get on an American submarine without a pass from the head of the Navy Department." Therefore, when fortune favored the *Times* with an opportunity to peek behind the scenes through the eyes of no less a personage than Lawrence Spear, the editors hastened to take advantage of it. Although Electric Boat had seen such lean years that Henry Carse, a banker and prominent director, had resigned from the board in 1913, the coming of the war, with the European orders it brought, had quickly fattened the firm up, and Carse had returned two years later as president. In the five months from December 1914 to May 1915, the stock tripled in value, from $24 to $73 a share, and two months later it reached $186.

With the aid of tables, the chief designer and engineer of Electric Boat presented the progress of the submarine from 1900 with its 53-foot length to the current vessel at 230 feet, from "a frail craft of 75 tons to a boat of almost 1,000 tons, and of an increase in cruising activity from 200 to 3,000 knots [sic]." Forty times as much horse-power—2,000 as against 50—drove the boats at a surface speed of 17 knots as against 6. The specifications of these current U.S. submarines were similar to those of Arnauld de la Perière's famous *U-35*.

Submarines of more than 800 tons belonged, said Spear, among "the submarines of tomorrow." Those less than 800 tons he divided into three types: (1) local- or harbor-defense; (2) coast-defense; and (3) offensive. At the present time, Spear noted, it appeared to be U.S. pol-icy to "employ submarines extensively for coast defense purposes"; he predicted that "in view of the great distances which separate us from most of our probable enemies, and certain special characteristics neces-sary for the offensive type," in the immediate future "at least two quite separate types will be employed, one of which we designate as the 'de-fensive submarine' and the other as the 'fleet submarine' "—the latter a boat with a high surface speed and a long effective radius, intended to accompany the battle fleet in operations. One such boat was now un-der construction, Spear said, with another authorized. In speaking of the fleet submarine, Spear was enunciating a dream that would engage and bemuse submariners for years to come: that of the submarine play-ing an important role in the clash of great ships and thus requiring very high speeds. The chief problem lay in getting enough power from diesel engines to produce speeds of 25 knots or more.

Spear's discussion took place amid a complicated scene. In 1915, in-dulging in its perpetual tendency to dabble in the details of various technical realms (defense, nutrition, pharmaceuticals), Congress had approved the construction of two extralarge submarines capable of at-taining speeds as high as 25 knots, with a required minimum of 20. The trouble was, however, that nobody could design a diesel engine that could drive a boat at more than 19 knots. Hence, in March 1916, the navy would be reporting to Secretary Daniels that it had not suc-ceeded in obtaining a single bid for such a contract. Since, under the terms of the act, the secretary could not spend the appropriated funds without requiring the 20-knot minimum, he would have to ask the House Naval Affairs Committee to produce a revised bill, lowering the minimum speed to 19 knots. The navy took comfort from their belief that no foreign navy had any submarines that could do more than 17 knots. Spear, who was actively grappling with the problem at Electric Boat, even suggested that "notwithstanding its serious disadvantages for submarines, designers may in the immediate future be forced to employ a steam plant" to meet the demand for a high surface speed, but that solution would, he conceded, introduce a number of other problems.

Well aware that Simon Lake, like Teddy Roosevelt, always had an opinion ready to give the press (and, as the pronounced underdog in his rivalry with Electric Boat, Lake needed all the publicity he could get), a reporter sought him out in Bridgeport to ask whether he considered American submarines a success. Speaking with reference to accidents that had recently occurred on maneuvers, Lake sang his rival Spear's song, observing that the failures had happened because "too many demands for surface speed have been made. Now surface speed is a good thing to have, but the ironclad specifications of the Navy Department disregard the circumstance that we have not developed a submarine engine for the great speed demanded." The existing 11-knot engines, however, he considered perfectly adequate for the slow, defensive boats.

Lake then went on to a theme of his own: He also considered these engines capable of powering boats that would fulfill a dream of his, the creation of a supply line of 2,500-ton submarines carrying freight to England. Having no doubts that the Germans would continue their U-boat campaign, he said in July 1915 that if the war lasted two more years he expected them to "succeed in cutting off all travel to England on the surface of the sea"; if the British were to avoid starvation, they would have to be provisioned by submarine. Besides that, "new methods of conserving the air supply and food supply mean that passengers will be safer in the undersea boats than in liners which are subject to the fate that overtook the *Lusitania*."

With this outlook, Lake naturally responded with great excitement to the crossing of the Atlantic by the big submarine *Deutschland* in 1916, hurrying down from Bridgeport to Baltimore to inspect the wonder for himself and to preach his gospel of maritime underwater commerce. "For twenty-five years I have been urging commercial submarines," he declared, "but no one seemed to think such an idea practical."

Seemingly always embattled in one controversy or another, Lake and his company had always suffered from its junior status, while Electric Boat used its political clout on Capitol Hill to secure domination of the submarine field. But, as navy officials liked to point out, Lake made his own problems worse with inefficiencies in management and production that raised unit costs beyond what seemed reasonable. In 1918 Lake asked the navy to allot to his company a fair share of new construction; he did, indeed, hold one ace in his hand, his Busch-Sulzer diesel engines, far more reliable than those from his big competitor's Nelseco plant. Then came the end of the war, however, and with it a profoundly shrunken market for the wares of submarine builders. It also revealed a dismal record for the U.S. submarine force: Though the navy had dispatched "offensive" boats to European waters, they had proved to have neither the size nor the stamina to do the job; the final reckoning showed not a single enemy ship sunk by a U.S. submarine.

As Lake and some other observers pointed out, the government would be ill advised to put all its eggs in Electric Boat's basket. But another alternative offered itself: The navy had its own yards, as at Portsmouth, and it could build its own submarines while still doing business with Electric Boat. This move represented something of an act of defiance directed at the company, which "lobbied for the appropriations, designed the vessels, and then proceeded to build its own designs," while it "intimated," said a Bureau of Engineering official, that the navy did not know as much about submarine construction as the company and, in effect, should not waste its time trying to do the job. "In fact, if you look up history," commented a construction officer, "you'll find that the Navy Department frequently didn't ask for submarines, but they were put in the bill anyway, due to political pressure from this organization." The navy also made complaints at times about sloppy workmanship and the company's use of inferior materials.

In the postwar era, Simon Lake's firm, which did little besides build submarines, declined into its terminal phase, lingering for only a few years. But Electric Boat would face lean years of its own. Its leaders were willing to tackle almost any kind of project, however, and in the end the company's diversity would save it.

ARMS AND THE NATIONS

n the early afternoon of November 11, 1921, in the marble amphitheater of Arlington National Cemetery, President Warren G. Harding officiated at the burial of America's Unknown Soldier of the World War. In each of the victorious Allied countries the idea of the "unknown soldier"—an unidentified body taken from a military cemetery—had assumed great emotional significance as the national symbol of sacrifice. This Washington ceremony had been preceded by a parade down Pennsylvania Avenue, with troops and bands, with the president and General Pershing striding immediately behind the black coffin, followed by Vice President Calvin Coolidge, other officials, and military and naval officers. Still farther behind, in a single open carriage, rode a shrunken, huddled figure bracing himself with a cane, Harding's predecessor, the stroke-wasted Woodrow Wilson, whose dream of American participation in a great League of Nations had collapsed in postwar Washington.

"I can sense the prayers of our people, of all peoples," President Harding declared in his remarks at Arlington, "that this Armistice Day shall mark the beginning of a new and lasting era of peace on earth, good will among men." For once in the world, such standard rolling rhetoric did not appear to have been spoken in a vacuum. By 10:30 the next morning a crowd of 1,300 men and women, with the aid of some pushing and shoving, had gathered in Memorial Hall, the Washington meeting place of the Daughters of the American Revolution, to take seats in the galleries and boxes that surrounded the central floor area, where stood a large U-shaped table covered with the standard diplomatic green baize. Those who now filed into the hall to take their places at this table—former prime ministers and foreign secretaries, generals and admirals, French, Japanese, Portuguese, British, and others—were, before the eyes of the world, coming together in a most unusual conference.

Just the year before, out in the Pacific Ocean, Japanese naval forces had occupied the island of Yap, in the Carolines group, some 1,200 miles east of the Philippines and about the same distance north of New Guinea. Suddenly, with the greatest war in history barely over, the Pacific seemed to be moving toward becoming the cockpit for the acting-out of another rivalry, this one between the United States and Japan. Despite the seeming insignificance of tiny, isolated Yap, Americans became alarmed over the seizure of the island, and there was even talk of war. Rumblings were also heard about building a U.S. Navy second to none to enforce freedom of the seas, so that never again would Britain or anybody else be able to interfere with American merchant ships sailing the world's oceans. And Britain and Japan were bound by an alliance: What did this portend for the United States in the future?

To head off a new naval arms race, President Harding invited nine countries with significant navies to Washington to discuss the limitation of naval armaments and the control of new agencies of war such as poison gas, and also to deal with all questions concerning the Pacific and the Far East. After opening the proceedings, the president, who liked the idea of arms limitation but had little detailed knowledge of such matters, turned the meeting over to the secretary of state, the stately Charles Evans Hughes. The secretary startled the gathering of distinguished international delegates by putting aside orotund rhetoric and pious generalities, producing instead a set of concrete proposals that called for the nations not only to cease building ships but also to scrap many that were already in service; the secretary named actual countries and actual ships, including seven U.S. battleships then on the ways. The assembled delegates sat in shock at the sight and sound of such unorthodox behavior. As a British military correspondent observed, the American secretary of state had just "sunk more ships than all the admirals of the world had sunk in a cycle of centuries." Behind Hughes's words stood the unarguable fact that the United States spoke from strength, having the wealth and resources to build the world's mightiest navy if it should choose to do so, and, after a stunned moment, the galleries exploded in an outburst of applause, with hats waving, handkerchiefs fluttering, neighbors hugging one another and slapping each other on the back.

As finally agreed after three months of generally amicable negotiations, the powers established a ten-year "holiday," as everybody called it, on building capital ships (battleships and battle cruisers), with those that were retained having to conform to a U.S.-British-Japanese ratio of 5:5:3 in permissible tonnage, with France and Italy each at 1.67. The advent of a new type of vessel, the aircraft carrier, raised a problem of definition: Was it a capital ship? The delegates answered the question by putting the carrier in a category of its own and applying the 5:5:3 formula to it.

In another important realm, however, the British had to accept a deep disappointment. Although at the time of the conference they maintained the largest submarine fleet in the world, they had learned in the World War that the lurking danger these vessels presented to their island greatly outweighed any advantage they themselves could gain from their use, and thus they argued at Washington for the complete abolition of the submarine; it was effective only as a commerce raider, they insisted, and in this role only if it ignored international law. In presenting this view, the British representatives were proving themselves faithful to the Admiralty opinion advanced more than a century earlier by Lord St. Vincent, who had opposed any dealings with Robert Fulton concerning the submarine and, according to a popular story, had called the prime minister, William Pitt, "the greatest fool that ever existed to encourage a mode of war which those who command the sea do not want and which, if successful, will deprive them of it."

While not objecting to the imposition of limitations on submarines, the Americans replied to the British argument by noting that the submarine had a legal and effective role against warships that involved no violation of international law, and a French admiral had earlier said that "because a man shoots another man with a rifle, does that mean that we abolish the rifle?" The Americans proposed as a solution to apply the capital-ship ratio to submarines as well.

But the French, pointing out that they had accepted a smaller battle fleet than the Anglo-American powers or Japan, refused to accept a smaller submarine force, too. The chief French delegate declared that "the submarine is the only arm that allows a country without a large navy to defend itself on the sea"; further, he said, "the barbarous use that was made of the submarine by a belligerent condemns this belligerent, not the submarine." In making this argument the French received some support from Italy and Japan, and even from the United States, and the conference therefore adopted no limits of any kind on submarines; a country might build and deploy them as it wished. But in a sort of footnote document, the signatories declared that their submarines would obey the rules of warfare that applied to surface vessels (i.e., would operate with restrictions), but the French refused to agree.

Succumbing to intense American pressure, the British did not renew their alliance with Japan; instead, a new treaty glossed over the whole business by creating a four-power consortium of the United States, Britain, France, and Japan to maintain the status quo in the Pacific. This British defection, as the Japanese viewed it, caused deep resentment in Tokyo, although the government signed the treaty; the British dominions with Pacific interests, Canada and Australia, however, highly approved of the change.

Writing about the Washington Conference a decade later, a proponent of disarmament called it "more promising for the world than any one before or since," yet in actual fact the negotiators had made no progress at all in any field of armament they took up except, as traditionally had been the case, the naval realm. Ships always seemed easier to point to and control than anything else, and the powers in Washington were able to reach the ratio-based agreement on relative strengths. Despite achieving only limited success, the major countries would continue in following years to meet and discuss limitations on armaments.

To some extent, the victors of the Great War engaged in this ongoing effort because they had incurred a vague moral obligation to do so: In the Treaty of Versailles they had partially rationalized the disarmament they imposed on Germany by pledging to follow up this step with advances toward the disarmament of everybody else, including themselves. Throughout the 1920s conferences and committees concerned with the question became increasingly familiar and increasingly drearier features of the international scene. "The technical aspects of the disarmament problem," wrote a historian in that era, "were constantly pushed into the background by fear, jealousy, national pride, and economics."

With the 1922 Washington Treaty due to expire at the end of 1936, a far more significant naval conference opened in London in January 1930, three months after the great Wall Street crash and the onset of the Great Depression. This meeting came about partly because the United States and Britain now found themselves led by two pacifists, President Herbert Hoover and Prime Minister Ramsay MacDonald; both heads of government wished above all to save money and neither had any inclination to quibble over the details of naval discussions. Within three months the delegates had produced the London Naval Treaty, which for the first time established limits on submarines: The United States, Britain, and Japan could each build submarines to a total tonnage of 52,700; this parity, though disliked by the U.S. Navy, reflected the actual situation at the time. The treaty also reaffirmed rules for submarine warfare, the old familiar code calling for securing the safety of passengers in commerce-raiding operations. The French and the Italians, vying for superiority in the Mediterranean, refused to sign the treaty; France had built herself into the strongest underwater power, with more than forty modern oceangoing boats and, intending to maintain that position, never accepted any limitations on submarines.

On May 21, 1935, the German Navy, known under the republic established in 1919 as the Reichsmarine (the navy of the realm), received the bristling new name Kriegsmarine (the war navy), reflective of the public militancy of the Nazi regime, and a few months later its vessels received a matching new banner dominated by the swastika. In June, acting entirely on their own, the British took a strange step in relation to this self-assertive Nazi Germany, concluding an agreement whereby the Germans could build up to 35 percent of the tonnage of warships allowed to Britain by the London Naval Treaty and up to 45 percent of the submarine tonnage. The figure of 35 percent came from Adolf Hitler himself, who apparently believed that it would give Germany a navy equal to that of France. The agreement, which contravened the Treaty of Versailles and which the British entered into without even consulting the French, "created a formidable outburst of indignation in the French capital"—hardly surprisingly, since its provisions removed any practical or public relations restraints on German naval construction, because they authorized building in quantities sufficient to keep shipyards busy for years to come. Making use of a term that would soon become as common as *peace* or *war,* the American diplomat Norman Davis told President Roosevelt that the British did not wish to "overlook the possibility of exercising a moral influence over Germany to bring about an *appeasement* [italics supplied] which would avert an ultimate war" and, he added, "which is all to the advantage of France as well as themselves." The French, however, did not share their friends' ideas about what was good for them.

At a second London conference, which opened in December 1935 (indeed, on the seventh of the month), the Japanese caused a great stir. They would no longer, they declared, accept any inferiority in ship tonnage but must have parity in all types, including battleships. When the American and British delegation leaders, Davis and Anthony Eden, who had just become foreign secretary, gave an unfavorable reply, the Japanese walked out of the meeting. So ended the era of disarmament discussions and arms limitations, and with it all attempts to set ceilings on the size of navies and thus to limit the construction and deployment of submarines, with the odd exception of the formal constraints accepted by the Germans in their new agreement with Britain.

But the British, continuing to show faith in the written word and the diplomatic signature, made one more attempt to impose curbs on the submarine. If they could not circumscribe these craft in nature and number, they could at least insist on everybody's adherence to the old Prize Ordinance, as expressed in Article 22 of the London Naval Treaty, under which a submarine in confrontation with a merchant vessel must conduct itself exactly as if it were a conventional warship, carefully searching the vessel and placing its passengers in "a place of safety."

The United States, Britain, and Japan had solemnly bound themselves to these rules in 1930. Sometimes, it was true, submarines could conform to such strictures, as they had often demonstrated during the World War, but often they could not do so without exposing them-

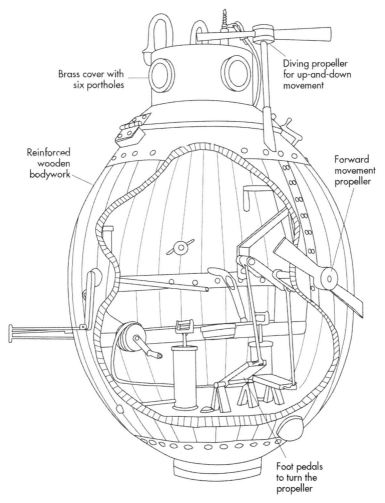

Brass cover with
six portholes

Diving propeller
for up-and-down
movement

Reinforced
wooden
bodywork

Forward
movement
propeller

Foot pedals
to turn the
propeller

David Bushnell's *Turtle:* John P. Holland called this pioneering Revolutionary War craft "by far the most effective submarine boat" built before Holland's own work a century later.

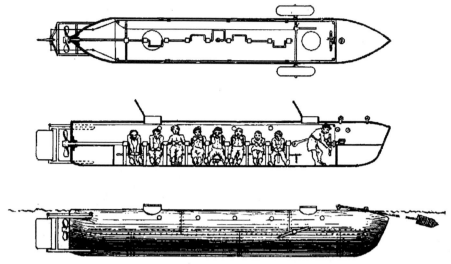

A nineteenth-century artist's view of the Confederate submarine *H. L. Hunley,* which became the first submersible vessel to sink a hostile ship and also the first submersible to be lost in such a confrontation.

Though not dressed in standard nautical style, John P. Holland posed in the conning tower of his boat *Holland VI,* which in 1900 became the U.S.S. *Holland.*

The *Holland* had not yet joined the navy, but in this 1899 drawing showing her at her moorings, she is flying the U.S. jack as well as the ensign.

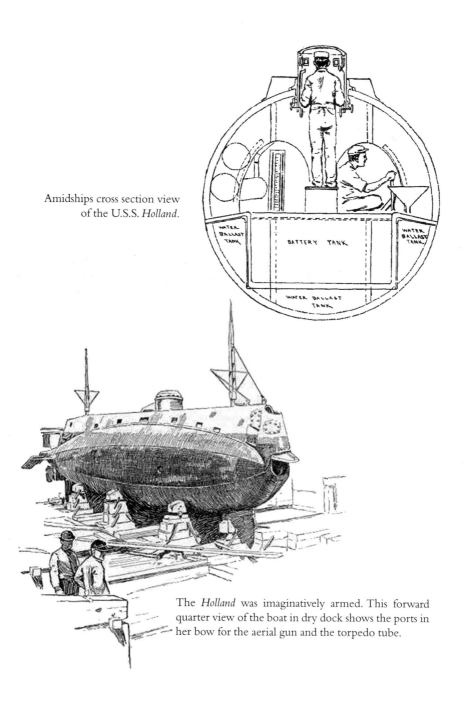

Amidships cross section view
of the U.S.S. *Holland*.

WATER BALLAST TANK

WATER BALLAST TANK

BATTERY TANK

WATER BALLAST TANK

The *Holland* was imaginatively armed. This forward
quarter view of the boat in dry dock shows the ports in
her bow for the aerial gun and the torpedo tube.

Simon Lake, the submarine's "other father" as Holland's rival in the 1890s and later, contributed influential ideas to the development of underwater craft.

With its wheels intended to allow running on the seabed, Simon Lake's first experimental submarine, the little *Argonaut Junior,* resembled a wagon more than a boat.

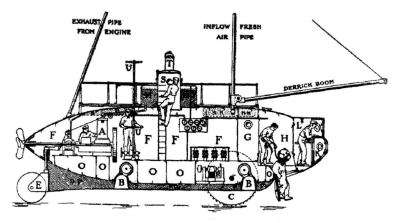

Lake's first important boat, the senior *Argonaut,* shown here in longitudinal section, was driven by a 30-horsepower gasoline engine.

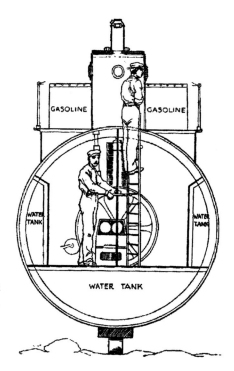

The *Argonaut* shown in amidships cross section.

Despite her ungainly appearance, the *Argonaut* proved eminently seaworthy, once making a surface voyage of 1,700 miles.

A pioneering torpedo expert as a young officer, Admiral Alfred von Tirpitz became the creator of Imperial Germany's modern fleet.

Kapitänleutnant Otto Weddigen created a worldwide sensation in September 1914 by sinking three patrolling British cruisers in a single attack.

The *U-9*, the famous submarine commanded by Kapitänleutnant Weddigen in his assault on the Royal Navy cruisers.

Germany's big submarine *Deutschland* was the talk of the town on the U.S. east coast in the summer of 1916. She represented a remarkable attempt to circumvent the British blockade.

During the World War I era, the U.S. Navy created the design of the S-boats (shown here is the *S-47*), submarines that had constant troubles but nevertheless went on to serve in World War II.

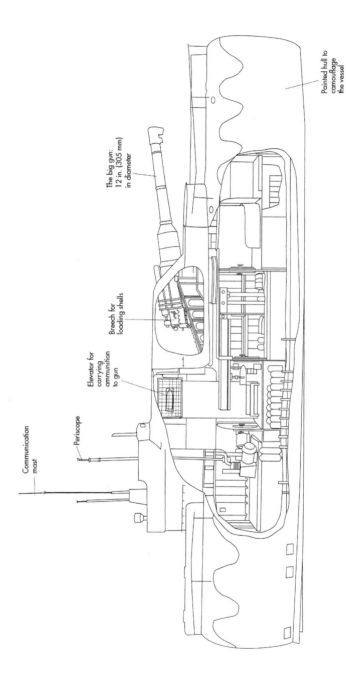

Communication
mast

Periscope

Elevator for
carrying
ammunition
to gun

Breech for
loading shells

The big gun:
12 in. (305 mm)
in diameter

Painted hull to
camouflage
the vessel

British M Class: Converted from the survivors of K–class tragedies as the Great War ended, these large boats were essentially monitors (one–gun battleships). Unfortunately, they inherited the jinx of their K–class sisters. Of the three built, two went down in accidents.

Designed during the late 1920s, the U.S.S. *Nautilus* represented one of the American entries in the big-submarine game. She went on to play various roles during World War II.

Fittingly enough, the U.S.S. *Gato*, the namesake of the standard World War II fleet boat class, joined the navy in December 1941.

Admiral Karl Dönitz (dark uniform, with sword) is very much the chief in this gathering of planning officers.

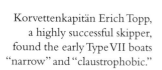

Korvettenkapitän Erich Topp, a highly successful skipper, found the early Type VII boats "narrow" and "claustrophobic."

Members of a U-boat crew enjoy the chance for fresh air as the submarine moves awash off the European coast.

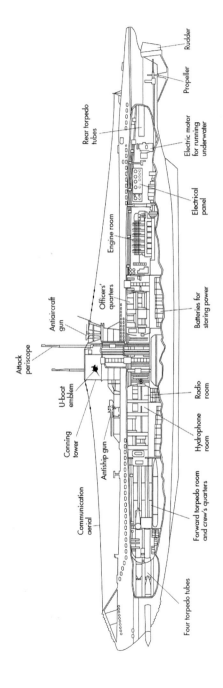

Attack
periscope

Antiaircraft
gun

Rear torpedo
tubes

Conning
tower

U-boat
emblem

Officers'
quarters

Engine room

Propeller

Rudder

Communication
aerial

Antiship gun

Electric motor
for running
underwater

Electrical
panel

Batteries for
storing power

Radio
room

Hydrophone
room

Forward torpedo room
and crew's quarters

Four torpedo tubes

Type IX U-boat: Though not "claustrophobic" like the early Type VIIs, these versatile larger boats were not nimble enough to satisfy Admiral Dönitz.

The adventurous Korvettenkapitän Reinhard Hardegen, skipper of the *U-123,* led the way in the Germans' 1942 onslaught off the U.S. east coast.

After sinking nine ships in American waters, Jochen Mohr, commander of the *U-123,* wrote a verse mocking President Franklin D. Roosevelt.

Lieutenant Moon Chapple's old S-boat (the *S-38*), operating in the Philippines, scored one of the earliest U.S. submarine kills of the Pacific war.

selves to the heavy risk of destruction by surface gunfire. Hence the effect of abiding by the rules would be, as the Germans had discovered more than twenty years earlier, to eliminate submarines as serious commerce raiders and confine them to their role as warships. To accomplish their purpose, the British circulated among the powers, like a round-robin property lease, what they called the London Submarine Agreement. The United States gave strong support to this effort, hoping, as Undersecretary of State William Phillips explained to FDR, to gain the acquiescence of France and Italy and ultimately of "all the nations of the world, if possible." On November 23, 1936, the Third Reich joined the company of signatory nations.

Thus, as the world moved into the tensions and crises of the late 1930s, the submarine had preserved its status as a legal weapon of war, but the nations had explicitly bound themselves to employ it with scrupulous care for the rights of others. Ever since its arrival in the navies of the world in the early years of the twentieth century, this idiosyncratic, hybrid vessel had posed complex questions of purpose and use both for its admirers and for its detractors. Now, the nations had in effect defined it as a warship and prohibited the use of it as a commerce raider. That was the way matters stood at the beginning of September 1939.

16

BOATS AND BUILDERS II

iscussions and doubts about the nature and functioning of the submarine continued in the United States into the years following the World War, fueled by the realization that American technology had not produced a design that could fulfill the navy's desire for boats that could operate successfully as warships making up part of the fleet or supporting it, that is, as the cherished fleet submarines. For one major point, fleet submarines would have to reach and sustain speeds of 17 or 18 knots; otherwise, they could not keep up with the standard surface ships. But the admirals chose to reject the most obvious alternative, the kind of role that had almost enabled Germany to cut Britain's ocean lifeline in 1917; commerce raiding of that kind was dismissed as, in effect, ungentlemanly.

In 1919 a series of U.S. submarines designated the S class made its first appearance with the commissioning of the *S-3*. These boats, the first American submarines designed by the navy rather than by private industry, came in three varieties, which had similar performance but differed in various characteristics. Of the first three S-boats, the *S-1*, built under the auspices of Electric Boat at the Fore River Shipbuilding Company yard at Quincy, Massachusetts, and commissioned in June 1920, was the "Holland type." The *S-2*, built by Simon Lake's company at Bridgeport, Connecticut, and commissioned in May 1920, was called, reasonably enough, the "Lake type." The *S-3*, built at the government yard at Portsmouth, was the "government type." The essential difference between the Holland and Lake types remained the method of submergence, with the Holland boats capable of diving like the inventor's favored dolphins and Lake's boats employing the "even keel" method, although making some use of diving planes. After re-

178

ceiving the *S-2,* however, the navy required Lake to build its succeeding boats to the government design, which employed the Holland
method of submergence. The most visible difference between the
government-produced *S-3* and its sisters was its size: 231 feet in overall
length, with a surfaced displacement of 875 tons. The *S-2* was just 207
feet and 800 tons, the *S-1,* 219.5 and also 800.

Despite the high hopes the navy held for these boats, they proved to
have numerous technical problems, notably but far from exclusively
with the engines. At the same time the navy was studying, with increasing admiration, the intricacies of a group of commandeered
U-boats that had been brought across the Atlantic for this purpose. On
examining these arrivals from Germany, the U.S. officers decided that,
while they were clearly inferior to American boats in the quality of the
submarine's internal environment, or "habitability" (one of the relatively positive points of the new S-boats at that stage of submarine development), they otherwise outclassed the U.S. boats in every respect.
This realization shocked a number of the American officers: "It seemed
that the German experience rewrote the rules of the game," noted the
historian Gary Weir. All this contradicted the general impression
among Americans that the United States built submarines second
to none.

In his 1915 reflections, Franklin Roosevelt had noted "the well
known fact that the propelling and operating mechanism is in such an
experimental stage that frequent accidents occur—these are the evils
of any new apparatus, witness the automobile of fifteen years ago." But
the time was not far distant, he said, when the submarine would be "as
dependable as any other high powered vessel." Now, four years later, he
welcomed the chance to benefit from the German experience. When
the navy sought to give Electric Boat and other private industry suppliers some of the machinery and devices from the U-boats, to serve as
models and as subjects for research, the assistant secretary modified the
plan to make the distribution a matter of lending rather than giving;
the navy itself would keep ownership of the German hardware.

Seeking a solution to the submarine problem—which "ranged from
diesel and motor malfunction to severe periscope vibration, poorly designed air compressors, and inferior ventilation systems"—some officers

argued that the navy must cease leaving the design and construction of submarines to private industry and take a larger part in the whole process. For some years a battle would continue to rage between the navy and Electric Boat over the questionable reliability—and the reasons for this uncertainty—of the submarine diesel engines, and in the early 1930s the navy would begin producing its engines under license from a German manufacturer. Given the lines drawn between government and industry, "the Navy's mission to develop and build warships and industry's desire for profit and growth were certainly legitimate ambitions," as Weir noted, "but, at least at the outset, they were also completely incompatible."

All these questions, however, involved more than a cold war between the navy and civilian suppliers; something of a schism also existed between the seagoing officers and the navy technical bureaus, which did not share engineering decisions with the men who were going to use the resulting product—a disjunction that would make itself felt twenty years later in a dramatic and tragic way. The discontented officers received important support from Admiral Sims, who had returned from England to reassume his official chair in Newport as president of the Naval War College. The sheer obviousness of German superiority also made itself increasingly felt and thus furthered the development of consensus among the contending parties. Strikingly, the chief of the Bureau of Engineering said in 1927: "We find in general that departures from German practice get us into trouble and that the trouble can generally be cured by strict adherence to German practice."

Shortly afterward—despite the fact that the design dated from 1916, more than a decade earlier—the navy adopted a U-boat, the 1,175-ton *U-135*, as its prototype for the next period of construction. Interestingly, this sizable submarine (its submerged displacement was 1,535 tons) was a *U-Kreuzer* (U-cruiser) designed as a long-range commerce raider. This seemed an odd choice as a model for a navy that was purportedly seeking a fleet submarine, not a large commerce raider, but, perhaps only half-consciously, the planners were acknowledging the problems inherent in the quest for a high-speed fleet submarine—for instance, the bigger the engines, the less the room for other features and hence the lower the level of habitability. In any case, many officers by now had begun to believe that the navy would never produce submarines that could keep pace with surface ships and that they should take a fresh look at the mission of these unique vessels.

In view of the fact that U.S. submarines would of necessity operate across the far reaches of the Pacific, range, habitability, and reliability ranked at the top of the list of desiderata; speed and maneuverability, though certainly desirable, shared second place. From somewhere, everybody seemed to agree, the navy must obtain something better than the old S-boat. The crew of a submarine must be reasonably comfortable and rested in order to meet the challenges of duty. Air quality became of first importance, in view of the striking fact that one person breathes one cubic foot of carbon dioxide into the air every hour; the gas had to be efficiently removed from the environment of the submarine if the members of the crew were to remain alert. Navy scientists devised chemical methods of dealing with the problem.

Another very important advance came in 1935 when the authorities, in view of the undoubted fact that many submarine operations would occur in tropical and subtropical waters, approved a trial air-conditioning installation in the *Cuttlefish* (SS-171). This boat, contracted for in 1931 and the first submarine produced by Electric Boat since the World War, ended a thirteen-year drought during which Lawrence Spear exerted himself, with significant success, to keep together the company's team of irreplaceable designers, specialists, and skilled workers. The *Cuttlefish* also became the navy's first partially welded submarine. Since the most marked effect of air conditioning is to lower humidity, the reduction in condensation on the boat's interior surfaces more than justified the allocation of space to the new systems, not only from the point of view of the crew's comfort but also, and importantly, because it reduced hazards to the vital electrical systems resulting from excessive moisture. Working within the severe limits of submarine space, the engineers could not solve all the problems related to habitability, but they indeed made long strides from the days of the World War. One great factor in the improvement was the navy's full involvement in the creation of its boats, in contrast to the earlier domination by private industry.

During the 1920s the U.S. Navy also joined what was seen as an international trend to larger and larger underwater craft, notably with the *Argonaut* (SS-166), a 385-foot giant of 2,710 tons' surface displacement (4,000 submerged) that would remain the biggest U.S. submarine built until the post–World War II era. Some years earlier, in one of his periodic reflections on the submarine of the present and the future, Spear had expressed his basic conservatism with his approving prophecy that the U.S. Navy would keep "in the middle of the road, thus avoiding all sudden radical changes," but by 1927 he appeared to have mellowed enough to accept the idea of a boat of 3,000 tons serving as an active and wide-ranging offensive weapon.

Launched in that same year, the *Argonaut* owed her size partly to her intended use as a minelayer, although few officers actually had much interest in employing submarines for this purpose. The big submarine was followed in 1929 and 1930 by two other comparably sized giants, the *Narwhal* and the *Nautilus,* but thereafter the trend turned in another direction, for the United States and for other countries as well.

A British foray into the realm of the oversized submarine led to a series of unbelievable disasters. Though designers conceived the Royal Navy's K-class boats during the World War as a response to rumors about the power and speed of forthcoming German boats, none of their remarkable troubles came from encounters with the enemy. Designed to be fast as well as large, an entry in the perpetual race for an effective fleet submarine, the K-class boats could reach 23 or 24 knots (they were faster than battleships of the time), but only because they were powered by steam turbines, the possibility glumly foreseen by Lawrence Spear in 1916; no diesel engine yet existed that could drive a 2,000-ton boat at such speeds.

But steam power brought with it extremely undesirable complexities. Before the boat could begin a dive, just as in the old days before 1900, the crew had to shut down the boilers, the funnels had to be retracted into their housings, and all the openings around funnels and ventilators had to be sealed. The entire procedure took about five minutes, ten times as long as was required for a diesel boat to execute the dive routine, and an American observer timed one dive at eleven long minutes. There were just "too many damned holes." The K-boats had their habitability shortcomings, too; the temperature in the boiler room could reach 160°. Thus nothing had changed in the world of steam.

The *K-3* began the parade of problems that turned into a series of disasters by burying herself in a mud bank, 130 feet down, off Portsmouth while the captain was showing her off to a special guest, the Duke of York, who two decades later would become King George VI. A few months on, this time in a heavy sea, she made another undesired plunge, again burying her nose. At just about the same time, her sister boat, the *K-2,* suffered an explosion in the engine room; the crew had trouble dealing with the resulting fire because somebody had forgotten to install the fire extinguishers. As for the *K-6,* she proved reluctant during her diving trials to return to the surface. After two or three more incidents of the kind, dockyard workers began objecting to taking part in any dives on K-boats.

But matters turned far more serious in January 1917, when the aptly numbered *K-13* headed out from her base for diving trials off Scotland, carrying, besides the crew, a number of executives from the builder, civilian guests, and Admiralty officials. From the beginning, the day did not go well. The *K-13* first ran aground and then, back on course and undergoing a test dive, sprang a leak. During the lunch interlude aboard an accompanying tender, two of the civilians, more prescient than the rest of the company, informed the skipper of the *K-13* that they were through for the day and would remain on the surface.

In the late afternoon, disregarding a gauge that seemed not to be working properly, the officers sent the boat into its first official dive. Almost immediately the boiler room began flooding (the troublesome gauge was supposed to show whether the boiler room ventilators were closed), and the submarine plunged to the bottom, 55 feet below the surface of the bay. The engine room quickly flooded and fire knocked out the electrical system. Spotting bubbles breaking the surface, a nearby submarine alerted the authorities ashore, who responded with unbelievable sluggishness.

Six hours went by before anybody dispatched a rescue mission, and it arrived with no plan of action and no effective equipment. Finally, a day and a half after the ordeal began, rescuers were able to connect air hoses to the downed boat, and a day later forty-seven survivors, of the eighty men who had been on board, were brought out to safety.

This nightmare did not end the misadventures of the K–boats, not even those of the *K-13*. In February 1918, having cast off the shadow of her past, the refurbished boat, now redesignated the *K-22*, took part in a training exercise in which two squadrons of K–boats sailed as fleet submarines with a battle squadron. The results gave little encouragement to the proponents of the submarine as a warship operating in concert with larger vessels. Forced to avoid a collision with a minesweeper flotilla that suddenly appeared before them in the gathering darkness, the submarines scattered like chickens, and in the confusion the *K-22* proved that her change in number had not changed her character. She rammed another K–boat and then was herself rammed by a destroyer, while a cruiser smashed into another submarine. Altogether, in what amounted to perhaps the greatest accident in the history of the submarine, two boats went to the bottom and three others, together with two surface vessels, suffered damage. Stubbornly, or perhaps only through inertia, the Admiralty ordered six more of these demonstrably useless boats, though only one actually went all the way through production to become commissioned.

All this did not augur well for the large submarine—the underwater cruiser—but in the late 1920s the French Navy carried this line of construction to what would seem, until well along in World War II, its ultimate with the *Surcouf,* an experimental giant of 3,250 tons' surface displacement (4,300 submerged). Armed like a small cruiser, the *Surcouf* bristled with firepower: two 8-inch guns, which gave her the possibility of slugging it out with an enemy in a surface battle, and an antiaircraft battery. To extend her range of reconnaissance, she also carried a small seaplane. But all the elements intended to turn her into a mini-surface ship contrived to detract from her performance as a submarine, rendering her slow to submerge and an easy-to-spot hulking presence below the surface; like the big American boats, she handled more like a truck than a roadster. (She would come to a disappointing end, going down in the Gulf of Mexico in February 1942 after a collision with an American freighter.)

Expensive, and handicapped by their limited maneuverability, such submarine cruisers exerted little appeal for the Americans. "Naval designers concluded that the size and heavy deck guns [two 6-inchers] were more of a burden than a benefit to the combat submarine," observed the naval historian Theodore Roscoe.

■ ■ ■

During the mid-1930s a special U.S. Senate committee attracted much attention with an investigation into the role played by American munitions makers in the World War. The results of the war, which at first had been merely disappointing and now appeared more disastrous with every passing day, had deeply disillusioned Americans, since the great struggle had not only failed to make the world safe for democracy but seemed merely to have created opportunities for Fascism and Communism to rise and flourish. Surely, thousands or perhaps millions of people felt, some identifiable and sinister person or persons were to blame for America's becoming involved in this disaster.

Then, in March 1934, *Fortune* magazine published an explosive article detailing shady relationships between European arms manufacturers and politicians; perhaps, it was thought, such tie-ups had existed in the United States, too. The chairman of the investigating committee, Senator Gerald P. Nye of North Dakota, believed so, and passionately: In their drive for profits, American armaments manufacturers, in collusion with Wall Street (which in the 1930s lived in a state of continual defensiveness after having produced the crash of 1929), had dragged the United States into the war. "In public affairs," one historian observed, "it is not the accuracy but the force of a belief that counts."

The Nye committee's hearings led directly to the passage of the Neutrality Acts of 1935–37, which in some respects reflected William Jennings Bryan's warning to Woodrow Wilson in 1915 about money as the worst of all contrabands. The legislation forbade American firms to trade with belligerents, banned loans to belligerent governments, and required foreign governments to pay for military items before they could leave the country.

Prominent executives in defense industries hence found themselves traveling to Washington to appear before Nye and his committee. The Electric Boat Company naturally figured in the drama, and in September

1934 Spear, President Henry Carse, and another executive underwent questioning by the senator and his colleagues. Committee staff members produced documents said to show that Electric Boat and its old British partner, Vickers, had worked together to dominate the world submarine marketplace. The spotlight turned on South America, where Electric Boat was working to obtain submarine orders from Peru, while Vickers, according to testimony, devoted its efforts to convincing the government of Peru's rival, Chile, of its need for a new submarine flotilla. Spear cautioned the managing director of Vickers, Sir Charles Craven, to continue talking "nothing but British construction as far as Chile was concerned"; if Vickers succeeded in its dealings with Chile, Electric Boat could then quietly collect its share of the profits. It was also implied in testimony that the U.S. naval mission in Peru was working closely with Electric Boat to help the company obtain the contracts.

To lighten the picture presented by these goings-on, Electric Boat's representatives declared that their operations in foreign countries kept the United States up-to-date on submarine developments elsewhere. Though the answer seemed somewhat on the thin side, and the evidence seemed to indicate that Vickers and Electric Boat had cheerfully tried to promote a low-level arms race between Peru and Chile, not even a zealot like Senator Nye could make a leap from there to claim that the two companies had performed any such feat as dragging their respective countries into war with the German Empire. Certainly American business had laid heavy bets on an Allied victory between 1914 and 1917, and some of its practices then and later were less than admirable, but for Wilson the U-boat remained the agent of decision.

The Nye hearings, however, would not by any means constitute the last appearance of Electric Boat in public controversy.

■ ■ ■

Tonnage posed a special consideration for naval planning during the 1930s because of the limits imposed by the London Naval Treaty of 1930; U.S. planners had to decide how best to use the navy's allotment of 52,700 total submarine tons. By 1936, after intensive discussions on all aspects of the long quest for the fleet submarine, American naval opinion had made its choice: a boat of approximately 1,450 tons, with an overall length of about 308 feet and a surface speed of 21 knots (9 knots submerged). The new *Salmon*-class boats would serve as the models. The family of new "S"-boats (not to be confused with the earlier S class), which would include *Sargo, Stingray, Sturgeon*, and twelve others, were a few knots faster and a few feet longer than the preceding "P"-class of fleet submarines, *Porpoise, Perch*, and eight others. Curiously enough, even though the navy had required Simon Lake to give up his own approach in building the later S-boats and Lake's company had disappeared only a few years later, the developing fleet submarines bore important marks of Lake's thinking not only in the decking and superstructure, which reflected Lake's desire to produce good performance on the surface, but also in the double hull, with the ballast tanks outside the pressure hull. Holland's dolphin thus wore a very effective disguise, which it would keep for a number of years.

Since Congress refused to allow the navy the option of building all the boats, those of the *Salmon* class would come both from Electric Boat and from the Portsmouth and Mare Island naval shipyards. But in this new expansion, the navy took a much stronger line than in the World War, when industry had in effect dictated terms and procedures. This time poor workmanship and the use of inferior materials would bring substantial fines. Electric Boat "now confronted a Navy willing and able to have its own way by playing the role of senior partner." At the same time Assistant Secretary of the Navy Charles Edison acknowledged that working with the federal government, with its frequent changes of policy and requirements, often posed problems for private industry, and he took a number of steps to put ship design and procurement on a businesslike basis. After war began in Europe and danger loomed for the United States, Edison, who as the son of the world's most famous inventor took a special interest in technical matters, responded by helping Electric Boat undertake a sizable enlargement of its facilities to meet the new demands on the navy. The navy no longer had to work within limits on its size, for the London Naval Treaty had now, of course, gone to join the Treaty of Versailles in the graveyard for dead documents.

■ ■ ■

"The headline 'S-boat Sinks,'" commented a naval historian, "was frequent in the American press between the wars." Two such disasters not only attracted great attention but combined to produce important results. In September 1925 the *S-51*, proceeding on the surface with hatches open, went down in Block Island Sound after being rammed by the *City of Rome*, a coastal steamer. The collision flung nine of the crew into the sea, but the inrush of water drowned the remaining twenty-seven men at their posts as the boat sank in two minutes, flooded throughout.

A little more than two years later, on December 17, 1927, an accompanying destroyer smashed into the *S-4*, a boat that had begun its life seven years earlier with severe engine problems, as she unexpectedly surfaced after a run off Cape Cod. For a while after the *S-4* sank, a diver could pick up tapping sounds from survivors, both forward and aft, but would-be rescuers found themselves as helpless as those who had first responded to news of the plight of Britain's *K-13*. The officers who took charge of rescue attempts tried to save the crew of the *S-4* by blowing out her ballast tanks with compressed air and thus bringing her to the surface, but all efforts—complicated by a storm that blew up—failed, leaving forty men dead.

The lasting importance of the two S-boat disasters became clear in the spring of 1939, when within little more than a week both the U.S. and British navies suffered major submarine accidents. On May 23, on the nineteenth and last of the preliminary sea trials of his boat, the skipper of the submarine *Squalus* (SS-192) took her out into the Atlantic off Portsmouth for a crash dive. Everything went off properly, with the boat reaching a 50-foot depth in record time, until a sudden call came from the engine room: "Take her up! The inductions are flooding!" The main induction valve, the air intake, had not closed completely before the dive began and, in addition, the "Christmas Tree" indicator panel (so-called because of its red and green lights) had failed to show that the valve had remained open. Water poured into the stern compartments, and the boat sank to the bottom; the depth gauges read 240 feet.

Now began a drama different from the stories of the lost S-boats.

After the *S-4* tragedy, two young navy officers had begun working on devices to make survival not only possible but likely in such situations. Lieutenant Charles Momsen, known (not remarkably for those days) as Swede, began experimenting with an underwater breathing apparatus—a mask, a nose clamp, and a rubber chamber filled with oxygen. Using this pioneering SCUBA gear, which became known as the Momsen lung, a submariner, given a slow-enough ascent to avoid the bends, could survive from depths of at least 150 feet.

The *Squalus* had settled deeper, however, in 240 feet of water, and in this situation the rescuers called for the invention created by another lieutenant, Allan McCann. After the sinking of the *S-4,* while Momsen was developing his escape device for crew members to employ, McCann had set to work to create a diving bell, a tank that could be affixed to a special escape hatch on a sunken submarine. Controlled by a two-man crew in an upper compartment, this rescue chamber was reeled down a wire guideline placed in position by a diver. Even with the use of McCann's chamber, the rescue effort on the *Squalus* proved harrowing and exhausting. While the cable was lifting the last group of sailors to safety, it jammed, leaving the men suspended for a time in midwater until the problem was corrected. But, though the twenty-six men sealed in the engine room had been drowned, all of the thirty-three in the forward section had returned safely to the surface. None of them asked for transfer from the "Diving Navy." The *Squalus*, like these thirty-three crew members, survived to fight another day.

The *Squalus* rescue presented a curious historical sidelight. In later years many people developed the impression that Momsen's lung rather than McCann's chamber had saved the crew—probably because Momsen came to the scene as part of the rescue team. Each of these officers deserved great credit for his work, of course, and it was especially noteworthy that each had insisted on using himself as the subject in all the hazardous experiments needed to test and perfect these devices.

An unpublicized hero of the operation was the Portsmouth naval designer and constructor, Captain Andrew McKee, who not only worked out the detailed salvage plan but managed to persuade all the officers involved to follow it. (McKee would become legend in the submarine force for knowing "every part of every submarine by its first name." One officer said that, if somebody "recommended that the potato masher be moved six inches to the right or left, he'd go down and talk to the cook about it.")

Following almost immediately in the wake of the *Squalus* rescue, on June 1 a remarkably similar tragedy struck the Royal Navy. On the submarine *Thetis,* in the Mersey off Liverpool, an officer opened the door of a flooded torpedo tube, and the resulting inrush of water sank the boat with all hands. The McCann rescue chamber had, of course, become famous around the world during the preceding days, but nobody had yet had time to act on the lesson taught by the rescue of the *Squalus* survivors. Following these disasters, the British then moved to create an escape device, a so-called self-contained system that differed considerably from both Momsen's and McCann's inventions.

■ ■ ■

In September 1940 the U.S. Navy brought the Manitowoc Shipbuilding Company of Wisconsin into the submarine fold, to supplement the efforts of the Electric Boat Company. Both would begin production of the seventy-three boats of the navy's new standard for what it still called the fleet submarine, the *Gato* class (SS-212–SS-284). The *Gato* was commissioned just three weeks after Pearl Harbor.

The *Gato*s were 311 feet long, with a surfaced displacement of 1,525 tons; they had a speed on the surface of 20 knots and could carry a crew of as many as eighty-five. The ten 21-inch torpedo tubes were divided six in the bow, four in the stern. The early members of the class carried a 3-inch deck gun, later versions a 4-inch or even 5-inch gun. With minor modifications, the *Gato*s would serve as the U.S. fleet submarine throughout the looming war as the first boats of the class were building. (And every one would bear the name of a fish, a principle of nomenclature that would give currency to many a name never before seen outside an ichthyological dictionary.) Besides the fleet boats, the U.S. Navy would also operate a number of the older S-boats, which, despite all their ailments, had to join in the action at the outset of the war in the Pacific and would prove valuable again two or three years later.

Much had changed since the first American war submarine experience a quarter of a century earlier. During the intervening years, the collaboration and the clashes between naval officers and Electric Boat executives had created the climate in which U.S. submarines had evolved. The continuing tug of war had made it plain that simple ideas about government and industry engaged in a cozy alliance could hardly begin to cover the situation and in fact could be quite misleading. Now, "after being completely dependent upon private industry in 1914, the Navy—not industry—controlled the design and construction process by the eve of the Second World War."

The development of the boats themselves, though incremental rather than revolutionary, had created craft substantially larger, more versatile, and more habitable than those described by Lawrence Spear in his 1915 paper. Though still not suitable for anyone suffering from claustrophobia, the new boats were a hundred feet or more longer, they carried crews of up to eighty instead of twenty-five, they could go a hundred feet deeper (and thus have less to fear from depth charging), and they were 5 or 6 knots faster. By the end of 1941, guided by an evolved concept of the submarine as a vessel capable of operating independently across oceans, the planners, designers, and builders had created the fleet submarine that would carry the load for the United States in the crisis now at hand.

WORLD WAR II:
THE STRUGGLE FOR THE ATLANTIC

The Battle of the Atlantic was the dominating factor all through the war. Never for one moment could we forget that everything happening elsewhere, on land, at sea, or in the air, depended ultimately on its outcome. . . .

—Winston S. Churchill

PART IV

LIEUTENANT LEMP'S GREAT DECISION

A strange mixture of violence and hesitancy marked the first three days of September 1939. On August 23 Nazi Germany and the Communist Soviet Union, universally believed to be mortal enemies, had startled the world by signing a nonaggression pact that officially made them friends, if not actual partners. Two days later, knowing that the German-Soviet treaty had prepared the way for Hitler to make war on Poland, the British government proclaimed a formal alliance with the Poles, thus confirming an earlier guarantee given after the Germans had occupied Czechoslovakia in March. On August 31 these public acts were followed by Hitler's signing of his Directive No. 1 for the Conduct of the War, and early the next morning the Führer's troops, tanks, and aircraft flung themselves on Polish defenders in history's first *Blitzkrieg*. The Germans aimed at achieving a quick success in this lightning war, smashing their victims before the western allies, Britain and France, could offer much effective aid and thereby, perhaps, leading the western powers to abandon a war that would rapidly have become pointless. The Poles placed the few hopes they nourished for survival on Allied attacks in the West that might at least draw some of the German strength away from the firestorm roaring across their homeland.

For two days, however, the Allies took no military action, while serving the Germans with ultimatums demanding that they withdraw from Poland. Not having begun a war just to abandon it the same weekend, Hitler dismissed the ultimatums, and on Sunday, September 3, Britain and France formally declared war on the Reich. In another notable event of the third, Winston Churchill returned to the Admiralty as First Lord, the post he had been forced to give up a quarter of a century earlier after the failure of the Allied attempt to seize Gallipoli and force the Dardanelles, an operation whose failure had dogged him ever since.

During the two days of last-minute attempts to restore the peace, the Polish forces had taken fearsome punishment from the Wehrmacht, on the ground and in the air. But, aside from some essentially meaningless operations by the French in the neighborhood of their northeastern frontier ("Movements are progressing normally," read a typically vague statement in one communiqué), the declarations of war brought no Allied actions on the ground or in the air. Not only did the French Army stand quietly along the front with Germany, but, for their part, the Germans, busily engaged in the east, abstained from launching any air attacks against either Britain or France. The French even asked the British not to try bombing Germany, so that the enemy would not retaliate upon French war factories, which lay open to attack. Thus, while Hitler proceeded to crush Poland, the western allies continued to do nothing, contenting themselves with dropping propaganda leaflets intended to persuade the Germans to mend their ways.

As this astonishing period, which nobody had anticipated, continued, it received various designations and nicknames—Twilight War, for one. It was the American tag, however, that achieved the greatest currency and proved lasting: the Phony War.

Twilit and phony as it was on land, however, the new war presented a different picture at sea. In his first official action back at the Admiralty, Churchill asked the director of naval intelligence for a report on the strength of the German U-boat force. He made this request in response to an event that occurred only three hours after he had first sat down at his familiar desk with his old wooden map case from the first war still hanging on the wall behind it.

■ ■ ■

During late August, as events on the Continent moved toward war, Americans and Canadians in Europe on business or on vacation began scrambling for accommodations on westbound passenger ships. Damon Boynton, a thirty-year-old professor at Cornell, who had gone to England to further his studies in pomology (fruit growing), hastily booked passage on the *Scythia,* but when the line canceled that sailing he found a third-class berth on the *Athenia.* "It was crowded," he said later. "There were extra bunks everywhere—in smoking rooms, in writing rooms. My cabin had two extra bunks. Most of the passengers were women and children." Managing to acquire accommodations on the *Athenia* seemed to represent great good luck for the last-minute passengers. A vessel of 13,581 tons, built in 1923 and owned by the Donaldson Atlantic Line, she had through the years built up such a reputation as a cozy family ship that many regular transatlantic travelers preferred her to any other liner. The squeeze came now not only from the greatly increased demand but from the withdrawal of several vessels from passenger service to be fitted out as troopships or armed merchant cruisers. The most renowned of these was the *Queen Mary,* but the *Athenia* acquired a number of passengers who had been booked on the *Caledonia.* These included a group of six socialite young women from Houston, who had been traveling in England and Scotland. Numbered among others on board were the wife of the mayor of Saratoga Springs, New York; the baby daughter of the renowned German and Hollywood film director, Ernst Lubitsch; a professor of journalism at Syracuse; and a young man who had just graduated from Washington and Lee. The *Athenia* also carried 155 refugees from various countries in Central and Eastern Europe who had managed to get out from under the looming Nazi terror. When the ship sailed from Glasgow, she left behind on the pier a number of Canadians and Americans who had vainly hoped to get a berth at the eleventh hour.

With 420 passengers on board, the *Athenia* departed from her dock on the Clyde at noon on September 1, bound first for Belfast, where she picked up another 136 passengers, and on to Liverpool, where a further 546 passengers came aboard. At 4:30 in the afternoon of September 2, now carrying a total of 1,102 booked passengers, the 155 refugees, and a crew of 315, the liner departed from Liverpool, sailed back through the North Channel, and headed out into the Atlantic, bound for Montreal.

The next morning, when word came that Britain and Germany were now at war, the skipper, the resonantly named Captain James Cook, making his fourteenth crossing in the *Athenia,* ordered a lifeboat drill, although the passengers had already taken part in the obligatory drill held shortly after sailing. Following Admiralty instructions, Captain Cook also took another—and significant—step, ordering the crew to prepare for darkening the ship at sunset, when even the navigation lights would be dimmed.

Sunset that day, which came at about seven o'clock, found the *Athenia* some 200 miles west of the Hebrides, proceeding at 16 knots, with her hatchways now blacked out and her lights dimmed. At 7:39, with twilight heavy, the masthead lookout saw white tracks in the water, about 250 yards away, aimed at the ship and streaking toward it. With the torpedoes so close and moving at a 40-knot clip, his cry to the bridge could not have any effect on the event. One of the torpedoes slammed into the side of the ship and exploded, immediately killing some of the passengers and some of the crew and wounding others. Captain Cook moved quickly to have the lifeboats manned, loaded, and lowered, and gave the order to abandon ship.

A variety of vessels turned in their courses in response to the *Athenia*'s distress call, including the Norwegian tanker *Knute Nelson;* the yacht *Southern Cross* (owned by the famous Swedish industrialist Axel Wenner Gren), and, somewhat farther away, an American freighter, the *City of Flint.* Listening stations in Britain also picked up the signal, and the Admiralty ordered three destroyers to speed to the scene. Though some problems occurred in the loading and handling of the lifeboats, and one of them was smashed by the propellers of the *Knute Nelson* when it was pulled under the stern of the vessel, this ship, the Wenner Gren yacht, and two of the destroyers rescued a total of 1,305 passengers and crew. The passengers lost numbered 112, sixteen of them children; deaths of crew members totaled nineteen.

During the rescue struggle, bizarrely, a great pod of whales appeared, circling and plunging around the boats. Lifeboats with flares dotted the surface, and from all directions came desperate cries for help. On the *Southern Cross,* which picked up about four hundred survivors, a young woman who had just been hauled to safety screamed "My baby!" and leaped back into the sea. The Wenner Gren yacht also offered a happier scene, when, from a lifeboat that had capsized more than once, crewmen pulled a small gray-haired woman, the nurse of

Ernst Lubitsch's ten-month-old daughter; she had the baby clutched at the back of her neck where, as much as possible, she had kept the child out of the cold water.

The news of the sinking, coming just hours after the war began in the West, produced a sensation on both sides of the Atlantic (292 of the passengers were reported to be Americans). The *Athenia* was immediately declared to have been the victim of a torpedo. Seemingly mindful of all the discussion of the *Lusitania* that had gone on through the years, Steve Early, President Roosevelt's press secretary, pointedly declared that the ship carried refugees, not munitions; of course, since the *Athenia* was bound westward, not toward Britain, she would hardly in any case have been loaded with weapons and explosives.

"The World War practice of torpedoing passenger ships at sea," noted the *New York Times,* "renewed so soon after the declaration of war, caused anxiety to spread over the breadth of the Atlantic." In the House of Commons, members denounced the Germans for the "outrage" and "crime" committed by the U-boat. Commentators pointed out that, in connection with the Anglo-German Naval Treaty of 1935, Germany had expressly accepted the provisions of the London Naval Treaty of 1930 binding the signatory powers to follow the long-established cruiser rules and thus forbidding attacks without warning and without making provision for the safety of the victims' passengers and crew.

The rescue ships carried the survivors to Galway and Glasgow, where they were welcomed and interviewed by officials, including the U.S. consuls; in Glasgow, Consul-General Leslie Davis had the assistance of young John F. Kennedy, son of the American ambassador to Great Britain. In Galway, Captain Cook declared: "There's no doubt about it. My ship was torpedoed. The torpedo went right through the ship to the engine room and completely wrecked the galley. Passengers were at dinner when the torpedo struck the ship and the explosion killed several."

Even before Captain Cook arrived in Galway, the world had paid little attention to the rapid German denial of culpability or to the contention that the *Athenia* must either have hit a floating mine or been done in by a boiler explosion—and still less to the later assertion that "it is likely that a British submarine fired the torpedo as a propaganda measure to influence United States neutrality." It was not a U-boat captain but Winston Churchill, as always throughout his career serving as a lightning rod, who should bear the blame, declared Joseph Goebbels's propagandists. But this notion had little impact outside the Axis world. To most people, the sinking of the *Athenia* meant, beyond any question, that the Germans, whatever documents they might have signed, had taken up where they had been forced to leave off in 1918: The submarine had reappeared as a commerce raider, and it would be unrestricted warfare once more. But the story had more to it than that.

In the early evening of September 3, the submarine *U-30*, commanded by Oberleutnant Fritz-Julius Lemp, was patrolling her operational area, a box on the map 200 miles by 180 miles, northwest of Ireland. Twelve days earlier, in anticipation of the outbreak of war, fifteen other submarines had departed from their bases at Kiel and Wilhelmshaven, proceeding north along the coast of Norway, westward in the waters between the Shetland and the Faroe Islands, and out into the ocean. On August 22 the *U-30* had departed Wilhelmshaven to join its fellow boats, and one more, the *U-27*, had come along the next day. Once out into the ocean, the U-boats had lain in wait for the expected fateful signal, which indeed came on Sunday, September 3. Now that the war had begun, the U-boats moved southward to patrol their assigned areas.

As darkness fell that day, Lemp surfaced to perform a diesel boat's ever-present chore of charging the batteries (Type VII boats were good for 90 underwater miles at most on a charge). Surfacing also gave the crew a much-craved bonus of fresh air and some of its fortunate members a chance to escape topside for a while from their cramped existence amid the cables, pipes, and machinery below. In just a few minutes the skipper sighted a dark shape approaching, less than 10 miles away. He recognized it as a passenger liner but also noted that, unlike normal passenger ships, which rode the waves lit up like hotels, it was dark except for its dimmed running lights. Curious, too, Lemp thought, was the ship's course, somewhat north of the normal track. Perhaps, in this large and darkened vessel, he was confronting not an innocuous passenger steamer but an armed merchant cruiser. And such a cruiser counted as a warship and hence as a legitimate target for a U-boat's torpedoes.

As it happened, the course of the approaching ship put the *U-30* in a favorable spot for attack. Diving, still not quite sure whether or not to go ahead, Lemp maneuvered the submarine into firing position and peered through the periscope, and now, like an addict who cannot resist the call of the drug, he was hooked. Firing all four bow tubes at the darkened ship, Lemp saw one strike her in the side and explode.

Soon, moving away on the surface, the U-boat captain heard the distress calls from the *Athenia* and, with the exhilaration of the attack now fading, realized just what he had done: He had sunk a large British passenger liner. He decided not to report the sinking to headquarters but to wait and deliver the news personally to the Kommodore of Submarines, Captain Karl Dönitz. He could expect to find himself in very hot water when he returned to Wilhelmshaven, because the Führer himself had decreed that U-boats must conduct submarine warfare in strict compliance with prize rules and the London Submarine Agreement: No U-boat should attack any merchant ship without first challenging her and making sure that her passengers and crew had made their way safely into the lifeboats. In spectacularly blatant fashion, Lemp had just disobeyed this clear and explicit order.

The news of the sinking thus caused consternation in Germany as well as in Britain and the United States, though for different reasons. After Hitler heard the news, he ordered the issuing of the denial, and with some legitimacy, since not only had his order forbidden such an attack but Lemp also had not reported; nobody knew where he was, and the sinking had occurred somewhat north of the *U-30*'s assigned patrol area. As the story took shape in the newspapers in the succeeding days, of course, nobody of any nationality could long harbor doubts about what had really happened. The Führer did not wait for discussion and debate, however, but immediately ordered the U-boat command to notify all boats at sea that "on no account are operations to be carried out against passenger steamers, even when under escort." The last proviso indicated the seriousness of Hitler's purpose, since, as in the first war, a ship sailing with escort lost its legal neutral or noncombatant status and became as valid a target as a battleship. The Führer soon added still another point: U-boats must not attack any French ships at all.

The order forbidding the unrestricted submarine attacks that had characterized the first war came not from any sudden reverence Hitler had developed for his own pledged word but from his desire to keep matters essentially calm in the West. The developing Phony War suited his aims perfectly, while his legions subdued the Polish forces and prepared the stage for a "peace offer," which, as the victor in the east, he could graciously make to Britain and France. These powers, after all, had gone to war to aid Poland and had failed to make any attempt to do so, and now, with that country erased from the map, what would be the point in any further fighting?

Oberleutnant Lemp returned to Wilhelmshaven on September 26 to find the Kommodore awaiting him on the pier. After hearing Lemp's account and thus for the first time finding out exactly what had happened, Dönitz ordered the young man into an airplane and off to Berlin to report to the commander in chief of the navy, Admiral Erich Raeder himself—fortunately for Lemp, not to the Führer. By this time, more than three weeks after the sinking, the Germans had woven an entire fabric of denials and explanations exculpating U-boats from any involvement in the attack on the *Athenia*. They now made a possibly fateful choice: Instead of recanting and admitting that a U-boat captain had indeed made the attack but had done so in violation of strict orders, they decided (apparently with little deliberation) to stand by their story. This decision meant, in turn, that the authorities could not subject Lemp to court-martial for his flagrant disobedience of an order that had come from the highest level of government, because the attack had officially not taken place at all.

After a brief period of cabin arrest, Lemp, with no charges possible against him, simply returned to duty as a U-boat skipper. To protect the denial, the authorities removed the smoking-gun page from the *U-30*'s logbook and replaced it with an innocuous entry that made no mention of the *Athenia* and gave a false location for the U-boat at the time of the sinking. The cover-up operation required this step because, though these logs bore a "secret" classification, they were prepared in eight copies and made available for use in training crews.

The British had held some hope that if the Germans resorted to un-restricted operations by submarines, they would move only gradually in this direction and that they might even exercise some general re-straint in attacking undefended ships. But, thanks to one lieutenant in one U-boat, the first day of war saw those hopes blown sky-high. It seemed obvious to everybody who looked that the Germans had sunk the *Athenia* out of their familiar old *Schrecklichkeit* (frightfulness). Thus, at the very beginning of hostilities, the question of convoy arose again.

■ ■ ■

A submariner to the marrow of his bones, Karl Dönitz, like many other senior officers on both sides in the new war, had been formed by his experiences in the first war, even though in the closing days he had missed the chance to test his ideas about simultaneous attacks by sub-marines on convoys. On returning home in July 1919, Dönitz decided to stay in the navy when the director of personnel assured him that, in spite of the prohibition of submarines imposed by the Treaty of Ver-sailles, Germany would soon have them again. During his time in U-boats, Dönitz had in his own way developed the kinds of strong feelings that characterize submariners worldwide: fascination with "that unique characteristic of the submarine service, which requires a submariner to stand on his own feet and sets him a task in the great spaces of the oceans" and with "that unique spirit of comradeship en-gendered by destiny and hardship shared in the community of a U-boats crew," in which "every man's well-being was in the hands of all and where every single man was an indispensable part of the whole." Every submariner, Dönitz believed, had "felt himself to be as rich as a king and would change places with no man."

The power of this mystique ensured Dönitz's remaining loyal to the U-boat arm, even though for the next fifteen years his country would have no submarines and he would spend the time learning the han-dling of surface warships. Rising to command of the cruiser *Emden,* he managed to pursue his own special approach to tactics by simply creating analogues between surface craft and submarines, emphasizing maneuvers that would give a weaker adversary the prospect of pre-venting a superior enemy from taking full advantage of his strength

204 · THE SUBMARINE

(even harking back to the Black Sea raids in 1915) and stressing night operations, which give the weaker opponent "the protective mantle of darkness, from which he can suddenly emerge and behind which he can equally quickly retire again." His experience convinced him that knowledge of surface tactics should always be required of a submarine commander and, conversely, that an admiral in charge of convoys ought to have had experience in the submarine service.

During the early 1930s Dönitz had as his immediate superior a fellow submariner from the Great War, the adventurous and intrigue-minded Captain Wilhelm Canaris. "We used to refer to him as the man with many souls in his breast," Dönitz said. "We did not get on with each other." In January 1935, with the Nazi government now in power for two years, Canaris made an important change of jobs, returning to his World War cloak and dagger field by becoming head of the Abwehr (armed forces intelligence). He took this step even though he disliked and distrusted Hitler, and in time, in an almost convoluted way, he would allow his office to become the center of an anti-Nazi group. On the other hand, Dönitz, who always spoke and wrote in the style of the bluff professional officer, had no involvement in such matters. Like many other high-ranking officers, he pursued his duties while accepting what he saw as the accomplishments of National Socialism and crediting Hitler with achieving them. For him, Canaris was merely the intelligence chief whose service "failed throughout the war to give U-boat Command one single piece of information about the enemy which was of the slightest use of us."

Dönitz also acquired a new job in 1935. After the conclusion of the Anglo-German Naval Agreement, Admiral Raeder picked him to command the resurrected Reich U-boat arm. The fifty-nine-year-old Raeder, who now enjoyed the prospect of having a real fleet to command, had led his class at the naval academy, had served on the Kaiser's yacht *Hohenzollern,* and under various titles had presided over the navy since 1928; Hitler had confirmed him in the post earlier in 1935. (A conservative professional, the admiral possessed the notable distinction of being the last officer in any navy anywhere to wear the formal wing collar with his day uniform.)

Where critics in democratic countries considered the naval treaty an

ill-advised move for the British, Dönitz looked at it through the other
end of the telescope. Submarines played only a minor role for the
British, who had no likely opponent dependent on sea commerce
(Dönitz was thinking only of Europe), and thus, for him, the granting
of permission to build to 45 percent of the Royal Navy total, about
two-thirds that of France, could not be considered much of a conces-
sion; though 45 was the highest percentage mentioned in the treaty, it
represented the lowest tonnage. Even the 100 percent figure did not
impress Dönitz. Although completely devoted to submarines, he saw
himself "being pushed into a backwater" as commander of the tod-
dling U-boat arm, but, as he later conceded, "subsequent events"
proved that his opinion was quite wrong.

Despite his early doubts, Dönitz noted, "body and soul, I was once
more a submariner." Involving himself thoroughly in every aspect of
his new responsibilities and drawing on all his experiences and ideas, he
exerted firm control over both tactical and technical developments
and, characteristically, he did not neglect the psychological side: "One
of the first things I had to do was to rid my crews of the ever recurring
complex that the U-boat, thanks to recent developments in British antisubmarine defense, was a weapon that had been mastered." In the
realm of construction, Dönitz, who took command in October, found
himself with twelve of the small Type IIA coastal boats (250 tons), either on hand or about to be completed. These made up the first operational flotilla of the new navy, operating as the Weddigen Flotilla (in
homage to the North Sea hero of 1914), commanded by Captain
Dönitz himself.

Approving and refining the work the navy had put into the Type VII
boat (he did not actually supervise construction), Dönitz sought to establish it as the standard submarine, considering it the design that
would make the most efficient use of the tonnage granted under the
agreement with Britain. Type IIs—small, lightly armed, and slow—did
not fit into his operational design, and Type Is, though larger than the
VIIs, had poor handling characteristics. The Kriegsmarine, he felt, must
resist the temptation, common in all countries, to "possess ever bigger
and more powerful warships." He saw the characteristics of the Type
VII—reasonable maneuverability, quick diving time, fairly high speed,

with the capacity for twelve or fourteen torpedoes—as coming close to meeting his "somewhat conflicting demands," especially when modified, at the cost of an additional 17 tons, to carry enough fuel oil to increase its range from 6,200 miles to 8,700. (These tonnage figures for the various boats may be misleading, since they are based on the displacement formula adopted by the signatories to the 1922 Washington treaty, which does not include carrying capacity.) The VIIC, the standard boat, had a surfaced displacement of about 760 tons (870 submerged) and was about 220 feet long, with a beam of 20 feet; it could do 17 knots on the surface and 7.6 submerged.

Although war games and studies in the late 1930s had indicated to the naval staff that Germany would need a fleet of 300 U-boats to defeat Britain and the Royal Navy, at the outbreak of the war—which came five years earlier than Hitler had led the military commanders to expect—Dönitz commanded a fleet of only fifty-seven submarines. Of these, only twenty-two (Type VIIs and Type IXs) qualified as oceangoing, suitable for operations in the Atlantic; seventeen of them had been deployed at the outset, covering the approaches to Britain. The other thirty-five (Type IIs, dubbed "Dugouts") could do little more than patrol the coasts and act as training submarines. Thus, curiously, Germany had not gone into the war with the numbers a U-boat campaign would require, and Britain had begun while lacking the defenses such a campaign would demand.

18

U-BOATS IN TROUBLE

In September 1939 the British fleet base at Scapa Flow became the object of special interest to the Germans and of varied kinds of scrutiny by them. On the eleventh of the month Captain Dönitz received an aerial photograph showing warships lying at their anchorages; the captain of one of the coastal "dugout" submarines also gave the U-boat fleet Kommodore a report on Royal Navy patrols and on weather conditions in the area. Dönitz then asked for further pictures, and on September 26 he received a thorough set taken by a reconnaissance aircraft.

The great base in the Orkneys north of Scotland, though "a bleak, dismal, God-forsaken place," held both practical and symbolic significance for the German Navy. Not only had it served as the home of the chief opponent in the 1914–18 war but it had also defeated the attempts of U-boats to penetrate its defenses; two of them had been lost in the effort. Then the terms of the armistice in 1918 had required their crews to sail most of the vessels of the High Seas Fleet—ten battleships, six battle cruisers, numerous lighter vessels, and all submarines— across the North Sea and turn them over to the British, who assembled them in Scapa Flow; in 1919 further indignities imposed by the Treaty of Versailles forced the Germans to deliver eight more battleships and many other vessels. On June 21, perhaps to conform to an old *Kaiserliche Marine* tradition whereby a German warship should sink herself rather than surrender, the crews ran up battle flags and, having opened the sea cocks of their ships, presided over the literal disappearance of the German Navy beneath the waters of Scapa Flow. Now, in 1939, the rebuilding that had slowly begun in the 1920s and had accelerated under Hitler had still produced nothing comparable to the powerful surface fleet Admiral von Tirpitz had created early in the century. Much, therefore, would be demanded of the submarine force.

Though Dönitz dreamed of mounting an operation against the Royal Navy that would succeed where his first-war predecessors had failed, he feared the power of the currents in the area of the Orkneys; the *U-16*, the coastal submarine that had provided him with the report, had herself been caught in a 10-knot current and, being forced to hold steady, her captain, Lieutenant Wellner, had spent the time observing the situation around him. Besides, after their initial alarums in 1914 the British had built up the defenses of Scapa, and surely it had remained a secure shelter for the fleet. Reluctant to let the idea go, however, the U-boat chief questioned Wellner and came to the conclusion that an operation to sneak into Scapa Flow and attack battleships in their berths might just be possible, though success would require extreme daring, skill, and even luck.

Dönitz had his man in mind, a skilled professional whose personality he greatly admired, a man "full of zest and energy and the joy of life, wholly dedicated to his service and an example to all who served under him." This officer, Lieutenant Commander Günther Prien, skipper of the *U-47*, had won his chief's admiration in prewar days with observations like "I get more fun out of a really good convoy exercise than out of any leave." He also had the widest experience of all the U-boat commanders, having served in the merchant marine and qualified as a ship's master. A fellow submariner credited him with just the qualities the Scapa Flow operation would demand: "a cool head, robust nerves, intelligence, and, above all, a zestful and daring spirit."

Summoning Prien to his office, the Kommodore described the assignment, handed Prien the material he had collected, and gave him forty-eight hours to decide whether he would accept. Probably not to any great surprise on Dönitz's part, Prien returned with an affirmative answer. Study of the problem had shown that he would have to make his approach through Kirk Sound, a narrow passage connecting Holm Sound with Scapa Flow itself and constituting the northernmost entrance to the base. The task would require the most precise maneuvering in order to squeeze between the two blockships in the channel, but the advantage this entrance offered an attacker was the absence of nets or any other obstructions. The operation would take place on the night of October 12–13, to combine the darkness of the new moon with suitable tides; the plan called for going into Kirk Sound on the rising tide, so that if the U-boat ran aground, it could float off.

Concerned to maintain absolute secrecy, Dönitz told nobody except Admiral Raeder about the operation, and Prien maintained comparable silence. He did not even break the news to his crew until early in the morning of the attack, as the *U-47* lay on the North Sea floor off the Orkneys. The men had wondered what kind of patrol they were engaged in, since they carried much less than the usual supply of fuel and food and they had noted with surprise how the skipper had made no attempt to molest ships passing in the distance. During the afternoon Prien noted in the log the "superb" state of the crew's morale, and at 7:15 that evening he gave the order that started the submarine rising to the surface. Now, however, as if reaffirming the uncertainty that can attend even the most carefully calculated military operation, nature presented not the much-desired and planned-for darkness but a brilliant display of the Aurora Borealis: streaked with lights, the sky glowed with almost midday brilliance.

Despite this unexpected development, Prien decided to go ahead with the attack—the men were fired up, and who could know what the Northern Lights might do tomorrow night?—and proceeded on the surface into Kirk Sound. When a rip tide seized the boat, Prien was ready for it, but the twisting and jockeying took all his concentration, and at one point the U-boat grazed one of the blockships. Looking to his right, the captain could see a man riding a bicycle along the coast road. Then the bay opened out, and he shouted below: "We're inside Scapa Flow!"

Peering to port, toward the main anchorage, Prien did not see the expected line of battleships; they had gone to sea. Off to the north, however, "could be seen the great shadow of a battleship lying on the water, with the great mast rising above it like a piece of filigree on a black cloth. Near, nearer—all tubes clear—no alarm, no sound but the lap of the water, the low hiss of air pressure and the sharp click of a tube lever. *Los!* Fire!" Prien had identified the shadow as the battleship *Royal Oak,* and from behind it protruded the bow of another vessel the captain identified, wrongly, as the battle cruiser *Repulse*. There came an explosion, and a column of water rose high in the air; only one of the five torpedoes had hit, and Prien believed that the *Repulse* had been its victim. Exceeding even his own reputation for coolness, Prien then took his boat on a cruise around the harbor while the crew worked to reload the torpedo tubes for a second attack. Meanwhile, incredibly, nothing stirred in Scapa Flow; no lights flashed on, no shots were fired, no destroyers churned across the bay. What had happened to everybody?

Then, in twenty minutes, the sweating crew finished their reloading, and the captain took the U-boat back toward the battleship, closer this time, and fired a salvo into it. This time the torpedoes ripped the bottom out of the vessel, smoke and water rose toward the sky, and entire gun turrets and great chunks of armor plate descended on the water in an awesome rain of steel. In less than two minutes the *Royal Oak* capsized and sank, going so quickly that she carried 786 men to their deaths.

Fleeing a destroyer that seemed to have him cornered but then turned away, Prien squeaked back through the channel and out into the sound and then moved on to the North Sea. "After leaving Holm Sound," he said in his report, "observed great anti-U-boat activity (with depth charges) in Scapa Flow. Was greatly bothered by brilliance of northern lights." Before the attack, a cartoonist in the crew had produced a drawing showing "Harry Hotspur," as the men called the skipper, as a bull with his head down and smoke curling from his nostrils. Now, as the *U-47* cruised southeastward, a small party wielding paint brushes climbed outside and soon, on the side of the conning tower, the boat bore a new symbol: The Bull of Scapa Flow.

When Prien and his crew returned to Kiel, they saw waiting for them not only Dönitz, the commodore, but Admiral Raeder himself. The grand admiral came aboard, shaking the hands of the crew and awarding each one the Iron Cross, Second Class, while honoring Prien with the First Class. The day proved profitable for Dönitz as well; the commodore was being promoted to rear admiral, with the new title Flag Officer, Submarines. Prien's day was completed by a flight to Berlin, with a triumphal parade and an interview in the Chancellery with the Führer, who presented the young man with the Knight's

Cross of the Iron Cross. The U-boat skipper had become Germany's first hero in the new war.

It had been almost exactly twenty-five years, from October 17, 1914, since the alarm had spread through the fleet at anchor that a German submarine had penetrated Scapa. This time, confronted with an actual explosion, the commanders had failed to realize what had happened, so secure did they feel in their harbor. But this time an invader had actually come, and once again the fleet would leave Scapa to seek other moorings. That fact, rather than the loss of the battleship, represented the most important strategic result of Prien's remarkable feat.

■ ■ ■

It was not the *U-47,* however, that could claim the first sinking of a major British warship in the new war. Just a month earlier, with hostilities under way for two weeks, Lieutenant Otto Schuhart in the *U-29,* patrolling in the Western Approaches to England, began his morning by tracking a large liner he believed to be a troop ship and then, to his great surprise, found himself head-on with another large vessel coming straight toward him—nothing less than a Royal Navy aircraft carrier. Warily watching for air escorts, Schuhart spotted two planes flying sweeps, but neither saw the *U-29.* Then, when the carrier in turning presented her flank to the U-boat, Schuhart fired a spread of torpedoes, relying on guesswork, he said, because "the vast size of the target upset all normal calculations and in any case I was looking straight into the sun." Crewmen also noted the sweat running down the skipper's face as, his eye to the periscope, he watched the torpedoes streak toward the target. He had just started to dive when a series of explosions echoed through the *U-29,* so heavy that he thought the boat had suffered damage. But all the sounds came from the carrier.

The next morning, returning from taking a look at Scapa Flow, where as the new First Lord he had reacted with concern on discovering the limited nature of the precautions against submarine and air attack, Churchill saw with surprise that Admiral Pound had come to meet him at Euston station. Pound's look was "grave," Churchill noted, and he said, "I have bad news for you, First Lord. The *Courageous* was sunk yesterday evening in the Bristol Channel." The *Courageous* was an old ship, Churchill reflected, but much needed at the time. Nevertheless, he spoke words of comfort to the admiral; he had been through these things before, he said; they were what happened in war. But of the 1,260 men of the crew of the *Courageous,* more than five hundred were drowned, including the captain, who went down with his ship.

Just three days before, also in the Western Approaches, the *U-36* had engaged in a similar confrontation with another aircraft carrier, this one the 28,000-ton *Ark Royal.* Lieutenant Commander Gerhard Glattes, the U-boat skipper, fired three torpedoes of a new type, with magnetic pistols, or detonators, designed not to explode on contact with the hull of a ship but to be set off under the keel by the "influence" of the ship's magnetic field, thus outflanking the side armor plating. But all three torpedoes detonated prematurely, doing no damage to the *Ark Royal* while sending up columns of water that drew the attention of the carrier's destroyer screen; the escorts soon found and destroyed the U-boat, though the crew members were saved. The misfiring of the torpedoes in this attack marked the beginning of a problem that would soon call for Dönitz's full attention. Even so, the ability of his U-boats to get within firing range of fully escorted important warships like the *Courageous* and the *Ark Royal* represented good news for the U-boat commodore, because it suggested that he might not have much to fear from a much heralded device the British had developed to smell out submarines underwater.

The Royal Navy called the invention *asdic.* The name supposedly came from the Allied Submarine Detection and Investigation Committee, said to have been set up in 1917, though no subsequent trace of such a committee has ever been found; a Royal Navy captain involved in antisubmarine work explained the origin of the word as the ending -ic added to the initials ASD (for Anti-Submarine Department). Later to become universally known by its American name, *sonar* (*sound navigation and ranging*), this development, it was believed, would henceforth make life too dangerous for submarines attacking surface ships. Sonar indeed represented a definite advance in the detection of hostile vessels; unlike the old hydrophones, it could detect even an unmoving submarine, because it was active, emitting a series of pings that would bounce off an object and back to listening earphones. But at the time it had a maximum range, in favorable conditions, of only about 1,500 yards and gave accurate readings neither for bearing nor for range (it could be off by as much as 25 yards, a significant figure in relation to the effectiveness of depth charges); nor could it discriminate between echoes from a submarine and those from some other object. Its effectiveness also suffered in rough weather.

▪ ▪ ▪

Since his first weeks back at his old Admiralty desk, Winston Churchill, full of plans and proposals as always, had kept his strategic eye on the long coastline of Norway, stretching southward from the Arctic Circle to the latitude of Scotland. What concerned the First Lord was the nature of this jagged coastline—small islands set off from the mainland by an inland waterway that ran in Norwegian territorial waters. To the Germans the Leads, as the waters were known, offered a highway for the transport of iron ore from Swedish mines southward to the mouth of the Baltic Sea, safe from hindrance by the Royal Navy; to Churchill the Leads represented an obvious challenge, a German supply line that the British must try to choke off. "If it were possible to stop this traffic," a German officer later noted, "then German war industries would starve for lack of steel, and Allied victory would be merely a question of time." For months Churchill strove to persuade his colleagues in the Cabinet to approve the sowing of mines in the Leads, but his advocacy of this use of British seapower could never overcome their objections to mounting an operation that so clearly would violate Norwegian neutrality.

During these same months Admiral Raeder and the German naval staff likewise paid much attention to strategic questions presented by Norway, at first wondering nervously whether the British were likely to invade the country and thus provide themselves with bases close enough to the Baltic to threaten U-boat training bases and then, as time went on, deciding that such Allied action was highly probable. Particularly after the Russians began a war with Finland on November 30, the Germans entertained well-founded fears that the Allies might try to provide help to the Finns by way of northern Sweden and, in the process, seize the iron mines for themselves; Allied control of Norway would also threaten and perhaps even cut off German access to the open ocean.

On the other hand, if the Germans should take control of Norway with its long coastline, they would not only secure the Leads but provide themselves with ocean bases that would greatly weaken British attempts at a blockade on the model of the first war. An invasion staged in Norwegian waters under the noses of the British Home Fleet seemed an audacious idea for the Germans to contemplate with their limited surface forces, but the more or less open discussion in Allied countries of the Norway project (even including stories in British newspapers) led Hitler to summon an infantry general, Nikolaus von Falkenhorst, to a morning meeting on February 21 at which the Führer charged the general with planning and leading an invasion of Norway. On leaving the Chancellery, Falkenhorst, who professed to know nothing about Norway, had a bit of lunch and then dropped into a bookshop to pick up a pocket atlas so that he could begin drawing up his plan.

On April 3 the British Cabinet finally rewarded Churchill's persistence by granting the Admiralty permission to mine the Norwegian Leads; the operation was to begin in five days. Since the Germans might well counter with a riposte of some sort, the authorities also agreed that detachments of Allied troops should take part in the operation by occupying Norwegian ports, thus denying them to the enemy. Early in the morning of April 8, according to plan, British destroyers laid a minefield in the channel leading to Narvik, the port in northern Norway at which the iron-ore ships began their southward journey. But after that, the plan unraveled. Later in the day northward-bound German warships were sighted off the Norwegian coast, and in a carefully planned operation German vessels began landing units at the key ports the British had intended to occupy. Fresh from invading Denmark on April 9, the Germans moved with "surprise, ruthlessness, and precision" to take control, in forty-eight hours, of all the principal Norwegian ports. The Phony War had come to its end.

On March 4 Dönitz had received orders from Naval Headquarters to keep all U-boats at home, canceling all sailings, and to ensure that

U-boats already at sea did not engage in any operations in the Norwegian area. The next day, having gone to a meeting at the Admiralty in Berlin, he learned the details of the invasion plan; the U-boats would take part by protecting the ships from enemy attack when they arrived at the target ports, and they were also to oppose any enemy attempts at landings intended to dislodge German forces. As a third task, submarines would attack enemy naval forces that tried to interfere with communications between Norway and Germany.

To fulfill these duties, Dönitz, realizing that along this complex coastline he could not be strong everywhere, decided to group his units as *masses de manoeuvre,* as if they were reserves, ready to intervene wherever threats should arise. But, since he still did not have as many of his workhorse Type VII U-boats as he believed necessary to perform the tasks assigned to his command, he turned to the submarine school for its six small submarines, which he added to the team, and he also ordered the commanders of two new U-boats to end their trials and get ready for action. These arrangements would give him a total of thirty-one boats, large and small, for use in operations off Norway. For secrecy, a number of them would sail with orders not to be opened until they had reached their assigned areas.

The Royal Navy also entered the underwater action. With German supply ships moving through the waters off Norway like ordinary merchantmen, the British dispatched submarines to the area: small vessels like 640-ton S-class boats and larger, long-range boats like the 1,500-tonners of the *Porpoise* class; the Royal Navy also employed T-class submarines, 1,100-ton boats made especially formidable by their bank of ten forward-facing torpedo tubes. These boats came with orders to sink merchant ships on sight, that is, to wage unrestricted warfare.

Though the Germans did not have sonar, their antisubmarine patrols had the advantage conferred by the increasing hours of daylight as spring lengthened into summer. Finally the British withdrew their submarines from the Skagerrak and neighboring coastal waters, but before they left the area, one of the *Porpoise*-class boats, the *Seal,* claimed an unfortunate place for herself in the annals of the war. On May 5 she ran afoul of one of the mines she had just laid in the Kattegat, suffering damage that made it impossible for her to submerge. Her plight rendered her an easy conquest for a German seaplane, and she thus became the only British submarine to be captured by the enemy during the war. But by the end of June Royal Navy submarines had sunk nineteen enemy ships, amounting to 89,000 tons.

Major fighting developed in the Narvik area, with the British seeking to take the town from the Germans. (If General von Falkenhorst had begun his operational planning in an impromptu fashion by buying a pocket atlas, British bomber pilots could outmatch him in the improvisation department; in seeking some of their targets in Norway, they were using as their guide the 1912 edition of Baedeker's *Scandinavia*.) On April 15 Dönitz ordered U-boats, including Günther Prien's famous *U-47*, to reconnoiter the area to find which of the possible fjords would be the scene of the expected British landing.

The early hours of the next morning saw Prien quietly at rest in his chosen fjord, watching through his periscope as British destroyers moved to and fro on ceaseless patrols. A major event of some kind, Prien decided, was about to occur. Late in the afternoon, as he was about to surface and move away to recharge the batteries, he and his men heard strange clanking noises that seemed to echo throughout the boat. Carefully they took the *U-47* up so that the periscope barely broke the water, and when the skipper took a look he saw with amazement that his boat was facing an array of cruisers and transports, about eight ships in all; the strange noises had obviously been the rumbling of their anchor chains. Dönitz had indeed picked the right spot for action by his daring ace skipper; Prien pointed out to the crew that they had more targets here than they had seen in their incursion into Scapa Flow.

As Prien peered through the scope, he saw small boats carrying troops and supplies from ships to shore and then returning to load up again. He realized immediately what a great and even pivotal opportunity lay before him. If he could sink these ships, the Allied troops would find themselves marooned on these barren rocks, with no visible or invisible means of support; the whole campaign in Norway might turn on the events of the next few minutes. At this range, with these fat targets, how could he miss?

Carefully, with everything in order, the *U-47* fired a spread of four torpedoes, one for each of the two cruisers and two more for two of the transports. "Ships stretched in a solid wall before me," said Prien, and officers and crew listened eagerly, waiting as nothing happened, and nothing continued to happen. No explosion came. This appalling failure could not be due to errors of calculation, Prien was sure; his men knew what they were doing, and the longest range was only 1,500 yards.

After midnight, following an interval for charging the batteries as well as for reloading, Prien returned to the fight, this time on the surface, sending out four more torpedoes. All missed again, and as the *U-47* turned to go, Prien, furious, had two bad moments: A crunching noise told him that the boat had run aground, and at the same time, thunderously proving that it could detonate if it managed to collide with something, one of the torpedoes smashed into the shore and exploded in a geyser that signaled to Prien probable doom from the guns of the cruisers. But deft handling of the boat, and the luck that seemed to accompany him, succeeded in getting the *U-47* free of the shore, down the passage of the fjord, and out into the open sea. The angry skipper had an account to settle with the ordnance department and its torpedoes. "As the result of the explosion of one of [the torpedoes] at the end of its run," he reported to Admiral Dönitz with some understatement, "I was placed in a most awkward predicament and was pursued by destroyers coming from all directions."

The admiral had already realized that his U-boats were in trouble. Since the beginning of the campaign in Norway they had achieved little success. Even earlier, torpedo failures had "given rise to very considerable anxiety," but the rate had surged in operations off Norway. The problems seemed to afflict torpedoes with magnetic detonators, like those that had failed even to damage the *Ark Royal;* more than half of these seemed suddenly to have begun producing premature explosions. The development of the magnetic detonator in the period between the wars had been considered an important advance by submariners, but on April 11 Dönitz reluctantly ordered his captains to switch to the old contact exploders, though they were less deadly than the magnetics, that is, when the magnetics did what they were supposed to do.

But the admiral's hope that he had found the solution to the problem lasted only a few days. Against the big ships in the fjord, Günther Prien had used torpedoes with contact exploders, and they too had completely failed. Dönitz now began an investigation into the whole torpedo problem, and to bridge the gap until his diagnostic study produced results, he gave his skippers a series of complicated orders to guide them in their use of torpedoes. He felt little faith in these new procedures himself, however, saying that their very complexity "exposed for all to see how completely we and the various technical departments were at a loss to find any explanation for these torpedo failures." He really felt that "to all intents and purposes" the U-boats had no weapon.

The torpedo failures seemed to involve three kinds of behavior: (1) Whether having contact or magnetic pistols, torpedoes ran too deep, thus missing the target ship or, in the case of magnetics, not coming close enough to activate the detonator. (2) Magnetics experienced frequent malfunctions during their running, the result often being premature detonation. (3) Contact exploders, supposed to be set off when they hit the hull of a ship at almost any angle, were in practice proving unreliable at any angle of incidence less than 50°.

The search for cures proved long and hard, and it involved not only unpleasantness between the U-boat arm and the Torpedo Directorate but finally court-martial proceedings against some of those who had designed and tested the weapons. Much of the overall difficulty could be traced to the failure of the torpedo experts to subject their devices to realistic and rigorous testing before supplying them to the fleet; in particular, they had not realized that variations in the intensity of the earth's magnetic field between one place and another would affect the performance of the delicate magnetic exploder. "It was only gradually that the causes of failures became known," Dönitz later noted, "particularly as the connection between the faulty, deep running of the torpedo and the failure of the pistol mechanism rendered it all the more difficult to trace the type of failure which had occurred." As matters would turn out, Dönitz and his aces would not be the last submariners during the war to face critically significant problems with torpedoes. Future antagonists of the Axis could have benefited mightily from a good long peek over the admiral's shoulder as he went about making his diagnosis and solving his problem.

19

ATLANTIC RAIDERS: THE "HAPPY TIME"

On June 22, 1940, meeting in the old railway car in the Forest of Compiègne in which the plenipotentiaries had signed the armistice that ended the Great War, French and German representatives staged an encore performance, signaling the official end of hostilities between their two countries in this second war. The very next day an important visitor appeared in Lorient and several other ports along the Biscay coast of Brittany. Admiral Dönitz had in fact fixed his eye on these coastal prizes as soon as he realized that the battle in northern France would not bog down in stalemate, as had happened in 1914, but that the Germans were headed toward quick and clear-cut victory. Several weeks earlier, at the admiral's command, a number of mechanics and other submarine maintenance personnel had been assigned to a special train, which, stuffed with torpedoes, sat waiting for the call to action.

At the beginning of June, only three weeks after the campaign began and without waiting for an end to the fighting, Dönitz had dispatched staff officers to France with orders to visit the Biscay ports as soon as the German Army took the area, to judge their suitability as U-boat bases. Now, on June 23, the admiral himself came to take a good look and make up his mind whether to send that special train, with its technicians and its torpedoes, rolling westward to these ports.

Dönitz had strong reasons for hoping that he would like what he saw. The armistice agreement—a de facto *Diktat,* in retaliation for the indignities imposed on Germany at Versailles twenty-one years earlier—established the conquerors in occupation of the entire Atlantic and Channel coastline of France, thereby changing, even revolutionizing, the strategic situation in the Atlantic for both of the new dimensional fighting arms. In the air, the Luftwaffe could now mount serious and possibly decisive attacks on England from fields near the Channel in northern France and Belgium. Earlier, despite all the talk at the time of Munich in 1938 and at the beginning of the war in September 1939 about the imminent danger of the annihilation of London from the air, no such possibility had actually existed, because of the limited range of Luftwaffe bombers and fighters.

For Atlantic raiding operations, the Germans of 1940 had created a situation beyond the fondest dreams of Kaiser Wilhelm and Admiral von Tirpitz and indeed far beyond any fantasies of their own. No longer squeezed by geography, they now had the naval independence conferred by their new Atlantic sea frontier (and, in the bargain, they had eliminated the powerful French navy as a foe). Dönitz called the possible new bases "an exit from our 'backyard' in the south-eastern corner of the North Sea," noting that "the danger that enemy measures on a grand scale might prevent the U-boats from putting to sea would no longer exist, for such measures, if possible at all, could only be carried out in the shallow waters of the North Sea." At the same time, the Biscay bases would offer the U-boats enormous practical advantages, far more than had come from the occupation of Norway. By moving their homes close to the arena of action, relieving them of the need to reach the open sea by making the long passage through the North Sea and then circling north of Scotland, the new bases would increase the range of the boats by as much as 2,500 miles or their endurance by many days.

At this point, in June, Dönitz needed to achieve the greatest yield possible from his U-boats, which now numbered only twenty-nine available for operations out of the total of fifty, a smaller fleet than he had commanded at the beginning of the war; the rest of the boats had to serve as training vessels for the crews of the new submarines under construction. Basing themselves on the new ports would also spare the U-boats the lethal danger from patrolling craft and mines always posed in British waters. Now, Dönitz felt, even his tiny and slow 250-ton Type II coastal boats would be able to operate in the Atlantic.

The admiral saw even further advantages in the Biscay prospect. These ports would offer new repair yards, thus relieving some of the pressure on German facilities, which then could turn most of their attention to building new U-boats. In view of all these points, Dönitz did not take long to make up his mind in favor of the move. It could lead to decisive results: The navy must take, "as swiftly as it could and by every means it possessed, the greatest and most comprehensive advantage possible" of this remarkable improvement in its strategic position. Immediately all the relevant branches of Dönitz's command set to work to turn a series of French ports—Brest, Lorient, St. Nazaire, La Pallice, La Rochelle, Bordeaux—into U-boat bases, organizing facilities for supplies of fuel, food, and water and for minor repairs. (St. Nazaire, situated at the mouth of the Loire River, had a special feature that made it attractive as a naval base: a huge drydock that, having been constructed for one of the largest ocean liners in the world, the *Normandie,* could handle the biggest warships.) Next would come the more thorough organization of facilities for complete refit of U-boats, but the admiral had no intention of delaying the transfer from German bases until the completion of this task. His boats had now recovered from the rigors of the Norwegian campaign, and on July 7, just a bit more than two weeks after the signing of the armistice, the first boat, the *U-30,* came into Lorient from the Atlantic to take on food and munitions. Within a month work crews had Lorient ready to go into full service, and from this point on the Bay of Biscay and not German waters became the home of U-boats operating in the Atlantic.

Like other commanders of submarine forces of any country, Dönitz felt the strong pull of comradeship with the crews of his boats, and he also kept a keen awareness of the short time many of them had to live; hence he had made it a point not only to greet crews returning from patrols but also to present any decorations due (very commonly, the Iron Cross, Second Class) on the spot. Now, with the transfer of the U-boats to the new bases, he looked forward to moving his headquarters from Senkwarden, near Wilhelmshaven, to the Biscay coast, where he could keep in close contact with his men. But first a new task demanded his attention. Having amazed themselves as much as everybody else in the world by winning a complete victory in France in just six weeks, the Germans had to decide what to do next and how to do it. Thus they began to discuss Operation

Sea Lion, a proposed invasion of England; to plan it and, at least theoretically, to conduct it, all the high commanders were summoned to
Paris.

Nobody in the army, the navy, or the air force showed much enthusiasm for the project, as the leaders of each service put forward conditions the other two must meet before the operation could be deemed
feasible, and it is doubtful whether Hitler himself ever had any real intention of pursuing it beyond the talking stage. Dönitz supported Admiral Raeder's insistence that German forces must not attempt such an
invasion without complete control of the air in the operational area
and complete control of the English Channel as well. Since he considered neither condition at all likely to be fulfilled, Dönitz delivered
himself of his opinions and then, having set himself up comfortably in
a mansion on the Boulevard Suchet near the Bois de Boulogne, devoted himself to the war in the Atlantic and the training of new U-boat
crews. To achieve the aim of forcing Britain into peace negotiations,
which the admiral saw as the proper and realistic German objective, the
Kriegsmarine must mount a heavy assault on her sea lines of communication. "On them directly depended the very life of the British nation. On them, immediately, depended Britain's whole conduct of the
war, and if they were really threatened British policy would be bound
to react." Having gained the wonderful new strategic position conferred by the bases in Brittany, Germany should concentrate her entire
resources on waging the kind of war at sea that had now become possible. Deeming commerce raiding the only logical course to follow,
Dönitz intended to play his full part in pursuing it. He had become
perhaps the world's leading believer in the *guerre de course,* and he was
becoming increasingly able to put his principles into practice.

"Every morning on the stroke of nine," one of the admiral's staff
recalled, "he would enter the operations room and the operational staff
officer would deliver an account of the events of the night; he would
report on the signals received and dispatched, the details of boats due
to sail and those returning to base, and the developments of any operation currently in progress." Other officers would then present requests
for escorts, submit the latest intelligence reports, or discuss questions of
logistics and provide details of new boats. Like any other commander

with his staff, the admiral would break in with a question and often follow it up with an order.

At this point in the war, both the Royal Navy and the German submarine command appeared to consider themselves as operating at a disadvantage. The U-boats, with their effectively increased range, had begun to move into the mid-Atlantic from the Biscay ports at a time when the British had only enough escorts to reach 500 miles west of Ireland. The heavy cost in destroyers and smaller craft exacted by the Norwegian campaign, together with the need to guard the southeastern English coast against invasion, meant that a convoy often might be forced to sail with the protection of only one or two escort vessels; the danger of invasion likewise kept many Coastal Command aircraft patrolling the North Sea rather than the Atlantic.

At dusk one evening, in accordance with the practice he had quickly adopted of paying flying visits to the Biscay coast to keep in touch with his crews, Admiral Dönitz, together with staff officers, stood on the pier waiting for the return of a U-boat from patrol. The officers "never missed such an occasion, for each of them knew what it meant to find a welcome when your boat came back from an operation." Finally, in the deepening darkness, the submarine appeared, sliding into the harbor, her crew enjoying the opportunity to stand on deck without fear. After the boat tied up and the skipper reported the results of the patrol, modestly disclaiming any satisfaction at having sunk "only twenty thousand tons," Dönitz ordered him to muster the ship's company and then went aboard, his greeting—"Heil, U-Thirty-eight!"—evoking the chorused response "Heil, Herr Admiral!"

The navy's standard Type VII boats, 20 crowded feet across at the widest point, were gamy affairs, affording few washing facilities; special soap intended to work with sea water proved ineffectual, and the men had limited opportunities even for shaving; the pervasive dampness meant that wet clothes never truly dried out. Aside from the stink of unwashed bodies, the air held other heavy effluvia: the smell of decaying food and the odors from the only toilet in use, which had to serve all forty men on board (with space so precious, the second toilet usually became a storage bin). As one skipper put it, the crews were "the captives of our own smells." Unperturbed by such unpleasant details, Dönitz walked along the lineup of sailors with their beards and their rancid reek, and then he congratulated them all for having sunk more than 100,000 tons in only three patrols: "The credit for this splendid performance goes chiefly to your gallant captain. Lieutenant-Commander Liebe, the Führer has conferred upon you the Knight's Cross, and it is my pleasure to hand it to you." After the flag lieutenant clipped the decoration around Liebe's neck, the admiral shook his hand, stood back, and, raising his hand to his cap, called for "three cheers for Lieutenant-Commander Liebe!" As the voices sounded across the harbor, the U-boat skipper stood motionless at attention.

■ ■ ■

In the Battle of Britain, fought over the summer of 1940, the Luftwaffe failed to break the Royal Air Force, and it likewise failed to destroy civilian morale with its attacks on cities. In October, with Germany having proved unable to gain control of the air over southern England, the Führer abandoned (officially, postponed for the year) Operation Sea Lion and turned his whole attention eastward, toward Russia. Freed from his official duties concerning what he saw as an absurd project, Admiral Dönitz immediately fled Paris for the coast, establishing his headquarters in a seaside villa at Kernevel, near Lorient, requisitioned from a magnate in the sardine business. Here, in the quiet of the large room he commandeered as his office, he would put in much time pacing around and around the table, pondering the implications of the reports he received from captains back from patrol. The British, they said, were stepping up the protection of the convoys, "with more destroyers, more escort vessels, more star shells to lift the cover of darkness from the attacking U-boats," and the admiral would wonder whether he had done everything in his power to protect his own boats. In expressing these concerns, he would have appeared to an uninformed observer to be a commander losing a battle and doing anything he could contrive to salvage the situation. But such an observer would have drawn the wrong inference from the admiral's fussiness and obsession with detail.

. . .

Although the establishment of a convoy system had saved Britain from disaster in 1917, this hard lesson had not appeared to linger in the minds of naval leaders in the following years. "The public revulsion to war and slaughter after 1918," a naval historian and serving officer observed, "was perhaps a main cause of the failure of the British Admiralty to analyze the results of the German attack on shipping," analysis that would have proved the decisive effect of the convoy system. Beyond that, however, and despite its history of success through the centuries, the concept of convoy with its indisputable defensive flavor appeared to affront the British nautical mind. Its opponents in the 1920s and 1930s produced various reasons to believe that no preparations need be made for the employment of convoy in any future war. For one thing, many politicians and a number of naval figures thought that the maritime powers might well succeed in banning unrestricted submarine warfare by treaty. Indeed, such agreements did come into existence, and, as Churchill observed, "the ceaseless struggles and gradual emergence of Adolf Hitler as a national figure were little noticed by the victors, oppressed and harassed as they were by their own troubles and party strife."

Realistic observers could see, however, that the future of international agreements for the banning of any truly effective weapon could not be considered promising, especially after Hitler came to power in 1933. Unrestricted submarine warfare had proved so potent in the 1914–18 war that no country fighting an enemy whose existence depended on being supplied by sea could be counted on to deprive itself of this weapon, regardless of rhetorical considerations, and Britain, of course, offered a textbook example of such dependency.

With its great faith in asdic, however, the Admiralty professed no fears. Its officials told the Shipping Advisory Committee, the government body specifically responsible for the protection of shipping in wartime, that "the submarine menace will never be what it was before. We have means of countering a submarine which are very effective. . . . It will never be a fatal menace again as it was in the last war."

The German naval authorities appeared to have a contrary view of the future. From 1922 on, not awaiting the arrival of a Hitler, they had worked on developing and testing submarines, both coastal and blue-water, partly through a dummy design company they operated in the Netherlands. They had maintained a secret U-boat technical section, and they gained considerable knowledge from building boats for foreign clients. Such projects enabled them, for example, to study the value of welding, with its weight-saving qualities, as against riveting for hull construction. As soon as Hitler came to power, the navy began laying down submarines, and in June 1935 came the naval treaty with Great Britain, whose provisions included, to the surprise and dismay of observers in democratic countries, the granting to Germany the right to build submarines with a total tonnage equivalent to 45 percent of the British total (i.e., 24,000 tons) and, in a muddled clause, the right to construct a submarine fleet equal to Britain's if the circumstances called for it. The Admiralty looked on the agreement with considerable satisfaction, which prompted Churchill to comment in retrospect that "it is always dangerous for soldiers, sailors, or airmen to play at politics."

In 1936 the Admiralty drew further cheer from the German government's acceptance of the London Submarine Agreement, under which the signatories bound themselves to sink merchant ships only in accordance with international law and to assure the rescue of crews. As noted, strict adherence to these terms by any power maintaining submarine forces out in the ocean would really mean that this power had renounced commerce raiding, but, as Churchill said, "who could suppose that the Germans, possessing a great fleet of U-boats and watching their women and children being starved by a British blockade, would abstain from fullest use of that arm?" That statement possessed its essential truth, regardless of the presence or the absence of a Hitler.

All of these trends and tendencies together produced a damning effect: During the interwar years the Admiralty did little to produce the kinds of ships that could protect convoys. In early 1939, indeed, the navy had no plans, let alone the actual vessels, for a ship designed as an antisubmarine escort and no vision of producing such ships in the kind of intensive program that war would demand. Then, in April, after the German occupation of Czechoslovakia led the British to abandon their appeasement policy, Hitler denounced the 1935 naval treaty. The

Reich must now consider Britain a possible enemy, he informed his commanders, and a committee secretly set to work to formulate what came to be known as the Z Plan, which looked to war beginning in 1944 and called for a large conventional fleet (including six super battleships of 56,000 tons each) and 126 submarines.

Hitler's public denunciation of the treaty made it clear that he "was intent on war and that his main naval weapon was to be the U-boat." After mulling the matter over for two months, the Admiralty ordered fifty-six modified "whale catchers," intended to protect coastal shipping against air attack. The boats, known as Flower-class corvettes (*Pansy, Periwinkle,* and the like), would prove unstable in a heavy sea— "rolling their guts out on wet grass," as the expression went—and difficult to maneuver. The Admiralty also ordered a class of small destroyers, which came from the yards only slowly and, with their short range, did not prove effective in ocean service.

In one of the ironies that seem to occur almost daily in war, the sinking of the *Athenia,* though Lieutenant Commander Lemp had done it in error, left the Admiralty no choice but to institute convoy immediately, whether or not it could supply enough effective escorts. At the end of the first week of September, four days after the declaration of war, the series of outward-bound Atlantic convoys began— code-named OA (from Southend, at the mouth of the Thames) and OB (from Liverpool) to North America, OG to Gibraltar. On September 16 came a more portentous event, the sailing of the first eastbound convoy from Halifax; these convoys, designated HX, would serve as the vital link between the factories and farms of North America and the island nation that depended on imports for survival.

■ ■ ■

Even though Admiral Dönitz fussed over them every day, during the summer and autumn of 1940 his U-boats found themselves enjoying the best of the submariners' world, sinking tons upon tons of enemy shipping while themselves suffering only light losses. The U-boat fleet, not yet built up for the clash that Hitler had scheduled for 1944, found itself at war with an enemy ill prepared to defend itself against submarine attack, and the advantage went to the submarines; Dönitz's crews called the five months from June to October "the happy time." The skipper aces—Otto Kretschmer, Günther Prien (of *Royal Oak* fame), Joachim Schepke—led the way for the relative handful of boats, usually just twelve or thirteen, that destroyed 1,395,298 tons of shipping, an average of 279,060 tons a month (or about three freighters or tankers every day). They also became national heroes, as celebrated across Germany as the Red Baron and other air aces from the Great War.

The U-boats attacked ships sailing singly or those that had strayed away from their fellows in convoys, though often the convoys themselves made good targets, since the lack of British long-range escort vessels meant that many sailed with only limited protection. From about 200 miles out in the Atlantic the vessels were on their own as they sailed westward, though they were supposed to keep together for another day before dispersing to head for their North American destinations. Meanwhile, the escorts, having waited at the point at which they had released their charges to pick up incoming convoys, would accompany the new arrivals the rest of the way into western English ports. These eastbound convoys, which carried war materials to Britain, had protection all the way across, but in midocean this might consist only of a converted passenger liner with guns (an "armed merchant cruiser") that carried no antisubmarine weapons and was there to protect against surface raiders, not U-boats.

Before a convoy sailed, the captains of the merchantmen attended a conference ashore, in which every detail of the forthcoming voyage was discussed, the primary aim being to leave no room for anybody to make careless moves. Formations generally varied between six and nine columns, with up to five ships in each, emphasizing breadth rather than depth in the organization so as present as slim a profile as possible to a waiting U-boat. After steaming out of the anchorage in a straight line, ships would begin to creep up toward their allotted places. Each vessel flew flags indicating its assigned position; green and yellow flags reading "7-1," for instance, meant that the vessel had the first spot in the seventh line. Its orders called for it to maintain that position regardless of changing weather or any other considerations. In fog, a ship was to keep close to the ship immediately ahead, closer generally than 200 yards. To prevent the ocean equivalent of a highway rear-end collision, each ship except those in the last rank trailed a fog buoy, a cable stretched perhaps 400 feet astern, dragging at its end a funnel-like contrivance through which water would spurt up a few feet above the surface; a lookout truly needed an impressive attention span as well as sharp eyes. Once the convoy reached the open sea, much depended on the engineers. They would earn compliments if they saw to it that not a wisp of smoke rose above any funnel, but, above all, a ship had to keep station.

Yet nothing close to perfection could ever be achieved. The ships were diversified: "big ships and small, samson posts and cargo booms, freighters and tankers, new ships and old." And "the laboring engines grinding away in each of them were not capable of quite consistent performance, nor was the fuel absolutely uniform, and as time went on tubes might clog and valves might stick, so that the propellers the engines drove would not continue to turn at a uniform rate." The working of these variables might produce only small changes, "but in those close-packed columns of ships a few feet's difference in one minute could bring disaster in twenty." And beyond these variables stood "the human variable, the greatest variable of all." Lurking U-boats fed on stragglers; to stray was to take a long step toward suicide, yet stragglers there were.

In late August, a slow convoy, SC-2 (SC convoys were slower than those designated HX), departed from Halifax, expecting to meet its escort on the other side on September 6 for the final leg into port. But on August 30 the B-dienst (Beobachtungsdienst), the German naval cryptological branch, deciphered the message giving route instructions, and, handed this information, Admiral Dönitz responded quickly, ordering four U-boats to proceed to that location. Clustering submarines in this fashion represented no passing fancy on the admiral's part. Ever since taking control of the new U-boat service in 1935, he had looked to waging an unrestricted campaign and had never entertained the idea that in a future war the nations would abide by the treaty rules. But, though he intended for Germany to pursue again the submarine strategy of 1917 and 1918, he had his own ideas about the tactics needed to implement this strategy. In the first war, as he later wrote, he and a number of other officers had immediately realized that the introduction of convoy had rendered obsolete the role of the U-boat as a lone wolf prowling the seas, but no action had resulted. In 1918 he and Lieutenant Steinbauer had developed their own plan, which the mechanical problem with Steinbauer's boat had foiled, to make a coordinated attack on a convoy and to carry it out under the cover of darkness.

From 1935 on, basing his thinking and planning on his belief that, despite its name, the submarine was primarily a surface craft that had the useful ability to dive beneath the surface when necessary, Dönitz worked to train his officers and crew in a new kind of coordinated attack tactics, taking advantage of the submarine's tiny silhouette, hard for escort vessels to spot at night, and of its speed on the surface, much greater than that of the ships making up the convoy. "Tactical formations of the most varied character were tried out in a very large number of training exercises and maneuvers," noted one officer, "and from them there eventually emerged a formation in a concave curve. Into this the enemy would penetrate, the U-boat which first sighted him would maintain contact, while the U-boats on the more distant rim of the curve would act as a support group." The method came to be known as the *Rudeltaktik* (pack tactic). In time, the pack would acquire a more specific identity, becoming not simply any kind of pack but a *wolf pack*.

Until September, however, the Germans had not possessed enough U-boats to make coordinated attacks possible; Kretschmer, Prien, and Schepke had run up their gaudy totals in individual strikes. Dönitz and his experts, as they faced "the daily problem of the U-boat dispositions," saw their challenge as always the same: "What is the best way of spreading a small number of boats over the widest possible area, so as to cause the maximum damage to the enemy?" The problem seemed acute, because the "wide gaps in the ring round Britain" could not be closed until the boats now under construction should come into service in 1941; besides, the "desperate shortage of aircraft" so limited air reconnaissance that "the U-boat operations staff had to rely upon a sort of sixth sense of their own."

When headquarters received a message indicating that a U-boat had made contact with a convoy, the commander in chief dispatched messengers to the radio room with explicit instructions calling in other submarines for the assault. Then the men at headquarters would wait and speculate, building pictures from the fragmentary reports they would receive from the attacking boat, as they wondered about the weather out in the ocean and the strength of the convoy escort. Boats kept in remarkably close touch with headquarters, even radioing such information as "enemy in sight, position xyz, course southeast, am attacking." This was as Dönitz wished: For him, radio served as an extension of brain and hand, an indispensable instrument of command and control.

The first demonstration of this procedure came on September 6. Though Dönitz did not yet command enough submarines to put into practice his full wolf pack tactics, he was able to employ his long-planned technique of radio control to assemble a group to harry the fifty-three ships of Convoy SC-2 as it approached the point at which it would meet its escorting vessels. First sighted on September 6 by the U-65 (despite the best efforts of the engineers, this miscellaneous collection of freighters announced its approach with columns of smoke), the convoy escaped harm when a destroyer and a corvette drove the enemy submarine away.

The surcease proved only temporary, however. Later that night Lieutenant Commander Hans-Gerrit von Stockhausen, skipper of the U-65, not only reappeared but brought with him the U-47, with the redoubtable Günther Prien. Undeterred by the turbulence produced by a storm that had blown up, Prien charged into action, making exactly the kind of night surface attack preached by Dönitz, and quickly put fatal torpedoes into a 5,000-ton cargo ship. Though the convoy tried to maneuver to escape the marauders, the U-47's skipper was just beginning to get warmed up. Taking his boat into the middle of the convoy, he singled out another 5,000-tonner, this one (as he could not know) loaded with steel and linseed oil, and in a few minutes had sent her to the bottom. Hiding in the open, like the purloined letter, he did not take long to choose, attack, and sink still another freighter.

When morning came, RAF Sunderland flying boats appeared, and, having given a precise demonstration of Admiral Dönitz's nocturnal principles at work, Prien, along with Stockhausen, readily retired to the bottom to wait unmoving, like a vampire, for the return of night. That next night another U-boat reported contact with the convoy, and, reentering the one-sided fray, Prien knifed into the heart of the convoy and sank a merchantman. In the early hours of the ninth the *U-28,* commanded by Lieutenant Commander Günter Kuhnke, inflicted the fifth and final loss on the convoy when he torpedoed a small British freighter.

Never having imagined such an assault, the escort and convoy officers could only react to it with confusion and do little to stem it. They had not experienced a true attack by a wolf pack—such calculated attacks were still to come—but they had felt the deadly force of the first coordinated action ever mounted by a submarine command. Succeeding convoys encountered even greater fury on the part of Dönitz's gray wolves. HS-72 lost twelve ships, SC-7 sixteen, and by the end of 1940 the central issue in the war had become clear to the leaders on both sides: The Atlantic Ocean would be the decisive theater. Dönitz believed that Germany could win if her sea and air forces could destroy 700,000 tons of Allied shipping a month; the British Admiralty calculated that the country could not sustain losses of more than 600,000 tons and considered even that figure extremely tight. The Battle of the Atlantic was shaping up, not only as the key to victory, but also as an unrelenting fight to the death, a battle whose tides would ebb and flow over the years with changes in resources, information, and technology.

20

DÉJÀ VU IN THE NORTH ATLANTIC?

During the morning of September 4, 1941, the American destroyer *Greer*, eastward bound for Iceland and some 200 miles out from Reykjavik, received a warning from a British patrol aircraft that a U-boat lay in its path. Although the United States was not at war with Germany and thus did not qualify as an official shooting participant in the Battle of the Atlantic, the destroyer's skipper, Lieutenant Commander Lawrence H. Frost, did not seek to avoid this potential trouble spot but immediately sent his old World War four-piper speeding toward it, and when he reached the position he ordered the engines slowed while his sonar operator listened for sounds from the U-boat.

What did Frost have in mind? As the captain of a warship of a neutral country, why was he taking part in the raging ocean battle between the British and the Germans, attempting to locate a German submarine and then, when he succeeded, broadcasting his position (which was also the U-boat's position) for every ship and airplane in the area to pick up? When a British aircraft arrived, its pilot asked Frost a pointed question: Did he plan to attack the U-boat? No, Frost did not; his orders did not include making attacks on a German vessel, unless the German shot first at his ship. In that case, said the Royal Navy skipper, the *Greer* should step aside and allow him to make the attack, which he promptly proceeded to do, dropping four depth charges over the spot occupied by the submerged U-boat. Running low on fuel, he then turned back toward his base, leaving the submarine apparently undamaged.

As the U-boat moved on, the *Greer* shadowed her for three hours, continually broadcasting her position, while the U.S. officers no doubt wondered where had all the British sub-killing destroyers gone. Finally, turning, the submarine fought back at her pursuer; lookouts on the *Greer* sighted, dangerously close, an impulse bubble, the big air ball that rises when a submarine fires a torpedo. The U-boat had apparently aimed by her sound equipment and thus had not raised her periscope. It was a close miss, but the attack meant that the *Greer* could now make an attack of her own; the crew rolled eight depth charges over the stern, but, though green geysers splashed up from the sea, none of the charges seemed to have produced results.

When a British destroyer did finally arrive on the scene, her captain proposed to Frost that the two ships make a coordinated search for the U-boat. The American skipper declined the offer, however, telling the British captain that his orders would not permit it. Well, then, said the Briton, "now *you've* got a phony war." About two hours later, the *Greer*'s sonar reported another contact, and more depth charges were dropped, but with no visible results. The destroyer then resumed her journey to Reykjavik.

■ ■ ■

The British skipper had made a fair point with his gibe at Captain Frost. American actions in the North Atlantic in the autumn of 1941 raised the question whether a new phony war, with the United States and Germany as the participants, had actually developed, or whether it was a phony peace, war in disguise, with the United States taking part at Britain's side without making its involvement official—tracking U-boats, for instance, but not actually attacking them.

Certainly the Royal Navy needed all the help it could get in the battle to sustain the North Atlantic lifeline against the assaults of Admiral Dönitz's U-boats, now growing in numbers because the new construction ordered at the beginning of the war was coming along to take its part in the fleet's operations, and still more boats were beginning to move in the production pipeline; an average of about ten new submarines appeared each month. In the first two months of the year winter gales had held sinkings by U-boats to sixty ships, for a total of 323,565 tons, but March promised to produce totals more satisfactory to Dönitz. Though the numbers increased as anticipated, March also produced unexpected events that would influence the way the ocean battle would henceforth be fought.

In the evening of March 6, Günther Prien's *U-47* spotted the westbound British Convoy OB-293 and passed the word to other U-boats. One of those coming to join the grim party was Otto Kretschmer's *U-99*, which very efficiently sank a tanker and fatally wounded another ship. Prien himself had no success that first night, and, approaching the next night during a heavy squall, found himself surprised by a British destroyer, with his crash dive being followed by depth charges that sent the daring ace and his crew permanently to the bottom of the sea.

Just a week later, after Fritz-Julius Lemp in the *U-110* sighted the eastbound Convoy HX-112, a ferocious fight ensued, with Otto Kretschmer and Joachim Schepke taking part. After escorts beat off early attacks, Kretschmer bored into the midst of the convoy to sink three tankers and two freighters and damage still another tanker. Having expended all of her torpedoes, Kretschmer's *U-99* then withdrew from the scene of the action. Moving up to take her place, Schepke's *U-100* was picked up by the radar of a British destroyer, which chased the submarine and then rammed her as she began to dive; the blow crushed the famous skipper as he stood at his post in the conning tower. As for Kretschmer, when he left the paradoxical safety of the surface to submerge, he thus rendered his boat detectable by the sonar operator on a destroyer, the H.M.S. *Walker*, skippered by a U-boat fighter who would become a legend, Captain Donald Macintyre. Depth-charging by the *Walker* forced Kretschmer to return to the surface, where he and thirty-nine members of his crew were forced to surrender. They became prisoners of war, as they would remain for the next four years.

Thus, in a horrible ten-day span, Admiral Dönitz lost his most effective commanders, his three greatest stars. This loss had more than sentimental significance. It marked "the close of the period of individual brilliance," observed a British official historian, "with all that it had meant in inspiration to their fellow U-boat captains." The U-boat chief would now modify his methods, giving himself the actual tactical command of the submarines as they made their attacks instead of simply bringing the boats together with the convoys and then leaving the conduct of the battle to the individual skippers.

Though this method of massed attacks would prove powerful, running up impressive totals of ship sinkings, its results nevertheless would often prove disappointing during the summer of 1941. Puzzled, having no inkling of the reason, Dönitz could not have imagined that he should put the blame on his own style of command. Yet many of his orders were being heard and understood not only by his skippers out in the North Atlantic but also by a remarkable group of British intelligence officers and academics of various stripes located in a Victorian mansion, Bletchley Park, in the English Midlands. This organization held, as its central secret, the ability of its cryptanalysts to read the output of the principal German enciphering machine, which bore the name Enigma and was employed by all three armed services. The intelligence produced by this operation became known as Ultra.

Nothing so simple as "breaking the German code" characterized the work of Bletchley Park. Though the teams that worked at such pursuits in "the Park" and elsewhere were commonly known as codebreakers, they were dealing primarily with ciphers, a mathematical and far more complex affair. Intellectual laborers now inspired, now plodding, they attacked encrypted messages plucked from the air by listening stations, trying by various techniques to find the meaning hidden in scrambled letters whose pattern did not repeat itself. Just how scrambled the letters from the Enigma could become is suggested by the fact that, with one version of the machine, the German operator had 105,456 possible ways to set it before transmitting a message, and the machine had numerous other complexities as well. Many factors determined whether some messages could be read or would remain impenetrable, and the picture changed from day to day.

In the summer of 1941, Bletchley Park enjoyed considerable success with naval Enigma, partly owing to an encounter on May 8 between the H.M.S. *Bulldog* and Fritz-Julius Lemp's *U-110*. The *Bulldog* depth-charged the U-boat, which rose to the surface; crewmen expected to hear the skipper order them to save the code equipment, but to their surprise he gave only the order to abandon ship. Lieutenant David Balme,

238 · THE SUBMARINE

a languid but effective young officer, led a party aboard the U-boat and, picking up an array of secret material, returned to the destroyer. The crew all became prisoners.

Though success with ciphers generally depended on making specific discoveries or breakthroughs rather than on achieving sweeping results from a single coup, the easily conducted U-119 operation proved valuable for the codebreakers while remaining unknown to Dönitz, who could only presume that the submarine with its secrets had been lost. Soon the Bletchley teams were reading the messages in what was called the Heimisch (Home) key within three days and often within a few hours; Bletchley called this key "Dolphin." The success with U-boat Enigma enabled Admiralty officials to spend much time sitting at Dönitz's elbow as he issued his orders to his gray wolves. Even aside from the information supplied by code breaking, Dönitz's acting as a tactical commander, almost in the manner of Frederick the Great overlooking a battlefield from horseback, inevitably put a great deal of information into the hands of his enemies. The working of the wolf-pack principle, or even calling in two or three submarines to make a joint attack, demanded streams of messages from the U-boats: reports on the size, course, and speed of the convoy, on the weather, and on the condition of the submarines themselves. While these reports were furnishing the admiral with the information he needed to make command decisions, the heavy signal traffic also enabled the British, through radio direction finding (which they developed to an elaborate degree), to locate the boats, often in time for a convoy to be rerouted, even if the particular messages could not be decrypted.

Dönitz, however, did not lack cryptological resources of his own. The B-dienst experienced considerable success with the British standard naval code early in the war. Increasingly, cipher machines, as well as ships themselves, were engaging in duels in the ocean battle. As for the boats, in the summer of 1941 Dönitz began to have as many as thirty-two submarines at sea, enough to launch his full-blown wolf pack principle and to keep Bletchley Park busy. The admiral regarded the ocean battle as still in its early stages, since he looked forward to amassing a total of three hundred boats, which would enable him to put a hundred at a time on patrol; that total could win the war. As it was, his force had sunk 2 million tons in nine months, and in March, on Admiral Raeder's urging, Hitler gave permission to extend operations farther westward in the Atlantic, beyond the areas closer to England in which the Royal Navy supplied convoy escorts. The need to correspondingly extend the escorts became urgent. The British must have help, and, of course, it could come from only one source.

After the fall of France in June 1940, nervous Americans of various political persuasions had begun to contemplate the possible effects on the United States of a victory by the Nazi Reich over Britain and to discuss measures the country might take to prevent this ghastly eventuality from happening. In response to an urgent request from Churchill, FDR, after considerable legalistic head scratching by administration experts, announced on September 3 the exchange of fifty World War–vintage destroyers for leases for naval and air bases in British possessions in the western Atlantic, from Newfoundland to Trinidad. The principle that supplying the sinews of war to Britain represented the best defense of the United States became the basis of administration policy, and in a radio speech in December the president crystallized the theme in his famous declaration that the country must become the "great arsenal of democracy."

Continuing the efforts he hoped would help Britain win the war without the United States having to intervene directly, FDR won passage of the Lend-Lease Act, adopted on March 11, 1941, which allowed the administration to transfer war matériel to any country whose defense the president deemed vital to the defense of the United States. Obviously, little likelihood existed that such supplies sent across the ocean would ever be returned, but nevertheless FDR, in typical fashion, compared these transactions to a Hyde Park resident's lending a neighbor a garden hose to put out a fire in his house: "I don't say to him before that operation, 'Neighbor, my garden hose cost me $15; you have got to pay me $15 for it.' " No, said Roosevelt, "I don't want $15—I want my garden hose back after the fire is over."

Taking the next logical step in the process of giving Britain all aid short of war, the Americans moved to become increasingly involved in making sure that the lend-lease goods arrived safely at their destination on the other side of the Atlantic. On March 20, 1941, Secretary of the

Navy Frank Knox presented the president with a memorandum that explained how the process would work. The plan called for "placing in convoy as much as possible of the shipping in question," and the Navy Department originally intended to provide support and escort forces that would accompany merchant ships all the way across the Atlantic. "We have begun intensive training of forces for all of this work," Knox told Roosevelt, but he would appreciate the opportunity "to have six to eight weeks for special training." During the next two months, however, the plan became transformed into a more efficient arrangement whereby U.S. escorts would cover the convoy route from Newfoundland as far as Iceland.

On May 17 Admiral Harold R. Stark, chief of naval operations, sent President Roosevelt a covering memo concerning an encounter that had occurred not long before out in the Atlantic. It began with a sentence that could have come from a novel of intrigue: "So far as I know only two people in the Navy Department know about this, my Aide and myself, and I am enjoining strict secrecy." The admiral went on to say, "Whether or not the Skipper did the right thing I admire his decision and feel like patting him on the back." In other words, Stark was suggesting that the skipper in question had acted in true sailorly fashion, but perhaps in doing so had contravened U.S. policy.

The accompanying material, which consisted of reports that had begun with the commander of a destroyer division off Iceland and had climbed all the way up the chain of command, described an incident that had begun at about 7:30 in the evening of April 10. The destroyer U.S.S. *Niblack* picked up an SOS from a torpedoed Dutch freighter, which reported that it was sinking rapidly. The *Niblack,* commanded by Lieutenant Commander E. R. Durgin, set off to render assistance, and next morning, having sighted three small boats, lay to to pick up their occupants. As the crew were hauling up the last of the sixty men (the entire complement of the ship, as it turned out), the *Niblack*'s sonar operator reported what definitely appeared to be a submarine approaching for attack. Commander D. L. Ryan, commander of the destroyer division, ordered Durgin to "attack instantly as the most effective method to escape damage." When the *Niblack* reached the presumed position of the U-boat, the crew dropped three depth charges at ten-second intervals and then, considering its work done, hightailed it away from the area at 28 knots. This incident, as Admiral Stark was well aware, might have the most serious consequences, since it marked the first action by an American warship in what was still considered a European war.

Rear Admiral A. L. Bristol, Jr., commander of the Atlantic Fleet Support Force, did not receive the *Niblack*'s report until she returned to base at Newport, Rhode Island, on April 28. Because more than two weeks had passed since the incident and also because "the matter was an established fact," Admiral Bristol decided to let the story stop there. But later a rumor about the encounter seemed to have arisen, and Bristol therefore started Commander Ryan's report on its climb up the ladder that ultimately took it into the president's study.

Referring to the conduct of the skipper of the *Niblack*, Admiral Stark told Roosevelt that "it takes no stretch of the imagination to consider that he was acting in pure self-defense against an oncoming enemy." Admiral Ernest J. King, commander in chief of the Atlantic Fleet—through whose hands the reports passed on their journey—suggested to Stark the need to consider what action German submarines might now take when they encountered U.S. naval vessels. Stark showed little concern, telling FDR, "It is my understanding that German submarines have instructions to 'beat it' just as fast as they can if they see a man-o-war coming over the horizon; their mission being only to attack shipping." What Hitler had actually ordered would prove a much debated point in the West in the coming weeks.

■ ■ ■

Iceland represented a prime geographic prize, a midocean base for ships and aircraft protecting convoys and, in time, for organizing those going over the top of Europe to North Russia, and in June the United States agreed to relieve the British garrison on the island. The first American units arrived in July, not because the local inhabitants wanted them in their country any more than they had wanted the British, who had moved in a year earlier, after the German occupation of Denmark, Iceland's mother country. The premier agreed to the plan only after "considerable heat" had been applied by Winston Churchill, and barely in time: The first U.S. ships were already steaming into the harbor of Reykjavik. With a touch of wartime flexibility, the U.S. Navy stretched its charts just enough to redefine the Western Hemisphere as including Iceland, thus almost insinuating that the country constituted part of North America, which required protection by the United States. Occupation by Germany, declared Admiral King, would threaten America and American shipping, though very little likelihood existed of Germans arriving in Iceland to occupy the country. Even if they had the navy, the transport shipping, and the other needed resources, they had just taken on a full-time job in the East, having invaded the Soviet Union on June 22; Iceland's only invaders would be the British and the Americans.

The Newfoundland conference between Roosevelt and Churchill in August, most remembered for the drafting of the Atlantic Charter, produced agreement on close cooperation between the U.S. and British navies, adopting the plan for the Americans to escort convoys to the Mid-Ocean Meeting Point, south of Iceland. (As it happened, this practice would begin just about two weeks after the incident between the *Greer* and the U-boat.) The convoys would wear a fig leaf of neutrality, because in theory they operated between two U.S. bases—the mainland and Iceland—though "shipping of any nationality [might] join such United States or Iceland flag convoys."

■ ■ ■

As matters seemed to stand in the late summer of 1941, a U.S. warship could track a U-boat and could direct British attackers to the spot, but could not make an attack herself. Confusing, indeed: The skipper of the *U-652*, Lieutenant Georg-Werner Fraatz, did not know until the news became general a day or so later that the pursuer he had attempted to sink on September 4 was an American ship. Even a good look at the *Greer* might not have made the situation perfectly clear to Fraatz, because this destroyer was one of more than fifty retired flush-deckers hauled out of the "bone yard" at the Philadelphia Navy Yard early in the war and reconditioned; most of them, identical to the *Greer,* had gone to Britain in the "destroyers-bases deal" worked out by FDR and Churchill, and now sailed the North Atlantic as Royal Navy vessels on convoy duty.

The U.S. Navy announcement of the attack on the *Greer* omitted some signficant details. Describing the *Greer* as "en route to Iceland with mail," the navy said that she had reported that "a submarine had attacked her by firing torpedoes which missed their mark. The Greer immediately counterattacked with depth charges. Results are not known." The press accurately described, however, the destroyer's role as part of the Atlantic patrol, which was supposed to keep watch for the presence of potentially hostile craft. When the wife of the *Greer*'s thirty-nine-year-old skipper learned from a radio news broadcast that her husband's ship had been attacked, she picked up the telephone and called the Navy Department. Her husband was unharmed, the officer on duty told her, adding, "Somebody out on the ocean sure has rotten aim—and it's a good thing."

On Capitol Hill, senators of varying persuasions limited themselves to restrained comments. Pat McCarran, the cantankerous veteran from Nevada, commented, calmly enough, "We've been sticking our nose out so far that we can expect anything." No one, interventionist or isolationist, seemed to feel that the incident might lead to war with Germany, though interventionists wanted to reserve comment until they had more facts. When FDR got the news of the attack, he realized that it suited his purposes perfectly. On September 11 he would deliver a speech in which he would explain the new policy on convoys; now the *U-652*'s two torpedoes seemed to give him precisely the justification for orders, already issued to the fleet, to shoot German war vessels on sight. In the speech FDR, using information supplied by the navy, accused the Germans of "piracy legally and morally" and declared that the time for "active defense" had come: "When you see a rattlesnake poised to strike you, you do not wait until he has struck before you crush him."

The *Greer*, Roosevelt said in his speech, had been proceeding on a legitimate mission when the U-boat fired on her "without warning and with deliberate design to sink her." FDR had received this first impression from a navy memorandum, but he, Congress, and the public

had been thoroughly misinformed; nor did statements made in Reykjavik by officers and crew of the *Greer* make for an accurate picture,
some of them having even indicated that British aircraft had come to
the defense of the destroyer while she was under attack. In a letter
written at the behest of the Senate Naval Affairs Committee, Admiral
Stark corrected the record, revealing that, far from waiting to ambush
the *Greer,* the U-boat was trying its best to escape the unwanted attentions of the destroyer, which was radioing details of latitude and longitude to all listeners, including British destroyers. Admiral Dönitz
considered all this highly improper, and the Germans released an in-
dignant and quite accurate demurrer; Dönitz later quoted with approval a statement by two U.S. historians that it was "difficult to regard
as justifiable the indignation with which news of the episode was received in American official and private circles." After all the harassment
the U-boat had received, they observed, "it would have been surprising
if the envisaged victim had not in the end turned on its tormentor."
But, of course, the president's shoot-on-sight order stood.

Strangely, not much in the way of reaction to the incident came
from London. For more than a year, the British leadership had called
for and worked for greater American intervention and even full participation in the war. But now that an actual provocation, or what appeared as one, had happened, Londoners seemed to miss what would
seem an obvious point: an attack on a U.S. ship might give American
opinion a powerful shove in the direction of war. Instead, after two
years of war people seemed more inclined to consider the torpedoing
of a ship too commonplace an affair to call for much attention. One
London newspaper did observe, however, that the torpedoing "provided the reminder that America needed that the war was near her
shores."

Some Washington officials devoted their attention to the largest
question raised by the incident: Had Hitler decided to force the issue
and start an all-out war with the United States? Indeed, would the submarine once again, as a quarter of a century earlier, serve as the force
propelling America into a great European war? In actual fact, a beleaguered U-boat captain trying to save his boat had apparently caused no
change in U.S. policy, but, for all the Americans knew, the skipper had

acted on direct orders from Berlin. That seemed to be the general opinion, a conclusion quite in accord with the tendency that has shown itself throughout history for those who speculate about the causes of events to overestimate the part played by purpose and underestimate the influence of accident. In any case, nobody had ever established rules for waging an undeclared war.

■ ■ ■

In contrast to the *Greer,* the U.S. Navy had in the *Kearny* one of its newest and finest destroyers. Displacing 1,630 tons, this ship was laid down in 1939 and had been commissioned on September 14, 1940. She carried the standard 5-inch battery and ten torpedo tubes, and was constructed with full compartmentalization and a double hull to cut down possible torpedo damage to her inner skin; a true greyhound, she could do 40 knots. Her captain, Lieutenant Commander Anthony L. Danis, had an interesting background; an airshipman in the days when many air enthusiasts looked on the glamorous dirigibles as the craft of the future (at only five-foot-two, he seemed almost lighter than air himself), he had survived the crashes of both the *Akron* and the *Macon,* disasters that, together with the fiery death of Germany's *Hindenburg,* at Lakehurst, New Jersey, had led to the abandonment of the navy's dirigible program.

During the night of October 15–16 the *Kearny,* along with four other destroyers, responded to a call for help from Convoy SC-48, eastbound from Canada and now some 400 miles south of Iceland, which had run into a heavy concentration of U-boats—in fact, an organized patrol line consisting of thirteen submarines and stretching southeast from Cape Farewell, Greenland. A storm had scattered the convoy; even the ship of the convoy commodore had become a straggler, and the U-boats had fallen on their prey with the ferocity that justified the name "wolf pack."

Still new at the game, the Americans quickly saw that they had a great deal to learn about tactics. Taking station at nightfall on October 16, they found themselves much closer to the merchantmen than were the U-boats, which attacked at ranges up to 5,000 yards; nor did the destroyers yet carry radar gear, and the U-boats lay outside sonar detection range. When a stricken ship went up in flames, the glow lit up the *Kearny*, making her a perfect target for a shot from the periphery of the scene, and then a torpedo tore into her starboard side. Her builders had done their work well, however, and her crew was able to control the damage; she returned to Reykjavik under her own power. Standing by was another destroyer of the division, the U.S.S. *Greer.*

First reports indicated, at least by omission, that the attack had caused no casualties, but unfortunately the omission proved just that: The torpedo had exploded in a fire room, killing eleven men and wounding twenty-four. Some naval authorities declared that the blow that struck the *Kearny* would have sunk a less strongly built ship.

The torpedoing of the *Kearny* represented the first attack on a U.S. warship since Roosevelt had issued his shoot-on-sight order. Lieutenant Joachim Preuss, skipper of the *U-568*, believed he was attacking a British rather than an American destroyer, though in the midst of a battle at night this consideration seems such a nicety that it suggests some morning-after thinking. (A retired U.S. chief of naval operations explained the attack on the *Kearny* as an assault on a patrolling ship, miles out in the ocean, "intended by the Nazis to strike fear in American hearts.") In the German-American version of the Battle of the Atlantic, the Germans had drawn first blood. But "since there were no drafted men in the Navy at that time," observed one of FDR's confidants, "there was no great popular indignation against Hitler for the attacks on the destroyers; but what is most important is that neither was there any serious popular indignation against Roosevelt for his responsibility in thus exposing our ships." The New York chairman of the anti-intervention America First Committee commented, however, that Americans could hardly expect that "our war vessels" could "hunt the ships of any nation and escape attack." Not only was the "war party" eager for the attacks, he said, but these attacks were not coming fast enough to satisfy these interventionists.

A few days later, General Robert E. Wood, the leading figure in America First, called for the president to appear before Congress and request a definitive vote for peace or war. The general, the head of Sears Roebuck, had no doubt about the result of such a vote—nor did FDR. Some of his associates might like the idea, but he knew better.

Just two months earlier, the bill to extend the period of service of army draftees had barely passed in the House of Representatives, squeaking through by only a single vote, and that vital vote may have owed something to the speed with which Speaker Sam Rayburn banged his gavel to end the session. Congress would beyond any doubt vote no on war. Above all, apart from formal decisions on war, the president could risk nothing that might endanger his chief concern, his program of all-out aid to Britain, which he had characterized as America's first line of defense.

The drama of U-boats and U.S. destroyers had thus far featured two acts: A submarine had fired at a destroyer and missed, and another submarine had wounded a destroyer but not sunk it. Now would come the third act.

■ ■ ■

At daybreak on October 31 out in the North Atlantic about 600 miles west of Ireland, a destroyer officer lay half awake, lulled by the quiet of the sea. In an instant, everything changed, when a loud explosion brought him upright: "I know instantly that it is a torpedo and not a depth charge," he noted in his journal. Within seconds he was on deck, while General Quarters sounded. The victim, he saw immediately, was not his ship but one about a mile ahead. "With a terrific roar, a column of orange flame towers high into the night as her magazines go up, subsides, leaving a great black pall of smoke licked by moving tongues of orange. All the ship forward of No. 4 stack has disappeared."

These destroyers formed part of a group of five escorting HX-156, a fast convoy that had departed Newfoundland on October 23. The destroyer that had just been hit, an old four-piper named the *Reuben James,* had suffered a fatal blow, with her forward magazine probably having gone up to produce the explosion that blew off the fore part of the ship as far aft as the fourth stack. As her sister destroyer approached, the stern of the *Reuben James* rose straight up and then slid slowly beneath the surface. "A moment, and two grunting jolts of her depth charges toss debris and men into the air. Suddenly my nostrils are filled with the sickly stench of fuel oil, and the sea is flat and silvery under its thick coating."

The destroyer had now reached the survivors, looking "like black shiny seals in the water." The crew prepared lines for heaving and rigged cargo nets over the side. Officers and men then went over the side to help the sailors struggling in the water, while one survivor called, politely, "A line, please, sir!" But, after more than an hour's effort, with two survivors still bobbing in the water immediately astern, the sonar picked up a submarine, and all the destroyers went on the move. Later they came back, hoping that all the men who had been flung into the water had been picked up by one ship or another.

The after part of the *Reuben James* sayed afloat only about five minutes, and when it sank to the level set for its depth charges, several of them exploded, killing men floating in the water. Only forty-five of the ship's complement of 160 survived; the list of survivors did not include the skipper, Lieutenant Commander Heywood L. Edwards, a Texan who had captained the 1928 U.S. Olympic wrestling team, or any of the other officers. Now, what might have happened to the *Greer,* and to a limited extent had actually happened to the *Kearny,* had finally and totally occurred: A German torpedo had sunk an American warship, with heavy casualties. Not a tough new ship like the *Kearny,* the *Reuben James,* it was said, had "met the fate that all sailors [had] long agreed a destroyer faced if hit by a torpedo."

If the Americans wanted an issue on which to make war, they could now claim to have it. The news of the sinking caused the standard stir on Capitol Hill and in Washington generally, but in a press conference not held in response to the sinking FDR took a low-key approach to the incident. He seemed surprised, in fact, when a reporter asked whether it would lead to the breaking of diplomatic relations with Germany, and, when asked whether "this first actual sinking" would make any difference in the international relations of the United States, he calmly replied that he did not think so—the destroyer was merely carrying out its assigned task; in other words, the torpedoing of a vessel on routine convoy duty must be regarded as an inevitable incident. Curiously enough, a German government spokesman in Berlin made just the same point. If the *Reuben James* was participating in a convoy, he said, "it was no wonder that she was torpedoed. A convoy is an English affair and whoever participates in it becomes part of an English formation."

Administration leaders felt confident, however, that the sinking of the *Reuben James* had guaranteed them a safe majority in the vote to amend the Neutrality Acts, and this hope quickly proved correct. Within a week Congress had authorized the arming of all American merchant ships and had abolished the restriction that kept U.S. shipping out of European waters; now the navy could escort American cargoes all the way to British ports. But the U-boat that had destroyed the *Reuben James,* as FDR had made clear even before Washington had learned any of the details, had not blasted the United States into war or even into breaking relations with Germany.

Many in Washington felt that the decision for war would be (and, some thought, had already been) made in Berlin, with the Führer supposedly having decided that the United States would cause him less trouble as an outright foe than as a threatening so-called neutral. They held this belief even though, under the Tripartite Pact signed by Germany, Italy, and Japan, a signatory power could count on the aid of the others only if it should be attacked by another country, not if it did the attacking. Washington seemed unable to visualize what had actually happened in the encounters with the U-boats or to realize that they had not become engaged in a campaign aimed at U.S. warships. No one in America could know, of course, that in a meeting with Admirals Raeder and Dönitz following Roosevelt's shoot-on-sight declaration the Führer had waved away Raeder's request for freedom of action for his U-boats; they should take defensive action, said Hitler, only if they were being attacked.

So it was that both the president and the Führer were treading very carefully, in a pattern quite unlike the scenes that had involved Woodrow Wilson and Kaiser Wilhelm a quarter of a century earlier. As for the American public, commented Robert E. Sherwood, they had a "sort of tacit understanding" that "nobody was to get excited if ships were sunk by U-boats, because that's what got us into war the other time. It has been said that in 1914 the French were prepared for the war of 1870, and in 1939 they were prepared for the war of 1914. It could be said with equal truth that in 1941 the Americans were fully prepared to keep out of the war of 1917." The submarine had constituted the great political fact of the World War. But now, with all-out war about to come to the United States again, it would come in a fashion far different from that of 1917, and far more spectacular. And the submarine would take its place at the center of the story.

RAIDERS IN THE FAR WEST

The Axis alliance of Germany, Italy, and Japan did not constitute any kind of integrated team. In the evening of December 7, 1941, news that an event of the highest conceivable importance had occurred—the Japanese had attacked the U.S. fleet at Pearl Harbor—came to German ears as a total surprise. Hints in a secret telegram from Tokyo that a clash with America might "come sooner than anyone dreams" had proved a little too vague and elliptical to give the Germans any picture of what was about to happen. But the Kriegsmarine command received the news of the strike with great satisfaction, as a devastating blow against the troublesome Americans with their undeclared war in the Atlantic, and the German admirals, who did not control their own air arm, could not help noting with envy that Japanese naval air power had produced in two hours the kind of results the Luftwaffe, in two years of trying, had failed to obtain against Britain.

Since the news came as a genuine surprise, Admiral Dönitz found himself with no U-boats in American waters to follow up Hitler's declaration of war on the United States four days after Pearl Harbor. Under the terms of the Tripartite Treaty, Germany did not have to join Japan in war against the United States, because the Japanese had not been attacked. But, in thus expressing his readiness to move from the frustrating state of undeclared war to the more conventional plane, the Führer had revealed that, like the German High Command in 1917, he did not fully appreciate what war with the United States would involve. Nor did his naval war machine stand ready to advance into heavy action against the Americans. Dönitz, however, knew what a rich opportunity the virginal American waters would present, and he suggested that twelve U-boats be immediately dispatched to operate across the Atlantic.

Even after two and a half years of war, the U-boat arm had only about ninety submarines in service, with twenty-six consigned to the Mediterranean and four stationed off the coast of Europe; of the rest, more than fifty were undergoing repair and refit. But even if the numbers were relatively small, the American coast offered such rich pickings that Dönitz "confidently expected great things of these twelve boats. American waters had hitherto remained untouched by war." No U.S. convoy system existed, and whatever antisubmarine methods the Americans had developed would be untried and ineffective. But this great harvest season would not last long; the Americans, having now to organize themselves on both sides of the world, would quickly gain experience and would certainly establish effective convoys in the Atlantic. His men had the opportunity now for a second "happy time," but they must act fast and make the most of it.

Hitler and Raeder saw the situation differently, however, and to Dönitz's frustration the grand admiral, refusing to release boats from the Mediterranean, granted only six for transatlantic operations. As it turned out, only five would be ready for the quick blow—an operation called *Paukenschlag* (Drum Roll)—that Dönitz, making the best of the situation, planned to strike along the North American coast between the St. Lawrence River and Cape Hatteras. The attack would begin on Tuesday, January 13.

One day earlier, however, the westward-bound *U-123* encountered the British steamer *Cyclops* some 300 miles out in the Atlantic. Deciding that one single day surely could not make a great difference to anybody, and that the admiral would surely agree with this point, the skipper, Lieutenant Commander Reinhard Hardegen, fired two torpedoes at the steamer, hitting her and sending her stern-first to the bottom. A day ahead of schedule, *Paukenschlag* had begun.

Hardegen's real revelation came when he arrived at the approaches to New York. "It's absolutely unbelievable," the skipper said to the second officer, as they stared through the night at what looked to be a great city in peacetime, marveling at the truly incredible array of colorful lights shining from signs and buildings, all across the harbor, and even from ships in the bay. "I have the feeling," Hardegen said, "that the Americans are going to be very surprised when they find out where we are." His opinion quickly proved to be sound. When a hapless oil tanker presented itself to the U-boat, Hardegen decided to give it two torpedoes, and there came two explosions and a fire that reddened sky and water. When the radioman picked up the distress signal from the tanker, he reported to his incredulous skipper that the ship's captain thought he had struck a mine.

"You're certain they're saying 'mine'?" Hardegen shouted. "A mine! What assholes!"

Hardegen and his fellow U-boat commanders worked their way south toward Cape Hatteras, feasting off the incredible abundance that presented itself to them. Following the basic Dönitz principles—lying low during the day, attacking on the surface at night, carrying the assault close up to the ships—the skippers quickly produced an unprecedented box score that completely fulfilled their mentor's expectations. *U-123* netted nine ships totaling 53,175 tons (besides the damaged tanker); *U-130* (Commander Kals), six ships, 36,993 tons, and one ship damaged; *U-66* (the fittingly named Commander Zapp), five ships, 33,456 tons; *U-109* (Lieutenant Commander Bleichrodt), five ships, 33,733 tons. Of the five skippers, only Lieutenant Commander Folkers, in the *U-125,* proved a disappointment, as he accounted for only one ship, of 5,666 tons. But the grand total for the second half of January amounted to 163,201 tons, a truly remarkable tally when compared with the monthly totals of all sinkings by U-boats for November and December of 100,000 tons.

All along the Atlantic coast in the early months of 1942, new kinds of lightning flashed in the night sky to the east, explosions rumbled across the water, and vacation beaches became littered with bodies, empty lifebuoys, and charred lifeboats. Even as late as June 15 the hundreds of families holidaying at Virginia Beach could stand and watch U-boats methodically go after two large freighters. Drawing lyrical inspiration from the reports of such spectacles, Admiral Dönitz told a German correspondent that "bathers and sometimes entire coastal cities are witnesses to that drama of war whose visual climaxes are constituted by the red glorioles of blazing tankers."

Such drama had not come as a complete surprise. Some time earlier one prophet, the almost aptly named mayor of Baltimore, Clifford B. Cropper, had scoffed at gloomy forecasts that the war would hurt Maryland's tourist business. Instead, the mayor declared, submarine activity off the beaches would create a great new tourist attraction for shore resorts. Indeed, when the war did arrive residents and businesses in coastal areas seemed determined to help the lurking U-boats. For six miles along the ocean edge, Miami and its suburbs continued to light up the night sky, turning freighters and tankers into perfect targets by silhouetting them against the glow; blackouts, the locals said, would ruin the winter tourist trade. Similar attitudes prevailed northward along the coast.

The double-barreled fatuity of Mayor Cropper—in holding his view in the first place and then in publicly expressing it—and the public's refusal to turn off the lights along the coast demonstrated how much Americans had to learn about war and how selfish many of them could be while absorbing the lessons. The federal government's own conduct showed a disgraceful lack of political will in the face of clear necessity. Dimout along the coast did not come until March, and New York was allowed to cling to its lights, with Times Square staying bright, until military authorities finally issued an order in June. A tanker crewman pulled from the water off New Jersey told the press that some twenty of his shipmates had been lost because "it was lit up like daylight all along the beach. That submarine was right there, waiting for the first boat to come along."

Crewmen of the merchant ships outlined in the city lights sometimes had to fight for their lives in oil scum an inch or more thick, which spread faster than they could swim, struggling to keep from swallowing the muck or taking it into their lungs and ducking beneath it when the waves flamed in fiery patches. At various points along the coast people could hear gasping cries coming from the water; a teenager on Ocracoke Island, off the North Carolina coast, saw as many as four and five ships ablaze at a single time, and on a winter Florida night the funeral pyre of a torpedoed tanker could be seen by anybody who stepped outside a cabaret for a breath of ocean air. On one occasion, Hardegen, in an oddly compassionate gesture, took his

U-boat inshore of a burning victim so that shells from his deck gun would not threaten spectators on the beach.

"The Battle of the Atlantic," Secretary of the Interior Harold Ickes declared, "is being fought with oil and will be won with oil," but during the winter and spring of 1942 this black gold appeared to symbolize the loss of the battle, as it poured uselessly from the torpedoed tanker ships into the waters of the Caribbean and of the Atlantic off the East Coast.

Strangest of all was the behavior of the United States Navy. Single destroyers sailed up and down the traffic lanes with such regularity, said Admiral Dönitz, that "the U-boats were quickly able to work out the timetable being followed." Merchant skippers used their radio as freely as if no deadly enemy lurked anywhere, frequently signaling their position and thus helping the U-boats create a detailed picture of shipping in the area. During one January night alone, U-123 sank three large ships and blew a hole in a fourth. In concrete terms, such a night's activity meant that, besides three or four ships, the Allies had typically lost at least forty-two tanks, eight 6-inch howitzers, eighty-eight 25-pound guns, forty 2-pound guns, twenty-four armored cars, fifty Bren-gun carriers, 5,210 tons of ammunition, 600 rifles, 428 tons of tank supplies, 2,000 tons of stores, and 1,000 tanks of gasoline. To create similar losses by air attack (on ground targets), the enemy would have had to mount 3,000 successful bombing sorties.

A patrolling destroyer did not necessarily enjoy immunity from attack by a U-boat. At 6:45 in the evening of February 28, Admiral Stark informed the president in a telephone call that, in the early morning darkness of that day, the U.S.S. Jacob Jones had not only been hit but also almost literally destroyed by two torpedoes, one of which had blasted her in the bow and the other in the stern. Then, as these parts of the ship were sinking, the depth charges exploded, which, said the admiral, probably accounted for the heavy loss of life. The survivors had been taken to the hospital in Cape May, "where they cannot talk to anyone." Stark bluntly told Roosevelt that no press release about the sinking had been issued and that it "should be kept quiet for the present."

On April 11, as the U-123 cruised in shallow water off northern Florida while nursing her last remaining torpedo, lookouts spotted a patrolling destroyer (the U.S.S. *Dahlgren*), and Hardegen, trying to get away from a U.S. aircraft and intending to head for deeper water, ordered a dive. Before the *U-123* could get far, however, the *Dahlgren's* approach made any action too hazardous. But as the U-boat sat quietly, with engines off, at a depth of about 70 feet, a series of depth charge hammer blows gave jolting evidence that the Americans had spotted her. Water began coming in through seams and stuffing, and the watch officer realized the helplessness of knowing that "the enemy is above you and has the power to kill you, and you cannot do anything but wait."

When Hardegen decided that the crew must abandon the boat, he led the way up the ladder to the hatch, as submarine protocol required, but a fresh pass by the destroyer caused him to pause, pondering the possibly gruesome effects of being hit by an exploding depth charge on his way to the surface: "If he were to drop more depth charges, I would be dead at once." The crew waited silently as the churning propeller noises passed overhead and then—Hardegen could not imagine why—the destroyer left the scene and went on her way. (Later, Hardegen learned that, having spotted leaking oil and shattered wood from the U-boat's deck, the American captain decided that he had sent the submarine to the bottom and could therefore conserve his stock of depth charges.) Now the boat could surface and the crew could make repairs, though only one engine would function. With this task accomplished, Hardegen headed for deeper water, where he saw a target of opportunity for his final torpedo: a sugar freighter en route from Cuba to New York. The single shot, the only one he had, sufficed for the job, but even now the *U-123* had not finished her course of destruction; the boat's deck gun accounted for three more merchant ships, giving Hardegen a total of nineteen victims in his North American activities as he headed for the Bay of Biscay ports, whose possession by the Germans had furnished Admiral Dönitz's submarine campaign with its real sinews. In the first six months of 1942 the U-boats would bag some four hundred ships in their North American *Feindfahrt*, more than two a day.

Continuingly frustrated at Hitler's refusal to see the strategic importance of *Paukenschlag,* Dönitz had nevertheless extended it south to the

Caribbean, and the second happy time continued on its frolicsome course. After sinking nine ships, Jochen Mohr, captain of the *U-24*, signaled to the admiral:

> The new-moon night is black as ink.
> Off Hatteras the tankers sink.
> While sadly Roosevelt counts the score—
> Some fifty thousand tons—by
>   MOHR

The British, who after almost two and a half years saw themselves as seasoned veterans of war, reacted with horror to the carnage in what they termed "the far west." Many of the weakly protected ships swelling the U-boats' bag in the Caribbean, the Gulf of Mexico, and the western Atlantic flew the British merchant ensign and were manned by British crews, and, apart from the human costs of the sinkings, the island needed those endangered supplies to survive. On February 6 Winston Churchill raised the question of "the very heavy sinkings by U-boats" in a letter to FDR's principal confidant, Harry Hopkins. In March the prime minister declared that "the situation is so serious that drastic action of some kind is necessary," and a few days later President Roosevelt offered the sheepish response that "my Navy has been definitely slack in preparing for this submarine war off our coast."

The U.S. Navy had made some prewar effort at preparedness; trawlers, cutters, and private yachts had been collected and armed so that they could serve on antisubmarine patrol, but Admiral King, who had become commander in chief of the navy, insisted that destroyers could not be spared from their transatlantic duties to serve in coastal convoys. (Hardegen even presumed that the available destroyers stayed in harbor instead of going out on patrol.) Alas for Admiral King, the fifty four-stacker destroyers swapped to Britain in 1940 had left U.S. service forever, but on February 10, in a sort of reciprocal gesture, the British agreed to send the U.S. Navy twenty-four antisubmarine trawlers and ten corvettes, manned by experienced crews.

Convoy still offered the obvious prime answer to the U-boat menace, just as it had for transatlantic traffic during the preceding two years and had, in fact, ever since it had proved itself after the debates at the Admiralty in 1917. Early in 1942 Admiral King declared, defensively but accurately enough, that an unescorted convoy was worse than no convoy at all, but he seems to have believed at the time that only destroyers could serve effectively as escorts. Sending individual vessels to hunt submarines worked no better than it had in the first war, however, when President Wilson said of U-boat seekers, "They despaired of hunting the hornets all over the farm." On March 12, 1942, Rear Admiral Adolphus Andrews, commander of the Eastern Sea Frontier (the U.S. Atlantic coast), wrote the president and Admiral King asking for blanket authority to obtain various kinds of small craft and fit them out as rapidly as possible for antisubmarine service. FDR gave the idea his immediate approval, telling the secretary of the navy that Andrews should be allowed to go ahead "without having to go through the old rigamarole of referring plans, specifications, etc., to Washington." Andrews also noted that a few of the promised British trawlers had now arrived and had immediately been sent to sea on patrol duty. Nevertheless, some weeks would pass before Admiral King would fully awake to the problem and the answer, and some months would pass before the Americans acquired enough escort vessels to create an interlocking coastal convoy system.

In the emergency, the president, who as a Hudson Valley squire liked to describe his business occupation as "tree farmer," took a direct part in anti–U-boat efforts. In the first war his superiors had rebuffed his advocacy of small submarine chasers, but now he occupied a position in which no one dismissed any of his ideas out of hand. Returning to his old concept, except that the boats would be larger, he pushed for the construction of large numbers of escort craft (ECs), as the chasers were called: boats of 173 feet or 110 feet. Production was distributed among a large number of mostly family-owned shipyards nationwide, and by April builders had completed twenty-four, with thirty-six more scheduled to be finished by May 1. Scouring the forests of the Northeast for tall, straight oak trees, the navy found two thousand mature staghead oaks on FDR's own estate. Represented by a Syracuse University silviculturist, the estate arranged (presumably at a competitive price) for a Connecticut sawmill to take three hundred of the oaks, which were squared into keels; most of them then went across the Hudson to a shipyard in Kingston, where within a few weeks they had become the ribs of subchasers that would shortly head down the river and out to sea. The men aboard them would not be happy; these little boats tended to roll and pitch, making even veteran sailors miserable, and most of these crewmen were reservists (and were called the "Donald Duck Navy"). But one U-boat commander noted that the ECs posed a particular danger because their tiny silhouettes often did not show up in periscopes.

Rummaging through its cupboards for anything that might help stem the German sea invasion, the navy found several World War I–vintage R-class submarines and gave them the mission of catching U-boats on the surface and ("hopefully," said one skipper) sinking them. The crews made "short patrols of about two weeks' duration," said this skipper, Lieutenant Commander John S. Coye, Jr., "because we didn't have any air-conditioning like the modern submarines have, and you didn't carry much fresh water." The boats were "small and cramped, and we usually had extra people aboard, because we were training them to go and get qualified" to take over the new submarines being built. "You just barely had enough fresh water to brush your teeth." His boat, the *R-18,* could shoot torpedoes, the skipper said, as though the point might have been in question, and "for a boat that old it was probably safe."

Despite his relative faith in the soundness of the boat, Coye had a narrow escape from disaster off Bermuda in the spring of 1942. Just before dawn one morning, while patrolling in a "submarine sanctuary" (an officially safe zone in which air attacks on boats were forbidden) the *R-18* became the target of a U.S. Navy plane that came roaring in, ignoring both the recognition signal Coye fired and the American flag tied to the periscope. Coye dived, but bombs from the plane smashed the forward trim tank, flooding it. The damage did not prove fatal, and Coye later learned that the flier, who had sighted a U-boat a few days earlier but had failed to attack it, had become a man on a mission: He would not make that mistake again.

The depredations of the German submarines and the shortage of combat aircraft in these months led to a special role for civilians with the activation of the Civil Air Patrol (CAP), made up of civilian sport fliers; they used their own planes and received no pay. Charged with reporting any submarines they saw, they proved particularly helpful in spotting wreckage and lifeboats. Finally covering up to a hundred miles offshore, they released army and navy planes for long-range submarine search. Unaware that CAP planes carried no weapons, U-boat captains would try to hide from them by diving when caught on the surface. Once, off New Jersey, a submarine plunged into the muddy bottom and became stuck fast, while the CAP plane circled overhead, radioing for help, but none came. This and similar incidents won the civilian airmen permission to carry depth charges or light bombs. By the end of the war they had bombed fifty-seven U-boats, sinking several of them. It proved to be dangerous work: twenty-six pilots were killed in action.

■ ■ ■

In London, the naval information from all sources poured into the Admiralty's Operational Intelligence Centre (OIC), specifically the section called the U-boat Tracking Room, presided over by a barrister in uniform, Rodger Winn, who had come on board just before the war began. A polio victim whom the disease had left with a hunchback and limp, Winn had devoted all his brains and training to the study of U-boats, their patterns and habits, and had achieved striking success; the tracking room could essentially be considered his creation. Since he also possessed considerable gifts as an advocate, his superiors regarded him as just the man—indeed, the only man—to carry out a crucial assignment: to go to Washington to bring British intelligence experience to bear on the raging disaster the U-boats had created in American waters.

Winn's brief called for him to demonstrate to the newcomers to the war the importance of a coordinated intelligence system and to explain that one did not have to consider it a baffling proposition to keep track of enemy submarines and predict their movements. He could show them a theory that worked; he had the results to confirm it. The Americans might well prove stubborn and defensive, the British thought, and

Winn had the right combination of qualities to win the argument and provide the needed technical guidance.

As it happened, Winn fared remarkably well on his assignment, though his first encounter in Washington seemed to give substance to British fears about American attitudes. At the outset, Rear Admiral Richard S. Edwards, Admiral King's deputy chief of staff, intimated to the visitor that the Americans wished to learn their own lessons. Here Winn had a bit of luck, because, acting on the exaggeratedly simple idea that Americans react well to blunt speaking, he fired back, "The trouble is, Admiral, that it's not only your bloody ships you are losing. A lot of them are ours." Fortunately, Edwards took no offense but responded in the way Winn expected, laughing and conceding that the visitor might have a point.

Then, ushered into King's office, Winn also did well with the fleet commander in chief, a formidable bear who gave him a thoughtful hearing despite his general dislike of the British. After the interview, King issued orders for the immediate establishment of a submarine tracking room on the Admiralty model. "Once convinced," commented a veteran of the Operational Intelligence Centre, "the Americans moved with a speed and efficiency that was surprising to anyone accustomed to the ways of the admiralty. Before Winn left Washington . . . the necessary accommodation had been found and the additional staff required were being selected."

To direct this new staff, the navy chiefs chose a tall, slim officer from Maryland, Commander Kenneth A. Knowles (Naval Academy '27), who had been retired in 1938 because of nearsightedness; happy to contribute, Knowles noted that in this assignment he would not need the kind of keen eyesight required to maneuver a destroyer doing 35 knots. In July he went off to London for a sort of internship in the Citadel (the bunker housing the Operational Intelligence Centre) with Winn, whom he found "utterly brilliant," with "things so beautifully laid out." When he returned to Washington, the period of close Anglo-American cooperation in naval intelligence truly began. The two officers had a cable reserved exclusively for them, and they exchanged messages every day. "Frequently, with his brilliant wit, he would try to push me around a bit," Knowles said, "and I would come back at him. We had a nice working relationship."

Intelligence, along with convoy and countermeasures, constituted the keys to victory over the U-boats. But, for all their accomplishments, Winn's tracking room and Knowles's new situation room could not make up for the gap in intelligence that had opened up on February 1, 1942, when the friendly Dolphin key had fallen silent. The Germans had changed sea creatures, and the new and unreadable naval operational key received the Bletchley designation "Shark." Put less metaphorically, the enemy had added a fourth rotor to the standard three of the machine (thus multiplying the number of possible settings by 26). If the convoys were to flourish, they would need the help of all the countermeasures that could be devised, and Shark must be tamed.

■ ■ ■

The higher authorities in all countries had a way, not always applauded by the chiefs of their submarine forces, of taking boats off patrol to perform various kinds of special missions. These vessels seemed ideally suited to serve as vehicles for smuggling people and small cargoes, and thus, in the evening of June 12, 1942, Lieutenant Commander Hans-Heinz Linder, skipper of the U-202, found himself making a landfall off the eastern end of Long Island. A veteran of action in the North Atlantic, Linder wished only to unload his passengers and cargo as efficiently as possible and then return to the hunt for Allied freighters and tankers.

Putting the men and their impedimenta off in an inflatable rubber boat manned by two sailors, Linder waited until the crewmen returned and then, preparing to go, found his boat stuck on a sandbar. Veiled by heavy mist, the U-202 succeeded in avoiding detection until morning, when flood tide allowed the skipper to free her and proceed to sea.

On shore, the four Germans changed into civilian clothes and buried their cargo, an array of wooden boxes containing explosives and timing devices. The team had come to the United States with the mission of blowing up defense factories, particularly light-metal plants making aircraft materials. But almost immediately, accosted by a young Coast Guard beach patrolman made curious by hearing German voices drifting through the fog, the four would-be saboteurs began losing the game. They had plenty of money (these men and another German team together carried more than $150,000) and they began clumsily by offering the patrolman a cash bribe, which he pretended to accept, only to call headquarters as soon as he left the scene. But even that development proved irrelevant. On his own, one of the German agents took the startling step of boarding a train to Washington to explain the operation to no less a figure than J. Edgar Hoover himself. The Abwehr, it appeared, had not screened its saboteurs with much care; the defector, one Georg Dasch, professed loathing for the Nazis.

The other team of four agents landed from the *U-584* at Ponte Vedra Beach near Jacksonville, Florida. The members of both teams had all lived in the United States and worked as waiters, machine-tool workers, painters, chauffeurs, and butlers, and all spoke English. But, owing to Dasch's defection, none of their experiences would prove of any value. Dasch succeeded in meeting with a senior FBI agent, and as the result of his information the bureau had rounded up both groups, north and south, by June 27. Operation Pastorius, as the mission was called, had not only failed, it had completely collapsed. Six of the eight agents were executed in August; Dasch and another agent who had joined him in defecting received prison sentences, which, after the war, were commuted by President Truman.

Later in 1942, the British and the Americans mounted a smuggling mission of their own that turned into one of the more captivating adventures of the war. This took place in late October, shortly before the launching of Operation Torch, the Anglo-American invasion of French Northwest Africa. The Allies hoped to win the support of the local French authorities and thus to carry out unopposed landings in the area, but the political situation was enormously complicated, as French politics had been generally since the surrender of 1940. To attempt to foresee what would happen when the invasion came and what military and political developments might follow it, General Eisenhower, the commander of Torch, dispatched his deputy, Lieutenant General Mark Clark, to Africa to meet with an American diplomat, Robert Murphy, and a young French resistance general, Charles Mast.

With the area constantly patrolled by Vichy French and Axis forces, a submarine provided the only possible way to sneak Clark into the area for the meeting, which would take place at an isolated farmhouse on the Mediterranean coast about 75 miles west of Algiers. A problem arose from the fierce French opposition to British participation in negotiations, or even in the invasion itself, but since the Americans had no submarines in the area, the 872-ton H.M.S. *Seraph* (Lieutenant Jewell) was pressed into service and for the time being flew the U.S. ensign. Clark and his accompanying officers duly appeared at the farmhouse, but while the meeting was under way local police banged on the door and then burst into the house; Clark and the American officers with him fled to the wine cellar, while Murphy lightened the scene by posing as an inebriated guest at a raucous party. As it turned out, the police had no concern with high policy but were responding to rumors that genuine smugglers were using the house; Arab servants had tipped off the authorities in the hope of receiving a reward for leading them to stolen goods. Clark and his companions had to make a hasty exit and run for the beach, with the result that the tall and lanky general arrived at the agreed spot lacking his trousers. When he later met with reporters, Clark seemed to enjoy reliving his adventure, a mission special both for the *Seraph* and for the general.

22

MASSACRE IN THE NORTH

"The Arctic was new to us in the *U-255*, and strange," recalled the skipper, the twenty-seven-year-old Lieutenant Reinhard Reche, "and strange it remained for as long as we were there." Off Jan Mayen Island, far north of Iceland, the sea was "like silk, covered with a fluff of fog. Everything seemed intangible and mysterious. Strange birds followed the boat. The sun rarely broke through clearly enough to take a sight." It was the last week in June 1942, and with the sun always above the horizon "one lost all feeling for time; only the regular changing of the watch and the succession of meals told how late or early it was. But even then—was it breakfast or supper you were eating?" And vision never stayed clear for long, because "some kind of a shower would blot it out, usually snow. And those eternal curtains of fog!"

Indeed, everything in the Arctic seemed nebulous to Reche, including the movements of the Allied supply convoy for which the *U-255*, a VIIC 769-ton Atlantic U-boat, and a picket line of accompanying submarines—*Eisteufel* (Ice Devil)—of the Northern Waters Flotilla lay in wait in those northern waters. Then, out of one of the fog curtains, the faint shapes of two warships, probably destroyers, appeared, only to vanish after a brief chase. Next the *U-255*'s radio picked up a report from a boat that had established contact with the convoy and then lost it again.

Since the convoy was believed to be headed in the direction of Bear Island, making a wide sweep around the north of Norway to avoid attacks by German land-based aircraft on its way to North Russia, the *U-255* set off at high speed on a course that might lead to interception of the array of merchant ships and their sizable flock of escorts. The sound gear began providing evidence of the convoy's presence in the area and suddenly, as the fog started to lift, "there it was, the convoy served up on a plate before us!" A corvette appeared, belching black smoke, and then another, forcing the U-boat to dive, but before it did Reche noted that "the escorts were having their work cut out shepherding the convoy and in those conditions it can't have been an easy job, holding a bunch of civilian skippers together" (an unconscious echo of one of the chief objections to instituting convoy raised by British Admiralty officials twenty-five years earlier).

For a full day the *U-255* rushed ahead toward what the skipper hoped would prove a favorable position for attack, but during that time the convoy changed course, so that all the submarine could spot was a destroyer in the port screen, while the merchantmen passed safely by unseen. But presently "the sky was full of aircraft, all ours, heading northward," and several hours later a flight of torpedo bombers followed this first wave, while an observation plane guided the U-boats to the convoy. "We could see the masts of sinking ships," Reche said, "with escorts standing by." Diving, the *U-255* covered the last stretch underwater, and when she surfaced again the escorts were making off, leaving their charges to look out for themselves.

In a while the *U-255* picked out as a victim a huge freighter ("a choice morsel indeed") while receiving reports of other U-boat attacks on other lone ships. The escorts had all fled the field, leaving the merchant ships, helpless as chicks, to scatter as best they could and hope that fate would allow them to survive. Reche bagged his chosen target, the *Alcoa Ranger*, 10,800 tons ("some hors d'oeuvre!"), and his crewmen handed bread and water to the survivors in the lifeboats and indicated for them a course across the Barents Sea for the far-off, frozen, and uninhabited Soviet island of Novaya Zemlya, the nearest land. Reche surmised that the Luftwaffe air strike had forced the convoy to take the desperate step of dispersing. But he was quite wrong.

■ ■ ■

The series of convoys from the West to Murmansk and Archangel ranked among the most bitterly debated Allied operations of the entire war. At bottom, this ferrying of supplies through Arctic waters flanked for hundreds of miles by German airfields and ship anchorages amounted to a political act. Many Allied strategists had few illusions about the outlook of their surly, if intermittently jovial, partner in the East. They did not feel that they could afford to forget how Stalin had remained Hitler's faithful colleague from the concluding of their surprise agreement in August 1939 until June 22, 1941, when the Germans had roared eastward onto the great Russian plain. Stalin had leaned over so far backward to avoid involvement in the war that his border forces were swiftly trampled by the onslaught of the Wehrmacht. As hard as many of them tried, Western analysts could not see into Stalin's mind, but his past behavior made it reasonable to consider the possibility that he might aim at getting out of the war at the smallest cost, leaving Germany and the western powers to go on with it; perhaps, if he had luck with him, he could even pick up some chips here and there.

In this context, Roosevelt and Churchill agreed on the urgency of countering that nightmarish prospect with more than simple words of encouragement and talk of future activities. In these earlier years of the war, only Russia stood in a position to do real damage to the German Army, as the prime minister pointed out. The western powers must do everything they could, even if it might lack logistical justification and should prove arduous and wasteful, to demonstrate their wholehearted support for a Soviet war effort becoming increasingly desperate as Wehrmacht pincers encircled whole armies and Russian cities fell to the advancing enemy. Even given all that, Churchill, as head of the government responsible for the actual operating of the convoys and closer to the specific problems facing the Admiralty, had his doubts.

On August 21, 1941, within two months of the German attack, the first convoy sailed from Iceland for Murmansk, a primitive hellhole in extreme northwest Russia, on the Kola Inlet of the Barents Sea; an ice-free port, it had come into being twenty-five years earlier, when Russia's World War I armies found their normal supply routes choked off by German power. This inaugural convoy consisted of only seven merchant ships, but it carried Hurricane fighter planes—the real if unheralded stars of the Battle of Britain—as well as rubber, tin, and other urgently needed raw materials. By the end of the year, fifty-three cargo ships had reached North Russia; their deliveries, in fact far more than symbolic, included almost 600 tanks, 800 airplanes, and 1,400 vehicles, as well as 100,000 tons of general military supplies.

This success, accomplished without the loss of a single cargo ship, came in good part because the Germans allowed it to happen. They seemed to be looking elsewhere, not realizing the treasures that were slipping past the North Cape and into the hands of their Soviet ene- mies, who in spite of predictions by most of the military experts, Al- lied as well as German, had failed to collapse before the German fury. (The western political experts, Roosevelt and Churchill, felt less sur- prise than their military advisers.)

Early in 1942 the convoy picture began to change. For some time the Führer had been nursing one of his famous "intuitions," a mode of thought that, disconcertingly often, had proved more accurate than the most careful analyses produced by the army and navy staffs. This time Hitler feared that, with the United States now in the war, the Allies might assault his long, exposed Norwegian flank, a concern not lacking some basis in fact. In October Churchill had informed FDR that he planned a "descent upon the Norwegian coast" to distract the enemy from British operations in Libya; the idea received no support from the prime minister's military and naval advisers (in fact, they hooted at it), but Churchill nevertheless kept the idea alive. A Norwegian landing, Hitler declared, must be repelled at all costs, a task befitting his surface ships. Hence the new battleship *Tirpitz,* the almost identical twin of the once mighty and now vanished *Bismarck* (sunk in the Atlantic in May 1941), received orders to go north to Trondheim, at the top of the Norwegian bulge. The other available capital ships would accompany her, and submarines and torpedo-bomber squadrons would protect the surface vessels. The U-boats quickly acquired coats of white paint, and crews embellished their conning towers with the figures of polar bears.

Thus, inadvertently, the Germans set the stage for heavy assaults on the Murmansk convoys. German plans and Allied worries at this time both focused on the *Tirpitz.* A worthy namesake of the old admiral with the heavy eyelids and the billowing fork beard, the battleship dis- placed 43,000 tons (slightly more than the *Bismarck*), which made her the largest capital ship ever built in Europe and bigger than any American battleships except those of the final World War II giant class, the *Iowa* and her sisters, including the renowned *Missouri*. She carried eight 15-inch (380mm.) guns, the largest caliber the Germans ever employed, and could reach 31 knots, only about half a knot below the maximum of a commerce raider like the battleship/battle cruiser *Scharnhorst*. Despite some inadequacies in her armor protection, the *Tirpitz* had to be considered formidable in every way: She could break out to spread terror in the Atlantic, she could menace the convoys with their escorting warships bound for Russia.

As the spring days of 1942 grew longer and longer, the Admiralty's worries about the convoys grew proportionately with the sunlight. Despite Lieutenant Reche's first impression of northern weather, these latitudes offered few periods in which the cargo ships and their escorts could slip unobtrusively through the sea, and sometimes even hazy weather would help the German air attackers; a thin layer would form perhaps a thousand feet above the water, providing a perfect shield for Luftwaffe bombers. Having suffered the perhaps unique experience of losing two flagships in just two weeks, Rear Admiral Stuart Bonham-Carter had no doubts about the unwisdom of maintaining the convoys in the existing conditions. "If they must continue for political reasons," he wrote, "very serious and heavy losses must be expected," and he added, "We in the Navy are paid to do this sort of job but it is beginning to ask too much of the men of the Merchant Navy." In a letter to Admiral King, Admiral Pound judged the convoy situation "a most unsound operation with dice loaded against us in every direction." "All realised that a disaster was likely," wrote an Admiralty staff officer, "but when and on which convoy would it fall?"

These forebodings came from the professional naval officers. The politicians knew the dangers, too, but on their visits to their map rooms they saw the power of the Wehrmacht's 1942 offensive on the Eastern Front, with bulges swelling toward the Caucasus and the Volga and a still unfamous Stalingrad. The Russians were crying for a second front, partly because they devoutly wished for one, but also because making incessant demands gave them the possibility of getting other things they wanted, like the convoys, and in Britain thousands of ordinary citizens joined in the clamor. The United States pushed for a second

front, too, until these wishes dissolved in the glare of inescapable military and logistical fact: The seasoned troops and the needed equipment
did not exist. Thus, failing the second front, the Americans pushed all
the harder for the Arctic convoys, and the Admiralty in Whitehall felt
the convergence of all these pressures.

■ ■ ■

In the middle of the afternoon of June 27, 1942, the largest Murmansk
convoy yet assembled began its single-file departure from the rock-
framed harbor of Hvalfjordur, on the west coast of Iceland, bound on
a 2,000-mile journey that would take these ships far north, around
Bear Island, a forlorn outcropping lying between the North Cape and
Spitsbergen, and then south again into the Kola Inlet—that is, if all
went well. "Like so many dirty ducks they waddled out past the nets
and out to sea," wrote a watching diarist, the dashing Hollywood star
Douglas Fairbanks, Jr., now a lieutenant on an escorting cruiser, the U.S.S.
Wichita. "No honors or salutes were paid to them as they passed,
such as there are for naval vessels. But everyone who was watching
paid them a silent tribute and offered them some half-thought
prayer."

The freighters, the core of the whole operation, numbered thirty-
six. With them sailed three specially fitted-out rescue ships, and two
oilers carried fuel for the destroyers, which had the assignment of
fending off U-boats. The bonanza the merchantmen carried for the
Russians, lashed on decks and crammed into holds, included 156,492
tons of American Lend-Lease matériel: almost three hundred airplanes,
almost six hundred tanks, and more than four thousand trucks, as well
as supplies of varied kinds. Even though the North Russian convoys
served political and psychological ends, these thirty-six merchant ships
did not sail merely as symbols: They hauled enough equipment to put
several divisions in the field.

Despite the tactical disadvantages of sailing in the summer, the crews
of the ships in this convoy could at least feel some relief that they
would not have to contend with the gales that struck convoys in winter, with waves, driven by winds roaring all the way from Greenland
across the thousand miles of Arctic sea, that might tower 70 feet high.

Spray would freeze solid as soon as it hit the decks and rigging; a ship would quickly find itself encased in a foot-thick layer of ice. In the darkness a lookout had no function, since he could not even see the bow of his own ship. Sometimes, when men returned to their quarters below, with tears frozen on their cheeks, their eyebrows and eyelashes would thaw out and fall off. Nevertheless, the darkness and the hurricane-force winds conspired to keep the Luftwaffe's fliers out of the air.

The convoy bore the designation PQ-17 (according to legend that may have been true, the code identification *PQ* simply happened to be the personal initials of some functionary in the Admiralty). Twenty-two of PQ-17s freighters were American, with crews made up partly of young men fresh from the Merchant Marine Academy but mostly of veteran sailors, some of whom had already escaped from ships torpedoed by U-boats or sunk by gunfire from surface raiders. They made their living by serving on merchant ships—had done it for twenty or thirty years, in many cases—and when, a few months earlier, the ships had been caught up in a war, so had they; but they had not asked for it. "We weren't fighting men when we started out," said one veteran of Arctic convoys, "but just a simple bunch of guys that you'd find in any union hall or along any dock in an American port."

The authorities provided the convoy with three types of protection: (1) a *close escort* of destroyers, corvettes, and antiaircraft ships; (2) *close support* from four cruisers (two U.S., two British), with their destroyer screen; (3) the *distant covering force,* including two battleships, an aircraft carrier, and other vessels. One of the battleships, the brand-new U.S.S. *Washington,* like the two U.S. cruisers had joined the Royal Navy on loan because operations elsewhere in the world had left the British short-handed at home. For the first time in the war, a substantial American force had sailed under British operational command.

The commander in chief of the Home Fleet, Admiral Sir John Tovey, a statesmanlike figure and an outspoken sailor whose bluntness displeased Winston Churchill (the prime minister had spoken of him as a "stubborn and obstinate man"), virulently opposed the continuation of the Arctic convoys during the season of the midnight sun. As commander of the distant covering force, he made the strength of his

272 · THE SUBMARINE

feelings evident when, after reading the minutes of a June 4 meeting concerning the possibility of increasing the convoys, he protested to Admiral Pound that the record contained a gross understatement of the objections he had raised. The First Sea Lord promised to have the minutes amended.

Thus far, for almost a year now, the Allies had enjoyed relative luck in the Arctic. They had experienced casualties and sinkings, like the misadventures of the luckless Admiral Bonham-Carter with his two cruiser flagships, but no great catastrophe had struck. This luck, Tovey declared, could not hold. Sooner or later would come "sheer bloody murder."

■ ■ ■

At the end of May 1942, Grand Admiral Raeder paid a visit to Admiral Otto Schniewind, commander of Naval Group Command North, aboard the *Tirpitz* in her berth at Trondheim. The Führer, like the Kaiser before him, dreaded the thought of losing a great ship or even of having it suffer damage; the *Bismarck* had been lost on her first foray into the open sea, and that fate must not befall her sister. Raeder, for his part, had not been convinced early in 1942 that the *Tirpitz* would be best employed in attacks on convoys. But in March the authorities had ordered the giant battleship out on what proved a fruitless search for a PQ convoy, and on her way home she had been assaulted by a swarm of torpedo bombers from the British aircraft carrier *Victorious*. The inexperience of the attacking fliers in carrying out this kind of operation, together with a good measure of pure luck, had enabled the *Tirpitz* to escape unscathed. But the near miss had shaken the Germans.

On June 18, nine days before Convoy PQ-17 sailed from Iceland, the Admiralty received some vital information, which came not from the Ultra codebreakers but from Swedish intelligence operatives listening in on German landline telephone messages to headquarters in Norway. This source declared that the Germans had made plans for an all-out attack on the next North Russia convoy, using U-boats, bombers, and surface ships. "Surface ships" was bound to mean the *Tirpitz*.

Just before the Home Fleet sailed on its distant-covering mission, Admiral Pound, speaking on the telephone to Admiral Tovey at Scapa

Flow, made a final point. If the convoy seemed to confront direct danger of attack by surface ships, said the First Sea Lord, the Admiralty might intervene and order it to scatter. Scatter! Tovey reacted with shock. If the convoy were to lose its close order, its network of mutual support, it would be stripping itself of its basic protection and of its very definition. The freighters would become individual lost sheep, wandering through the sea before the covetous eyes of Admiral Dönitz's wolves in their Arctic white.

For four days PQ-17 plowed through the Arctic swells at its 8-knot pace, the forward motion so slow as to seem almost imagined, the gray rows of ships holding steady on station. The Admiralty had given PQ-17 a path farther to the north than recent convoys had taken, because in summer the Arctic ice pack retreated. The changed routing made the journey longer but kept the ships farther from the Luftwaffe bases in northern Norway. Even though it was the warmest time of the year, deep green floe ice, chiseled into fantastic shapes, lay on the rolling sea. Some of the pieces stood 20 or 30 feet high; seamen on deck could feel the chill from them as they drifted past. The fog buoys trailing behind the ships would crunch along the floes or leap over them, and sometimes the tow lines would snap.

Early in the afternoon of July 1, aircraft engines sounded in the fog astern, and soon there appeared a big four-engine Focke-Wulf Kondor, one of the planes that served as eyes for the U-boats. And where their reconnaissance aircraft spotted targets, there the wolves would soon appear. Indeed, that same evening the German admiral radioed Lieutenant Reche and two other U-boat skippers a simple order: "Shadow."

■ ■ ■

Admiral Sir Dudley Pound turned sixty-five in 1942, a vigorous age for many men but not for the First Sea Lord. His severe arthritis often granted him only fitful sleep as he lay on his camp bed in his office, where he spent most nights, and some days he appeared to be exhausted, utterly worn out. As the war went on, the admiral's health steadily ebbed; his exhaustion seemed mental as well as physical. In spite of his condition, Pound had a continuing way of intervening in the operations of fleets at sea, often on small details. Though certainly extreme and unhealthy, and upsetting to members of the Naval Staff, this practice did not actually violate British tradition, which, far more than American, allowed for intervention of the high commands of both the army and the navy even in operations in theaters far distant from the central authorities; the American way, on the other hand, seemed, studiedly or not, to reflect the federalism of the country's governmental and political structure. One reason tempting Pound to intervene in operations was simply the availability of information about the enemy, thanks to Ultra.

While PQ-17 was proceeding on its course, Admiral Tovey, one of the line officers who had great faith in intelligence (commanders varied in their views of it), pressed the Admiralty not only for the latest information about German movements but also for word about just when he could expect such information; since the time required to decrypt Enigma ciphers varied, this request did him credit as tactician and commander. Early in the morning of July 3 the admiral received big news: *Rösselsprung* (Knight's Move) was scheduled to come that day (the codebreakers even supplied the operational code name). This meant only that German battleships had left Trondheim on their way north to temporary bases from which they could assault the convoy, not that they were ready to attack. Although air reconnaissance had spotted PQ-17 on July 1, the six U-boats that had answered the Kondor's call had been driven off by the convoy's close destroyer escort. Initially, in fact, the Germans had misjudged the situation by mistaking Rear Admiral Louis Hamilton's escorting cruiser force for the distant covering battleships and ordering the U-boats to seek it out, but they quickly abandoned the pursuit of the phantom target and specifically pursued the convoy's merchantmen. In the evening a Luftwaffe torpedo bomber attack had failed to sink a single one of the freighters. Then fog had shrouded PQ-17, so that the convoy survived without a casualty until the early morning of July 4, when a lone torpedo bomber struck an American merchantman through a hole in the fog.

Heavier action then came at about 8:15 in the evening, when the radarscope on one of the escorting destroyers showed a line of blips on the horizon. A few minutes later one of the antiaircraft ships began signaling the approach of eight bombers, then ten, then twelve, then eighteen. Finally the loudspeaker roared: "Good God, there's twenty-five!" The U.S. destroyer, normally part of the screen for Hamilton's cruisers but just at that time visiting the convoy to refuel, unhooked from the oiler and dashed into action, circling the convoy, putting up such devastatingly accurate fire that the attackers jettisoned their torpedoes and fled the scene. On the other side of the convoy, however, the assaulting Heinkels had scored three hits; nevertheless, a wave of optimism, even self-congratulation, swept through the escorts. U-boats had failed, now marauding bombers had been repelled, and no sign of surface attack had been seen. Perhaps PQ-17 was going to make it.

◼ ◼ ◼

The central scene in the drama of command unfolded at about the time the torpedo bombers were attacking the convoy, with Admiral Pound and Commander Norman Denning, director of the Operational Intelligence Centre, as the actors. From intelligence intercepts the OIC had learned that the *Tirpitz* had arrived at nine o'clock that morning at Altenfjord, the advance base. Ominously—perhaps—the message added, "Destroyers and torpedo boats ordered to complete with fuel at once." When these supporting ships had filled up, what was to happen? When would the *Tirpitz* sail? Or had she sailed already? If she had, she could, the staff estimated, reach PQ-17 by two o'clock the next morning.

The First Sea Lord came to the Citadel behind the Admiralty, to take a personal look at the situation. A "concrete ship," as Commander Kenneth Knowles characterized it, the Citadel ranked as the most secret part of the British naval operation. An array of machine guns protected it against attack, and on short notice it could be flooded. Its inhabitants "worked themselves to death. They were poorly fed, and they didn't see the light of the sun for years. They were just like moles down there."

Not only was Admiral Pound ailing and weary, he was constitutionally taciturn; he did not arrive at decisions by means of give-and-take debate. Sitting down on a stool in front of the main plotting table, he asked Denning a blunt question: "Do you know if *Tirpitz* has put to sea?" As the founding father of the OIC, five years earlier, with the special duty of keeping watch on the German surface fleet, Denning understood the nuances of the situation as well as anyone could. The codebreakers had not yet cracked the naval Enigma cipher for that day, so that if the *Tirpitz* for some reason had sent a message indicating that she had *not* sailed, Denning would not yet know of it. But he had relevant evidence nevertheless: A battleship at sea received a regular flow of messages from headquarters ashore, in the Kriegsmarine as in the Royal Navy. But monitoring posts had picked up no such radio transmissions. Besides, patrolling British and Soviet submarines had sent in no sighting reports. Denning and his colleagues therefore felt confident that the super-battleship had not left the shelter of the fjord. Accordingly, Denning replied to Pound: "If *Tirpitz* has put to sea, you can be sure that we should have known very shortly afterwards, within four to six hours."

Not satisfied, Pound then swung his hammer a bit more heavily: "Can you assure me that *Tirpitz* is still at anchor in Altenfjord?"

A pioneer in methods of ship plotting, Denning had no doubt that he was right, but he had no smoking gun to display. No, he told Pound, he would only have firm evidence after the *Tirpitz* had sailed. Ultra decrypts should shortly be coming through that would, he believed, confirm his view that the battleship had not left harbor.

Pound fired a third question: "Can you at least tell me whether *Tirpitz* is ready to go to sea?"

She would not leave for a few hours, Denning said—he was sure of that because her destroyer escorts had not yet come out to make an antisubmarine sweep, an activity the watching Allied submarines would certainly have spotted.

When, within a few minutes, the expected Ultra decrypts began arriving, they contained nothing to suggest that the *Tirpitz* had sailed, although, not surprisingly, they did not say that the big ship had *not* put to sea. Admiral Pound went off to a staff meeting, at which the fate of PQ-17 would be settled. Denning, deeply disturbed, remained at his post. What else ought he to have said to the First Sea Lord? Should he have pointed out that negative intelligence as well as positive intelligence can tell a valid story? On other occasions, negative intelligence (the absence of orders to ships at sea, for instance) had been accepted by the Admiralty, which had acted in accordance with it and with good results. In the present situation, Denning attached great significance to one particular negative: Since the *Tirpitz* had arrived at Altenfjord, British listening posts had picked up no message in the *Offizier* (most secret) setting of naval Enigma, as would certainly have been the case if she had sailed. But Admiral Pound had not asked for any opinions, any background facts, any qualifying thoughts. He made his decisions in his own way.

At 8:30 the intelligence pipeline produced a decrypt containing what amounted to positive proof that the *Tirpitz* had not sailed at midday. The German command had told the U-boats off the North Cape that they need not worry about encountering any of their own heavy ships that day; the only battleships they would see would be British—targets to be destroyed. The OIC sent this news to the First Sea Lord, but he had already made up his mind. His orders went out from the Admiralty at 9:36.

■ ■ ■

With his First Cruiser Squadron, Admiral Hamilton, a genial, pipe-smoking career officer widely known in the Royal Navy as "Turtle," kept watch over PQ-17 at distances varying from 10 to 30 miles. Some minutes past 9:30 in the evening of July 4, an explosive message from the Admiralty arrived on the bridge of Hamilton's flagship, the cruiser *London*.

MOST IMMEDIATE. CRUISER FORCE IS TO WITHDRAW TO WEST-WARD AT HIGH SPEED.

In a few minutes came a second order:

IMMEDIATE. OWING TO THREAT OF SURFACE SHIPS CONVOY IS TO DISPERSE AND PROCEED TO RUSSIAN PORTS.

And then a third:

MOST IMMEDIATE. MY 9.23 OF THE 4TH. CONVOY IS TO SCATTER.

The "my" in the third message meant Admiral Pound himself. This message added nothing to the second but simply represented an emendation of "disperse" to "scatter"—no clustering; neither verb represented good news for the merchantmen. Hamilton reacted with shock. The desperate orders meant first that the convoy would lose its covering force and second that the cargo ships were being sent off individually into the crepuscular Arctic night. To Hamilton, and to Admiral Tovey as well, this could mean only one thing: The Admiralty had acquired information that for some reason it had not yet passed on. The *Tirpitz* had gone to sea, perhaps was almost on the convoy. At any moment her superstructure might appear on the horizon. A battle loomed in prospect, one that in its first stages would pit just the four cruisers against the superbattleship.

But there was no shooting, no enemy surface ship. Instead, about five hours later, Tovey received another message from the Admiralty: "It is not known if German heavy forces have sailed from Altenfjord," but they could hardly have done so before noon of July 4. Another message indicated the caution of the Germans: They might perhaps believe that a battleship was accompanying Hamilton's four cruisers. And it appeared that the enemy had not succeeded in finding out the whereabouts of the Home Fleet, the distant-covering force. Tovey knew the thrust of these points: The enemy would not risk sailing until they knew just what they were up against.

But this information came too late for PQ-17. Amazed, disbelieving, the men on the merchant ships had watched the four cruisers sail off westward, abandoning them in the night. (The action puzzled the German authorities, too: What were the British up to?) To the dismay of the officers and crews of the merchantmen, the destroyers took it on themselves to go with the cruisers. This defection directly affected the men on the merchant ships, because, while the supporting-force cruisers might have other obligations, it was the destroyers that represented the line of defense against U-boats. The men could not know that the destroyer-escort commander believed that he was joining the cruiser force for the battle he expected at any moment. Even the small anti-submarine craft scattered.

Some of the freighters proceeded individually, some out of desperation clubbed together. Already on the edge of the pack ice, they could go no farther northward. The dispersal point was 240 miles from the North Cape and more than 450 miles from the forbidding coast of

Novaya Zemlya, and the enemy would be right with the freighters while they tried to reach it. Even when hailed from Allied ships, the shattered crewmen in the lifeboats and on the rafts often refused to leave them. The ships would soon be sunk anyway. What was the point of coming aboard? At first the German U-boat commanders could not believe their remarkable good fortune, but they quickly rallied, spreading the word about the rich and easy rewards.

So dense did the traffic become that Reinhard Reche in the *U-255* found himself having to fire at a target hastily because another ship loomed up almost on top of him. But he had no need to chase either of those because, "conveniently," a third put in an appearance and "this time the torpedo found its mark." Now everything turned to be fun. "We got up the ammunition," the skipper said, "and the sailors were allowed to amuse themselves gunning her from the surface with the 88-millimeter. They left the good ship *Cleopatra* a blazing wreck." The deck gun soon claimed another victim, and by this time, Reche thought, "the area must be getting a bad name." Deciding to move on to intercept ships that had escaped the inferno, he took his boat southwest to a position athwart the route to Archangel.

Bizarrely enough, a rickety old Russian biplane came zooming in, forcing the *U-255* to dive, and the skipper took her off to the north where, in accordance with orders, she combed the area for stragglers from the convoy. Reche and his men now made an interesting find, an abandoned Dutch ship stuck in pack ice. She had been torpedoed, and the crew had obviously left in a hurry; breakfast still sat on the table. More important, German sailors found a metal box containing the new operational codes for convoys and a list of the ships that had made up PQ-17. The Germans, said Reche, were thus "able to announce the fate of the famous PQ-17 before even the enemy knew it himself." Even though they had not literally destroyed the entire convoy, the Germans had scored a great triumph, to which Reche and his boat contributed the sinking of three freighters (four, including the abandoned wreck of the Dutch *Paulus Potter*), for a total of about 18,000 tons.

Returning from Murmansk, Convoy QP-13 had found itself under air attack in the vicinity of Bear Island. Then, as suddenly as they had appeared, the bombers vanished, a welcome development that then

280 · THE SUBMARINE

produced a good measure of anguish when the crews heard, from the south, the noise of battle and realized that the real Luftwaffe target was a fat new eastbound convoy that had arrived in the area and was now undergoing sea and air assault. For two days the explosions sounded until, as the seamen correctly concluded, the convoy had been wiped out.

■ ■ ■

When the dimensions of the slaughter had become clear, Winston Churchill told his touchy Soviet ally, "with the greatest regret," that he and the Admiralty had "reached the conclusion that to attempt to run the next convoy, PQ 18, would bring no benefit to you and would involve dead loss to the common cause." Indeed, out of nearly 600 tanks in PQ-17, almost 500 had been lost. Stalin fired back a "rough and surly answer": His "naval experts" considered the British reasons "wholly unconvincing"; he had "never expected" such a decision.

For the prime minister, however, the reckoning meant that the entire vexed question of the Arctic convoys must be reconsidered, and the government immediately took the decision to suspend all these convoys for some weeks, until the days grew shorter. The final count for PQ-17 showed twenty-four of the merchantmen sunk by German attack (earlier, two of the ships had suffered other difficulties and been forced to return to port). The adventures of the survivors comprised a saga of life rafts and small boats, like those from the *Alcoa Ranger* setting out across the Barents Sea, and for many that grim chapter represented death only postponed. In the final accounting, just eleven of the cargo ships reached Russia; the last straggler, the freighter *Winston-Salem,* would not turn up until July 28. Of the dispersal and its consequences, Rear Admiral Samuel Eliot Morison, the American official historian, said, "There has never been anything like it in our maritime history." In his official dispatch Admiral Tovey, not overstating the case, declared that "the order to scatter the convoy had been premature; its results were disastrous." Though it had not come quite in the form he had expected, the assault proved to be the "sheer bloody murder" he had foreseen.

Even before the revelation of the Bletchley Park operation and its Ultra secret in the 1970s enabled commentators to go back and look over Pound's shoulder in July 1942, American naval opinion had blamed the admiral for ignoring the well-known German pattern of refusing to risk surface ships in actions with convoy escorts of even cruiser strength, let alone battleships. As a German admiral later observed: "It is remarkable how a mere report of the possible appearance of the *Tirpitz* and her accompanying destroyers could so influence the situation." Pound's actions also demonstrated the truth of the age-old point that information from intelligence has no value apart from its proper use; fortunately for the Allies, Ultra intelligence from naval Enigma would have a great part to play in the drama of the coming months.

Beyond the immediate scene, Admiral King's disgust over the pointless and ungallant employment of the *Washington,* one of the only two new United States battleships, and of the two cruisers led him to withdraw these ships and transfer them to the Pacific for action against Japan, the use he had originally intended for them. Henceforth, King, as an observer mildly put it, viewed combined U.S.-British naval operations with disfavor. He was said by some to have declared that none of his ships would ever again sail under a British admiral.

The Führer published a statement of his own praising the conduct of *Rösselsprung* and ordered his observations included in a training manual issued to the fleet. It bore the tragically appropriate title *Convoy Slaughter in the Arctic Sea.* Before another North Russian convoy would sail, the British would take a number of protective measures, including establishing bases for patrol planes outside Murmansk, enhancing the defensive power of merchantmen, and assigning more warships to escort duty, though the Admiralty would reject Churchill's proposal to assign practically the entire Home Fleet to the task of fighting the next convoy through.

During the course of the war the Western Allies would send forty-two convoys through Arctic waters to Murmansk and Archangel; of the 848 ships involved, sixty-five would succumb to attack by U-boats and Luftwaffe aircraft. The westbound convoys, which numbered thirty-six, would lose forty of their total of 735 vessels. Thus, overall, the North Russian convoys lost 105 ships, a figure grim in itself but one that throws into sharp relief the nightmarish outlines of the toll—more than two-thirds—the enemy took on the merchant ships of PQ-17. The floor of the Barents Sea remains today a great junkyard with the carcasses of thousands of trucks, tanks, and aircraft, a loss to the Allied cause equal to what it would have suffered in a major battle. For the U-boats it had proved to be a rare feast, beginning with Lieutenant Reche's tempting hors d'oeuvre.

■ ■ ■

Just by her presence in the North, the *Tirpitz* had created a calamity for the Allied cause and an embarrassment for the Royal Navy. The British found the long shadow cast by the great battleship intolerable, and they resolved to invade her fjord and do their best to put her out of business. (Churchill's personal irritation showed itself in a carping message to Admiral Pound: "Is it really necessary to describe the *Tirpitz* as the *Admiral von Tirpitz* in every signal? This must cause a considerable waste of time for signalmen, cipher staff, and typists. Surely *Tirpitz* is good enough for the beast.") The instrument of attack the British chose was a kind of craft that had aroused little interest in the United States but exerted considerable appeal for the British and also for the Italians: the midget submarine.

In this same year, 1942, the Royal Navy had developed a two-man, battery-powered "human torpedo" called the Chariot, modeled after an Italian midget that in the previous year had sunk three cargo ships at Gibraltar and, in an audacious attack, had severely damaged two Royal Navy battleships in Alexandria harbor. Attacks by Chariots, however, failed to damage the *Tirpitz,* and the British moved on to the "X-craft," a larger vessel that was actually a 45-foot submarine with a crew of four. In a procedure reminiscent of David Bushnell's method of attack in 1776, the X-craft would sneak up on its intended victim and a diver would leave the vessel to place charges under the hull of the ship. Forced to wait out the summer 1943 midnight-sun season, the British made their move in September. On the twenty-second divers from two X-craft (out of six that had set out on the mission) succeeded against remarkable odds in reaching the *Tirpitz* and planting charges that went off under her keel, damaging her enough to set her up for aerial attacks that partially crippled her. Transferred to the port of Tromsö, the *Tirpitz* succumbed to the blows of a British bomber force on November 12, 1944.

23

"TOO MUCH FOR THE HUN"

arly in the morning of March 5, 1943, a line of merchant ships began moving down the North River (mariners' name for the lower Hudson), through the upper and lower New York bays, and out into open water; four Canadian Navy destroyers accompanied these vessels. As the war developed, Canada had assumed perhaps half of the Allied escort burden, "building many scores of warships and merchant ships, some of them thousands of miles from salt water, and sending them forth manned by hardy Canadian seamen to guard the Atlantic convoys." Beyond the Ambrose Lightship the merchantmen began assembling in convoy formation, in accordance with the instructions the skippers had received the previous day at the sailing conference, at which they had also been given some idea of what they might expect from U-boats on the coming passage of the North Atlantic. This convoy bore the designation SC-122, meaning that it was the one-hundred-twenty-second in the series of eastbound slow convoys; it would sail at a pace of about 7 knots.

Behind SC-122 would come two faster convoys, HX-229 and HX-229A. Altogether this collection of ships would number 141, with thirty-one of them joining the convoy from Halifax. Most were of British registry, but twenty-nine were American, and a number of other countries were represented in the total. Altogether the ships carried almost a million tons of cargo, from munitions to tanks and aircraft to wheat and frozen beef—all of the kinds of goods that not only enabled Britain to keep fighting but also had to be sent across the ocean to be stockpiled for a future Allied invasion of the Continent. During the afternoon of the next day the weather, which had been favorable enough, turned more typical for the North Atlantic at this time

284

of year, with heavy rain and strong winds that blew themselves up into a gale. At this season commodores of convoys could hardly maintain the tight patterns favored by the planners, and the light of morning showed that during the night the storm had scattered the ships over a wide area of ocean. At midday, when the escorts, moving busily like sheep dogs, had brought their charges back together at the prearranged rendezvous point, eleven proved to be missing, though only one turned out to have serious problems.

On March 8, one of the faster convoys, HX-229, sailed from New York, to be followed the next day by HX-229A; both of these missed the big storm. Aboard the merchantmen, as the crewmen went about their work—four hours on, four hours off, seven days a week—life quickly took on its quiet, even boring standard routine. Off duty, sailors played cards, shot the bull, and read. The boredom could vanish in an instant, giving way to restrained tension, if any kind of activity— a scout plane, a distress call from a ship—suggested the presence in the area of U-boats, and General Quarters might sound at any time. If you worked in the black gang, down in the engine room, one veteran re- called, you could feel yourself intimately close to the frigid water out- side, with only a thin steel curtain between the two of you, and in the event of trouble "you don't know if you'll get out. All the time, you're expecting." During these weeks of the war, the North Atlantic formed a giant arena that seemed to be crammed with convoys. In addition to SC-122 and the two HX-229s, Admiral Dönitz's U-boats had as po- tential targets two earlier eastbound convoys, SC-121 and HX-228, and two westbound, ONS-169 and ON-170. The ocean arena likewise served as the stage for a much larger number of U-boats than for- merly; the increased production the admiral had looked forward to in 1941 and 1942 now allowed him to maintain his desired force of more than a hundred on patrol at a time. Since the beginning of the year Dönitz had held the chief responsibility not simply for the submarine arm but for the entire navy; in January, after a stormy session with Hitler, Admiral Raeder had insisted on resigning as commander in chief, and the Führer had called for the U-boat chief to replace him. This unlooked-for elevation to the top level meant that Dönitz had been required to transfer his work from his seafront headquarters in

Lorient to navy headquarters in Berlin, but he nevertheless kept the U-boat operational reins in his hands.

In the realm of radio intelligence, a major change had occurred: After a blackout of ten months Bletchley Park had regained the ability to decrypt messages in the Enigma Shark key. This happy event had come in good part as the result of the Royal Navy's capture, on October 30, 1942, of a U-boat in the Mediterranean. As had happened in earlier instances, like the seizure of Julius Lemp's *U-110,* and unlike what had happened once in 1940, when a similar great opportunity had been lost because sailors looted the German boat before responsible officers could intervene, the navy recovered a code book. This development, together with German carelessness in the use of the Enigma with the fourth rotor (they never seriously questioned their belief in the invulnerability of the machine to attack by cryptanalysts on the other side), by the beginning of December 1942 had enabled the Allied codebreakers to begin eavesdropping on operations again. Bletchley had actually divined the wiring of the fourth wheel in December 1941 when a German operator, using a four-wheel Enigma before it officially went into service, sent a message employing the four and then retransmitted it using just three wheels. This blunder would not have given the Ultra teams the ability to read Shark right off—new equipment was required, for one thing—but, nevertheless, delay at Bletchley had meant that in February 1942 naval Enigma ceased to be a source of information for the Allies for almost the entire year.

With a hundred U-boats at sea, Rodger Winn's U-boat Tracking Room received intercepted signals in great streams between Admiral Dönitz and his U-boats. Increasingly, Allied convoy escorts could locate the boats by means of sophisticated radio apparatus called "Huff-Duff" (HF/DF, or high-frequency direction finding). Installed in ships beginning in 1941, HF/DF could rapidly obtain a bearing even on signals too brief to be picked up by ordinary direction-finding gear. Its contribution to the Allied cause in the antisubmarine war probably equaled that of radar.

On March 14, informed by Ultra that a wolf pack was shadowing the westbound ON-170, the Admiralty ordered SC-122 and HX-229 to move out of harm's way and onto a more southerly course. But then the U-boats proceeded to abandon the ON-170 project and move toward the new anticipated track of the two big eastbound convoys. The eruption of another gale now favored the Allied ships, as this new storm held up the arrival of some of the U-boats, allowing SC-122 for the moment to slip unseen through the gap in the picket line. But on the morning of March 16 along came HX-229, and the arrival of these ships found the wolf packs ready for them.

Two years earlier, in their graduation ceremony in the main square of the Naval Academy at Flensburg, the group of newly minted ensigns had received a challenge from the speaker. "The time has come for you to show what you have learned," said this admiral. "You will prove yourselves for the sake of your country. You will take on England wherever you find her ships, and you will break her power at sea. You will win victory." Although these young men had heard such words many times before, one officer remembered, "the call to glory or death had lost none of its exciting challenge." And then, with a bow to the rival across the North Sea, the admiral closed with a suitably edited version of Lord Nelson's signal at Trafalgar: "This day Germany expects every man to do his duty."

Though some members of the class found themselves assigned to vessels ranging from minesweepers to battle cruisers, the majority received orders for the U-boat service. Now, in 1943, events had put one of these young men, Lieutenant Herbert Werner, in a situation that might give prophetic force to the graduation speaker's words about breaking England's power. The weather had disrupted the convoys, turning them into a great, scattered fleet of merchant ships, and within two days Dönitz had realized that what he had taken to be a single convoy, SC-122, actually was two, giving him a huge potential bag of far more than a hundred ships. To make the most of this fantastic opportunity, he sent out a torrent of messages, ordering eighteen U-boats to concentrate on HX-229 and thirteen on SC-122.

Sailing through the night, through snow squalls and against strong winds, Werner's *U-230* "beat the sea to spray and foam." At 10:40 lookouts spotted shadows "the size of bugs" moving along the hazy moonlit horizon some four miles ahead. "It's the whole herd," the lookout called, and the *U-230* moved up from the southwest to cut into the starboard flank of this huge herd. Then, proceeding parallel to the convoy, the U-boat found two destroyers coming uncomfortably close, turned away through the rolling sea, and then turned back again, moving into firing position. Almost awed, the men on the U-boat stared as the procession of shadows passed before them, so thick that "their masts stuck up along the horizon like a heavy picket fence." The target, they realized, constituted one of the largest convoys ever to sail the Atlantic. With destroyers closing in, the skipper cried, "Exec, select your targets!"

Werner shouted into the hatch, "Tubes one to five, stand by! Ready . . . ready . . ."

"What are the fellows astern doing?" the worried captain called. Those destroyers could end the career of the *U-230* on the spot.

Werner, carefully aiming, did not want to tell the captain that the destroyers were gaining on them. "Holding steady," he said.

But the time was up. "Exec, shoot!" cried the captain.

Werner pulled the lever five times, and immediately the captain spun the boat around to head toward the tail of the convoy and away from the destroyers. As the U-boat smashed through the waves, Werner and his comrades "heard the terrific rumble of three hard explosions. Blinding flashes revealed cargo ships, destroyers, and trawlers." Racing away into the winter darkness (on this patrol the boat had now used up all of her torpedoes), the men on the *U-230* saw two freighters break apart, while another drifted away, out of sight. Throughout the night flashes lit up the sky in the distance and the detonations of torpedoes rumbled across the water.

Realizing that a slaughter was taking place out in the ocean, officers at the Admiralty in London looked desperately for reinforcements to strengthen the convoy's slim escort, and even though realizing the futility of the gesture in view of the distance and the storms in the Atlantic, they ordered three destroyers they found in Iceland (two American, one British) to rush to the scene. Meanwhile, on the scene, U-boat after U-boat performed just as the *U-230* had, slashing into the jumbled herd and overwhelming the escorts. The defenders had no chance to rescue seamen from torpedoed ships, who had to be left to freeze in the icy water, a process that would not take long. The Admiralty dispatched long-range aircraft to help the defenders, but constant snow showers blinded them.

The carnage went on in a "gigantic holocaust" until the morning of March 19, when the U-boats had run out of fuel and torpedoes and the convoys had come within 600 miles of Northern Ireland and thus within range of land-based antisubmarine aircraft. "Only then," Werner noted in a later reflection, "did the infernal battle come to a halt." Dönitz accurately called the operation "the greatest success ever achieved in a single convoy battle," characterizing it as "all the more creditable in that nearly half the U-boats involved scored at least one hit." In this triumph the wolf packs had sent to the bottom twenty-one ships of 140,842 tons, while suffering not a single loss. Overall, in this Black March, the first ten days had seen forty-one ships lost, and in the second ten days forty-four more went down, with the total exceeding half a million tons. As Churchill famously said, "The Battle of the Atlantic was the dominating factor all through the war. Never for one moment could we forget that everything happening elsewhere, on land, at sea, or in the air, depended ultimately on its outcome, and amid all other cares we viewed its changing fortunes day by day with hope or apprehension." Now, deeply shaken after the great convoy battle, some Admiralty officials put convoy itself into question: Perhaps it could no longer serve "as an effective system of defence." On the other hand, who had an alternative to offer? Nobody came forward.

Behind the influence of the storms and the power of the dozens of U-boats Dönitz now could assemble into his wolf packs loomed other great questions: How did the admiral know when to switch his U-boats from one part of the sea to another? How did he so often seem to know just where to find a convoy?

■ ■ ■

In August 1940 a unique British mission had arrived in Washington. Led by a physicist, Sir Henry Tizard, this mixed group of scientists and military officers had come with a small but priceless cargo, the secrets of devices that could help win the war. Tizard, who had formerly served as the chief adviser of the Air Ministry on air defense, owed his availability for the mission to the simple fact that when Churchill became prime minister, he brought with him his own personal scientist and statistician, and this bottle had room for only one scorpion; therefore, Tizard (objectively speaking, a superior scientist to Professor F. A. Lindemann, Churchill's man) had to go, but on departing he created the great conception of what would be known as the "Tizard Mission," which had as its aim the creation of a reciprocal, secret-sharing relationship with the Americans, which the British would launch with their cargo, including what one American scientist enthusiastically called "the most valuable cargo ever brought to our shores." This device was the cavity magnetron, a type of vacuum tube that would make possible microwave (centimetric) radar; this invention would lead to the development of airborne radar. The fitting of effective radar sets into aircraft first proved its value in defending against night air attacks on England, but by 1943 the airplane-plus-radar combination was yielding increasingly good results in the hunt for U-boats. After leading his group to a brilliant and lastingly significant success in the United States, Tizard had returned home to find that the government still had little use for his services. He was said not to be bitter, and then, within two years, he managed to get back into the main arena by becoming involved in a controversy with Lindemann.

Also in 1943 the new members of the surface antisubmarine family, destroyer escorts, would join the fleet. These ships carried 3-inch guns and, because of their greater maneuverability, actually proved more effective than destroyers against U-boats.

In still another development, this one pushed by Roosevelt against not only the lack of enthusiasm but also the actual opposition of his navy chiefs, escort carriers (dubbed "baby flattops") quickly proved their worth in the convoy battle by revolutionizing aerial surveillance. Independent "hunter-killer" groups, not tied to a particular convoy and based on an escort carrier, searched out and destroyed U-boats.

Altogether, by the middle of 1943 a profusion of inventions, devices, and tactics had begun to play key parts in the antisubmarine war. Ships on the prowl for submarines carried such weapons as the U.S. Hedgehog and Mousetrap and the British Squid, different types of ahead-throwing devices that could enable a ship to increase the effectiveness of depth charging by attacking a U-boat before reaching it. One

U-boat commander later said that everything together made the entire Atlantic seem to be under surveillance. As another captain summed it up: "The Allied counteroffensive at sea had struck with unexpected and unprecedented force. The British and Americans had quietly, steadily massed their forces. They had increased their fleet of fast corvettes, built a number of medium-sized aircraft carriers and converted a number of freighters into pocket-sized carriers, assembled squadrons of small planes for carrier duty as well as huge armadas of long-range land-based bombers" (particularly B-24s); no longer were there gaps in aerial protection. "Then they hit with frightening precision."

This officer did not know about the technical devices involved in this Allied success, but he knew and felt the results: In May, just two months after the great convoy slaughter, the Allies sank forty-eight U-boats. Though much travail and many sinkings remained, the tide had now turned in the Battle of the Atlantic. Everything together, said Admiral Sir Max Horton, the World War I submarine ace who now presided over the protection of convoys in British waters as commander of the Western Approaches, had become "too much for the Hun." The enemy might "wriggle as much as he likes, but the inherent disabilities of a submarine if properly exploited will reduce our losses in convoy to a reasonably small factor." That was spoken by a sailor who knew his submarines.

■ ■ ■

How had Admiral Dönitz possessed so much information about the whereabouts of Allied convoys? In the realm of cryptological intelligence, the Allies and the Germans turned out to have been locked in a strange, unconscious, continuing dance, with each party looking over the other's shoulder, but with varying timing and success. While Bletchley Park was having its adventures with Dolphin and Shark, Germany's B-dienst had moved on from its original success with the basic British code to crack Naval Cipher No. 2. After the United States entered the war, realizing the increased importance of the cipher, the veteran chief of the B-dienst's English section, Wilhelm Tranow—quietly famous for never forgetting the movements of a ship, even years after the fact—led his analysts in what, within a month, became a successful attack on Naval Cipher No. 3 (which, since this was not a true cipher, involved not breaking an encrypting system but reconstructing a code book).

The Germans gave No. 3 the official designation Frankfurt, but gleefully nicknamed it the "convoy cipher." Now, most of the time, they not only could read the convoy sailing telegrams but also could know in what areas the British believed the U-boats to be prowling and hence would avoid. This was the kind of information that had enabled Dönitz to send his U-boats after SC-122 when it had switched course from the northern track to the southern to avoid them. His uncertainty about the presence of HX-229 came simply from its sailing telegram's having presented the decoders with a few problems, so that he did not receive it as quickly as usual.

To crack messages encrypted on the Enigma, Bletchley Park used high-speed machines, originally inspired by the trailblazing Polish mathematicians, called Bombes (after an ice-cream dish favored by one of the Poles). Concerned at the losing battle in the Atlantic in 1942, and miffed over the British failure to make good on a promise to deliver a Bombe to Washington, the Americans went ahead with plans to make their own Bombe and announced to the British that they would mount their own attack on naval Enigma and produce a huge number of Bombes (360) to crack these ciphers. After some discussion, negotiators agreed on a total of a hundred for the Americans; a team at the National Cash Register Company in Dayton, Ohio, headed by a remarkably talented engineer, Joseph Desch, overcame a number of problems to develop a highly effective Bombe. In another result of the discussions, the Americans sent a contingent to work permanently at Bletchley.

Once Bletchley Park had again begun reading Shark, the dance with Dönitz became as intimate as a tango. Shark told the Allies where the U-boats were and what they were doing, while Frankfurt revealed details about the convoys and about what the British knew of German movements. Possibly a great deal of trouble could have been saved during this period, with little difference in the results, if neither side had bothered with ciphers at all. But after the spring battles the dance—belatedly—turned into the last tango. Bletchley Park became convinced that Shark decrypts contained information that could have come only from messages in the Royal Navy's own Cipher No. 3. Evidence of this problem, with its crucial significance, had existed for some time, but the Admiralty had moved and continued to move with culpable sluggishness before finally facing the issue—particularly culpable behavior since Commander Laurence Safford, one of the most important American cryptanalytic pioneers, had pointed out to his British colleagues the cipher's vulnerability. Although the Admiralty had available as an alternative the American Typex machine, which proved invulnerable to German attempts to break it, the British rejected it.

No one would know how many lives the Cipher No. 3 fiasco cost the Allied nations, but, as it was, in convoy operations overall perhaps one seaman in five perished. In any case, the availability of the Shark decrypts led Admiral King to push the use of decrypted material to make specific attacks, such as on refueling ("milch cow") submarines on which the U-boats depended. "With the information currently at our disposal," said a memorandum produced for King's staff, "we are now able to determine up to a week or ten days in advance the exact position of the refuelling area."

The obvious danger accompanying such an approach caused a good bit of perturbation at the Admiralty, with Admiral Pound sending King "expressions of alarm" concerning the danger of compromising the intelligence by making pinpoint use of it. King believed, however, that he could properly blunt the danger by employing such tactics as wrapping the attack on milch cows within a general attack on all U-boats. Besides, he felt with all his stubborn strength that the great rewards justified the running of some degree of risk.

Thus a measure of delicacy characterized relationships in intelligence matters between the Allies as they waged the Battle of the Atlantic. The stage had therefore been set for an eruption on the part of Admiral King if any American indiscretion threatened the security of the Ultra secret. And on June 4, 1944, one of the most celebrated exploits of the naval war did exactly that. Operating 150 miles off the coast of Rio de Oro, in west Africa, a hunter-killer group based on the escort carrier *Guadalcanal* and commanded by Captain Daniel V. Gallery focused on the *U-505*, homeward bound from patrol. Depth charges from the destroyer *Chatelain* forced the submarine to the surface, her crew abandoned her, and a boarding party from the destroyer *Pillsbury* took her over. Not only had the group performed the remarkable feat of capturing an intact submarine, but they now had in their possession the boat's two Enigma machines, codebooks, and other secret materials.

Commanders at the level of Captain Gallery received information based on Ultra intelligence, as King wished, but it came in disguised form, so that no one knew what sources had provided it. Hence the captain did not suspect that in seizing the German submarine with its decrypting equipment he had put Allied signals intelligence at possibly grave risk. Horrified when he received the news, King made sure that the prisoners picked up from the boat were kept in ignorance of the situation and led to believe that the submarine had sunk. For the duration of the war her survival was kept a secret from everybody else, so that the Germans would conclude that she had become just one more casualty in the anti-U-boat war, having carried her cryptological secrets with her to the bottom of the sea.

■ ■ ■

The last U-boat to surrender in World War II was *U-977*, commanded by Lieutenant Heinz Schaeffer. A teenager when Hitler came to power in 1933, Schaeffer had grown up under the Nazi regime and been thoroughly indoctrinated by it; hence, as he cruised off England in the early days of May 1945, he simply could not believe it when a radio message from headquarters told him the unthinkable had happened: The Reich had surrendered unconditionally. Had not Admiral Dönitz declared to his crews: "We shall fight to the very last man. We shall never surrender"? Surely, after all his fine words, the Grossadmiral could not have "sunk so far as to send out official orders to surrender." Hence Schaeffer told his men in all sincerity that the Allies must have obtained the submarine cipher and were sending false messages telling boats to surface and disarm.

The skipper then persuaded his crew to sail with him to Argentina, a tortuous journey that demanded much dodging of ships and aircraft and spending sixty-six consecutive days underwater. The *U-977* arrived on August 17, 1945, after the war had ended everywhere, in the Pacific as well as in Europe. The Argentine government interned Schaeffer and his men, treating them well, before turning them over to the Americans, who took everybody to Washington. Schaeffer underwent continual grilling from investigators who believed that the *U-977* might have served Adolf Hitler as the vehicle that carried him from Germany across the Atlantic to an unspecified new Berchtesgaden. But Schaeffer had no idea where the Führer might be. He was merely a disillusioned U-boat captain, and he was finally allowed to go home.

■ ■ ■

Out of 2,200 Atlantic convoys, U-boats sank 2,779 merchant ships, for a total tonnage of 14,119,413, along with 148 warships. On the German side, the U-boat crews paid the highest price wrung from the members of any service for any country: Of the 39,000 men who sailed in Admiral Dönitz's eleven hundred U-boats, 28,000 died at sea.

WORLD WAR II:
THE PACIFIC PRIZE

A strong merchant marine was vital to the economy and warmaking potential of the island nation of Japan. Its ships imported oil, iron ore, coal, bauxite, rubber, and foodstuffs; they exported arms, ammunition, aircraft, and soldiers to reinforce captured possessions. When submarines succeeded in stopping this commerce, Japan was doomed.

—Clay Blair, Jr.

PART V

24

SURPRISE AND SHOCK

s he approached the island of Oahu and the U.S. naval base at Pearl Harbor a few minutes before eight o'clock on the morning of December 7, 1941, Commander Mitsuo Fuchida of the Imperial Japanese Navy gazed with amazement at the spectacle below. Taking his aircraft down through a layer of overcast, Fuchida saw before him "the whole U.S. Pacific Fleet in a formation I would not have dared to dream of in my most optimistic dreams." How could the Americans have left themselves so profoundly vulnerable to attack? Did they not remember what had happened just under thirty-eight years earlier, on February 8, 1904, when the Japanese, under Admiral Heichiro Togo, had unleashed a squadron of torpedo boats on the Russian Pacific Fleet lying in harbor at Port Arthur—"without previous declaration of war or notification of hostilities." As for the Japanese themselves, they not only remembered that attack but commemorated it: The flagship of Admiral Chuichi Nagumo, commander of the Pearl Harbor strike force, flew Admiral Togo's old flag from the Russo-Japanese War, thus dramatizing the retrospective role of Port Arthur as a dress rehearsal for Pearl Harbor.

Commander Fuchida, the leader of the air strike, reported to his superiors that the attack had achieved full tactical surprise, a development not really expected by the commander in chief of the Combined Fleet, Admiral Isoroku Yamamoto, who had planned this daring operation: Surely at some point the attackers would be sighted and the American commanders alerted. But the admiral had turned out to be quite wrong.

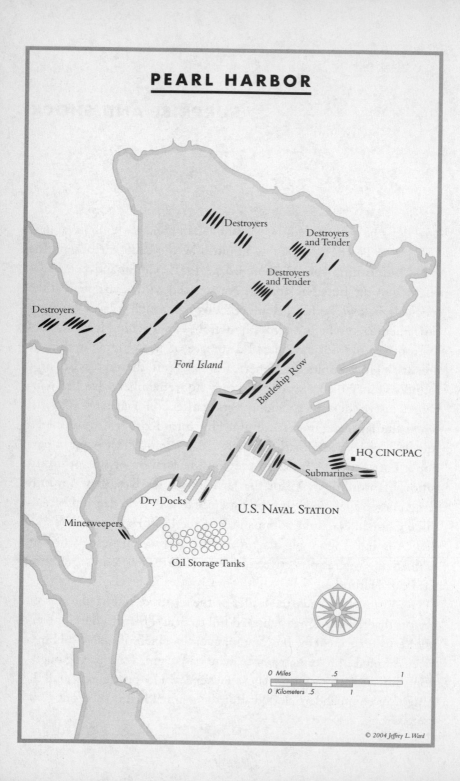

PEARL HARBOR

Destroyers

Destroyers
and Tender

Destroyers
and Tender

Destroyers

Ford Island

Battleship Row

HQ CINCPAC

Submarines

Dry Docks

U.S. Naval Station

Minesweepers

Oil Storage Tanks

0 Miles .5 1

0 Kilometers .5 1

© 2004 Jeffrey L. Ward

■ ■ ■

The Japanese attack on Pearl Harbor came after two decades of mutual suspicion and overt enmity across the Pacific. Much of this hostility related to China. For an array of reasons having to do with everybody from missionaries to shippers and merchants, Americans had long maintained a special interest in this vast and troubled country. For some, China seemed the object of sentimental concern, almost filling the role of a worthy but poor relation, to be worried over and propped up as much as possible. The Japanese seizure of the region of Manchuria in 1931 disturbed the Americans, though no action was taken against it, and in the summer of 1937 the Japanese launched the so-called China Incident, in reality an all-out war against their far larger but divided and disorganized neighbor. American friends of China, President Roosevelt and members of his administration prominent among them, looked on with dismay, while taking whatever limited financial and other measures they could contrive to help China.

In May 1940 (coincidentally, just as the land war in Europe was exploding with the German invasion of the Low Countries and France), FDR took a fateful decision. Hoping, by showing the American flag in the Pacific, to deter any further Japanese aggression, such as moves against British, French, and Dutch possessions in southeast Asia and the East Indies, the president ordered what was then called the U.S. Fleet to transfer from its West Coast bases to Pearl Harbor, in the Hawaiian Islands. The fleet commander, Admiral J. O. Richardson, raised vehement but unavailing objections to basing his ships on a relatively undeveloped facility 2,000 miles from the mainland, and in February 1941 Admiral Husband E. Kimmel, a highly regarded, aggressive officer, succeeded him, with the new title Commander in Chief, U.S. Pacific Fleet.

It was at just this time that Admiral Yamamoto, Japan's principal naval strategist, set his staff to work on a deadly countermove to FDR's ploy—the daring plan for a surprise attack on U.S. forces in Hawaii by aircraft flown off carriers. With a fondness for gambling amounting perhaps to a compulsion, the admiral not only spent hours at *go* and *shogi* (Japanese checkers and chess) but also, during two tours of duty in the United States, at Harvard and in Washington, had become expert at bridge and poker. Since aircraft carriers were still little tried in war, the plan to attack Pearl Harbor and other installations on the island of Oahu, which was Yamamoto's own original conception, represented a supreme gamble, an attempt to win the greatest battle, by unorthodox means, at the outset of war. In 1940 the British had supplied something of a precedent with their successful November torpedo plane attack on the Italian battle fleet in the harbor of Taranto. This feat, though demonstrating to thoughtful observers that the carrier with its aircraft had become the dominant force in naval war, did not compare in scope and complexity to the Pearl Harbor operation.

Yamamoto, whose years in America had made him thoroughly aware of the economic power and potential military might of the country, told the Naval General Staff that if the government was determined to pursue a course leading to war with the United States, Japan's only chance for victory lay in defeating the U.S. fleet at the outset. In this way, Japan, in its push for the riches of southeast Asia and the East Indies, could secure its flank—no American fleet would be left to imperil the imperial southward drive—while building up its security area before America could put itself on a war footing. In late 1940, having made it plain to the premier, Prince Konoye, how strongly he opposed war with the United States, the best Yamamoto could offer was the prescient statement: "If I am told to fight regardless of consequence, I shall run wild considerably for the first six months or a year, but I have utterly no confidence for the second and third years."

■ ■ ■

In the early days of December 1941, in accordance with the role assigned to them in Admiral Yamamoto's plan for the attack on Pearl Harbor, twenty-seven of the Imperial Navy's large, oceangoing I-class submarines lay off the Hawaiian Islands, ready to go after any U.S. ships that attempted to escape from the onslaught by moving out into the open sea. Five of these boats had an unusual purpose: They would launch the "Special Naval Attack Unit," midget submarines with the mission of making their way into the harbor and joining the carrier aircraft in the assault on the U.S. battleships moored along Ford Island in the center of the harbor. These midgets, each of them only about 45 feet long, carried two-man crews and two small torpedoes. Since, even after being modified for the Hawaii operation, they had a cruising range of no more than 150 to 200 miles, they had been carried across the Pacific to a spot near the arena of intended action on the decks of mother ships, the I-boats. On each deck the midget nestled behind the conning tower, held to her mother by four heavy clamps.

At 0342 on December 7, with the moon breaking through cloud, a sharp-eyed lookout on the U.S. minesweeper *Condor* spotted a periscope rippling the water outside the entrance buoys of Pearl Harbor. Alerted by the *Condor,* the skipper of the destroyer *Ward* began a radar sweep of the surrounding waters but failed to make a contact. This early morning overture to a yet unanticipated drama had not ended, however. At 0630 the *Ward*'s helmsman saw what looked like a small submarine and roused the captain, Lieutenant William W. Outerbridge; by 0645 Outerbridge was reporting to naval headquarters that the *Ward* had "attacked, fired upon, and dropped depth charges upon sub operating in defensive area." The *Ward* had also attempted to ram the sub, and after seeing a patch of oil Outerbridge had concluded that this particular intruder had been sunk.

After receiving Lieutenant Outerbridge's report, the admirals at Pearl Harbor argued back and forth, unable to decide whether to consider the whole incident anything more than a false alarm. Even if it was genuine, concluded Rear Admiral Claude C. Bloch, who as commandant of the 14th Naval District actually held the responsibility for the operation of the base, the sighting probably signified only an isolated submarine attack and nothing larger, even though a midget could not have made its way from Japan on its own but had to have come on a mother ship, and therefore Outerbridge's quarry quite likely was part of a purposeful operation. In any case, Admiral Bloch, though informing Admiral Kimmel, saw no reason to tell the army commander in Hawaii, Lieutenant General Walter C. Short, that a navy destroyer had just sunk a Japanese submarine at the entrance to Pearl Harbor; Bloch later said, with notable understatement, that in failing to pass the news on to Short, he "had been absolutely wrong." (The failure to share information and the lack of coordinated army-navy plans for the defense of Oahu, astonishing as this behavior has always seemed to commentators, in reality constituted no more than a typical instance of territorial rivalry between the army and navy; their mutual hostility and the condescension with which each has always tended to view the other are facts as old as the existence of the separate services.)

One hour and ten minutes after the *Ward's* encounter with the midget submarine, as Pearl was coming to life on what was supposed to be a quiet Sunday morning, the first wave of Japanese planes began dropping torpedoes whose fins had been specially fitted with wooden baffles to keep them from running into the shallow bottom of the harbor. So effective did these torpedoes and accompanying bombs prove that within just half an hour the attackers had, for the time being, destroyed the American power represented by Battleship Row.

Of the five midget submarines involved in the attack, however, one went far astray and ran aground on a reef on the other side of Oahu, owing to the failure of its gyroscope. It thus fell into American hands, thereby producing the first Japanese prisoner of war, Lieutenant Kazuo Sakamaki, who swam ashore and surrendered; nor did any of the others return to their mother boats. Although at least one midget had managed to sneak into the harbor, none exerted any discernible influence on the operation. Admiral Yamamoto originally had excluded midget submarines from participation in the operation because their short range meant that they could not be recovered.

After the midget crews pleaded for the opportunity to share in the great endeavor, however, the admiral agreed to the plan to modify the boats to extend their range, and thus they received the chance they coveted (even though, in actual fact, recovery could not really be considered likely). When Yamamoto, a man who habitually wore a grave expression, heard that none had returned, he reportedly looked even more somber, saying, "I would never have sent them, if I'd known we'd achieve so much with air units alone."

■ ■ ■

Even when the first Japanese bombs fell on U.S. installations, the Americans on the ground could not accept the evidence of their eyes and ears but believed that the top brass must have ordered an amazingly realistic surprise drill. As described in the novel *From Here to*

Eternity, it was only when soldiers at Schofield Barracks saw a fellow GI machine-gunned by a strafing Japanese fighter that they realized that "thems real bullets that guy was usin." How could such an incredible event have happened?

Commander Fuchida, Admiral Yamamoto, and those GIs at Schofield Barracks would all have felt even greater surprise had they known of the remarkable achievements of American codebreakers. In the summer of 1940 a team of army Signal Intelligence Service cryptanalysts led by Frank Rowlett had performed a truly wondrous feat. Working to decrypt Japanese diplomatic messages—exchanges between the Foreign Ministry in Tokyo and embassies and consulates around the world—encrypted in what was dubbed the Purple cipher, the army team, through sheer logic and mathematical analysis, created a machine that could break Purple though no Americans had ever seen the Japanese machine or any part of it. A navy cipher expert later declared that "the army's solution of the Purple machine was the masterpiece of cryptanalysis in the war era." The chief signal officer felt such admiration for his codebreakers that he called them magicians, and consequently the intelligence produced by cryptanalysis came to be designated Magic.

Though the Japanese employed Purple to keep in touch with their diplomats overseas, these messages at times carried information of great military and naval relevance. On September 24, notably, the Foreign Ministry asked the Japanese consul general in Honolulu to keep Tokyo informed about what ships were in Pearl Harbor and where and how they were moored, and the ministry continued to ask questions on the same subject. Other intercepts during this time revealed Japanese curiosity about the Canal Zone, Manila, and even Seattle and San Diego. But, some officers wondered, did the highly detailed queries about Pearl Harbor have special significance?

Other Magic intercepts tracked a curious series of messages relating to Japanese-U.S. negotiations then being conducted in Washington over possible stabilization of the situation in the Pacific. The Foreign Ministry gave the Japanese envoys deadlines for reaching an agreement with the Americans. The date of November 25, said one message, must be considered "absolutely immovable," but the foreign minister nevertheless granted the envoys a four-day extension when they urgently requested it. But no more: "[T]his time we mean it," the foreign minister now declared; "the deadline absolutely cannot be changed. After that things are automatically going to happen."

On the morning of December 7, "things" did indeed happen, and they came without warning, just as had been the case at Port Arthur. According to classical U.S. Army doctrine, the process of intelligence consists of three steps: collection, evaluation, and dissemination. With respect to collection, the Magic team had done inspired, unparalleled work, even though they had to labor within the constraints imposed by a skimpy, Depression-era budget, but the Americans lacked a comparable organization for evaluating and disseminating the information that Magic produced. Army and navy officers, performing the task on alternating days, carried briefcases with the intercepts deemed important to high-ranking figures, civilian and military. No system of thoughtful analysis existed, however; far from it: the security-conscious intelligence officers required each recipient to read through the message quickly, ask any questions on the spot, and then hand the message back. Besides, the Purple messages gave no actual operational details; material of that kind would come from messages in one of the Japanese naval ciphers, with which U.S. Navy cryptologists had achieved success from time to time but which tended to change.

Nevertheless, the Purple messages gave the Americans a clear indication of the Japanese state of mind: Hostilities were clearly going to begin soon, somewhere. Actually, the messages confirmed what the average naval officer and even the ordinary civilian newspaper reader could hardly fail to know, as the negotiations between United States and Japan proceeded fitfully through the autumn: Hostilities between the two countries loomed as a likely possibility, one that could turn into reality any day.

Beyond that, U.S. Navy war games had more than once demonstrated the feasibility of a successful attack from aircraft carriers on the island of Oahu; December 7 provided resounding confirmation of the results of these games.

In view of all these points, no one should feel any surprise that the causes and culpabilities and alleged cover-ups relating to Pearl Harbor would form the subject of an endless and frequently ferocious debate, producing fifteen or twenty books in every succeeding decade. When all was said and done, however, the most likely central explanation for the failures of intelligence, analysis, and command came from the forthright Admiral Kimmel himself: "I never thought those little yellow sons of bitches could pull off such an attack, so far from Japan." And, of course, the two countries were officially at peace, a consideration that still counted for something in those days. The Japanese success dramatized, at bottom, a failure of expectations. As Admiral King put it, the commanders in Hawaii were living with an "unwarranted feeling of immunity from attack," a feeling, as the record shows, of which Hawaii had no monopoly. The admirals and generals wrapped in this feeling of immunity might have suffered a truly personal shock had Admiral Yamamoto not dropped from the plan one of his earlier ideas: the employment of landing parties to seize U.S. officers, thus, he supposed, depriving the Americans of leadership. As it happened, however, December 7 saw the ablest U.S. commanders (notably Vice Admiral William F. Halsey and Rear Admiral Raymond A. Spruance) at sea, but certainly the loss of a number of second-level officers would have hampered the functioning of the Pacific naval bureaucracy.

But more important than the fact of surprise was the nature of the objective it had achieved. Yamamoto aimed not at the destruction of Pearl Harbor itself but at the annihilation of the U.S. heavy ships. For this pivotal reason the attackers gave all their attention to Battleship Row, which they effectively destroyed. But they left untouched the base facilities that had been built up in the prior two years—the oil storage depots and the maintenance and repair shops. They also ignored a sizable area on the southern edge of the harbor—the submarine base.

In concentrating on the battle fleet to the exclusion of other naval targets, the Japanese left intact an installation of now almost unrivaled importance and one that in recent years had been developed to a high level of excellence. The submarine base included machine shops and repair facilities for the submarine force, supply depots, a torpedo plant, arrangements and equipment for training, housing for 2,500 men, officers and crew, and, extending long fingers into the harbor, piers for submarines and auxiliary vessels. For the boats the base constituted the vitally important center for refit and resupply, and for their officers and crews it provided the stage for continuing training and development of technique. If they had suddenly been deprived of their base, U.S. submarines would have found themselves orphans in the middle of the Pacific.

■ ■ ■

As the Japanese torpedo planes swept in from the southeast on their run toward the eight battleships in Pearl Harbor, they roared just past the submarine base, like trespassers taking a short cut across a front yard. At the moment the base was host to five of the twenty-two submarines attached to the fleet (out of the overall U.S. total of fifty-one). These were the *Cachalot, Cuttlefish, Dolphin, Narwhal,* and *Tautog,* the others being scattered on various assignments from California to the Central Pacific (and some of these having, in reality, only a paper connection with Pearl Harbor); these five were all undergoing overhaul.

Along with the approach of the invading planes there came, from army installations close by, the heavy sound of explosions. The *Tautog's* duty officer this Sunday morning, Lieutenant Barney Sieglaff (Naval Academy '31), felt that this realistic exercise fitted in perfectly with the boat's recent activities. The *Tautog* (SS-199), one of the *Tambor* class of twelve fleet submarines that immediately preceded the *Gato* class and were similar in size, had been commissioned a year and a half previously. She had arrived at Pearl Harbor on June 6, 1941, and on October 21 had departed, with the *Thresher,* for the first-ever simulated wartime patrols carried out by the Pacific force. She had returned to Pearl on Friday, just two days earlier, having spent fifteen to sixteen hours submerged on each of thirty-eight consecutive days of the forty-five at sea. The members of the crew had come home ready for rest and recreation, and the boat itself ready for repair and refit; that weekend most of the men were off on liberty. The *Tautog* lay at its pier inert, tied to land by electric cables and water lines, and existing in anything but a fighting condition.

As one of the speeding planes turned, the men on the *Tautog* and the other submarines saw that all the noise and excitement came not from a drill but from the real thing: The aircraft bore the red sun of Japan. This was war! Immediately rapping out orders, Sieglaff pulled together a gun crew; sailors broke out weapons and passed ammunition up from below. Quickly the *Tautog's* .50-caliber and .30-caliber machine guns went into action, though the 3-inch deck gun proved to be frozen, somehow waterlogged from her recent mission and unable to elevate skyward.

The improvised gun crews on the *Tautog* and the older *Narwhal* (SS-167), one of the products of the navy's 1920s flirtation with size (she had a surfaced displacement of 2,730 tons), blazed away at a torpedo plane, as did a destroyer moored nearby. The intruder exploded in flames and crashed offshore from the base.

As a V-formation of torpedo planes flashed overhead, tracers from the *Tautog's* after .50-caliber and starboard .30-caliber machine guns signaled the path of hits that slashed into the fourth aircraft in the enemy formation. As Torpedoman Second Class P. N. Mignone, Gunner's Mate First Class I. H. Dixon, and Electrician's Mate First Class W. E. Floyd poured their fire into the plane, they saw it begin to come apart in an explosion and then fall in a fiery nosedive into the channel. Minutes earlier the two submarines had shared in the first American kill of the Pacific war; now the *Tautog* had made the first singlehanded kill by a U.S. submarine in World War II.

For the submariners, watching the horrifying onslaught on the battle fleet as if they had box seats in a gigantic coliseum, seeing the fire and smoke and hearing the explosions, the world had turned upside down this Sunday morning. Suddenly it had become imperative for the scattered boats of the Pacific submarine force to get together and get ready to fight.

The first of the submarines expected at Pearl Harbor was the *Thresher,* a *Tambor*-class boat like the *Tautog,* which was two days behind the *Tautog* in returning from their patrol exercises off Midway Island. When her skipper, Lieutenant Commander W. L. Anderson (Naval Academy '26) received the radio dispatch with the news of the Japanese attack, the boat was proceeding homeward, some 50 miles west of Oahu, under the escort of the destroyer *Litchfield*. Then came a tangle of timing. Intending to submerge until night came, Anderson relieved the destroyer of its escorting obligation to allow it to join a passing task force that had set out to scour the sea for any Japanese vessels that might have been involved in the attack. But just as the *Thresher* was about to slip beneath the surface, a message came from the submarine chief at Pearl Harbor, Rear Admiral Thomas Withers, Jr., ordering her not to release the escort. Anderson immediately radioed the *Litchfield* to arrange a meeting point, at which the destroyer and the submarine would rendezvous in two hours' time.

At the appointed moment Anderson brought the *Thresher* up to periscope depth, saw the familiar four stacks of a World War I–vintage destroyer, and surfaced. Immediately, however, the destroyer turned into firing position for its forward 5-inch gun and began raining shells on the submarine. Clearly, it was mistaken identities all around, as the destroyer was not the *Litchfield* and the *Thresher* was not a Japanese boat. Anderson desperately dived deep, fortunately having suffered no damage from the barrage of unfriendly fire. After the destroyer broke off its attack and moved on, Anderson contacted Admiral Withers, who arranged for the gate in the Pearl Harbor antitorpedo net to be opened at 0600 the next day, but when the *Thresher* tried to come in, she was this time assaulted by U.S. Army aircraft. Finally, a destroyer came out to meet the submarine, and after a gingerly exchange of recognition signals, the new escort led the *Thresher* into the harbor. By now it was midafternoon.

The story had one particularly sad aspect. Anderson had urgently hoped to reach Pearl Harbor on December 7, because early that morning a seaman had been slammed to the deck by a large wave, suffering not only a broken leg but serious internal injuries. But next morning, while the U.S. bombers were keeping the *Thresher* trapped beneath the surface, the seaman had died. Other submarines managed to make it to Pearl without having to survive attack by angry and none-too-careful American defenders, though several had a close shave. The *Gudgeon,* a *Tambor*-class boat (SS-211), which was near Oahu when the Japanese blow fell, received orders to rendezvous with three P boats (from the mid-1930s—*Plunger, Pollack,* and *Pompano*), arriving from refit at Mare Island, the navy yard on the northern arm of San Francisco Bay. The work at Mare Island had included the installation of degaussing gear, to protect the boats against magnetic mines and torpedoes, and something that directly symbolized transition from peacetime to wartime conditions—the removal of the conning tower doors. ("Believe it or not," said one of the officers, "we had glass windows in our conning towers!")

Even after having spent two months at Mare Island, the *Pompano* had developed engine trouble as she approached Oahu. To be sure, the supply people at the navy yard could hardly be described as infallible; one submarine's requisition for a case of toilet paper came back stamped ITEM CANNOT BE IDENTIFIED. Sailing together, all three submarines lagged behind schedule, a benign failing on the part of the *Pompano,* since otherwise she would have appeared at the entrance buoys in Pearl Harbor at six o'clock on the morning of December 7. At about eight o'clock the radioman appeared in the conning tower with news of the Japanese attack, and not long afterward the three submarines were dodging Japanese aircraft, which the submariners presumed were strafing the boats on the way back to their carriers.

After two nights and a day submerged, as the three boats lay offshore, they fell under the roving eyes of edgy air corps pilots, who after the Japanese strike looked on anything unfamiliar as definitely hostile. The resulting order to bomb these boats fortunately came to the attention of Admiral Withers in time to prevent an actual attack. Until Tuesday morning, when the *Pompano* entered the harbor, those on board had not known just what had happened there two mornings earlier. They saw a navy fighter that had crash-landed, then smoke rising from Hickam Field and Ford Island and the battleship *Nevada* beached. "Then we turned the corner," said Lieutenant Slade Cutter (Naval Academy '35), the *Pompano*'s executive officer, "and saw battleships this way and that way—the masts—all of them didn't sink on an even keel." Moving closer, they saw the *Oklahoma* and the *Utah* upside down, and the *Arizona* still burning. He saw people on the pier, Cutter said, but "we couldn't get people to handle our lines. It was like they were all in a daze."

One of those on the pier did not suffer from stupor, however. Having heard that his friend Cutter was aboard the *Pompano,* Tom McGrath, a guard on the academy football team just two years before, when Cutter served as assistant line coach, had come down to meet him. Mc-Grath, a "red-headed Irishman," wore a pair of khaki shorts, sandals, a .45, and nothing else; all his clothes, as Cutter learned, had gone down with the *California,* on which he served as signal officer. During the attack he had been up on the signal bridge, firing his pistol at the Japanese planes. Invited to lunch by Cutter, McGrath declared, "I want to go out on the first ship that's going out after those bastards!"

The commanding officer, Commander Lewis Parks, overheard this fiery statement from his cabin, just aft of the wardroom.

"Young man, do you mean that?" Parks said.

When McGrath fired back a brisk, "Yes, sir," Parks got up, left the boat, and went to Admiral Kimmel's headquarters, a short walk away. When he came back, in about fifteen minutes, he said simply, "Son, you're a member of the *Pompano* crew."

Parks made this decision even though McGrath was not a submariner and had undergone none of the specialized training that had evolved through the years to fit an officer or an enlisted man to serve underwater. Such decisiveness, however, marked Parks, an outstanding commander, a tough leader, and a pioneer in tactics who made a deep impression on Cutter and other officers who served under him. "A lot of tough skippers didn't have any esprit de corps," Cutter said. "They didn't have the qualities of leadership that Parks had." His officers "learned everything from him, not from submarine school. It helped out later in the war. It helped me sink ships."

Later arrivals at Pearl Harbor, coming from here and there (*Tambor, Trout, Argonaut,* and *Triton*) had easier going than the earlier group. These nine new boats, together with those that had been in harbor at the time of the attack, constituted the force with which Admiral Withers would begin taking this new war to the enemy. In deciding how to make the most effective use of their submarines, however, the Americans had some history to reckon with.

Tom McGrath saw his desire fulfilled right away. On December 17 the *Pompano* departed from Pearl Harbor, heading westward for Truk and Wake Island.

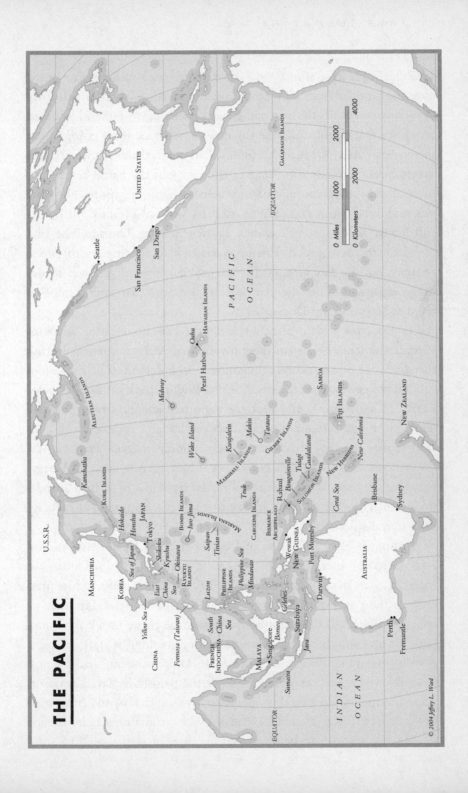

THE PACIFIC

U.S.S.R.

MANCHURIA

KOREA

Yellow Sea

CHINA

Formosa (Taiwan)

East China Sea

South China Sea

FRENCH INDOCHINA

MALAYA

Singapore

Sumatra

Borneo

Java

Surabaya

Celebes

Sea of Japan

Hokkaido

Honshu JAPAN

Shikoku

Kyushu

Tokyo

RYUKYU ISLANDS

Okinawa

Luzon

PHILIPPINE ISLANDS

Mindanao

Philippine Sea

BONIN ISLANDS

Iwo Jima

MARIANA ISLANDS

Saipan

Tinian

CAROLINE ISLANDS

Truk

BISMARCK ARCHIPELAGO

Rabaul

Bougainville

Wewak

NEW GUINEA

Port Moresby

Darwin

AUSTRALIA

Perth

Fremantle

Sydney

Brisbane

Coral Sea

SOLOMON ISLANDS

Tulagi

Guadalcanal

NEW HEBRIDES

New Caledonia

Kamchatka

KURIL ISLANDS

ALEUTIAN ISLANDS

Seattle

San Francisco

San Diego

UNITED STATES

PACIFIC OCEAN

Midway

Wake Island

Kwajalein

MARSHALL ISLANDS

Makin

Tarawa

GILBERT ISLANDS

SAMOA

Fiji ISLANDS

NEW ZEALAND

HAWAIIAN ISLANDS

Oahu

Pearl Harbor

EQUATOR

GALAPAGOS ISLANDS

INDIAN OCEAN

EQUATOR

0 Miles   1000   2000

0 Kilometers   2000   4000

© 2004 Jeffrey L. Ward

■ ■ ■

Less than three days after Pearl Harbor, far to the southwest, air power gave the world a fresh and startling demonstration of its effectiveness against warships. In the preceding weeks, seeking to establish a deterrent force that might cause the Japanese to pull back from going to war in southeast Asia, Winston Churchill had coerced the Admiralty into dispatching the battleship *Prince of Wales* to join the battle cruiser *Repulse,* already at Ceylon, and basing them both on Singapore. The force was under the command of Vice Admiral Sir Tom Phillips, a tiny man "all brains and no body," widely known as Tom Thumb. The plan called for the new aircraft carrier *Indomitable* to accompany the *Prince of Wales,* but she ran aground on leaving the shipyard and had to undergo repairs. Lacking the planned air cover, the two capital ships arrived at Singapore on December 2.

On December 8 (local time), less than two hours after attacking Hawaii, the Japanese began their invasion of Malaya, a massive effort that, from the outset, overwhelmed the British defenders of the peninsula. In the evening of that day, Admiral Phillips took his ships (labeled Force Z) northward in search of reported enemy troop convoys. Though he had requested local air cover, he later received a disconcerting message from his headquarters ashore: FIGHTER PROTECTION ON WEDNESDAY TENTH WILL NOT, REPEAT NOT, BE POSSIBLE. This negative development came as the result of the rapid loss of British airfields in northern Malaya. Hoping at least to enjoy the advantage of surprise, the admiral sailed on.

During the early afternoon of December 9, the Japanese submarine *I-65,* on station in a picket line of twelve strung northward along the Malayan coast from Singapore, sighted Force Z and reported its presence to the commanding admiral. Unaware of this development, of course, Phillips, after continuing for some time, turned back for home, but next morning he received a report from his chief of staff in Singapore of enemy landings along the coast. Despite having had by now more than two years' experience of war, the British displayed amateurishness in the conduct of this operation, rivaling that of the Americans in the Pearl Harbor disaster. Concerned with maintaining radio silence, Phillips appears to have believed that his chief of staff would presume that the report of the landings would send Force Z coastward to try to stop the enemy action and would therefore automatically order fighter protection from Singapore for the force. Nothing of the kind happened: The chief of staff, drawing no conclusion at all about Phillips's possible response to the report of the landings, took no action.

Presently, reconnaissance showed Phillips that the report of the landings was a false alarm. Later in this strange and tragic story, the authorities learned that a herd of water buffaloes had wandered into a minefield, causing Indian troops in the area to believe that the explosions they were hearing signified the beginning of a Japanese operation. Phillips, who earlier had spoken of the value of air cover but nevertheless seemed determined to spend the day wandering about the South China Sea without it, now sailed northeastward to investigate news of a junk or a barge towing a string of smaller boats.

Here, at 1130, a squadron of nine twin-engine Japanese bombers found Force Z. Their bombs bracketed the *Repulse,* doing no grave damage; it was the arrival of torpedo planes that determined the fate of the British ships. The *Prince of Wales* suffered a mortal wound, and newly arriving torpedo bombers soon did in the *Repulse,* which took a series of hits and turned over and sank. Any hope of air cover from Singapore vanished when it came to light, after an hour had gone by, that nobody had thought to tell the base about the Japanese attack and ask for help. The ill-starred "Tom Thumb" Phillips went down with his ship. After receiving the terrible news in a telephone call from the First Sea Lord, Churchill felt thankful to be alone: "In all the war I never received a more direct shock." Having destroyed the only capital ships remaining to the Allies in the Indian Ocean or the Pacific after Pearl Harbor, the Japanese appeared supreme "over all this vast expanse of waters."

Aside from its strategic implications, the destruction of Force Z dramatized a profound development in sea warfare. At Pearl Harbor, and in the earlier British action at Taranto, the respective attackers had performed like marksmen in shooting galleries, with the targets sitting unmoving, unable to take any kind of evasive action. But the loss of the *Prince of Wales* and the *Repulse* represented a new kind of fact: They were the first warships ever sunk by aircraft while steaming at sea. The

Japanese commander, Admiral Nobutake Kondo, had expected to need his battle fleet to finish the job begun by the planes, but the deadly work of the torpedoes left nothing for the big ships to do. This battle in the South China Sea, together with two great American-Japanese engagements in the coming months, would provide absolute proof that the future had arrived. (Even so, Admiral Phillips posthumously had a defender in Admiral Thomas C. Hart, the veteran submarine specialist who now commanded the U.S. Asiatic Fleet, who conceded that Phillips's "gallant attempt was called reckless and foolhardy" but maintained that the big guns of Force Z had represented the only chance to stop the Japanese invasion of Malaya.)

In spotting Force Z and setting in motion the process that led to the epochal British catastrophe, the submarine *I-65* also played a part in starting an entirely different chain of ideas and events. The shocking disappearance from the scene of the *Prince of Wales* and the *Repulse,* seeming to underscore Britain's impotence in the Pacific, left Australians—always conscious that their best troops were far off fighting in North Africa—feeling naked to their enemies, with no mother country in a condition to succor them and perhaps not even concerned to do so. In words tinged with bitterness, the Australian prime minister, John Curtin, declared that his country "would now look to America, free of any pangs as to [her] traditional links or kinship with the United Kingdom."

But America had many questions to answer, too.

"EXECUTE UNRESTRICTED WARFARE"

On the Thursday following the Japanese attack, the first Pearl Harbor submarine ready for action, the brand-new *Gudgeon* (SS-211), set forth on patrol, under the command of the thirty-eight-year-old Lieutenant Commander Elton "Joe" Grenfell (Naval Academy '26). This fleet boat arrived off the southeast coast of Kyushu, at the Bungo Suido, the southern entrance to the Sea of Japan, on January 2, three weeks after departing Pearl Harbor. Owing to the haste with which the authorities had sent her on her way, the crew had a variety of tasks to perform to complete her preparations. In particular, she had gone to sea with some of her torpedoes not in the "fully ready" condition, and the men had to finish this task and perform thorough daily checks on this important cargo, examining the gyroscopes, the air flasks, and the other functional features of these complex machines.

After arriving on station, the officers and men of the *Gudgeon* began to discover the many points of difference between the targets offered in peacetime torpedo practice and the challenge presented by unfamiliar ships, of indefinite size, in strange waters; but in Robert "Dusty" Dornin (Naval Academy '35), the fire control officer, Grenfell had a highly capable associate who in peacetime practice had set a record for accuracy with the Torpedo Data Computer (TDC), the prized electromechanical device that translated information on the course, bearing, and speed of a target ship into settings for the torpedoes.

On December 31, on the way to her station, the *Gudgeon* sighted and tried to catch a freighter, her first potential target, but after a twenty-five-minute pursuit Grenfell gave up hope of attaining firing position; in fact, the *Gudgeon* could get no closer than about 8 miles. Grenfell also had to remember his firm and explicit orders requiring him to economize on torpedoes. On January 4 he fired two torpedoes at another target, a coastal freighter, at the long range of about 2,600 yards, but missed; he believed that this failure was due to the range and also to the small size of the target.

After five more days had passed without sighting a ship—where was everybody in what was supposed to be a congested seaway?—the *Gudgeon* sighted masts on the horizon and began an approach, but a chase brought the submarine no closer than 5,000 yards, and the freighter moved away. Just before midnight, about seven hours later, lookouts spotted a fresh target, a darkened freighter of about 5,000 tons. With the moon rising, the ship presented an inviting silhouette; Grenfell ordered a surface attack. Turning in order to give the stern tubes a 90° track angle, the *Gudgeon,* orders or no orders, fired three torpedoes at the freighter at an estimated range of 2,500 yards, and then Grenfell sensed the gratifying shock of an explosion. The crewmen in the after torpedo room, feeling two thuds, thought that two torpedoes had hit the target, and the sound man reported "explosive reverberations." Skipper and crew believed that their boat, the first to leave Pearl Harbor on patrol, had scored its first kill.

■ ■ ■

During the period between the world wars, the U.S. Navy had consistently seen Japan as its foe in a future war, and many of those who speculated about the future took it for granted that the conflict would begin with a Japanese attack launched before a formal declaration of war. The studies envisioned an ensuing wide-ranging naval conflict, with the Americans slowly pushing the foe back toward the home islands until his advance outran its logistical limits. At this point the Japanese would attempt to settle the issue by delivering a heavy counterpunch— battleships versus battleships. Depending on the outcome, either the Americans would propose negotiations or, if the Japanese lost, the home islands would undergo blockade and then surrender.

It would be a big-gun war. Like many other observers, some of the influential Naval War College thinkers saw no role for submarines in connection with the fleet; they could best serve as scouts. As for commerce raiding, the theoreticians believed that it should be carried out by light cruisers, not submarines, although in general they had little faith in this tactic; as disciples of Mahan, they saw commerce raiding as the tool of the weaker power in a conflict. For the submarine, they saw no attack role at all. But some of the officers in the submarine force had other ideas. Withers, then the commander of a submarine division, advocated operations along the line of the U-boats of the Kaiser's navy, that is, sending the submarines out on offensive patrols; but during the 1920s and most of the 1930s the navy did not possess boats capable of performing this role 4,000 or 5,000 miles from Pearl Harbor across the Pacific to the Philippines or Japan. Though the new fleet submarines began arriving at the end of the 1930s, no doctrine had jelled by the time of Pearl Harbor; certainly, none of the planners, neither those who still believed in the idea of the fleet submarine nor those who did not, had ever dreamed that the United States would enter on war with no battle fleet for submarines to sail with.

Admiral Dönitz had sent his boats into action in the Atlantic with a theory and a tactical plan. Though at the outset Hitler had forbidden unrestricted attack on commercial traffic, Dönitz had felt no doubts that Germany would turn to unrestricted warfare and that it must do so if it wished to have any hope of winning the war; treaty obligations could no longer count. The United States, bound by the same agreements, came into the war with questions rather than a doctrine. If a submarine pursued a merchant ship, should the commander follow the old prize rules out in the Pacific? After the shock of the Japanese attack, few officers at Pearl Harbor felt any urge to treat the enemy according to niceties drawn up in peacetime. So the simple message that arrived in Hawaii from Admiral Stark's headquarters in the middle of the afternoon of December 7 received a highly approving welcome:

EXECUTE UNRESTRICTED AIR AND SUBMARINE WARFARE AGAINST JAPAN.

The issue that had divided the councils of Imperial Germany for three years, the conduct that had drawn the eloquent and angry denunciations of Woodrow Wilson and finally led him to take his country into war, had ceased to exist for the United States within six hours of the coming of this new war. The London Submarine Agreement had also ceased to exist, except perhaps for the Japanese, though the Americans had not made the unrestricted order public. The decision did not come as a surprise or simply as the result of anger at the Japanese. During 1941 everybody understood, noted Commander John Wilkes, "that a directive for unrestricted warfare could be expected within the first week after the outbreak of hostilities." At least theoretically, Joe Grenfell or any other skipper, if captured by the Japanese after sinking a merchant vessel without warning, would have no rights and could legitimately be hanged as a pirate. Admiral Withers signed a to-whom-it-may-concern paper explaining to any potential captors that the skipper was merely following orders. How effective such a document might have proved to be remains an interesting question.

■ ■ ■

Despite the carte blanche conferred by Admiral Stark's order, the submarines in the first patrols from Pearl Harbor did not have sinking merchant ships as their primary mission. Fearing that the Japanese might return, this time with an invasion force, Admiral Kimmel ordered Withers to send the submarines out as scouts, with some of them, including the *Gudgeon,* going all the way to Japanese waters. These first long, slow patrols produced disappointing results. Since in fact no invasion force existed, the skippers could hardly be faulted for failing to find it, but they produced only a short list of actual sinkings (and postwar research would trim it even further).

This experience revealed the existence of several problems in the submarine force. The parsimonious practices of the 1930s had instilled habits of frugality deep in the minds of the high command. Since at the time Pearl Harbor had only a limited supply of torpedoes, a skipper, instead of firing a three-torpedo spread as standard doctrine, must not expend more than two on a freighter or a tanker, and one, the authorities said, would be better. This requirement obviously increased the chances of missing the target altogether, and it stepped up the demands on the captain himself, though Admiral Withers's concern became understandable when one realized that he had on hand only about a hundred torpedoes, with a limited quota of replacements due in the coming months.

Withers, remembered by Slade Cutter as "a fine old gentleman," represented a stodgy prewar command generation, Cutter thought, not attuned to modern war. But it was true that, unlike some of the other implements of war, torpedoes did not readily lend themselves to stepped-up mass production even by experienced workers and certainly not by patriotic newcomers to industry; Rosie the Riveter was not likely to be soon joined in war work by Tillie the Torpedo Maker. A beautiful, intricate, nineteenth-century-style machine made to tight tolerances, the torpedo—whatever its merits as an explosive device would turn out to be—came from the hands of the craftsperson, not from a fast-moving assembly line. Especially following the Depression years, admirals tended to hoard these machines, each of which cost as much as several automobiles. True to his principles, Withers frowned on Grenfell's having used two torpedoes on such a minor target as a 1,500-ton coastal freighter and three on the 5,000-tonner believed at the time to have been sunk.

Part of the difficulty came from the central fact that everybody on a submarine was performing in a war for the first time. Coupled with that, the skippers had been enjoined to operate with extreme caution—for instance, not to travel on the surface within 500 miles of a Japanese air base. Their peacetime training had put great stress on this kind of circumspection in relation to aircraft, with commanders urged not even to come to periscope depth in making attacks but to stay well below the surface and find the enemy by means of sonar. Yet, despite the prewar emphasis on caution, the superiors at Pearl Harbor would chastise returning commanders for lacking aggressiveness (though all but one got medals, too). Withers faulted Grenfell for spending only twelve days on station—the assigned area of potential attack—out of a total of fifty-one days for the whole patrol. This "terrific overhead in time," the submarine force commander said, could have been cut by the use of "efficient" lookouts, which would have enabled Grenfell to spend more time on the surface en route to the target area. Withers also criticized Grenfell for keeping the *Gudgeon* submerged until 2100 each night, an unproductive use of evening darkness that could have been spent in recharging the batteries and in possible night action. Many of the skippers were rapped for being too eager to dive, thus avoiding action, and, like Grenfell, for not making night attacks on the model developed by the now acknowledged expert, Admiral Dönitz, in the Atlantic.

Lew Parks, certainly as skilled as a skipper could be without having previously experienced war, encountered a severe technical problem, which first showed itself off Wotje, an island in the Marshall group about halfway between Hawaii and New Guinea. The *Pompano* fired two torpedoes at a Japanese destroyer, or destroyer-size vessel, only to have both explode just after leaving the tubes. In addition to absorbing the shock effects of this inadvertent depth charge, the *Pompano* now had to deal with the onrushing destroyer; Parks fired two more torpedoes, but both missed. All the submarines, said Cutter, were "handicapped by the terrible torpedoes." Even when these weapons performed as intended, they lacked the range, speed, and hitting power of Japanese torpedoes. At the beginning of the war, however, the Americans had no awareness of these relative deficiencies.

The torpedoes the *Pompano* carried were not the newer Mark XIVs, with magnetic exploders, but the older, contact-exploder Mark Xs, a product of the World War I era packing limited punch and barely able to outrun many destroyers. Another attack by the *Pompano* during her first patrol proved Cutter's point. Reconnoitering off Wotje, Parks encountered a large transport, the *Kamakura Maru,* which had been a luxury liner before the war. "We were supposed to get any ships we could," Cutter said, and they fired two torpedoes; then they dived to escape depth charging, and when they surfaced again no transport was in sight. They reported a sinking—"we heard the hits and saw the splash of water, so Parks assumed it was going to be sunk." But "we didn't know what a torpedo hit sounded like," and Parks and Cutter did not realize until later that two duds had simply bounced off the hull and thus had caused the splashes. "It's just a crime that Parks didn't have a good submarine with good torpedoes, because he would have made a killing out there," Cutter said. "He was aggressive."

Grenfell and Dornin likewise proved wrong in their belief that they had sunk a 5,000-ton freighter off Japan; the torpedoes had failed them, too. But on January 27, in a surprising turnabout, their boat pulled off a significant coup. Operating on instructions based on radio intelligence from the navy's codebreaking operation at Pearl Harbor, the *Gudgeon* lay in wait northwest of Midway for three far-ranging submarines returning from a mission that had seen them firing shells at oil refineries and other targets in southern California, the first enemy attack on the U.S. mainland since the War of 1812. "At 0900, the sound operator reported fast screws on the port bow," Grenfell reported. "The O.O.D. was making a periscope operation at that time and training it on the sound bearing" and there, about 5,000 yards off, he saw a submarine running fast on the surface. Taking over the periscope, Grenfell determined the boat to be Japanese by its profile and by the forward location of the deck gun.

Just seven minutes after the first report from the sound operator, the *Gudgeon* fired three torpedoes from the bow tubes at the Japanese submarine, the *I-173*. The crew felt "two distinct thuds" and heard reverberations a little under two minutes after firing; when these reverberations died away, no propeller noises could be heard from the submarine. Grenfell hence believed that two torpedoes had struck it, but Dornin did not think they had sunk it; Grenfell did not claim a kill. But he was wrong again: The Japanese boat had not simply dived, it had sunk, and it never broadcast another signal from its radio. The *Gudgeon* had rung up a double achievement: the war's first sinking of a Japanese warship, aside from the midgets at Pearl Harbor, and the first sinking ever of an enemy warship by an American submarine.

■ ■ ■

Five thousand miles southwest of Pearl Harbor, in the early hours of December 8, 1941 (local time), the U.S. submarine *S-39* (SS-144), one of the oldest boats in service, lay quietly at anchor in Nin Bay, off the Philippine island of Masbate. At 0330 an excited machinist's mate rushed into the wardroom and, waking up the drowsing duty officer, showed him a message a radioman had just taken down. From there the ensign and the machinist's mate both went scrambling up on deck where, on that hot night, most of the crew had chosen to sleep. Moving through a maze of canvas cots, the machinist's mate spotted the skipper, Lieutenant James W. Coe (Naval Academy '30), his red hair shining in the moonlight.

When Coe read the brief message, he said simply, "Make all preparations to get under way."

The message came from Admiral Thomas Hart, the commander in chief of the United States Asiatic Fleet: JAPAN STARTED HOSTILITIES. GOVERN YOURSELVES ACCORDINGLY. In less than half an hour, with everything stowed away, the S-39 had headed for her patrol area to begin action in the war everybody in the Philippines, perhaps Admiral Hart more than anybody else, had been expecting.

Traditionally based at Shanghai, with the primary mission of looking after American interests in China, Admiral Hart's fleet had moved to the Philippines in the autumn of 1940, since its commander, having no doubt about the approach of war, believed that he must avoid being bottled up in a Chinese river and that coordination with General Douglas MacArthur, the former U.S. Army chief of staff who commanded Philippine Commonwealth forces, had now become his most important task.

In a way unimaginable to later generations, American defense efforts in the years leading up to World War II had to subsist on the thinnest of diets. Pleading, in his earnest way, for money in testimony before a Congressional committee in 1939, for instance, General Marshall praised the new 37mm gun the army had developed, but added, sadly, "We consider [it] very fine, but at present we have only one gun." An obvious target like the Philippines had only two radar sets in operation and depended for attack warning on Filipino air watchers with access to telephones or telegraphs.

Certainly Hart's Asiatic Fleet could not be considered a robust enterprise. Overall, at Manila and other bases, it consisted—aside from minesweepers, gunboat refugees from China, and auxiliary ships of various kinds—of one heavy cruiser, two light cruisers, twelve old destroyers, and a squadron of six PT boats. On December 1, just a week earlier, the fleet had also officially acquired as a component a new command called Submarines, U.S. Asiatic Fleet, commanded by Captain W. E. Doyle and consisting of the seventeen submarines of Squadron Twenty, already on hand, and twelve newly arrived late-1930s S-class boats (*Salmon, Spearfish,* and sisters, including the *Sailfish,* the resurrected and renamed *Squalus*), not to be confused with the old S-boats, designated as Squadron Two. The chief of naval operations had ordered these boats dispatched from Pearl Harbor to Manila to support the active defense of the islands that was coming to be expected; the new command now included half of all the U.S. submarines in the Pacific.

Though three-fourths of these were modern boats, Captain Doyle also had under his command six of the old S-boats from the World War I era, with their well-known technical deficiencies, which had long concerned Admiral Hart. In 1921 Hart had led ten S-boats on a cruise from Portsmouth to Manila to join the Asiatic Fleet. It was the first trans-Pacific crossing for American submarines and the longest venture any had yet undertaken; previously, boats had been carried to the Philippines lashed to the decks of colliers. No matter what S-boats had been able to accomplish years earlier, the navy called on them now simply because it needed every submarine it could scrape up; small (about 850 tons) and slow (12 to 14 knots on the surface), an S-boat seemed to proclaim its lack of status by having as commanding officer a lieutenant rather than a lieutenant commander, like the fleet boats.

The shortcomings of S-boats actually represented something of a badge of honor for those who served on them and who proudly claimed the name "pigboat" for their craft (because of "foul living conditions"), even though others considered the name generic for all submarines, deriving from the ancients' idea of the dolphin as a sea pig.

■ ■ ■

The Japanese moved efficiently to achieve the lofty goals they had set for themselves in the first phases of the Pacific war: destruction of the U.S. Pacific and Asiatic fleets, of British seapower in Southeast Asia, and of Allied airpower in the area. With these objectives accomplished, the high command believed, the imperial march of conquest could move forward unimpeded.

The attack on Pearl Harbor and the sinking of the British Force Z in the South China Sea provided two quick successes, both of them not only shocking and tragic but highly embarrassing for the Allies. But the annals of human mortification can yield nothing equal to what happened to U.S. air strength in the Philippines. Although the Americans held the responsibility for the defense of these islands, the United States lay more than 6,000 miles away and even Hawaii nearly 5,000. U.S. planners had long expected that a serious Japanese attack would force the defending American and Filipino troops into a stand on the Bataan peninsula; their aim would be to hold Manila Bay.

Meanwhile, according to the planners, the U.S. fleet would be advancing across the Pacific, defending troop convoys, engaging in big-gun battles with any Japanese fleet sent out to oppose it, and preparing to seize the islands back from the invaders, with Manila Bay as the arena from which to mount the counteroffensive. In one of the kinds of unintended consequences that always accompany any complicated act of policy, however, the Washington Naval Treaty had left Japan with the most powerful force in the western Pacific, and it had further hampered the United States by forbidding the strengthening of any bases, like Guam and Manila, lying west of Hawaii. Hence the Americans appeared to have strategic commitments on which they simply could not make good.

In the summer of 1941, however, the planners began to take a more cheerful view of the prospects of resisting a Japanese assault, thanks in good part not only to General MacArthur's vigorously expressed faith in the troops under his command but also to the idea that a strong force of B-17s could put up an active defense on its own and possibly even deter the Japanese from attacking. If General Marshall sent Fortresses, as promised, then it seemed that Manila Bay might well be secure. Marshall, impressed by the possibilities of heavy bombers, saw to it that four groups (sixty-eight planes each) were allotted to the Philippines, with one more group in reserve, and promised still more out of future production. The assembly line for defense still moved at a slow prewar low-budget pace, and these figures represented plans, not yet actual aircraft. But by December, thirty-five Fortresses had joined MacArthur's command, not a great number but nevertheless amounting to half of all the U.S. heavy bombers stationed anywhere overseas. In the second half of 1941, Marshall had, in fact, devoted his chief effort to building up the defenses of the Philippines, but the great distances involved and the shortage of available shipping made the development move haltingly. Even so, in the first week of December the Philippines had a stronger complement of combat aircraft than any other U.S. base, including Hawaii and Panama.

At about three o'clock in the morning on December 8 in Manila, an army signalman picked up a commercial radio report that was quickly relayed to General MacArthur: The Japanese had attacked Pearl Harbor. Shortly thereafter the chief of the War Plans Division, telephoning from Washington, discussed the situation directly with the general and declared that he "wouldn't be surprised if you get an attack there in the near future." General Hap Arnold likewise warned MacArthur's air commander, Major General Lewis Brereton, to expect an air attack. Brereton, who had just arrived in Manila in November, had expressed strong concern about the shortage of antiaircraft guns in the area. Sending heavy bombers without providing antiaircraft protection, he had observed before leaving Washington, amounted to probable suicide.

Though the officers in Washington naturally felt impelled to make their points, they can hardly have believed that their colleagues would fail to draw the obvious and ominous implications for the Philippines from the Japanese action in Hawaii. Nevertheless, at 12:20 P.M., more than nine hours after MacArthur had learned of the Pearl Harbor attack, a force of Japanese bombers and fighters flying from Formosa caught MacArthur's aircraft, fighters as well as bombers, spread out on the tarmac of Clark and Nichols fields, the air force bases, just like General Short's aircraft on Oahu (which had been bunched together in the thought that they could thus be more readily protected against possible sabotage). Fog over Formosa had forced the enemy to delay the raid, planned for dawn, and they were "very worried," said a Japanese air officer, that the Americans would have dispersed their planes by midday. They need not have been concerned. In the attack MacArthur lost half of his most important airplanes ("on the *ground*, on the *ground!*" cried a dismayed FDR when he received the news) and thus at the outset of their effort the Japanese had effectively fulfilled the objective of destroying U.S. airpower in the region.

Many reasons were put forward for this debacle, none of them carrying much conviction. One, however, smacked of mystery: For more than six hours Brereton had sought in vain to talk with MacArthur about launching a raid on Formosa with the B-17s that had been so earnestly sought from Washington. He apparently did not receive the desired permission from MacArthur's imperious gatekeeper and chief of staff, Major General Richard K. Sutherland (who had followed Dwight Eisenhower in that position), until almost eleven, for whatever reason. Before Brereton could organize and launch any attack—or, actually more important, just get his sitting ducks in the air and dispersed—the Japanese had arrived over Clark and other army fields with their bombs.

MacArthur himself offered little in the way of explanation of this catastrophe. Since he never admitted inadequacy of any kind, let alone actual error, he displayed no embarrassment and seemed to feel no need to justify or even explain his actions. "The inclination of his staff," reported the journalist John Gunther, "is to blame a subordinate officer for this botch and blunder." In any case, the general, unlike the commanders on Oahu, could hardly have claimed to have been surprised; not only had Pearl Harbor already happened, many hours earlier, but the Japanese had given thorough warning of their intentions by bombing northern Luzon earlier that morning. In one way or another, the suicide General Brereton had foreseen had occurred.

Even though General MacArthur and his subordinates did not rush to claim responsibility for the debacle, rumors in Manila quickly combined with lively reporting to produce the inevitable sneaky evildoer, a standard figure at the scene of any World War II disaster: the fifth columnist (fear of such subversives had also haunted the army commanders in Hawaii before the attack). Instead of military unpreparedness and inadequacy, it was "scores of fifth columnists and traitors" who aided the Japanese to destroy the air force by such deviltry as igniting flares at the corners of Nichols Field to outline it as a target. One "good Joe" bartender was largely responsible for the debacle, according to one reporter, because through his "powerful short-wave transmitter in a room back of the bar" he radioed details of the airfields to the Japanese. What amounted to vigilante justice was said to have triumphed, however: A "grim sergeant from the 26th Cavalry" stormed into the bar with a tommy gun, and when he came out the good Joe and all his employees were dead.

Few people wanted to face the central simple truth about the catastrophes at both Oahu and Luzon: Everything about them, from the sluggishness of senior commanders to the heedless handling of important messages by low-ranking officers and enlisted personnel, showed that the army and the navy still dwelled in a peacetime 1930s world, in which nobody would presume to take advantage of the United States.

However the public may have reacted to the fifth-column stories, the essential facts were that MacArthur had lost his air force, his Philippine Army would quickly prove nothing like as effective as he had proclaimed it to be, and, of course, no U.S. fleet would now come steaming across the Pacific from Pearl Harbor or anywhere else to succor the islands. What was left? Not much, besides Admiral Hart's small force, with its complement of elderly S-boats.

■ ■ ■

When a young ensign had joined the old *S-39* in 1940, he recalled having heard that "S-boats weren't exactly queens of the sea, possessing none of the amenities of the larger, newer, faster fleet submarines." (The *S-39* had been laid down in January 1919 in San Francisco and commissioned in September 1923. She had made the long trans-Pacific voyage in the autumn of 1924 and had served with the Asiatic Fleet ever since, operating out of Manila in the winter months and out of Tsingtao, on the China coast, during the summers.) Within a few hours of coming aboard, this ensign "had already experienced the *'39*'s lack of air conditioning, the Rube Goldberg complexities of her head, and the primitive shower facilities." He also remembered a statement quoted from an official 1925 report: "[E]xperience in maneuvers indicates that these vessels cannot be considered as a satisfactory type of fleet submarine."

Another arrival decided that "from machinery to furniture, the old boat was as beat-up as the leftovers at a church rummage sale." But neither of these young men had felt any desire to transfer. Of one it was said, "he was damned glad to be aboard," and of the other, "he was hooked and happy."

One day, some time before Red Coe took over as commanding officer of the S-39, the chief engineer went over to the Cavite navy yard, on Manila Bay, to discuss the details of a scheduled overhaul with the engineering duty officer. Some time later he returned to the boat, seething and, said Lieutenant Roy Klinker, the gunnery and torpedo officer, with tears in his eyes. What was the problem? Klinker asked.

"That goddamned assistant planning officer over there turned down every one of my work requests!"

Klinker had heard that an old superior of his, a famously penny-pinching specialist in ship construction and repair, had been assigned to Cavite; "engineering duty only" meant that an officer had opted out of the line of command to concentrate on technical matters. "What's his name?"

"Rickover."

"Ah-ha," said Klinker, who immediately saw the solution of the problem. Lieutenant Commander Hyman Rickover, he had learned from his earlier association, reacted best to treatment with a heavy dose of his own strong medicine. Putting the engineer's specific points into a reply as bristling as Rickover's brush-off, Klinker allowed the S-39's skipper "a few beers and a little ruminating" before inducing him to sign the letter and send it off. Rickover, "though nitpicking and squawking as usual, finally honored the requests." The S-boat would be the beneficiary of Klinker's insight.

The U.S. defense plan, which took a realistic view of Admiral Hart's limited assets, recognized that the fleet had no chance of standing up to an attack by Japanese battleships and carriers and therefore called for its principal ships, the cruisers and destroyers, to sail southward to the Indian Ocean, out of danger. The submarines would remain, acting as the principal naval defenders of the islands, watching for and resisting enemy landings. But by maiming U.S. air power—the bases as well as the aircraft themselves—the Japanese attackers had delivered a particularly powerful blow to the submarines, because in at-

tempting to defend the Philippines the boats would now have to operate in shallow coastal waters as clear as the Caribbean with no air cover
to fend off enemy bombers. They would form unmistakable targets.

■ ■ ■

Just before one o'clock in the afternoon of December 10, a force of
Japanese bombers, with fighter escorts, appeared over Cavite navy yard.
With little to fear from American interceptors, the fighters found few
protective chores to perform, while for two hours the bombers, cruising beyond antiaircraft range at 20,000 feet, rained destruction on the
base, as "Admiral Hart looked on in helpless rage. . . ." Fire swept
through the entire yard, consuming, as well, a third of the town of
Cavite itself. So confidently did the Japanese do their work, Hart
noted, that "if they were not completely satisfied with their aim, they
held their bombs and kept making runs until they were satisfied."

Admiral Hart had already scattered his cruisers and destroyers, and
for some days the submarines had been patrolling just as if war had already been declared. The *S-35* had been sent to Bolinao Harbor to
stand by for patrolling in Lingayen Gulf, and the *S-39* had been ordered
to Sorsogon Bay; two other S-boats waited in harbor with orders to be
ready for immediate action, and they went out as soon as word came of
the Japanese attacks on Oahu and other U.S. island bases, Midway and
Wake Island. Without waiting for orders from Admiral Stark in Washington, or even from Admiral Hart, Captain Doyle had told the skippers to "conduct unrestricted warfare on anything that flies the
Japanese flag or that you recognize as Japanese." There would be no
stop-and-search procedure, said Commander Stuart "Sunshine" Murray, who had come to Manila with the S-class submarines from Pearl
Harbor. "We knew," he said, "that the Japanese merchantmen were
armed, and we were not taking any chances on it." Admiral Hart accepted the *fait accompli*.

The remaining submarines received orders for various patrol positions, and when the air assault began those that were still at home
rather than out on patrol churned away from the harbor as fast as they
could go, diving as soon as they reached deep water. Two S-class boats,

however, had less mobility. The *Seadragon* was just finishing overhaul, while the *Sealion* was a stage or two behind, with her engines dismantled. On the very first enemy pass, as one or more bombs hit the wharf at which the *Seadragon* lay, the machine gunners made futile efforts to damage the attackers. Before the enemy planes could return, Lieutenant Commander R. G. Voge (Naval Academy '25), skipper of the *Sealion,* said to Lieutenant Commander William E. "Pete" Ferrall (Naval Academy '27), skipper of the *Seadragon:* "You know, I think we're damn fools staying up here on the bridge." Ferrall agreed, and both cleared the boats topside. All of Voge's people went below into the control room, but on the *Seadragon* a few stayed up in the conning tower.

This time the attackers struck hard. Almost together, two bombs smashed into the *Sealion.* The first wrecked the conning tower area, and fragments from this explosion not only wounded three men in the control room but sliced into the conning tower of the *Seadragon,* lying next door, almost decapitating Ensign Samuel H. Hunter, Jr., who became the first American submariner to die of enemy action in World War II.

A moment later the second bomb exploded in the *Sealion's* engine room, killing four crewmen. Water poured in and the boat quickly sank by the stern, coming to rest on the bottom about half underwater. Since the attack had destroyed the repair facilities at Cavite, the authorities had no choice but to declare the *Sealion* a casualty of war. To keep her from falling into Japanese hands, Commander John Wilkes, who took over as the Asiatic Fleet's submarine commander on December 10, later ordered her destroyed. She thus entered history as the first U.S. submarine lost in the war.

For the *Seadragon,* however, destiny had other plans. Moving through the Japanese firestorm came the rescue vessel *Pigeon* (which happened to be in the yard because her steering gear had needed repairs and also happened to have an enterprising skipper, the renowned diver Lieutenant Commander "Spittin' Dick" Hawes). The *Pigeon* passed a line to the submarine, which now carried the *Sealion's* crew as well as her own, and pulled her away from her berth and into a position in which she could then maneuver. Proceeding out into the bay under her own power, she received a remarkable temporary patch job on the spot. She then went on to the Dutch naval base at Surabaya, Java, where she received more thorough repairs, and on December 30 she left on her first wartime patrol.

BATTLE: BOATS VS. INVADERS

With no air cover, no heavy ships, and now no main base, the U.S. Asiatic Fleet, as Admiral Hart memorably declared, had to face the Japanese invaders of the Philippines "like a man with bare fists fighting a killer with a tommygun." These bare fists were the fleet's six S-boats and twenty-three later-design submarines, and they were missing some of their punch, because the Japanese attacks on Manila had destroyed more than two hundred torpedoes, a loss that would constitute only one aspect of an unfolding and dismal torpedo story for the Pacific fleet.

The *S-39* had left Manila Bay on December 1, and Red Coe, like all the other skippers, had taken with him some basic advice from Captain Doyle. Though the war would not begin for a week, Doyle had made it clear that the boats had a war mission and that they might well find themselves in contact with Japanese warships. On these first patrols, Doyle said, commanding officers were to "use caution and feel their way because it was felt that this patrol would be the most dangerous and would also be the most informative as to enemy methods." Skippers should use great care not simply to save themselves and their crews but to bring back knowledge that could help others.

When Coe received Admiral Hart's war message on December 8, his boat lay in position to move right to her patrol station, the San Bernardino Strait, which divides the long, thin southeastern peninsula of Luzon from the next island, Samar. On December 11, at Legaspi on Albay Gulf, near the end of this peninsula, the Japanese, in carrying out their systematic invasion of the Philippines, landed an infantry battalion. In support of the operation, two minelayers sowed some three hundred mines in the San Bernardino Strait. During the day enemy

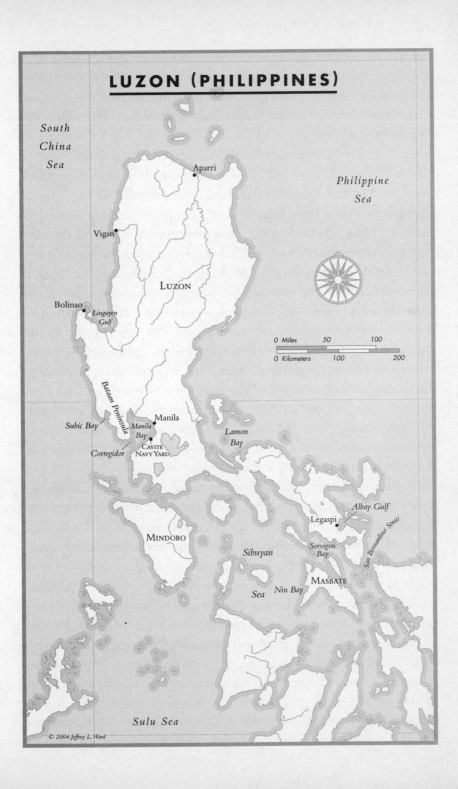

LUZON (PHILIPPINES)

South
China
Sea

Philippine
Sea

Aparri

Vigan

LUZON

Bolinao
Lingayen
Gulf

0 Miles   50   100
0 Kilometers   100   200

Bataan Peninsula

Subic Bay

Manila
Bay   Manila

Corregidor

CAVITE
NAVY YARD

Lamon
Bay

MINDORO

Sibuyan

Sea   Nin Bay

Legaspi

Albay Gulf

Sorsogon
Bay

MASBATE

San Bernardino Strait

Sulu Sea

© 2004 Jeffrey L. Ward

destroyers accompanied these activities with heavy and frequent random depth charges, and as the detonations came closer the men on the
S-39 began to feel like deliberately chosen targets. Even though they
knew better, they still had to dive and stay down, while the enemy pre-
empted their territory.

After the boat had surfaced early the next morning, December 13,
crewmen saw a Japanese submarine almost next door. The S-39 dived
immediately, and then, in the darkness, a game of stalking began, with
the Japanese boat's active sonar (S-boats did not have this equipment)
bouncing pings off the S-39 for more than an hour before finally fading away. But further action came along immediately. A few minutes
before 0600, Ensign Charles Hendrix, on the periscope, spotted a
Japanese merchant ship on the port bow, at a range of about 12,000
yards. Red Coe rushed to the bridge, wearing only shorts, and immediately ordered Battle Stations Submerged. The entire party in the
control room then began the elaborate approach and firing procedure,
involving the approach officer, diving officer, assistant approach officer, plotting officer, the chief of the boat, the bow planesman, the stern
planesman, the helmsman, the quartermaster, the trim manifold man,
the blow manifold man, the telephone talker, a messenger, and the con-
trollerman—altogether, a third of the boat's company. The S-39 was
about to make her first attack on an enemy vessel.

Bearings and ranges changed as the target ship, identified from the
navy's guide to Japanese merchant silhouettes as a 5,000-ton freighter,
zigged and zagged. Finally, after twenty-one minutes, with the boat on
the firing bearing, Coe ordered two torpedoes fired. After a little more
than two minutes, he believed that he saw the freighter list and begin
going down by the stern. But he had no time to linger. One of the destroyers escorting the convoy, having picked up the submarine's
periscope, fired a shot that splashed into the water nearby.

Taking the S-39 down, the skipper ordered her rigged for silent running. Strangely, however, though the destroyers began tracking and
pinging, no depth charges came. Probably, Coe decided, the destroyers
did not know whether the submarine they were tracking was American or their own boat (the one the S-39 had earlier evaded), and, for
her part, the Japanese submarine, if she had not left the area, had to

consider the possibility that these searching destroyers might be Americans looking for her.

An hour and then another passed, while all the crew except the helmsman and the planesmen sat immobile, to conserve energy and the fading air and to make as little noise as possible: "[A]ching eyes had become red-rimmed and filmy. . . . Increasing headaches were acting as a barometer of decreasing air quality inside the pigboat. Men who had been florid from heat were paling out from lack of oxygen. Nobody complained because there was no point in it. An S-boat was a great leveling agent; all suffered equally."

Finally the pinging began fading away, the *S-39* slowly surfaced, and when a quartermaster opened the hatch the foul air blew out with a rush. Then, with the boat beginning to get under way, fresh air poured in. One officer remembered that men realized for the first time that air has a taste: "They opened their mouths and gulped it. They rolled it around their tongues. They smacked their lips over it."

The next day, amid rain and fog, the Japanese convoys continued to arrive at the entrance to Albay Gulf, but despite *S-39*'s best efforts, the destroyer screens kept their charges invulnerable. The invasion proceeded here as successfully as elsewhere in the islands; for the moment the Japanese seemed invincible. After being summoned back to Manila, the men of the *S-39* learned a curious fact about themselves as they proceeded northward. The Japanese radio propagandist dubbed Tokyo Rose informed them that the *S-39* had been sunk, building on this supposed fact to try to persuade other submariners to abandon the fight. The *S-39* remained very much afloat, however, despite suffering from some mechanical problems, but it was an appallingly transformed Manila to which they returned, with the orderly, well-kept buildings at Cavite reduced to burnt-out rubble and continuing Japanese air raids confining submarines to the bottom of the bay during daylight hours.

Clearly the end was approaching for the Pearl of the Orient, as Manila was long known. Having landed at three points in northern Luzon on December 10, the Japanese struck their main blow on December 22 with a landing at Lingayen Gulf north of Manila on the west coast. Hardly a surprise attack, since the gulf had long seemed to planners the likely place for the expected principal Japanese landing, the operation nevertheless began almost undetected, with only one U.S. submarine, the *Stingray*, on hand to pick it up and no watchful cordon spread out westward to give advance word. Without such notice the Americans had no chance to deter or damage the invasion fleet, but Hart and Wilkes did not appear to have considered this use of submarines, though the operational doctrine built up during the preceding decades put heavy emphasis on such a defensive role for the boats. (Wilkes blamed the blindness on the Japanese destruction of U.S. patrol planes, which had been expected to supply submarines with information about enemy movements.)

At the same time, however, a picket line of submarines might well fail to catch sight even of a large fleet of enemy heavy ships. In any case, the Japanese found no attackers on hand when they arrived at Lingayen. Only after the *Stingray* signaled the enemy landing did Wilkes rush other submarines to the scene, but the game had already been lost; the boats could not operate effectively in the shoal waters of the bay.

Nevertheless, the old *S-38*, one of the boats sent by Wilkes, managed to make herself felt. Laid down in January 1919 and commissioned in May 1923, the *S-38* had served with the Asiatic Fleet since November 1924. Commanded by Lieutenant Wreford "Moon" Chapple, a sturdily built varsity football player and heavyweight boxer at the Naval Academy ('30), the *S-38* sneaked behind the Japanese destroyer screen, in shallow, 30-foot water, amidst razor-sharp reefs and rocks, and into Lingayen Gulf in the early hours of December 22.

At first light Chapple made a periscope sweep of the scene and immediately focused on an array of tempting targets, a group of enemy transports. Hardly sitting ducks, however, the ships enjoyed the protection of active destroyers that dashed around them in a defensive ring. Nevertheless, the *S-38* moved into firing position, and, picking out four targets, Chapple fired four torpedoes—all he could shoot without reloading—and scored no hits. At that range—1,000 yards—it hardly seemed possible, but the skipper presumed that the error was his, and when the crew had reloaded he set the torpedoes to run at 9 feet rather than 12. Chased from her spot by a pinging destroyer, the *S-38* moved farther into the bay, where Chapple fixed on a true sitting duck, a

5,455-ton transport riding at anchor, 500 yards off. Thirty seconds later came an explosion that literally rocked the boat; the *S-38* had claimed her first victim and the Japanese vessel settled to the bottom of the bay. Chapple's adjustment of the torpedo setting had worked perfectly, but having earlier experienced the frustration of missing a fat target with a well-aimed torpedo, he became one of the first in what would prove to be a long parade of frustrated submarine skippers in the Pacific who would soon engage in fierce battle with the navy's ordnance experts.

After torpedoing the freighter, the *S-38* went as deep as she could in the shallow bay (about 80 feet), while relays of "ash cans" (depth charges) began exploding in the surrounding waters. One sailor characterized the detonation of a depth charge resounding inside a submarine like the ring of a sledgehammer against a boiler, with the listener's head inside the boiler. In one attempt at evasion, the *S-38* thrust herself into a mud bank at 80 feet, then coasted up the bank to 57 feet, where she remained stuck. This difficulty, from which she later managed to extricate herself, marked the first of a harrowing series of problems that beset the boat, including the kind of heat and sweat and stink and lack of air that had beset the *S-39* off Legaspi, as destroyers and small boats pursued her in her attempts to survive and then make her way back to base. At one point during the boat's fourteen-hour stretch on the bottom, things seemed so desperate that Chapple ordered the sound man to turn off his apparatus. "I figured—and the men figured—that we were pretty helpless," Chapple said, "that we probably were going to get it, and what was the use of knowing exactly when." When they finally could surface in darkness, "Ensign G. W. Forbes said we certainly had given the Japs 14 hours of hell. Everybody laughed, and the tension relaxed." The next day brought a similar ordeal, only this time it stretched to eighteen hours.

"Depth bombs, groundings, underwater collision, a broaching, mechanical maladjustments and an internal explosion [her after battery blew up]," said an official historian, "had been defeated by all hands and a boat remarkable for stamina." Of course, life on an S-boat would never be easy.

Chapple and the *S-38* made the only kill recorded by the submarines belatedly sent to attack the Japanese landing at Lingayen (and it entered the rolls as the second U.S. submarine sinking of the war). After sighting the invasion force, the patrolling *Stingray* had taken no further action, firing no shots at any target, a performance Captain Wilkes deemed so unsatisfactory that, when the boat returned to Manila, he relieved the skipper of command. Overall, noted the official historian, "one transport out of an armada which numbered more than 80 ships does not stand as impressive on the record."

On Christmas Eve, General MacArthur bestirred himself, almost at the last minute, to inform Admiral Hart of his decision to declare Manila an open city to spare it pointless destruction; army headquarters would move to the fortress island of Corregidor at the mouth of Manila harbor. "This was the first intimation," said Captain Wilkes, that Hart "had received of any possibility of such action," and it gave the navy almost no time to assemble the vitally important supplies, spare parts, and oil stocks that had been dispersed around the metropolitan area.

Hart then decided to command his force from Java, and arranged to leave Manila in a patrol seaplane that had been hidden in a stand of mangrove bushes on a lake to protect it from Japanese bombers, but just before he arrived the next afternoon an enemy attack destroyed this aircraft and another that was also supposed to perform ferry service. (Afflicted, like everybody else, with a touch of the fifth column virus, Hart wondered how the enemy could have known about the planes unless told by fifth columnists, "of which the Philippines seem also to have had their share"; he also ascribed part—certainly not all— of the Japanese success at Pearl Harbor to "the failure to suppress the fifth columnists on Oahu.") The admiral settled for a week's journey to Java aboard the submarine *Shark*. Captain Wilkes temporarily transferred his submarine headquarters to Corregidor, but within a week the constant Japanese air raids on "the Rock" had proved the utter impracticability of this move. Without further deliberation, Wilkes decided to follow Hart to Surabaya. Commander James Fife, Jr., Wilkes's chief of staff, led another party of officers to an alternate base at Port Darwin, on the northern Australian coast. On evacuating Corregidor, the submarine command loaded the boats as full as possible of people and material, but some officers and enlisted men remained behind; most of the spare parts would end up dumped into the water. Wilkes asked the commandant to "make every effort to destroy" the secret Mark VI magnetic torpedo exploders that had to be left on the Rock. As later experience would show, a shrewder move might have been to leave them on display for the Japanese to find and try to use.

When the *S-38* returned on December 26 from her Lingayen Gulf action, Moon Chapple accordingly received orders for Surabaya. For the time being, at least, the *S-38* and all the other submarines of the Asiatic Fleet would have new home ports, either Surabaya or Port Darwin. The once quiet Dutch base in Java, now overwhelmed by its greatly expanded responsibilities, presented a welter of linguistic, mechanical, and procedural confusion, and Darwin proved to be a sunscorched and isolated red-dirt town with hardly so much as a stray dog moving along the main street. ("When you're there a few weeks," said one American, "you find yourself talking to yourself. After that, you find yourself talking to the lizards. After another couple of weeks, you find the lizards talking to you. Then you find yourself listening.")

From these unlikely lodgings, working with the eight Dutch and two British submarines in the area, U.S. boats tried to help in the defense of the Indies, but these efforts met with failure. Despite all the work of the Allied submarines in Southeast Asia, the Japanese shook them off and continued on their conquering path. "Even if all their attacks had succeeded," commented a British admiral, "it is doubtful whether they would have done more than impose a slight delay on the Japanese advance." On March 3 Roosevelt's naval aide summarized the situation in a bleak memorandum for his boss: "Japs nearing south coast of Java by sea in addition to three landings on north shore and the rest of the Indies had fallen to the invaders." The Dutch admiral commanding had ordered surface forces to withdraw and would rest the naval defense of Java on submarines (this thought represented a bit of wishful thinking; the campaign in the East Indies had in fact ended). The memo ended on a forlorn note: "MacArthur has nothing to report."

■ ■ ■

After accomplishing their initial conquests, the Japanese dispatched submarines on striking missions south and west, one squadron crossing the Indian Ocean to the coast of Africa. When seaplanes on a reconnaissance run found H.M.S. *Ramillies* in the harbor of Diego Suarez, at the northern tip of Madagascar, the navy loosed midget submarines that sneaked into the harbor and torpedoed the battleship. A similar reconnaissance of the eastern Australian coast produced an unsuccessful attempt to attack cruisers in the harbor of Sydney, and seaplanes from submarines even investigated Puget Sound, at Seattle, for possible victims. Earlier, the three submarines that would have a fatal encounter with Joe Grenfell and the *Gudgeon* had fired shells at oil refineries and other targets in southern California. Lying in the channel off Santa Barbara, one of the boats spent forty unmolested minutes lobbing 5-inch shells at oil installations and a nearby bridge, though with a remarkable lack of accuracy. These missions had little effect on the course of the war, aside from the damage done to beachfront real estate values in Santa Barbara, but they offered the Allies impressive examples of the scope Japanese submarine operations could achieve.

As history had already demonstrated to the Allies, submarines, despite doctrines long and stubbornly held, did not perform well in a defensive role: "It is always extremely difficult to put them in the right place and their strategic deployment to meet enemy moves is invariably slow." In February a bizarre controversy arose between skippers and higher authorities over an order requiring a submarine to make a radio report before beginning an attack. The submariners pointed out that "this procedure would almost certainly nullify any possibility of successful attack," and they asked that the standard doctrine of attacking first and then reporting remain in force; headquarters gave its approval. It was also true, Wilkes could not help commenting, that such reporting would have had no point in any case, since no air or surface forces existed in the area to take advantage of any information that submarines might offer. Overall, submarines as warships had endured a strikingly rough initiation in the Pacific encounters of December 1941 and into 1942, inflicting little harm on enemy warships, and in the southwest the loss of their bases and of most of their torpedoes had compounded their tactical and technical difficulties.

But if the submarine had accomplished little as a warship and had not yet made a mark as a commerce raider, it quickly began to demonstrate its handiness when called on for some kinds of specialized missions; in fact, "special mission" came to be the standard term for such operations. Not surprisingly, efforts to supply aid to embattled Corregidor assumed early prominence, even though such errands had their critics because they took the boats away from patrol and hence from possible confrontation with the enemy. In late January the *Seawolf* delivered 37 tons of .50-caliber ammunition to the Rock and ferried out twenty-five army and navy pilots; a few days later the *Seadragon* appeared, with the mission of evacuating twenty-one codebreakers and other army and navy personnel, together with 2 tons of submarine parts and 1.5 tons of radio equipment. Just the day before, the *Trout* had also returned to Luzon waters to deliver antiaircraft ammunition to the Rock and carry away not people but 20 tons of Philippine government gold and silver.

In two separate visits in late February the *Swordfish*, skippered by Chester C. Smith (Naval Academy '25), came to pick up Philippine President Manuel Quezon, his family and associates, and the U.S. high commissioner to the Philippines, Francis B. Sayre, and his official party. "You're going out with an ace submarine skipper," the admiral commanding on Corregidor assured Sayre. "He'll get you through." The mild-mannered but effective Smith did indeed perform as advertised.

After the surrender of Singapore on February 15, Commander Wilkes tapped Red Coe and his *S-39* for a mission to rescue a group of British refugees, including an air vice marshal and a rear admiral, who had landed on a tiny island called Chebia, in the South China Sea. The American authorities had picked up this information from an SOS sent out by members of the party who apparently were at the same time dodging Japanese searchers. Eluding swarming enemy patrols, the *S-39* raced (in S-boat terms) to the island, covering 90 miles in twenty-three hours, even risking some early morning travel on the surface. Arriving just after midnight on March 1 but seeing nobody on the moonlit beach, Coe took the *S-39* inshore and by blinker gun signaled her presence, taking the chance that, if spotted by foe instead of friend, the *S-39* could dive to safety; Coe had decided that rescue was impossible without risk. Repeated efforts that night and the next produced no replies, nor did a two-man landing party, which boldly went ashore with guns at the ready, encounter either British or Japanese. But, studying a line of shoe prints leading down to the water's edge, the Americans concluded that the Japanese had beaten them to the island. "We were sorry for those people," Coe said later, with understated feeling. "The Japanese prisons were tough."

One instance of a submarine transportation run took a curious turn and ended in a disappointing if instructive confrontation. It involved the adventure-prone Moon Chapple, who in mid-February moved up from his exhausted *S-38* to replace the exhausted commander of the *Permit,* one of the midthirties P-boats that were somewhat smaller than the later and standard *Gato*-class fleet submarines (301 feet long, 1,282 tons). The *Permit's* official ship history reports that she departed from Surabaya on her fourth patrol (and first under Chapple) on February 22 for the southern Philippines and, it notes, a trip on to Corregidor, where she "landed several thousand rounds of ammunition. After leaving the Rock she headed South, patrolling the southern Philippines en route to Australia."

The special interest in this account comes from the information that does not appear between those two sentences—facts some of which the writer of that history may well not have known. The *Permit* had been directed to Corregidor to evacuate General MacArthur with his entourage (FDR had ordered him to leave the losing battle and continue the war from Australia), but while Chapple was en route to the Rock, the general decided not to wait for him and made what became his famous departure from the Rock in a PT boat. New instructions told Moon to connect with MacArthur's boat and the three others accompanying it off the island of Panay, but arriving there, Chapple discovered that once again the general had stood him up. He found one of the PT boats, however, which lay incapacitated with an engine breakdown, and after taking on board the fifteen-man crew destroyed the boat with gunfire.

Proceeding to Corregidor, Chapple did indeed offload the ammunition, as the history stated, and he also unloaded some of the PT boat's crew. Then he received a new assignment, one having the highest importance: The *Permit* was to evacuate thirty-six members of the Station Cast codebreaking operation who had not gone with the *Seadragon* on February 5. A third and final group of twenty-one officers and men would hang on at Corregidor until April 8, when the *Seadragon* would return to carry them to Australia. (The Cast group had been divided into three teams—each including linguists, cryptanalysts, and radiomen—so that they could operate independently of each other.)

With everybody he was now responsible for, including part of the PT crew and a few other officers and enlisted men from Corregidor, Chapple found his boat crammed with 111 bodies, some of them possessing unique importance. He therefore reacted with astonishment when the naval officer commanding on Corregidor ordered him, not to proceed with the utmost expedition to a safe harbor in which to offload his codebreakers, but instead to conduct a patrol off Manila Bay. Patrolling meant, of course, subjecting everybody on the boat to the risk of death or—perhaps worse for the keepers of high secrets—capture by the Japanese. Nevertheless, Chapple dutifully obeyed this foolish order, even to the extent of attacking a trio of destroyers that approached from astern instead of simply trying to elude them. The resulting depth charge attacks kept the *Permit* deep underwater for an entire day, with the heat growing ever more intense and the oxygen supply shrinking, before she could get away under cover of darkness. The ship history laconically notes that, after leaving Corregidor, the *Permit* "headed South patrolling the southern Philippines en route to Australia," where, with the crumbling of the situation in the Indies, she would now be based. For its location, much too close to the Indies that were falling into the hands of the Japanese and for a variety of other reasons, including the great depth immediately offshore (which meant that any vessel sunk in harbor could not be salvaged), Darwin had been found wanting as a base. Hence the *Permit* headed for Fremantle, on the southwestern coast, arriving on April 7 at the end of an adventurous and varied 38-day patrol.

Captain Wilkes, moving from Surabaya, had arrived at Fremantle a month earlier and established his headquarters in a downtown office building in nearby Perth, the metropolis of Western Australia. But he rolled out no red carpet for Moon Chapple, who had merely succeeded in overcoming a variety of unforeseeable circumstances and hardships to complete a mission of vital importance. Instead, after delivering a standard-style chewing-out to the newly arrived skipper, Wilkes even reported him to Washington for having allowed the admiral at Corregidor to load his boat with far too many passengers. ("Previous directives from this command," Wilkes said stiffly, "had limited total number of passengers to twenty-five and on this occasion the Commanding Officer, PERMIT should have protested the carrying of one hundred and eleven persons in his ship.") Wilkes in fact would have done well to pray that his carping report would not come to high-level attention at the Navy Department: Admiral King had personally ordered the evacuation of all the Cast personnel, both because he feared what they might reveal under torture if they fell into the hands of the Japanese and also because he deemed them of vital importance to the continued prosecution of the war; they must therefore be carried away from Corregidor by "any means of transportation."

The unique nature of Moon Chapple's passengers appeared to mean no more to Wilkes than to the by-the-book admiral on Corregidor who had ordered Chapple to conduct a needless patrol en route to a safe harbor. Such attitudes demonstrated the truth, increasingly evident in early 1942, that traits identified with success and advancement in rank in peacetime often count for nothing in war; Wilkes's obstinacy seemed closely akin to the mentality of the petty officer at Pearl Harbor who demanded a written order before he would open a gun locker for sailors who wanted to shoot back at the attacking Japanese planes. The men on that Sunday solved the problem by smashing the lock.

Even in wartime the navy in general continued its policy of rotating and reassigning officers, and in April 1942, apparently for such bureaucratic reasons rather than for any high-level dissatisfaction with his performance, Captain Wilkes received orders to return to the United States, where he would receive the Distinguished Service Medal and take command of a new cruiser, the U.S.S. *Birmingham*. Certainly Wilkes had faced enormous problems in the Southwest Pacific, with his small collection of refugee submarines responsible, in some degree, for covering a vast area of ocean, and with the torpedo problem that played no favorites: Those on the S-boats had the failing contact exploders, while those on the fleet submarines had the frustrating magnetic exploders. In May Wilkes turned these troubles over to his newly arrived successor, Rear Admiral Charles A. Lockwood, a cheery and energetic officer who had served in the submarine force since the first war and had been much involved in questions of design and equipment, had commanded a submarine division and served at the Navy Department as the top submarine officer, and then had been posted to London as naval attaché, where the American entry into the war found him. Arriving on a cold and rainy afternoon, the new commander thought the streets of Fremantle "could have been those of a typical Kansas boom town." Even to so dedicated an optimist, the strategic outlook seemed to share this bleakness.

■ ■ ■

Shortly before the United States was thrust into the war, Roy Benson, then the executive officer of the *Nautilus,* attended a highly secret briefing in which he and his skipper learned about a new device for torpedoes, the magnetic "influence" exploder, which, because it could be set to detonate the torpedo just under the keel of the target, was supposed to break the unprotected back of the ship. This was the Mark VI exploder. At a similar session in submarine school, a young ensign, Ned Beach, watched closely as the officer conducting the demonstration passed a magnetized steel rod over the mechanism, causing a satisfying click. But then Beach thought of a question: What would keep the exploder from going off too soon if the torpedo was fired at a big ship with a big magnetic field? The designers had taken that possibility into account, the demonstrator said; the exploder would cause detonation immediately after the torpedo passed the magnetic field's highest value, just past the line of the keel. Unfortunately, said Beach, that response was untrue and merely a facile answer to a question that happened to hit on a serious problem.

But, being supplied with torpedoes with magnetic exploders, said Benson, "we had to figure out approximately how much water the target drew and set torpedo depth about ten or fifteen feet below." After the United States entered the war, American skippers, while having no idea that in all these problems and details they were step-by-step recapitulating the German experience, discovered that the torpedoes ran deeper than they were set to run, so deep that the magnetic needle felt no "influence" and hence was not deflected, and the torpedoes did not explode. In one case Benson noted, a skipper fired one shot, hitting and stopping a tanker, and then, seeking to finish it off, fired nineteen more torpedoes without scoring a single hit—"could not get anything to explode." These torpedoes featured dual ignition; either the magnetic exploder or contact with the target would set them off. But neither method worked, though nobody yet realized why.

As for the magnetic exploder, the higher authorities decreed that skippers must follow procedure, setting the depth at about 40 feet, rather than giving in to any desire to compensate for what they believed to be torpedo error by setting the depth at a low figure like 10 feet. The problem was simply that the higher-ups did not believe the complaints uttered by skippers returning from patrol. Since no proof of the deep running could exist, of course, the admirals, in their adversarial way, could simply blame the misses on faulty aim.

"But at my level," said Benson, "we lieutenant commanders in command of submarines knew very well that setting them to run under the keel was not productive." Therefore some skippers (Benson with a wink would not admit having been one) worked out a silent collaboration with the torpedo men, who would set the torpedoes to run at 10 feet while pretending they were set for 40. "Many of the early skippers produced nothing and were transferred out of the submarine service," Benson said. "The only reason they didn't produce anything was the magnetic exploder didn't let them."

These problems, which were severe and highly significant, arose in December 1941 and January 1942 and would continue for many months, in one of the greatest scandals of the war and one that did not find final resolution on all counts for the astonishing time of almost two years. What made the higher-ups so determined not to credit reports from men who had employed these weapons in actual confrontations with the enemy?

The Bureau of Ordnance had developed the Mark VI contact exploder at its Newport Torpedo Station shortly after the first war. In May 1926, in a highly secret test, a Mark XIV torpedo fitted with the magnetic exploder succeeded in sinking an obsolete submarine. But this success came only on the second try; on the first go, the torpedo passed under the ship without detonating and continued on its way. Expressing satisfaction with this success (only, after all, a 50 percent rate), officials of the bureau decided to keep their secret closely held and provided the fleet with torpedoes fitted with practice warheads, a policy that lasted into 1941, until the bureau began sharing the secret in restricted meetings like the one the officers from the *Nautilus* attended. Between 1926 and the Pacific patrols of early 1942, in consequence of this policy, nobody had fired a single torpedo with a Mark VI exploder at a single ship hull; the magnetic exploder went to war with only one unconvincing test behind it in sixteen years. It remained "so secret that nobody could work on it," said Lieutenant Paul Schratz, torpedo officer in the *Mackerel*. "To install or remove one, only the torpedo officer and one torpedoman's mate were allowed in the torpedo room, and we weren't allowed to touch the exploder insides."

In Germany, the skimpy, unrealistic testing of torpedoes had earned some ordnance officials severe censure and even court-martial. But the material bureaus of the U.S. Navy—Ordnance, Supply, Yards and Docks, and others—had a long history of operating as almost independent fiefdoms with close ties to Congress, though a navy reorganization in 1915 (which created the post of chief of naval operations) had acted as something of a curb on this freedom. The bureau chiefs generally remained, however, energetically territorial and bureaucratically skillful, and had little fear of encountering the degree of unpleasantness experienced by their counterparts in the Third Reich. Certainly the U.S. Navy moved more slowly than the frustrated and angry Admiral Dönitz had done not only to solve the torpedo problem but also even to define it. The Bureau of Ordnance officers chose to see the problem as lying not with themselves but with submarine commanders and their torpedo crewmen, who were presumed to be employing the exploder improperly but not wishing to admit it.

In early 1942 Japanese submariners were likewise engaged in soul-searching exercises. The Imperial Navy had supplied its boats with what most observers considered highly effective "oxygen" torpedoes, so termed because the propulsive power came from hydrogen peroxide, oxygen in its most compact form. These missiles moved through the water at high speed without giving off a wake, but the extreme volatility of peroxide posed a constant risk of explosion that the Americans, though engaging in experiments with such torpedoes, had not really wished to take. Japanese skippers appreciated the performance of their weapons but complained about their tendency, at shallow depth settings, to leap out of the water, revealing their approach to the enemy (a problem with any torpedo). The submariners also wanted something better than contact exploders; like the Germans and the Americans, they had heard the false but seductive call of influence. Slower and more stable torpedoes could be more effective than the present type, the Japanese skippers said, if they had a "magnetic type exploder that would make them detonate beneath a ship if they passed under it."

However, the existing submarine torpedo, the Type 95, Mod-1, with contact exploder, carried far more punch, and at greater distances, than the American Mark IV. The Japanese had also developed an effective electric torpedo. For issue to surface ships the Imperial Navy could claim to have the deadliest torpedo in the world, the oxygen-propelled Type 93, introduced in 1933. Much rumored about in the West before its existence was confirmed, it became famous as the Long Lance. (Though no Japanese disasters were attributed to the explosiveness of hydrogen peroxide, the later record of H_2O_2 would contain appalling tragedy.)

Finally, after admitting that perhaps the magnetic exploder might have a problem or two, the U.S. Navy Bureau of Ordnance dispatched experts from Newport to the Pacific. They proceeded to modify a batch of torpedoes to make them more sensitive. "As it turned out," said Lieutenant Commander John Coye, Jr., who had transferred from the Atlantic battle to the Pacific, "they made them so sensitive that if the torpedo depth control wasn't perfect, if it would wiggle a little bit, then that would destroy the magnetic field and that torpedo would explode." On patrol, carrying some of the first of these modified torpedoes, Coye encountered an unescorted seaplane tender and fired four of the torpedoes at this ideal target. Two of them exploded prematurely ("prematured"), thus alerting the men on the tender, who maneuvered to avoid the other two. Exactly the same thing happened in another attack on a tender, the torpedoes prematuring just 30 or 40 yards from the target. "This not only gave your position away and it not only didn't sink any ships," said Coye, "but it was bad for morale."

Captain Wilkes had paid full attention to the torpedo problem. Noting that the torpedoes on hand before the war had been fitted with influence exploders, except for the Mark Xs in the S-boats, Wilkes said that during December nobody had blamed premature explosions on a defect in the torpedoes, but that after the first of the year it became clear "that torpedoes in general were not functioning properly and that this factor contributed to the poor results obtained during the early stages of the campaign." It was only after January 1 (and after skippers like Moon Chapple had discovered it for themselves) that the Navy Department informed him that his crews could expect the Mark X torpedoes to run 4 feet deeper than set.

Wilkes also commented on the experience of the *Sargo,* which during December and early January had fired thirteen torpedoes with magnetic exploders at close range and under good conditions and yet had failed to make a single hit. So ineffectual had the attacks been, in some cases, that the targets did not even appear to know that anybody had fired at them. Wilkes had presumed that such failures by skippers stemmed from buck fever, now that they found themselves in an actual war, together with inexperience in firing at actual ships. But some officers wondered whether the Japanese might not know all about the Mark VI exploders and so might have equipped their ships with countermeasures that neutralized the magnetics. Reluctant to put the blame on the torpedoes and exploders themselves, Wilkes saw possible merit in the countermeasures idea. It also began to become clear, he said, that the Mark XIV torpedoes with the magnetic exploders were running much deeper than set; in addition, captains expressed serious concern about the number of premature explosions. The skipper of the *Sargo* had reacted to a premature, which came with the very first torpedo he fired, by having the magnetic exploder inactivated. Calling this move a mistake, Wilkes decided that torpedoes should be set to run no deeper than 10 feet—in other words, should be set as if they were fitted with contact exploders—but that the magnetics must not be inactivated.

The Bureau of Ordnance weighed in, on February 2, with a firm opinion on the side of the magnetic exploders. Torpedoes fitted with them, said the bureau, would inflict such heavy damage on target ships that concern about the prematures must not lead to inactivation of the influence feature. Wilkes also noted that technical problems with the design and maintenance of torpedoes had contributed to the high total of failures. More personally, he pointed out that crews operating out of Java during February and March could not perform at their best because they had been forced to sail without having adequate preserved food to carry them through long patrols. Nor had the United States government helped in this area, since prior to December 7 requisitions for vitamins had not been filled; night vision, in particular, suffered from this lack. With reference to the well-being of crews, Wilkes also commented that Darwin had offered no possibility for improving rest camps, while Perth was big enough so that he saw no need for such camps.

Despite all the technical and material problems, some of the fault lay with people themselves. Some of the submarine commanders simply had not measured up, and Wilkes had found it necessary to relieve them. He believed, however, that the problems with these skippers demonstrated not so much the failure of the individual as the failure of the peacetime system for selecting submarine commanding officers. A bit acidly, he observed that the system lacked an elementary requirement: a "native ability to hit with torpedoes."

Despite all these considerations, as Admiral Lockwood would quickly see, the torpedoes themselves remained a central problem for all submarines in the Pacific, whether based in Australia or in Hawaii. When, after her second patrol, a long reconnaissance to the south and west, the *Tambor* reported a number of surprising misses in an attack from a favorable firing position, Rear Admiral Robert H. English, who had succeeded Admiral Withers as Commander Submarines Pacific Fleet at Pearl Harbor, conceded that "the exact causes of the misses" could not be precisely determined, but he managed to find a possible specific explanation for each one; his opinions definitely did not favor the skippers.

Lockwood saw the inadequacy of the whole design, but the problem presented a particularly frustrating aspect: The torpedoes functioned as designed just often enough to confuse the issue. Whatever they might think at Pearl Harbor, Lockwood decided to take action for his own area of command when Red Coe, who had moved up from the old S-39 to become captain of a fleet submarine, the *Skipjack* (SS-184), returned from patrol with scathing comments about the situation with the torpedoes. It was pointless, said Coe, to "make a round trip of 8,500 miles into enemy waters to gain attack position within 800 yards of enemy ships only to find that the torpedoes run deep and half the time will fail to explode." This information could be more readily collected right at home, Coe said bluntly, without involving the enemy. Taking him up on the idea of staging a test, and thus challenging the barons of the Bureau of Ordnance, Lockwood and his chief of staff, Captain James Fife, bought a large net from a local fisherman, moored it in King George Sound, and had Coe's boat attack it with dummy torpedoes. The spotting of the holes would show whether the "fish" were running at the set depth.

By the time of the test in June, U.S. submariners on patrol against the Japanese had fired more than eight hundred torpedoes, but until now no one had been willing to subject even a single one of them to testing. Conducted over two days, Lockwood's experiments showed that torpedoes were running at an average of about 11 feet too deep. The bureau gave the resulting report a frosty reception—"instead of thanking us, they scorned our inaccurate approach," said the disgusted but probably not thoroughly surprised Lockwood. These field tests, however, began a process that, involving Admiral King himself, finally, in August, produced an admission from the bureau that the depth-control mechanism suffered from bad design and did indeed need to be modified. The skippers who had already proceeded on the assumption that they were right and the Bureau of Ordnance wrong could

354 · THE SUBMARINE

now claim vindication, but, just like Admiral Dönitz, his predecessor in conflicts with the suppliers of weapons, Lockwood found that solving one problem did not relieve him of all worries. Having the torpedoes run closer to the surface seemed to increase both the number of premature detonations and the frequency with which the fish would strike a hull with a dull thud rather than an explosion. As for the magnetic exploder, "it must have been known in the Department," Lockwood said, "that both the British and the Germans had abandoned this type of unreliable exploder early in the war, yet our experts clung to it 'like grim death to a dead cat' for many months more"; in fact, Lockwood himself showed considerable reluctance to part with it and still hoped that cures could be found for its deficiencies. The contact exploder was producing its own problems as well, and the torpedo factories were still not turning out the numbers needed if the United States intended to wage serious campaigns using submarines as warships against the Japanese Navy and as commerce raiders hounding freighters and tankers—the vessels that kept the resource-shy empire supplied with the materials without which it could not wage war.

SUBMARINES AT MIDWAY

he Allied war against Japan differed fundamentally from the struggle for Europe. Water, not land, served as the primary stage for the action, with fighting ranging over the vast Pacific, often focusing on groups of small and widely separated islands; many of these islands were actually no more than atolls, tiny rings of coral surrounding shallow lagoons. In May 1942 one of these tiny spots on the map suddenly assumed commanding importance. On the twelfth of the month, U.S. Navy codebreakers at Pearl Harbor decrypted a Japanese message containing what would appear at first glance to be remarkably innocuous information: Imperial naval intelligence had learned that an American station in the Pacific, designated AF in the message, had reported a shortage of fresh water. The Japanese interest in this seemingly minor fact immediately took on major proportions as a vindication of Lieutenant Commander Joseph Rochefort, head of the Combat Intelligence Unit on Oahu.

The Japanese had changed their naval cipher on the day of Pearl Harbor, but during the spring American codebreakers on Oahu and in Washington had managed to achieve a good deal of success in reading enemy messages. "There were often gaps in the readable text of messages," one officer noted, "but, even if no more than a word or two of a message could be decrypted, it was sometimes significant." In early May the unit had decrypted messages indicating that Japan intended to assault AF, and from all the evidence he and his listeners and cryptologists had collected, Rochefort had believed— had, indeed, been sure—that AF meant Midway, an atoll with two tiny islands, 1,100 miles northwest of Oahu, almost on the International Date Line. A patrol plane base lying all by itself, Midway was nevertheless close enough to Hawaii to possess strategic importance (as Admiral Nagumo put it, "Midway Island acts as a sentry for Hawaii").

But not everyone, in Oahu or in Washington, agreed with Rochefort. If the Japanese were mounting a major push, as all the messages indicated, many felt that Midway hardly seemed the most likely target. Designations of other points (AL, AO, AOB) also appeared in the intercepts. Some saw the supposed operation aimed at Hawaii, others feared for the West Coast. The higher-ups at Op-20-G in Washington, the navy codebreaking and traffic analysis operation, convinced themselves that the Japanese would mount a significant invasion of the outer Aleutian Islands, the long, rocky chain curving out into the ocean south and west from Alaska.

Instead of wasting time in repetitive arguments, Rochefort devised a plan to prove to skeptics what he already held as a certainty. After he presented his idea to the Pacific Fleet's top intelligence officer, Lieutenant Commander Edwin Layton, who had held this post at the time of Pearl Harbor but escaped blame for the tragedy, Layton, an admirer of Rochefort's work, took the plan to Admiral Chester Nimitz, who had succeeded the unfortunate Admiral Kimmel in command of the Pacific Fleet. It called for Midway to send a message to Pearl Harbor, in the clear, reporting an urgent need for fresh water because its distillation plant, which made drinkable water from salt water, had suffered an explosion. Eager for solid evidence and willing to accept a measure of risk (the Japanese might ask themselves why Midway had not sent its message in cipher), Nimitz agreed to Rochefort's plan. Then, two days later, Rochefort's team intercepted the message showing that the Japanese had taken the bait. AF was low on water, they reported, and thus the enemy had confirmed Midway as the target of a great impending eastward thrust. It bore the code name Operation MI.

▪ ▪ ▪

Even before Pearl Harbor, Admiral Yamamoto and his colleagues in the Japanese high command had drawn up ambitious plans for 1942. On November 1, 1941, Combined Fleet Operation Order No. 1 outlined a series of "areas that are to be rapidly occupied or destroyed, as soon as the war situation permits."

1. Imperial forces would seize Port Moresby, on the southern coast of New Guinea, and the island of Tulagi, a thousand miles eastward in the Solomons group. With these bases secured, the navy could control the Coral Sea area, including northeastern Australia.
2. The forces would capture Midway. The U.S. fleet (still intact, of course, a month before Pearl Harbor) would come out to defend Midway against the attempt, Yamamoto believed, and thus find itself in battle with the Combined Fleet, which would defeat it.
3. Simultaneously, the navy would deceive the Americans as to their real purposes and lure U.S. strength away from Midway by attacking Attu and Kiska at the tip of the Aleutian Islands.
4. Japanese forces would cut the line of communications from the United States to Australia by seizing New Caledonia, the Fiji Islands, and Samoa.

The imperial high command seethed with continual dispute between army and navy leaders, but this consensus plan would serve everybody's purposes. With these victories won, Japan would have established a defensive perimeter around its Greater East Asia Co-Prosperity Sphere, the official aim of its war effort, and in view of the establishment of this new order in Asia, the western powers would surely prove open to a negotiated peace.

Despite all the great and obvious differences between the Japanese and their German allies, the two shared a tendency to overestimate the strength of their respective countries and, particularly on Japan's part, to assume victory in a planned battle before the action had even begun. In World War I Germany found itself fighting a coalition of powers that dwarfed it in size and resources (just as Russia dropped out, the United States came in), and in the second war the Germans had managed to put themselves in that strikingly unfavorable situation again. Even though respecting the latent power of the United States, the Japanese in their planning operated on the complacent assumption that fate would always respect their wishes, although the paradoxical Yamamoto tended to agree with a fellow officer who believed that "it was obvious in terms of figures which side would have the advantage if Japan and America were to indulge in unrestricted competition, but that didn't matter to people infatuated with the 'Way of the Gods.' "

For a time after Pearl Harbor, fate indeed seemed to favor the Japanese as they moved outward to their planned perimeter. By February 15 they had taken Malaya and Singapore, by March 1 they had driven Allied naval forces out of the Netherlands East Indies, by March 7 they had evicted British forces from the capital of Burma, by April 9 they had won the surrender of the Bataan peninsula on Luzon in the Philippines and within two months would have completed the conquest of the islands. On December 10 they had overwhelmed the small U.S. garrison on Guam, 1,500 miles east of the Philippines, and on December 23 they had taken Wake Island, some 2,500 miles west of Hawaii, after heroic resistance by U.S. Marine defenders (a significant loss for the U.S. submarine force, for which the island had been intended as a forward base).

In April and early May, however, this march of maritime conquest encountered two different but important surprises. On April 18, to the amazement not only of the Japanese but also of most Americans and the rest of the world, U.S. B-25 bombers attacked Japan itself, hitting military installations in Tokyo and four other cities. B-25s were Army Air Force aircraft, land-based planes; where in the world could they have come from? In a press conference, President Roosevelt, who in December had ordered the services to find a way to strike back at Japan as soon as possible, declared in typical fashion that the attackers had taken off from Shangri-la (an imaginary Tibetan paradise described in the popular 1933 novel *Lost Horizon* and appealingly presented in a movie based on the book). Apparently having no readers of English novels on staff, Dr. Goebbels's Berlin radio stolidly reported that the aircraft had come from the American base at Shangri-la, "otherwise unidentified."

But the planes in this raid, led by the famous and flamboyant flier Lieutenant Colonel Jimmy Doolittle, had actually come from the deck of the aircraft carrier *Hornet*; volunteer pilots had rehearsed the operation at an air force base in Florida and had never flown off a carrier until the day of the performance itself. This unprecedented operation had the full and active support of Admiral King, who in the aftermath of Pearl Harbor wanted to demonstrate to the world that the U.S. Navy could be aggressor as well as victim (and who had no idea that anyone would give even temporary credit to Shangri-la). From Admiral Nimitz it required steady nerves, since he had to watch two of his irreplaceable carriers (the *Enterprise* accompanied the *Hornet* to supply air cover) disappear westward on a venture that had been dictated from Washington and, as Admiral Halsey, the task force commander, commented, would "need a lot of luck." Admiral English sent the submarine *Thresher,* skippered by Lieutenant Commander William L. Anderson (Naval Academy '26), to help with the project by patrolling off Tokyo and flashing weather reports. (While engaged in this duty, the *Thresher* became involved in confrontations with various Japanese submarines and freighters, sinking one of the latter.)

Coming after many weeks of losses and retreats in the Pacific, the Doolittle Raid, as it quickly became known, gave American morale an enormous boost, which perhaps would have constituted justification enough for the effort and expenditure it involved, the risks run in removing the two carriers from the Central Pacific, and the losses that inevitably occurred. It also caused appreciable if not great losses to Japanese installations. Far more important, it produced a moral shock to the Japanese people, who had grown up in the assurance of their inviolability, and sent a wave of profound embarrassment through the high command. ("It's a disgrace," noted Yamamoto, "that the skies over the imperial capital should have been defiled without a single enemy plane being shot down.")

Unexpectedly, the homeland, whose boast was that never in its history had it been invaded, had proved to be vulnerable to direct attack, with the emperor himself possibly in danger. And, remarkably, one of these strange brown American aircraft had flown past a passenger plane carrying the prime minister, Hideki Tojo, and members of his staff on a local inspection tour, though the B-25, intent on its mission, had paid no heed to the transport. A situation like that could not be tolerated. Clearly, the existing defense perimeter of the empire must be pushed outward and the homeland made secure.

■ ■ ■

After the Pearl Harbor disaster, to nobody's surprise, Washington had relieved Admiral Kimmel of his command. Whatever his justifications or deficiencies, Kimmel had suffered the greatest reverse that fate could inflict on an admiral: He had lost his fleet. He had understood the implications immediately, during the first wave of the attack. When a machine gun slug smashed through his office window, slicing his tunic and stinging his chest, the admiral said to a nearby officer, "It would have been merciful had it killed me." In selecting the new Pacific Fleet commander, President Roosevelt told the secretary of the navy, "Tell Nimitz to get the hell out to Pearl and stay there till the war is won."

Hence, at ten o'clock in the morning of December 31, 1941, the freshly four-starred Chester W. Nimitz raised his flag in the submarine *Grayling,* a new boat that had just come in from California; no stranger to the base, the admiral had supervised its construction twenty years earlier. "He liked to say that he assumed command aboard a submarine because the Japanese attack had left no other sort of deck available at Pearl Harbor," observed his biographer, but "he may have been influenced by the fact that he wore the submariners' dolphins himself." Indeed, early in his career Nimitz had commanded, successively, four submarines and had become something of an expert on diesel engines. In 1912 he had even lectured at the Naval War College at Newport, though he offered no new insights but expressed the conventional wisdom of the time that the submarine should serve as an instrument of defense and an auxiliary to the battle fleet.

A few years before the war, in a conversation with his son (who in a few years would also become a submarine skipper), Nimitz had come forth with a remarkable look into the future. The United States would be involved in a war with Germany and Japan, he believed, and the conflict would begin with the defeat of American forces in a surprise attack. Since the commanders would then be "thrown out," Nimitz wished to have won sufficient prominence by this time to be considered for one of the top commands. Now that all this had come true, he could hardly have been surprised that, when he told his wife about his appointment, she responded: "You always wanted to command the Pacific Fleet. You always thought that

would be the height of glory." Yes, darling, he said in effect, but that
was then and this was now—and now the fleet lay "at the bottom of
the sea."

As Admiral Kimmel could have testified, that statement had considerable force when applied to the battleships, with the attack having either permanently or temporarily put all eight out of action, and in
much of the thinking of the day the battleship still ruled the waves.
More important, however, as would gradually become clear, was the
timing: The Japanese strike, for all the planning that went into it, had
come on a day when the three Pacific Fleet aircraft carriers all happened to be at sea on various missions—mundane missions, at that, not
anything calculated to have them safely away from home as a security
measure. The *Lexington,* engaged in ferrying marine fighter reinforcements to Midway, did, however, have the additional charge of scouting
the northwestern approaches to Hawaii. The *Enterprise* was returning
to Pearl Harbor after having delivered fighters to Wake Island, and the
Saratoga had gone to the mainland for maintenance. But the absence of
the three carriers from Pearl Harbor on December 7, together with the
attackers' failure to assault the submarine base, meant that, denied on
the surface, the Americans would have the opportunity to fight back in
the Pacific in both of the new twentieth-century dimensions—submarines beneath the surface and aircraft above it—though few observers
yet discerned the new shape naval war was about to take.

A few days after taking command of the fleet, Admiral Nimitz paid
a visit to a curious sort of office situated beneath a new wing of 14th
Naval District headquarters. A long room hidden away, like a bank
vault, behind a heavy steel door, it looked something like a messy version of an insurance company bullpen with lines of desks and filing
cabinets, with folders piled on chairs and on the floor. The room also
housed an array of equipment unusual in 1942: keypunchers, sorters,
collators, and machine printers. As Joe Rochefort, the officer in
charge, showed the admiral around this drab and secret domain, informally called Station Hypo (for "H" in the phonetic alphabet in use at
the time), he explained that it was one of two satellite operations of
Op-20-G in Washington; the other branch, called Cast, operated on
Corregidor Island in Manila Bay.

As a Naval Academy graduate ('05), Nimitz had been trained for leadership, and in various posts through the years since, including a tour in command of a battleship division, he had gained wide experience. A quiet, personable Texan who led by consensus and firmness rather than any sort of bluster, he had built himself into an effective figure of command, though his boss, the stubborn and bullying Admiral King, used to vex himself with the disturbing thought that Nimitz had sometimes been known to give favorable consideration to army points of view; he therefore felt the need to keep an eye on the new Pacific commander. Nimitz concluded the session at Hypo by thanking Rochefort politely but saying little about his impression of the operation. Commander Layton, Nimitz's intelligence officer, had developed great admiration and respect for Rochefort and his team, an attitude that Nimitz came increasingly to share. Responsible for a vast ocean area and possessing severely limited forces, the admiral, who fortunately did not belong to history's sizable company of egotistical and dogmatic commanders but listened well and learned quickly, realized that radio intelligence might provide him with something of a counterbalance to Japan's material superiority in the Pacific.

In mid-April, in response to information from Magic, Nimitz dispatched the carriers *Lexington* and *Yorktown* to the Coral Sea, where the enemy was mounting an advance toward Australia (the *Enterprise* and the *Hornet* had not yet returned from the raid on Japan). Having completed their first round of planned conquests, the Japanese had now begun Point 1 of the November 1, 1941, Combined Fleet order, the attacks on Port Moresby and Tulagi (Operation MO). Rear Admiral Frank Jack Fletcher commanded the countering U.S. task force. The resulting meeting between U.S. and Japanese fleets, in the first days of May, offered a vivid reminder of the lesson taught by the sinking of Force Z in December; indeed, it produced a startling and historic phenomenon—the first naval battle ever in which the ships never fired a shot at each other. Aircraft now played the role of the big guns.

Japan won a tactical victory in the Coral Sea, with only a light carrier being sunk, while the Americans suffered a loss they could ill afford, the carrier *Lexington,* together with a destroyer and a fleet oiler.

Strategically, however, the palm went to the Americans, because the Japanese, though having landed on Tulagi at the outset, abandoned their attempt to take Port Moresby: Operation MO thus represented their first failure since they had launched their march of conquest in December. Besides that, U.S. planes had damaged two carriers sufficiently to put them out of action for a month or more. The *Yorktown* suffered severe damage as well, and if she proved unable to take part in further operations without lying up for time-consuming repairs, Admiral Nimitz would find himself facing the next major enemy operation with only two carriers to call on, inasmuch as the *Lexington's* sister ship *Saratoga*, torpedoed on January 11 by a Japanese submarine, would not return for five months.

■ ■ ■

The idea of attacking Australia had appealed to the Japanese Naval General Staff far more than to the officers at Combined Fleet headquarters; as was frequently the case, the two groups had different emphases and interests. Well before the Coral Sea battle, Admiral Yamamoto had developed the plan for the operation he favored, the advance to Midway. Then, on April 18, came the surprise attack of Doolittle's raiders on Tokyo and the four other cities. This shock silenced all opposition to the Midway operation (some high-ranking Japanese officers believed that Shangri-la was actually Midway), though various dissidents still muttered their private doubts.

Paradoxical as always, Yamamoto, though the author of the plan, even expressed doubts of his own, writing on May 27 that he would be at sea for about three weeks in overall command of the operation, "not that I'm expecting very much of it." A small but curious incident had occurred two days earlier at lunch during a final conference on the admiral's flagship, the giant battleship *Yamato*. A cook, unconcerned about any sailorly superstitions, presented sea bream broiled in *miso* (fermented bean paste), even though the expression "to serve with *miso*" had the popular meaning "to make a mess of things." The chief orderly thought he saw Yamamoto's expression change when he was served; the admiral made no comment, but "if he had been a more hot-tempered type, he could easily have flung the whole dish at my head."

By May 27 the carrier task force commander, Admiral Nagumo, had traversed thousands of miles of ocean; after Pearl Harbor he had taken his striking force from Rabaul to the Marshall Islands and westward as far as Trincomalee on the coast of Ceylon. He now set out for a second go at the primary enemy, the United States, leading his four flattops, with their escorting battleships and cruisers, out of Hiroshima Bay, through the Bungo Suido between Kyushu and Shikoku, and into the Pacific. Two days later Yamamoto, the overall commander, followed with the battleship fleet.

As usual, the Japanese had devised a complex operational plan that called for several different fleets and forces (in this case, six) to play important parts. In essence, Nagumo's striking force had the charge of knocking out U.S. air and sea forces in the Midway area. After it had achieved this result, the troops of the landing force, protected by another fleet, would take control of the little island group, and then Yamamoto's Main Body with its battleships would join with Nagumo's force to smash the expected American counterattack. As the happy result of this encounter, the Rising Sun banner would fly over Midway, and the U.S. carriers would have gone to the bottom of the sea; Hawaii and even the American West Coast would lie open to the imperial forces.

■ ■ ■

Long-cherished U.S. military and naval doctrine called for a commander to base operational planning on the enemy's capabilities rather than on his presumed intentions. Bolder than his quiet demeanor would suggest, however, Nimitz was breaking with tradition. Trusting in the codebreakers and what they had told him about the Japanese plan for the Midway operation, CINCPAC, with remarkable courage, resisted the importunities of army colleagues in Hawaii and some naval intelligence officers in Washington who saw Oahu, not scrawny, relatively insignificant Midway, as the likely Japanese target, or who pointed to Alaska.

Nimitz and his staff had devised a counter plan to make the best use of the skimpy U.S. forces available to resist the expected Japanese advance. Under the command of Admiral Spruance, the two carriers *En-*

terprise and *Hornet,* together with cruisers and destroyers, would take station some 300 miles northeast of Midway, a position putting them on the Japanese flank but out of range of enemy search planes. Logically, these would have been the only carriers available for the battle. But Nimitz also had ideas about the *Yorktown,* which, battered in the Coral Sea battle, chugged into Pearl Harbor on May 27, trailing an oil slick that stretched back for 10 miles. Examination in drydock showed the extent of the ravages wreaked by a bomb that had penetrated the carrier's vitals.

The bevy of experts who came to slosh around in these vitals in hip boots included Admiral Nimitz himself, and when the technicians told him that repairing the ship would be at least a ninety-day job, the admiral gravely replied that they must have her ready to sail in just three. The navy yard's specialist in hull repair could do nothing but gulp and say, "Yes, sir." The possibly crucial moment in the war had arrived far earlier than anyone would have dreamed, and to meet it Nimitz had to draw on everything he could get. (Even in the rush to repair the carrier her crew was not forgotten: Among the many entries on the list of replacements appeared a new freezer for the soda fountain.) Admiral Fletcher continued in command of the *Yorktown* task force.

Submarines would have a part assigned to them in the great forthcoming battle, and they would play it in fleet operations; so, to some extent, the fleet boats would actually have the chance to perform in accordance with the name admirers of the concept had long ago bestowed on them. Admiral English, who had just relieved Admiral Withers as ComSubPac (Commander Submarines Pacific), divided his available boats into three task groups. Twelve, making up Task Group 7.1, would lie in wait in a huge wedge west of Midway, where they could sight and possibly intercept elements of the Japanese fleet. Task Group 7.2 (three submarines, called the Roving Shortstops) would take station somewhat north of a line from Midway to Oahu, where they could watch for any enemy strike aimed at Hawaii. Task Group 7.3, with four boats, would cover the area directly north of Hawaii. Thus the plan took into account the concerns of those worried about a direct Japanese drive on Oahu.

Not all of these boats were fleet submarines. Two of them, the lumbering twins *Nautilus* and *Narwhal,* belonged to the oversize V-class series conceived in the 1920s and designed for long-range service. Giants of 3,900 tons' submerged displacement, stretching 370 feet in length with a beam of 33 feet, the *Nautilus* and the *Narwhal* each carried a crew of ninety and armament formidable enough to be called a battery: two 6-inch guns. Despite their power, however, these boats represented an evolutionary dead end in submarine design; in the 1930s the navy submarine chiefs had opted for the smaller, nimbler, and cheaper boats in the line of development that led to the fleet boats of World War II.

The *Nautilus* was laid down in May 1927 at Mare Island and commissioned on July 1, 1930 (and subsequently designated SS-168). "Now the strange thing was that I had heard," said Lieutenant Commander Roy Benson, the executive officer of the *Nautilus* in early 1942, "that there were two ways to do things in the submarine business. One was the way the *Nautilus* did it and the other was the way everybody else did it. She was sort of left-handed." Part, at least, of this reputation seemed to stem from the boat's great size, which essentially tied her with the *Narwhal* and the *Argonaut,* and with the French *Surcouf,* for the world mark and set her off from the other boats in the fleet.

In July 1941 the *Nautilus* had been ordered back to California for modernization, a process that included replacement of its "great big German rock crushers" (its two 47-ton MAN engines) with four General Motors engines and installation of air conditioning and improved radio equipment. During such an overhaul, Benson commented, the boat's officers and many of the petty officers had an important part to play, keeping an eye on those carrying out the changes and repairs to ensure that things were done right. Benson himself received the news of the attack on Pearl Harbor while checking work down in the pump room of the *Nautilus* with a representative of the shipyard. While at Mare Island the *Nautilus* also acquired a new skipper, Bill Brockman, a husky star athlete at the Naval Academy ('27).

Even if the changes had not given her the friskiness of one of the new fleet submarines, the *Nautilus* counted as an available boat, and the battle plan put her in Task Group 7.1, screening Midway. Though she had returned from Mare Island in April, she had not arrived ready for action because even after her long stay in the navy yard she had come in trailing an oil slick. When word came that the operation was imminent she lay in drydock having the leak repaired, but, working around the clock, the yard had her ready to depart Pearl on the morning of May 24.

By the morning of June 4, English's submarines had all taken their assigned positions. The deployment of Task Group 7.1 resembled an arc in layers, with the *Cuttlefish* far out on the point, 450 miles west of Midway. Some 200 miles closer in, the *Grenadier*, the *Gato*, and the *Dolphin* made wide sweeps. Fifty miles inside this arc, *Gudgeon, Grouper, Grayling, Trout,* and *Tambor* were covering the area and with them, in the middle of the arc, was the *Nautilus*. Backing up the defense, only about 60 miles west of Midway, patrolled the *Cachalot* and the *Flyingfish*.

The submarine task force became directly involved in the action at 0700, when the *Cuttlefish* radioed that it had made contact with a Japanese tanker. After making its report, it dived, fearing air attack, and did not regain contact. But this was to be "the day" in the Pacific, the kind of *Tag* the German officers drank to in the days before World War I. As for the submariners below the waves, a historian later characterized their mood: "Breakfast? Not with stomach muscles as tight as whalebone corsets, throats dry and teeth gritty from the tension of waiting." The 312-foot fleet boats each carried a normal complement of five officers and fifty-five enlisted men, all of this team having to live and work amid the machinery and munitions squeezed into the hull. The officers, in addition to the skipper, included the exec, the fire control officer (who operated the Torpedo Data Computer), the engineer and diving officer, and "George," the most recent Submarine School graduate, who handled the officers' equivalent of scut work (commissary and other unassorted duties). The enlisted crew included several chief petty officers, veteran specialists who were often in their fifties and on occasion might be as old as sixty-five; the senior petty officer, called the chief of the boat, filled a role comparable to that of an army first sergeant. Everybody—torpedomen, electricians, gunner's mates—had a special job, except for the youngest seamen just beginning their service. As the closest thing to a medical expert on board, the pharmacist's mate (always, like a small-town druggist, called Doc) had special responsibilities that might even, if the crunch came, require him to perform an appendectomy.

With spaces having to serve double or triple functions, the officers slept in the forward battery compartment, two to a stateroom; the captain had his own stateroom, with a narrow bunk and a tiny desk. Chiefs bunked at the aft end of the forward battery compartment, while the rest of the crew slept jammed into a bunk area or in bunks rigged over the torpedoes. The ward room, above the forward battery compartment, provided a conference and working area for the officers as well as serving as the dining room. The enlisted men's mess, over the after battery compartment, could handle about half the crew at a time. Watches for everybody were four hours on, eight hours off, and when off watch the men had plenty to do, keeping the machinery functioning at top efficiency. Of course, they had time for a card game and also for a particular favorite of submariners, acey-deucey, a form of backgammon. "In keeping with navy tradition," as one veteran said, "all hands drank gallons of weak coffee and ate hearty, wholesome meals."

■ ■ ■

Not a single one of the submarine pickets spotted Admiral Nagumo's striking force, but as the Japanese carriers reached their assigned position about 150 miles northwest of Midway and began launching their bombers for the assault on the island, they were sighted by Catalina PBY planes of Midway's search patrol, which had been hampered by clouds (spotting the enemy array, said one of the fliers, was "like watching a curtain rise on the Biggest Show on Earth"). Then, while the Japanese bombers were attacking the island, B-17s and other planes from Midway returned the favor but did little damage to Nagumo's force; though theoreticians had believed that the big bombers would produce good results against ships, the Fortresses, in fact, failed to score a single hit. As for Midway, the Japanese attacks inflicted heavy damage but did not put it out of commission as an air base.

Admiral Chester W. Nimitz, a submarine veteran, took over the U.S. Pacific fleet on the last day of 1941. Though after Pearl Harbor his command lacked battleships, it still had its submarines.

"Uncle Charlie" Lockwood, commander of the U.S. Pacific submarine force, always met his crews when they returned from patrol.

Newlyweds: Mush Morton,
the future skipper of the *Wahoo*,
and his bride pose for their
official portrait (1935).

Periscope view: The *Wahoo* sinks a Japanese freighter.

Periscope view: The *Wahoo* does in an enemy destroyer.

Triumphant homecoming: The *Wahoo* enters Pearl Harbor with enemy flags and a broom atop the attack scope, indicating a clean sweep on her patrol.

The *Gato*-class submarine *Flasher* destroyed 100,231 tons of Japanese shipping, the top total achieved by a U.S. boat in World War II.

Bob Hall, the nineteen-year-old *Parche* cook who made a commodore cry.

Cream puffs: Submariners typically enjoyed the best food in the U.S. Navy.

The target: A torpedoman paints a Rising Sun on a tin fish.

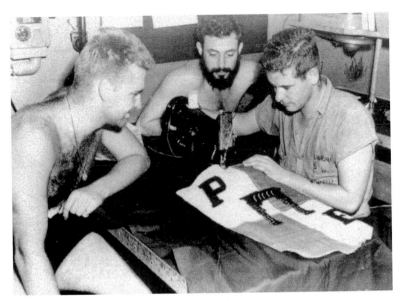

Crewmen of the U.S.S. *Parche* work on their battle flag: *P* plus an arch plus *E*.

Parche crewmen show off a Japanese life preserver fished from the sea.

July 1944: Periscope view from the U.S.S. *Archerfish* shows ships off Iwo Jima during a U.S. raid on the island—early action in what would be a long campaign against the islands in this group.

Commander Joseph Enright, skipper of the *Archerfish* in November 1944, recorded the biggest kill ever made by a submarine.

In five patrols as skipper of the U.S.S. *Tang,* Dick O'Kane sank twenty-four enemy vessels, making him the top U.S. skipper of the war.

Tang crewmen created an outstanding record in their "lifeguarding" rescues of downed U.S. airmen.

The U.S. postwar submarine *Tang* (SS-563) and her five class sisters included numerous features adapted from the German Type XXI U-boats.

January 21, 1954: The U.S.S. *Nautilus,* the world's first nuclear submarine, slides down the launching ways at Groton, Connecticut.

Having fun:
Edward Teller and
Rear Admiral
Hyman Rickover
sit at the controls
of an SSN.

Success story:
Rear Admiral
William Raborn with
his great achievement,
the Polaris missile.

Seen here on her commissioning in August 1961, the *Thresher,* the U.S. Navy's first deep-diving attack submarine, was lost off New England in April 1963.

As attack submarines, the *Los Angeles*-class ships could carry the fight to an enemy on land with cruise missiles and to ships with Harpoon missiles. They also carried advanced capability torpedoes.

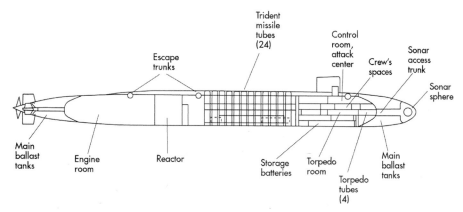

Ohio Class: These eighteen boomers, which began entering the fleet in 1981, served as the basic U.S. strategic submarine force.

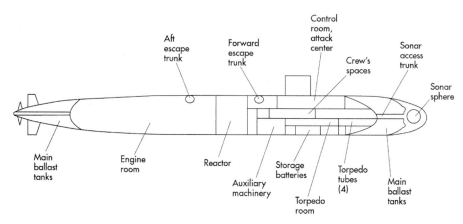

Los Angeles Class: The major class of U.S. fast attack submarines, these fifty-three ships joined the fleet between 1976 and 1996.

Following the *Los Angeles* class came the three-member *Seawolf* class, including besides the namesake ship (*above*) the *Connecticut* and the *Jimmy Carter.*

Preview: A close-up look at construction activities at the Electric Boat yards in Groton, Connecticut.

Sleek but doomed, the Russian attack submarine *K-141,* named the *Kursk,* lies at her mooring. On August 12, 2000, tragedy would strike.

Now, between 0900 and 1030 of the fourth, would come one of the most dramatic and most significant reversals of fortune in the history of warfare. Central to this drama stood the fact that the Japanese had been unable to carry out a planned reconnaissance of Oahu, intended to confirm their expectation that the U.S. ships lay quietly at their berths. Nagumo therefore proceeded on the unconfirmed (and, of course, unconfirmable) assumption that this was the case. Sure that he would not need to call on the ninety-three aircraft he had ordered to stand by armed with bombs and torpedoes to take care of any U.S. ships that might turn up, the admiral therefore felt free to respond to his flight leader's call for a second strike on Midway by ordering these planes rearmed with incendiary and fragmentation bombs.

As crewmen rushed to perform this task, a search plane reported sighting American warships off to the northeast. Thrown off balance by this development that contravened all expectations, Nagumo hesitated, then ordered the ninety-three planes rearmed again, this time to attack ships. But the launching had to be put on hold so that the carriers could recover the planes returning from bombing Midway.

While Nagumo dithered, and his ships continued steaming toward Midway, aircraft from the *Enterprise* and the *Hornet* were winging toward his force. Then came a grim chapter in the annals of courage. Nagumo ordered a 90° turn, to head toward the U.S. ships, and as the result the dive-bombers and fighters from the *Hornet* never found his force. But determined to press the attack, the *Hornet's* Torpedo Squadron 8 with TBD-1 Devastators, already on the edge of obsolescence, went in against the enemy carriers without fighter escort and were wiped out, all fifteen of these two-seater aircraft being shot down.

In the next phase of the action, the U.S. naval aircraft attempted no coordination but simply attacked as they arrived on the scene. First came the torpedo squadron from the *Enterprise,* which lost ten out of fourteen. Bombers from the *Yorktown* now arrived, to lose all but four. Of forty-one Devastators launched in the battle, only six made it back home. And, for all the incredible bravery these young men displayed, not a single one scored a hit on a Japanese ship.

It was now 1024, and the Japanese appeared to have won a sweeping—and, indeed, a devastating—victory. But then, within two minutes, Lieutenant Commander C. Wade McClusky, the *Enterprise* air group commander, arrived with two squadrons of SBD dive-bombers. With the planes of Nagumo's fighter cover preoccupied with the lower-level American attacks, the unmolested dive-bombers pounced like eagles from on high on the carriers *Kaga* and *Akagi,* each with its deck as congested as a used car lot. Having no way to defend themselves, both carriers were destroyed, *Akagi,* Nagumo's flagship, dying almost immediately, *Kaga* staying afloat, but abandoned, until evening. At this point the *Yorktown*'s dive-bomber group came screaming from the skies onto the carrier *Soryu,* which took three half-ton bombs and within minutes would break in two and sink into the 2,600-fathom depths of the Central Pacific.

Within just six astonishing minutes Japan's bright victory had literally exploded. This incredible drama had a unique eyewitness, Ensign George Gay, the navigation officer of Torpedo Squadron 8. While Gay had been making his run in to the target, a carrier, his radioman had been killed and he himself hit by a machine gun bullet in the upper left arm and by shrapnel in his hand. Then another shot knocked out his left rudder pedal, and his plane, having just passed over the deck of the carrier, careened into the water. As it began to sink, Gay slid the hood open and rose to the surface. Next to him floated a black rubber seat cushion; when strafing Zeros appeared, he held the cushion over his head. Sailors on a Japanese destroyer spotted him and ran to the rail to point him out to others, but no one shot at him. The sole survivor of the thirty men who had made up Torpedo Squadron 8, Gay spent the whole day bobbing in the water, a spectator in the middle of one of the greatest battles in history. He saw the flames consume the *Kaga,* the *Akagi,* and the *Soryu.* He saw the *Hiryu,* farther away, fleeing the inferno northeastward. Then, during the early afternoon, Gay saw a different kind of sight—a new element in the battle.

For seven hours that day, the big *Nautilus* had stalked Japanese ships. At 0825, rising to periscope depth, she had found herself in the middle of the enemy fleet—"ships all over the place." Her attempt to torpedo a battleship "was the first time anybody on board had been involved in firing a torpedo war shot; that is, with an explosive head," Roy Benson said. Brockman took the boat down to a depth of about 250 feet, and "immediately we also had a baptism in depth charges and what they sounded like." On returning to periscope depth shortly afterward, Brockman saw a scene "never experienced in peacetime practice. Ships were on all sides, moving across the field at high speed and circling away to avoid the submarine's position." A cruiser passed over them, and "flag hoists were going up, blinker lights were flashing and the battleship on our port bow was firing her whole starboard broadside at the periscope."

At 1253, scope up again, Brockman had spotted a burning carrier; "she was lying to in the water and didn't look as if she was moving." Then, laboriously, proceeding underwater at only 4 knots, the *Nautilus* had begun to cross the 8 miles separating her from this "choice target." Brockman checked the identification books to make sure that the target was not American. Definitely not, he decided; it was probably the *Soryu*. At about 1400 he fired three torpedoes, which headed straight for the carrier. "We got three explosions and there was increased smoke and fire," Benson recalled. "Then aircraft flew over and dropped bombs. We sneaked away." Later on in the war, Benson said, they would not have done anything exactly the way they did that day. "We'd never have sneaked away. We would have stuck around, but you have to learn."

From his water-level post, George Gay heard the explosions that broke out on the ship and saw the flames spring up. He later confirmed the submarine's kill. But was he right? Were Brockman and his officers right when, coming to periscope depth and seeing no carrier where a carrier had sat before they attacked it, they claimed a kill. "There wasn't anything there, not even smoke or fire." Certainly Brockman displayed outstanding leadership that day, for which later he received the Navy Cross. But postwar analysis, which drew on both U.S. and Japanese sources, determined that Brockman had fired at the *Kaga,* not the *Soryu*. Two of his torpedoes missed and the third, though hitting the target amidships, failed to explode (the story that was becoming increasingly familiar for U.S. torpedoes at the time). "It was such a glancing blow," said the *Kaga's* flight officer, who had taken to the water from the already stricken ship, "fired at such an angle that the torpedo bounced off the side of the ship and circled lightly." The collision shattered the torpedo's air flask, which, in an unpredictable development, floated away and was transformed by several members of the *Kaga's* crew into a temporary life preserver. The hits George Gay saw were probably two or three of the internal explosions that racked the *Kaga* during the afternoon, before she went down at dusk. As for the *Soryu,* she had indeed succumbed to the blows of the *Yorktown's* dive-bombers.

Unbeknownst to Brockman and his crew, the *Nautilus* had played a special role in the battle. The destroyer *Arashi* had busied itself depth-charging the *Nautilus,* an activity that caused her to become separated from the Japanese fleet. As her skipper headed toward the carrier, the destroyer was spotted by Commander McClusky, who adopted the same course, which took him straight to Nagumo.

The final chapter for the Japanese carriers came in the afternoon, when scouts from the *Yorktown* sighted Nagumo's fourth flattop, the *Hiryu,* as it fled northwestward. Dive-bombers summoned from the *Hornet* and the *Enterprise* soon turned the carrier into a platform of fire, and by evening she was drifting, abandoned. Earlier, however, aircraft from the *Hiryu* had struck the biggest Japanese blow of the battle by damaging the *Yorktown* so severely that Admiral Fletcher abandoned her, transferring his flag to the cruiser *Astoria.*

The aftermath of the great battle saw an odd but inadvertently effective contribution from the U.S. submarine *Tambor.* In the still-dark early hours of the next day, June 5, this boat, commanded by Lieutenant Commander John Murphy, Jr. (Naval Academy '25), still on station about 90 miles west of Midway, sighted a force of enemy ships—four cruisers and two destroyers—headed for the island. Though Murphy, of course, had no way of knowing their orders, the cruisers had the mission of bombarding Midway's air facilities to cover the retreat of Nagumo's fleet, as a sort of Parthian shot at the Americans by Admiral Yamamoto.

In the moonlight the enemy likewise spotted the *Tambor,* which followed the force for some time before establishing definite identification of it as Japanese; then Murphy sent out a contact report. Soon, as dawn lightened the sky, the skipper ordered the boat to dive. When he came up to periscope depth again, he saw, to his surprise, only two cruisers instead of four. Although he had not succeeded in getting into firing position, the Japanese at least partially had done his work for him. After the U.S. submarine had been sighted, the Japanese task force commander had ordered the cruisers to make an emergency turn to port. While the *Mikuma* was executing the turn, the *Mogami,* which either had not received the signal or had not interpreted it properly, continued to plow straight ahead and smashed into its sister ship, rupturing a fuel tank and shattering its own bow.

In view of this last disaster, Yamamoto had abandoned the project of bombarding Midway and had ordered the other two cruisers, the *Suzuya* and the *Kumano,* to withdraw northwesterly at high speed, leaving the wounded pair to proceed on their own at about 17 knots. During the day these cruisers fought off aircraft from Midway, but on June 6 planes from the *Hornet* and the *Enterprise* caught up with them, sinking *Mikuma* and severely damaging *Mogami.*

That same afternoon saw the most important action by any submarine in the whole drama of Midway. Unfortunately for the Americans, the submarine belonged to the enemy. Early in the morning of June 5 a Japanese seaplane had spotted the *Yorktown,* which, though disabled, seemed salvageable and was slowly proceeding under escort back to Pearl Harbor. Though the Japanese scout plane had sighted the carrier, it had miscalculated the position, and the submarine *I-168* spent June 5 vainly searching for its intended victim. But early the next afternoon the *I-168* encountered the carrier with its escorts and, deftly getting itself into firing position, released four torpedoes; two slammed into the *Yorktown* and one hit the escorting destroyer *Hammann,* which split in two as it sank, with its exploding depth charges adding to the damage inflicted on the *Yorktown.* Devoted work by salvage crews had enabled the carrier to survive the earlier damage, but now she had suffered mortal wounds. At first light the next morning, "with her loose gear making a horrible death rattle," she rolled over and went to the bottom. With the aircraft carrier now unmistakably having usurped the battleship's place as the sovereign of war at sea, the *Yorktown* represented a serious loss for the United States, but in the overall battle the Americans, despite the appalling casualties suffered by the air groups, had won a near-miraculous victory, preserving their own fleet while stopping the Japanese advance in the Central Pacific.

Like all miracles, this one had a key, which Admiral Nimitz succinctly summed up as "early information of the Japanese movements": the codebreaking of Joe Rochefort and his team. But for all his efforts, even Nimitz could not win a medal for his Magic wielder; office politics and rampant jealousies at Op-20-G in Washington saw to it that Rochefort never received recognition for one of the greatest contributions anybody made to the Allied cause in World War II. He had committed the capital sin of being right when people who considered themselves more important, and who knew how to play the power game, had been totally wrong.

■ ■ ■

Events during the ebb and flow of the great battle showed how much all the participants had yet to learn about fighting three-dimensional war. Aircraft crewmen on scouting missions had trouble identifying what they saw (they commonly took ships to be larger than they were) and reporting its position. The crews of land-based planes encountered navigational problems, and, despite prewar expectations, their bombing of ships proved almost totally ineffectual (although, at the time, reports and news stories indicated just the opposite, not from any deliberate falsification but simply owing to the difficulty of telling, from high up, exactly what happened on the surface of the water; a measure of optimism may have been involved here, as well). Much of the action by the carrier air groups was improvised, as, to some extent, was the composition of the groups themselves (the *Yorktown*'s air group was made up of men from three different carriers), and tactics and aircraft both needed improvement. The heroism of the fliers, however, shone beyond cavil or parallel. Before the battle, Lieutenant Commander John C. Waldron, the organizer and skipper of the *Hornet*'s Torpedo Squadron 8, had told his men: "I actually believe that under these conditions we are the best in the world." With respect to bravery, no one could doubt it.

Submarines had problems identifying and reporting the movements of enemy vessels similar to those encountered by fliers. In the encounter with the Japanese group of four cruisers that included the *Mogami* and the *Mikuma,* Commander Murphy sent off a vague report of contact with "many unidentified ships," with no mention of a course—information from which Admiral Spruance inferred that the enemy might still intend to invade Midway. Several hours later Murphy clarified his information, accurately characterizing the two remaining cruisers and reporting their westerly course. But during this time Spruance had deployed his force north of Midway to attack the invasion force as it moved in; by midmorning, however, it had become clear that no invasion was forthcoming: Murphy's first report had simply sent the American forces on a wild-goose chase. This skipper, who lost his command as the result of his sketchy reporting, later wrote: "We should have made an opportunity . . . to amplify our initial report, but we didn't."

War produces remarkable peripeties, however, and in switching attention from a possible pursuit of the westward-fleeing Japanese to attack on the Midway invasion force, Murphy—unintentionally, to be sure—had guaranteed that the American carriers would not come under the big guns of Yamamoto's battle fleet at night, an encounter that would hold the possibility of total disaster. In any case, Spruance, a thoughtful and balanced commander, neither rash nor nervously cautious, had no desire to be caught in an ambush. In this and other situations during the winding-down days of the battle, Spruance had always to be mindful of the not altogether simple instructions Nimitz had issued before the carrier forces had left Pearl Harbor. "You will be governed by the principle of the calculated risk," said CINCPAC, "which you shall interpret to mean the avoidance of exposure of your force without good prospect of inflicting, as a result of such exposure, greater damage to the enemy." Win the battle, if you can, but don't lose the fleet. In World War I Churchill had characterized Admiral Jellicoe as the only commander on either side who could "lose the war in an afternoon"; circumstance had just placed Spruance, a bolder spirit than Jellicoe, in much the same role in the Pacific. He assessed the position with great accuracy.

Spruance had his own problems with inaccurate and incomplete reports from scouts. During air attacks on the wounded *Mogami* and *Mikuma* on June 6, the admiral sent out two observation planes with the mission of identifying the enemy ships, one of which had earlier been, characteristically, mistakenly described as a battleship. When the pilots returned, Spruance personally grilled them. Just what were these Japanese ships that were standing up so stubbornly to air attack? "Sir, I don't know," responded one pilot with singularly ill-timed casualness, "but it was a hell of a big one." The other pilot gave an equally vague answer; he hadn't remembered to take his ship recognition cards with him. Furious, the normally contained Spruance gave the two young men what has long been officially known in all the armed forces as an ass-chewing.

With the sinking of the *Mikuma,* Spruance deemed the Battle of Midway at an end. He had faithfully fulfilled his instructions from Admiral Nimitz, and, though they might not yet realize it, those who had worried about possible Japanese attacks on Hawaii and California could henceforth sleep serenely. The strike on Pearl Harbor on December 7 had represented a defeat in which the Americans had appeared as amateurs in the business of war; though Midway had likewise revealed a variety of kinds of amateurism, this time the amateurs had won, and won stunningly.

Lieutenant Commander Mike Fenno's submarine *Trout* (SS-202) figured in the last footnote to the Battle of Midway. On June 9 crewmen fished two forlorn figures from a floating hatch cover, survivors of the *Mikuma*. When the *Trout* arrived at Pearl Harbor "it took an hour and a half," according to one officer, "before they could get the marines over to take the prisoner off, and they wouldn't let anybody aboard until the prisoner was removed." Actually, both prisoners were involved, and their capture, or rescue, gave this boat the distinction of being the first U.S. submarine in the Pacific war to take Japanese prisoners.

Following the Battle of Midway, the U.S. and Japanese navies entered on what Admiral Frederick Sherman later described as a time of stalemate, which was broken after a year and a half by the Allied capture of Tarawa in the Gilbert Islands. Though some important naval battles took place in late 1942 and most of 1943, particularly around Guadalcanal in the Southwest Pacific, neither side could obtain much more than temporary control of the air or the sea, and almost another year would go by before the two fleets would engage in an action with capital ships. Submarines, however, would find themselves increasingly busy, as the Americans went about learning what the Germans had discovered more than twenty-five years earlier: These boats had severe limitations as warships in battle with fleets, as Midway had strongly suggested, but as commerce raiders pouncing on freighters and tankers they could become the deadliest vessels on or in the sea.

28

WAR MISSION FOR THE GIANTS

The big, slow, and unfashionable *Nautilus*, the only U.S. submarine to play a conspicuous part in the memorable action at Midway, soon received, together with her sister *Argonaut,* a new sort
of challenge. The opportunity came, in part, because of developments
on the other side of the world.

Even before the United States entered the war, the Americans and
the British had agreed on a "Germany first" strategy: The Allies would
concentrate on defeating Hitler, who posed the most immediate threat
to their security, before turning their attention to the other major Axis
power. In U.S. command circles, this approach became known as Plan
Dog, because of its effective statement by Admiral Stark in November
1940 in a memo to President Roosevelt; Stark's alternative D [or Dog]
called for an offensive in the Atlantic combined with a defensive pos-
ture in the Pacific. After Pearl Harbor and Hitler's declaration of war
on the United States four days later, the principle continued to seem
eminently sound, because Germany was the only country with which
all the members of the alliance were at war. But it was also true that
Plan Dog had won general acceptance before Americans knew that
they would be blasted into war with Japan. Might not U.S. leaders now
change their minds in response to public cries for revenge for this "unprovoked and dastardly attack," as President Roosevelt called the Pearl
Harbor strike?

To the relief of the jittery British, however, American leaders did
not abandon Plan Dog. In lengthy meetings in Washington that began
on Christmas Eve, the Allied chiefs of staff agreed that, though much
had changed since earlier staff conversations, "our view remains that
Germany is still the prime enemy and her defeat is the key to victory.

Once Germany is defeated, the collapse of Italy and the defeat of Japan must follow." This meant, said the chiefs, that "only a minimum of force necessary for the safeguarding of vital interests in other theatres should be diverted from operations against Germany." Even so, this agreement did not and could not mean that the Allies, and certainly not the United States, would make no effort against Japan for an indefinite time. Indeed, on the sea, within a little more than five months, the Coral Sea and Midway had profoundly changed the shape of the Pacific war. But, though Admiral Nimitz displayed initiative in dispatching carrier forces to the Coral Sea, both this engagement and Midway were strategically defensive battles, checking the Japanese in the Southwest and the Central Pacific. The aggressive Admiral King now wanted more than that; the enemy, he believed, would not calmly sit on its possessions, watching its imperial perimeter, waiting for the Americans to act at times of their own choosing. Nimitz agreed; he favored an operation in the Solomon Islands to take Tulagi, with its great natural harbor, which the Japanese had seized on May 3. General MacArthur, commander of the Southwest Pacific Area, proposed a more ambitious operation aimed at capturing Rabaul, which, with its two fine harbors, gave the Japanese domination of the entire New Guinea area and posed a continuing threat to Australia.

While discussion of these projects took place, the Americans found themselves involved with the British in the "transatlantic essay contest," as one participant dubbed the running dispute over the U.S. proposal to make a landing on the northwestern French coast (Operation Sledgehammer) in the autumn of 1942 to succor the hard-pressed Russians. Since the bulk of the forces involved in such a risky, longshot operation would necessarily be British, Churchill and General Sir Alan Brooke, chief of the Imperial General Staff, took the lead in determining its fate, and—at first evasively, then emphatically—they rejected the plan; they had long favored, instead, landings in Northwest Africa. British defeats in Libya and Egypt by General Rommel's Afrika Korps made a fresh commitment on the Continent even less likely.

For General Marshall, Sledgehammer possessed significance far beyond its immediate purpose; he saw the mounting of it as a guarantee that the Allies would then push forward with the major landing on the

Continent in 1943, which he believed to be the key to winning the war in Europe. A move into Africa would represent the kind of diversion he deplored. If there was to be no action in Europe in 1942, then perhaps the United States should turn to the Pacific and undertake decisive operations against Japan. But FDR, whose wishes had inspired Admiral Stark's Plan Dog, insisted on action against Germany, if not in Europe then somewhere else, in 1942. As the generals only slowly came to understand, the president could not allow a whole year of war to pass without direct confrontation with the enemy that was most dangerous, even though it was not the one that had attacked the United States.

But MacArthur, King, Nimitz, and others in the Pacific pressed for action against the Japanese; King, for one, had little real regard for the thinking behind Plan Dog. Planning meetings in London produced a small bonus for the Pacific commanders with an agreement to make some aircraft and shipping committed to the buildup in England available for offensive operations in the Pacific. In March the Joint Chiefs had included in their recommendations that the United States should contain the Japanese in the territory they now held and should attempt to reduce them through attrition by submarines and carriers. But by July, with the Japanese fleet weakened by the rout at Midway, American plans had become more ambitious. Looking to the ultimate seizure of New Guinea and neighboring islands, the Joint Chiefs issued a directive that included operations to capture Tulagi and to occupy the rest of the Solomons group. Rabaul would have to come later.

In July the Japanese, seeming to anticipate the coming American actions, busied themselves with the construction of airstrips at Rabaul and at spots on neighboring islands, including Bougainville in the northern Solomons. An American scout plane also observed work beginning on a landing strip on an island lying southeastward, at the end of the Solomons chain, 22 miles south of Tulagi. This obscure island, chosen by the Japanese because, unlike its nearby neighbors, it offered a flat plain large enough for a landing field though it presented few other attractions, was Guadalcanal. The news of the Japanese activity demanded a quick American response, and thus Guadalcanal became the place in which U.S. forces undertook their first offensive of the war. A place of almost uniquely repulsive characteristics, Guadalcanal sweltered in a miasma arising from slime and thick, rotting jungle vegetation so potent that the official navy historian coined the term *faecaloid* to describe the stink.

To support the landings on Guadalcanal, Admiral Nimitz produced a scheme that might have come from the brain and pen of Admiral Yamamoto, with his fondness for diversionary schemes and operations ancillary to a main endeavor. At 0900 on August 8, in accordance with Nimitz's orders, the big submarines *Nautilus* and *Argonaut* departed Pearl Harbor for the Gilbert Islands, some 2,000 miles to the southwest. Bill Brockman, who had made a name for himself at Midway and added to it with a successful mission to the coast of Japan, remained in command of the *Nautilus,* which also served as the command ship of the task group (7.15) under Commander John M. Haines, a prewar sub skipper and a survivor of the battleship *Maryland* on December 7. Lieutenant Commander John R. Pierce (Naval Academy '28), a former S-boat skipper, commanded the *Argonaut,* fresh from Mare Island, California, where she had been fitted out for special duties.

At 0300 on August 16, eight days after leaving Pearl, the *Nautilus* arrived off Little Makin Atoll, and at first light began conducting a periscope reconnaissance of its objective, Butaritari, the main island of Makin Atoll, which lay not only 2,000 miles from Hawaii but 1,200 miles from Guadalcanal. (As his chief guide, Brockman had a map based on 1888 German research with additional information from a 1902 British survey, a level of preparation reminiscent of the British in Norway in 1940.) The *Nautilus* and the *Argonaut* had come to this spot, far from the fighting on Guadalcanal, to play the indirect role in the battle Admiral Nimitz had assigned to them. The giants had been transformed into troop transports, thereby becoming the first submarines ever used for this purpose. They carried two companies of marines, who were to carry out a raid on Makin to draw a measure of Japanese attention away from Guadalcanal.

The marines involved in this diversionary operation belonged to the 2nd Raider Battalion, commanded by the kind of unique character that war tends to produce. This officer, Lieutenant Colonel Evans F.

Carlson, who would earn lasting linguistic fame by giving the expression "gung ho" to the English language, had created this commando-type unit over the objections of many senior Marine Corps officers who, in the time-honored way of orthodox elders, disapproved both of charismatic juniors and of the creation of elite units; in the Marine Corps, particularly, this seemed blasphemy, since the corps was considered elite in itself. A man of wide experience, the lean, sharp-featured Carlson had served two tours of duty in China in the 1920s and 1930s, and after becoming acquainted with FDR had been ordered back to that country as a military observer; in this role he sent the president his comments on politicians, diplomats, and generals, and he made a trek into the Chinese interior to witness Chinese Communist operations against the Japanese. Some of the methods and tactics he had observed there influenced his thinking when he formed his Raiders. This experience also gave him the motto "gung ho," an expression which more or less meant "work together."

To transform themselves into troop transports, the *Nautilus* had given up most of her torpedoes and the *Argonaut* (the only U.S. submarine designed as a minelayer) had lost her minelaying facilities, the freed spaces being filled by tiers of bunks and by the added air conditioning equipment made necessary to service 221 breathing new bodies. Even so, as the group commander noted, "with the ship sealed up for diving the air . . . is rapidly vitiated and in the course of a submergence of more than 10 hours resort must be had to the use of soda-lime and oxygen," and in this tropical area body heat and high humidity tended to overwhelm the air conditioning equipment (problems that had, indeed, concerned the design and construction experts when they were experimenting with the *Cuttlefish* in the 1930s, even without considering the challenge that would be posed by loading a hundred or more extra men on a boat). The need to conserve the water supply meant that bathing did not form part of the routine while the *Nautilus* made her way to Makin. As the brightest spots in the day, the marines had morning and afternoon exercise periods on deck, outings that also served literally as breathers. The benefits, Commander Haines had decided, justified taking the risk in having a large number of men on deck in daylight hours.

■ ■ ■

In making their early morning reconnaissance of Butaritari, the Americans noted that "almost no distinguishing features existed," but they were able to make preliminary judgments about the set and drift of the current in the intended area of the landing, finding the waters much choppier than they had been told. They attempted to reconnoiter the alternate landing beach, at Ukiangong Point on the southern tip of the island, but strong currents and potent riptides made the task impracticable in the few hours available for it.

At 2116 that night, during a heavy rain squall, the *Nautilus* effected its rendezvous with the *Argonaut* at the designated Point Affirm; the task group commander passed on to the new arrival the final plans for the assault. The two boats then proceeded together to Point Baker, the chosen spot of disembarkation, the marines rigging their rubber boats and shouldering their gear en route. While the skipper fought the current to keep the *Nautilus* clear of a reef, the boats were put over the side in accordance with the schedule, despite an unanticipated problem: "The noise from the surf and the wash from the limber holes of the ship rendered interboat communication by voice difficult." In the resulting confusion, the boats left for the beach en masse instead of in two groups as planned. All eighteen made it to the designated Beach Z, however, except one that landed alone some distance off and two that landed north of the main body. But they did it with difficulty and in ragged fashion, as the surf drowned the Evinrude gasoline motors that powered the boats. Then, as soon as they landed, an accidental burst from a marine's submachine gun broke the silence. Now, facing enemy fire for the first time in the war, the marines received a hot reception from Japanese snipers, who were said by island natives to have been waiting in position in treetops for three days. So thoroughly had the snipers concealed themselves that the Americans soon realized they would have to shoot the branches off the trees in order to get them, a procedure Carlson considered "a most uneconomical operation."

After putting off the landing force, the submarines moved clear of Point Baker, taking position about 4 miles offshore. At 0513 communication was established with Carlson's men ashore, and thirty minutes later the colonel sent a terse message: "Everything lousy!" Just a few minutes afterward, however, Carlson had cheered up, reporting that "situation expected to be well in hand shortly." A little more than an hour and a half later, the colonel radioed for fire support on the Ukiangong area, where he believed the Japanese had stationed reserves.

At 0703 the *Nautilus* opened up with her two 6-inch deck guns, firing twelve salvos (twenty-four rounds) which did "considerable" damage to the reserve area, though the *Argonaut* for some reason had failed to get the word and did not join in. Carlson also asked the *Nautilus* to take under fire a merchant ship in the lagoon anchorage. This request presented quite a challenge, as the target was out of sight, 7 miles away, "no point of aim in deflection was presented due to lack of distinguishable landmarks, and the Nautilus' own position was only approximately known." Nevertheless, the range was computed and, during firing, was continuously shifted to cover the harbor as thoroughly as possible. Remarkably, this attack not only sank the freighter but also, as a bonus, disposed of a 1,500-ton patrol boat. Although some of the marines witnessed the destruction of the two craft, Brockman and the *Nautilus* would never receive official credit for these sinkings.

After landing and moving inland, the marines spread out over the island, killing most of the forty-four-man garrison. During the day of August 18, between midmorning and 1730, four flights of enemy planes came over, bombing Butaritari and neighboring islets and bringing reinforcements. These successive flights caused the *Nautilus* and the *Argonaut* to spend much of the day submerged, giving the crews a chance to make up for sleep lost in the preceding day and a half.

The operation being a hit-and-run raid (get in, inflict maximum damage and pick up what information you can, get out), withdrawal had been set for 1930, high tide and thus supposedly the most favorable time for getting the rubber boats over the reef. The attempt to return to the submarines produced the most harrowing part of whole operation; battling the incoming waves in the boats "provided a struggle so intense and so futile that it will forever remain a ghastly nightmare to those who participated." When the motor refused to work, "paddling rhythmically and furiously for all we were worth we would get over one roller only to be hit and thrown back by the next before we could gain momentum." Boats filled to the gunwales, the marines bailed, then tried to swim and pull the boats, which capsized, and finally Carlson ordered his boat back to the beach, where he found most of the other boats together with exhausted men.

Some of the boats had made it to the submarines by 2130, and in the morning one was sent back with a message telling Carlson that if the coming of enemy aircraft forced the *Nautilus* to submerge, she would return at 1930 and remain on station. That evening, finally, all but thirty marines had been collected; these men were believed to have been killed in the fighting. But in actuality, nine of them were alive and would become prisoners of the Japanese. Taken to Kwajalein, with Tokyo as the ultimate destination, they received good treatment from the Japanese for six weeks, until the commander, Vice Admiral Koso Abe, became weary of serving as their host and summarily ordered them beheaded. After the war the admiral was tried for this atrocity, and hanged.

■ ■ ■

What had the navy learned from the operation? It had accomplished its primary mission, which Commander Haines, taking a down-to-earth view, defined as the destruction of enemy troops and installations on Makin, but at a higher cost in men and equipment than had been anticipated. Among the reasons, the task group commander cited the ship-shore communication problems, the difficulty of clearing the reef with the rubber boats on the attempted return to the submarines, the inflexibility of the general plan, and (hardly surprising for this early-day effort) inexperience and inadequate training. In future operations, to be sure, it would also be desirable to avoid notifying the enemy of your arrival by accidentally discharging a weapon. Amateurism had marked this pioneering effort, at the very beginning of the amphibious Pacific war, but with further experience, greater firepower in the hands of the raiding parties, and the employment of more submarines, Haines saw the possibility of carrying out successful raids on strong and well-defended enemy island stations.

Carlson shared Haines's objection to inflexible plans and time limits: "The time limit for withdrawal should be determined by the commander ashore in accordance with the dictates of the situation there."

The effectiveness of the enemy snipers made a deep impression on the colonel, who called for the training of Americans in this peculiar skill, and to counter Japanese marksmen he wanted to give his men more M-1 rifles instead of the light and inaccurate tommy guns. But these were details. Like Haines, Carlson believed that raids from submarines could have a great future. They could be used to "confuse the enemy, pull him off base and open the way for the drive of a larger force against vulnerable and vital points." The colonel also brought back a bit of philosophy from Makin. It was "a truth as old as the military profession," he said, that "no matter how bad your own situation may appear to be, there is always the possibility that the situation of the enemy is much worse."

On returning to Pearl Harbor, where the task group was greeted by bands and cheering sailors, Colonel Carlson introduced a wounded young officer, Lieutenant W. S. Le François, to Admiral Nimitz, as Major James Roosevelt, the Raider battalion's executive officer (and FDR's eldest son), stood nearby. Ill at ease in the presence of top brass, the lieutenant managed to say, "I hope the admiral is pleased with the results of our efforts."

"Very pleased," replied CINCPAC. "Very pleased—a very successful raid." But nobody could yet know one big negative result the raid would produce. Because it had exposed the vulnerability of the Gilberts, the Japanese would quickly move to build up their defenses in this island group. In operations during the following year, notably at Tarawa, the marines would discover with what deadly effectiveness the enemy had acted.

. . .

In its efforts during 1942 to employ the submarine in the long-cherished role of warship vs. enemy warships, the U.S. Navy would encounter severe and even maddening problems, but during the year, nevertheless, submarines would sink two Japanese cruisers, a seaplane carrier, four destroyers, and six submarines. Off Guadalcanal, Japanese submarines would enjoy their greatest success of the war, sinking the aircraft carrier *Wasp*, as well as damaging the *Saratoga* and the battleship *North Carolina*. U.S. submarines proved useful in rescue and reconnaissance, and they carried out various special missions (notably, of course, the raid on Makin Island), but they were destined to make a monumental contribution to the Allied success in the Pacific war in quite a different way—the way the admirals had traditionally frowned upon and made light of. But it would prove to be the indispensable way.

29

THE STAR AND THE TORPEDOES

hen the new fleet submarine *Wahoo* (SS-238) returned to Pearl Harbor from her first patrol, her commander did not receive an enthusiastic reception from his superiors. The skipper, Lieutenant Commander Marvin "Pinky" Kennedy, who had been patrolling off Truk during September and early October 1942, reported success with a sizable freighter but failure to exploit two significant contacts and two other contacts that had been more fleeting.

On September 30 an aircraft tender had eluded the attentions of the *Wahoo*, though, said Kennedy, "the Japs were just begging someone to knock off this Tender, but it was not our lucky day." Six days later the *Wahoo* encountered a light aircraft carrier Kennedy mistakenly took to be the *Ryujo* (which had been sunk a month earlier in the Eastern Solomons), accompanied by two destroyers, but his approach "lacked aggressiveness and skill," as he put it, and "he watched the best target we could ever hope to find go over the hill untouched at 0800." Admiral English commented solemnly that it was "unfortunate that the *Wahoo* failed to press home an attack in this instance. Opportunities to attack an enemy carrier are few and must be exploited to the limit with due acceptance of the hazards involved." The captain did not disagree. Not the jaunty sort of fellow his nickname might suggest, he had expressed his remorse after letting the supposed *Ryujo* escape. "We're going to take *Wahoo* back to get someone in command who can sink ships," he said to his executive officer, Lieutenant Dick O'Kane. "We're never going to win the war this way."

But when the *Wahoo* departed for her second patrol, at 0900 on November 8, Kennedy remained captain. He had, after all, produced results no worse than those of many other skippers at the time. He also

388

had a talented wardroom, including O'Kane as exec and Lieutenant George W. Grider as the engineering officer. When these two had met upon becoming shipmates, O'Kane, a native of New Hampshire, liked Grider's "pleasing southern manner," but Grider had not returned the compliment. Though he found O'Kane likable and a hard worker, he also saw him as "overly garrulous and potentially unstable" and "a little out of touch with reality."

The wardroom also had a new face, a PCO (prospective commanding officer). An officer would attend a short course at PCO School, focusing on the use of torpedoes, and then, as a finishing touch, would go on a patrol as a PCO to observe everything that went on before being assigned to his own boat. The PCO on the *Wahoo*'s second patrol was Lieutenant Commander Dudley Morton, a product of an Ohio Valley town who had been known ever since his academy days as "Mush," some said from his Kentucky accent, others from his habit of talking with a cigar stuffed into his mouth. Morton thoroughly applied himself to his learning assignment, constantly roaming about as much as such a feat is possible on a submarine, "his big hands reaching out to examine equipment, his wide-set eyes missing nothing." Grider noted that "the tiny wardroom always brightened when Mush squeezed his massive shoulders through one of the two doorways and found a place to sit. He was built like a bear and playful as a cub."

Since Morton had no responsibility on this patrol, he could be one of the boys to officers and enlisted men alike, and the crew loved him. But occasionally, when Morton would express an opinion about tactics and ways of carrying the fight to the Japanese, Grider would wonder whether this popular PCO might not be just a little too aggressive. O'Kane, who disapproved of Kennedy's style and had expressed disappointment at his continuing in command, welcomed Morton as an officer of Kennedy's rank on whom the captain could lean for advice.

On this second patrol, the *Wahoo* accounted for one 5,000-ton freighter (though at the time everybody believed that she had sunk two ships), while letting several other targets escape with no attack being made. Kennedy indicated again in his second report that in at least one case he had failed to "appreciate the true nature of the approach" needed. When Morton and O'Kane wanted him to follow up on a missed opportunity with another effort, he declined. Hence the crew arrived in gloomy spirits at Brisbane, their base for the next patrol, having "missed the really big game," as Grider put it. But they soon had a new commander as well as a new home; the boat Mush Morton would command would be the *Wahoo* herself.

■ ■ ■

As the year 1942 ended, the record showed that, despite all the problems with the torpedoes, some U.S. submarine skippers had come back from patrol with good results. Operating in Japanese waters in August and September, Thomas "Burt" Klakring (Naval Academy '27) in the *Guardfish* sank five merchant ships (16,709 tons), the record number for the year. Charles Kirkpatrick ('31) and his *Triton* equaled this record, with total tonnage of 15,483. The tonnage award went, however, to Chester Bruton ('26) with a total of 20,400 on a patrol in the *Greenling* off Honshu (and, in the bargain, a small aircraft carrier damaged). Actually, the palm for the year could be awarded to Creed Burlingame ('27), except that the patrol straddled the end of 1942 and the beginning of 1943. This skipper, a "dynamic leader" much loved by his crew, took his *Silversides* from Brisbane to Pearl Harbor by way of Truk and ran up one of the best totals for a single patrol of the war (four ships for 27,798), his bag including a 10,000-ton tanker. Another good total was turned in by Robert Rice ('27) on the first patrol of the *Drum*: four ships for 20,000 tons.

Japanese home waters and the adjacent East China Sea clearly offered the commerce raiding submarine force the greatest opportunities for good hunting. That fact could hardly be considered surprising, since the direct trail from Southeast Asia and the Indies to the seat of the imperial war machine led through those waters. Perhaps, if Admiral Nimitz and his submarine commanders and the forces based in Australia decided to capitalize on this reality, the Americans could enjoy their own version of a happy time. They had not yet shown much evidence of having an overall strategic plan, however, and the totals run up by Burlingame and his fellow successful skippers were hardly typical; many boats returned from patrol having bagged not a single ship. All in all, a year after Pearl Harbor the unrestricted campaign Admiral

Stark had ordered against Japanese shipping "did not promise to be more than an irritation to them."

■ ■ ■

When Dudley Morton was a youngster in a village outside Owensboro, Kentucky, his friends knew him as the most daring of them all, the boy "who would take his bicycle to the highest part of the hill" and come roaring down, "who was venturesome and would take any chances." He was, a cousin said, "fearless, maybe reckless." Later, his parents moved to Florida; he graduated from high school in Miami and became a member of the class of 1930 at Annapolis.

During the "second happy time" the U-boats enjoyed in early 1942, Morton had commanded an old R-class boat in the Atlantic and then, as relief skipper on another old submarine, the *Dolphin* (which he deemed worn out beyond usefulness), had become embroiled in a controversy with Commander John Haines, who in consequence attempted to transfer him to surface duty. Morton's fame as a football star at the Academy saved him, however, and thus he entered the PCO pool.

Morton unofficially took command on the day the *Wahoo* arrived at Brisbane, and he immediately issued two orders that won applause from the crew members who carried them out. The silhouettes of enemy ships posted around the boat were to be ripped down and replaced by glossy prints of starlets and bathing beauties, which he produced from a traveling bag and turned over to the boat's yeoman (ship's clerk) for posting. He had picked them up in Hollywood, where he had gone to serve as technical adviser on the submarine film *Destination Tokyo,* and thought they "might be just the thing to bring along on a war patrol."

For his second order, the new skipper told the yeoman, Forest Sterling, to lose the captain's mast book, the docket of disciplinary offenders. "Don't deep-six it," Morton said, "but somehow get it lost while I am skipper. We won't be needing it on my boat." Indeed, he displayed an unorthodox approach to discipline. Before taking the *Wahoo* out for the first time, he told the crew that if anybody wanted to challenge him, he would take off his bars and they would see who was the best man. He also gave the men another choice: He intended to be aggressive as a commanding officer, he said ("[W]e're going to kill the SOBs"), and he offered anyone who wished to leave the chance to do so, without prejudice. In this speech to the crew, Morton gave terse expression to his credo: "We will take every reasonable precaution, but our mission is to sink enemy shipping."

The *Wahoo* was certainly going to be a different boat now, and when she sailed on her third patrol her husky skipper had a unified crew behind him. "The officers acted differently," said Sterling. "The men felt differently." Morton "was a natural-born leader," and "everybody on ship was glad to follow him wherever he would go." He was "positive, intolerant, quick to denounce inefficiency if he thought it existed," said a friend in Kentucky, but he was "precise by nature, absolutely fearless and possessed of a burning desire to inflict damage upon the Japanese enemy."

The new skipper formally assumed command of the *Wahoo* on the last day of the year 1942, and at 0900 on the following January 16 she moved away from her mooring and headed for the open sea. When her escorting destroyer turned back, she sent the message: "Good luck. Good hunting." Morton clearly took these standard sentiments to heart.

Jimmy Fife, who had just taken command of the submarines operating out of Brisbane, had given the *Wahoo* the assignment of reconnoitering Wewak on the northeast coast of New Guinea, en route to patrol in the waters off Palau in the Carolines. Morton urbanely described Wewak as "a more or less undetermined spot"; his point did not represent an exaggeration, since nobody on the boat knew which tiny dent on the coastline might be Wewak. In lieu of charts (maps) of the harbor, however, a motor machinist in the crew offered a cheap school atlas he had picked up in Brisbane, and in it appeared a map with a wrinkle marked "Wewak." Working together, with an old camera and toilet paper, officers and crew created a blown-up chart of the area, showing a roadstead surrounded by four islands.

To reach the spot, Morton drove the *Wahoo* on the surface, wanting to save time so that he could not only "reconnoiter" the area but invade the harbor. "A couple of months before," Grider commented, "the idea of entering an enemy harbor with the help of a high-school geography would have struck me as too ridiculous even to be funny." But Morton had said that he wanted "to see what's there."

After arriving at this obscure coastal site, the *Wahoo* crept between islands and through the harbor for half a day, keeping out of sight of patrolling Japanese small craft. Nine miles inside the harbor, O'Kane spotted a destroyer lying at anchor, flanked by several small submarines. The executive officer was on the periscope, normally the place of the skipper, because Morton had instituted an arrangement whereby he and O'Kane would perform as "co-approach officers," with the exec making the approach observations and the captain handling the conn (that is, getting the boat to the point at which O'Kane could shoot). At PCO school, Morton had noted that while he made periscope observations and then tactical decisions based on the observations, the instructors could record quicker and better decisions because they did not have to concern themselves with mechanics. Adapting this arrangement to actual battle conditions, Morton felt, would give him a better grasp of the overall situation, and O'Kane naturally appreciated this mark of confidence.

As the *Wahoo* prepared to attack the unsuspecting Japanese vessel, Grider found himself marveling at the change he saw now in O'Kane. "It was as if, during all the talkative, boastful months before, he had been lost, seeking his true element, and now it was found. He was calm, terse, and utterly cool." But at this point the destroyer began to move, and, said Grider, "the only sensible thing to do was to get out. Later, perhaps, we could get a shot at her in deep water." But Morton quickly fired a spread of three torpedoes, all of them missing; then a fourth missed as well. Now the enemy ship came straight on toward the submarine.

"That's all right," called Mush. "Keep your scope up and we'll shoot that SOB down the throat." The officers had talked about down-the-throat shots (in which the submarine would fire at the target vessel while it came directly toward its attacker) in wardroom bull sessions, said Grider, but nobody had expected to find himself in such a situation. "I felt an almost uncontrollable urge to urinate," said the yeoman Sterling, as the destruction of the *Wahoo* seemed imminent.

Morton loosed her two remaining forward torpedoes and then took the boat down to try to escape the inevitable depth charging that would come. When they had reached about 80 feet, they heard "a mighty roaring and cracking, as if we were in the very middle of a lightning storm." Everybody knew what that meant—the destroyer's boilers were pouring steam into the sea. "We hit the son of a bitch!" came the cry.

When the submarine came back to periscope depth, everybody with a camera had the chance to snap the scene through the scope. The destroyer had broken in two, with its bow down and sinking. As Mush described it: "To insure maximum likelihood of hitting with our last torpedo in the forward tubes, withheld fire until range was about 800 yards. This last one, fired at 1449, clipped him amidships in twenty-five seconds and broke his back. The explosion was terrific!" This feat represented Morton's first sinking of an enemy ship, but he already seemed to have divined that the admirals back in port loved to read patrol reports with sentences like that last one.

Now it was time for the *Wahoo,* her so-called reconnaissance of We-wak completed, to get out of this tortuous and previously unknown harbor. As a plane tried to bomb her, she succeeded in making her escape by using sonar echoes off reefs and beachheads to navigate: "No difficulty was experienced," Mush reported calmly; the young sailor on the sound equipment had earned his pay that day.

The next day proved to be a quiet interlude, featuring a humanitarian gesture by the men of the *Wahoo.* At 0800 the submarine encountered a sampan with a crew of six Malays, feeble and seeming on the point of starvation. Communicating by sign language, the fishermen indicated that three of their group had died. *Wahoo* gave them oranges to combat scurvy, fresh and canned food, bread, and water, and, as O'Kane said, "sent them on their way with a wave and a prayer."

The following morning, just twenty-four hours later, presented a sharply contrasting scene. At 0757 a lookout on the *Wahoo* spotted a streamer of smoke on the horizon; this giveaway plume turned out to mark the presence of a convoy consisting of a tanker, two freighters, and a large troop transport, with no escorting warships anywhere in sight. After the approach was made, Mush fired two torpedoes at the first freighter, registering two hits, and two at the second freighter, switching his fire so fast that the first fish missed; the second torpedo, however, found its target.

At 1047, with the transport offering itself at a perfect 90° angle, the *Wahoo*, at 1,800 yards' range, fired a spread of three torpedoes from her forward tubes, two of them delivering powerful punches that stopped the ship. One of the freighters then began churning toward the submarine like a warship on the attack. Morton responded with two down-the-throat shots, one of which hit but failed to stop the determined attacker. The *Wahoo* took evasive action. Then, said Morton, "there followed so many explosions that it was impossible to tell just what was taking place." After coming back to periscope depth, observers on the submarine saw that one freighter had sunk, the intrepid second was under way but with steering trouble, and the transport lay dead in the water. Mush fired a torpedo that passed under the middle of the transport, failing to explode, while crewmen on the ship shot at the *Wahoo* with deck guns and rifles. At 1135 Mush loosed a second torpedo, at a more favorable angle, and the resulting explosion "blew her midships section higher than a kite. Troops commenced jumping over the side like ants off a hot plate. Her stern went up and she headed for the bottom." Morton added: "Took several pictures."

Recharging the batteries while doing his determined best to destroy all the troop boats that carried survivors from the transport, Morton was forced to let the wounded freighter and tanker sail away, but he later renewed the chase. He scored a hit on the tanker and believed that he had sunk it, and at 2113, having pursued the freighter for another hour after torpedoing the tanker, fired the last two torpedoes at his quarry—having no time to waste, since the sweep of a searchlight signaled the approach of an escort vessel.

Before Morton fired the final torpedoes, Grider said to another officer: "If either of those torpedoes hits, I will kiss your royal ass." After seeing the freighter sink, an event that made his self-determined fate inescapable, Grider had to play his part in "the most unusual ceremony ever performed in the conning tower of the mighty *Wahoo*." O'Kane would later recall one of Morton's guiding principles: "Tenacity, Dick. Stay with the bastard till he's on the bottom."

In a letter to his cousin Sam Morton in Owensboro, Mush gave a chatty description of his activities: "We just had the 'gol darndest' series of fights with the Japs anyone ever heard of. To say it was exciting would be putting it mildly." The nerves in his shoulders, he said, stayed knotted up for several days. "The Japs fought back savagely, but we were so fierce and determined that we did not stop until we had destroyed all we sighted, including thousands of tons of shipping, hundreds of troops, and a man-of-war." The submarine stuck to them, he said, "until they were all destroyed."

On the trip back to Pearl Harbor, the crew spruced up the boat while the officers worked on their various reports. As executive officer, O'Kane proofread these documents before they were turned into mimeograph stencils by Sterling. He had been reading patrol reports for about a year, O'Kane commented, but Morton's narrative was the first one he had seen that devoted a paragraph to the officers and men. Of his executive officer, Morton said: "O'Kane is the fightingest naval officer I have ever seen and is worthy of the highest of praise. I commend Lieutenant O'Kane for being an inspiration to the ship."

■ ■ ■

After each engagement with the Japanese, Morton had dispatched a brief account of it to ComSubPac and had received replies bearing praise from the highest brass on Oahu. Among the remarkable features marking the adventures of the *Wahoo* was the rapid expenditure of all of her torpedoes on targets, which came so quickly that this 23-day outing could be reckoned perhaps the shortest successful patrol of the war. Captain "Babe" Brown, acting as temporary ComSubPac after the death of Admiral English in an airplane crash, declared that the "most aggressive manner" in which the *Wahoo* had carried out her attacks "clearly demonstrates what can be done by a submarine that retains the initiative." The squadron commander called the performance "an epic of submarine warfare." The day of the prewar-style skipper— engineering-oriented and technically competent but trained to be cautious and to wait for a target to present itself (like the *Wahoo*'s first skipper)—had now given way to the era of the hunter, technically competent as well but devoted to seeking out and fighting the enemy.

As the *Wahoo* approached the submarine base on February 7, those on the bridge and on deck saw waiting crowds on the pier, including dignitaries, bands, and reporters. The signalmen on the submarine had run up eight tiny Japanese flags on one of the halyards, one flag for each enemy ship believed sunk (as was common, postwar analysis would lower the total), and on orders from the captain crewmen had lashed a broomstick to the periscope, telling the world of a clean sweep. It became, said O'Kane, the most photographed broom in the world. With her swashbuckling name fitting perfectly with the flash and dash of her skipper, the *Wahoo* had become the most famous submarine in the temporarily not so Silent Service. Like Ruby Keeler's character in the old musical film *42nd Street*, the boat had gone out an obscure performer and had come back a star. And so had her skipper.

■ ■ ■

Beginning on February 23, the *Wahoo's* fourth patrol of the war (the second with Morton as skipper) took her to the East China and Yellow seas, by way of Midway. The results again demonstrated both the skipper's boldness and his thoroughness: In a true commerce raiding operation, the *Wahoo* sank nine freighters and tankers, the highest total achieved on any patrol up to that time and the second-highest of the entire Pacific war. "The intelligent planning and sound judgment of the Commanding Officer in making his decisions enabled the WAHOO to outsmart the enemy, retain the initiative, and inflict a considerable amount of damage." Morton's habit of cruising extensively on the surface, a practice that enabled the boat to spend more time covering her patrol area, earned particular and approving note. "During this patrol," declared the squadron commander, "the outstanding aggressiveness and the magnificent fighting spirit of the captain, officers, and crew were largely responsible for the splendid results obtained." Those commenting on Morton's report, however, took note of the reported "faulty torpedo performance."

The next patrol, to the Kuril Islands, the chain extending north from Hokkaido to Kamchatka, brought a bag of two freighters and a tanker, and once again Morton's aggressiveness and his strategic and tactical judgment won praise from his superiors, this time from Admiral

English's successor, Admiral Lockwood. The three patrols under Morton, Lockwood noted, established "a record not only in damage inflicted on the enemy for three successive patrols, but also for accomplishing this feat in the shortest time on patrol." The commander of Submarine Squadron Ten, however, paid full attention to Morton's problems with torpedoes. At one point, describing an attack on a convoy, Morton fired a spread of which the first "prematured after a 51 second run halfway to the target." The second torpedo "was evidently deflected by the premature or failed to explode. The third torpedo fired at the foremast hit the point of aim but failed to explode." Both sound operators, Morton said lyrically, "reported the thud of the dud." "Such erratic performance following determined and aggressive approaches," said the squadron commander, "must have been a source of keen disappointment to the Commanding Officer and personnel of the WAHOO."

Because the boats operated mostly in the far western Pacific, said Lockwood's chief of staff, Sunshine Murray, "our really busy hours of hearing from the submarines were from about midnight on." He and Lockwood split up the time so that one or the other would always be present at headquarters at peak time, and generally both of them were on hand. Admiral Nimitz, the old submariner, often went down to headquarters at three or four o'clock in the morning to read dispatches, so that he would be thoroughly ready for the morning conference at nine. Once, handling a message before it reached either Lockwood or Murray, the admiral immediately sent an answer. The submarine *Darter* had requested permission to move from its patrol area to one that seemed more promising, and CINCPAC replied: "Yes, my darling Darter, you shouldn't oughter, but since you wanter, approved. Nimitz." Murray noted that, though phrased differently, that was the answer he or Lockwood would have given. "Of course," he added, "all the submarines got the message also and got a big kick out of it."

Lockwood and Murray kept CINCPAC and his staff fully informed about the activities of the submarine force, in order to avoid any mixup in relation to operations of the surface fleet. A submarine had a "moving haven," a rectangle of water about 10 miles wide and 50 miles long, that advanced at its estimated speed toward its destination. A skipper had to report any deviation from his course, so that a new haven could be formed around him and all ships could be notified of the change. Otherwise, his submarine represented "free bait" for depth bombs from his own side's surface forces or aircraft.

On October 3, 1944, for example, such a fate apparently struck the *Seawolf* as she was carrying out a special mission in Philippine waters. Running a day behind schedule, owing to heavy seas, she apparently fell victim to an information gap, which led to depth charging by a destroyer escort. In the search of the scene for bodies or wreckage, Emerson Grossman, a third-class torpedoman on the old *S-47*, fished an oily dollar bill from the floating wreckage. On the same day, in the same area, another destroyer escort almost did in Admiral Nimitz's "darling *Darter*" but backed off when the submarine skipper, Lieutenant Commander David McClintock, was able to supply not only a convincingly American name but a convincingly named home state.

■ ■ ■

In June 1943, after much discussion, Admiral Lockwood had reluctantly agreed with his submariners about the need to deactivate the frustrating and unreliable magnetic exploders on the torpedoes and had obtained Admiral Nimitz's agreement. One skipper, Chuck Triebel (Naval Academy '29), had even written a letter to the secretary of the navy, as Slade Cutter recalled, in which he demanded the court-martial of Rear Admiral "Spike" Blandy, chief of the Bureau of Ordnance; Lockwood apparently intercepted the letter. Not only did Triebel's message get through, however, but so did Triebel himself; Lockwood dispatched him to Washington to work with the bureau on improving torpedoes.

Lockwood's successor as submarine commander in the Southwest Pacific, Rear Admiral Ralph Christie, remained a true believer in the magnetic exploder, a view not unrelated, perhaps, to the time the admiral had spent at Newport, where he had midwifed what the Bureau of Ordnance had regarded as the magnetic marvel. Christie viewed the matter with intense seriousness, not only forbidding crews to tamper with the exploder mechanism but ordering the torpedo shop to put paint over the screws that any potential miscreants would have to remove in order to deactivate the device. Admirably united against the high brass, however, the torpedomen and the workers in the torpedo shop circumvented Christie's detective scheme; the men in the shop would give a submarine crew a small can of paint in the color of the day so that, after removing the screw and deactivating the exploder, they could touch up the blemished spot.

After having the exploders modified, said one of Christie's skippers, Lieutenant Commander Norvell Ward, the admiral was sending crews out with torpedoes that "barely got out of the tubes and were barely armed before they started going off. That was the end of magnetic exploders in SoWestPac." (Speaking of his own problems with the magnetic exploder, Admiral Dönitz would later point to the "uncritical attitude adopted by the Torpedo Experimental Establishment toward its own achievements.")

Mush Morton's fourth patrol, which came after a complete overhaul at Mare Island, began on August 2 and produced far more than "keen disappointment." In ten attacks, torpedoes missed the target, broached, or failed to explode on impact. At one point Morton simply noted: "Damn the torpedoes." The *Wahoo,* which was operating in the Sea of Japan, failed to inflict any damage on the enemy, except for sinking three sampans by gunfire. On August 18, Morton, unused to failure and disgusted by the inadequacy of the tools with which he had to work, radioed Lockwood for permission to return to Pearl Harbor to have the torpedoes checked; Lockwood assented the next day. The *Wahoo* broke all records with the speed of its return home: eleven days.

"Mush was boiling mad," Lockwood said. "He had found plenty of targets but a combination of deep running and duds had broken him down." Though frustrated and furious, Morton weakened his argument with Lockwood by describing how he had adopted a new procedure. Trusting in his accuracy, though he no longer had O'Kane as his co-approach officer (his exec was getting his own boat), he had fired single torpedoes rather than spreads, a method that gave his superiors the opportunity to make such points as "torpedo spreads must be used to cover possible errors in date or possibility of duds." It happened, however, that another normally successful skipper, Benny Bass in the *Plunger,* had undergone almost the same experience in the Sea of

Japan, except that after various fiascoes with duds and misses, he did manage to claim a freighter as a victim. Another skipper, Dan Daspit in the *Tinosa,* peppered a 19,000-ton ship with eleven torpedoes, all with contact exploders and all duds. Like Morton, he brought home a few to show his superiors.

The famous Captain Swede Momsen suggested a test of the contact exploders, in the style of the experiments Lockwood had supervised in Australia the previous year concerning the depth at which torpedoes were running. A submarine fired three Mark XIV torpedoes against a cliff, two of which exploded and one of which simply bounced off the rock and went to the bottom. Its recovery by a truly heroic diver, who had to find and tackle a live missile, immediately led to the solution of the mystery.

"We were the only navy in the world that had the firing pin vertical," Cutter explained. "There was a ring sitting on these four supports for it, and if it got bumped in any direction, the ring would be released. It would fall off, and a spring would take the firing pin up." Two fulminate of mercury caps in the booster would be set off by "two tits on the firing pin that would hit these caps and explode." That would set off the booster, which in turn would set off the main charge. The problem came from the failure, under some conditions, of the vertically moving firing pin to strike the caps with enough force to explode them, as when, ironically, the torpedo hit the target at the theoretically ideal 90° angle. But when the impact occurred at a small angle, all went well. As Lieutenant Commander John Coye put it, "We found that if you took the ideal shot and hit the target 90 degrees (that is, what we call a 90 track, hit it right abeam), this would deform the contact exploder." Hence the skippers received instructions to try for the oblique angle or to set torpedoes to run so that they hit on the turn of the bilge. But, said Coye, "it is pretty difficult to know where the turn of the bilge is, and odds are the torpedo isn't going to run at its exact set depth anyway."

Those instructions were supposed to serve only for the short term, however, until a redesigned mechanism became available. A whole team at Pearl Harbor went to work on the problem and within three weeks had produced an "acceptable, safe and sure-fire contact exploder."

Thus, finally, irrefutable evidence had vindicated the submarine skippers on all three counts against the torpedoes and all three problems had now been solved. In October captains could set out on patrol with new confidence. Lockwood came to Midway, now serving as a submarine base along with Pearl Harbor, to demonstrate the new exploder to an assemblage of skippers.

The captains also had the choice of a new weapon, the Mark XVIII electric torpedo, which had been under development by Westinghouse since 1941 but had run into various problems and even needed further work after the first ones arrived on Oahu. This torpedo, Lockwood said, "was a 'Chinese copy' of the German electric torpedo," but, "unfortunately, we had felt it necessary to improve on the model and, in so doing, had run into difficulties." Though this new torpedo ran somewhat more slowly than the standard steam torpedo, it derived its power from a bank of battery cells and thus had the great advantage of producing no gases to create a telltale wake. Lockwood gave his captains their choice of the steam or electric model, and the latter ultimately became the favorite.

■ ■ ■

Mush Morton wanted to go right back to the Sea of Japan, but with better torpedoes than those that had failed him, and with some reluctance Lockwood agreed. The admiral felt that his ace skipper might need time off, but, he decided, how could he deny this fighting wish? With a load of the new electric Mark XVIIIs, still in the trial stage, the *Wahoo* departed on September 9 on what Mush regarded as simply the second part of his previous patrol. When they stopped at Midway, mail flown in from Pearl Harbor contained orders for Forest Sterling to go back to the United States for advanced yeoman's school, and saying good-bye to his shipmates, Sterling stood on the pier and took in the last line cast off, watching as the *Wahoo*'s tops disappeared below the horizon.

About ten days later, taking the long way around, the submarine passed through La Perouse Strait, north of Hokkaido, and headed for her patrol area in the southern Inland Sea. On September 29, October 5, October 6, and October 9 she sank merchant ships—three freighters and a passenger steamer—for a total of 13,000 tons. These sinkings left Morton with an overall bag of nineteen ships sunk, which would stand as the third-highest total in the Pacific war, a particularly impressive achievement since it came before sound, properly functioning torpedoes became available.

On October 11 a Japanese shore battery fired on a surfaced submarine, which then dived, and various aircraft and submarine chasers, attracted by an oil slick and employing bombs and depth charges, mounted a heavy assault on the boat. ComSubPac expected a radio report from the *Wahoo* on or about October 23. It never came.

"It just didn't seem possible that Morton and his fighting crew could be lost," said Lockwood. "I'd never have believed the Japs were smart enough to get him." Taking all the time allowed, the admiral finally had to give in and add the *Wahoo* to the list of boats overdue and presumed lost; it was, he said, the most difficult task he ever faced. "Uncle Charlie" made it a point to greet his submarines when they came back from patrol, but never again would he stand on the pier watching the *Wahoo* "steaming in with a broom at her masthead and Mush Morton's fighting face, with its wide grin, showing above the bridge rail."

30

MEDALS OF HONOR

On July 24, 1943, at the Portsmouth Navy Yard, a young woman named Betty Russell banged a bottle of champagne against the bow of the submarine bearing Hull Number 384 and christened this new *Balao*-class vessel *Parche*. The name, obscure as it was, held some promise: The navy bureaucracy had called the boat after a small but clever butterfly fish gifted with a knack for finding its way through the most intricate passages of coral reefs. Four months later, in a ceremony presided over by Rear Admiral Thomas Withers, the commandant of the yard and former submarine chief at Pearl Harbor, the U.S.S. *Parche* became commissioned as a vessel in the United States Navy.

Among the original members of the crew, though technically not a "plank owner" because he had not yet arrived at Portsmouth when the boat was commissioned, was Bob Hall, a lean and lanky nineteen-year-old from Castine, Maine. Without having any particularly strong feelings in the matter, Hall had chosen to enlist in the navy rather than wait for his draft board to send him off to army basic training. Similarly, when given the chance to volunteer for duty in submarines he had accepted it, though he had never previously felt any strong interest in that service. The pay was 50 percent higher than the normal rate, but that factor did not govern Hall's decision. He found something appealing about the idea of submarines, he said. "I had a cousin who was a paratrooper. He wouldn't go down in a submarine. I wouldn't jump out of an aircraft."

After boot camp, Hall went off to Submarine School at the submarine base at Groton, Connecticut, upstream from the yards and shops of the Electric Boat Company. Here both officers and enlisted men

learned about problems they would likely face as submariners and acquired a variety of practical skills: plotting an underwater course,
learning the workings of diesel engines, getting familiar with gear like
periscopes and hydrophones. After completing the six-week course
(three months for officers), the volunteers proceeded to duty assignments.

Because the life of a submarine and everybody on board depended
on the actions of the entire crew, each officer and enlisted man had to
demonstrate his thorough and instantaneously available knowledge of
submarines. After reporting aboard, he received a "qualification" book
with his assignments and answers: test pressures of the main ballast
tanks, names of all the piping systems (internal salvage line, impulse air
lines, and so forth), details of pyrotechnics, location and name of every
hull opening, and seemingly countless other details—fittings, levers,
switches, valves. "Our lives were so interdependent, dependent on
every man knowing his job," said one submariner, "that no lack of enthusiasm was tolerated as we studied all aspects of submarine operation, patrol, and warfare." Only after thus qualifying did a crewman
receive his dolphin insignia, the symbol of a true submariner.

At the start of this whole process, however, even before taking any of
the substantive classes at Submarine School, a candidate had to show that
he could deal with the basic medium of the submariner's trade, deep
water, which could veil a boat from an attacker but also had the power to
crush it like a bug. Water pressure at great depths could produce searing
pains in a man's ears or give him sudden heart trouble, and a student had
to demonstrate to the instructors that he could take it and survive. First
he went into the decompression chamber, in which he was subjected to
50 pounds of pressure. If he passed that test, he moved on to a tall silo
marking this unusual campus; this 138-foot tower, which contained 100
feet of water, was the escape tank, which would induce claustrophobia in
many people in the general population but rarely did so in those who
had chosen to sail in submarines. Almost all candidates passed this examination, which called for them to descend to the bottom of the huge
tank and then make a mock escape using the Momsen lung.

Bob Hall did all the work at Submarine School and passed all the
tests, and in due course found himself ordered to the *Parche* at

Portsmouth. One of the few members of the crew who had not yet acquired a specialty, he thought he might like to become a baker. In the independent and often isolated world of the submarine service, food held a place of unique importance.

■ ■ ■

The skipper of the newly commissioned *Parche,* Lieutenant Commander Lawson P. Ramage, came from the Pacific, where he had commanded the *Trout* (SS-202) on patrols off Truk and in the Solomons and the South China Sea. A native of Monroe Bridge, Massachusetts, "Red" Ramage, thirty-five, grew up in upstate New York. After graduating from the Naval Academy in 1931, he served in destroyers and on the heavy cruiser *Louisville* before going to Submarine School in 1935. He had sea duty on the *S-29,* and early in 1942 he returned to sea on the *Grenadier* and, as the result of some musical chairs changes in command, soon found himself skipper of the *Trout,* which had won a measure of fame by carrying the Philippine government's gold reserve to safety.

Ramage quickly saw the truth in all the talk going around about faulty torpedoes. After he fired three fish at an enemy destroyer with no visible results, he saw sailors running out of the cabin and peering over the side to see what had caused the strange thumping noises. Crew members on a submarine had no way of knowing how well the skipper could shoot, he said, but "those of us who were looking through the periscope were fully convinced that the torpedoes were running hot, straight, and true." A friend reported a failed attack by saying of his intended victim, "I clinked him with a clunk," an observation that would become famous in Australian circles.

Before going on his next patrol, Ramage joined the growing cacophony of complaints against Captain Christie, the torpedo expert. He gave Christie a "deliberate needle" by telling him that the torpedoes could not be relied on, and quickly found that "any disparaging remarks about [them] were not countenanced at all." Christie huffed that it was "all just small talk," saying that "people are trying to berate these torpedoes and there's nothing to it." He would not listen to any suggestions, and the situation became tense enough for Christie's helpful aide to hustle the forthright Ramage out of the office before real trouble could develop.

In going to "new construction" (that is, being assigned to a new boat) at Portsmouth rather than at Electric Boat, Ramage was getting a new "heavy hull" boat, capable of diving to greater depths (400 feet as against 300 feet) than those being produced in Groton. He arrived in July, and in accordance with navy custom had several months' opportunity to make a number of suggestions, drawn from his combat experience, about features and details to be added to the boat. On December 11 Portsmouth officially completed the *Parche* and signed her over to the navy. After several weeks of drills and trials, the new boat departed for Pearl Harbor, stopping for two weeks en route at Key West to serve as a training target for antisubmarine warfare crews.

After the *Parche* arrived in Hawaii on March 5, her officers and crew spent most of the month in various kinds of training, including something new for the U.S. fleet: exercises in performing as part of a "coordinated attack group." After limited, on-and-off experiments in previous months, the U.S. Navy had decided to develop its own version of the wolf pack, and this training involved the *Parche* working with the *Bang,* another new submarine, and the *Tinosa*. The American adaptation of the idea differed from Admiral Dönitz's approach in a number of ways, calling for a small group that would depart from port together and would operate on its own rather than a large group summoned from all sides when a convoy was located. This concept took into account two basic points of contrast with the scene in the Atlantic: The American submarines were working in a bigger ocean and they were opposing smaller convoys. Though based on the idea that the submarine would no longer operate as a lone wolf, the concept still did not go all the way to turning the boats into pack animals with detailed direction from a higher authority, and thus it did not risk giving the enemy the opportunity to turn radio signals against the senders. At the same time, radio messages drawn from U.S. Ultra intelligence many times told submarines where to find victims. Overall, the American doctrine, when practiced successfully, would tend to produce cooperation rather than tight control, and it left the skippers with a good measure of the independence they prized.

Under Captain George Peterson, newly arrived from the Atlantic theater, the fledgling wolf pack departed Pearl Harbor on March 29. Because the *Parche* had an experienced skipper and she was heavy hulled, the division commander made her, in essence, his flagship. This was not the first of the 1944 wolf packs but it ranked among the earliest, and en route to Midway, where the pack would stop for fueling, Peterson and Ramage discussed tactics. The navy had decided on three as the suitable number of boats for a wolf pack with the idea that one submarine would attempt to get into position ahead of the target, on either bow, and the third boat would act as the trailer, going after laggards and picking off cripples. If the convoy should reverse its course, then the trailer would be in position to attack it in front. Peterson and Ramage agreed, however, not to allow this idea to act as a straitjacket on the group. They divided the patrol area into 60-mile squares, with each boat having a 20-mile lane 60 miles long. When a boat made contact with enemy shipping, she could then summon the others.

After leaving Midway for the Luzon Strait south of Formosa (Taiwan), the patrol proved so uneventful that in the afternoon of April 18 Ramage noted in the log: "Picked up sky lookout—Bird (genus: unknown; sex: undetermined; habits: not altogether proper) which took station on #1 periscope." The tedium continued, with only a few aircraft sightings, until the twenty-ninth, when the *Bang* reported a convoy at 50 miles' distance. The three boats rushed to attack, with the *Parche* scoring a hit, but no one received credit for a sinking.

On the morning of May 3, when the *Tinosa* radioed contact with a convoy consisting of seven ships, the *Parche* sped north to intercept it. At 0100 on May 4, having reached firing position, the *Parche* attacked the leading ship, scoring three hits, and she put two more torpedoes into the third freighter; both went down. Overall, the group sank seven cargo ships, totaling 35,000 tons; the *Parche* received credit for two of the *maru*s. "The advantage of the wakeless [electric] torpedo was realized," Ramage reported, "when four of these torpedoes were fired in daylight attack on a 10 ship convoy which maneuvered but could not effectively avoid [them]."

The division and squadron commanders and Admiral Lockwood all expressed full approval of Ramage's handling of the *Parche* and, speaking of coordinated attacks, the admiral praised Captain Peterson for providing "a perfect example of the manner in which such attacks should be made." Ramage approved of Peterson as well, since he "would take any suggestions" and "left the individual operation of the boats to the skippers."

But things were about to change. For her next patrol as part of a wolf pack, the *Parche* would again serve as the command post of the leader, and the boss this time would be the formidable perfectionist Lew Parks. "It was a different sort of ball game with him than it was with George Peterson," Ramage said. "We went through quite a long ritual with him because he was pretty much of a stickler for detail and everything else." Beyond that, Ramage could never have imagined what would happen when they returned to their previous patrol beat, the busy operational area south and southwest of Formosa that would become known as the campus of "Convoy College."

■ ■ ■

Red Ramage had given the performance of his crew high praise in his first patrol report. The men returned the compliment: From their point of view, the skipper was proving to be reasonable and pleasant as well as a capable commander, and his boat could truly be called a happy ship; one sailor later said that "togetherness" was what impressed him most about serving on the *Parche*. But, though the skipper represented a presence, the men normally did not have a great deal of contact with him, except after a battle, when he would come through the boat and talk with everybody.

Bob Hall had no regrets about his choice of the submarine service. He had no special training for the job he wanted—indeed, he had never done any cooking at all—but he apprenticed himself to the cooks and, as one chronicler said, he "mess-cooked his way into the Baker ratings, so he never learned the ways of navy cook school." Some home cooking was just what the boys needed, Hall had decided, and accordingly he had brought along an old family cookbook.

For Hall, the galley represented a kind of separate world. He had no earphones to plug into the communication system, and he often would have no idea what was happening topside. One morning he stood at his stove, happily putting to use one of his mother's recipes. As a treat for his shipmates, he had decided to prepare good New England fried mush. As the cornmeal sizzled in the hot fat, a cloud of dense black smoke suddenly arose from the pan and was immediately sucked into the ventilating system, which whirled it throughout the boat. Since the air was reasonably clear where he was standing, Hall failed to realize that a problem existed. In a few moments, however, the skipper appeared, wanting to know what had happened. To his great credit, when he saw the scene he did not administer a chewing-out to the apprentice cook, whose actions had put the *Parche* in some jeopardy, since the boat was being forced to surface in these enemy-controlled waters to change the air. Ramage merely said the only reason Commander Parks had not come back personally to chew him out was that he had "tears in his eyes as big as horse turds and he couldn't see anything." But Hall quickly realized that there would be no more mush on the menu.

■ ■ ■

As Ramage liked to say, the boats making up the pack this time were the *Steelhead* and the *Hammerhead*, with the "redhead" in the *Parche* rounding out the group. Since wolf packs had begun to acquire alliterative nicknames, the pack had been dubbed Parks' Pirates, but, said Ramage, "I was more or less inclined to refer to it as the 'Head Hunters.' "

En route to her patrol area, after leaving Midway on June 17, the *Parche* sighted and sank a 1,500-ton picket boat by gunfire. Less than thrilled by playing host to a dominating supervisor, Ramage found himself amused when "our so-called wolf pack commander came up on the bridge with all his movie equipment and was recording the whole thing in color," though it indeed turned to be "quite a spectacular show."

On July 4 Ramage, preparing to make a night surface attack, had to take the boat down to escape gunfire from two cruisers and depth-charging by their accompanying destroyer. Otherwise, the patrol proved essentially a bore for the entire month, except for a note of excitement provided by an enemy aircraft carrier that zigged at the right time and thus escaped a torpedo attack.

But at the end of the month, nearing the expiration of her allotted days on patrol, everything changed for the *Parche*. Early in the morning of July 30, the *Hammerhead* radioed a report of a contact with a large convoy, as many as fifteen ships, but this and subsequent reports did not enable either the *Parche* or the *Steelhead* to find the enemy vessels. Pacing the bridge and glowering, Ramage was reported by crew members to be in "a hell of a mood." If the *Hammerhead's* reports were accurate, then the *Parche* should be picking up the convoy on her own radar. But nothing showed. When the next morning broke, Ramage noted that "it finally dawned on us that we were the victims of another snipe hunt." And the worst side of that was that the misinformation had come from a sister ship.

Running low on fuel, the *Hammerhead* said good-bye to her disgruntled fellow wolves and set off for Fremantle. Not wanting to return to base without having fired even a single torpedo, Parks and Ramage received permission to extend the patrol. During the day of July 30, the *Parche* and the *Steelhead* (commanded by Commander Dave Whelchel) searched the area, as Japanese patrol planes kept a continual eye on them. At 1025 Ramage spotted smoke, and a little more than an hour later it had turned into five separate columns. But as the convoy altered its course, the *Parche* lost contact with it until after dark, at 2014, Ramage surfaced and received a report from the *Steelhead* giving a location for the ships. But they did not show up on the *Parche's* radar. Four hours later the *Steelhead* sent another contact report, which indicated that the convoy had made a radical change of course, and at 0115 the desired radar contact came, dead ahead.

Running on the surface at top speed, Ramage took the *Parche* toward the quarry. At 0332 Whelchel opened the attack, firing six torpedoes at a tanker and a freighter, observing hits on both. He then withdrew to reload the torpedo tubes. Ramage no longer had that problem, because on the first patrol the *Parche's* torpedo officer had convinced him that he and his crew could reload while the submarine was speeding on the surface in contact with the enemy. Contrary to all theories about the danger involved, with a torpedo possibly getting loose ("they're just like a greased pig"), the experiment had worked, a development that had immediately stepped up the submarine's fire-power, and it set a precedent for the submarine force.

Now came the action that quickly became famous throughout the service as "Ramage's Rampage." Driving toward the flank of the convoy, Ramage saw, in the glare of flares sent up by some of the ships, several cargo vessels and three busy escorts. Finding his "present position untenable," Ramage turned away from one escort headed his way and swung behind another, the first of a series of moves that made the helmsman giddy, confused the enemy, and put the *Parche* between the escorts and the convoy itself. At the same time, the convoy had done a turnabout and now was headed directly for the submarine. Swinging away from a freighter that just missed it, the *Parche*, still on the surface, bored into the heart of the convoy. Putting one stern shot into the freighter, Ramage fired four torpedoes at a tanker, then three more at a second tanker. The first one sank in minutes, the second, although hit, managed to limp out of the line of fire. Then the *Parche*, surrounded, shot at the encircling ships and received heavy fire from them. "We were so close they couldn't angle their guns down enough to fire at us," Bob Hall said, "so close that Americans and Japanese were yelling insults back and forth," with the *Parche* twisting and weaving like the clever little fish whose name she bore. The Japanese became so befuddled that they were firing at themselves in the middle of the convoy.

With a "small fast job" coming in with intent to ram, Ramage "called the engine house to pour in all the oil they had—the other fellow had the right of way but we were in a hurry." As she crossed in front of the Japanese ship, the *Parche* cleared by no more than 50 feet. Then, with a big cargo ship looming up ahead, the *Parche* could save herself only by firing a down-the-throat salvo. The first torpedo missed, but the second and third hit home. Swinging around to bring the stern tubes to bear, Ramage fired a final shot, the last of the nineteen the *Parche* loosed that morning, and the target ship started her plunge to the bottom.

With escort vessels buzzing dangerously close, "Captain Red" called down to the conning tower: "Set course 330 degrees true, and let's put a little distance between us and this hornet's nest. Dawn's beginning to break."

Having returned to action, the *Steelhead* attacked two ships fleeing the carnage, sinking one of them. Though some of the enemy merchantmen believed at the time to have been sunk actually were able to leave the field, the *Parche* and the *Steelhead* together accounted for five of the cargo ships sunk, totaling 39,000 tons. After a quiet day submerged, the two submarines began their journey back to Pearl Harbor. After studying Ramage's report, Admiral Lockwood's staff credited the *Parche* with seven sinkings, but in that dramatic, close-punching night surface action what held the most importance was not the numbers but the way the fight was waged. Ramage's Rampage became famous throughout the submarine force.

Questioned about the action, Ramage said to a reporter, "I got mad." But anger alone could not have created this one-of-a-kind performance; Ramage had also drawn on preparation, remarkable seamanship, and the always needed measure of luck. Lockwood, who termed Ramage's fight "one of the outstanding actions of submarine warfare to date," nominated Ramage for the Congressional Medal of Honor, and the idea won approval in Washington. The citation took note of the important part played by the two torpedo reloads, and it said of Ramage: "In the mounting fury of fire from the damaged and sinking tanker, he calmly ordered his men below, remaining on the bridge to fight it out with an enemy now disorganized and confused." After the forty-six minutes of violent action, the *Parche* and her "valiant fighting company" retired "victorious and unscathed."

Ramage received the medal in a ceremony in the president's office. Like many other persons seeing FDR for the first time during 1944 or 1945, Ramage felt shock at his appearance. In profile the president's face was gaunt, and he seemed "practically on his deathbed."

A British officer observing American submariners in action reported that "with their up-to-date radar and their short-range ship-to-ship telephony, they had brought the art of wolf-pack tactics to a pitch finer than anything achieved by the German U-boats in the Atlantic.

When the Americans invaded the Philippines and the Japs responded by sending large naval forces to the area, one of the U.S. submarine wolf-packs in one night sank a Kongo-class battleship and a heavy cruiser, hit another cruiser with four torpedoes, and made sighting reports of two other battleships and cruisers."

■ ■ ■

Like Mush Morton, Dick O'Kane received command of a submarine with a keen and memorable name. When the *Wahoo* departed on her final patrol in September 1943, her former executive officer had gone back to the United States, where, at Mare Island, he oversaw the final stages of the construction of the U.S.S. *Tang* (SS-306). On her trials, said the skipper, "she performed as if she'd been at sea a year," and on January 22, 1944, O'Kane took the boat out on her first patrol, with the waters off the Japanese island fortress of Truk, in the Caroline Islands, as her assigned area.

By the autumn of 1943 the Americans had created what could justly be considered a new and powerful navy—a new *kind* of navy—featuring carriers, assault vessels of various types, and other shipping that would ensure the success of major amphibious invasions. Along with the warships came a seemingly endless procession of merchant vessels to meet the unprecedented challenge of supplying these operations across the Pacific. Now the Americans could begin a great push toward positions in the western ocean from which to attack Japan directly, by air and if necessary by invasion. In January 1944, as a part of the campaign in the Central Pacific, navy flying boats would bomb Wake Island, which the Japanese had held since the early days of the Pacific war, to neutralize it as a factor in the forthcoming U.S. attack on the enemy strongpoint of Kwajalein, in the Marshall Islands.

Tang's rookie captain had received a two-phase assignment for this operation. First, the *Tang* would perform what the navy called lifeguarding service. This new idea involved just what the name said: Submarines took station to rescue aviators forced to make crash landings. In collaboration with Rear Admiral Charles Pownall, commander of carrier forces in the Central Pacific, Admiral Lockwood had informally set up lifeguarding for an island operation the previous August, by detailing the *Snook* to stand by, ready to pluck any downed fliers from the sea. "Just the knowledge it was there," said Pownall, "would boost the morale of the aviators."

Snook's lifeguarding efforts did not prove to be needed in the August air strike, but by the next winter the service had become well established with worked-out operating procedures. Later, the navy and the air force developed the organization further, to enable submarines to rescue B-29 crews coming from raids on Japan itself. Submarines on lifeguarding duty acquired their own designation, the Lifeguard League, which later split into the National and the Texas Leagues to reflect the fact that two tactical groups of submarines were now involved. Overall, lifeguards would rescue 504 members of air crews. (On September 2, 1944, off Chichi Jima in the Bonins group north of Iwo Jima, the submarine *Finback,* responding to calls from fighter planes, picked up a pilot who had been in the water for two hours after parachuting from his burning Grumman Avenger torpedo bomber. The pilot, Ensign George H. W. Bush, noted that the submarine's crewmen "fixed [him] up in grand style." The highlight of the 30 days he spent on the *Finback* was the admirable food—"steaks, chicken, ice cream, etc." The captain, Lieutenant Commander Robert R. Williams, Jr. [Naval Academy '34], received high praise as well. In all her service, the *Finback* rescued five downed fliers.)

Tang's lifeguarding duty off Midway passed quietly, and, released from this assignment on February 6, she proceeded toward Truk to take up the second part of her assignment. A little after midnight on February 17 she made sound contact with Japanese surface ships, clearly a convoy fleeing the raid on Truk. The *Tang* and two other submarines had been informed by an Ultra message of this small convoy, which had a destroyer escort. To avoid the destroyer, O'Kane took the boat down to 500 feet, brought her up again in a favorable position to attack a large freighter, and fired three torpedoes from the stern tubes into the target. He had chosen to use the standard procedure whereby the skipper made the periscope observations and also conned the boat, rather than the method Morton had devised, and also he was now firing the torpedoes with no supervisor. All of them hit (torpedoes truly were different now) and the fat *maru* seemed to disintegrate as he

416 · THE SUBMARINE

watched through the periscope. O'Kane then dived away from the depth charging that followed, and later tried for another kill but could not overtake the convoy to get into firing position. He had, however, racked up his and the *Tang's* first sinking, giving the submarine her baptism of fire as a commerce raider, and he had also given more than a suggestion that he could carry on the aggressive tradition established by his captain and partner, Mush Morton.

On February 22 O'Kane found himself in a similar situation off Saipan, the object of a heavy attack by carrier-borne aircraft. This time it was a three-freighter convoy that turned up, and, attacking on the surface, the *Tang* loosed a salvo of four torpedoes that, again, seemed to pulverize the target, which sank in just moments. Fleeing the escort, the relentless *Tang* then came back to the convoy, dodging the destroyer, and fired four torpedoes into another freighter; with the fish performing perfectly, the ship went to the bottom. The next day, after dogging another convoy in heavy weather, O'Kane added two more cargo ships to his bag. He crowned his first patrol with another sinking early on February 26.

O'Kane had shown himself a resolute skipper and a crack marksman; no doubt, he was maturing and changing from the somewhat mercurial officer George Grider had sailed with. On his first outing he had accounted for five merchant ships, amounting to more than 21,000 tons.

In April, the *Tang* not only carried out another lifeguarding assignment but, in the process, set a record not of destruction but of rescue. Off Truk, operating under enemy fire and moving around the area like a very large waterborne ambulance, taking full advantage of fighter air cover, the *Tang* pulled twenty-two downed fliers from the water, a record that would stand for more than a year. The *Honolulu Advertiser* called it "one of the lustiest, thrill-packed stories of the war, almost fantastic in its revelation of courage and skill."

On June 8, 1944, the *Tang* moved away from her pier at the submarine base, down the channel from Pearl Harbor, and into the open sea, headed out on her third patrol. This one would take her to the shallow waters of the East China Sea, off southern Kyushu. At about eleven o'clock at night, June 24, the radar operator reported a contact—"a mess of ships." Looking at the screen for himself, O'Kane saw "a jumble of blops." None stood out for size, as a battleship would, but "they were ships and we'd take them as they came." Continuing to practice his fondness for operating on the surface, O'Kane took the *Tang* into what seemed a cloud of escorts—twelve of them—screening six large ships. Having infiltrated the pack itself, the *Tang* fired salvos at two of the big freighters, and by some alchemy, as records would later show, emerged from the seven-minute engagement having sunk four ships. Then, seeing in the distance the glow of the lights of Nagasaki, O'Kane turned to head for deeper water.

Five days after this sweep, the *Tang* began a series of individual sinkings in the Yellow Sea that added six ships, all but one freighters, to her bag. Returning to Pearl Harbor with ten ships accounted for, the *Tang* had become the first and only submarine to sink that many vessels in one patrol; the tonnage total, 39,160, also ranked as the highest merchant tonnage total for a single patrol. This did real damage to the enemy: The figure, achieved by just one submarine, equaled between 35 and 40 percent of the monthly tonnage turned out by all Japanese shipyards.

Not only did O'Kane set the record with the ten ships sunk on his third patrol, but by sinking seven ships on the *Tang's* fifth patrol he claimed third place on the list. Between these two performances came Mush Morton's nine sinkings on the *Wahoo's* fourth patrol. Thus the old *Wahoo* team held combined honors with twenty-six enemy ships accounted for in three patrols, and right behind came George Grider, in the *Flasher,* with six, a total shared with four other skippers. The aggressive spirit of the *Wahoo* indeed lived on.

O'Kane ended the Pacific war as the overall champion in number of ships sunk, with twenty-four, and ranked second in tonnage with 93,824. But he did not end the war as skipper of the *Tang.* On September 24 the submarine departed Pearl Harbor on her fifth patrol; she would be operating in the Formosa Strait, between Taiwan and China, a congested area that offered obvious danger and obvious rich pickings. In his now established fashion, O'Kane began on the night of

October 10–11 with a pair of sinkings and then, on October 23, took on a convoy of merchantmen and escorts. Boring in on the surface, he stirred up a "ferocious free-for-all" as he torpedoed seven vessels, three of which sank; the others suffered serious damage. A day later the *Tang* went back on the attack, this time assaulting a military convoy carrying troops and aircraft to Leyte in the Philippines. Again, in a night action, the *Tang* operated on the surface, producing the usual results; at this point, still only a month out of Pearl Harbor, O'Kane and his men had racked up the seven sinkings that would give this patrol third place in the record.

So furious had been the *Tang*'s performance on this patrol that she had only two torpedoes left. Firing again at one of the damaged ships, a troop transport, O'Kane sent the final two on their way. One of them smashed into the limping troopship, but the other "broached in a phosphorescent froth only yards ahead of *Tang*'s bow, turned sharply left, and commenced porpoising in an arc" off the boat's port bow. Before the *Tang* could get out of the way of this sudden demon, the missile struck her in the stern in a violent explosion. The result-ing wave washed the skipper and everybody else on the bridge into the sea; the *Tang* sank immediately, coming to rest 180 feet down, with those of her crew in the shattered rear compartments struggling for-ward. Amid the pounding of depth charge attacks, thirteen members of the crew got out of the boat through the escape hatch, and eight of them reached the surface alive. Since the depth was far below the supposed limit of the Momsen lung, some of the others, it is thought, did not believe it possible to save themselves. Still others simply could not. Five of the eight who made it to the surface survived through the night, swimming until a Japanese vessel picked them up in the morning.

Of the nine members of the party on the bridge, O'Kane and two others were able to swim till morning; they had with them an officer who had been in the conning tower when the rogue torpedo hit and had managed to grope his way to the hatch and escape. O'Kane and his companions spent the rest of the war in a Japanese prison camp. After the war, on visiting the recuperating O'Kane in a U.S. hospital, Ned Beach, who turned up everywhere, expressed shock at the sight of his friend, wasted away to 85 pounds. If the war had lasted a few days longer, Beach thought, O'Kane would have died. Instead, he survived to receive the Congressional Medal of Honor, become a rear admiral, and tell his own story.

■ ■ ■

Besides Red Ramage and O'Kane, five other submarine officers received the Medal of Honor. The first to be honored was Commander Howard Gilmore, skipper of the *Growler* (SS-215), which suffered a severe collision with a Japanese ship on February 7, 1943. When the crew of the ship opened up on the *Growler's* bridge with a machine gun, severely wounding Gilmore, crew members tried to carry the skipper to safety, but, realizing that any delay might cost lives as well as the loss of the boat, Gilmore ordered the bridge cleared and then uttered the unforgettable cry: "Take her down!" Reluctantly, the executive officer complied.

Captain John Cromwell, a division commander and passenger on the *Sculpin* in November 1943 when she received fatal injuries from a Japanese destroyer, elected not to abandon ship but to go down with her, in order to avoid the possibility of capture and subsequent torture that might induce him to divulge high-level secrets, including Ultra codebreaking.

Sam Dealey, the "destroyer killer" and fifth-ranking skipper in number of ships sunk (sixteen), was lost with the *Harder* in action off Luzon in August 1944.

The other two Medal of Honor recipients, Commander Eugene Fluckey and Commander George Street III, survived the war. Fluckey (Naval Academy '35), who received credit for sinking 95,360 tons of Japanese shipping, enabling him to claim the top spot (outdoing O'Kane by about 500 tons), often acted in imaginative ways, such as turning up unpredictably to bombard shore installations; he won the Medal of Honor for actions in the eleventh war patrol of the *Barb* (SS-220), in the Formosa Strait and the East China Sea. On January 24, 1945, he took his boat up a narrow channel and into a harbor on the China coast, sinking one merchantman (according to postwar analysis) and apparently damaging various others. Though hard numbers

420 · THE SUBMARINE

counted, flair was important, too. "This patrol," wrote Admiral Lockwood, "should be studied in detail by submarine personnel."

On her first patrol, in April 1945, the *Tirante*, commanded by Lieutenant Commander George Street (Naval Academy '37), who was
making his own maiden patrol as a skipper, sank six enemy vessels
and damaged a number of others. After surviving a severe depth-
charging attack, the *Tirante* produced her most spectacular result in
her attack on a 10,000-ton tanker during a harbor invasion, when "a
great mushroom of white blinding flame shot 2,000 feet into the air
and a thunderous roar nearly flattened the crew of *Tirante*." Turning
to escape, the submarine fatally torpedoed two frigates as she fled the
harbor.

■ ■ ■

In spite of the tonnage triumphs scored by American submarines in
the role of commerce destroyers, fate reserved the most spectacular
victory of all for one boat pitted as a warship against another and vastly
greater warship. Though it came months before the end, this victory
represented a fitting capstone to the fighting in the Pacific. It also came
with more than the usual ironies.

In November 1943 a rookie skipper named Joe Enright had taken a
new boat on her first patrol but, in his own eyes, had failed to perform
properly, having allowed the 25,000-ton carrier *Shokaku* to escape unscathed from a promising encounter. On returning empty-handed
from Japanese waters, Enright had put forward a most unusual request:
He asked to be relieved by an officer who could do a better job. His
request granted, he served in relief crews and then went off to Midway
as executive officer of the base. But shore duty did not represent his
idea of fighting the Japanese, and he prayed to get back into action.
This time, he vowed, he would be more flexible, less guided by caution
and formal rules.

On November 29, 1943, the new *Balao*-class submarine *Archerfish*
(SS-311) arrived at Pearl Harbor, and within a month she had departed
on the first of four patrols she would have under two skippers. For her
fifth patrol she would have still another new captain, an officer whose
nerve and skill at the poker table had so impressed a submarine divi-

sion commander that he was deemed ready for action again. Commander Enright (Naval Academy '33) was getting back into the war.

Her crew regarded the submarine as such a special boat that they liked to give the name a distinctive spelling, *Archer-Fish,* which in consequence often appeared in official documents; yet after a year she had only one confirmed kill, a small coast defense vessel, to show for her efforts. On October 30, 1944, the *Archerfish* departed Pearl Harbor on her fifth patrol, the first under Joe Enright. She had a double mission, to render lifeguard service and to operate an offensive patrol, but the lifeguarding took on special importance because she and other submarines would be supporting the first American B-29 raids on the Japanese home islands.

After November 24 and 27 Superfortress attacks saw no fliers having to be hauled from the water, the *Archerfish* turned to regular patrol duty outside Tokyo Bay. At 2048 during the night of November 28–29, Enright's radar operator reported a blip at about fourteen miles, and the *Archerfish* started to approach on the surface on the starboard side, then backed off as an escort appeared. Less than an hour later the blip could be translated into nothing less than an aircraft carrier, though it was not one that could be identified. That anonymity came from the Japanese government's effective effort to keep the secret that, after Midway, it had decided to turn a giant battleship, the sister of the *Yamato* and the *Musashi,* into a carrier. Upset that the Americans were now able to bomb the homeland, the Japanese authorities had decided to move the great ship, named the *Shinano,* from the Yokosuka Naval Shipyard on Tokyo Bay to the quieter waters of the Inland Sea. She was finished and had been commissioned, but considerable fitting-out remained to be completed.

Four escorts, Enright now realized, shielded the carrier as she steered southeastward, and after some maneuvering, he reported, "from here on it was a mad race for a possible firing position. His speed was about one knot in excess of our best, but his zig plan allowed us to pull ahead very slowly." For six hours the *Archerfish* tracked the *Shinano,* until at 0316 came the crucial zig. With the giant ship now unwittingly headed straight for him, Enright began firing his bow tubes. The rest was, indeed, history. Just before eleven o'clock the next morning, having taken four hits, the *Shinano* slid beneath the shallow coastal waters; her entire active life had consisted of sailing across Tokyo Bay and just 65 miles out to sea.

When Enright returned to Pearl Harbor, he received warm praise for having conducted a "successful night attack on a large enemy carrier" (he was granted credit for 28,000 tons) and thus having conducted a "highly successful patrol." Poker may have been the game that had given Enright the chance to impress the division commander, but neither he nor Lockwood nor anybody else yet realized that the *Archerfish* had triumphed in an all-night chess match with the largest warship ever built by any country and the largest ship ever sunk by a submarine. This giant carrier had a steel flight deck 30 centimeters thick, placed over a layer of concrete; she could, the Japanese believed, simply shrug off any bombing attack. But she fell to a lone submarine. The *Archerfish* sent just one ship to the bottom on that patrol, but that extraordinary kill, 59,000 tons, gave her the top total for a single Pacific patrol.

■ ■ ■

Fighting right up till the end, which would come sooner than anyone could know, the Japanese launched a kind of minioffensive in the Southwest Pacific that gave them the last significant warship victory of the war. Since the Japanese surface force had ceased to be a factor in the fighting, this attack was brought by submarines (six I-class boats that carried *kaiten,* one-man midget submarines) on their decks. On July 24, 1945, one of these "human torpedoes," from the *I-53,* sank a U.S. destroyer escort guarding a convoy. The Japanese struck their heavy blow five days later, when the *I-58* encountered an American heavy cruiser in the Philippine Sea. This cruiser, the *Indianapolis,* had earlier served as Admiral Spruance's flagship, had suffered severe damage by kamikazes off Okinawa, and on July 16 had arrived back in the western Pacific after undergoing repairs in the United States. On this return voyage she had carried elements of the atomic bombs from San Francisco to the U.S. base on the island of Tinian.

Sailing without escort and not zigzagging, relying on her speed to protect her in these waters in which Japanese vessels no longer seemed to pose any serious threat, the *Indianapolis* was spotted, shortly before midnight on July 29, by the *I-58*. Two torpedoes crashed into the cruiser's hull, and twelve minutes later she rolled over and sank. There followed one of the bitterest tragedies of the Pacific war. Of the crew of 1,199 some 300 to 350 went down with the ship, but the others made it into the water, which was heavily infested with sharks. But no help was dispatched for almost four days, because, through a sad series of bungles, the navy lost track of the ship: Nobody missed it. Finally, by chance, a patrolling plane spotted life rafts, but by the time the rescue took place only 316 men had survived the gruesome ordeal.

The sinking of the *Indianapolis,* coming just a little more than a week before the top secret cargo she had brought to Tinian arrived over Hiroshima, represented a major if unavailing submarine victory for the beleaguered Japanese navy and the last major loss suffered by the Americans in World War II.

■ ■ ■

In his final report, Admiral Lockwood stated that U.S. submarines in the Pacific had sunk some 10 million tons of Japanese shipping (4,000 vessels). Though the list included a battleship, eight aircraft carriers, and twenty cruisers among the victims, almost all of the 4,000 ships sunk were merchantmen: The deadly commerce raiding submarines had destroyed three-fifths of the Japanese commercial fleet. On April 13, 1945 (a crewman remembered the date because on that side of the world it was the day FDR died), the submarine *Bashaw* surfaced in the South China Sea after a depth charging to see the Japanese destroyer that had pursued her riding some distance away, not making headway, unable to attack again. Clearly, she could go nowhere because she had run out of fuel, an eloquent testimonial to the commerce raiding achievements of the U.S. submarine force in the Pacific.

The submarine force lost fifty-two boats, on which 375 officers and 3,131 enlisted men had served. As with the submarine services in other countries, the U.S. casualty rate—about 22 percent—ranked as the highest for any branch of service, though far below the German figure of about 72 percent.

In talking about submarine skippers, veterans of Pacific action tended to mention a common theme. The captains they admired were aggressive, but ahead of such characteristics as personality, knowledge, and background, these submariners ranked focus on the job to be done: The successful skippers, they said, were all business. In Admiral Arleigh Burke's words, they were "neither timid nor reckless." They were efficient.

THE COLD WAR:
THE NUCLEAR GUARANTEE

The goal toward which all engineers are striving is the perfection of a submarine having a surface speed of 25 knots, an economical cruising radius of 10,000 miles, a submerged speed of 20 knots at least, and a far more formidable armament than that borne today. To ensure the fulfillment of these specifications within a reasonable space of time, some sensational discovery or startling new development is imperative.

—Frederick A. Talbot (1915)

PART VI

31

TOWARD THE TRUE SUBMARINE

"I declare this keel well and truly laid." Standing on a temporary platform in front of a construction cradle in the south yard of Electric Boat, President Harry S. Truman spoke these words to a crowd of some ten thousand dignitaries and interested citizens. Just before making his declaration, Truman had inscribed his initials on a curved steel shell, the keel plate of a new kind of submarine that, like others before it in fact and in fiction, would bear the name *Nautilus*. The foreman of the welders then took his torch and burned the president's initials into the steel. Truman next flashed a signal to crane operators who began lifting the shell into the cradle in which the *Nautilus* would be assembled. Behind the president on this sunny day, an array of diesel-powered fleet submarines dotted the gleaming Thames River.

This keel-laying ceremony took place on June 14, 1952, and Truman apologized to the residents of Groton for having previously told reporters that he was coming to the better-known town of New London to speak. "I know how you feel," Truman told his listeners. "I get tired of having Kansas City given credit for being Independence." More seriously, the president declared: "The day that the propellers of this new submarine first bite the water and drive her forward will be the most momentous day in the field of atomic science since the first test bomb was exploded in New Mexico seven years ago." The world could now move into a new age, said Truman, were it not for the failure of the Soviet Union to cooperate with other countries. "They have sought to sow disruption and distrust among free countries," the president declared. "They have used threats and riots, bloodshed, and outright aggression in their attempt to expand their empire. They have left us no choice except to look to our own defenses."

· · ·

The spectacular ending of World War II in the ashes of Hiroshima and Nagasaki, just seven years earlier, had left the victorious American and British leaders puzzled and uneasy. The victory over the Axis powers had been as complete as the Romans' final defeat of Carthage, but what would come next? What direction would the postwar world take, and how would the unleashed power of the atom shape it? Within just two years the international picture had taken on grim but clear outlines. On March 5, 1946, Winston Churchill had called the world's attention to the "iron curtain" across Eastern Europe, and in September 1947 the Communists announced the establishment of the Communist Information Bureau (the Cominform), an organization intended to impose a common political line on all the Communist parties of the Soviet sphere. At the initial meeting the keynote speaker, Andrei Zhdanov, Joseph Stalin's chief ideologue, declared that since 1945 the world had become irrevocably divided into an imperialist camp, led by the United States, and a progressive socialist camp, led by the Soviet Union.

Though people in the West would define these so-called camps quite differently, the fact of the division obviously had profound implications for Western ministries and departments of defense and their armies, navies, and air forces—most notably for the United States, as the largest and by far the wealthiest country. Legislation adopted in 1947 consolidated the War and Navy Departments into the Department of Defense and created a third branch of service, the air force. The great question would now become: In this new world of the Cold War, what could and should the new department seek to do? Well might the navy, in particular, ponder these questions. Through all the great changes in technology that characterized the twentieth century, high officials of the U.S. Navy lived in fear that outside interests— generally, the army and politicians allied with it—might seek to do away with their branch of service. The army itself enjoyed perfect security: It operated on land and was needed both to hold territory and to occupy conquered territory. No one proposed to abolish the soldiers; you could not have a war without them. And the air force had the glamour of novelty; it had not only made prominent and much publicized contributions to winning the war in Europe but had supplied the mighty Superfortresses that dropped the atomic bombs on Japan and thus introduced the world to the nuclear age; the fliers would unquestionably play a prominent role in any new defense profile that successive administrations and Congresses might decide to adopt.

To be sure, however, the navy could make strong claims of its own. Entering the war as the second largest in the world (after the Royal Navy, the instrument by which Britannia had long ruled the waves), the U.S. Navy emerged as incomparably the mightiest fleet in history, with an unparalleled record of victories and a variety of other accomplishments. Japan, the long-foreseen antagonist, had been faced and completely beaten—just as the gloomy but insightful Admiral Yamamoto had feared—and had disappeared as a power in the Pacific. Aircraft from the great array of American fast carriers had shielded amphibious landings and swept the seas clean of enemy war vessels, and the great fleet of commerce raiding submarines had literally put Japan out of business, dispatching three-fifths of the empire's merchant fleet to the bottom of the sea and thus becoming the single most important factor in Japan's surrender.

History had long made it plain, however, that moments of triumph tend to be highly perishable. Fleet submarines that had roamed the ocean soon found themselves going into scrap yards or, like the *Parche* and others, detailed to Bikini atoll, in the reaches of the Pacific, to serve as guinea pigs in tests of the effects of nuclear explosions. At Pearl Harbor on December 7, 1941, the battleships that reigned as kings of the sea had been blown out of action by the Japanese attack, but their loss did not mean defeat for the United States. The navy had quickly seen that these ships no longer could claim to be the heart of the fleet; that position now went to the aircraft carriers, as the Coral Sea and Midway soon demonstrated and, indeed, as had been indicated by the success of the Pearl Harbor strike itself, carried out by aircraft from carriers.

The existence of the navy depended on tangible and changeable objects—the ships themselves—and, as the fate of the battleship had shown, these objects could fade in importance, quickly become old-fashioned, and even disappear. Might not the navy, some of the admirals and their civilian supporters feared, disappear along with them? The question took on particular importance because, after the war, a wave of demobilizing and economizing swept over all the services, even while the new conflict with the Soviet Union was hardening. "The postwar Navy was in bad shape," noted James Earl Carter, Jr., then a young ensign. "It was a time of great discouragement because we were undermanned, the nation was relaxing after a long and difficult war, and funds allocated for naval operations were meager." At the same time, one great fact, the atomic bomb, dominated all discussions. Many air force advocates held that the bomb had rendered most past strategic thinking useless in the new age and that national defense could now depend on a strategic air arm carrying nuclear weapons; the navy might best serve as a seagoing transportation service. One point became painfully clear: Since the atomic bomb had become the great prize, both the navy and the air force wanted it and were determined to get it.

During the war the army and the navy had often seemed as hostile to each other as to the nation's official enemies. Seeking to counter this mentality, to increase the efficiency and effectiveness of both services, and to wring the most out of lean postwar military budgets, the Truman administration had proposed the unification of the armed forces. But, haunted by their sense of insecurity, which included the fear that the air force would always in any interservice debate join its vote to that of its parent, the army, the navy's admirals and the secretary, James Forrestal, opposed the creation of the single Department of Defense, and at most were agreeable only to a weak central organization; in September 1947, nevertheless, Forrestal, who had won some concessions from the apostles of unification, became the country's first secretary of defense.

Reacting to air force claims on the atomic bomb, the admirals declared that, if the Russians should assault Western Europe, only carrier-based aircraft could provide tactical support for operations against the invaders. More important, the navy began to take a hostile look at a new air force project, the B-36 strategic bomber being put forward as the country's primary nuclear weapons delivery arm. The largest warplane ever built, this aircraft represented a transitional design with its six pusher piston engines assisted by four small jets. It figured in controversy even inside the air force, since in most respects it appeared to be yesterday's airplane heralded as the weapon of the future: a propeller-powered giant for the jet age. The B-36 first flew in August 1946 and went into operational service in June 1948.

The admirals fought back with a colossus of their own, a supercarrier called the *United States,* which would be able to operate anywhere in the world to deliver nuclear attacks on an enemy. One air admiral suggested to his superiors that they "start an aggressive campaign aimed at proving the navy can deliver the atom bomb more effectively than the air force can." What followed could only be called an unseemly brawl, an epic turf war inside a Defense Department that had just been created partly to lift the services above such battles.

In March 1949 President Truman, now in office on his own after his win over Thomas E. Dewey the preceding November, chose a veteran party politician, Louis A. Johnson, to succeed the able but now mentally ill Forrestal as secretary of defense. With the army and the air force exchanging confusing claims about the merits of their approaches and making dubious statements about Soviet air strength and capabilities (much exaggerated by navy representatives), Johnson received instructions from Truman to cut defense spending. The secretary then decided to deal with more than one problem at one blow by scuttling the fledgling supercarrier. Outraged, the admirals now trained their big guns on the gigantic B-36, which, in delightful irony, the air force had christened the Peacemaker in honor of its deterrent role. The interservice war moved into the newspapers and congressional committee rooms; the navy brought in Admiral King and the stars of the great Pacific victory—Nimitz, Spruance, and Halsey—but Johnson's decision stood and the supercarrier disappeared from the navy estimates.

The admirals then turned on one of their own, the hapless chief of naval operations, Admiral Louis Denfeld, accusing him of having failed to wage the war with proper zeal and dedication; in fact, the navy's toughest advocate proved to be not the chief but the vice chief of naval operations, Admiral Arthur Radford, a flier and strong proponent of naval aviation. In a final congressional turn, however, Denfeld, a well-liked but not forceful officer, a compromiser expected by many to deliver a fangless statement, had surprised his audience by echoing Radford's attack on the B-36, though he knew that this defiance of the secretary would end his career. He held office not quite two weeks longer.

It was a dark hour for the navy, too, but unlike Admiral Denfeld, the service would have a new chance to prove its worth. Salvation, in two very different forms, lay immediately ahead. In the one case, events across the Pacific would suddenly give the navy a new lease on life, when the North Korean invasion of South Korea, beginning on June 25, 1950, inaugurated a large-scale war. Demonstrating the inevitability of the unexpected, the countries involved would fight the war on the model of World War II, employing conventional weapons and carefully and explicitly avoiding the use of nuclear forces. The effectiveness of the U.S. Navy's carrier-based air power and ability to bombard enemy positions with big guns, and its delivery of a successful amphibious invasion like those during the preceding war, ended attempts to turn the service into nothing more than a transportation agency. Many of the ships hurriedly brought out of mothballs for service in Korean waters owed their readiness for action to the thoroughness and persistence of the inspector general of the 19th (Mothball) Fleet, the pesky Engineering Duty Only officer named Rickover who some years earlier had kept a miserly watch over the spare parts at the Cavite navy yard.

The other kind of salvation for the navy involved forces much more fundamental, with implications that would radiate far into the future.

■ ■ ■

In 1946 Vice Admiral Edward L. Cochrane, head of the U.S. Navy's Bureau of Ships, began a push to find ways to increase the underwater speeds of submarines. On the surface, improved diesels would now drive fleet boats at more than 20 knots, but, submerged, the old limitations still held: The storage batteries could produce only about 8 knots, and that speed just for an hour, or if endurance was the prime consideration, 3 knots for 36 hours. In the latter part of the war, the Germans' development of the snorkel *(Schnorchel)* breathing tube had allowed the

use of the diesel engines underwater, but for Cochrane and the committee he put together (including Admiral Lockwood, who was now
serving unhappily as the navy's inspector general), this represented only
an improvement, not a fundamental advance. The tube sticking up out
of the water could readily be seen by crewmen on an opposing destroyer, it presented various technical problems, and the noise of the
diesel engines could be picked up by sonar at long ranges. As the Allies
discovered after the war, the Germans had also created, but had not had
time and resources to complete and put into service, a class of U-boats
that could be driven underwater by steam turbines powered by hydrogen peroxide (*Ingolin,* it was called). Such power plants could produce
unprecedented submerged speeds, up to 25 knots, but the Americans
found their endurance of just six hours too limiting, and the Ingolin itself too volatile; in some respects, employing it would have been like
going back forty years to the days of gasoline.

The Navy did, however, pay full tribute to the Germans' outstanding streamlined Type XXI boats in two ways: by using the design as a
model to improve existing fleet boats in what was called the Guppy
program (for Greater Underwater Propulsive Power) and by building
new boats on the same model (the *Tang* class, taking its name from
Dick O'Kane's lost boat and also honoring five others that had not returned from patrol in the Pacific: *Gudgeon, Harder, Trigger, Trout, Wahoo*).
The presumption that the Russians were making similar use of the
Type XXIs they had acquired in eastern Germany provided much of
the pressure for the navy program.

Because the emphasis on greatly increased submerged speeds
brought new hydrodynamic challenges, the navy constructed a research
submarine, the *Albacore,* whose teardrop shape seemed to turn the
clock back half a century to John Holland's porpoise profile. In his designs Holland had emphasized underwater performance, sometimes
not showing much concern about surfaced characteristics. Now, after
years of development in which the submarine with its superstructure
and decking had resembled an ordinary surface craft and most of the
time performed as one, Holland's original idea was coming to the fore
again.

But Admiral Cochrane and his successor, Rear Admiral Earle W.

Mills, had more fundamental scientific and technical possibilities in mind: a generational leap, the equivalent of developing a super-Ingolin. When consulted by the committee, Ross Gunn, superintendent of the Division of Mechanics and Electricity of the Naval Research Laboratory (NRL), which during the war had developed the hydrogen peroxide torpedo, confirmed the view that the volatility of peroxide indeed made it unsuitable for propelling a submarine. But Dr. Gunn made an interesting point: Since 1939, not long after he had learned of Otto Hahn's splitting of the atom in experiments at the University of Berlin, he had believed and said that harnessing the power of the atom would enormously increase the range, and hence the effectiveness, of a submarine. Gunn had also drawn inspiration from a meeting with Enrico Fermi, the brilliant Italian émigré physicist whose interest focused on creation of a controlled nuclear chain reaction; supported by a $1,500 grant from Admiral Harold Bowen, the head of the NRL, Gunn had put various researchers to work on methods of separating the fissionable uranium 235 from the basic U-238. A physicist at the Carnegie Institution in Washington, Philip Abelson, came to the NRL and, together with Gunn, developed what became known as the Abelson-Gunn process for producing uranium hexafluoride, which was used to extract the isotope U-235. This project, not the famous Manhattan Engineer District (the Manhattan Project, as it became commonly known), actually constituted the first federal effort in the nuclear realm, and by late 1942 it had created an isotope separation plant. By the summer of 1944 NRL had built a much larger plant at the Philadelphia Navy Yard, whose output Gunn hoped to use to construct the core of a submarine nuclear power plant.

But the Manhattan District and its work on the atomic bomb held such a dominant position in the field that the NRL, which only had second-class status, found itself forbidden to produce the isotopes, though the Abelson-Gunn process accounted for some of the fissionable material that went into the Hiroshima bomb. With the war over, Gunn pushed on with further investigation of nuclear power and its uses, though he found progress difficult because of the security blanket in which the navy swathed the whole subject. He received valuable assistance from a newcomer to the NRL, Commander Robert Olsen, assigned to the laboratory as submarine liaison officer. An experienced submarine skipper (*Angler*, SS-240), Olsen—known, inevitably, as "Swede"—took up the nuclear cause and developed a close relationship with Abelson, who returned to the NRL from Oak Ridge, where he had spent a few weeks. Resenting the second-class status in which NRL nuclear research seemed stuck, Abelson announced his intention of returning to the world of civilian science as soon as his contract with the navy expired. Realizing that the NRL could hardly afford such a loss, Olsen after considerable discussion persuaded the physicist, who had a strong interest in submarines, to hang on with the prospect of achieving a historic first. "He told me he'd do it for the boys in the Submarine Service," Olsen recalled for Lockwood some years later, "if I'd see to it that it got into submarines first and not aircraft carriers first."

Deciding that the time had come to counter the atomic secrecy inside the navy, with the war now over some three months, Gunn with the enthusiastic help of Olsen invited about thirty higher-ranking officers to attend a presentation in which they could learn about nuclear energy and the outlook for nuclear-powered submarines from the two men who had developed the eponymous Abelson-Gunn process. This pioneering meeting took place at the NRL on November 19, 1945, and a few months later, after Admiral Cochrane's Bureau of Ships committee had sought Gunn's advice on improved methods of propulsion, the various interests and forces in this area came together in a full-dress session, with a report produced by Abelson serving as the stimulus and centerpiece.

"If I live to be a hundred," Lockwood said, "I shall never forget that meeting on March 28, 1946, in a large Bureau of Ships conference room, its walls lined with blackboards which, in turn, were covered by diagrams, blueprints, figures, and equations which Phil used to illustrate various points as he read his document, the first ever submitted anywhere on nuclear-powered subs." To Lockwood it all sounded like pages from Jules Verne, and it was in fact a manifesto for the nuclear submarine. Abelson opened with a series of "showstoppers," as Lockwood justly called them. The "atomic-powered submarine," Abelson told his audience, most of whom were new to this subject, could operate at 26 knots submerged, an incredible speed and one that could be maintained not simply for several hours but indefinitely, because the power unit would require neither additional fuel nor oxygen. The atomic material would not work directly in a turbine, in some exotic new fashion, to produce propulsion; in essence, the nuclear reactions would produce heat (just as coal or oil had traditionally done) to turn water into steam, which, through a system of pipes, would power the engines of the submarine. Oxygen for breathing could be replenished by electrolysis or chemical methods. The vision that thus captivated nuclear enthusiasts was that of the world's first true submarine, a vessel that not only could remain submerged indefinitely but that would have its true home under the surface of the sea, that would have a single power plant for surface and subsurface operation, and that could perform at high speed in all operations.

The 26-knot speed, Abelson declared to his rapt audience, represented merely a beginning. "With better power conversion, machinery and hull design, there is no reason why the speed should not go up to approximately 40 knots using screw propellers"; Abelson even envisioned jet propulsion that might push the submarine over 60 knots. He also suggested a role and purpose for this marvelous new vessel: "To function offensively, this fast submarine will serve as an ideal carrier and launcher of rocketed atomic bombs." Atomic power appeared so promising, Abelson declared, that the navy should directly proceed to set up a research and development program. He recommended that the Navy Department place a special NRL task force in charge of carrying out the plan. He also, and pointedly, called for cooperation between Manhattan District nuclear scientists and the navy "under a presidential directive if need be" and, finally, for the building of a nuclear submarine by the navy according to the recommendations of the task force.

Lockwood and his fellow committee members gave Abelson's stunning report an emphatic endorsement and forwarded it to the Bureau of Ships, which naturally greeted it with the same enthusiastic approval and moved it on up to the chief of naval operations, now Admiral Nimitz. Though, according to Lockwood, Nimitz added his endorsement and passed the report to Forrestal, then secretary of the navy, this line of development and progress came to its end. In the confusing, transitional year of 1946, the services vied for power and weaponry, and the civilians were now asserting primacy with the creation of the Atomic Energy Commission (AEC), which received control of the production of nuclear materials, the manufacture of nuclear weapons, and the development of nuclear reactors. On its own, the NRL could not produce a nuclear ship, and the new commission, which took legal possession of the field on January 1, 1947, did not find itself in a position to approve the development of a reactor to power such a ship; the ideas and efforts of Gunn and Abelson thus seemed to swirl away in the shifting Washington scene of the day.

The navy did not surrender all hope, however, as two developments in June 1946 demonstrated. Not intending to allow the work of Gunn and Abelson to be wasted or forgotten, and definitely intending to secure for the navy a share in any nuclear future, Admiral Mills let two contracts for research into the metals most suitable for use in a power reactor. More striking was the arrangement reached between the navy (Admirals Mills and Bowen) and the Manhattan District (the AEC had not yet taken over the field) for five officers to take nuclear training at Oak Ridge, where the plan was to build an experimental reactor with the involvement of the armed services and private industry, thus making each group acquainted with nuclear technology; the navy representatives would become the potential leaders of any nuclear navy that might develop. From a list of nominees drawn up by Captain Albert Mumma of the Machinery and Design Division of the Bureau of Ships—a man of considerable scientific background and a stronger proponent of nuclear propulsion than Mills—the admiral selected Lieutenant Commanders Louis H. Roddis, Jr. (who at that moment was out at Bikini, assisting with the atomic bomb tests), Miles A. Libbey, and James M. Dunford, each of them a graduate of the Naval Academy with a further degree from MIT. A fourth officer, Lieutenant Raymond H. Dick, a top-of-his-class metallurgist, came from Ohio State. Mumma had also suggested that Mills choose Captain Harry Burris, a very able officer, as the senior officer of the group. Instead of Burris, however, Mills picked Captain Hyman Rickover.

"Captain Rickover did not particularly relish assignment to the nuclear energy project," as Mills recalled their conversation, though some persons thought otherwise. The captain, Mills said, "argued over the wisdom of his assignment to the project by me as such action might damage his future career." Certainly Rickover did not know, and did not profess to know, anything about nuclear physics or nuclear engineering. But, paying no attention to any carping, the admiral sent his reluctant warrior off to the atomic town in Tennessee.

■ ■ ■

In brusquely rejecting the overhaul requests of the *S-39*'s engineer officer at the Cavite navy yard in the Philippines, back before the war began, Lieutenant Commander Hyman Rickover had delivered a characteristic performance. In a similar fashion he told the skipper of the *S-41* that the navy had made a mistake in allotting as much as $7,000 for overhaul of that old boat and that he would see to it that cuts were made. In both cases Rickover displayed a miserly reverence for federal dollars and even pennies (the implication that the authorities had succumbed to the lure of extravagance in their allotment for the *S-41* lacked even the faintest plausibility), and he had done it in an abrasive way that, at least in one case, had brought the supplicant almost to tears of frustration.

Before Rickover drew the assignment to Cavite in 1937, he had spent a few months in exercising the only independent command he ever had, of a venerable minesweeper and tug, the *Finch,* attached to the Asiatic Fleet, about as obscure a rustbucket as the navy possessed. For an officer who had aspired to command a submarine, this post had a deadeningly terminal quality, but for a time Rickover put his crew to work "overhauling the machinery, cleaning bilges, removing rust, scraping old paint, and repainting," attempting to make the ship serviceable. But at the age of thirty-seven, Rickover realized that his destiny did not lie in the direction of command of his own ship, and he applied for and was granted Engineering Duty Only status; he immediately received orders for transfer to Cavite.

Rickover had reached this point after an unusual career in the navy. Born in Russian Poland and growing up in Chicago as the son of Jewish immigrants, he had an unusual enough background for an Annapolis midshipman in the second decade of the twentieth century. Roy Klinker of the *S-38,* who had contact with Rickover through the years, knew that his acquaintance's natural truculence, of which there seemed to be a goodly supply, had been rubbed raw by treatment he received from fellow midshipmen at the academy, where most so-called ethnic groups were scantily represented. Agreeing that some prejudice did indeed exist, Arleigh Burke, who was at the academy at the time, said that nevertheless Rickover "arrived looking for trouble."

Rickover did well but not remarkably in "four years of grind and little or no social life" at Annapolis, graduating in the top quarter of his class. It was not until 1930, eight years after leaving Annapolis, that he received the assignment he coveted to the submarine service; in the meantime he had earned a master's degree in electrical engineering from Columbia, thus acquiring the basis for his later move to E.D.O. status.

After service on the *S-9,* he went as executive officer to what some officers considered the worst boat in the navy, the *S-48,* the largest of all the S-boats and one that had never functioned well in any department. In sending Rickover to this submarine, those who handed out the assignments "may have hoped that a driving executive officer would help ferret out some of her problems and correct them." But that was not the way the experiment turned out. Rickover made great efforts to do the job, which called for him in effect to act as the personnel manager, but "in the process he established himself as a despot who could never be satisfied." He harassed his subordinates unmercifully, and unpleasant stories about him spread throughout the submarine force, a tight community of shared acquaintanceships like those in a small town.

The *S-48* experience proved transformative for Rickover's career and perhaps for himself, effectively ending his chances of receiving a submarine command of his own, and when returned to sea duty he found himself out of the submarine force and on the battleship *New Mexico* as assistant engineer officer. Devoting himself to what proved a successful effort to lash his men into a performance good enough to win the battleship engineering competition, he earned the esteem of the skipper and, to no one's surprise, the dislike of everybody else. So intently did he focus on efficiency and economy that, according to a widespread and credible legend, he once walked into the stateroom of a junior officer who sat reading a book, unscrewed the bulb from the lamp by the officer's chair, stuck it in his pocket, and walked away. Rickover's successor as assistant engineer officer, Lieutenant Commander F. A. Edwards, found it his first task to soothe the sailors whom Rickover had left with a "legacy of fear."

In June 1939, promoted to commander, Rickover returned to the United States to take up assignment as assistant head of the Electrical Section of the Bureau of Ships. The attack on Pearl Harbor gave him the opportunity to show what his highly individual combination of traits could accomplish. In supervising the remarkable repair of battleship electric motors containing miles of wiring encrusted with saltwater and oil residues, a task considered impossible by everybody else, Rickover drew on his driving power, his miserliness (why should the navy buy new motors when he could fix these?), and a third and developing element: a lust for perfection. "We were all aware," said Ned Beach, then a young submariner, "that in the *California* something very difficult had been accomplished."

Throughout the war Rickover served as head of the Electrical Section. One of his assistants later described him as "not the best technician" but "an excellent administrator," who had "the ability of getting himself surrounded with nothing but the finest of people," and as the result the section ran up an outstanding record in its production of power and lighting equipment for the fleet. This record rested in good part on the minute attention Rickover and his closely associated staff gave to each of the thousands of electrical devices and components that went into the ships, including redesigning them as the captain thought it necessary. Rickover's own inspections turned up such lemons as "circuit breakers that would pop open when the ship's guns were fired, cable that would leak and carry water through bulkheads to control switchboards, new electrical motors built according to specifications dating back to the 1920s, and junction boxes that would emit poisonous gases in submarines when fires occurred" (and noxious gases had indeed posed a problem for submarines ever since the installation of the first storage battery in an underwater craft half a century earlier).

Through his particular approach, Rickover created a unique relationship with private industry, which supplied all those parts he examined so closely. As the war developed, he insisted that contractors accept bureau staff members almost as partners in the design and production of components, with banishment from the table threatened for anybody who did not measure up. In thus creating something of a joint operation on a concrete level, Rickover extended his power from his own official naval realm into the civilian world. He sought control over every aspect of the operation, and gained a good measure of it. He also added another kind of personal touch: Since in his dealings with suppliers he invariably proved to be a man of his word, he became able to begin something of a custom of working with companies to get projects launched on his say-so, without the formality of a contract.

Although Rickover left the bureau in April 1945 for staff duty in the Pacific Fleet service force and then took command of the naval repair base on Okinawa, Admiral Mills remained impressed with the captain's way of reaching his goals, especially perhaps his obsession with detail, a central point in a completely new field like nuclear propulsion (so new that no one even knew whether the fuel on which the whole undertaking would depend would even become available). Also, appropriately, Rickover had a background in submarines, even if some of the experience had been unhappy. Mills, like Rickover, had an engineering degree from Columbia and thus had a shared perspective with the captain, whom he had now known for six years. The admiral either did not fully realize, or simply chose to disregard, Rickover's obvious compulsion to irritate everybody with whom he had any dealings, and in June 1946, just three months after Phil Abelson's delivery of his report with its detailed look into the possible nuclear future of the submarine, Mills made his fateful choice of Rickover to lead the small naval delegation to Oak Ridge. To cushion the impact of his selection of the unpopular Rickover, Mills did not give the captain any command authority over the others. Unfazed, Rickover would move to acquire the power in his own way, by angling for the responsibility of making out the fitness reports of the group. He would get it.

"THE PRICE THAT WOULD BE PAID"

The scene at Oak Ridge quickly took on a collegial aspect with its mixture of scientists and engineers from Westinghouse, General Electric, and other corporations, besides the army and navy representatives. Because his rank as a navy captain put him just behind the army colonel in command of operations for the Manhattan District, Rickover appeared on the organizational chart as deputy director of operations. But he spent his time reading and talking, cramming as if he were beginning all over again at the Naval Academy, and since the project lacked much direction, with various civilian and military participants having differing aims and interests, Rickover began to act as naval group leader and driver, even though he could be sure that his juniors had been warned about him and even though they had knowledge that he lacked in advanced mathematics and physics.

In any case, Rickover, no scientist, had no interest in research; he approached the situation as a pragmatic engineer, seeking to find out just what he and the other navy representatives needed to know in order to accomplish one specific purpose: the development of a nuclear power plant for a ship. During their stay at Oak Ridge, however, the navy team produced under Rickover's supervision a series of valuable reports on the status of nuclear power. The subjects "ranged from the metallurgical, chemical, and nuclear properties of beryllium to the problems associated with shielding personnel from radiation," and at Rickover's strident insistence the writers presented their ideas in clear and correct English. But the joint atomic pile project went nowhere.

During the summer of 1947 Rickover led his naval group on a tour of atomic installations across the country, so that they could see for themselves the actual state of knowledge about power reactors. "There's nobody in the navy who knows anything about this stuff except us," he declaimed. "And the goddamned AEC [Atomic Energy Commission] has just one guy with any experience with reactors. One! And he's not an engineer, he's just a physicist." The trip proved to be a huge success and brought many new acquaintances, like Walter H. Zinn, director of the Argonne National Laboratory; Ernest O. Lawrence, the Nobel Prize winner who had invented the cyclotron; and the physicist Edward Teller, then at Los Alamos. On the basis of their experiences, the members of the naval group prepared plans for the construction of a nuclear-powered submarine and submitted them to the authorities.

But then came bad news. The members of the group, which had evolved into a tight band with Rickover firmly at its head, received new and separate assignments. This change came as a result of Admiral Mills's effort to answer the overall question of nuclear power for the navy by setting up an orthodox staff system to deal with it in all its aspects. Nothing could have pleased Rickover less; he had hoped to create his own reactor group within the Bureau of Ships. Instead, he found himself, with his report filed away, assigned to Mills's staff as an assistant dealing with nuclear propulsion.

■ ■ ■

For some time during 1946, the continuing group of naval officers known as the Submarine Conference had devoted serious attention to the service's need for improved boats, which would possess greater submerged speed and range (i.e., endurance). The snorkel-equipped submarine they saw as only a transitional solution, good just until detection methods should improve, as they unquestionably would. Though they liked the German closed-cycle idea (like the hydrogen peroxide U-boat), they considered the nuclear power plant as the only true and lasting answer. The next day this program received the approval of Admiral Nimitz, and Admiral Mills integrated the responsibility for developing it into his new staff arrangement by assigning it to the coordinator and deputy coordinator for nuclear matters (which included work on explosives as well as power generation); the latter officer was Mills's longtime associate, the well-educated and knowledgeable

Captain Mumma. But what could happen until the Atomic Energy Commission, which held undisputed authority over all nuclear research and development, decided on its direction and picked its priorities? The Bureau of Ships could talk about a future but it could not design one.

Admiral Mills's arrangements ran counter to Rickover's desires and his developing view of the ways things ought to be done and of his own destiny. If the nuclear submarine became his cause, as it indisputably had done, then the navy must realize it and must give him the freedom to establish his own independent operation, responsible for this and for nothing else, and not hinder him in driving ahead with his mission. Mills's arrangement reflected a merely conventional approach, as Rickover saw it, but it perhaps also reflected the importance to the navy of the atomic bomb in its rivalry with the army. Propulsion for ships might well have to wait its turn until explosives had reached full development. Nobody opposed nuclear propulsion, but nobody seemed to realize that a nuclear power plant could well be a matter not of eight or ten years but of only three to five, and that if the navy needed salvation from peril at the hands of the other U.S. armed services, then nuclear propulsion could be the instrument to provide it.

Rickover spent the autumn of 1947 as a sort of atomic gadfly, attending conferences at Oak Ridge and the Argonne laboratory, following work at General Electric on a liquid metal (as against water) heat transfer system (literally getting the heat from the reactor to make the steam that would drive the turbines), and following developments at the all-powerful if still confused AEC. Making the best of his position on Mills's staff, Rickover began crafting a plan that would create a project closely involving the navy and the AEC. Over weeks and months of writing and rewriting letters and persistently conducting negotiations, he took full advantage of the navy's fear that the AEC would do nothing for it to stage what would amount to a coup: He won approval for the kind of organization he wanted.

His work began modestly, as the Bureau of Ships liaison officer with the AEC. Once again, it was Admiral Mills who waved the necessary wand, though he did not choose Rickover without hesitation. Once Mills gave Rickover a free hand, his zealous nominee "would out-work, out-maneuver, and out-fight the Commission, its laboratories, and the Navy. He would threaten, cajole, and even insult those who stood in his way." Mills recognized that Rickover would probably embarrass him many times, but he "was ready to do what the situation demanded." Mills did not need scientific contributions from Rickover; he needed his man's raw drive, his hectoring and harrying and obsessive concern with the tiniest details.

After making the appointment, Mills redid his organization of the bureau by creating the nuclear power branch, known as Code 390, with Captain Rickover as its head. Mills chose Rickover in July 1948 and as he expected, "Rickover seized the initiative from the day of his designation" as head of the branch. The new branch chief operated out of quarters in an old and grimy so-called temporary building like many others that blighted the Mall area at the time; his office itself had once been a ladies' room and took on added glamour from a plastered-over bullet hole in one wall (there before Rickover arrived).

Within six months Rickover's group had acquired its much desired second organizational lodging by becoming established in the Atomic Energy Commission division of reactor development. Just as he had planned it, the captain now found himself in the happy position of dealing with the navy on behalf of the commission and of dealing with the commission on behalf of the navy. "Yes, we'll write Navy letters," Rickover had earlier said to the exuberant Jim Dunford, who was delighted at the possibilities of the situation. "But we'll send them up through the chief of BuShips, through the chief of naval operations to the secretary of the Navy and the secretary of defense. Strictly kosher. And yes, we'll answer them from the AEC, but we'll get sign-offs from the director of reactor development and then the AEC commissioners. I'm dead serious about this, Dunford. If I catch any of you bastards trying to cut corners on this, I'll slaughter you."

Though the pathway to the first nuclear submarines would have its falls and rises, it now lay straight ahead, beginning with all the work involved in converting the research and development office into the core of a nuclear shipbuilding program. The rises would consist of Rickover's enlisting of Electric Boat and Westinghouse as the builders of the first ship and its propulsion plant, respectively, and in general of his characteristic steady extension of his sphere of power. Rickover had negotiated an arrangement with GE to develop a nuclear plant using liquid metals as the heat-transfer medium, but he also wished to push ahead with a propulsion plant that would use a water-cooled reactor and a high-pressure water heat exchanger to produce the steam that would actually drive the turbines.

Westinghouse had an energetic president who, having failed to acquire a large jet engine contract, was looking elsewhere for a way to build up the company's prestige in new realms of technology. Since Westinghouse scientists had attended the Oak Ridge sessions, the nuclear power plant seemed an ideal answer for the company's aspirations. After making the deal with Rickover, Westinghouse assigned a physicist named Charles Slack to the project as technical director. (Together with his brother, Francis, an early experimenter in atomic energy, Slack received an honorary doctorate from Marietta College in 1952, one reason being, according to Charles, that the presenter had the wonderful chance to comment that the college had given degrees to many stuffed shirts but never before to a pair of Slacks.)

At the outset of the project, Rickover summoned Slack to Washington to "learn how the Navy operates." But, said Slack, "I soon found out that his real purpose was to convince me of the necessity of taking all orders directly from him, bypassing my superiors at Westinghouse." To achieve complete domination over the personnel of the division, Rickover "had the habit of issuing arbitrary minor orders and then following them up relentlessly until eventually they were executed. By this means he let it be known that you might as well carry out his orders immediately, no matter how irrelevant or unethical they might be, since you would have to do it at some time in the future anyway." One of the Westinghouse engineers habitually wore a straw hat and a bow tie, leading Rickover to declare that "no one who dressed that way could be a good engineer"; eventually, the man was fired.

Most remarkably, as time went on Rickover maintained firm control over the selection not only of engineers and technicians but of those who would operate the boats, thus beginning to establish a generation of the navy's brightest young officers that would bear his stamp. If he objected to a navy proposal, it was said, wearing his other hat he could simply deny the reactor to the navy. Altogether, Rickover's operation, both extensive and intensive, controlling both hardware and personnel, had no parallel in navy annals and perhaps no parallel anywhere else. He even forced a reorganization of Electric Boat, and, as Slack remembered, he "surveyed the technical personnel from Westinghouse from every possible angle and then would order the company to transfer the best technical people to the Atomic Power Division"; Slack believed that this practice caused Westinghouse to lag behind other corporations for the next ten years.

Overall, Rickover was progressively performing a feat that could stand comparison with the achievements of the federal bureaucracy's greatest empire builder, J. Edgar Hoover, and perhaps in some respects he even exceeded the master. In taking over so promising a field as nuclear propulsion, Rickover had ingeniously circumvented the normal bureaucratic way by "carefully attending, from the very first, to acquiring autonomy before he acquired resources."

The most notable of all the slips on the pathway to nuclear success would come from Rickover's own problems with the navy. Though he obviously loved something about the service, he scorned its habits and protocols and would even argue that the Naval Academy should be shut down unless it could do a better job of teaching engineering. Like officers in all countries and services (for instance, the marine officers with their distaste for Colonel Evans Carlson's gung-ho raiders), most navy officers disapproved of separate, elite groups and operations, which was precisely the kind of instrument Rickover had created. Higher officers did not like juniors who told them they were wrong and then went out and proved themselves right. Rickover's operation also—and no doubt necessarily—ran counter to the navy's fundamental principle of rotation, with officers holding a wide variety of assignments and never taking root in one place; the officer, indeed, was expected to be capable of serving where and when needed. And nobody liked Rickover's personal style, though Admiral Mills patiently endured it for what he considered higher purposes. Rickover seemed to turn reporters into walking thesauruses, as they trotted out adjectives to describe him: "difficult" (by far the mildest), "dour," "irascible," "abrasive," "astringent." One officer fresh from a rough session offered a quasisurgical explanation of the problem he had encountered: "The only thing wrong with Rickover is that when they circumcised him they threw away the wrong end."

Slade Cutter, who ended the Pacific war tied with Mush Morton for second place in Japanese shipping tonnage sunk and held various posts in the postwar navy, believed that Rickover used obnoxious behavior as a tool to get the attention of listeners. (Though the choice of such a method of achieving this goal might raise a number of questions, no one could deny that it worked.)

One time, Charles Slack said, Rickover declared that "the height of his ambition was to be able to play two giant corporations against each other, and while he would have preferred General Motors and U.S. Steel, General Electric and Westinghouse would serve very well for his purpose." When Slack complained about Rickover's practice of sending strong, even slanderous, and completely contradictory criticisms of employees to the higher executives of the two companies, he received the reply: "My method of accomplishing things is to start out with a fact and then I use that fact in whatever way is necessary to accomplish the desired end." Did morals and ethics and impugning personnel not enter the picture? "Not if they interfered with getting the job done."

In 1952, weary of Rickover and his ways, the reigning admirals received their golden chance to rid themselves of him. Previously passed over for promotion from captain to rear admiral, Rickover would have his second and last chance in 1952: If not chosen by the selection board, the navy's mechanism for arranging promotions (adopted in 1916 as a great advance on simply proceeding on the basis of seniority), he would face retirement in 1953. One day during this time, Rickover, who had come to New London to speak to submarine officers about the nuclear program, asked Sunshine Murray why the board had not selected him. Murray, who commanded the Atlantic submarine force, had known Rickover since the 1920s, and he bluntly said that "flag officers are required to get along with people," something Rickover could not do. The lecture he had just delivered, Murray said, demonstrated the point. Although he had come to seek recruits for the nuclear program, he had angered his listeners by calling them "stupid and dumbbells," not bright enough to learn nuclear physics.

"To give Hyman credit," said Murray, "he sat there for about a minute without saying a word, and then he said, 'Thank you very much. I'm going back to Washington.'"

In the second go-round, Rickover seemed to be failing again, being presented as the engineering specialist who lacked the broad experience traditionally given high importance with respect to promotion (though engineering duty officers did not actually compete with line officers for promotion), until the center of the storm drew on a critical source of power in just the way J. Edgar Hoover had perfected: He brought in Congress, notably Senator Henry M. "Scoop" Jackson of Washington, a strong supporter. Rickover also had an effective admirer in the press, Clay Blair, Jr., a young reporter for *Time* magazine.

As the result, the navy found itself "blackjacked into keeping [Rickover] by congressional leaders who threatened to block the promotion of every admiral in the United States." (The officer deprived of his anticipated star by this legislative intervention was Captain F. A. Edwards, Rickover's long-ago successor on the *New Mexico*. Edwards, who had later dealt with Rickover at the Bureau of Ships and did not trouble to disguise his feelings, characterized Rickover as "the most disagreeable, noncooperative naval officer" he had ever known; indeed, "he was a bastard of the lowest order.") With his promotion in hand, together with the success his operation had achieved in producing a nuclear reactor, Rickover "could now move with a new confidence and a new sense of independence toward building a nuclear Navy."

"If the government had a project which was all-important," said Slack, "they could pick no better man than Rickover to undertake the setting up and starting of such a project. It must be so vital to the welfare of the country, however, that the many careers that would be ruined, other projects sabotaged, the general lowering of morale in many areas and the frustration of Navy personnel must be recognized as part of the price that would be paid. It must also be recognized that no branch of the government could have more than one such person working at any one time."

■ ■ ■

Sailors have their superstitions, and on the morning of January 21, 1954, the fog began lifting, the clouds parted, and the winter sun suddenly appeared just before the wife of the president of the United States swung a bottle of champagne at the bow of the great new *Nautilus*. The omens for this pioneer nuclear submarine seemed bright and auspicious enough to satisfy any seaman.

When the nine-car special train from Washington had pulled into Electric Boat's shipyard at Groton, the raw fog hung thick enough to obscure the 340-foot profile of the *Nautilus* as she sat on the ways. Some 12,000 people—Electric Boat employees and their families—had gathered in the bleachers set up alongside, to be joined by the party from Washington, led by Mamie Eisenhower, together with representatives of various companies involved in the project and a huge array of print and broadcast reporters. Heading up to the launch itself was a series of speeches from dignitaries: John Jay Hopkins, president and chairman of the board of General Dynamics (the new umbrella company of which Electric Boat formed a division) as the builder; Gwilym A. Price, president of Westinghouse, as the maker of the reactor; Admiral Robert B. Carney, chief of naval operations; Admiral Lewis L. Strauss, chairman of the Atomic Energy Commission. Beyond the *Nautilus*, "as marvelous a product as she is," said Admiral Carney, he looked to succeeding generations of atomic-powered submarines and surface ships. "Nautilus will probably appear to our sons and grandsons as a quaint old piece of machinery which introduced the transition to a new age of power," but now, the admiral said, the fleet was "hungry to put her to work."

Giving general praise to those in science, industry, labor, and government whose teamwork had created the new vessel, Carney mentioned by name only one person, Admiral Rickover. During the proceedings, in which he took no part, Rickover sat stiffly in the front row on the launching platform, looking uncomfortable in the characteristic way of persons who are preoccupied with themselves. Since he never appeared at his office in anything but civilian clothes, friends expressed surprise at seeing him at a public function in his uniform.

Splendidly appareled in a black jersey dress with surplice bodice, mink coat, pink gloves, and flowered pinwheel bonnet of pink straw, Mamie Eisenhower, who had spent some time in the private quarters of the White House practicing for her task by smashing water-filled wine bottles, awaited the arrival of the appointed hour. From a cat-walk high above the launching cradle, a voice shouted: "Hit it good and hard, Mrs. Eisenhower." Smiling, Mamie hefted the bottle and made a slight adjustment in her grip. Her escort, Ned Beach, now serv-ing as the president's naval aide, had carefully choreographed the cere-mony, allowing intervals for greetings and photo opportunities, in order to time the climax with high water in the Thames River. But a few minutes early, to Beach's dismay, the ebullient and excited Hop-kins pulled Mrs. Eisenhower to her feet and crying "Let's go and do it, Mamie!" led her to the designated spot. After some confusion, the ship suddenly began to move rapidly down the ways, and with a champi-onship swing on the striking plate Mrs. Eisenhower declared: "I chris-ten thee *Nautilus.*"

"As the champagne frothed about the ship's bow," wrote a reporter, the "little gray man in the front row of dignitaries breathed a long, easy sigh of relief when the *Nautilus* began to move." It represented, the re-porter believed, Admiral Rickover's "greatest hour."

■ ■ ■

On September 30, 1954, during her long series of builder's trials, the *Nautilus* joined the U.S. Navy, becoming the first commissioned nu-clear ship in any navy (SSN-571). She began her first sea trial, on Jan-uary 17, 1955, with a simple and memorable message from the skipper, Commander Eugene "Dennis" Wilkinson, a reserve officer who had played a part in the sinking of the Japanese admiral Kurita's flagship at Leyte Gulf in October 1944: UNDER WAY ON NUCLEAR POWER. Car-ried out under the keen eyes of Rickover and a corps of navy experts and representatives of the companies that had built the boat and the re-actor, the test proved completely successful. Three days later the *Nau-tilus* made her first dive and on February 28, after a long series of shallow dives, Wilkinson took her into her first deep-sea dive off the coast of Maine. In his reflections on the submarine written forty years earlier, Franklin Roosevelt had likened the undersea craft to the whale, each of which suffered from the fatal flaw of having to come to the surface to breathe and thus subjecting itself to danger at the hands of its enemies. But the *Nautilus* had overcome this original weakness of the submarine; the nuclear engine had made her a permanent fish, needing no surface exposure, no free air.

One advantage the *Nautilus* gained from her nuclear power plant was space. In a World War II fleet submarine, the batteries and the fuel tanks took up almost half of the room inside the hull, but having to carry no supply of fuel, the *Nautilus* had relatively spacious accommodations for her personnel. In particular, each sailor had an individual bunk, instead of having to double up ("hot-bunk"), and the wardroom and the crew's mess were much larger than on a standard submarine. Still, to anyone not a submariner, the stack of bunks looked tight, and obviously an occupant had to decide, before sliding into his 20.5-inch space, whether to sleep on his back or his stomach.

The prophecy that nuclear vessels would be able to sail literally for years without needing refueling came gratifyingly true with the *Nautilus,* which recorded more than 62,000 miles before her nuclear core was replaced in February 1957. Five months later Commander William R. Anderson, a Pacific veteran of patrols in the *Tarpon, Narwhal,* and *Trutta* and later skipper of the postwar *Wahoo,* succeeded Wilkinson as commander of what Rickover insisted was too big and important to be called a boat, in the traditional fashion for submarines. The *Nautilus* and vessels like her were *ships.*

In early 1956 Anderson had been serving as an instructor at the Submarine School in New London when he received a summons from Rickover's office. Like most other naval officers, Anderson had been fascinated by the creation and early success of the *Nautilus,* and he eagerly went down to Washington, though having no idea what the admiral might want with him. "I didn't know," he said, "but I could think of no place on earth where I would rather work." Working in the nuclear program involved surviving one of the admiral's notorious grillings misleadingly described by the mild term "interviews," in which he often shouted at candidates and threw them out of his office.

("He took great pride in being able to evaluate people," said Charles Slack, "but his methods were extremely unorthodox and many times he was far off the beam.")

Commander Anderson's session occurred on a Saturday afternoon, Rickover's favorite time for staging these ordeals, and, though Anderson encountered problems during the interview, he was spared one notably unorthodox feature Rickover, as a self-taught psychologist testing the mettle of interviewees, had frequently used: a chair with the front legs cut down so that the candidate would be tipped forward. To this feature the admiral added his habit of flicking the venetian blinds open, forcing the candidate to stare into the glare as he tried to stay sitting upright. During these goings-on, Rickover would fire unpredictable kinds of questions at the sensorily bombarded candidate. "You can't concentrate or think straight," said Jim Dunford, "and you end up making a complete ass of yourself."

One story Anderson had heard involved Rickover's asking a candidate a curious hypothetical question: If the citizens of Washington had to liquidate either the young officer or the city's lone street cleaner, which one would he choose?

"Myself, of course," the candidate replied with admirable modesty.

Banging his fist on the desk, Rickover exclaimed, "That's the wrong answer!" The naval officer could serve as a street cleaner, he explained, but the street cleaner could not be a naval officer without being trained.

After another officer had told Rickover about some of his mountain-climbing adventures, the admiral asked the young man whether he could climb Goat Mountain. Wherever that mountain might be, the officer gave his assurance that he could do it. If he could return the next morning with proof of having climbed Goat Mountain, Rickover said, he would be hired. Goat Mountain turned out to be a hump of landscaping concrete in the mountain goat cage at the National Zoo, and the next morning the officer arrived with a Polaroid photograph of himself on the "mountain," the feat having been recorded by a Japanese tourist who had waited to snap the picture while the officer scurried over the fence and up the promontory. Rickover made good on his promise.

454 · THE SUBMARINE

One candidate recalled what happened after he made a guess at the population of his home town, Vallejo, California. Rickover's secretary consulted an atlas and then quickly gave the figure to the admiral. "Rickover looked across the desk and shouted in his reedy voice: 'Goddamn, I told you I just wanted the truth. Don't answer me unless you know what you're talking about.' "

Once, however, a young man fresh from the Naval Academy put on a dazzling performance of his own. Asked whether he could think of an act that would make the admiral angry, the candidate said that he could. Rickover told him to go ahead and do it. The young man extended his arm and swept papers and everything else off the admiral's desk onto the floor. Rickover could not afford to react with anger—at least, visible anger. He accepted the candidate.

Despite this lone setback, Rickover had managed to carpenter one of the best of worlds for himself, one in which he often acted like a kind of Iago, engaging in the "motive-hunting of a motiveless malignity," but could indulge this irascibility by clothing it in the guise of socially useful psychologizing.

The officers undergoing interviews by no means were the only sufferers. "He is unusually hard on his technical people," said an official who dealt with the Rickover organization at close range. "He treats them all as if they are all covering up. All of them feel the pressure, and the more responsibility they have, the more pressure they get. He expects them to work twenty-four hours a day and to have no other interest in life, not even their family."

If you were involved in the naval nuclear project, regardless of whether you worked for the navy or for a private contractor like GE or Westinghouse, you were de facto Rickover's employee. Henry Stone, the general manager of GE's Knolls Atomic Power Laboratory, recalled a summer evening when he and his children were fishing in the middle of a lake and he suddenly saw "what appeared to be a commotion on shore, with lights waving." Bringing the boat in, he was informed that he had a telephone call at the owner's house. "It was Admiral Rickover," Stone said, "complaining that I was out fishing while he was still working hard. I do not know how he found that number; it wasn't even known to me."

Telephoning indeed amounted to a way of life for the admiral. He told Stone that he expected to be called every Monday, Wednesday, and Friday. "This was a no-win request," Stone said, "because if you had nothing to report you were accused of not knowing what was going on, and if you reported a problem chances were you were getting hell for that."

When he accompanied Rickover on checkup visits to the Idaho Reactor Test Facility, located out in the desert 60 miles from Idaho Falls, Stone and any colleagues from the Knolls laboratory would drive separately, following the admiral's car so that if, as often happened, Rickover became angry at something that was said and had one of his own party thrown out of the car, the Knolls group could pluck the victim from the desert.

"Sure he has driven good people away," one engineer said. "He handed out crap that a lot of good people didn't want to take, but then there is a liability to excellence. That's the thing that Rick has done that's more important than anything else—he has conveyed a commitment to excellence." Just as important, thought Ted Rockwell, an associate from the Oak Ridge days, Rickover's driving power drew and held engineers because it gave them the opportunity to achieve tangible results from their dreams. And they were, of course, engaged in work of great importance.

Even after admitting all the stresses and problems involved in dealing with Rickover, Stone described himself as still a supporter. "When a difficult design or test is completed successfully the first time," Stone said, "that provides great job satisfaction. To be a member of a team that is successful and respected also provides a lot of job satisfaction." Especially, "when a ship finally goes to sea (and you may even be on sea trials witnessing it) and it meets all its specifications the first time, that provides immense satisfaction."

"I was saturated with cold sweat," said a former submariner, Jimmy Carter, recalling his interview. When Rickover asked how he had stood in his class at the Naval Academy, Carter proudly replied that he had been fifty-ninth in a class of 820. "I sat back to wait for the congratulations—which never came. Instead, the question: 'Did you do your best?'" Carter started to say yes but then realized that, like anybody else, of course he had not done his best. He "finally gulped and said, 'No, sir, I didn't always do my best.'"

Turning his chair around to end the interview, Rickover put one final question that left Carter "shaken": "Why not?"

■ ■ ■

Commander Anderson had been ordered to report to Rickover's office at eight o'clock in the morning, but during the preceding evening he received a telephone call from a member of Rickover's staff who told him the interview had been postponed until late afternoon. So devious was Rickover considered to be that Anderson began wondering whether the change in arrangements simply represented a trick to see whether he could be persuaded to disregard orders by a call from somebody he did not know. He resolved to report as ordered at eight.

As it happened, the call had been genuine, and Anderson spent most of the day sitting and observing the tone and pace of the operation, which was characterized by the kind of frenzy that suggested to him people thoroughly involved in what they were doing. After he had entered the admiral's famously austere office and begun talking, giving Rickover the details of his Tennessee boyhood and his education, Anderson ran into what seemed to be a fatal stone wall. Asked to list the books he had read in the past two years, he froze, unable to think of even one. Later, back home after a dismal trip up from Washington, he took his wife's suggestion that he compile a reading list and send it to the admiral. Although convinced that by his silence he had completely ruined any chance he had to join Rickover's operation, he felt the list would at least show that he was not "completely ignorant." Rickover never told him that the letter had saved him, but there seemed little doubt about it. It was also true, however, that the interviews represented only the last step in a process of digging that gave the admiral thorough knowledge of the candidates before he met them.

Anderson took up his appointment in the admiral's shop, entering on a self-designed course of study and also helping to manage the interviews, which continued on their unorthodox course. One afternoon a young man burst out of Rickover's office, came running down the hall, and, stopping at Anderson's desk, asked to use the telephone.

Then he wanted the Yellow Pages, saying that he needed to find a pet shop. Used to anything, Anderson sat quietly as the candidate made arrangements to buy a cat and then directed the young fellow to a likely spot on Constitution Avenue to pick up a taxi. But at this point Rickover's secretary rushed up to the desk, collared the candidate, and took him back to the admiral's office. As Anderson later learned, Rickover had upbraided him for saying, in answer to a direct question, that he did not like cat meat even though he had never eaten any of it. He had therefore decided to find out whether he did or not and report. Although this display of initiative earned him another bawling out— what the hell was he planning to do to a helpless little cat?—it apparently helped him get into the program.

After he "learned to talk back" to Rickover, Anderson said, the two "got along quite well," and he received the appointment as captain of the world's first nuclear submarine when Dennis Wilkinson completed his tour. Later in the summer of 1957 the new skipper took the *Nautilus* on a voyage along the north polar ice cap and under it to a latitude only 180 miles from the North Pole. In the fall of that year came an event that amazed the world, upset American politicians, and impressed scientists: the Russians' putting into orbit of Sputnik I, the first artificial earth satellite. Although the secretary of defense, Charles E. Wilson, downplayed the feat by terming it nothing more than "a neat technical trick," everybody else saw it as more than that—for one thing, it presented convincing evidence of the power of Russian rockets—and the United States entered on a concentrated effort to catch up.

In the summer of 1958, Anderson and the crew of the *Nautilus* did their part to help rebuild damaged American prestige. On August 1, back in the polar region, Anderson found the Barrow Sea valley, a deep trench off Point Barrow, Alaska, and only sixty-two hours later the ship had reached the North Pole. Like Wilkinson, a believer in simple messages, Anderson took note of the historic moment by signaling the chief of naval operations: NAUTILUS 90 DEGREES N.

President Eisenhower expressed his pleasure and satisfaction at the feat by having Anderson flown to Washington for a reception and the presentation of a Presidential Unit Citation (never before awarded in peacetime). But the event produced an odd footnote. When Anderson asked who would be present, he was told that "just four or five senior people, civilian and navy, from the Pentagon" had been invited, and Rickover was not one of them. "It was too late to do anything about it," Anderson said, but immediately after the ceremony and press conference ended, he had himself driven to Rickover's building, where he went inside to pay his respects to the admiral. "I didn't want to come to Washington and not stop to see you," he said.

"I'm really quite moved, Anderson," Rickover replied. "That was awfully nice of you."

Anderson was "really sweet the way he came to see Rickover after the thing at the White House," said Rockwell, who had been listening, along with Rickover, to the radio coverage of the event. "It was a little gutsy and a very nice thing to do. It made a real impression on Rickover."

■ ■ ■

Coming along behind the *Nautilus* at Electric Boat was her sister, the *Seawolf* (SSN-575), launched in July 1955. This vessel had the sodium-cooled reactor built by General Electric, which offered theoretical advantages over the less glamorous pressurized-water plant installed in the *Nautilus,* but for a variety of reasons it proved unsatisfactory and after two years it was replaced by a plant like that in the *Nautilus.* Then came the *Skipjack* (SSN-585), which represented an achievement that would have thrilled John Holland could he have dreamed of it. The *Nautilus* and the *Seawolf,* prototypes revolutionary in their power source, featured hulls conventional in design and would produce no magical speeds. But the *Skipjack,* the first production nuclear submarine, wrapped its power plant in an *Albacore*-style porpoise hull that made it, at least for its time, the ultimate underwater creature, with a submerged speed of 30 knots; this class of attack submarines included five other ships.

There was also the giant *Triton,* as big as a light cruiser, with two reactors, each driving one propeller. The largest submarine that had ever been built (447 feet in length), the *Triton,* commanded by Ned Beach, would make a spectacular shakedown cruise, a voyage around the world completely submerged. Asked later whether he would have stopped the cruise if he had been forced to shut down one of the reactors, Beach declared: "No, indeed! we were going to finish that trip if we had to do it rowing the ship with oars."

President Eisenhower wanted to have this globe-circling achievement in his bag when he attended a summit conference with Soviet Premier Khrushchev in Paris in May 1960, and the *Triton* made her desired contribution, returning on schedule from her 83-day, 36,014-mile voyage. The summit conference adjourned as soon as it opened, however, broken up by Khrushchev after Eisenhower admitted he had known about the flight of a U-2 surveillance plane that a Soviet rocket had shot down over Sverdlovsk; the Soviet premier had put the aircraft on show in Moscow as an example of American iniquity. Ike's press secretary, the able and effective Jim Hagerty, ruefully told Beach: "Of all the things we'd planned for the summit meeting with Khrushchev, you're the only one to come through." Beach wondered what the other items might have been.

During this period, as it happened, the Soviet premier was devoting considerable attention to his own submarines. In a speech delivered just a few months earlier, on January 14, in which he announced the formulation of a new military doctrine, Khrushchev had declared that the traditional navy had lost its significance but that "the submarine fleet is acquiring great importance." No admirer of "coffins," as he called large surface ships, the Soviet premier together with his planners had a dual mission in mind for the new underwater fleet: to attack NATO carrier strike forces, in the event of war, and to disrupt western sea communications. The logic of this strategy acknowledged the West's great dependence on ocean transport, in contrast to the geopolitical situation of the Soviet bloc, tied together by land traffic. In some ways, the Russians in operating under this doctrine would be following the German example of the two world wars.

As a great land power, the USSR had previously produced quantities of submarines but had put little emphasis on submarine strategy, and these craft had not played important roles during the war. But on January 30, 1945, Lieutenant Commander Alexander Marinesko, in the *S-13*, earned a grim and spectacular distinction for himself and his boat. At the beginning of the year, as the Red Army advanced toward

East Prussia, the Germans had mounted the greatest evacuation of a population ever seen, employing large passenger liners to move troops and civilian refugees out of the immediate grasp of the Russians. Into Marinesko's sights on the thirtieth came the liner *Wilhelm Gustloff,* loaded to utter capacity with between six and eight thousand people. The *S-13* fired a salvo of four torpedoes, three of which hit their target, and the *Gustloff* went to the bottom of the Baltic Sea; German ships in the area picked up possibly a thousand survivors. The death toll in this sinking made it the greatest maritime disaster of all time. Less than two weeks later, for good measure, Marinesko torpedoed and sank the *General Steuben,* with 2,700 more people dying in the freezing sea. In this brief but remarkable span the Soviet skipper had thus accounted for about ten thousand lives.

This awesome demonstration of the power of the submarine had few consequences in Soviet thinking until the advent of Khrushchev, in the mid-1950s, which occurred in parallel to the American development of nuclear-powered vessels. Khruschchev's first important decision, made necessary by the Americans' success with nuclear propulsion, called for canceling a diesel building program inherited from Joseph Stalin, who had died in 1953. With the emphasis on nuclear power, however, came the beginning of a series of troubles. In 1957 an experimental Soviet submarine, the *M-256,* conducting tests in the Gulf of Finland, experienced some undefined problem that led its captain to make a strange decision. The boat was close enough to land so that she could have been beached, but the skipper, apparently believing that making such a defeatist move would have landed him in serious trouble, chose instead to let the submarine sink, and all aboard died. (This incident, as was generally the case, was not reported during the Cold War, but in 1997 survivors of crew members commemorated the fortieth anniversary of the disaster with public funeral ceremonies.)

In attempting to create a nuclear navy to match the developing American fleet, the Soviets encountered endless difficulties. Whereas the Americans had quickly decided to stick to pressurized water around the nuclear core, the Soviets stayed with liquid metals, despite their volatility and their capacity to become radioactive. Many of the Soviet ships also were perhaps not built to demanding tolerances; in

1959 a skipper refused to take one of the early nuclear vessels out to sea because he considered it unsafe.

In the United States, however, the era of the nuclear submarine had begun auspiciously. Thanks to Rickover, said Bill Anderson, this development had come perhaps five years earlier than would otherwise have been the case. That judgment represented a common opinion, but one officer expressed strong disagreement with it. Admiral Mumma believed that Admiral Mills had erred greatly in 1946 by choosing Rickover rather than Harry Burris to lead the navy group at Oak Ridge. "My personal opinion," said Mumma, "is that the nuclear program could have been done twice as fast with Harry Burris" and "with everyone on a happy, constructive team." In addition, Mumma claimed, Rickover hampered the program by refusing to train successors; instead, he did the opposite, "killed them all off, chopped their heads off one after another." This kind of feud seemed beyond resolution, though Mills himself subsequently expressed regret at his choice, but in any case, with the nuclear submarine now a reality, another great challenge awaited the Americans and the U.S. Navy—a challenge whose answer, combined with the nuclear submarine, could shape the strategic picture in the world long past the foreseeable future.

33

ADMIRAL BURKE MAKES A CHOICE

s the commander of a destroyer squadron in the Pacific in 1943, Captain Arleigh Burke carried out his missions with notable speed and flair. Called on to help in the invasion of Bougainville, in the Solomons group, he led his force in a sweep around the island, shooting up enemy airfields while the marines stormed ashore. Burke's destroyers likewise played an aggressive part in follow-up operations, and in the course of these activities the commodore acquired a lasting legend. Ordered to stop the Japanese in their evacuation of another island, so the story went, he headed his ships toward the objective while warning American transports in his path: "Stand aside. I'm coming through at 31 knots." His destroyers reached the island in time to sink three enemy transports, and when Admiral Halsey heard the story, Captain Burke had acquired his lasting nickname: "31-Knot Burke."

Thus the legend, which perfectly fit Burke's style. But in fact 31 knots represented no fast-stepping for a destroyer; in reporting his speed to headquarters, Burke had simply let it be known that he was squeezing 1 more knot than he had previously achieved out of weary ships much in need of maintenance. The message went to Captain Ray Thurber, Halsey's operations director, whose reply opened with the jocular salutation: "31-Knot Burke." Reporters seized on the nickname without knowing the story behind it, and hearing it at home, the public, thinking that 31 knots must be fast indeed, "pictured Burke as a hotshot, hell-for-leather destroyerman, which of course he was."

Stationed in Washington after the war, this dashing officer had to temper the flamboyance he had shown at sea as he served in the office of the chief of naval operations, which he found stolidly unreceptive to new ideas. Not only a fighting sailor but also something of a specialist in ordnance and explosives (and, like many of his peers, holder of a master's degree in engineering), Burke directed a study that tried to discern the nature of future warfare and to fit the navy into the picture the group produced. During the late 1940s and early 1950s, the navy was spending much of its energy not only in defending the United States but also in fighting its running battle with the air force over the role each would play in relation to nuclear weapons.

In early 1955 Admiral Carney, a firm leader who had seen ample action in the Pacific as chief of staff to Admiral Halsey, found himself losing his battles in Washington. Appointed chief of naval operations (CNO) in 1953, he encountered serious problems with the Eisenhower administration's new secretary of the navy, Charles S. Thomas (previously assistant secretary of defense for supply and logistics), who felt that "the navy was too slow in adopting a lot of new ideas, mostly in weapons systems." Carney believed in modernizing the navy, too, but apparently he moved at too slow a pace to please Thomas. Hence, in April, Arleigh Burke found himself summoned to a meeting with the secretary. He wanted a CNO who would push forward, Thomas said, a chief who would generate support for the needed advances. This conversation with its obvious purpose did not please Burke.

"I was a very junior rear admiral when I was appointed," he said, "and I didn't really want the job very much—didn't want it at all, as a matter of fact, at that time." Though he was fifty-three, Burke felt concern that, in choosing an officer as junior as he was (he ranked ninety-third on the list of line admirals), the civilian officials were implying that the navy lacked good senior officers, a view with which he strongly disagreed. Besides, if he were to become CNO he wanted first to have had the chance to command a fleet. However, Thomas made it plain to the admiral that the question had already been decided. Philosophically accepting his surprising fate, Burke noted that the decision was "very complimentary" and he was highly honored.

In June he went to work, though not yet officially in charge. Moving through the Pentagon world, talking to a variety of officers, he created a list of problems facing the navy that expanded into a collection of some fifty notebooks, one notebook for each problem: the army, torpedoes, personnel (promotion and assignment), and so on. Among them Burke included weapons systems. "Surface-to-air missiles were coming along fairly well then," he commented, noting his experience with them when he had been head of research for the Bureau of Ordnance; that, as it happened, was a specific area of interest to Secretary Thomas as well.

In this sphere, of course, the air force–navy fight over the delivery of nuclear weapons on enemy territory took the central place, a controversy Burke had seen close up as the air force got its B-36 while the navy lost its supercarrier. (Burke's involvement in the controversy reportedly delayed his promotion to rear admiral.) The air force still based its claim to primacy, if not exclusivity, on its bomber force, because ballistic missiles were still untried. The army was working hard on its missile, the Jupiter, while the air force, not wanting to be caught short in the unmanned-delivery derby, was developing its Atlas, its Titan, and its Thor.

A ballistic missile is so called because, after it lifts off with the thrust from its engine, it proceeds according to the laws of motion in following the course on which it is aimed, just like a shell from a high-angle gun; it reaches a peak and then falls forward onto the target, without any outside control affecting its movement. These missiles grew out of the German V-2, the first rocket-powered ballistic missile ever used in war. Though the V-2 had only a short range and other limitations, the damage it inflicted on southeastern England in 1944 indicated the great possibilities of such weapons, and immediately after the end of the war the Western Allies and the Soviets scoured Germany to collect scientists and engineers to take eastward or westward for participation in the creation of truly ultimate weapons: rocket-powered missiles topped with nuclear warheads. One of the prize catches in this manhunt— Wernher von Braun, the notable rocket pioneer who had led in the development of the V-2—went into hiding until he could give himself up to Western troops.

Writing out his own analysis, Burke concluded that "if they could get a high specific impulse [thrust] from a good fuel and could get a reasonable-sized warhead, ballistic missiles were going to replace air-

craft for the delivery of large quantities of nuclear weapons." Beyond
that, missiles fired from fixed bases were highly vulnerable: "three great
big beasts sitting on a launching pad." So, decided the admiral, "a mobile ballistic missile would have tremendous advantages." And what
had greater mobility than a ship? But his own missile specialists did not
give these thoughts a very cordial welcome. Work on missiles would
take money away from programs that were far more practicable, they
declared. As their central point, they noted that all the missiles under
development at that time were liquid-fueled (because solid-fuel engines lacked the power to fire nuclear warheads over long distances):
They were big, too big for all practical purposes, and they were highly
dangerous, with their volatile and explosive mixture of alcohol and liquid oxygen. And how would you target and fire a "movable" missile
from a platform that, being a ship, had no fixed location and was pitch-
ing and rolling in the sea?

Yes, Admiral Burke said, he and his experts saw tremendous numbers
of problems, but at least they did not have a "damned bit" of pressure
from politicians. The navy had already modified ships, both submarine
and surface, to carry the short-range Regulus I, which was not a ballistic missile but resembled a jet plane with a warhead and was a direct
descendant of the German V-1 buzz bomb. Yet "nobody outside of the
navy gave a damn or thought anything at all about a ballistic missile at
sea," because of the great problems that would have to be overcome to
make such an effort successful. Burke asked his people a simple question: "Could a strategy of ballistic missiles at sea be useful for the
United States?" Not only for the United States, came the answer, but
for the navy. "Of course, there was no thought of submarines then,"
Burke said, "because you couldn't put a Jupiter in a submarine. It was
a very large liquid-fueled missile." Indeed, the absurdity of the idea
was obvious: Missiles were launched vertically, and a Jupiter stood 65
feet tall.

Since the other services had put in a great deal of work on missiles,
Burke decided to join one or the other in research and development
instead of attempting to start a brand-new navy program. He would
have had only limited chances of winning approval for such a program

from Eisenhower and the secretary of defense, in any case, because the administration had decided to limit the number of ballistic missile programs to four, and the air force had already won approval for its three.

In talks with air force missile experts, the admiral made a striking proposal: "I want about a foot in your missile [the Thor] to put in the equipment that's going to be needed for a navy missile," and he offered to share costs for research. But the air force turned him down. As he remembered it, they said they had nothing to gain from such a partnership and they were doing just fine as things stood. To be sure, some air force officers had no desire to see the navy develop a strategic missile, which would represent an incursion on air force turf, though later some did offer help to Burke's project.

The army experts proved more forthcoming, however, telling Burke that if he would pay for it, they would give him his foot of space in the Jupiter missile. This step offered immediate advantages to both the army and the navy, however the relationship might turn out, by seeming to ensure the future of the Jupiter. Thus, despite all the weighty drawbacks of the liquid-fueled rockets, Burke prepared to move ahead, and on November 8, 1955, the secretary of defense established the joint program. Though the agreement represented the navy's commitment to liquid-fueled missiles, naval specialists still looked to developing solid propulsion.

Admiral Burke had no intention of trying to run the naval side of the project himself: "I was my own missile man for several months, and I couldn't handle it and do anything else." He was speaking only of preliminary investigation, of course, not of the actual project, which loomed up as a vast enterprise requiring the involvement and contributions of various navy bureaus, numerous industrial corporations, and scientists and engineering specialists from many areas.

■ ■ ■

Despite the pressure put on the navy by Secretary Thomas and Admiral Carney's consequent departure from office, the Eisenhower administration had spent its first two years making no decision at all about defining American strategy. In 1954 the National Security Council had created the Technological Capabilities Panel, chaired by James R. Kil-

lian of MIT, to look at the overall question, but Ike had ignored the resulting report for another year. In 1954 and 1955, in the early days of
the era of Nikita Khrushchev, the Soviet government displayed a series
of impressive strategic bombers (called in the West Badger, Bear, and
Bison) that began to stir up fears in the United States of a "bomber
gap" and would lead the air force to win funding for a great expansion
of its bomber fleet. Rocketry attracted Khrushchev as well, and in
pushing the development of missiles he encountered some opposition
from his army generals, who wanted a more orthodox balance of
forces, a view somewhat similar to that of Admiral Carney. But the
missile program had taken a path that would lead to the firing of the
first Soviet ICBM 5,000 miles across Siberia in August 1957, an event
followed in two months by the launching of Sputnik I.

Finally, in September 1955, shortly after Admiral Burke took over as
chief of naval operations, information about the Soviet progress in
rocketry from a CIA National Intelligence Estimate ("Soviet Capabilities and Probable Programs in the Guided Missile Field," October
1954) and other sources led the president to order the armed services to
begin carrying out the recommendations of the Killian Report, which
were not beyond controversy. The committee recommended a three-
part strategy for missiles: (1) The air force should speed up the development of its Atlas intercontinental ballistic missile (ICBM), a weapon
with an intended range of 5,000 miles; (2) the army should develop an
intermediate-range ballistic missile (IRBM); and (3) the navy should
develop an IRBM to be launched from a ship at sea. Ultimately, if all
went well, the Americans would possess three separate nuclear delivery
systems capable of striking the Soviet heartland: the air force's strategic
bombers, the ICBMs, and the missile-carrying nuclear ships.

With respect to its third point, the Killian Report mandate clashed
with the views of the many officers and experts who saw no way to
solve the problems involved. Neither the ship nor the missile existed,
and some believed that such a usable missile could never exist; nor did
they seem to see the transformative nature of the achievement, if it
could be realized in submarine form. In any case, Eisenhower's order
represented confirmation of Admiral Burke's efforts, but the committee
had stated goals only, not designs or methods or sources of financing,

and the tightfistedness of the president and of the secretary of defense, "Engine Charlie" Wilson, was well known.

Who should—who could—direct this project that seemed to present a range of ultimate challenges? "I studied the flag list and I went over every flag officer every night," Burke said. "One of the things I would do when I got home would be to go over that damned list." He looked further down, through the list of captains. *"Who could it be?"* he asked himself. Ideally, the man would have technical ability, but certainly he would be a hard worker and a good organizer. "He had to be a salesman, he had to be able to separate the important things from the unimportant things, and he had to know what he was doing." Burke also wanted a flier, because aviation problems arose in building missiles and, perhaps more important, because the project would take some of the emphasis away from carriers and he wanted full cooperation from the Bureau of Aeronautics, which not only had hoped to serve as home base for the program but also had independently proposed a naval strategic missile program. Burke was looking, in short, for a paragon—some said, even a messiah.

■ ■ ■

During the last few years before the United States came into the war that became World War II with the Japanese attack on Pearl Harbor, William "Red" Raborn, a navy flier in his midthirties, was concerning himself with problems relating to gunnery and the deficiencies he saw in pilots coming along. "It was my dream to teach people to shoot fixed machine guns from fighter planes better," he said, "and also to teach them to dive-bomb better." After spending two enjoyable years at Pensacola flight school on his gunnery mission, he drew assignment to long-range patrol planes based in California. These big flying boats could haul tremendous loads, but Raborn noted one deficiency: They carried little in the way of ordnance and hence had no offensive punch; specifically, they had no way to carry torpedoes. Yet in wartime these aircraft would range hundreds and thousands of miles from their bases, and they might well have the chance to sink enemy ships—if they had the weapons to do it with.

The planes did have bomb racks, one on each wing, and, said

Raborn, "I took it on myself with the cooperation of people in other parts of the navy locally in San Diego to adapt surface-ship torpedoes so that they could be carried on the wings of patrol planes." The Torpedo Station did its part in preparing the torpedoes, and Raborn and his ad hoc team fitted box fins to the tails to give these birds some aerodynamic qualities. While Raborn flew the planes, doing the testing, he had an associate flying alongside photographing the operation so that it could be fine-tuned. After achieving success, Raborn sent in a report to the Bureau of Ordnance, describing his work, complete with pictures showing the sequence from the dropping of the torpedo to its impact on the target.

"We got a blistering letter back, telling us that these actions exceeded our authority. Such things were not a matter for the fleet to experiment with. This was my first brush with entrenched bureaucracy." Undaunted, though disgusted with an attitude with which Pacific submariners dealing with the bureau over the torpedo problem would soon become discouragingly familiar, Raborn and his friends proceeded to create a device that could be fitted into the bomb racks and would carry depth charges, one under each wing. He seems not to have sought approval from BuOrd (Bureau of Ordnance), but when his wing of patrol planes was deployed to Pearl Harbor in mid-November 1941, the admiral in charge of aviation units took one look and ordered the immediate manufacture of racks to carry both torpedoes and depth bombs. On the morning of the Japanese attack, a patrol plane, outfitted with Raborn racks, attacked an enemy submarine trying to enter Pearl Harbor—the first American use of aerial depth charges. Later in his career Raborn would find himself on the other side of the hill as assistant to the head of the Bureau of Ordnance for all aviation ordnance.

■ ■ ■

"Those fellows made a real impression on all us dusty dry kids with sand in our hair," Red Raborn said, looking back to the day when two immaculately clad Naval Academy midshipmen appeared in his home town in Texas-Oklahoma border country. Inspired by the image presented and, like many other boys in the American heartland, by glamorous visions of ships and oceans, the teenage Raborn—an open-faced and solidly built young man, looking, as he always would, like a square-jawed cherub—responded to the urge to apply for Annapolis and won admission in 1924. Interested not only in ships and oceans but in airplanes flying from those ships, and further inspired by Charles Lindbergh's Atlantic crossing in 1927, Raborn determined to become a naval aviator. An eye problem, however (possibly caused by nothing more than a sleepless night), caused him to fail the physical examination, but pursuing his goal while serving on a battleship and then two destroyers finally won him his wings in 1934.

Following the Pearl Harbor attack, during which a Zero pilot almost caught him with a machine gun burst, Raborn received the job of training air gunners, a task in which he showed his customary ingenuity in developing practical devices and teaching methods. He directed his ordnance crews as they fished the machine guns out of the burnt-out hulks of the patrol planes and set them up on stands, from which they could fire at sleeves towed overhead. He also had his crews remove gun turrets from torpedo and patrol planes and set them up on mounts for target practice, the idea always being to train men to use the equipment they would actually be using in the air. After his school had graduated some thousands of aerial gunners, Raborn found himself presented with a medal and summoned to Washington, where he became the navy's director of aviation gunnery training.

He later had a different kind of opportunity to shine when, back in the Pacific as executive officer on the carrier *Hancock,* he won a Silver Star for his leadership in fighting the fires caused by the explosion of a Japanese bomb. Though the bomb had blown a large hole in the deck and fires threatened to do in the ship, Raborn and his crews, in the midst of blinding smoke, so effectively suppressed the flames and patched up the deck that the *Hancock* was able to land her planes returning from a mission. Like everything else, Raborn reasoned, firefighting was a matter of preparation, equipment, and teamwork, and the experience seemed to show that "men will work harder for a leader who can bring them out looking real good—and if he can make them proud of what they're doing."

In Washington after the war, Raborn moved into the stronghold of his old foes, the Bureau of Ordnance, as director of work on guided missiles and other air armaments (the Terrier, Tartar, and Talos antiair-craft ship-based missiles and air-to-air rockets). The outbreak of the Korean War sent him back to the Pacific, where he commanded the aircraft carrier *Bairoko*. In just a year the navy pendulum swung again, bringing Raborn back to the United States, first to the Naval War College in Newport and then to the Pentagon as assistant director of the Guided Missiles Division; here he worked on the development of the Regulus and the solid-fuel air-to-air Sidewinder, which homed on its target through an infrared guidance system.

Raborn would have one more sea command, the carrier *Bennington,* and one more crisis—off Rhode Island, when a huge tank containing hydraulic fluid exploded, setting off a chain of secondary explosions and filling the ship's ventilating system with noxious fumes. With the fires threatening the store of bombs, the *Bennington* clearly faced mortal danger. But, just as had happened on the *Hancock,* the crew fought disaster both heroically and effectively, and the skipper was able to bring the ship into port. Speaking with reporters, Raborn gave the credit for the salvation of the ship to the previous skipper for having infused the men with the fighting spirit. But, as he did not say, they were now his men.

In 1955 Raborn reached flag rank, and in November he received the summons to Arleigh Burke's office.

■ ■ ■

"If this thing works," Admiral Burke said, "you're going to be one of the greatest people that ever walked down the pike. If it fails, I'll have your throat."

In looking back on that meeting, the chief of naval operations may have exaggerated the force of his language, but he had the essence of it clearly enough. Raborn had been "summarily jerked" out of his post in Norfolk, as operations officer for the commander in chief of the Atlantic fleet, and told to get up to Washington overnight. Now, sitting across the desk from the chief of naval operations—a man not quite four years older than he was, just senior enough to have had a higher level of responsibilities during the war—Raborn knew that he had not been summoned to the Pentagon to discuss a possibility that he might accept or might reject. As he mildly put it, "The job was explained to me and I was told to go to work."

Admiral Burke had picked his man after great care and consultation. Raborn had done all the kinds of things Burke wanted done now, but, of course, he had done them on a far smaller scale. He had displayed the personal qualities Burke sought—the talents and the toughness, the leadership and the diplomacy. Like Burke, he had experience in dealing with technical matters (though not an engineer) and a strong background in ordnance; he had even shown himself to be an inventor, and he had a gift for imaginative improvisation. As the ship historian of the *Bennington* commented, "He was appointed because of his ability and his reputation for getting along with people in stressful situations."

But could he do the job before them now, as big a job as the navy could have given anybody? "It couldn't be done by fear," Burke said. The project needed a leader "who could get things done without creating a fight and without demanding things. We've had enough—" He broke off his sentence. "Like Rickover, for example."

The Bureau of Aeronautics and the Bureau of Ordnance had both wanted to serve as the organizational home of the new project. Raborn would not be concerned with the bureau's hierarchy, however, but would be working outside the chart, directly under the chief of naval operations and the secretary of the navy as the director of an entirely new and unprecedented entity, the Special Projects Office (SPO), created on November 17, 1955, by the secretary. Burke made a bow to both bureaus, however, by choosing as director a flier who had worked in ordnance.

Aside from his relative organizational independence, Raborn also had what became known as his "hunting license," a letter from Thomas, joined by Burke, stating that "if Rear Admiral Raborn runs into any difficulty with which I can help, I will want to know about it at once, along with his recommended course of action. . . . If he needs more people, those people will be ordered in. If there is anything that slows up this project beyond the capacity of the Navy and the department, we will immediately take it to the highest level and not work our way up through several days." The navy had never before in its history granted such authority to anybody. Burke told Raborn that he could pick forty officers—anybody he wanted—and that he had full authority to give orders to any bureau. But the chief of naval operations accompanied this impressive warrant with a warning: "You use that authority once, and you ruin the program, because you've got to get willing support." Involvement resulting from command would not be good enough: Admiral Burke definitely wanted no more Rickovers.

That was just as well on other grounds. Though Rickover did not state his position clearly, he seems at the time to have opposed research on a fleet ballistic missile (FBM, as it came to be known) because he saw it taking some of the always limited funds away from his nuclear submarines.

■ ■ ■

In the seven years since he had moved into the grubby temporary quarters known as Building W, Admiral Rickover had seen his nuclear power kingdom spread out through much of it. The building lacked all amenities and probably could not have fended off condemnation by the municipal authorities, but, as two reporters observed, "every time someone moved out, someone else who needed office space moved in." Some space had become available in late 1955, and the navy's housing authorities, unconcerned with policy and personalities, assigned two small rooms to the Special Projects Office.

On Monday, December 5, Red Raborn and Commander William Hassler of the Bureau of Ordnance, the only two officers yet on board, opened their new headquarters. Faced with the challenge of assembling a staff of officers and civilian experts and building a great project from scratch, Raborn moved fast, leaving the office after an hour's talk with Hassler to make the rounds of the Pentagon, creating interest in the project and even enthusiasm for it. This kind of diplomacy became part of the daily calendar. Though Secretary Wilson had given the navy no extra money for the project, Admiral Burke had assured Raborn that he could recruit anybody he wanted, from any billet or station, and that proved to be the case. Rank and civil service grades disappeared as considerations.

In accordance with the normal pace followed by weapons development, the Defense Department gave Raborn a delivery date of 1965 for his seagoing Jupiter missile system. That schedule hardly seemed to fit the need; they were going to do much better, he told his staff early in the game, and "by a hell of a lot." Along with rank and grade, normal hours would be forgotten. Raborn established a five-and-a-half-day work week, which quickly became a de facto six-day and seven-day week. He wisely ruled out the convening of any meetings unless they were truly necessary, and he cut down on coffee breaks.

"Put your hand on the back of your neck," he would say to his people. "All right, you feel it? That's what we're trying to save. That's what this program is all about."

In creating his team, Raborn sought people who wanted to be part of it. He spoke of national need and patriotism without affectation, and as a salesman (one of Admiral Burke's desiderata) he proved everything the chief could have hoped for. Engineers, accountants, executives—he scoured the navy for top people, and he got almost all of those he sought. He took to the road, spreading his gospel to high-level executives, factory managers, and workers.

In recruiting staff members, he sometimes approached his quarry with an evangelical persuasiveness; on other occasions his recruiting methods had a crisply direct quality. Some time after the project had begun, looking for a chief scientist to replace the original holder of the job, Raborn telephoned a man he wanted for the post, John Craven, who had turned down the offer when it had been made by the departing chief. Craven had thought that as a GS-12 in the civil service, he ranked too far below the GS-18 rating the position called for.

"Why won't you be my chief scientist?" Raborn asked.

Craven began to explain that he could not become a GS-18 overnight.

Raborn interrupted him. "Are you trying to tell me what I can do and what I can't do?"

"No, sir."

"Well, then, are you going to be my chief scientist?"

"Yes, sir."

"Very well. Report in the morning."

It quickly began to become apparent to everyone involved that in Red Raborn, Admiral Burke had given the Special Projects Office precisely the leader it required. Staff members noted how, with his technical experience, he could soak up masses of material and "find the single critical obstacle which had to be overcome." Presented with a problem, he could offer a solution, and he could make up his mind quickly. "He picked the best approach, the best man, the best contractor unerringly." Even though he was not a technical expert, Vice Admiral Thomas Weschler pointed out, "he still knew how to get the best out of people in that field, as well as the industrialists, who were usually the senior executives of their companies. He worked with them and had them as energetic and enthusiastic for the program as though they were [junior officers] working for the skipper of a hard-driving squadron. He was superb. He really had the leadership knack." "His program got hot right from the start and stayed hot," said a senior staff member. "And there was only one reason—it was Raborn. The man has incredible luck."

Luck? It appeared to be more the central quality that makes one general or admiral win battles that others would likely lose. Raborn gave the staff great responsibilities and the authority to exercise them. In return he demanded candor: Whatever the bad news, he wanted it straight; that way he saved time and avoided many mistakes. He dealt with contractors just as directly, and they soon learned to consider a handshake deal as good as a written contract.

Overall, Raborn's optimism and energy spread throughout the project; conventional thinking had no place in the SPO or any organization associated with it. When a navy accountant "sought to apply the usual bureaucratic delays to FBM contractor requests, he was told that he would be immediately transferred to another, less desirable assignment if he attempted to do so again. 'Think big or get out' was the message."

"One of the reasons why so many people want this program to succeed so much," said one of the program managers, a little later, "is they want to prove that a guy like Raborn can run one. You don't *have* to be a son of a bitch."

34

THE REIGN OF THE BOOMERS

On Tuesday, November 15, 1960, a new U.S. submarine, the nuclear-powered *George Washington*, moved down the Cooper River, in Charleston, South Carolina, and headed for the open Atlantic. There, 65 miles out, this vessel would make her first dive as the first ballistic missile submarine to enter active naval service and go on patrol. She bore the designation SSBN-598, the letters standing for "submarine ballistic missile nuclear."

Behind the creation of this ship-and-missile system lay five years of extraordinary effort. Though not everyone had applauded the rocket-sharing arrangement the army had made with the navy to create the Jupiter missile, since it would certainly interfere with this weapon's unfettered development by requiring drastic changes in its configuration, Secretary Wilson had made the plan official on the preceding November 8. But Admiral Raborn and his associates still had all their doubts about the actual possibility of handling and launching a nautical version of a liquid-fueled missile. The prospect seemed nightmarish. Even on land, fueling of such a missile called for rigid precautions, with everybody except the members of the fueling crew cowering in a concrete-and-steel blockhouse a quarter of a mile from the site, and when they finished the job the members of the fueling crew made their own quick departure from the vicinity. Fueling aboard ship offered no such options. "Conceivably," observed Raborn, "you'd be in more danger from that than you would if you were under fire from the enemy." In tests with mockups, navy people projected the grim possibilities if a swell or a rougher sea caused the missile to topple over. If the liquid oxygen spilled out, the ship would explode as soon as the LOX (as it was called), now turning into a gas, encountered even a single spark. As for underwater craft, putting these missiles in the confined spaces of a submarine "would make an internal combustion engine out of the whole submarine." Solid-propellant missiles also possessed another appeal for the navy: by their nature they lift off much more quickly than liquid-fueled missiles.

The navy representatives candidly let the army team know that their marriage with the navy might prove short-lived, because the SPO was continuing to pursue research into the much desired solid fuels. Researchers also sought to approach the problem from the other end by shrinking the warheads the missiles would carry. Here Edward Teller, the "father of the hydrogen bomb" and an early proponent of missiles on ships, pointed out that those in charge should proceed on the assumption that warheads would continue to follow the established pattern of progressive reductions in weight, and he essentially promised such an outcome. He put his view in a striking question: "Why use a 1958 warhead in a 1965 weapon system?"

By the autumn of 1956, progress in solid-fuel development had reached such a point that Secretary Wilson authorized the navy to cease work with the Jupiter and to proceed with the development of a solid-fuel IRBM; the decision also carried the fateful order to make application to submarines the first priority. In a meeting on December 8, after Raborn had presented his plan, complete with slides, pointing out how it would constitute a bargain compared with the cost of the Jupiter for the navy, Wilson said, "Well, Admiral, you've shown me a lot of sexy slides this morning, but I tell you that last slide where you showed that tremendous saving was the sexiest slide of all."

Wilson's approval of the switch to solid fuel actually came before technological developments warranted it (perhaps this was a matter of Raborn's faith and evangelism), but the technology developed in good time, as Teller had foretold, though not without many discouraging stresses and outright failures. "We came up with a very, very much smaller missile carrying a respectable warhead," Raborn recalled, "and which would be entirely safe to put into submarines," which was what he really wanted to do. "It was very obvious to us that putting ballistic missiles in surface vessels was not nearly as attractive as putting them in submarines, because, one, the submarine was more difficult to find,

and, secondly, if we could launch it while the submarine was submerged the missile would have a very stable platform," because at even
a few feet below the surface the water is much calmer than it is at the
surface.

The project still faced skepticism from some of the admirals, because
"launching a missile from a submarine while it was submerged was an
entirely new idea." When the team's scientists encountered problems
and failures, doubters pointed to the likely impossibility of creating the
desired kind of big, powerful solid-fuel missiles, and superiors would
wonder whether Raborn was trying to move too fast, but Admiral
Burke stood behind his man. Thus began the Polaris program. Raborn
himself gave it its name.

In one of the most striking innovations to come out of the Special
Projects Office, Admiral Raborn and his team produced managerial
concepts that spread to other agencies in all fields. Many a participant
in social programs, for example, has had to learn how to apply the approach called PERT (program evaluation and review technique); pert
even became a verb ("pert it out"). This technique was developed by
Gordon Pehrson, an expert on organization and one of the seemingly
endless array of top people Raborn recruited.

Not everyone took to the Saturday morning PERT sessions with
their charts covering the walls of the meeting room, however. In the
office of Captain Grayson Merrill, Raborn's first technical director,
Pehrson was known as "Omar the chart maker." Merrill considered
Raborn a "superb salesman" who "inspired confidence in superiors,"
and he respected Raborn's ability to "spot officers and civilians with
the qualifications that he needed and recruit them into SPO." Raborn
also gave his technical director full freedom in his daily operations, but
in 1957 Merrill retired, somewhat dissatisfied with Raborn's style of
management and feeling burned out. But the two of them had worked
together well for two years, he said, and "who can argue with the success of Polaris?"

In a later study of the Fleet Ballistic Missile Program from the "bureaucratic and programmatic" point of view, a scholar noted that in
his book he intended to describe "a government program which
worked, a public bureaucracy which was successful." He added, "In

doing so I will attempt to show what we can reasonably expect from government."

"The phenomenal abilities of Red Raborn and his staff," noted an executive in the weapons system world, "catapulted the country into a five-year lead over the Soviets in the most critical weapon in the strategic arms inventory." This great success amounted to "a folktale in the American tradition."

With the team he put together, a German naval historian commented, Raborn "registered an achievement well-nigh unprecedented in the history of industrial management."

Admiral Burke declared: "The Polaris success is due primarily to Red Raborn and the people he chose, because he made it work."

Besides Raborn, Admiral Weschler said, much credit was due Captain Levering Smith, an expert in solid propellants, who became technical director in 1957. The Polaris program, Weschler noted, was the first time that anyone took what was essentially major R&D and laid it out as a production schedule. As somebody said, "They took ten miracles in a row, gave them a timetable, and achieved it."

■ ■ ■

Originally, the hull of the new *George Washington* had been designated *Scorpion,* but Admiral Raborn and the other decision makers—moving ship, missile, and all systems ahead simultaneously and also responding to the impact of Sputnik I and Sputnik II—had not waited to create a new submarine to carry Polaris, and for the time being they had also settled for a shorter-range missile than planned. Crews cut the *Scorpion*'s hull apart in order to add a 130-foot section that would house sixteen Polaris missiles, each of which had the power to destroy an enemy city and could be launched from deep in the sea; the submarine also doubled in displacement, from 3,000 to about 6,000. Since President Eisenhower had chosen to name the ships of the Polaris fleet after distinguished Americans, the *Scorpion* switched species and became a tribute to George Washington. The class would include *Patrick Henry, Henry Clay, Ethan Allen,* and ships honoring other figures from Thomas A. Edison and the Hawaiian king Kamehameha to Francis Scott Key and Will Rogers. Launched on June 9, 1959, and commissioned on

December 31, the *George Washington* had a surfaced displacement of just over 6,000 tons; submerged, the figure was 6,888. In the spirit of John P. Holland, her submerged speed outdid her surfaced speed by half: 30.5 submerged to 20 surfaced. She carried a crew of 112.

Previously, on July 20, the *George Washington* had demonstrated her readiness for service. After firing two Polaris missiles, she radioed another in the series of historic reports from nuclear submarines: "FROM OUT OF THE DEPTHS TO TARGET—PERFECT." Though some of those in the world who knew her secrets seemed slow to grasp the point, in combining almost limitless endurance with almost perfect invisibility, she represented not merely an advance but a transforming fact in the world power game. And this fact had come along five years earlier than originally projected, and under budget as well.

In an official statement the navy, after helpfully noting that the Polaris had taken her name from the North Star, described the star's namesake as "a two-stage ballistic missile about 28 feet long, 4½ feet in diameter, and weighing about 30,000 pounds. It is powered by solid fuel rocket motors and guided by a self-contained inertial guidance system independent of any external commands or enemy interference. Each motor exerts thrust through four nozzles in the motor base. Thrust vector (direction control) is exercised by devices called jetevators. The solid-fuel Polaris is relatively simple to manufacture and requires little upkeep and maintenance in storage. The little attention required can be provided readily."

Taking note of the initial range of 1,200 nautical miles, the navy statement indicated that within the next few years developments would more than double the reach of the Polaris, extending it to almost 3,000 statute miles. The new system would give the United States "a virtually invulnerable and powerful war-deterrent force capable of striking almost any potential enemy target in the world with nuclear warheads."

The United States now possessed and had deployed the ideal vehicle; on May 6, 1962, in the first test of the kind, the submerged *Ethan Allen* fired a Polaris missile armed with a nuclear warhead that detonated high above the Pacific. Now the entire system had proved itself.

Land-based missiles could be targeted by an enemy and "hardening" of their sites offered little guarantee of invulnerability, whereas a Polaris submarine had the waters of the world as her site. As Admiral Raborn would say to a congressional committee, the ocean represented "the world's best medium of concealment." "Polaris," said the editors of the *Navy Times,* "obviously has rewritten the books on naval warfare," and in this new world a new strategy would be required.

The leading strategist for Polaris was the "soft-spoken, silver-haired" Rear Admiral Ignatius J. Galantin (Naval Academy '33), a native of Illinois. Galantin had commanded the *Halibut* in the Pacific in World War II and as "a skilled and aggressive leader" had won the Navy Cross. Summing up the role of the Polaris submarine, the admiral observed that "after all, we are really seeking to control, not necessarily to destroy. Here, in the efficiency of its deterrent role, is where the Polaris submarine is most useful." With its high degree of invulnerability, the nuclear missile submarine, Galantin saw clearly, could act as a stabilizing rather than aggressive force in the international situation. The admiral was thus looking past the immediate, horrifying fact of the destructive power these vessels carried to the deterrent effect they could exert on aggression. And, somewhat unusually for that day, while not denying the Russians' traditional suspicion of other countries, he did not "wholeheartedly accept the premise that the U.S.S.R. [was] aggressively minded."

This Polaris revolution meant, however, that war had truly become a matter of totality. The missile submarine could not by its nature inflict selective or limited damage on an enemy. If it should send out its deadly messengers, the ship and the country would become totally committed. But in the great series of paradoxes that characterized the Cold War, the existence of a missile-bearing submarine made it unlikely that the messengers would be released. It meant that, as Raborn put it, "conventional war would be the only type we would have to fight."

For the first time, a nation had built an important warship that would not serve naval purposes. Admirals Rickover and Raborn had now created the context in which all the world's politicians and strategists would function throughout the Cold War and beyond.

■ ■ ■

By the early 1960s the U.S. Navy had begun regular patrols out of Holy Loch, an inlet of the Clyde, near Glasgow, Scotland. Patrols had lasted for two months during World War II, just like these Cold War patrols, but with one great difference: the earlier boats did the great bulk of their roaming on the surface, diving as necessary to meet particular situations or take advantage of particular opportunities, but the essence of these new true submarines and their mission was the stealth provided by their ability to live seemingly forever in the deep.

The development and deployment of Polaris submarines did not come as good news in Moscow. Even the Americans had not expected to have a ballistic missile submarine in service before 1965, and the Russians had focused their defensive efforts in the naval realm on fending off the threat from U.S. supercarriers. They had nothing with which to counter this new missile platform that could skulk deep in the ocean. Four developments, each remarkable in itself, had united to make Raborn's project succeed—(1) proven nuclear propulsion, (2) reliable solid rocket propellant, (3) inertial shipboard navigation development, and (4) miniaturization of nuclear warheads—and they had come together with remarkable simultaneity.

The Americans had created the world's first "boomer," as the ballistic missile submarine would become known. Its Polaris would proceed to evolve through two models into the A-3, with three 200-kiloton warheads and a range of 2,800 miles. In the early 1970s the Polaris would give way to the larger Poseidon, an ICBM that carried multiple, independently targeted warheads and could hit any spot on earth. These weapons became known as MIRVs, for Multiple Independently Targeted Reentry Vehicle.

"With the help of an extensive espionage effort and the work of Soviet scientists," said two authorities on the Soviet armed forces, "the Soviet Navy made rapid progress in developing its own version of this new weapon of warfare." K. U. Kraynyukov put it a bit more complacently in *Spravochnik Ofitsera*: "The creation of an oceanic nuclear submarine fleet, armed with nuclear missile weapons, marked a new qualitative jump in the development of the Soviet armed forces." Although the Soviets deployed stopgap submarines (the Hotel classes), the first real evidence of the jump appeared in 1967 with the Russian boomers dubbed the Yankee class by Western analysts, carrying sixteen SS-N-6 missiles (the decision for sixteen had no particular engineering significance for the U.S. Navy, but the Americans and their Soviet rivals both seemed to regard that number as the proper standard). In reality, however, the Soviets had not done quite as well as Kraynyukov claimed. The SS-N-6 missiles used liquid fuel, with all its attendant inefficiencies and hazards, and even fifteen years later the Russians did not seem to have developed a completely satisfactory, sufficiently powerful solid-fuel engine to power rocket launches from submarines. Thus Admiral Raborn's project, with its almost maintenance-free weapons, had given the Americans a very long lead over the Soviets. When the Russians introduced the Delta I ICBM submarines in 1972, they also carried liquid-fuel missiles.

In the 1970s the Americans developed the classic strategic missile submarines, the *Ohio* class. These big boomers (560 feet long, 18,700 tons submerged, carrying a crew of 155) entered service, beginning with the *Ohio* itself in 1981, to serve as launching platforms for the potent new Trident ICBM: first, the Trident I, with a range of 4,500 miles, and then, from the *Tennessee* in 1989 onward, the Trident II, with a range of more than 7,000 miles. The *Ohio*-class ships, which would progressively join the fleet through the 1990s, all bore the names of states except SSBN-730, which honored Senator Henry M. Jackson. (This congressional figure was chiefly responsible for keeping Admiral Rickover on active duty, though officially retired, until the wildly implausible age of eighty-two, the all-time record for the U.S. Navy and possibly for any modern armed service anywhere, with the notable exception of Field Marshal Helmuth von Moltke, the Prussian general who defeated Napoleon III and served as chief of staff until the age of eighty-eight.)

The ultimate strategic weapons of the twentieth century, the *Ohio*s had a difficult birth, assaulted as they were by antinuclear protesters who broke through a fence at Electric Boat and splashed blood on the hull of one of them. Much worse and more protracted, "a bitter, vicious fight over inflation, costs, claims, and counterclaims put the shipbuilder, the Navy, and Congress in a triangular free-for-all from 1976 until 1981. Work stoppages, strikes, and, as one report suggested, 'alcoholism, drugs, and sex' all found their way into the Trident controversy." Disturbed at reported cost overruns, Rickover had become embroiled in the fight with Electric Boat. This proved to be the conflict that would lead to the old admiral's forced departure from the scene.

Administrations and various admirals had been trying to rid themselves of Rickover since the Kennedy presidency. As Senate majority leader, Lyndon Johnson had helped Scoop Jackson protect the admiral, but after three years in the White House, LBJ had agreed with his secretary of the navy, Paul Nitze, that Rickover should retire—he had attacked Nitze and the secretary of defense, Robert S. McNamara, before a congressional committee. Johnson said, in effect, that if Nitze could pull it off, he could have what he wanted. When Nitze went up to Capitol Hill to make his case to a group of senators and representatives, however, he found himself in a lions' den; his hosts, all Rickover acolytes, had thoughtfully invited the admiral himself to sit in and hear what Nitze had to say. "The atmosphere," said an informed person who preferred to remain anonymous, was, " 'What in Christ's name do you mean being disloyal to Admiral Rickover?' The only question was whether they would impeach Nitze."

Rickover survived this and other attempts to remove him, as one Washington reporter saw it, because he had "both understanding [of] and contempt for the federal bureaucracy." Once, when he had drawn fire from a variety of groups and politicians and Congress as usual had rushed to save him, Representative Jim Lloyd of California offered a memorable defense: "Mr. Chairman, I am not prepared to sail into the teeth of Rickover's excellent batting average compared to that of the others with braid on their sleeves. He is a different drummer." In the teeth of a barrage like that, what could opponents do except reel back in confusion and defeat?

Rickover had not only crafted an empire, he had launched a cult—the "program," his operations were called—which, like any other sectarian entity, had both its true believers and its disillusioned apostates and existed in constant collision with groups outside its system of beliefs and practices. As the result, both its genuine great achievements and its genuine problems often became lost in the smoke of battle, both open and behind the scenes.

Kept in place by the will of Congress, Rickover could exert continuing control over the navy because leaders like Admiral Burke and Admiral Raborn did not aim at lifetime power, but came and went in the traditional way of the armed services. Rickover, said one official, "just sits there," and while he was sitting there he was picking the commanding officers, the executive officers, and the engineer officers of every nuclear submarine and thus creating "Rickover's Navy." Rickover "just simply was a discredit to the navy and to officers and men in general," Captain Edwards strongly believed, "yet he got what he wanted later on by kissing the asses of various congressmen and senators."

Some of the admiral's high-handed actions through the years had, however, dimmed his luster. In the 1960s and early 1970s, when deep submergence vehicles were attracting much interest, Rickover acting almost as a one-man Bureau of Ships produced a nuclear-powered vessel, the *NR-1*, which he foresaw as the first of a class of nuclear research deep divers that could lead to operational submarines. The secrecy with which he carried out the project—a degree of circumspection unusual even for him—the cost overruns, and the ambiguous explanations he offered legislators and others combined to embarrass a supporter here and there. The *NR-1* survived not as a warship but as a sort of deep-sea utility vehicle, wielding its big claw to perform chores like recovering a lost missile from the sea bottom.

But it was in 1982 that the huge flap over the *Ohio* ships enabled Ronald Reagan's secretary of the navy, John F. Lehman, Jr., to end the admiral's sitting. Rickover, whom nobody had ever charged with involvement in any kind of bribery, admitted having taken "small gifts" from General Dynamics. On a visit to the company one day, he had admired a horn-handled fruit knife and remarked that he would like to have a dozen of them. Company staff members swung into action, sending the knife to a laboratory which identified the horn as having come from a rare Asian buffalo. The company immediately ordered a supply of the horn and assigned some of their craftsmen the chore of producing the desired knives. Rickover also received a diamond necklace, jade earrings, and other "trinkets," as he called them, which went either to his wife or to the wives of members of Congress; the whole take amounted possibly to $60,000. In accepting these gifts, Rickover felt that, just as he could ignore all other normal rules because of his unassailable belief in his own judgment, he could also accept presents from contractors because his own rectitude was so strong that no material consideration could weaken it. "Did I ever favor General Dynamics or any other contractor?" he asked. In fact, having foolishly taken the gifts, Rickover had ferociously attacked General Dynamics for fleecing the government out of hundreds of millions of dollars. When the reporter who broke the story about the gifts came to talk with Rickover, he saw only two pictures on the wall in the old man's office: one of John Lehman, who had forced his retirement, and one of Lehman's predecessor, Edward Hidalgo, who had maneuvered a settlement favorable to General Dynamics and other shipbuilders and very costly to the taxpayers.

"You might ask me why they're up there," Rickover said.

Dutifully, the reporter asked.

"Two biggest goddamned fools who ever ran the navy!"

When the reporter returned for a later interview, he saw that the admiral had added a portrait of Benedict Arnold to the wall above the other two.

■ ■ ■

Despite the uproar that attended the birth of the *Ohio* class, by the end of the Cold War eleven of these ships had joined the fleet, and seven more followed after 1990. Each carried twenty-four Tridents and could stay on patrol for seventy days. In the 1980s the Soviets introduced the *Typhoon*, a class of monster nuclear-powered submarines, the largest such craft in the world. Each displaced more than 21,000 tons and had a 75-foot beam. Created to carry SS-N-20 ballistic missiles, these submarines would have been frightful, difficult-to-damage opponents in any conflict. Yet the *Typhoon*'s bulk did not truly figure as an asset, since it made these boats harder to maneuver and easier to detect than the Americans' *Ohio*-class boats. The size, commented one international team of analysts, reflected "the weaker Soviet technological level rather than its real strength, just as the 'largest watch or tape recorder in the world' is not necessarily the best." But, of course, the existence of these nuclear-powered submarines armed with ICBMs, always on the prowl in the oceans of the world, constituted one of the most urgent facts of life in the Cold War. Instead of roaming as much as the American submarines, however, Soviet boomers concentrated under the Arctic ice; their builders fitted them with a "hard hat" fin on top to crack the frozen ceiling.

The difference in levels of efficiency between the American and Soviet boomer fleets strikingly revealed itself in the fact that the U.S. Navy, which in the 1980s usually had about half as many ballistic missile submarines as the Russians, nevertheless on any day deployed two or three times as many boats at sea, and the difference in warheads on station was about 3,800 to 800. *Ohio*-class boats roamed on patrol about two-thirds of the time; the Soviets had a rate of no better than 15 percent. Aside from engineering efficiency, one reason for this disproportion was the American system of maintaining two completely separate crews, the Blue and the Gold, for each submarine, so that one was prepared to go to sea as soon as the other arrived in port ready for liberty.

The *Resolution,* Britain's first contribution to Western nuclear deterrence, made her appearance in 1967. This 7,500-ton (surfaced) ship was followed by three sisters; each of these vessels carried sixteen American Polaris missiles. In the 1990s the government began retiring them, replacing them with the much larger Vanguards, which carry Trident II missiles. France also produced its nuclear-powered *Force de Dissuasion,* beginning in 1971 with the 7,500-ton (surfaced) *Redoubtable;* four sister ships followed through the 1970s. Like the British, the French began in the 1990s replacing their original submarine-launch ballistic missile vessels with more powerful successors, *Le Triomphant* class. The British boomers normally operated under the control of NATO, as they patrolled in the Atlantic. The French, who tended to keep three ballistic missile submarines at sea at any given time, maintained their deterrent on their own. These vessels constituted a fair warning that an attack on France would produce catastrophic results for the attacker. On the global scale, to be sure, the two superpowers were the chief antagonists.

∎ ∎ ∎

For three decades, the boomers operated in the context of what was called Mutual Assured Destruction, for years nervously known as MAD. According to this concept, countries would have enough sense and restraint not to attack each other if each possessed the power to destroy its adversary—and *would possess this power even after being hit by a first strike.* Nor did destruction have to be "assured" in some objective, technical sense; the overwhelmingly strong likelihood of it carried sufficient conviction for most strategists as well as for ordinary citizens. Here the light shone on nuclear submarines. Even a country with overwhelming first-strike power would have to fear a retaliatory attack by missiles launched from somewhere in the sea. This truth became increasingly convincing as missiles grew ever more powerful. At the end of the Cold War, the explosive force inside a single Trident missile could wreak devastation beyond the combined power of all the explosives detonated in World War II, including the two atomic bombs dropped on Japan, and a single boomer on patrol could carry twenty-four of them. A missile submarine crewman spoke simple fact when he called his boat "the third-most-powerful country in the world."

Readers of Tom Clancy will recall the amount of time attack submarines spent in listening for the sound of their quarry, and the consequent importance of silence, which Gary Weir termed "the common currency." Indeed, the essence of the missile submarine could be summed as three s's—silence, stealth, secrecy—enabling it to go anywhere and reach any target. In his conservatism, Admiral Rickover opposed the 1980s U.S. push for submarines that could go deeper in the ocean, driven by quieter power plants; they would be too expensive, the admiral declared, and too complicated. But as more and more effort was spent on silence, one of the major areas of attention proved to be the search for methods to shush the minuscule bubbles that formed around the propeller blades as they turned. The Russians became aware of these problems and of some possible solutions through information given them by the family spy ring headed by John A. Walker, Jr., a U.S. Navy chief warrant officer who acted out of the simplest motive: greed. Though the Soviets paid him more than a million dollars overall, the pinchpenny father gave his son and accomplice Michael no more than a thousand.

A boomer could go for twenty years without refueling, but the 165 men of the crew—three times the complement of a World War II fleet submarine—would hardly be happy, and of course the food might run out. To keep the men in good spirits, the cooks produced pizza day and burger day, and every Sunday they offered steak. Since a patrol might last as long as six months, the boomer carried tons of food; for an ordinary patrol of three months' duration it might bring along 1,500 pounds of prime rib and 1,500 dozen eggs, and for piquancy several hundred pounds of onions, with desserts to match.

"We're a big family when we're at sea," explained one skipper. Indeed, the scene on a boomer suggested the 165 people of a village stuffed into a tube as long as two football fields and 40 feet wide. Everybody would know everybody else's business, and of course rumors would spread freely. But, said the captain, "the ocean is a unifying taskmaster." Hence "depending on each other is the Number One thing we preach."

On all nuclear vessels, however, it was a family with two parts—the regular sailors and the nuclear crew members—and there was thus a suggestion, at least, of a class system. All nuclear specialists took the same training and, in fact, did not know until they had graduated what kinds of vessels they would serve on, surface ship or submarine. "The nuclear-trained people are pretty separate from the rest of the ship," said one nuclear sailor. "No one else can get into the propulsion plant. It's restricted to everyone else. The whole 'power train' is the responsibility of the nuclear people. No one else knows what goes on there. And, generally, the nuclear people get advanced more quickly than the nonnuclear people, and their pay is higher. There's a bonus. There's some resentment there."

Throughout the Cold War the level of the crew's morale always received careful attention from the authorities, though not actually from any fear that a berserk sailor might seize the firing controls and start World War III. The procedures and safeguards were well established and frequently had to prove themselves through test alerts. In such an alert or in an actual war situation, six officers had to agree unanimously before the captain and the weapons officer turned their keys, like a customer and a bank official opening a lock box, to arm the missile. One skipper, who had no doubt that his mission was to keep the peace, made it clear in discussion that if the United States had been attacked while his boomer was on patrol, he would have unhesitatingly followed orders to retaliate. The belief that this would happen he saw as the key not only to the mission but to the whole concept of peace through deterrence.

A decade after the end of the Cold War, a lady who belonged to a group touring the *Nautilus* at the Submarine Force Museum in New London asked a provocative question of the polite young officer leading the tour: What had happened to the eight or ten or however many boomers that used to patrol the oceans? The officer smiled as he told her that those ships, or their counterparts, still roam the seas with all their fearsome firepower, are out there every day ready for immediate response in case of attack on the United States. She seemed a little surprised.

35

KILLERS, SPIES, AND TRAGEDIES

At 6:23 in the morning of April 10, 1963, some 220 miles off Cape Cod, the U.S. attack submarine *Thresher* came up to periscope depth. It was a clear day with a calm sea, the wind at 7 knots, visibility excellent. Fresh from overhaul at the Portsmouth Navy Yard, the submarine, with 129 men aboard, had spent the day before in a series of shallow dives. Now, in water up to 8,400 feet deep, she was about to begin her test deep dives.

At 7:52 the *Thresher* told her escort, the rescue ship *Skylark,* that she had reached 400 feet, with no leaks to report. She then notified the *Skylark* that, in accordance with security regulations (to thwart any eavesdropping Russians), she would henceforth give the figure as "test depth minus X feet." At 8:35 she reported being at test depth minus 300 feet. At 8:53 she was nearing test depth. After two more routine messages, at 9:13 those aboard the *Skylark* heard something like: "Experiencing minor difficulties. Have positive up angle. Am attempting to blow." This meant that the submarine, with bow raised, was blowing air into her ballast tanks in an attempt to surface. The captain of the *Skylark* received no answer to his anxious query about the situation. At 9:17 the loudspeaker in the *Skylark*'s radio shack produced a rumbling noise, within which a voice could be heard saying nothing intelligible except, perhaps, "test depth."

For almost two hours the *Skylark* circled the area, trying to reach the *Thresher* on the underwater telephone and dropping hand grenades every 10 minutes (the signal to surface). No response came. While messages went off to New London and the Pentagon, lookouts scanned the water, and just before dusk one of them spotted an oil slick, with a few bits of cork and yellow plastic floating in it. In

Washington, having reluctantly recognized the inescapable fact, the chief of naval operations held a press conference, opening it with the grim words: "To those of us who have been brought up in the traditions of the sea, it is a sad occasion when a ship is reported lost."

■ ■ ■

In the new nuclear world, the submarine, which through two world wars had ruled supreme as the highwayman of the oceans preying on merchant ships, had found a new role for itself—essentially, had the new role thrust on it. In the first half of the twentieth century admirals on all sides had only with great reluctance conceded the central importance of the submarine as a commerce destroyer and had fought for years to build up its role as a warship, and now, only fifteen years after the end of World War II, the marriage of the nuclear power plant and the nuclear-tipped missile had rendered the submarine sovereign of the sea. For the first time, it could assert itself not merely as a sometimes valuable warship but as the queen of warships. The big boomer served as a platform for launching missiles, playing the role of battleship, and it had its destroyer screen in the form of the fast attack submarine, designed to strike and kill. In other wars the analogues of these hunter-killers found their victims chiefly among freighters and tankers; now submarines—enemy warships—took rank as the chief targets. The highest possible form of a childhood game was played out: The boomers would hide and the attack submarines would seek.

At the beginning of the nuclear era in the 1950s and into the mid-1960s, the U.S. Navy had the *Nautilus* and the *Seawolf,* prototypes but officially classified as attack submarines; four submarines of the *Skate* class, with a standard displacement of 2,848 tons; six submarines of the dolphin-shaped *Skipjack* class, standard displacement of 3,500 tons; and Captain Edward Beach's big globe-circling *Triton,* which had not been created as a hunter-killer but received the designation several years later.

The navy also had an important class of eleven 4,311-ton attack submarines that began with the *Thresher* (SSN-593), launched in July 1960. These ships, the navy's first deep-diving attack submarines, shared something of a distinction in that none were built by Electric

Boat; they came from Portsmouth and Mare Island and from two private shipbuilders. The *Thresher* with her thick hull and her array of silencing devices was the pride of the navy, the new attack submarine that, with her sisters, would protect the burgeoning Polaris fleet. She thus had great strategic importance. She carried a normal complement of ten officers and eighty-five men, and was armed with Subroc (submarine rocket) missiles—with a range up to thirty miles—and a rocket-boosted, acoustic torpedo with a nuclear warhead.

As the hearings into the loss of the *Thresher* would soon show, however, this vessel had been a naval protector with a flawed cutlass. Although in service only two years, she had spent nine months in overhaul at Portsmouth, where she had been built. Yet the results of heedlessness and sloppiness remained. Because the periscope control had been installed backward, pushing the "up" button would cause the scope to lower. One-fifth of all the valves in the hydraulic system operated backward, so that throwing a switch marked "Close" caused a valve to open. In a simulated emergency the crew needed 20 minutes, thanks to the scrambled valve controls, to cut off the flow of water that in a real situation could have done fatal damage in seconds. The air pressure system tended to leak.

Mistakes of this kind were supposed to have been corrected before the *Thresher* went to sea, but the testimony of crewmen who had been on leave at the time of the fatal mission and of other witnesses did not suggest that the navy yard had produced and maintained the ship with the greatest care and competence. Testing of 145 pipe joints in the submarine revealed that 14 percent were below standard, but a greater problem was that for brazed joints (as against welds) no satisfactory test existed. Hence the *Thresher* went to sea with almost *three thousand* other joints not truly tested. In his "twenty feet of the ship," as Ted Rockwell put it, Admiral Rickover allowed only welded joints.

It also seemed damning that, despite serious pipe joint failures in the *Thresher* and other submarines, the navy took no action to limit diving depth until the problem had been solved. And in the eight years since nuclear submarines had begun diving ever deeper, the navy had made no tests to determine whether ballast tanks could be completely blown at great depth to restore buoyancy. This, admitted navy officials, had been an error.

The inquiry concluded that at 9:12 something, somewhere broke— some joint or fitting in a pipe. It would not have to have been a large pipe to produce, at a depth of 1,000 feet, a stream that could fill a compartment in seconds, shorting out electrical equipment and possibly affecting the nuclear reactor. The *Thresher,* the authorities decided, must have imploded, crushed like an egg, settling to the bottom in a thousand pieces.

The whole tragedy represented a nightmare for Admiral Rickover, the public perfectionist, though he distanced himself from the ship construction side of the problem by criticizing "carelessness, looseness and poor practices that have obtained in our shipbuilding business." The "major point I want to make," he told congressmen, "is that the conditions which possibly led to the loss of the *Thresher* exist throughout the submarine design-and-construction program." With some disgust, Admiral Ralph James, chief of the Bureau of Ships, said that Rickover telephoned him to insist that "he was not the submarine builder, he was simply the nuclear-plant producer." (With respect to submarine design and construction Rickover liked to have it both ways, often speaking of his influence in these areas and then, when it suited him, denying that he had any such influence.) It was the only time, James said, that he had found Rickover "thoroughly dishonest." Loss of power from the nuclear plant from a "scram" (an emergency shutdown) could certainly not be ruled out as a cause of the disaster; in fact, a shutdown seemed likely to have been at least part of the cause. Regardless of his remarks to investigators and congressmen, Rickover took steps to reduce the time lag to restart reactors in other ships, from ten seconds to six. Admiral James suspected that the failure of a pipe joint had led to a scram, with consequent problems when crewmen could not rapidly restart the reactor.

But why had the action to blow the tanks not succeeded in providing the buoyancy that would have brought the *Thresher* up from the depths? The navy concluded later, after deepwater experiments with another vessel, that ice, collecting on filters, had clogged the pipes delivering the compressed air to expel the ballast from the tanks, similarly to the way specks of dirt can collect on the fuel filter of an automobile and completely stop the flow of gasoline.

Following the loss of the *Thresher,* the navy established the Subsafe program to ensure the safety of all other nuclear submarines. Experts reviewed construction techniques to bring about strengthening of submarine hulls; the ballast tank system was modified and methods of brazing joints were improved. Deep diving was forbidden until numerous detailed corrections were made. Despite unexpected costs, as the researcher Harvey Sapolsky pointed out, the Special Projects Office did not have to seek supplemental appropriations to apply Subsafe to the FBM fleet, because it maintained sizable contingency funds. After the completion of the Polaris project, the SPO had continued to exist and continued to maintain its high prestige; it served, Sapolsky said, "as the navy's investment bank for new ventures during this period. This was because it was funded for full expenses of the program plus expenses—because Congress had wanted to be sure it had the money to create the deterrent, which it did with admirable speed and efficiency. Hence it had the money to pay for the Subsafe plan." In the wake of the *Thresher* loss, the navy would now devote much attention to what became known as the deep submergence program.

■ ■ ■

The U.S. Navy introduced the *Thresher* class of sub-hunters in 1961 (3,750 tons' surfaced displacement; renamed as the *Permit* class after the loss of the *Thresher),* and followed these ships in 1967 with an enlarged version, the *Sturgeon* class (4,260 tons' surfaced displacement). In the mid-1970s came the major family of U.S. fast attack submarines, the *Los Angeles* class, displacing 6,900 tons submerged and 6,082 surfaced, capable of 32 knots underwater and carrying a variety of armaments— cruise missiles for attack on land and others for antiship use. Commissioned in November 1976, the *Los Angeles* herself was the first of this class of fifty-three. Each of them would bear the name of a city, except one, commissioned in 1984, SSN-709; this one would be called the *Hyman G. Rickover.*

In response to the American success with nuclear power, the USSR rushed the November-class of nuclear-powered attack submarines into production, beginning in 1958. Produced in such circumstances, such a complex craft and system were not likely to arrive without problems, and the Novembers had big ones: They were noisy and dirty, the noise rendering them easy to locate and the dirty aspect coming from frequent and hazardous leaks from the reactors powering them. In the late 1960s the Soviets produced a more satisfactory class, dubbed Charlie by NATO and consisting of nine Charlie Is (5,000 tons) and six Charlie IIs (5,500 tons). The Charlie II carried a cruise missile that could be fitted with either a conventional or a nuclear warhead and, as a first for the Soviets, could be fired while the boat was submerged. Charlies were followed by the much bigger Delta-class of the 1970s, which eventually totaled forty-four boats, most of them displacing more than 13,000 tons. The 1970s and 1980s also saw the creation of a whole family of Victors (I, II, III); these submarines were followed by the Akula-class, the first member of which was launched in 1984. In 1980 the Soviet Navy also introduced a class of large attack submarines intended to assault NATO surface vessels with cruise missiles. This class, which the navy termed "submarine cruisers," became known as the Oscar I when it was followed, beginning in 1985, by submarines labeled Oscar II; the Oscar I vessels displaced 12,500 tons submerged, the Oscar IIs 13,400. The latter group included eleven submarines, one of which was called the *Kursk*.

The line of fifty-three U.S. nuclear attack submarines that began in November 1976 with the *Los Angeles* saw its last member, the *Cheyenne*, join the fleet in 1996. In the next year came the *Seawolf*, the first of a new class of big 9,137-ton ships that also included the *Connecticut* (1998) and a third ship, the *Jimmy Carter* (2004). The ships stressed speed, power, and silence. As work progressed on the *Jimmy Carter* (SSN-23), the navy folded in advanced technology for special warfare, tactical surveillance, and mine warfare operations.

Called "quieting" or "silencing," the drive for maximum sonic elusiveness had been a constant as the Cold War progressed. Most noise came from geared machinery of all kinds, down to food processors and other galley devices. The sweeping solution was to put all geared machinery on a "raft" on springs; in addition, tolerances became tighter and tighter. The *Seawolf* proceeding at "quiet speed," according to the navy's director of nuclear propulsion in 1990 congressional testimony, would be as quiet as the *Los Angeles* lying in harbor. This same admiral called the *Seawolf* the most powerful warship in the world.

Then, following these ships in development, came the *Virginia*-class attack submarines, a true twenty-first-century group thoroughly based on computerized information systems and powerfully armed as well, equipped with vertical launch systems for missiles that ensure efficiency in attack. Each of these vessels displaced 7,700 tons submerged, with a length of 377 feet and beam of 34 feet; the speed and diving depth were disclosed only in very general terms, like a senator's assets: more than 25 knots and more than 800 feet. The *Virginia*s, designed for coastal as well as midocean operations, in the established American fashion possessed "maximum technological and operational flexibility," provided in good part by their supermarket of weaponry: Mark 48 CAPTOR mines, advanced mobile mines, and unmanned underwater vehicles. The contract for the six vessels in this class (at $8.7 billion representing the largest order for submarines in U.S. Navy history) went to General Dynamics, but the arrangement called for the work to be equally divided between Electric Boat and a subcontractor, its long-time competitor Newport News Shipbuilding. (At the same time, curiously, illustrating the persistence of problems in the defense industry, the Justice Department was extracting $100 million from Northrop Grumman, the parent of Newport News, to settle cases involving over-charging and the use of defective parts.)

The champagne bottle was swung against the bow of the *Virginia,* the class leader (SSN-774), by Lynda Johnson Robb, wife of former Virginia senator Chuck Robb, on August 16, 2003.

■ ■ ■

The year 1968 opened with a coincidence perhaps even more curious than the twin disasters in 1939 of the *Squalus* and the *Thetis,* which had happened just a week apart.

In mid-January the Israeli boat *Dakar* (Swordfish), a refurbished 1,820-ton conventional submarine just bought from Britain, set out from Haifa on her maiden voyage under the Israeli ensign after twenty years of service in the Royal Navy. Only three days out of port in good Mediterranean weather, the *Dakar* suddenly disappeared, leaving no hint of what had happened.

Search-and-rescue operations had just begun when an 850-ton French submarine, the *Minerve,* went down in the Mediterranean, during a training exercise, in an equally mysterious fashion. Some investigators thought at first that both losses might have been caused by undersea disturbances spreading from an earthquake in Sicily, but no actual evidence supported the idea.

The hunt for both boats proved not only difficult but impossible. Sonar searches produced no contacts, and after four days, when oxygen reserves aboard the submarines would have been exhausted, the authorities in both countries abandoned hope; 121 crewmen on the two boats were lost. Hope had always been slender, since the submarines had sunk in waters a mile deep and neither had a "collapse depth" beyond a thousand feet. If death came quickly, an account somberly noted, the men "either drowned or were crushed when massive undersea pressure wrenched the vessels' steel hulls." If the boats had remained intact, the trapped crewmen would have slowly suffocated.

Remarkably, the tragedies that struck the Israeli and French boats in January 1968 had large-scale parallels a few months on, events that this time seemed heavy with Cold War portents. In May, as the U.S. attack submarine *Scorpion* (SSN-589), a sister of the *Skipjack,* was nearing the end of a three-month mission, the navy diverted her from her homeward course across the North Atlantic to take a look at naval exercises the Soviet navy was conducting near the Canary Islands. Since under normal procedure the submarine would observe radio silence, nobody felt any concern about her until she failed to arrive as expected at her home port, Norfolk, Virginia, on May 27.

In view of her assignment to scout the Russians, much speculation suggested that she had clashed with some of the Soviet ships. John Craven, who had been commandeered by Admiral Raborn as chief scientist of the Special Projects Office and had continued his association with that office as well as engaging in other research projects, directed the search for the *Scorpion,* basing his work on data from underwater listening devices. After he suggested the probable location of the wreckage, the authorities sent out the U.S. research ship *Mizar* to find what remains she could. Towing two 35mm cameras along the ocean floor, the *Mizar* patrolled the area and returned with a set of photographs, remarkable at the time, showing the wreckage of the submarine lying in the depths, 11,000 feet below the surface. Since her collapse depth was 2,000 feet, rescue teams presumed that she had undergone a severe implosion thousands of feet before her remains reached bottom. Analyzing sound tapes from the continuous operation of SOSUS, the secret American array of underwater listening devices created to monitor the movements of Soviet submarines, and from other sources, investigators spotted a peak of noise that probably had come from some kind of explosion on the *Scorpion*.

Had the disaster been caused by a piping failure, a mechanical failure of controls, an irrational act by a crewman, the accidental explosion of a torpedo detonator, or something else—possibly hostile action? The experts studied the wreckage to see which causes might have produced the pattern on the sea floor. In the summer of 1969 they were able to take closeup looks through the eyes of the new deep submergence rescue vehicle (DSRV) *Trieste II* (named after the record-setting research submersible *Trieste,* invented by the Swiss designer Jacques Piccard).

When the govenment released the records of its investigation in 1993, they placed the *Scorpion* 200 miles away from the Soviet vessels when she sank. Nor, astonishingly, had she suffered an implosion; her remains lay on the bottom in two sections, making it clear that she had been filled with water before reaching the collapse point. An explosion had torn a large hole in one side.

Certainly the damage could have come from one of the games of "chicken" that formed regular parts of the routine for Cold War ships, with attack submarines occasionally sniffing each other out so closely that they collided. According to the documents, however, the "most probable" cause of the disaster was not an encounter with a Russian ship but the explosion of one of the *Scorpion*'s own torpedoes, which had become armed and then was jettisoned by the crew. But instead of streaking harmlessly away from the submarine, the navy suggested, the torpedo veered around and, in the strange homing behavior these weapons have displayed on and off through the years, headed back toward the *Scorpion,* hit her, and exploded. Or—an answer the navy liked less but that may well have been the correct one—the torpedo had blown up inside the submarine. Either way, a Cold War clash that never was? Presumably so, but nothing in that era seemed totally free of ambiguity.

What was not ambiguous, however, was the actual state of the *Scorpion.* Far from being a sleek creature of the sea, this submarine was actually a shabby and seedy boat, so rickety that the crew had taken to calling her the U.S.S. Scrap Iron. Close investigation by experts (unofficial but highly qualified) produced evidence that the problem lay in batteries that the navy ordered, paid for, and put to use, despite warnings about various weaknesses in the battery activators. Though Naval Ordnance did not admit it, it seems the classic story of the small, cheap part that destroys an expensive machine. In this case, the torpedo would have blown up inside the submarine, with gruesome results for all hands. But, whatever the cause, the navy's remedial steps proved so effective that the *Thresher* and the *Scorpion* had no American successors in the world's chronicle of lost submarines. As it was, the loss of the *Scorpion* appeared to be a tragedy of timing: New torpedo batteries, ready to be installed, were awaiting her return from that fatal patrol.

■ ■ ■

In the summer of 1974, out in the Pacific in waters three miles deep, an observer could have seen a unique American ship busily engaged in some sort of puzzling technical operation. Those in charge had told the media and other investigators that this 618-foot ship, named the *Glomar Explorer,* was engaged in deep ocean mining as one of the projects of the famous Howard Hughes, a billionaire so eccentric that any action ascribed to him would seem plausible. The *Glomar* was said to be extracting manganese ores from the sea bed for commercial use. Instead, however, the ship sat at the center of one of the many tangled intelligence stories that marked the era.

It began with a tragedy like that of the *Scorpion.* In March a 320-foot Golf-class Soviet submarine (conventionally powered, not nuclear, but carrying surface-launched missiles) exploded and sank not far off Hawaii, taking all hands with it. After some time U.S. Navy officials decided to locate the hulk if possible and extract any information that could be gleaned from it. John Craven took charge of the search for the lost Soviet vessel.

The Americans did not at first know that the Russians had suffered the loss of a submarine. The realization came from noting their efforts to find the boat, similar to those Craven and his associates would undertake to locate the remains of the *Scorpion.* The Americans also realized that if the Soviet boat had not sunk but the Russians did not know where it was, then both countries might have a severe problem on their hands: a freelance boat that, unlike the *Scorpion,* carried nuclear missiles. One way or the other, this possible rogue elephant must be found.

Employing the same kind of analysis of sounds used to find the remains of the *Scorpion,* the Americans put on their own search. An expert reported the discovery of the noise of an explosion and he could pinpoint the spot, which was in fact well away from the boat's presumed patrol area. Authorization to proceed with the search had to come from the highest levels of government, and it was indeed forthcoming.

Craven had the perfect tool at his disposal, the submarine *Halibut,* which dated from 1960; begun as a diesel-electric boat, she acquired nuclear propulsion while under construction. She later underwent another important change: Designed to carry three Regulus II missiles, she had a 90-foot hangar to accommodate these weapons, but by 1965 they had become obsolete and the navy's undersea intelligence arm won control of that inviting 90-foot space in this unique submarine. In the greatest secrecy, the *Halibut,* ostensibly a fast attack submarine, was transformed into a carrier of unmanned, underwater search vehicles, and to the crew the former hangar became the Bat Cave. In 1968 the *Halibut* was further modified to hold a huge cable reel that could lower into the depths a device containing sonar gear and a video camera.

In sniffing out the secrets of the sunken Soviet submarine, the *Halibut* seemed to have performed her part perfectly, extracting as much information as the site had to offer. Nevertheless, amid behind-the-scenes controversy about the purposes and need for the operation, the Nixon administration pushed the CIA into creating the *Glomar Explorer,* and six years after the tragedy the ship set forth on her mission, which many critics regarded as, at best, redundant.

In any case, the project did not long enjoy the protection of its cover story. In 1975, as William Colby, director of the CIA, later put it, "the Glomar project blew sky high" when details of the high-tech effort leaked to the media. Stories promptly appeared, telling the world how the *Glomar Explorer* had attempted to salvage the submarine by scooping it up from the bottom with a giant robotic claw.

As is commonly the case with intelligence operations, whether soundly based or otherwise, the precise truth and the full implications are not easily determined. Accounts in the press said, for example, that the great claw had begun to lift the submarine when the claw itself snapped, dropping its load back into the depths. But, as the Russians acknowledged in 1993, the *Glomar* recovered two torpedoes with nuclear warheads; the claw seems to have scooped up and held on to the forward part of the submarine.

The discovery was generally judged a true intelligence coup, since, as an American arms specialist said, "Bombs can be very different from one another. There's a good chance Soviet weaponry held big surprises for us."

■ ■ ■

One day in 1982, in the Sea of Okhotsk off the Kamchatka Peninsula, a Soviet ship scouring the bottom of coastal waters discovered and hauled up an object its commander had actually expected to find: a metal cylinder some 20 feet long, crammed with electronic devices. What the skipper perhaps did not expect to see was the identifying label helpfully affixed to the interior of the cylinder: PROPERTY OF THE UNITED STATES GOVERNMENT. Bureaucracies are justly famed for rigid adherence to routine and consequent lack of imagination, but in this particular case an objective observer might have supposed that the navy, which had put the cylinder in place, could well have departed from the procedure requiring government property to be properly labeled. Although the Russians could have had few doubts about the origin of the cylinder, it seemed a bit as if Mata Hari or Kim Philby had worn a name tag reading SPY.

The cylinder had been placed in that spot as part of another project featuring the U.S.S. *Halibut*. For some time, as Soviet submarines proliferated, Captain James F. Bradley, Jr., chief of the very secret undersea warfare division in the Office of Naval Intelligence, had sought a way to eavesdrop on Soviet communications, which, he reasoned, must lie open for the tapping as they encircled the country in cables. But these bundles of wire were no more than a few inches wide, needles on the vast haystack of the sea bottom. How to find them?

Late one evening, as he sat in his Pentagon office, Bradley found himself thinking back to his boyhood in St. Louis. In those days, he recalled, when his mother would take him on riverboat rides, he would see the banks of the Mississippi dotted with signs warning: CABLE CROSSING. DO NOT ANCHOR. If American boats needed such warnings, it suddenly became clear, Russian boats ought to need them as well. It was so obvious it must be true. If a U.S. spy vessel—indeed, the *Halibut*— could find such signs, then the navy could devise the equipment to tap into the cables. These wires would carry discussion of all kinds, details of plans and problems, not purely local but leading all the way back to Moscow. And the eavesdroppers on these conversations would not have to concern themselves with cracking codes and ciphers.

In 1971 the *Halibut* received still another in its parade of modifications; this time it acquired a decompression chamber for divers. In October the skipper, Commander John E. McNish, led his submarine off on its hunt for some of the most mundane objects that ever inspired a high-level secret operation, signs like those in rural areas warning about buried power or telephone cables. Sneaking into the Sea of Okhotsk, which lies between the long arm of Kamchatka and the Siberian mainland, the skipper of the *Halibut,* scanning the shore, saw exactly what Bradley had anticipated, a crossing warning in Cyrillic letters. The cable proved to be the line connecting the submarine base at Petropavlovsk to area headquarters at Vladivostok. The divers, with special training and special gear for deepwater operations, did not cut into the cable but laid the pod over it, so that it would pick up the signals by induction, like electronic osmosis. The *Halibut* had scored another of its triumphs, and the U.S. intelligence agencies had acquired an unrivaled source of information on Soviet intentions, plans, and activities. It was not instantaneous information, however, because missions were required to retrieve the recordings.

Two years later the *Halibut* returned to the scene with a much advanced wiretapping device powered by a remarkable plutonium-fueled minireactor; this pod could record as many as twenty channels simultaneously. In 1978 a newer special attack submarine, the *Parche,* commissioned in 1974, arrived in the Sea of Okhotsk to pay a service call, like a technician performing routine maintenance on computers in an office. In the same year the *Parche* tapped a Barents Sea communications cable linking the naval base at Severodvinsk with the headquarters of the Soviet Northern Fleet at Murmansk, a most significant source of information because of the importance of the Northern Fleet in relation to Europe and the Atlantic.

But then, along came one Ronald W. Pelton, a former cryptologist for the National Security Agency. The officers on the Soviet ship that had pulled up the U.S. pod from the bottom of the Sea of Okhotsk in 1981 knew what they would find because Pelton had sold the Russians the secret of the operation. His masters, never noted for their generosity with their contract employees, paid him $35,500.

The Barents Sea tap, however, continued to supply information to the Americans through the end of the Cold War. Pelton had not been cleared for that one.

■ ■ ■

In the next year a dramatic incident illustrated the kinds of problems plaguing the Soviet nuclear fleet. The reactor on the submarine *K-19,* on patrol in the Norwegian Sea, experienced a burst of radioactivity that heated the fuel rods to a temperature of 1,000°. Heroic sailors volunteered to enter the reactor compartment to work on the cooling system, finally succeeding, but at the dreadful cost of absorbing a hundred times the fatal level of radiation. They saved the ship, but within a few weeks nine crewmen had died of radiation poisoning.

Cleaned up, the *K-19* returned to duty, but in 1969 she became involved in one of the close encounters of the Cold War kind that by rights should have led to many more collisions than actually occurred. In this case the Americans apparently engaged in a cover-up as deliberate as any action of the kind taken by the Russians. The U.S. submarine *Gato*, operating in the Barents Sea in Project Holystone (closeup surveillance of the Soviet coast), collided with a submarine, the luckless *K-19*. Crew members of the *Gato* later said that they came as close as one mile to shore. Not wishing to admit anything about the operation, the Atlantic Fleet commander ordered the skipper, Captain Lawrence Burkhardt III, to prepare twenty-five copies of a top secret after-action report claiming that the *Gato* had abandoned her patrol two days before the collision took place because a propeller shaft had malfunctioned; the captain also received orders to prepare six copies of an accurate report, to be hand-delivered to the Atlantic Fleet command after his boat returned to its home port. Just whom the false reports were created for remained a good question; in any case, the navy was able to sit on the story for only six years before it leaked out. As for the poor *K-19*, once more repaired and returned to service, she went only three more years before a fire broke out, killing twenty-six crewmen.

In 1986 a leak in a missile silo (the working of the liquid fuel curse) on an elderly Soviet boomer, the *K-219*, led to an explosion and fires that rendered the vessel helpless. Part of a standard cordon the Russians maintained in the western Atlantic, the Yankee-class submarine surfaced off Bermuda, 1,200 miles from the American coast. Overheating froze the controls for the reactors, and a catastrophic explosion was averted when, again, heroic sailors entered a lethally radioactive reactor room to lower the baffles. The navy chiefs in Moscow forbade the skipper, Commander Igor Britanov, to accept American help and ordered him to keep the crew on board rather than allow them to transfer to a nearby Soviet merchantman, but when poisonous fumes continued to spread throughout the ship, eating at the seals of the door behind which the men had taken refuge, the captain decided to disobey his instructions and sent everybody out through the escape hatch. Later, after Soviet ships failed in an attempt to tow the vessel, Britanov himself abandoned ship just before she plunged to the bottom. Whether the *K-219* sank as the result of the damage she had suffered or whether the captain scuttled her remained a question whose answer Britanov kept to himself.

In April 1989 the Soviets lost another submarine, the *Komsomolets*, to a fire that spread from compartment to compartment, probably pushed by high-pressure air from a ruptured line. Forty-two of the sixty-nine members of the crew died, either on board or from hypothermia after having jumped into the icy waters of the Norwegian Sea. All in all, the Russians seemed continually plagued by fires, explosions, and problems with reactors, though gamely patching up even severely damaged craft and returning them to duty. Then, with the end of the Cold War and the breakup of the Soviet Union, came severe budget cuts for the navy. This, in turn, led to even more problems, caused by limited mainte-nance and poor training.

By the year 2000, reports on the condition of the Russian navy were making disturbing reading. The total budget for all the armed forces amounted to only $5 billion a year, compared with about $300 billion for the United States. According to reports in Moscow, routine maintenance in the navy had ceased to be routine and become more or less nonexistent; when it did occur, those performing it often did a sketchy job. Submarines frequently broke down and were spending most of their time at their bases. Crew members could not conduct routine military exercises. With the level of pay pathetically low, some-times not even a hundred dollars a month, and with even that amount not always forthcoming, the quality of the officer corps had sharply declined, and young sailors found nobody to teach them.

In the years following the collapse of the Soviet Union, the Russian navy decommissioned about 180 nuclear submarines. But it lacked the resources to dismantle most of these ships. More than a hundred of them lay tied up, deserted and rusting, at piers—deserted, even though many still had reactor cores on board.

Making use of a common expression, a former U.S. naval intelli-gence officer considered the Russian navy "an accident waiting to happen." On Saturday, August 12, 2000, the waiting ended.

■ ■ ■

Engaged in the largest Russian war games since the end of the Cold War, the forty-five-year-old Captain Gennadi Lyachin presided over a distinguished group in the control center of the nuclear submarine *K-141,* named the *Kursk* after the site of one of the greatest Red Army victories in World War II. Besides the officers who would normally be on duty, the *Kursk* carried five high-ranking representatives from headquarters, on board to observe the submarine's actions in the Northern Fleet maneuvers in the Barents Sea. This powerful Oscar II–class attack vessel, which had joined the fleet in 1995, carried an array of antiship missiles and rockets and a new bank of rocket-propelled torpedoes.

It was late morning on August 12, and a few minutes before 11:30 Lyachin received permission from the fleet commander to test-fire one of the new torpedoes at a chosen target. The launch would be one of the high points of the mission, and two technicians from the factory had come along to witness it. The firing would produce a burst of sound so deafening that crewmen left the watertight doors open between compartments to allow the impact to spread throughout the ship; this practice, though common, represented a breach of regulations. The torpedo employed highly volatile hydrogen peroxide fuel, not used by the U.S. Navy for more than thirty years. After the launch the *Kursk* would return to her home port, and the skipper would have a bit of leave to celebrate his son's twenty-first birthday. Just before the half-hour, Lyachin gave the order: "Fire!" And then everything became aftermath. The rocket fuel exploded—owing to a leak, the official investigation later concluded—rupturing the torpedo and shooting a geyser of fire combined with seawater onto the launch crew, incinerating them in seconds. The lethal fire-and-water mixture boiled backward through a hatch, killing everybody it touched. Vainly Lyachin gave orders intended to enable the *Kursk* to surface. But the hull had been breached, and then the fire reached a torpedo sitting in its rack, which exploded with the force of a ton of TNT.

Sonar tapes recorded by technicians aboard the U.S.S. *Memphis* (SSN-691), a *Los Angeles*–class attack submarine observing the Russian maneuvers, provided a reconstruction showing that two minutes and fifteen seconds after the original eruption of the fuel, a torpedo warhead exploded with force enough to tear a huge hole in the bow of the submarine, instantly killing most if not all of the crew. Actually, the force of the explosion roared backward through the hull until stopped by the heavy wall shielding the nuclear reactors. A tidal wave followed it, killing seventy-nine men, everybody in the front two-thirds of the submarine.

Diving toward the sea floor, 350 feet below the surface, the *Kursk* smashed into the bottom. With all systems having failed, the twenty-three survivors huddled in the darkened stern compartments. It was not yet 11:35.

∎ ∎ ∎

Nobody survived the catastrophe of the *Kursk,* and in spite of various early reports of men tapping on the hull, life was measured in hours rather than days after the first explosion. At 3:45 Lieutenant Dmitry Kolesnikov wrote in a note found on his body: "It's too dark to write, but I'll try by touch. It seems there is no chance, 10–20 percent." He concluded, "Mustn't despair," but despite his courage there was no escaping the noxious gases and the flooding. Speaking to the press a week later, Vice Admiral Mikhail Motsak, chief of staff of the Northern Fleet, confirmed the view that most of the crew died in the first minutes of the disaster, and he added, poignantly, that he still found it difficult to pronounce the crew beyond hope, "because I have known the submarine's commander for many years."

The Russian government responded to the tragedy with a curious mixture of embarrassment, paranoia, and seeming indifference. At first, having made no announcement about it for two days, officials even reported that it had occurred on Sunday rather than on Saturday, perhaps as a cover for a slow response. President Vladimir Putin, who had not learned that one of the inescapable responsibilities of a democratically elected politician is to make a rapid appearance at the scene of any catastrophe, chose not to interrupt his vacation in the Crimea and compounded his error by delaying requests for foreign help in rescue attempts. Even when he returned from the South, he did not rush to the Murmansk area to talk with the families of the crew; he did not appear, in fact, for almost two weeks. Russian officials also claimed that the disaster might well have resulted from a collision with an intruding Western submarine, a charge for which no evidence existed and which the prosecutor general ultimately withdrew.

Despite the public perception, Putin certainly would have been anything but indifferent in the wake of the tragedy. It was a bitter dose to swallow. The war games intended to display the power and prowess of the Russian navy had ended in a horrible and spectacular disaster that won the world's sympathy but not its admiration of the Russian government or its navy.

Looking back at his own career during the Cold War, an American admiral noted that living with the constant risk of danger like the accidental ignition of a torpedo had created a "bond of camaraderie" between the members of the American and Russian submarine forces that transcended national antagonisms. In truth, such a bond extended far beyond Americans and Russians, embracing from the earliest days of the submarine all those who chose to serve in these unique and often puzzling vessels. Whether allies or foes in war, submariners would meet and talk as friends almost as soon as the last shot was fired. Such is the profound mystique of the deep.

■ ■ ■

From the naval point of view, the century that began with the official recognition of the *Holland VI* by the United States Navy and ended with the tragedy of the *Kursk* could without undue exaggeration be called the Century of the Submarine. From their humble beginnings in the 1900s as poor relations of battleships and cruisers, vessels of only a hundred tons with dimly envisioned possibilities, these craft moved with remarkable speed into a position of dominance at sea. By their audacity and success they brought the United States into the Great War (not the intention of the masters of the U-boats, though they accepted the likelihood of it), and the presence of the Americans determined the outcome of this, truly the greatest war yet fought. To the surprise of almost all professional observers, the submarine through its power to destroy commerce had established itself as a potentially decisive weapon in war (one of the few prewar commentators who foresaw this development was Sir Arthur Conan Doyle, the creator of Sherlock Holmes).

A generation later, submarines again menaced the Anglo-American lifeline across the Atlantic, causing Winston Churchill to declare that "the U-boat attack was our greatest evil"; it demanded the productive might of America to stave off this possible defeat. Amazingly, in both wars the Germans made no preparations for the ocean campaign they actually fought, and they produced their dramatic results with only a handful of boats. The world could wonder what the outcome of either war might have been if Germany had possessed sufficient boats and crews to conduct a true full-scale commerce raiding campaign in the Atlantic. In the Pacific in World War II, the U.S. submarine force played the role of ocean highwayman, with decisive success. Together with mines, American boats all but destroyed the merchant fleet on which the island empire depended for its survival.

In the Cold War, once the submarine had found its determinative role with the birth of Polaris, it quietly brought a strange stabilization to the world arena, a risky and suspenseful balance that nobody could have desired but that miraculously succeeded. Indeed, as John Milton observed to Cromwell, "Peace hath her victories/No less renowned than war."

In the new century, with the great institutionalized East-West confrontation replaced by a swirl of hostilities and antagonisms between and among not only states but groups, some with nuclear weapons and many with nuclear aspirations, the boomers on their endless patrols could well find a new mission: serving as global sheriffs, ready to perform a rapid arrest from the sky on an incorrigible and menacing disturber of the peace, wherever on the surface of the earth this miscreant might be. Whether nuclear vessels themselves would undergo any kind of transformation brought about by breakthrough developments analogous to radar, jet propulsion, or the transistor remained for the scientists and their engineering colleagues to determine. In general, it is humbling for observers to recall that predictions about the future of war and weapons have a way of being far off the mark.

In the later years of the twentieth century and after, the peaceful probing of the ocean depths by explorers with a variety of ingenious submersibles brought back the hundred-year-old dream of Simon Lake, with his picture of submarines rolling across the sea bed and passengers walking about like explorers up above on dry land. Inevitably, celebrating a strange kind of ordinariness, a couple even said their wedding vows on the deck of the *Titanic*, 12,000 feet below the surface, and the immediate neighborhood appeared to be becoming not only crowded with people but also littered with such mundane detritus as soft drink cans. Simon Lake might not have approved of that.

Early in the new century the U.S. Navy found itself in unusual trouble. Having created the impressively named Surveillance Towed Array Sensor System Low Frequency Active sonar, a potent tool for detecting the presence of enemy submarines in an area, the navy came under attack by the Natural Resources Defense Council and other groups, which maintained that the intense and far-ranging sounds produced by the new system could harm whales and dolphins. The navy thus faced the danger of losing its five-year exemption from the Marine Mammal Protection Act. Perhaps, however, that problem represented a small debt the navy could repay the creatures whose hydrodynamic beauty had inspired the father of the submarine more than a century earlier.

EPILOGUE: ON ETERNAL PATROL

By its very definition, the U.S. Submarine Veterans of World War II was not the kind of organization that could exist in perpetuity, and inexorably the ranks of its membership grew thinner year by year. Finally it merged with the organization for younger submarine veterans. But well over half a century after the end of the war, the annual national convention of the World War II group was still drawing as many as fifteen hundred persons: the submariners themselves, wives, a sprinkling of grandchildren and great-grandchildren, and visitors from other countries who sailed under other flags. It is a long meeting, as conventions go, lasting from midweek until Sunday morning, and those in attendance—particularly the veterans themselves—spend much of the time in one of the host hotel's largest public rooms, which is supplied with sixty or seventy tables, each of which has as its centerpiece a plaque or banner bearing the name of a specific boat. Around the table, in a kind of continuing reunion, sit men who served on that boat—sometimes, nowadays, just two or three of them, and sometimes ten or more—men in their seventies or early eighties, quiet looking, conservative, seeming the essence of Middle America, the kind of men you might expect to see chatting in a barber shop or helping out at a Kiwanis picnic. They are casually dressed, but each wears a blue vest with gold trim, and the back of the vest bears the real story in gold letters: the name and hull number of the submarine (sometimes more than one) on which each served. To a student of the subject, these names represent legends sewn onto the fabric of the vests: ARCHERFISH . . . CREVALLE . . . RASHER . . . GUARDFISH.

"No one, save a power maniac, a sadist or a nautical romantic, can hold any brief for submarine warfare," declared Nicholas Monsarrat, who wrote *The Cruel Sea,* a fine account of the Battle of the Atlantic told from the perspective of a convoy escort commander. "It is a repellent form of human behavior . . . it is cruel, treacherous and revolting under any flag. We should like to know what it was like at the opposite end of the periscope, that we should understand what made these men tick—and, in ticking, kill."

How did they feel at the opposite end of the periscope, on boats whose crews did their best to sink the kinds of ships that Monsarrat's hero and all the other convoy commanders were guarding? Certainly the survivors around the tables at the U.S. convention express no revulsion or regret concerning their activities during the war. Quite the opposite: It takes a listener only a few minutes to realize that for these men reminiscence never grows old and the war remains yesterday. Their organization has among its purposes "to promote and keep alive the spirit and unity that existed among U.S. Navy submarine crewmen during World War II"; it is also supposed to foster sociability and good fellowship, and it clearly lives up to those aims.

A visitor who wonders why people volunteered for submarines receives an interesting answer from a Kansan named John Shaw, who is sitting at the *Bashaw* (SS-241) table. He chose the navy over the army in good part, he says, on the strength of an old World War I veteran who told the local boys about the messiness and the horrors of the trenches; service on the sea seemed to offer a much cleaner prospect. Besides, he had spent his life following four mules, and he welcomed the chance for a change. Why submarines? The Great Depression had been really grim in Kansas, and the service offered double pay. And, as it turned out, the food proved to be good, too.

Another *Bashaw* veteran, Gus D'Oranzio of Philadelphia, recalls his first experience with depth charging. To the chief of the boat, who was standing next to him, he said, "What the hell am I doing here?" The old chief said simply, "You'd better get used to it."

The *Tautog* ended the war as the champion submarine in numbers of ships sunk, and David Veder of Cincinnati recalls how the skipper, Barney Sieglaff (one of the three who captained the boat), had the habit of sticking a cigarette in his mouth and not removing it, while the ash grew longer and longer and bent over in an impressive droop.

Sieglaff did that not out of heedlessness, Veder explains, but to show, by the steadiness of the precarious ash, that he was perfectly calm and nobody had reason to worry about anything.

Bill Williams, who served on the U.S.S. *Ray,* thinks back to a day his boat was on station close to the Japanese coast on a lifeguarding assignment, when he and others were picking up the crew of a downed B-29. The copilot had managed to get out just before the Superfortress went under, but the pilot was crushed against the instrument panel; his friend could do nothing for him.

A better memory comes from the rescue of the crew of a PBM (patrol flying boat). The crew said their life rafts began capsizing in 40-foot waves until those on them realized that, if they quit bailing, the water they had shipped would stabilize their craft. Since night had fallen, the submarine's skipper, Lieutenant Commander Bill Kinsella, ordered the searchlight on and swept in an arc from bow to stern, but toward the sea, not the shore. The rescuers spotted the two rafts and threw lines to them. One flier became entangled in a line, so that when the submarine would go down in a trough the resulting wave would lift him up, and vice versa. The sailors finally managed to haul him in. Forty years later he had appeared at a *Ray* reunion with others who had been rescued, Williams said, and when he heard a description of the scene with a PBM crewman tangled in a line, he fervently said, "That was me!"

A visitor also stares with awe at the gold letters on the back of one jacket: WAHOO . . . HARDER . . . THRESHER. The *Wahoo,* lost with Mush Morton; the *Harder,* lost with Sam Dealey. The man in the vest had served on both boats and had survived to attend a convention more than half a century later. He had a broken leg that kept him off the *Wahoo* for her fatal patrol, the veteran explains, and illness had done the same thing when Dealey went out for the last time. When he reported to the *Thresher,* he warned the captain that he'd been on two lost boats and asked whether he was really wanted. "Come on," said the skipper, not hesitating.

What made the submariners tick? A U.S. admiral once observed that "the submarine force has always been a compact, cohesive segment" of the navy, and that its enlisted men, "all volunteers, seek the camaraderie and personal involvement they can have in the workings of a smaller, less formal, team," in "a force with a special esprit de corps." They still cherish the camaraderie and they still have the esprit de corps, and in listening to individual stories one sees that for many the comradeship began when the men realized, at the outset of their service, that in joining this arm, with its extra pay as well as its distinctive qualities and tight teamwork, they had graduated from the lingering rigors of the Great Depression to a better life they would share with others like themselves.

To speak of it as a better life is not to romanticize it. "War, obviously, is the least romantic of all man's activities," as the Civil War historian Bruce Catton once observed and as Nicholas Monsarrat would agree, "and it contains elements which the veterans do not describe to children." Still, like the old Civil War soldiers Catton is talking about, these submarine veterans as young men found themselves caught up in something vastly larger than themselves, and, despite any later accomplishments, it is true that what was most real in their lives took place when they were young. Far from being ashamed of it, they delight in reliving it. They take continuing and cheerful pride in the history their small force wrote from the day of the Japanese attack on Pearl Harbor when, as Admiral Nimitz said, submariners "held the lines against the enemy while our fleets replaced losses and repaired wounds." Indeed, said the World War II CINCPAC, "it was to the Submarine Force that I looked to carry the load until our great industrial activity could produce the weapons we so sorely needed to carry the war to the enemy."

The printed program of the conference concludes with an item that expresses much of the spirit of the occasion; lest anyone forget, there's a recipe for "navy bean soup for one meal on a U.S. diesel electric submarine": "In a 12–15 gallon pot, boil 2 gals water, add 6 lbs Navy Beans, 6 gals ham stock w/water, 8 ham bones. Cover & simmer 1½ hrs. Add 3 cups carrots, 4½ cups chopped onions, 2 tbsp pepper. Simmer 30 mins. Add 3 cups hard wheat flour. Stir & cook 30 mins." That should indeed have held sixty or so submariners, who, in their encased world, gave food the top place among their limited pleasures.

The convention also has its side of high seriousness. Every year, at ten o'clock on Saturday morning, all the participants come together in the grand ballroom of the hotel for a ceremony that forms the center-piece of the week, the memorial service for those submariners—374 officers, 3,131 men—said to be "still on patrol" on board 52 boats. It cannot accurately be described as a slick Hollywood production. The ceremony at one recent convention begins belatedly, and raggedly, as the presiding officer has somehow become involved in two or three other meetings that morning and finds himself, burdened with manila folders, running behind schedule. A high school ROTC color guard waits at the back of the ballroom and then, when all is set, marches forward for presentation of the colors.

The program features patriotic remarks and a notably long medley of patriotic songs rendered by a group of young people. Then comes the memorial service itself, the ceremony of the bell. As the president reads the name of each boat lost during the war, from *Albacore* through *Perch* to *Wahoo,* with the boat's number, and then adds the total lost— 86 men for *Albacore,* to 11 men for *Perch,* to 80 men for *Wahoo*— another veteran taps a large bell sitting at stage left. In actual fact, the reading does not go any more smoothly than some of the earlier parts of the program, with the names, the numbers, and the totals being given in varying orders, so that you cannot always tell which figure applies to which boat.

But none of these details really matter. The veterans are spending the week recalling a time in their lives filled with far more important experiences than most people ever know, and this memory is what counts.

What truly impresses itself on anybody sitting in the room is the re-peated *ting* of the big bell performing its official task, reminding the audience of the 3,505 U.S. submariners who perished during World War II. Or, as the veterans have it, their 3,505 fellow submariners who remain On Eternal Patrol.

NOTES

Abbreviations for sources of documents and other materials: NA—National Archives (U.S.); IWM—Imperial War Museum; FDRL—Franklin D. Roosevelt Library; USNI—U.S. Naval Institute; NHC—Naval Historical Center; SFL—Submarine Force Library.

vii *Epigraph:* Bennett, Foreword by Admiral Burke.

Chapter 1: The Peripatetic Coffin

page

3   Quotes from the *Post and Courier*, Charleston, August 9, 2000. Other points from interview with a spectator, Herbert Ping, from Philip Stern, from the Naval Historical Center, and from television coverage. See also *National Geographic*, July 2002, 82–101.

4   "The spectacle": Philip Stern, 177.

Chapter 2: Dreamers and Some Doers

9   Leonardo quoted, program of Submarine Veterans of World War II convention, August 2000.

12 The point about copper sheathing is made by Compton-Hall, *Submarine Warfare*, 92.

13 Never bashful, Fulton sent a copy of his canal book to George Washington, hoping with the president's support to return to America and develop a series of canals, but his timing failed him. Washington was just leaving office and, though he liked the book, he died before having had much chance to help the author promote his projects. Fulton mansion presented an imposing appearance: It still does today.

15 "The liberty of the seas": *Dunlap's History of the Arts of Design*, New York, 1834, quoted by Arthur Townsend, *New York Times*, July 18, 1915.

15 "crafty, murderous ruffian": *Naval Chronicle*, quoted by Compton-Hall, *Submarine Boats*, 82.

17 Movement of the Danish fleet: Alaluquetas, 254.

18 Fuel mixture from Alaluquetas, 254.

21 Thorsten Nordenfelt: His name is frequently rendered as "Nordenfeldt"; however, a contemporaneous (1906) Swedish who's who gives it as it ap-

pears in the text here. Both versions appear to be common; in fact, Thorsten's own grandfather seems to have preferred the spelling with a *d*.
21 "The Whitehead torpedo": Tirpitz, I, 37.

Chapter 3: The Dream Realized: Holland and Lake

23 "This event": Lloyd, 121. The reporter, looking back twenty years later, had his dates off by a year.
23 "the little cigar-shaped vessel": *New York Times*, May 17, 1897, quoted in Morris, 3.
24 "One man": Morris, 32.
25 Holland and his backers: In 1876, just as Wilhelm Bauer had done with the authorities in Schleswig, Holland demonstrated his approach to his revolutionary backers with a clockwork-driven working model about the same size as Bauer's. Unlike Bauer, however, he received not only approval but immediate promises of sizable financial backing, the sum amounting to perhaps $4,000. When he completed the actual boat, it seemed hardly larger than a model, since it was only 14½ feet long, with a 3-foot beam, and thus barely had room even for one operator.
26 "the navy doesn't like": quoted, *New York Times Book Review*, January 29, 1967, in review of Morris, *John P. Holland*.
26 "I call this boat": letter, Stephen Bonsal, *New York Times*, June 30, 1945. The following two quotes also come from this source.
28 "if he did not mind": quoted, George Davis, 32.
29 "the outcome": Frank Cable, quoted, Rodengen, 21.
30 He would build his own boat: Holland had already induced his company to support such a project (since his brain was the firm's only asset, the investors had to back him) and had begun work on it while feuding with the navy experts over the *Plunger*. Though the firm bore the name John P. Holland Torpedo Boat Company and the inventor held a substantial share of the stock, he did not have a controlling interest; he was an employee, serving as manager of the company, whose policies and operations were determined by the majority owners.
30 "That is what I want": quoted, Frank Cable, *The Birth and Development of the American Submarine*, New York: Harper, 1924, 112.
30 Performance figures from Jackson, 146.
30 *Holland VI* is well described in Gary W. McCue, *John Philip Holland (1841–1914) and His Submarines*, East Lyme, Conn.: The Holland Committee, 2000, published to commemorate the one hundredth anniversary of the U.S.S. *Holland*. See also McCue: John Holland Web site (www.geocities.com/gwmccue), and The Holland Project (McCue and Edward Popko: Worldcat database), devoted to creating digital reconstructions and simulations relating to the *Holland*. Further, see drawings of the *Holland* in this book, insert pp. 3 and 4.
32 "sea-devil" and "steel fish": quoted, Morris, 103, from *New York Herald*, April 15, 1898.
32 "if the [Spanish]": quoted, Richard F. Welch, *Military History*, October 1999, 16.

33 "You're blown": Robert A. Hamilton in "A Century of Innovation," Electric Boat Co., www.navyleague.org/seapower/electric_boat.htm.
34 "You might expect": Robert Hatfield Barnes, *United States Submarines*, New Haven, Conn.: H. F. Morse Associates, Inc., 1944, 26; quoted in Rodengen, 41.
34 "demoted": quoted, Richard F. Welch, *Military History*, October 1999, 16.
34 Few foreign corporations: Welch declares that none would deal with Holland.
36 *"Twenty Thousand Leagues"*: *New York Times*, July 11, 1916.
36 "the first submarine": *New York Times*, July 11, 1916.
40 "I am more interested": *New York Times*, June 19, 1915.
41 American named Alstitt: His work is described in Compton-Hall, *Submarine Boats*, 73.

43 *Part epigraph:* Hashagen, vii.

Chapter 4: "Those Damned Englanders"

45 "Horrible, horrible!": *New York Times*, June 29, 1914.
45 "the next war": One of the best known of Bismarck's many pithy observations, with the wording often varying. See, for example, the collection of Philip Johnston, Royal Military Academy, Sandhurst, www.philip johnston.com/links/links2me.htm.
45 Note on the beginning of the war: For three weeks, it had appeared that the issue could be localized and settled by negotiations between Austria and Serbia, with the other powers remaining calm, but before the month was out, the complex structure of power and interests that had kept general if increasingly uneasy peace on the Continent for more than forty years had proved unable to deal with this new challenge. Austria declared war on Serbia a month to the day after the assassination of Franz Ferdinand. The other great powers enlarged the conflict on August 1, when Austria's ally, Germany, declared war on Russia, the self-styled protector of the Balkan Slavs, and then set about invading Russia's ally, France, which had no Balkan concerns.
    When, in accordance with its long-established war plan, the German Army attacked France by way of Luxembourg and Belgium, in violation of a seventy-five-year-old treaty, Britain, having kept Europe and itself guessing for more than three days, entered into a state of war with Germany.
47 "big enough to constitute": Barnett, 118.
47 "modest aggregation": Wile, 3.
47 "My rise": Tirpitz, I, 33.
48 "he discovered": Wile, 4.
48 "an honorable, energetic": Admiral Knorr, quoted in Balfour, 203, from W. Hubatsch, *"Die Kulminationspunkt der deutsche Marinepolitik in 1912."*
49 "his amazing capacity": Wile, 3.
49 "I am just now": Seager, 214–15.
49 "grounded, collided": Seager, 257.
49 "had one navigational" and following quote: Seager, 36.
50 "the Caribbean": Mahan, *Influence of Sea Power upon History*, 33.

50 "keep their hands off": Champ Clark, quoted from *Congressional Record*, June 20, 1898; George Davis, 79.
52 "underhand, unfair": Admiral "Tug" Wilson, quoted in Legg, 13.
53 Officers' traditional view is discussed by Weir, *Building*, 5–6.
53 "I feel": quoted in Barnett, 117.
54 "If we had made": Tirpitz, August 23, 1914; I, 454. In actual fact, the Germans had made remarkable progress with their fleet in a short span of years, and the admiral could hardly have supposed that his country had the wealth and resources to produce and support a fleet equal to the Royal Navy while maintaining the most powerful army in the world. A British Admiralty white paper issued in September 1914 compared the figures: In 1905 Britain had spent £37,159,000 on naval armaments, to Germany's £11,300,000; by 1914 Germany had more than doubled its outlay, to £23,284,000, but the British figure had risen to £52,262,000. The intervening years had seen the development of the dreadnought, the "all-big-gun" ship that made previous battleships obsolete, and the British had made plain their determination to substantially outspend their rivals on these new kinds of ships.
55 "it would be dug out" and following quote: Marder, II, 48.
55 "everybody cheered" and "fairly slobbered": Marder, 54.
55 "an absurd fuss": Goldrick, 113.
56 "when we go out": Goldrick, 83, quoting Keyes's memoirs.

Chapter 5: "The Dreaded Little Submarine"

57 "I could see": Hersing's account, which appeared in the *New York World*, is quoted from Abbot, 133–34.
58 The admiral did not know: Marder, II, 58. Just five days before the U-9 came onto the scene, Commodore Keyes and a fellow officer had urged their superiors to move the squadron out of the North Sea and give it more suitable duties. At this meeting Churchill pricked up his ears when he heard an officer speak of the "live-bait squadron," and next day he urged the First Sea Lord, the admiral serving as professional head of the navy, to find a more suitable assignment for the old cruisers. The First Sea Lord agreed but allowed his subordinate, the chief of the naval staff, to talk him out of acting with any haste; the latter officer then responded to a spell of heavy weather by ordering the ships to confine their efforts to the southern part of the North Sea, the tight area known in nautical lingo as the Broad Fourteens. (The chief of the naval staff responded to Keyes's objection to this decision with a very bland "my dear fellow, you don't know your history. We've always maintained a squadron on the Broad Fourteens.") Because the rough weather was keeping destroyers in harbor, the cruisers would also, for the time being, perform their labors without the protection of a destroyer flotilla.
59 Weddigen narrative: Abbot, 133–34.
60 "chivalrous simplicity": Churchill, I, 352.
62 Newspaper quotes: *New York Times*, September 23, 1914.
62 Dougherty narrative and other details: *New York Times*, September 24, 1914.
64 A particularly poignant aspect of the tragedy brought especially bitter criti-

cism on the Admiralty and the First Lord. The sunken cruisers had been manned not by regulars but by members of the Royal Naval Reserve, some of them pensioners, most of them middle-aged men with families to support. Worse, each cruiser carried nine cadets from the Royal Naval College at Dartmouth, boys of fifteen and even fourteen, the "midshipmites." (There was nothing odd about these ages in themselves; Jellicoe, for instance, had entered the navy at thirteen.) Churchill noted ruefully that the Admiralty had assigned young cadets to the three cruisers and other such ships precisely because nobody expected these vessels to become engaged in battles.

64 New rules: quotes from the *New York Times*, September 26, 1914.

65 "One ship was sunk": Goldrick, quoting Bertram Ramsay, 134.

65 "You know we have": various sources, including Abbot, 139.

65 "What wonder": Abbot, 135–36.

66 Josephus Daniels quote: *New York Times*, September 16, 1914.

Chapter 6: Blockades for a New War

67 Quotes about the sinking from the *New York Times*, October 22, 1914.

69 "exploit without parallel": The phrase is that of the *New York Times*, September 23, 1914.

69 *E-9* details: Report of Proceedings, Appendix II, Chalmers, 253–54.

70 The Admiralty had long believed that swirling currents at Scapa would protect the base from submarine attack, although closer analysis showed that, once past the approaches, a U-boat would actually have clear sailing. Beyond that, neither Jellicoe nor his superiors in London had imagined that submarines could operate so far from their home bases. They had not had this belief all to themselves; the range and enterprise of the U-boats was as surprising to the German admirals as it was to the British.

70 "We are gradually": quoted, Churchill, I, 423.

71 "submarine successes": Tirpitz, September 25, 1914; II, 466.

71 Discussion of the development of commerce raiding rules draws particularly on Preston and Wise, 212–13.

72 "the flag covers": Mahan, *Sea Power upon History*, 84.

73 "efficient" and "manifest danger": Mahan, 85.

73 "whose strict observance": quoted, Fayle, I, 88.

74 "What made America's": May, 3.

75 Cautious British answer: Gregory, 65.

75 "For two hundred years": Mahan, 540.

76 "That made sense": Gregory, 66.

77 "blockade of Germany" and following quotes: Grey, 37.

77 Bernstorff quotes here and below: Bernstorff, 90.

77 The London rules had divided cargoes into three categories: (1) absolute contraband, which consisted of purely military goods like weapons and ammunition; (2) conditional contraband, which included goods that could serve both military and nonmilitary purposes (food and fuel, fodder, gold bullion); and (3) a free list (textiles, manures, unprocessed commodities like cotton and rubber that were immune from seizure). Germany and Austria-Hungary, as locked-up land powers that would hardly be patrolling the seas intercepting

merchant vessels and seizing cargoes, had little to lose in this exchange and declared that they would follow the rules if the Allies would do likewise.

77 As Captain Mahan might have observed if his narrative had extended beyond 1783, a British frigate, by stopping a smaller American frigate in a search for deserters from the Royal Navy, created an incident that could have moved the War of 1812 up five years to become the War of 1807.

77 "in her secure": Mahan, 84.

77 Wilson and House: Seymour, 303–304.

78 "a delusion": Mahan, 539.

78 "kept her fleet back" and "in effect a blockade": Tirpitz, II, 391.

79 "resources would diminish" and following figures: Renouvin, 10.

79 "a man who means well": Wile, 19.

80 "the economic life": Karp, 183.

80 Tirpitz to interviewer: *New York Times*, February 6, 1915.

80 "a blustering flourish": Tirpitz, II, 502.

80 Secretary Bryan, a pacifist as well as an apostle of neutrality, responded with disbelief when Bernstorff handed him the declaration. "He believed a submarine campaign of this nature to be unthinkable," Bernstorff wrote, "and my statements to be merely bluff."

80 "almost anything": Tirpitz, II, 392.

81 "a rather neat": *New York Times*, February 8, 1915.

81 Wilson's response: Seymour, 367.

81 Shipping quotes: *New York Times*, February 5, 1915.

Chapter 7: "My God, It's the *Lusitania!*"

82 Sumner quotes: *New York Times*, May 1, 1915.

84 "had entered upon a campaign": Robinson and West, 65.

84 Turner and Campbell quotes: *New York Times*, May 2, 1915.

85 "to provide destroyer escorts": Churchill, quoted, *New York Times*, May 11, 1915.

85 Operational orders: Thomas A. Bailey, "Documents Relating to the 'Lusitania,' " *Journal of Modern History*, 1936, 320–37.

85 Bauer orders from War Diary: quoted, Bailey, 324–25.

86 Details about Schwieger from Thomas interview with Lieutenant Rudolph Zentner: Thomas, 91–92.

86 "Certain necessary matters": Hashagen, 50.

87 Underwater stresses: Hashagen, 52–53.

87 "one of those jolly craft": Thomas, 81.

88 "It was dangerous": Zentner, quoted, Thomas, 85.

89 Sighting the *Lusitania:* Bailey.

91 The Manhattan shipping executive: details from R. L. Duffus, *New York Times*, April 16, 1924; other details from Duffus, *New York Times*, May 3, 1925.

91 "helpless souls": Diana Preston, "Torpedoed!" *Smithsonian*, May 2002, 65.

92 Frohman quote from many sources. The line comes from *Peter Pan*, which he produced in New York.

92 Vanderbilt no swimmer: "Riddle of the *Lusitania*," *National Geographic*, April 1994, 73.

92 Descriptive quotes from Schwieger's War Diary (Bailey).
93 "My God": interview with Max Valentiner, Thomas, 97.
93 "I could not have fired a second torpedo": Since Schwieger was not one of the chivalrous U-boat skippers (of whom there were a number) and never displayed concern about lives, military or civilian, lost in sinkings, some commentators have believed that he added this sentence some time later, after returning to Germany and becoming aware of the great stir his feat had aroused. The change may have been made by his superiors. In any case, Schwieger did not survive to sign the final, typewritten version; his later command, the *U-88*, was lost at sea, probably as the result of collision with a mine, perhaps British, perhaps German.
93 Schwieger quotes from War Diary (Bailey).

Chapter 8: A President Too Proud

94 "What will America": Arthur Davis, 89.
94 "spirit of commercial opportunism": Roosevelt, 23.
95 "The mind of man": Garraty, 50.
95 "the faculty": Lutz, 49.
95 "Presbyterian priest": Garraty, 46.
96 "if Germany": Seymour, I, 293.
96 "to aid": Baker, V, 116.
96 "greatly shocked" and "two torpedoes": *New York Times,* May 8, 1915.
97 London reactions to sinking: *New York Times,* May 8, 1915.
97 Quotes from Wilson's speech: Robinson and West, 256–61.
97 "Humanity first": *New York Times*, May 11, 1915.
98 "cheerfully into the future": Bernstorff, 13.
98 Newspaper survey: Abrams, 28.
98 Angry American: *New York Times*, May 11, 1915.
99 Turner on the weather: *New York Times*, May 11, 1915.
99 Turner "understood": Hickey and Smith, 294.
99 No fault found with participants: Lord Mersey did, however, find fault with nonparticipants, the officers of the cargo steamer *Californian*, who stood by at a distance estimated variously as 10 to 20 miles and watched the *Titanic* disappear. The master of the *Californian*, however, always denied that it was his ship that was seen from the *Titanic*.
99 Kaiser and Gerard: Gerard, *My Four Years*, 252.
100 The note: Robinson and West, 261, 265–66.
100 "money is the worst": Daniel Smith, 34.
100 During discussions concerning the American notes, Ambassador Gerard made what would become a famous riposte to a remark by Arthur Zimmermann, the undersecretary in the Foreign Office. Giving striking evidence that the messages Wilson had hammered out on his typewriter were having little effect on official German minds, Zimmermann, pounding the table with his fist, intemperately declared: "The United States does not dare to do anything against Germany because we have five hundred thousand German reservists in America who will rise in arms against your government if your government should dare to take any action against Germany."
    "We have five hundred and one thousand lampposts in America," Gerard

fired back, "and that is where the German reservists will find themselves if they try any uprising."

100 "even the German-Americans": Bernstorff, 144.
101 Wilson and "irregularity": Robinson and West, 264.
102 Status of *Lusitania* and *Mauretania: Naval Annual*, 1913, 229.
102 "Before the war": Abbot, 255.
102 Struggle had "witnessed the rapid discarding": Groves, 198–99.
103 "the Allies": Taylor, 46.
103 "Blockade and death": Groves, 182.
103 "The Americans unconsciously borrow": Bernstorff, 18–19.
104 "supplying arms and munitions": Tirpitz, II, 524; "the difficulty lies": Tirpitz, 556.
104 "Where participation": Groves, 198.
104 "to suspend all submarine": order quoted, Tirpitz, 416.
104 Tonnage totals: Marder, II, 345–46.

Chapter 9: From Folkestone to Dieppe

106 "no right to refrain": quoted, Birnbaum, 57.
106 "the one minister": Wile, 7.
106 The challenge to U-boat skippers is well discussed in Birnbaum, 64
107 Unfortunately, suffering from inadequate rehearsals, the production of *Goyescas* received some negative comments from reviewers, though the music was popular.
108 Pustkuchen believed the ferries no longer ran: This point is made by Tarrant, 280.
109 "The bridge is covered": quoted, Link, *Wilson,* IV, 228.
109 Lady from New York: quoted, *New York Times*, March 26, 1916.
110 "the discovery": Bernstorff, 248.
110 Wilson dispatched the note on April 18: Seymour, II, 238.
111 "The French politicians": quoted, Marder, II, 375.
112 Kaiser quotes: Abbot, 153.

Chapter 10: In the Med

113 Quotes from Arnauld: Thomas, 145.
115 "German submarine": Van der Vat, *Atlantic*, 28.
115 "underhanded": Parker, 28.
116 Q-ship encounter: Thomas, 145–46.
116 *Primola* encounter: Thomas, 151.
117 *Gallia* sinking: Thomas, 151–53.
118 "fish story": Thomas, 154–57.
120 "an almost unrivalled": Höhne, 15.

Chapter 11: "The Cursed Crowd"

124 "Where do you come from" and following description: *New York Times*, July 10, 1916.

125 The *Kopfstand* and other details of the voyage: König, 46–62.
125 "the most thorough": *New York Times*, July 11, 1916.
126 König interview: *New York Times*, July 11, 1916.
126 *Deutschland* specifications from Jackson, 58.
127 "I never saw": *New York Times*, July 11, 1916.
127 Bernstorff quotes: Bernstorff, 265–66.
127 Bernstorff and Wilson: Bernstorff, 267.
128 "peace without victory": discussed, Seymour, II, 417; speech quotes: *New York Times*, January 23, 1917.
128 "laboriously drafted": Renouvin, 57.
129 The Allies were dying for ideals: Seymour, II, 420–21. This idea is expressed in a letter from House to Wilson, written after a conversation between the colonel and a young British diplomat, Sir William Wiseman.
129 "even with the increasing war weariness": Renouvin, 58.
129 "All stood around": from the report of Rudolf von Valentini, chief of the Imperial Civil Cabinet, quoted in Birnbaum, 322.
129 Bethmann and Hindenburg: Ludendorff's notes on the noon meeting, from World War I Document Archive (www.lib.byu.edu) and *The General Staff and Its Problems*, quoted by Churchill, III, 224–25.
131 "I had the feeling": Bethmann-Hollweg in *Betrachtungen über den Weltkrieg*, II, 131–37, quoted by Churchill, III, 226.
131 "the distrust": Bernstorff, 389.
131 "the historian": anonymous review of *Russia Leaves the War* by George F. Kennan, *Times Literary Supplement*, January 4, 1957.
132 "the delivery of food supplies": quoted, Churchill, III, 227.
132 "the most important battle": Bernstorff, 389.
132 "Of all the grand": Churchill, III, 230.
132 "cursed crowd": Tirpitz, II, 552.
132 "Finis Germaniae": quoted, Birnbaum, 324.
133 Tirpitz on the Russian Revolution: Tirpitz, 442.
133 Churchill on Bethmann-Hollweg: Churchill, III, 227.
133 "warm friend": quoted, Bernstorff, 349.
133 "mental excitement": Gerard, *My Four Years*, 391.
133 Germany "could not hold out": Gerard, 375.
134 Text of the telegram: Deacon, 247.
136 Only five freighters: Fayle, III, 42.
136 "so marked an act of friendliness": Tuchman, 159.
136 "no other event": Link, *Wilson*, V, 454.
137 Wilson's speech: Abbot, 272.

Chapter 12: The Fight for Sea Shepherds

139 "We are ready": quoted, Sims, 58. Commander Taussig had a high-level connection with the Royal Navy, going back to 1900, when, as a midshipman, he had been sent to China in the American contingent of the international force assembled to rescue Western diplomats caught up in the Boxer Rebellion. Wounded in the fighting, Taussig made the acquaintance of a neighbor in the infirmary, a severely wounded British officer, Captain John Jellicoe. Twenty

years Jellicoe's junior, Taussig felt some surprise when, having barely arrived in Ireland, he was handed a letter of welcome from Jellicoe, who remembered him well. Jellicoe also made it plain that he was genuinely pleased at the arrival of the Americans, and he included a pointed comment: "We shall all have our work cut out to subdue piracy."

140 "knowing how highly": quoted, *New York Times*, September 29, 1936.
140 "Don't let the British": quoted, Trask, 55.
141 Sims with Jellicoe: Sims, 7–10.
141 "he viewed things": Sir Reginald Bacon, quoted, Marder, IV, 49.
141 the Allies might have lost the war: Similar thinking from the opposite point of view reigned at Pless castle. The definitely optimistic German High Command expected the war to end by July 1, or possibly to last a few weeks longer, until August 1.
141 Sims report: "First Cable Message," Sims, Appendix II, 374–76.
142 Jellicoe's summation: quoted, Marder, IV, 70.
142 "More Ships!": Sims, Appendix III, 381.
142 "could Germany": Sims, 29.
143 "There were those": Sims, 45.
143 "he did not like it": Daniels diary, April 9, 1917; quoted, Trask, 63.
143 "O for more": Trask, 64.
143 "a convinced": Trask, 64.
144 "Suddenly there is a scraping": quoted, Whitehouse, 93.
144 Vessels lost to U-boats: Hezlet, 88; tonnage lost: Fayle, III, 92.
145 "reasonable peace": Admiralty paper of March 24, quoted, Marder, IV, 114.
145 Sims to Daniels: Sims, 379.
146 "it will have more success": Mahan, *Sea Power upon French Revolution*, 217.
146 Convoy "is not recommended": quoted, Churchill, IV, 79.
146 "A single ship": Hezlet, 94.
146 Figures of losses: Whitehouse, 109.
147 Analysis of navy figures: Barnett, 194; Marder, IV, 150–51.
147 "The more experienced the Officer": Admiral Sir Alexander Duff, quoted, Marder, IV, 127.
148 "the British ought to convoy": Trask, quoted from the Daniels diary for April 25, 1917, 73.
148 "an experiment in this direction": Duff memorandum to Jellicoe, April 26; quoted, Marder, IV, 159.
149 admirals "had been convinced": quoted, Marder, IV, 167.
149 The Gibraltar convoy: Sims, 114–15.

Chapter 13: Ideas, Methods, and Triumph

150 The second flotilla: Sims, 76; June and July totals, Marder, IV, 275, note 28.
150 Hashagen recalled: Thomas, 220.
151 Destroyer's-eye view of action: Connolly, 92–107.
152 "we saw a smudge": Thomas, 220.
152 "The enemy has only": Hashagen, 187.
152 "No damn German's": Connolly, 103.
153 "They must have had you": Connolly, 107.

153 "by turning towards the sound": Captain T. G. Carter Papers, IWM.
154 "superior to anything": Sims, 203–204.
154 "I get my fingers": quoted, Morgan, 185.
154 FDR memo to himself: Assistant Secretary of the Navy, official file, FDRL.
154 "to call to fresh vigor": Halsey, 33.
155 "its natural prey": Halsey, 221.
155 Quotes from "Memorandum on Submarine Situation," May 24, 1917; Assistant Secretary of the Navy—official files: Submarine Warfare, FDRL.
156 French reply: Assistant Secretary of the Navy—official files: Submarine Warfare, Barrier North Sea, FDRL.
156 "the difficulties": De Chair to Roosevelt, July 12, 1917; Assistant Secretary of the Navy, official file, FDRL.
158 "the only big thing": Trask, 154
158 Sims quotes: Sims, 301.
159 "deeply conscious": Dönitz, 300.
160 "with the assistance" and following quote: Dönitz, 1.
160 having "robbed the U-boat" and following quotes: Dönitz, 4.
161 Merchant ship totals: Sims, 400.
161 Totals in final two paragraphs: Hezlet, 101–102.
162 Sims quote: Sims, 344.

163 *Part epigraph*: Langsam, vii.

Chapter 14: Boats and Builders I

166 "The submarine has come": handwritten draft of article, Assistant Secretary of the Navy, official file, FDRL.
167 "In all navies": *New York Times*, January 23, 1916.
168 "from 200 to 3,000 knots [sic]": This curious landlubberly use of "knots" as a measure of distance rather than speed may well have been put in Spear's mouth by an unsailorly reporter.
168 No foreign submarine could do more than 17 knots: *New York Times*, March 25, 1916.
169 First Lake interview: *New York Times*, June 19, 1915; interview, July 18, 1915.
169 "For twenty-five years": *New York Times*, July 11, 1916.
170 "lobbied for the appropriations": Weir, *Building*, 12. This study is an essential souce.
170 "In fact, if you look": Emory S. Land, quoted, Weir, 12.

Chapter 15: Arms and the Nations

171 Harding quote: Russell, 480.
172 "sunk more ships": Russell, 484.
173 "the greatest fool": This widely cited comment has been questioned by some because its only source is Fulton himself.
173 "because a man": Antier, 4.

174 "the submarine is" and following quote: Albert Sarraut, quoted, Antier, 25. The discussion here also draws on Hezlet, 110.
174 "more promising": Lefebure, 13.
174 "The technical aspects": Langsam, 204
175 The swastika: This Nazi Party symbol also became the centerpiece of the national emblem in 1935.
175 Hitler's belief concerning 35 percent: Eden, 155.
176 "created a formidable": Eden, 257.
176 Davis to FDR: February 18, 1936, PSF Subject File, Confidential, FDRL.
176 The British negotiations with Germany, Eden commented, provided a "classical example of the truth of Lord Salisbury's dictum that the methods by which a policy is executed in diplomacy are commonly as important as the policy itself." Eden was not yet foreign secretary and hence was not responsible for the making of the agreement.
177 "all the nations": Phillips to FDR, March 20, 1936, PSF, FDRL.

Chapter 16: Boats and Builders II

179 "It seemed": Weir, *Building*, 31.
179 "ranged from diesel": Weir, 35.
180 as Weir noted: Weir, 113.
180 "We find": Rear Admiral John Halligan, quoted, Weir, 39.
182 Figures on the *Argonaut*: Polmer, *American Submarine,* 41; Roscoe, *United States Submarine Operations*, 13.
182 Spear: *New York Times*, November 20, 1915, and November, 11, 1927.
182 Timing the dive: Harris, 248.
182 "too many damned holes": Chant, 29. The basic facts on the K-boat adventures are from Parker, 49–66.
184 *Surcouf* specifications: Jackson, 226.
185 "Naval designers": Roscoe, *United States Submarine Operations*, 13.
185 "In public affairs": Perkins, 96.
186 "nothing but British": *New York Times*, September 6, 1934.
187 "now confronted a Navy": Weir, 62.
188 "The headline": Polmar, 39.
189 Quotes about McKee: Schratz oral history, USNI.
190 Supplement the efforts of the Electric Boat Company: Electric Boat did not welcome this development, not simply because it would increase administrative costs but also because it would call for the company to make its secrets available to a business rival. The navy paid no attention to these arguments; it had plenty of work to keep both firms busy.
191 "after being completely dependent": Dean C. Allard, in Weir, ix.

193 *Part epigraph*: Churchill, *Second World War*, V, 6.

Chapter 17: Lieutenant Lemp's Great Decision

196 "Movements are progressing": *New York Times*, September 6, 1939.
197 "It was crowded": *New York Times*, September 14, 1939.

199 Early's comment: *New York Times*, September 4, 1939; also the following editorial statement.
199 "There's no doubt": *New York Times*, September 7, 1939.
200 "it is likely": *New York Times*, September 5, 1939.
201 "on no account": quoted, Peter Kemp, *Decision*, 6.
202 The authorities removed the page: The only known instance, says Harald Busch, of altering a U-boat's war diary, 2.
203 Dönitz observations: Dönitz, 5.
204 "the protective mantle": Dönitz, 6.
204 "We used to refer": Dönitz, 301.
204 "failed throughout": Dönitz, 277.
205 "being pushed" and following quote: Dönitz, 7.
205 "body and soul" and following quote: Dönitz, 13.
205 "possess ever bigger": Dönitz, 27.
206 "somewhat conflicting": Dönitz, 29.

Chapter 18: U-Boats in Trouble

207 "bleak, dismal": Whinney, 60.
208 "full of zest" and following quote: Dönitz, 175.
208 "a cool head": Busch, 12.
208 Approach to Scapa Flow: some details from U-Boat Command War Diary, quoted, Dönitz, 15 (softcover ed.).
209 Account of the attack based on Prien's report: quoted in Churchill, I, 491.
210 "After leaving Holm Sound": Prien report, quoted, Dönitz, 69.
211 "the vast size": quoted, Frank, 31.
211 Meeting with Pound: Churchill, I, 433–34.
212 Much heralded device: Dönitz's reflections, 74.
212 No trace of the committee: The point is made by Harris, 248. The following explanation comes from "Anti-Submarine Methods," Captain T. G. Carter Papers, IWM.
213 "If it were possible": Ruge, 77.
214 "surprise, ruthlessness": Churchill, I, 591.
215 British total: Hezlet, 127.
216 1912 Baedeker: Hinsley, I, 140.
217 "Ships stretched": Prien report, quoted, Dönitz, 85.
217 "As the result" and following quote: Dönitz, 85.
218 "exposed for all": Dönitz, 88.
218 "It was only": Dönitz, Appendix 3, "Causes of Torpedo Failures," February 9, 1942.

Chapter 19: Atlantic Raiders: The "Happy Time"

221 "an exit": Dönitz, 110.
221 Increasing U-boat range: The point is well made by Ropp, 234.
221 Availability of U-boats: point from Hezlet, 166.
222 "as swiftly": Dönitz, 110.
223 "On them directly": Dönitz, 115.
223 "Every morning": Frank, 83.

223 Limitations on escorts: Hezlet, 167.
224 U-boat's return described: Frank, 85–86.
224 Washing difficulties: Williamson, 10–11.
225 "captives of our own smells": Werner, 251.
225 "with more destroyers": Frank, 87.
226 "The public revulsion": Peter Kemp, *Decision*, 10.
226 "the ceaseless struggles": Churchill, I, 57.
226 "the submarine menace": quoted, Kemp, 10–11.
227 "it is always": Churchill, I, 137.
227 "who could suppose": Churchill, I, 140.
228 Z Plan figures: J. C. Taylor, 9.
228 Hitler "was intent": Kemp, 12.
229 Tonnage figure: Donald B. Steury in Runyan and Copes, 87.
229 Convoy organization: points from Reynolds, 20; Hague, 26.
230 "big ships and small" and following quotes: Forester, 4–5.
231 Lone wolf obsolete: Dönitz, 18–19.
231 "Tactical formations": Memorandum from U-boat commander, quoted, Dönitz, 20.
231 "the daily problem" and following quotes: Dönitz, 84.
232 "enemy in sight": Frank, 84.
232 Details of convoy attack: Rohwer and Hummelchen, I, 31, and Edwards, 22–24.

Chapter 20: Déjà Vu in the North Atlantic?

235 "now *you've* got": Whitehouse, 170.
235 Sinkings: total from Peter Kemp, *Decision*, 29–30.
236 Convoy actions: sources include Rohwer and Hummelchen, I, 84–85; Edwards, 48–49; Van der Vat, 201–203; Kemp, 30; Frank, 73–76.
236 "the close of the period": Kemp, 30.
237 Bletchley Park: background from Parrish, *American Codebreakers*.
239 "great arsenal": FDR speech, December 29, 1940, quoted, Rauch, 268.
239 "I don't say": FDR press conference, December 17, 1940, quoted, Rauch, 271.
240 "We have begun": Knox memorandum for the president, March 20, 1941, PSF Safe File, Navy, FDRL.
240 Concerning U.S. preparation for convoy operations: During this period of discussion, a U.S. staff officer, Captain Louis E. Denfeld, produced an analysis of the British convoy system to point out changes that would need to be made if the United States entered the war. The fact that this development did not occur in the immediately following months probably preserved a measure of Anglo-American harmony, since Denfeld found nine major deficiencies in British practices and procedures. He realized that the Royal Navy was spread very thin over the world, but it was "essential that the largest number of ships possible reach the British Isles in the shortest possible time, with as little loss as possible." The captain included a detailed list of recommendations having to do with the size and speed of convoys, the use of air escorts, and numerous other factors. (It is not clear that British officials ever saw this document.)
240 Stark to FDR: Memorandum, May 17, 1941, PSF Safe File, Navy, FDRL.

240 "attack instantly": Ryan to Rear Admiral A. L. Bristol, Jr., Commander Support Force, Atlantic Fleet, May 17, 1941.
241 "the matter was": Bristol endorsement to King, May 17, 1941.
241 "it takes no stretch" and following quote: Stark memorandum to FDR.
241 "considerable heat": Morison, I, 74.
242 "shipping of any nationality": King, Operation Plan No. 6 (July 19, 1941), quoted, Morison, I, 78.
243 Navy announcement: *New York Times*, September 5, 1941; also officer's comment.
243 McCarran comment: *New York Times*, September 5, 1941.
243 FDR quotes: Rauch, 282–89.
244 it was "difficult to regard": Langer and Gleason, 192.
244 "provided the reminder": *New York Times*, October 18, 1941.
246 "intended by the Nazis": William V. Pratt, *Newsweek*, October 27, 1941.
246 "since there were no": Sherwood, 381.
246 The New York chairman: John T. Flynn, *New York Times*, October 18, 1941.
247 Sinking of the *Reuben James*: Griffith Bailey Coale in Gannett, 412–13.
248 "met the fate": *New York Times*, November 1, 1941.
248 Comments on the *Reuben James* sinking: *New York Times*, November 1, 1941.
249 Hitler rejected Raeder's request: Dönitz, 193.
249 "sort of tacit understanding": Sherwood, 382.

Chapter 21: Raiders in the Far West

251 "come sooner": Parrish, *American Codebreakers*, 72. Foreign Ministry to Baron Oshima (Berlin), November 30, 1941.
251 German envy: Brézet, 247.
252 "confidently expected": Parrish, 142.
252 Hardegen quotes: Parrish, 141–42.
253 Sinking totals: Parrish, 143.
253 Dönitz quote: Frank, 116.
254 "it was lit up": *Newsweek*, March 30, 1942.
254 Hardegen gesture: Runyan and Copes, 161.
255 "The Battle": *Modern Marvels*, History Channel, January 29, 2002.
255 "the U-boats were quickly": Dönitz, 64.
255 Effects of losses: U.S. Navy training manual, quoted, Morison, I, 127–28.
255 Stark on loss of destroyer: Message note, February 28, 1942, Map Room File, FDRL.
256 "the enemy is above": "Lost Ships," *National Geographic Explorer*, July 23, 2000.
256 "If he were to drop": Hardegen interview, *Sharkhunters*, KTB #168.
257 Mohr verse: Frank, 116.
257 "the very heavy sinkings" and following quotes: Parrish, 146.
257 Hardegen even presumed: *Philadelphia Inquirer*, January 14, 1992.
258 "They despaired": quoted, T. J. Belke, "Roll of the Drums," USNI *Proceedings*, April 1983.
258 "without having": PSF, Navy File, FDRL.
258 Admiral King and convoy: Though King's conduct has generally been criticized, he won a stout defender in Clay Blair, who blamed Roosevelt for his

"stubborn and quixotic" refusal to support the production of destroyer escorts. In any case, however, this explanation would not account for such lapses as the rigid adherence to schedules (*Hitler's U-Boat War*, I, 451).

261 "The trouble is": Beesly, 114.

261 "Once convinced": Beesly, 114.

261 "utterly brilliant": Knowles interview, Parrish, 152.

262 The *U-202*: See Rachlis, 78–80; Blair, *Hitler's U-Boat War*, I, 603–605; *Time*, July 6, August 17, 1942.

263 Clark's adventure: Among the best sources is Murphy, 137–39 (Pyramid edition).

Chapter 22: Massacre in the North

265 "The Arctic" and following quotes: Reche in Busch, 111–12.

266 "there it was" and following quote: Busch, 114.

266 "the sky was full" and following quote: Busch, 115

266 "a choice morsel": Busch, 116

266 "some hors d'oeuvre": Busch, 117.

268 "descent upon the Norwegian coast": Churchill to Roosevelt, October 20, 1941, Churchill, *Second World War*, III, 344.

269 "If they must": quoted, Paul Kemp, *Convoy*, 54.

269 "a most unsound operation": Pound to King, May 18, 1942, quoted, Roskill, *War at Sea*, II, 115.

269 "All realised": Roskill, 130.

270 Fairbanks diary: quoted, Irving, 46.

270 PQ-17 cargo: from figures in Roskill, 143.

271 "stubborn and obstinate": quoted, Roskill, *Churchill and the Admirals*, 130.

272 "sheer bloody murder": quoted, Bekker, 274.

273 Scatter: This verb, along with *disperse*, would become the subject of much discussion relating to the ensuing convoy action. The essential difference was that *disperse* implied orderliness and *scatter* meant simply *sauve qui peut*.

274 The July 4 attack: well described in Kemp, 69–72.

275 "Destroyers and torpedo boats": Kemp, 74.

275 "worked themselves to death": Kenneth Knowles interview.

275 Pound and Denning: Many accounts of this fateful meeting exist. See, for example, Hinsley, et al., II, 217–19; Kemp, 73–75; Van der Vat, *Atlantic Campaign*, 284–85. The quotations are all reconstructions or approximations, since no minutes were taken.

277 Pound's orders went out: Hinsley, et al., II, 219.

277 Admiralty messages: Kemp, 75.

278 "It is not known": Hinsley, et al., 221.

278 joining the cruiser force: Peter Kemp, *Decision*, 75.

278 The dispersal point: Carse, 138.

279 Reche quotes: Busch, 117.

279 "able to announce": Reche, 118.

279 Reche total: Blair, *Hitler's U-Boat War*, I, 644.

279 Convoy QP-13: Carse, 135–36.

280 Churchill to Stalin: July 17, 1942, Churchill, *Second World War*, IV, 267–70; Stalin's reply: July 23, 1942, 270–71.

280 The last straggler: Rohwer, I, 232.
280 "There has never been": Morison, I, 186.
280 "the order to scatter": quoted, Roskill, 144.
281 "It is remarkable": Ruge, 274.
281 Churchill's proposal: Kemp, 78; Churchill, IV, 267.
282 "Is it really necessary": quoted, Gallagher, 12.

Chapter 23: "Too Much for the Hun"

284 "building many scores": Churchill, V, 121.
284 Convoy cargo: Middlebrook, 97–98 (book club ed.).
285 "you don't know": interview, Wilbur Von Braunsberg, Parrish, *American Codebreakers*, 157–58.
286 Decrypting Shark: Parrish, 156–57.
287 "The time has come" and following two quotes: Werner, 3.
287 "This day": Werner, 6.
287 *U-230* and the attack on the convoy: Werner, 129–31.
289 "gigantic holocaust" and following quotes: Werner, 132–33.
289 "The Battle of the Atlantic": Churchill, V, 6.
289 Admiralty concern: Roskill, *War at Sea*, II, 367.
289 For background of Tizard, see Snow; Clark; Crowther, 339–76.
291 "The Allied counteroffensive": Werner, 175.
291 "too much for the Hun": Horton, quoted, Chalmers, 192.
292 For the dispatch of the American contingent to Bletchley, see Parrish, Chap. 5.
293 Evidence of cipher problem: Hinsley et al., II, 554.
293 "With the information": undated [January 1943] memorandum, quoted, Dale C. Rielage, *Naval History*, December 2002, 32.
294 "sunk so far": Schaeffer, 201.
295 Sinking figures: Noli, 394.

297 *Part epigraph*: Blair, *Silent Victory*, I, xv.

Chapter 24: Surprise and Shock

299 "the whole U.S. Pacific Fleet": quoted, John Deane Potter, 98.
299 "without previous declaration": quoted, Blond, 150.
299 Surprise not expected: Agawa, 244.
302 "If I am told": quoted, Morison, III, 46.
302 Midget submarines: Morison, III, 95.
303 "attacked, fired upon": quoted, Roscoe, *U.S. Submarine Operations*, 5.
303 "had been absolutely wrong": quoted, Prange, 462.
304 "I would never": quoted, Agawa, 266.
305 "thems real bullets": quoted, Richler, 199.
305 Team of cryptanalysts: The chief of the SIS, Colonel William Friedman, was not directly involved in the Purple operation.
305 "the army's solution": Laurence Safford, quoted, Parrish, *American Codebreakers*, 56.

305 Japanese telegrams: Parrish, 71–72.
307 "I never thought": quoted, Prange, 460.
307 "unwarranted feeling": quoted, Morison, III, 129. In addition to the war games, during 1940 and 1941 various U.S. officers had also pointed to the possibility of such a strike, some in considerable detail, and early in 1941 the American ambassador to Japan, the experienced and highly capable Joseph C. Grew, had informed the State Department of talk in Tokyo about a surprise attack on Oahu. Magic supplied a thick file of information, but it could not on its own fit all the details into a comprehensive picture.
307 Points about submarine base: Roscoe, 7.
309 *Tautog* into action: Ship History, *U.S. Submarine Veterans, World War II*, II, 100.
309 The *Thresher*: Roscoe, 21; Blair, *Silent Victory*, I, 79–80.
311 "Believe it": Cutter oral history, USNI.
311 "Then we turned": Cutter oral history.
312 "I want to go": Cutter oral history.
312 "A lot of tough skippers": Cutter oral history.
314 "all brains": Leasor, 183.
314 Telegram to Phillips: Leasor, 188.
315 "In all the war": Churchill, *Second World War*, III, 620.
316 Hart's defense of Phillips: *Saturday Evening Post*, October 3, 1942.
316 "would now look to America": quoted, Thorne, 222.

Chapter 25: "Execute Unrestricted Warfare"

317 Patrol details from *Gudgeon* Patrol Report, 1 February 1942, NA.
318 No attack role for submarine: Buell, 52–53.
319 Withers's view: Weir, *Forged in War*, 3.
320 Wilkes: War Activities Report, NA.
321 "a fine old gentleman": Cutter oral history, USNI.
321 Withers's points: Report, Withers, February 4, 1942, NA.
322 "handicapped": Cutter oral history.
322 "We were supposed" and following two quotes: Cutter oral history.
322 "It's just a crime": Cutter oral history.
323 Sinking of submarine: quotes and account from *Gudgeon* Patrol Report, February 4, 1942, NA.
324 "Make all preparations": Gugliotta, 88.
324 Hart's message: Morison, III, 169.
324 "We consider": quoted, Watson, 151.
325 New command: War Activities Report, from Commander Submarines, U.S. Asiatic Fleet, to Commander in Chief U.S. Fleet and Chief of Naval Operations, April 1, 1942, NA.
325 "foul living": Gugliotta, 8.
326 Flying Fortresses: Morton, 39.
327 "wouldn't be surprised": quoted, Pogue, 233.
327 "very worried": quoted, Van der Vat, *Pacific Campaign*, 25.
327 "on the *ground*": quoted, Van der Vat.
328 "The inclination": Gunther, 38.
328 Fifth columnists: *Saturday Evening Post*, September 26, 1942.

329 "had already experienced": Gugliotta, 2.
329 "[E]xperience in maneuvers": quoted, Gugliotta, 3.
329 "from machinery": Gugliotta, 6.
330 "he was damned glad": Gugliotta, 3.
330 "he was hooked": Gugliotta, 6.
330 Encounter with Rickover: Gugliotta, 30.
331 "Admiral Hart": Morison, 171.
331 "if they were not": Roscoe, *Pig Boats*, 34. The unfortunate title of this book should not mislead the reader into regarding it as a popularization; it is, in fact, simply an abridgment, by Roscoe, of his *United States Submarine Operations in World War II.*
332 *Sealion* and *Seadragon*: Roscoe, *U.S. Submarine Operations*, 29–30.

Chapter 26: Battle: Boats vs. Invaders

334 "like a man": Roscoe, *Pig Boats*, 37.
334 "use caution": War Activities Report, from Commander Submarines, U.S. Asiatic Fleet, to Commander in Chief U.S. Fleet and Chief of Naval Operations, April 1, 1942, NA.
334 *S-39* attack: Gugliotta, 91–97.
337 "[A]ching eyes": Gugliotta, 98.
337 "They opened their mouths": Gugliotta, 99.
338 Wilkes blamed: War Activities Report.
339 "Ensign G. W. Forbes": *Reader's Digest*, August 1942, from *Collier's.*
339 "Depth bombs": Roscoe, 47.
340 "one transport": Roscoe.
340 Hart and fifth columnists: *Saturday Evening Post*, October 3, 1942.
341 "make every effort": Wilkes, War Actitivities Report.
341 "When you're there": *Reader's Digest*, August 1942, from *Newsweek.*
341 "Even if all their attacks": Hezlet, 194.
341 Naval aide memorandum: Map Room File, Box 41, FDRL.
342 "It is always": Hezlet, 195.
342 "this procedure": War Activities Report.
343 "You're going out": Roscoe, *U.S. Submarine Operations*, 81.
343 *S-39* Chebia Island mission: details from Roscoe, 81; Gugliotta, 143–46.
344 "We were sorry": quoted, Roscoe, 81.
345 The Cast group: Layton, 379.
346 "Previous directives": War Activities Report.
346 "any means": Layton, 379
347 Beach at demonstration: Beach, *Salt and Steel*, 59.
348 "we had to figure": Benson oral history, USNI.
348 "could not get": Benson oral history.
348 "But at my level": Benson oral history.
349 Exploder tests: Love, I, 614.
349 "so secret": Schratz oral history, USNI.
350 "magnetic type exploder": Orita and Harrington, 49.
350 "As it turned out": Coye oral history, USNI.
351 Wilkes discussion: War Activities Report.

353 "make a round trip": Blair, 250–51.
353 "instead of thanking us": Lockwood, *Down to the Sea*, 280.
354 "it must have been known": Lockwood, *Sink 'Em All*, 22.

Chapter 27: Submarines at Midway

355 "There were often gaps": W. J. Holmes, 86.
356 Nagumo quote: Morison, IV, 70.
356 Layton took the plan to Nimitz: Layton, 421.
356 The Midway plan has been widely discussed. See, for example, Holmes; Layton; Lord (*Incredible Victory*), Morison; E. B. Potter (*Nimitz*).
357 "areas that are to be rapidly occupied": quoted, Morison, IV, 6. See also Lewin, 84.
358 "it was obvious": Agawa, 202.
358 "otherwise unidentified": *Time*, June 1, 1942.
359 "need a lot of luck": Layton, 381.
359 "It's a disgrace": Agawa, 300.
360 "It would have been merciful": Layton (quoted from Pearl Harbor hearings), 300.
360 "Tell Nimitz": E. B. Potter, *Nimitz*, 23.
360 "He liked to say": Potter, 23.
360 Nimitz's lecture: Potter, 144.
360 Nimitz conversation with son: Potter, 1, and with wife, 12.
361 Nimitz's visit to Station Hypo: Holmes, 14; Potter, 77.
363 Shangri-la believed to be Midway: Morison, IV, 75.
363 "not that I'm expecting" and the *miso* incident: Agawa, 310.
365 The gulp: Lord, *Incredible Victory*, 34.
365 new freezer: Lord, 26.
366 "Now the strange thing": Benson oral history, USNI.
366 "great big German": Benson oral history.
367 "Breakfast?": Roscoe, *U.S. Submarine Operations*, 126.
368 "In keeping": Blair, *Silent Victory*, I, 87.
368 "like watching": Morison, IV, 103.
370 "ships all over": Benson oral history.
371 scene "never experienced": Brockman, quoted, Roscoe, 129.
371 Carrier spotted and following quotes: Benson oral history.
371 "There wasn't": Benson oral history.
371 "It was such": Morison, IV, 126.
372 Internal explosions: Lord, 297.
373 "with her loose gear": Morison, IV, 156.
374 "early information": Morison, IV, 156.
374 "I actually believe": *Life*, August 31, 1942.
375 "We should have made": Blair, 226.
375 Nimitz's instructions: quoted, Potter, 107.
375 Spruance and pilots: Buell, 147.
376 "it took an hour and a half": Cutter oral history, USNI.

Chapter 28: War Mission for the Giants

378 Plan Dog: Stark, memorandum for the president, November 12, 1940, FDRL. See discussion in Watson, 118–22.

378 "unprovoked and dastardly": Roosevelt, address to Congress, December 8, 1941; typescript of speech.

378 "our view remains": United States–British Chiefs of Staff, American-British Grand Strategy, December 31, 1941; PSF Safe File, Document No. 1, FDRL.

380 American plans more ambitious: Hayes, 141.

381 *faecaloid*: Morison, IV, 283.

381 Brockman's map: PSF: Makin, FDRL.

382 "with the ship sealed up" and "almost no distinguishing": Report of Task Group Commander (Haines), August 24, 1942, PSF, FDRL.

383 "The noise": Report of Task Group Commander.

383 "a most uneconomical": Report of Task Unit Commander (Carlson), August 21, 1942, PSF, FDRL.

383 "Everything lousy" and following quote: Roscoe, *Pigboats*, 160.

384 "considerable" and "no point": Report of Task Group Commander (Haines).

384 "provided a struggle" and following quote: Report of Task Unit Commander (Carlson).

385 Haines's recommendations from Report of Task Group Commander.

385 "The time limit" and following points: Report of Task Unit Commander (Carlson).

386 "Very pleased": S. E. Smith, 256.

Chapter 29: The Star and the Torpedoes

388 Kennedy quotes from Comsubpac Patrol Report No. 83, U.S.S. *Wahoo*—First War Patrol, November 1, 1942, NA. (*Note:* Quotes from patrol reports are the words of the submarine commander unless otherwise indicated.)

388 English comment: Comsubpac endorsement, Patrol Report No. 83.

388 "We're going": O'Kane, *Wahoo*, 60.

389 "pleasing Southern manner": O'Kane, 7.

389 Grider's comments: Grider, 22.

389 "his big hands" and "the tiny wardroom": Grider, 68.

390 "missed the really big game": Grider, quoted, *Owensboro Messenger-Inquirer*, n.d.

390 Sinking totals: assembled from Blair, *Silent Victory*, II, Appendix F, 875–96.

391 "did not promise": Hezlet, 212.

391 Descriptions of Morton: author's interview with Robert Rowe.

391 "might be just the thing" and following quote: Sterling, 50.

391 Morton's approach to discipline: Rowe interview.

392 "We will take": Sterling, 72.

392 "The officers acted": Sterling, 68.

392 "a natural-born leader": *Owensboro Messenger-Leader*, October 9, 1994.

392 "positive, intolerant": Paul Camplin (information from Rowe).

392 "a more or less": Patrol Report No. 83.

392 "A couple of months": Grider, 74.
393 "see what's there": quoted, Grider, 73.
393 instructors could record: point from O'Kane, 17.
393 "It was as if": Grider, 85.
393 "the only sensible thing": Grider, 82.
393 "That's all right": O'Kane, 138.
393 "I felt": Sterling, 81.
394 "a mighty roaring" and following quote: O'Kane, 139.
394 "To insure maximum" and following quote: Comsubpac Patrol Report No. 138, U.S.S. *Wahoo*—Third War Patrol, February 12, 1943, NA.
394 "sent them on their way": O'Kane, 142.
395 Attack on the convoy: Patrol Report No. 138.
395 "If either of those torpedoes": Grider, 107.
395 "Tenacity": O'Kane, 267.
396 "We just had": letter (February 1943) quoted in *Owensboro Messenger-Leader*, n.d., courtesy Robert Rowe.
396 "most aggressive manner": Patrol Report endorsement, February 12, 1943.
396 "an epic": Patrol Report endorsement, February 8, 1943.
397 Quotes from endorsements to Comsubpac Patrol Report No. 168, U.S.S. *Wahoo*—Fourth War Patrol, April 13, 1943, NA.
397 Quotes from endorsements to Combsubpac Patrol Report No. 184, U.S.S. *Wahoo*—Fifth War Patrol, May 29, 1943: Lockwood, May 29, 1943; squadron commander, May 22, 1943.
398 "reported the thud": Patrol Report No. 184.
398 "Sunshine": Murray oral history, USNI.
399 oily dollar bill: author's interview with Emerson Grossman.
399 Triebel letter: Cutter oral history, USNI.
399 touching up torpedoes: Bill Hagendorn, "The Torpedoes of WWII," *The Silent Service*, A&E Television.
400 "barely got out": Ward oral history, USNI.
400 Dönitz quote: Dönitz, 97.
400 "Damn the torpedoes": Comsubpac Patrol Report No. 246, U.S.S. *Wahoo*—Sixth War Patrol, September 8, 1943.
400 "Mush was boiling mad": Lockwood, *Sink 'Em All*, 117.
400 "torpedo spreads": Lockwood, Patrol Report, endorsement.
401 "We were the only navy": Cutter oral history.
401 "We found": Coye oral history, USNI.
401 "acceptable, safe": Lockwood, *Down to the Sea*, 294.
402 Lockwood to Midway: Cutter oral history.
403 "It just didn't seem": Lockwood, *Sink 'Em All*, 131.

Chapter 30: Medals of Honor

404 *Parche* facts: Chronological History (Hall collection).
404 Background information on Hall: author's interviews.
404 "I had a cousin": *Monadnock Home Companion*, July 25, 1997.
405 "Our lives": Carter, 55.
406 "those of us": Ramage oral history, NA.

406 "I clinked him": Ramage oral history.
406 Ramage and Christie: Ramage oral history.
408 Peterson and Ramage planning: Ramage oral history.
408 Ramage log entry: Patrol Report, NA.
408 Details of attack from *Parche* Ship History, *U.S. Submarine Veterans, World War II*; tonnage from Blair, *Silent Victory*, II, 572.
408 "when four of these": Patrol Report.
409 "a perfect example": Patrol Report, endorsement.
409 Peterson "would take any suggestions": Ramage oral history.
409 Comments about Parks: Ramage oral history.
409 "togetherness": from questionnaire sent to *Parche* veterans (Bob Hall).
410 Hall and mush: Hall interviews.
410 Wolf pack names: Ramage oral history.
410 "our so-called wolf pack": Ramage oral history.
411 "a hell of a mood": Farrell and Wilbur Cross, "Ramage's Remarkable Rampage," undated clipping, *True*.
411 "it finally dawned": Patrol Report.
411 Reloading torpedoes: Patrol Report.
412 Ramage's Rampage: Hall interviews; Patrol Report; Farrell and Wilbur Cross.
412 "We were so close": *Monadnock Home Companion*, July 25, 1997.
412 "small fast job": Patrol Report.
412 "Set course": Farrell and Wilbur Cross.
413 "I got mad": Roscoe, *U.S. Submarine Operations*, 346.
413 "one of the outstanding actions": Patrol Report, endorsement.
413 "In the mounting fury": Medal of Honor citation.
413 Description of FDR: interview of Ramage by Bob Hall and Joe Caruso, July 27, 1987.
413 "with their up-to-date radar": Young, 321–22.
414 "she performed": O'Kane, *Clear the Bridge*, 27.
414 "Just the knowledge": Roscoe, 465.
415 Lifeguarding details: Roscoe, 472–74.
415 "fixed [him] up": Bush, p. 50.
416 *Tang*'s first sinking: O'Kane, 77–82.
416 "one of the lustiest": story reproduced in O'Kane, 176.
417 "a mess of ships": O'Kane, 221.
417 *Tang* confirmed patrol figures: Blair, Appendix I.
418 "ferocious free-for-all": Roscoe, 420.
418 Sinking of *Tang*: O'Kane, 456, and Patrol Report.
418 "this patrol": Patrol Report, endorsement.
420 "a great mushroom": Medal of Honor citation.
420 *Archerfish* patrol details: Patrol Report.
422 Sinking totals: In its review of operations, the joint Army-Navy Assessment Committee (JANAC) slashed Lockwood's totals, as it also reduced figures from individual patrols, though the new figures may have understated the total somewhat. In any case, while cutting the number of ships sunk from 4,000 to about 1,300, JANAC reduced the tonnage by about half.
423 Destroyer out of fuel: eyewitness account by *Bashaw* veteran, author's interview.

425 *Part epigraph*: Talbott quoted in Kuenne, 177.

Chapter 31: Toward the True Submarine

427 Quotes from *New York Times*, June 15, 1952; details of the ceremony from the *Times* and the Associated Press, same date.
430 "The postwar Navy": Carter, 50.
431 "start an aggressive campaign": quoted, Parrish, *Cold War Encyclopedia*, 267.
432 Allies' study of German submarines and development of the GUPPY program: well discussed in Weir, *Forged in War*, Chap. 5.
435 "He told me he'd do it": Lockwood, *Down to the Sea*, 347. Along with Weir, Chap. 25 is an important source of information about the early nuclear era, and with personal touches. See also Blair, *Atomic Submarine*.
435 "If I live": Lockwood, 348.
435 Quotes from Abelson from his paper read at the March 28, 1946, meeting; Lockwood, 348–49.
437 Mills let two contracts: Weir, 160.
437 "Captain Rickover did not particularly relish": Mills interview, quoted by Lockwood, 350.
438 "overhauling the machinery": Beach, *Salt and Steel*, 181.
439 "arrived looking for trouble": Burke oral history, USNI.
439 "four years of grind": *New York Times*, July 9, 1986.
439 "may have hoped" and following quote: Beach, 180.
440 Removing lightbulb: Beach, 180.
440 "legacy of fear": Edwards oral history, USNI; Rickover discussed, 182–85.
440 "We were all aware": Beach, 182.
440 "not the best": Robert L. Moore, quoted, Weir, 166.
440 Rickover's inspections: Hewlett, 32.

Chapter 32: "The Price That Would Be Paid"

442 The subjects "ranged from the metallurgical": Rockwell, 41. For all aspects of Rickover, see Polmar and Allen.
442 "There's nobody" and following quote: Rockwell, 46.
444 nominee "would out-work" and following quote: Hewlett and Duncan, 76.
445 Rickover and Dunford: Rockwell, 45.
446 "learn how the Navy operates": Charles Morse Slack, unpublished memoirs, 1964, SFL. All material from Slack from this source.
447 "carefully attending": James Wilson, 185.
448 "The only thing wrong": quoted, Rudy Abramson, *Los Angeles Times*, February 26, 1977.
448 Rickover used obnoxious behavior: Cutter oral history, USNI.
448 Rickover and Murray: Murray oral history, USNI.
449 "blackjacked into keeping": Abramson.
449 Rickover "could now move": Hewlett, *Nuclear Navy*, 193.
450 Description of Electric Boat yard: *New York Times*, January 22, 1954.
450 "Nautilus will probably appear": Rodengen, 111.

450 "hungry to put her": *New York Times*, January 22, 1954.

451 Beach and the ceremony: Beach, *Salt and Steel*, 232–36.

451 "As the champagne frothed": Associated Press, January 22, 1954.

451 UNDER WAY: Rockwell, 190.

452 "I didn't know": Anderson, 20.

453 "You can't concentrate": Jim Dunford, quoted, Rockwell, 3.

453 The street cleaner: This anecdote is recounted by Anderson and various other persons who dealt with Rickover.

453 Goat Mountain: Rockwell, 4.

454 "Goddamn, I told you": Abramson.

454 Young man from Naval Academy: Drew and Sontag, 82.

454 "motive-hunting": This classic description of Iago's actions was delivered by the famous Harvard Shakespeare scholar George Lyman Kittredge.

454 "He is unusually hard": quoted, Abramson.

454 Stone material from interview and his written account.

455 "Sure he has driven": Abramson.

455 Rickover's driving power: author's interview with Rockwell.

455 "When a difficult": Stone e-mail message, December 31, 2002.

455 "I was saturated": Carter, 63–64.

456 Anderson's suspicions: Anderson, 20–22

456 Rickover's office and following details: author's interview with Anderson.

456 Rickover's process of digging: point made by Rockwell, interview.

456 The cat search and following quotes: Anderson interview.

457 Sputnik I "a neat technical trick": Parrish, *Cold War Encyclopedia*, 291.

457 NAUTILUS: hence Anderson's book title, *Nautilus 90 North*.

458 "just four or five" and following quotes: Anderson interview.

458 "I'm really quite moved": quoted, Rockwell, 250.

458 "really sweet": Rockwell quoted, interview by Rudy Abramson, January 15, 1997.

459 "No, indeed": Beach, "Warship," pbs.org/wnet/warship. See also Beach, *Around the World Submerged*; Beach interview, "We'll Go Around the World," *Naval History*, February 2003.

459 "Of all the things": Beach, *Around the World Submerged*, 282.

459 Khrushchev speech: Scott and Scott, 161.

461 Development had come five years earlier: Anderson interview.

461 Mumma believed that Mills had erred: Mumma oral history, USNI.

461 Mills expressed regret: Craven, 186.

Chapter 33: Admiral Burke Makes a Choice

462 "pictured Burke": E. B. Potter, *Admiral Arleigh Burke*. Potter's account corrects the long-believed story.

463 "the navy was too slow" and all other quotes: Burke oral history, USNI.

465 "nobody outside of the navy": Burke oral history.

466 Navy discussions with the army: Sapolsky, 21–23.

467 Soviet developments: Some points from Rohwer, *Superpower Confrontation*, 41–42.

468   a messiah: Burns, 193.
468   "It was my dream": Raborn oral history, USNI.
469   "I took it on myself" and following quote: Raborn oral history.
469   "Those fellows": Raborn oral history.
470   Raborn and gunnery: Raborn oral history; Baar and Howard, 86.
470   "men will work": Baar and Howard, 86.
471   "If this thing works": Burke oral history.
471   "summarily jerked" and following quote: Raborn oral history.
472   "He was appointed": Joseph L. Pires, U.S.S. *Bennington*, "Commanding Officers," www.uss-bennington.org.
472   Thomas-Burke letter: Baar and Howard, 86.
473   "You use that authority": Burke oral history.
473   Rickover opposed to FBM: Vincent Davis, cited by Polmar and Allen, 537.
473   "every time": Baar and Howard, 36.
474   "by a hell of a lot": quoted, Burns, 195.
474   "Put your hand": Baar and Howard, 43.
474   Raborn and Craven: Craven, 66.
475   "find the single": Burns, 196.
475   "He picked the best": Burns, 197.
475   "he still knew how to get": Weschler oral history, USNI.
475   "His program got hot": Burns, 197.
475   navy accountant: Sapolsky, 45.
475   "One of the reasons": Baar and Howard, 96.

Chapter 34: The Reign of the Boomers

476   "Conceivably": Raborn oral history, USNI.
477   "Why use a 1958 warhead": Teller, quoted, Sapolsky, 30.
477   Proceed with solid-fuel IRBM: history of the Jupiter Missile System, redstone.army.mil/history, 35.
477   "Well, Admiral": quoted, Raborn oral history.
477   "We came up with" and following quotes: Raborn oral history.
478   Merrill quotes: Merrill oral history, USNI.
478   "bureaucratic and programmatic": Sapolsky, 1.
479   "The phenomenal abilities": Burns, 221.
479   German naval historian: Rohwer, *Superpower Confrontation*, 46.
479   "They took ten miracles": Weschler oral history, USNI.
480   official statement: "Apocalypse Below," by the editors of the *Navy Times*, in Icenhower, 171.
481   "the world's best medium": Raborn oral history.
481   "soft-spoken, silver-haired": Icenhower, 172.
481   "a skilled and aggressive": from citation for Navy Cross.
481   "wholeheartedly accept": Icenhower, 173.
481   "conventional war": Raborn oral history.
482   Four developments: This point is succinctly made by Winkler, 27.
482   "With the help": Scott and Scott, 163.
482   "The creation": quoted, Scott and Scott, 163.

483 "a bitter, vicious fight": Dalgliesh and Schweikart, 3.
484 "What in Christ's name": quoted, Rudy Abramson, *Los Angeles Times*, February 26, 1977.
484 "both understanding": Abramson.
484 "Mr. Chairman": Abramson.
485 "just sits there": Abramson.
485 "just simply was a discredit": Edwards oral history, USNI.
485 Rickover and "trinkets": Tyler, 3–4.
486 "weaker Soviet technological level": Fieldhouse and Taoka, 54.
488 "third-most-powerful": *Modern Marvels*, History Channel, August 8, 2001.
489 "We're a big family": *Modern Marvels*.
489 "The nuclear-trained people": author's interview with Jon Tronc.

Chapter 35: Killers, Spies, and Tragedies

491 For details of the loss of the *Thresher*, see Bentley; Robert Gannon, *Reader's Digest*, May 1964; and the extensive coverage in newspapers and newsweeklies.
492 "To those of us": quoted, Gannon.
492 Background of the *Thresher* and her class: Hewlett and Duncan, Chap. 2, and Bentley, Chap. 6.
493 Heedlessness and sloppiness: details in *Time*, May 3, 1963.
494 Rickover quotes: *U.S. News and World Report*, January 18, 1965.
494 James on Rickover: James oral history, USNI.
494 Rickover reduces time lag: James oral history.
495 SPO funding: Sapolsky, 191.
496 *Seawolf* described: Admiral Bruce DeMars, quoted, Harris, 373, 375.
497 The *Virginia*-class attack submarines: press releases, General Dynamics, August 2003.
498 men "either drowned or were crushed": *Time*, February 9, 1968.
500 the problem lay in batteries: Drew and Sontag, Chap. 5.
500 *Glomar Explorer*: Parrish, *Cold War Encyclopedia*, 116.
501 Transformation of the *Halibut*: Craven, 135.
502 "the Glomar project": Parrish, 116.
502 "Bombs can be very different": Parrish, 116–17.
502 Information on the Okhotsk operation from Drew and Sontag and numerous follow-up stories in the press.
505 Preparation of reports: *New York Times*, July 6, 1975.
506 "an accident": Peter Huchthausen, *New York Times*, August 16, 2000.
506 Details of the *Kursk* disaster come from the *New York Times*; the Associated Press; *Time; Newsweek;* Jeff Wise in *Maxim* (December 2000); Burleson.
508 Kolesnikov quotes: Associated Press, November 3, 2000.
508 Motsak quote: *New York Times*, August 20, 2000.
509 "bond of camaraderie": Carlisle A. H. Trost, *New York Times*, August 20, 2000.
509 "the U-boat attack": Churchill, IV, 125.
510 Christopher Chant suggested that missile submarines could perform the "excision of 'loose cannon' " warfare capability (Chant, 115).

Epilogue: On Eternal Patrol

The material here comes from attendance at the 2000 convention of the Submarine Veterans of World War II, in St. Louis; from conversations; and from the printed program.

BIBLIOGRAPHY

This listing of sources includes only full-length books. All other materials—interviews, oral histories, documents, articles—are cited in full at the relevant points in the Notes.

Abbot, Willis J. *The Nations at War*. New York: Leslie Judge Co., 1918.

Abrams, Ray H. *Preachers Present Arms*. New York: Round Table Press, 1933.

Agawa, Hiroyuki. *The Reluctant Admiral: Yamamoto and the Imperial Navy*. Tokyo: Kodansha International, 1969.

Alaluquetas, Jacques. *Un loup gris dans l'Atlantique*. Paris: Jacques Grancher, 1999.

Anderson, William R., with Clay Blair, Jr. *Nautilus 90 North*. New York: World, 1959.

Antier, Jean-Jacques. *Les grandes batailles navales de la Seconde Guerre mondiale*. Paris: Omnibus, 2000.

Auchincloss, Louis. *Woodrow Wilson*. New York: Viking, 2000.

Baar, James, and William E. Howard. *Polaris!* New York: Harcourt Brace, 1960.

Bagnasco, Erminio. *Submarines of World War Two*. London: Cassell, 1973.

Bailey, Thomas A., and Paul B. Ryan. *The Lusitania Disaster*. New York: Free Press, 1975.

Baker, Ray Stannard. *Woodrow Wilson: Life and Letters*. 8 vols. Garden City, N.Y.: Doubleday, Page, 1927–1939.

Balfour, Michael. *The Kaiser and His Times*. New York: Norton, 1972.

Barker, Anthony J., and Lisa Jackson. *Fleeting Attraction: A Social History of American Servicemen in Western Australia During the Second World War*. Nedlands: University of Western Australia Press, 1996.

Barnett, Correlli. *The Swordbearers*. New York: William Morrow, 1964.

Beach, Edward L. *Around the World Submerged*. Annapolis: Naval Institute Press, 1962.

———. *Run Silent, Run Deep*. New York: Henry Holt, 1955.

———. *Salt and Steel: Reflections of a Submariner*. Annapolis: Naval Institute Press, 1999.

———. *Submarine!* New York: Henry Holt, 1952.

———. *The U.S. Navy: 200 Years*. New York: Henry Holt, 1986.

Beasant, John. *Stalin's Silver*. London: Bloomsbury, 1995.

Beaufort, J. M. de. *Behind the German Veil*. New York: Dodd, Mead, 1918.

Beesly, Patrick. *Very Special Intelligence*. Garden City, N.Y.: Doubleday, 1977; Ballantine edition, 1981.

Bekker, Cajus. *Defeat at Sea. The Struggle and Eventual Destruction of the German Navy, 1939–1945*. New York: Ballantine, 1955.

————. *Hitler's Naval War.* Garden City, N.Y.: Doubleday, 1974.

Bennett, Geoffrey. *Naval Battles of World War II.* London: B. T. Batsford, 1975.

Bentley, John. *The Thresher Disaster.* Garden City, N.Y.: Doubleday, 1975.

Bernstorff, Johann von. *My Three Years in America.* New York: Scribner, 1920.

Birnbaum, Karl E. *Peace Moves and U-Boat History.* Trans. Albert Read. New York: Archon, 1970; original Swedish edition, Almqvist & Wiksell, 1958.

Blackburn, Glenn. *The West and the World Since 1945.* 3rd ed. New York: St. Martin's Press, 1993.

Blair, Clay. *The Atomic Submarine and Admiral Rickover.* New York: Henry Holt, 1954.

————. *Hitler's U-Boat War.* 2 vols. New York: Random House, 1996.

————. *Silent Victory.* 2 vols. Philadelphia: J. B. Lippincott, 1975.

Blond, Georges. *Admiral Togo.* Trans. Edward Hymans. New York: Macmillan, 1960.

Blum, John Morton. *The Progressive Presidents.* New York: Norton, 1980.

Boatner, Mark M., III. *The Biographical Dictionary of World War II.* Novato, Calif.: Presidio Press, 1996.

Bosworth, Allan R. *My Love Affair with the Navy.* New York: Norton, 1969.

Boyne, Walter J. *Clash of Wings: Air Power in World War II.* New York: Simon and Schuster, 1994.

Brézet, François-Emmanuel. *Histoire de la marine allemande, 1939–1945.* Paris: Perrin, 1999

Broad, William J. *The Universe Below: Discovering the Secrets of the Deep.* New York: Simon and Schuster, 1997.

Brodie, Bernard. *A Layman's Guide to Naval Strategy.* Princeton: Princeton University Press, 1943.

Brown, Archie, ed. *The Soviet Union: A Biographical Dictionary.* New York: Macmillan, 1990.

Buell, Thomas B. *The Quiet Warrior* [Raymond A. Spruance]. Boston: Little, Brown, 1974.

Burg, David F., and L. Edward Purcell. *Almanac of World War I.* Lexington: University Press of Kentucky, 1998.

Burns, Thomas S. *The Secret War for the Ocean Depths: Soviet-American Rivalry for the Mastery of the Seas.* New York: Rawson Associates, 1978.

Busch, Harold. *U-Boats at War: German Submarines in Action 1939–1945.* New York: Ballantine, 1955.

Bush, George. *All the Best.* New York, Scribner, 1999.

Butler, John A. *Sailing on Friday: The Perilous Voyage of America's Merchant Marine.* Washington, D.C.: Brassey's, 1997.

Calvert, James F. *Silent Running: My Years on a World War II Attack Submarine.* New York: John Wiley, 1995.

Carse, Robert. *The Long Haul: The United States Merchant Service in World War II.* New York: Norton, 1965.

Carter, Jimmy. *Why Not the Best?* Nashville: Broadman Press, 1975; Bantam ed., 1976.

Chalmers, W. S. *Max Horton and the Western Approaches.* London: Hodder and Stoughton, 1954.

Chant, Christopher. *Submarines of the 20th Century.* London: Tiger Books International, 1996.

Churchill, Winston S. *The Second World War.* 6 vols. Boston: Houghton Mifflin, 1948–53.

————. *The World Crisis.* 5 vols. New York: Scribner, 1923–29.

Clancy, Tom. *The Hunt for Red October.* New York: Berkley, 1984.

―――. *SSN.* New York: Berkley, 1996.

―――. *Submarine.* New York, Berkley, 1993.

Clark, Ronald W. *Tizard.* Cambridge: M.I.T. Press, 1965.

Cline, Rick. *Submarine Grayback: The Life and Death of the World War II Sub USS Grayback.* Placentia, Calif.: R. A. Cline Publishing, 1999.

Coggins, Jack. *Prepare to Dive: The Story of Man Undersea.* New York: Dodd, Mead, 1971.

Coletta, Paola E. *Sea Power in the Atlantic and Mediterranean in World War I.* Lanham, Md.: University Press of America, 1989.

Collier, Basil. *The War in the Far East: 1941–1945.* New York: William Morrow, 1969.

Compton-Hall, Richard. *Submarine Boats.* New York: Arco, 1984.

―――. *Submarine Warfare: Monsters and Midgets.* Poole, Dorset, England: Blandford Press, 1985.

Conner, Claude C. *Nothing Friendly in the Vicinity: My Patrols on the Submarine USS Guardfish During World War II.* Mason City, Iowa: Sayas Publishing, 1999.

Connolly, James B. *The U-Boat Hunters.* New York: Scribner, 1918.

Coolidge, Archibald Cary. *The Origins of the Triple Alliance.* 2nd ed. New York: Scribner, 1926.

Cooper, John Milton, Jr., *The Warrior and the Priest.* Cambridge: Belknap/Harvard University Press, 1983.

Craven, John Piña. *The Silent War.* New York: Simon and Schuster, 2001.

Crawford, Steve. *Battleships and Carriers.* New York: Barnes and Noble, 1999.

Cremer, Peter. *U333: The Story of a U-Boat Ace.* London: Bodley Head, 1984.

Crowther, J. G. *Statesmen of Science.* London, Cresset Press, 1965.

Curtin, D. Thomas. *The Land of Deepening Shadow: Germany at War.* New York: George H. Doran, 1917.

Cutler, Thomas J. *The Battle of Leyte Gulf: 23–26 October 1944.* Annapolis: Naval Institute Press, 1994.

Dalgleish, D. Douglas, and Larry Schweikart. *Trident.* Carbondale: Southern Illinois University Press, 1984.

Davis, Arthur N. *The Kaiser as I Know Him.* New York: Harper, 1918.

Davis, George. *A Navy Second to None.* New York: Harcourt Brace, 1940.

Deacon, Richard. *A History of British Secret Service.* London: Frederick Muller, 1969; Granada ed., 1980.

D'Este, Carlo. *World War II in the Mediterranean.* Chapel Hill, N.C.: Algonquin, 1990.

Dönitz, Karl. *Memoirs: Ten Years and Twenty Days.* Trans. R. H. Stevens and David Woodward. London: Weidenfeld and Nicolson, 1959; Leisure Books paperback ed., n.d.

Dornberg, John. *Brezhnev: The Masks of Power.* New York: Basic Books, 1974.

Drew, Christopher, and Sherry Sontag. *Blind Man's Bluff.* New York: Harper Paperbacks, 1998.

Dunham, Roger C. *Spy Sub: Top Secret Mission on the Bottom of the Pacific.* New York: Penguin, 1996.

Eden, Anthony (Earl of Avon). *Facing the Dictators.* Boston: Houghton Mifflin, 1962.

Edwards, Bernard. *Dönitz and the Wolfpacks.* London: Brockhampton Press, 1999.

Enright, Joseph F., with James W. Ryan. *Sea Assault.* New York: St. Martin's Press, 1997.

Falls, Cyril. *A Hundred Years of War.* New York: Macmillan, 1953; Collier Books ed., 1962.

Farago, Ladislas. *The Tenth Fleet.* New York: Ivan Obolensky, 1962; Paperback Library ed., 1964.

Fayle, C. Ernest. *Seaborne Trade.* 3 vols. New York: Longmans, Green, 1920–24.

Ferrell, Robert H. *Woodrow Wilson and World War I.* New York: Harper and Row, 1985.

Ferro, Marc. *The Great War 1914–1918.* London: Ark Paperbacks, 1973.

Fetridge, William Harrison. *The Second Navy Reader.* Indianapolis: Bobbs-Merrill, 1944.

Fieldhouse, Richard, and Shunji Taoka. *Superpowers at Sea: An Assessment of the Naval Arms Race.* Oxford: Oxford University Press, 1989.

Foerster, Schuyler, and Edward N. Wright, eds. *American Defense Policy.* 6th ed. Baltimore: Johns Hopkins University Press, 1965.

Ford, Ken S. *St. Nazaire 1942: The Great Commando Raid.* London: Osprey, 2001.

Forester, C. S. *The Good Shepherd.* Boston: Little, Brown, 1955.

Frank, Wolfgang. *The Sea Wolves.* New York: Rinehart, 1955; Ballantine ed., n.d.

Franks, Norman. *Dark Sky, Deep Water: Firsthand Reflections on the Anti–U-Boat War in World War II.* London: Grub Street, 1997.

Fürbinger, Werner. *Fips.* Annapolis: Naval Institute Press, 1999.

Fussell, Paul. *The Great War and Modern Memory.* New York: Oxford University Press, 1975.

Gallagher, Thomas. *The X-Craft Raid.* New York: Harcourt Brace Jovanovich, 1971.

Gannett, Lewis. *I Saw It Happen: Eye-Witness Accounts of the War.* New York: Pocket Books, 1942.

Gannon, Michael. *Black May.* New York: HarperCollins, 1998.

———. *Operation Drumbeat.* New York: Harper and Row, 1990.

Garraty, John A. *Woodrow Wilson.* New York: Harper and Row, 1956; Perennial Library ed., 1970.

Gauss, Christian. *Why We Went to War.* New York: Scribner, 1919.

George, Alexander L., and Juliette L. George. *Woodrow Wilson and Colonel House.* New York: John Day, 1956.

George, James L. *The U.S. Navy in the 1990s.* Annapolis: Naval Institute Press, 1992.

Gerard, James W. *Face to Face with Kaiserism.* New York: George H. Doran, 1918.

———. *My Four Years in Germany.* New York: George H. Doran, 1917.

Gill, Charles Clifford. *Naval Power in the War: 1914–1918.* New York: George H. Doran, 1918.

Goldrick, James. *The King's Ships Were at Sea.* Annapolis: Naval Institute Press, 1984.

Gray, Colin S. *The Leverage of Sea Power.* New York: Macmillan, 1992.

———. *War, Peace and Victory:* New York: Simon and Schuster, 1990.

Gray, Edwyn. *The Killing Time.* New York: Scribner, 1972.

Gregory, Ross. *Walter Hines Page: Ambassador to the Court of St. James's.* Lexington: University Press of Kentucky, 1970.

Grey of Fallodon, Viscount. *Twenty-Five Years.* 3 vols. London: Hodder and Stoughton, 1928.

Grider, George, as told to Lydel Sims. *War Fish.* Boston: Little, Brown, 1958.

Groves, P. R. C. *Behind the Smoke Screen.* London: Faber and Faber, 1934.

Gugliotta, Bobette. *Pigboat 39.* Lexington: University Press of Kentucky, 1984.

Gunther, John. *The Riddle of MacArthur.* New York: Harper and Row, 1951.

Hague, Arnold. *The Allied Convoy System, 1939–1945.* St. Catherines, Ontario: Van-well Publishing, 2000.
Hale, Oron J. *The Great Illusion: 1900–1914.* New York: Harper and Row, 1971.
Halsey, Francis W. *Balfour, Viviani, and Joffre.* New York: Funk and Wagnalls, 1917.
Harris, Brayton. *The Navy Times Book of Submarines.* New York: Berkley, 1997.
Hashagen, Ernst. *U-Boats Westward!* New York: Putnam, 1931.
Hayes, Grace Person. *The History of the Joint Chiefs of Staff in World War II: The War Against Japan.* Annapolis: Naval Institute Press, 1982.
Herken, Gregg. *Counsels of War.* New York: Alfred A. Knopf, 1985.
Hewlett, Richard G., and Francis Duncan. *Nuclear Navy, 1946–1962.* Chicago: University of Chicago Press, 1974.
Hezlet, Sir Arthur. *The Submarine and Sea Power.* New York: Stein and Day, 1967.
Hickam, Homer H. *Torpedo Junction.* New York: Dell, 1989.
Hickey, Des, and Gus Smith. *Seven Days to Disaster.* New York: Putnam, 1981.
Hinsley, Francis Harry, with E. E. Thomas, C. F. G. Ransom, and R. C. Knight. *British Intelligence in the Second World War.* 5 vols. New York: Cambridge University Press, 1979–88.
Hinsley, F. H., and Alan Stripp, eds. *Codebreakers: The Story of Bletchley Park.* Oxford: Oxford University Press, 1993.
Höhne, Heinz. *Canaris: Hitler's Master Spy.* Garden City, N.Y.: Doubleday, 1979.
Holmes, Harry. *The Last Patrol.* London: Airlife Publishing, 1997.
Holmes, W. J. *Double-Edged Secrets.* Annapolis: Naval Institute Press, 1979.
Homewood, Harry. *Torpedo!* New York: McGraw-Hill, 1982; Bantam ed., 1984.
Howard, Joseph. *Our Modern Navy.* Princeton: D. Van Nostrand Company, 1961.
Hoyt, Edwin P. *The Lonely Ships: The Life and Death of the U.S. Asiatic Fleet.* Los Angeles: Pinnacle Books, 1976.
———. *U-Boats Offshore.* New York: Stein and Day, 1978.
———. *War in the Deep.* New York: Putnam, 1978.
Hutcheon, Wallace, Jr. *Robert Fulton.* Annapolis: Naval Institute Press, 1981.
Hythe, Viscount, ed. *The Naval Annual, 1913.* London: J. Griffin & Co., 1913; David & Charles reprint, 1970.
Icenhower, Joseph B. *Submarines in Combat.* New York: Franklin Watts, 1964.
Irving, David. *The Destruction of Convoy PQ. 17.* New York: Simon and Schuster, 1968.
Jackson, Robert. *Submarines of the World.* New York: Barnes and Noble, 2000.
Jones, Reginald Victor. *The Wizard War.* New York: Coward, McCann, and Geoghegan, 1978.
Kahn, David. *Seizing the Enigma.* Boston: Houghton Mifflin, 1991.
Karp, Walter. *The Politics of War.* New York: Harper and Row, 1979.
Keegan, John. *The Price of Admiralty.* New York: Viking, 1989.
———. *The Second World War.* New York: Viking, 1989.
Kemp, Paul. *Convoy: Drama in Arctic Waters.* London: Arms and Armour, 1993; Cassell Military Paperbacks ed., 2000.
———. *Submarine Action.* London: Sutton Publishing, 1999.
Kemp, Peter. *Decision at Sea: The Convoy Escorts.* New York: Elsevier-Dutton, 1978.
———. *Key to Victory.* Boston: Little, Brown, 1957.
Kennan, George F. *American Diplomacy 1900–1950.* Chicago: University of Chicago Press, 1951; New American Library ed., 1951.
Kennedy, Paul, ed. *Grand Strategies in War and Peace.* New Haven: Yale University Press, 1991.

Kimmett, Larry, and Margaret Regis. *United States Submarines in World War II*. Seattle: Navigator Publishing, 1996.

Kolyshkin, I. *Russian Submarines in Arctic Waters*. New York: Bantam, 1985.

König, Paul. *Die Fahrt der Deutschland*. Berlin: Ullstein, 1916.

Kuenne, Robert E. *The Attack Submarine: A Study in Strategy*. New Haven: Yale University Press, 1965.

Lafore, Laurence. *The Long Fuse*. Philadelphia: Lippincott, 1971.

Langer, William L., and S. Everett Gleason. *The Undeclared War*. New York: Harper, 1953.

Langsam, Walter C. *The World Since 1914*. New York: Macmillan, 1933.

Lawliss, Chuck. *The Submarine Book: An Illustrated History of the Attack Submarine*. Short Hills, N.J.: Burford Books, 1991.

Layton, Edwin T., Roger Pineau, and John Costello. *And I Was There: Pearl Harbor and Midway—Breaking the Secrets*. New York: William Morrow, 1985.

Leasor, James. *Singapore*. Garden City, N.Y.: Doubleday, 1968.

Lefebure, Victor. *Scientific Disarmament*. London, 1931.

Legg, Stuart, ed. *Jutland*. New York: John Day, 1967.

Levering, Ralph B. *The Cold War 1945–1972*. Arlington Heights, Ill.: Harlan Davidson, 1982.

Lewin, Ronald. *The American Magic*. New York: Farrar Straus Giroux, 1982.

Lewis, Eugene. *Public Entrepreneurship*. Bloomington: Indiana University Press, 1980.

Leyland, John. *The Achievement of the British Navy in the World War*. New York: George H. Doran, n.d.

Liddell Hart, Sir Basil. *History of the Second World War*. New York: Putnam, 1970.

———. *The Sword and the Pen*. New York: Thomas Y. Crowell, 1976.

Lindley, John M. *Carrier Victory: The Air War in the Pacific*. New York: Elsevier-Dutton, 1978.

Link, Arthur S. *Wilson*. 5 vols. Princeton: Princeton University Press, 1947–1965.

———. *Wilson the Diplomatist*. Baltimore: Johns Hopkins University Press, 1957.

Lloyd, Nelson. *How We Went to War*. New York: Scribner, 1919.

Lockwood, Charles A. *Down to the Sea in Subs*. New York: Norton, 1967.

———. *Sink 'Em All: Submarine Warfare in the Pacific*. New York: Dutton, 1951.

Lord, Walter. *Day of Infamy*. New York: Henry Holt, 1957.

———. *Incredible Victory*. New York: Harper and Row, 1967.

Love, Robert W. Jr. *History of the United States Navy*. 2 vols. Harrisburg, Pa.: Stackpole, 1992.

Lutz, Hermann. *Lord Grey and the World War*. Trans. E. W. Dickes. New York: Alfred A. Knopf, 1928.

Lyon, Hugh. *Modern Warships*. New York: Arco, 1980.

Macintyre, Donald. *Battle of the Atlantic, 1939–1945*. London: Lutterworth, 1970.

———. *The Naval War Against Hitler*. New York: Scribner, 1971.

———. *U-Boat Killer*. Annapolis: Naval Institute Press, 1956.

Macksey, Kenneth. *Military Errors of World War II*. London: Cassell, 1987.

Mahan, Alfred Thayer. *The Influence of Sea Power upon the French Revolution and Empire, 1793–1812*. Boston: Little, Brown, 1893.

———. *The Influence of Sea Power upon History, 1660–1783*. London: University Paperbacks, 1965. (Original pub., Little, Brown, 1890.)

Maloney, Sean M. *Securing Command of the Sea: NATO Naval Planning 1948–1954.* Annapolis: Naval Institute Press, 1995.

Manchester, William. *American Caesar.* Boston: Little, Brown, 1978; Dell ed., 1979.

Marder, Arthur J. *From the Dreadnought to Scapa Flow: The Royal Navy in the Fisher Era, 1904–1919.* 5 vols. London: Oxford University Press, 1961–70. (Vol. III, 2nd ed., 1978.)

Martel, Gordon. *The Origins of the First World War.* 2nd ed. London: Longman, 1996.

Mason, David. *U-Boat: The Secret Menace.* New York: Ballantine, 1968.

May, Ernest. *The World War and American Isolation 1914–1917.* Chicago: Quadrangle Paperbacks, 1959.

McCants, William R. *War Patrols of the USS Flasher.* Chapel Hill, N.C.: Professional Press, 1994.

McGruther, Kenneth R. *The Evolving Soviet Navy.* Newport, R.I.: Naval War College Press, 1978.

Members of the Department of English, History, and Government, United States Naval Academy. *American Sea Power Since 1775.* Chicago: J. B. Lippincott, 1947.

Middlebrook, Martin. *Convoy.* New York: William Morrow, 1976.

Middleton, Drew. *Submarine: The Ultimate Naval Weapon.* Chicago: Playboy Press, 1976.

Miller, David. *U-Boats: The Illustrated History of the Raiders of the Deep.* Washington, D.C.: Brassey's, 2000.

Miller, Nathan. *War at Sea: A Naval History of World War II.* New York: Simon and Schuster, 1995.

Miller, T. Rothrock. *A Ship Without a Name.* New York: Vintage Press, 1992.

Milton, Keith. *Subs Against the Rising Sun.* Las Cruces, N.Mex.: Yucca Tree Press, 2000.

Mitchell, Donald W. *A History of Russian and Soviet Sea Power.* New York: Macmillan, 1974.

Monsarrat, Nicholas. *The Cruel Sea.* New York: Alfred A. Knopf, 1951.

Montagnon, Pierre. *La Grande Histoire de la Seconde Guerre Mondiale.* Vol. I. Paris: Pygmalion, 1999.

Morgan, Ted. *FDR: A Biography.* New York: Simon and Schuster, 1984.

Morison, Samuel Eliot. *History of United States Naval Operations in World War II.* 15 vols. Boston: Little, Brown, 1947–62.

Morris, Richard Knowles. *John P. Holland.* Columbia: University of South Carolina Press, 1998. (Original ed., United States Naval Institute, 1966.)

Morton, Louis. *The Fall of the Philippines.* Washington, D.C.: Office of the Chief of Military History, Department of the Army, 1953.

Moyer, Laurence. *Victory Must Be Ours: Germany in the Great War 1914–1918.* New York: Hippocrene Books, 1995.

Muracciole, Jean-François. *Histoire de la France libre.* Paris: Presses Universitaires de France, 1996.

Murphy, Robert. *Diplomat Among Warriors.* Garden City, N.Y.: Doubleday, 1964; Pyramid ed., 1965.

Ninkovich, Frank. *The Wilsonian Century.* Chicago: University of Chicago Press, 1999.

Noli, Jean. *The Admiral's Wolfpack.* Trans. J. F. Bernard. Garden City, N.Y.: Doubleday, 1974.

Oberdorfer, Don. *The Turn: From the Cold War to a New Era.* New York: Simon and Schuster, 1991.

O'Kane, Richard H. *Clear the Bridge.* Novato, Calif.: Presidio Press, 1997.

———. *Wahoo: The Patrols of America's Most Famous World War II Submarine.* Novato, Calif.: Presidio Press, 1987.

Orita, Zenji, and Joseph D. Harrington. *I-Boat Captain.* Canoga Park, Calif.: Major Books, 1976.

Ott, Wolfgang. *Sharks and Little Fish.* New York: Pantheon, 1957; Ballantine ed., 1966.

Padfield, Peter. *War Beneath the Sea.* New York: John Wiley, 1995.

Paine, Lincoln P. *Warships of the World to 1900.* Boston: Houghton Mifflin, 2000.

Palmer, Michael A. *Origins of the Maritime Strategy.* Washington, D.C.: Naval Historical Center, 1988.

Parker, John. *The Silent Service.* London: Headline Book Publishing, 2001.

Parrish, Thomas. *Berlin in the Balance: The Blockade, the Airlift, the First Major Battle of the Cold War 1945–1949.* Reading, Mass.: Perseus, 1998.

———. *The Cold War Encyclopedia.* New York: Henry Holt, 1996.

———. *Roosevelt and Marshall: Partners in Politics and War.* New York: William Morrow, 1989.

———. *The Simon and Schuster Encyclopedia of World War II.* New York: Simon and Schuster, 1978.

———. *The Ultra Americans.* New York: Stein and Day, 1986; paperback ed., *The American Codebreakers: The U.S. Role in Ultra*, Scarborough House, 1991.

Perkins, Dexter. *The New Age of Franklin Roosevelt, 1932–1945.* Chicago: University of Chicago Press, 1957.

Philip, Cynthia Owen. *Robert Fulton.* New York: Franklin Watts, 1985.

Pogue, Forrest C. *George C. Marshall: Ordeal and Hope.* New York: Viking, 1966.

Poincaré, Raymond. *Messages.* Paris: Bloud & Gay, 1919.

Polmar, Norman. *The American Submarine.* Annapolis: The Nautical & Aviation Publishing Company of America, 1981.

———. *Guide to the Soviet Navy.* Annapolis: Naval Institute Press, 1985.

———, and Thomas B. Allen. *Rickover: Controversy and Genius.* New York: Simon and Schuster, 1982.

Porter, Bernard. *Plots and Paranoia.* London: Unwin Hyman, Ltd., 1989; Routledge paperback ed., 1992.

Potter, E. B. *Admiral Arleigh Burke.* New York: Random House, 1990.

———. *Nimitz.* Annapolis: Naval Institute Press, 1976.

Potter, John Deane. *Yamamoto.* New York: Viking, 1965.

Prange, Gordon W., with Donald M. Goldstein and Katherine V. Dillon. *Pearl Harbor: The Verdict of History.* New York: McGraw-Hill, 1986.

Preston, Diana. *Lusitania.* New York: Walker, 2002; Berkley ed., 2003.

Preston, Richard A., and Sydney F. Wise. *Men in Arms.* New York: Praeger, 1970.

Rachlis, Eugene. *They Came to Kill.* New York: Random House, 1961; Popular Library ed., 1962.

Rayner, D. A. *Escort: The Battle of the Atlantic.* London: William Kimber, 1955.

Reiners, Ludwig. *The Lamps Went Out in Europe.* Cleveland: World, 1966.

Renouvin, Pierre. *War and Aftermath, 1914–1929.* New York: Harper and Row, 1968. Translated from *Les Crises du XXe Siècle de 1914–1929* [Hachette, 1957] by Rémy Inglis Hall.

Reynolds, Quentin. *Convoy*. New York: Blue Ribbon Books, 1942.

Richler, Mordecai. *Writers on World War II*. New York: Alfred A. Knopf, 1991.

Robinson, Edgar E., and Victor J. West. *The Foreign Policy of Woodrow Wilson*. New York: Macmillan, 1917.

Rockwell, Theodore. *The Rickover Effect*. Annapolis: Naval Institute Press, 1992.

Rodengen, Jeffrey L. *The Legend of Electric Boat*. Ft. Lauderdale: Write Stuff Syndicate, 1994.

Rohwer, Jürgen. *Superpower Confrontation on the Seas*. Beverly Hills: Sage, 1975.

———, and Gerd Hummelchen. *Chronology of the War at Sea, 1939–1945*. 2 vols. Trans. Derek Masters. New York: Arco, 1972.

Roosevelt, Theodore. *America and the World War*. New York: Scribner, 1915.

Ropp, Theodore. *War in the Modern World*. Durham, N.C.: Duke University Press, 1959; Collier Books ed., 1962.

Roscoe, Theodore. *On the Seas and in the Skies*. New York: Hawthorn, 1970.

———. *Pig Boats*. New York: Bantam Books, 1949.

———. *United States Submarine Operations in World War II*. Annapolis: Naval Institute Press, 1949.

Roskill, Stephen Wentworth. *Churchill and the Admirals*. New York: William Morrow, 1978.

———. *The War at Sea, 1939–1945*. Vol. II. London: Her Majesty's Stationery Office, 1956.

———. *The White Ensign*. Annapolis: United States Naval Institute, 1960.

Ruge, Friedrich. *Der Seekrieg: The German Navy's Story 1939–1945*. Annapolis: Naval Institute Press, 1957.

Ruhe, William. *War in the Boats: My World War II Submarine Battles*. Washington, D.C.: Brassey's, 1994.

Runyan, Timothy J., and Jan M. Copes, eds. *To Die Gallantly: The Battle of the Atlantic*. Boulder, Colo.: Westview Press, 1994.

Russell, Francis. *The Shadow of Blooming Grove*. New York: McGraw-Hill, 1968.

Russell, Sir Herbert. *Sea Shepherds*. London: John Murray, 1941.

Saint Andrew's School Alumni. *World War II Stories*. Middleton, Del.: St. Andrew's School, 1995.

Sale, Kirkpatrick. *The Fire of His Genius*. New York: Free Press, 2001.

Sapolsky, Harvey M. *The Polaris System Development*. Cambridge: Harvard University Press, 1972.

Sasgen, Peter T. *Red Scorpion: The War Patrols of the USS Rasher*. Annapolis: Naval Institute Press, 1995.

Schaeffer, Heinz. *U-Boat 977*. New York: Norton, 1952.

Schoenfeld, Max. *Stalking the U-Boat: USAAF Offensive Antisubmarine Operations in World War II*. Washington, D.C.: Smithsonian Institution Press, 1995.

Schratz, Paul R. *Submarine Commander*. Lexington: University Press of Kentucky, 1988.

Scott, Harriet Fast, and William F. Scott. *The Armed Forces of the USSR*. Boulder, Colo.: Westview Press, 1979.

Seager, Robert, II. *Alfred Thayer Mahan*. Annapolis: Naval Institute Press, 1977.

Seth, Ronald. *The Fiercest Battle*. New York: Norton, 1961.

Seymour, Charles. *The Intimate Papers of Colonel House*. 2 vols. Boston: Houghton Mifflin, 1926.

Sharnik, John. *Inside the Cold War: An Oral History.* New York: Arbor House, 1987.

Sharpe, Peter. *U-Boat Fact File 1935–1945.* Leicester, England: Midland Publishing, 1998.

Sherwood, Robert E. *Roosevelt and Hopkins.* New York: Harper, 1948.

Shirreffs, Gordon D. *They Met Danger.* Racine, Wis.: Whitman, 1960.

Showell, Jak P. Mallman. *The German Navy in World War II:* Annapolis: Naval Institute Press, 1979.

Simpson, B. Mitchell, III. *Admiral Harold R. Stark: Architect of Victory.* Columbia: University of South Carolina Press, 1989.

Sims, William Sowden. *The Victory at Sea.* New York: Doubleday, Page, 1921.

Smith, Daniel M. *The Great Departure: The United States and World War I, 1914–1920.* New York: John Wiley, 1965.

Smith, Gaddis. *Britain's Clandestine Submarines, 1914–1915.* New Haven: Yale University Press, 1964.

Smith, S. E., ed. *The United States Marine Corps in World War II.* New York: Random House, 1969.

Smither, Roger, ed. *First World War U-Boat.* London: Lloyd's Register of Shipping/Imperial War Museum, 2000.

Snow, C. P. *Science and Government.* Cambridge: Harvard University Press, 1961.

Sokolovskii, V. D. *Soviet Military Strategy.* Trans. Herbert S. Dinerstein, Jean Gouré, and Thomas W. Wolfe. Englewood Cliffs, N.J.: Prentice-Hall, 1963.

Spector, Ronald H. *At War at Sea.* New York: Viking, 2001.

———. *Eagle Against the Sun.* New York: Free Press, 1985.

Sprout, Harold, and Margaret Sprout. *The Rise of American Naval Power 1776–1918.* Annapolis: Naval Institute Press, 1939.

Stafford, Edward P. *The Big E: The Story of the USS Enterprise.* New York: Random House, 1962; Dell ed., 1964.

Sterling, Forest J. *Wake of the Wahoo.* Placentia, Calif.: R. A. Cline Publishing, 1999.

Stern, Philip Van Doren. *The Confederate Navy.* New York: Bonanza Books, 1962.

Stern, Robert C. *Type VII U-Boats.* London: Brockhampton Press, 1998.

———. *U.S. Subs in Action.* Carrollton, Tex.: Squadron/Signal Publications, 1983.

Sweeney, Jerry K., ed. *A Handbook of American Military History.* Boulder, Colo.: Westview Press, 1996.

Syrett, David. *The Defeat of the German U-Boats: The Battle of the Atlantic.* Columbia: University of South Carolina Press, 1994.

Tarrant, V. E. *The Last Year of the Kriegsmarine: May 1944–May 1945.* Annapolis: Naval Institute Press, 1994.

———. *The U-Boat Offensive 1914–1945.* London: Cassell, 1989.

Taylor, A. J. P. *The Course of German History.* New York: Capricorn Books, 1946.

———. *History of the First World War.* New York: Berkley Medallion, 1966.

Taylor, Edmond. *The Strategy of Terror.* New York: Pocket Books, 1940.

Taylor, J. C. *German Warships of World War II.* Garden City, N.Y.: Doubleday, 1966.

Terraine, John. *Business in Great Waters.* London: Leo Cooper, 1989; Wordsworth ed., 1999.

Thomas, Lowell. *Raiders of the Deep.* Garden City, N.Y.: Doubleday, Doran, 1928; Sun Dial Press ed., 1940.

Thompson, Julian. *The War at Sea.* London: Sidgwick and Jackson, 1996.

Thorne, Christopher. *Allies of a Kind*. New York: Oxford University Press, 1978; paperback ed., 1979.
————. *The Far Eastern War: States and Societies 1941–1945*. London: Unwin Paperbacks, 1985.
Till, Geoffrey. *Maritime Strategy and the Nuclear Age*. New York: St. Martin's Press, 1984.
Tirpitz, Alfred von. *My Memoirs*. 2 vols. London: Hurst & Blackett, n.d.
Trask, David F. *Captains and Cabinets*. Columbia: University of Missouri Press, 1972.
Tuchman, Barbara W. *The Zimmermann Telegram*. New York: Viking, 1958; Dell ed., 1965.
Tyler, Patrick. *Running Critical: The Silent War, Rickover, and General Dynamics*. New York: Harper and Row, 1986.
Van Der Rhoer, Edward. *Deadly Magic*. New York: Scribner, 1978.
Van der Vat, Dan. *The Atlantic Campaign*. New York: Harper and Row, 1988.
————. *The Pacific Campaign*. New York: Simon and Schuster, 1991.
————. *Stealth at Sea: The History of the Submarine*. Boston: Houghton Mifflin, 1995.
Waller, Willard, ed. *War in the Twentieth Century*. New York: Dryden Press, 1940.
Ward, John. *Submarines of World War II*. St. Paul, Minn.: MBI Publishing, 2001.
Waters, John M., Jr. *Bloody Winter*. Princeton: Van Nostrand, 1967.
Watson, Mark Skinner. *Chief of Staff: Prewar Plans and Preparations*. Washington, D.C.: Historical Division, Department of the Army, 1950.
Weir, Gary E. *Building American Submarines 1914–1940*. Washington, D.C: Naval Historical Center, 1991.
————. *Forged in War*. Washington, D.C.: Naval Historical Center, 1993; Brassey's ed., 1998.
Werner, Herbert A. *Iron Coffins*. New York: Holt, Rinehart and Winston, 1968; Bantam ed., 1969.
Whinney, Bob. *The U-Boat Peril*. London: Blandford Press, 1986; Cassell ed., 1998.
White, John. *U-Boat Tankers 1941–1945*. Shrewsbury, England: Airlife Publishing, 1998.
Whitehouse, Arch. *Subs and Submarines*. Garden City, N.Y.: Doubleday, 1961.
Wile, Frederick W. *The Men Around the Kaiser*. Indianapolis: Bobbs-Merrill, 1914.
Williamson, Gordon. *Fighting Elite: U-Boat Crews 1914–1945*. London: Reed International Books, 1995.
————. *Grey Wolf: U-Boat Crewman of World War II*. Botley, England: Osprey Publishing, 2001.
Willmott, H. P. *The War with Japan: The Period of Balance, May 1942–October 1943*. Wilmington, Del.: Scholarly Resources, 2002.
Wilson, James Q. *Bureaucracy*. New York: Basic Books, 1989.
Winkler, David F. *Cold War at Sea*. Annapolis: Naval Institute Press, 2000.
Woodbury, David O. *What the Citizen Should Know About Submarine Warfare*. New York: Norton, 1942.
Woodward, David. *The Tirpitz and the Battle for the North Atlantic*. New York: Norton, 1953; Berkley ed., n.d.
Yoshimura, Akira. *Battleship Musashi*. Tokyo: Kodansha International, 1991.
Young, Edward. *One of Our Submarines*. London: Rupert Hart Davis, 1952; Granada ed., 1982.
Zubok, Vladislav, and Constantine Pleshakov. *Inside the Kremlin's Cold War*. Cambridge: Harvard University Press, 1996.

ACKNOWLEDGMENTS

As I begin to offer my thanks to all those who gave me help with this book, I wish to express one perhaps inevitable concern—that I may overlook somebody who deserves mention. Let me say, then, that I leave out nobody intentionally, and I hereby record my regrets for any omission. A book that requires any kind of investigation and research is to a good extent a collaborative enterprise, and I am deeply grateful to everybody who helped.

This listing of acknowledgments has two obvious beginning points: Wendy Wolf, executive editor of Viking, who proposed the book, and my agent, Stuart Krichevsky, who brought us together and made the arrangement possible. Wendy proved to be a thoroughly involved and stimulating—and often entertaining—editor with whom I have very much enjoyed working. As for Stuart, I cannot do better than to repeat what I have said on earlier occasions: He is devoted, imaginative, efficient, and cheerful—an ideal agent.

The unquestioned highest point during my work on this book was my attendance at the 2000 convention of the United States Submarine Veterans of World War II, and I wish to express my admiration and gratitude to all the veterans there with whom I spoke. They provided fascinating information on their lives and insights into the roles they played during the war, and beyond that they were remarkably outgoing and hospitable. The group from the old *S-47* welcomed me to their banquet table, and I quickly began to regard myself as a kind of honorary member of that crew. I felt even more so when one of the group, Emerson Grossman, lent me his irreplaceable scrapbook on the *S-47* and her adventures, and I confess to feeling considerable relief when it was returned safely to Emerson in Michigan. Among the many other submariners I spoke with at the convention, I wish to make special mention of Churchill Campbell, Gus D'Oranzio, John Hoppes, Kenneth W. Hull, John Shaw, and David Veder.

My contacts with the submarine veterans' group came as part of the remarkable help given me by Bob Hall, of Troy, New Hampshire, a loyal veteran of the U.S.S. *Parche* whose experiences as an underwater baker appear in Chapter 30. Such contacts actually constituted only a very small proportion of Bob's contribution to the book. Having assembled through the years an impressive documentary, magazine, and newspaper archive on the submarine war, he not only made all of this material available but also arranged it in a highly organized fashion, advised me in its use, and gave me copies of much of it. The Halls enriched this research by providing fresh coffee and the best imaginable blueberry muffins.

I am indebted to Robert Rowe, of Frankfort, Kentucky, for the use of material on the adventures of his cousin, Dudley "Mush" Morton, skipper of the U.S.S. *Wahoo*, and for personal information about the famous captain of this famous submarine; Bob provided insights I could have obtained from no other source. I thank Terri Furgason not simply for locating him but for discovering his existence.

For conversation and information professional and personal about the U.S. nuclear submarine program, I am grateful to Captain William R. Anderson (Ret.), Theodore Rockwell, Henry Stone, and John Tronc, the last-named a veteran of the nuclear navy. My thanks to my friend Fritz Heimann for arranging my contact with Mr. Stone, who provided wonderful personal reminiscences of Admiral Hyman Rickover.

The list of other persons who helped with various kinds of information includes Rudy Abramson; Debbie Anderson, daughter of the ingenious creator of World War II decrypting devices, Joe Desch; Daniel Beveraggi of Paris; Fregattenkapitän Lutz Bieber of the German Navy; Robert Brancaccio, a yachtsman with an eye for picture possibilities; John Bullen of the Imperial War Museum, London; Carolyn Holmes, who supplied a wartime letter from her father; John Isberg, formerly of the General Dynamics Corporation; Charles

McNutt; Ken Moody of Hyde Park, New York, a researcher who interrupted his own work to pass along information relevant to mine; and Herbert Ping.

I also wish to express my thanks for assistance and information to the librarians at the Franklin D. Roosevelt Library at Hyde Park and to Wendy Gulley at the Submarine Force Library, New London, Connecticut. I am also extremely grateful to the staff of the United States Naval Institute, Annapolis, Maryland, for their very great help with various kinds of original materials and photographs (their oral-history series constitutes a true national treasure). I would make mention here of Paul Stillwell, a fount of knowledge, and Susan Brook, and I would be guilty of a serious oversight if I did not place on this record my tribute to the incomparable helpfulness of Ann Hassinger.

For supplying other photographs, I am indebted to Darren Milford, to Diane Cooter of the Syracuse University Library, Department of Special Collections, and to Harry Cooper, the extremely cooperative president of Sharkhunters, Inc., and editor of its eponymous magazine, the "Official Publication of U-Boat History." I also thank Norman Polmar for permission to reproduce two drawings from his book *The Naval Institute Guide to the Ships and Aircraft of the U.S. Fleet.*

The maps were planned and projections chosen, in consultation with me, by Mark Wiljanen, director of the Geographic Information Systems Laboratory, Department of Geography, Eastern Kentucky University, with the assistance of Daphne Corbett, and were executed by Jeffrey Ward.

For their contributions to production of the book, I thank Cliff Corcoran and Sharon Gonzalez of Viking.

For technical help, I am indebted to Kurt Gohde and Anthony Basham.

As always, I—like everybody else who has written about war in modern times—wish to express my gratitude to and admiration of the veteran master of the subject, John E. Taylor of the Modern Military Branch of the U.S. National Archives. Likewise, as always, I am delighted to record my thanks to the hardworking and highly cooperative staff members of the libraries at Berea College, Eastern Kentucky University, and the University of Kentucky, who all have, through the years, extended every courtesy to me. For overall help in seeking out information, particularly on the Internet, I wish to thank my volunteer but very committed research aide, Lorrin Ingerson. For his thorough and devoted help in obtaining much of the archival material I have used in this book, I thank my Washington researcher Mark Tacyn, of College Park, Maryland. For his work digging in the riches of the Imperial War Museum, I thank Brian Meringer. For field help in Paris, particularly in connection with Robert Fulton's memorable experiments, I thank Ruth-Christine Knutson-Beveraggi. For research in archival text and photographic materials at the Submarine Force Library, I thank Nancy Coleman Wolsk of Transylvania University, Lexington, Kentucky.

In a more personal way, I thank Nancy for her continuing encouragement and advice, for sharing various adventures in research, and, above all, for always being there.

INDEX